palgrave advances in oscar wilde studies

edited by
frederick s. roden
university of connecticut

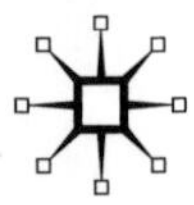

First published 2004 by
PALGRAVE MACMILLAN
Houndmills, Basingstoke, Hampshire RG21 6XS and
175 Fifth Avenue, New York, N.Y. 10010
Companies and representatives throughout the world

PALGRAVE MACMILLAN is the global academic imprint of the
Palgrave Macmillan division of St Martin's Press LLC and of
Palgrave Macmillan Ltd.
Macmillan® is a registered trademark in the United States,
United Kingdom and other countries. Palgrave is a registered
trademark in the European Union and other countries.

ISBN 1–4039–2147–4 hardback
ISBN 1–4039–2148–2 paperback

This book is printed on paper suitable for recycling and
made from fully managed and sustained forest sources.

A catalogue record for this book is available
from the British Library.

Library of Congress Cataloging-in-Publication Data
Palgrave advances in Oscar Wilde studies / edited by Frederick S. Roden.
p. cm.
Includes bibliographical references and index.
ISBN 1–4039–2147–4 — ISBN 1–4039–2148–2 (pbk.)
1. Wilde, Oscar, 1854–1900—Criticism and interpretation—History. 2. Authors, Irish—Biography—History and criticism. 3. Wilde, Oscar, 1854–1900—Chronology. I. Roden, Frederick S., 1970–

PR5824.P28 2004
828'.809—dc22

2004046699

10 9 8 7 6 5 4 3 2 1
13 12 11 10 09 08 07 06 05 04

Printed and bound in Great Britain by
Antony Rowe Ltd, Chippenham and Eastbourne

For my family: Arlene and Donald Roden and Joseph Portanova

contents

list of illustrations

acknowledgments

Special thanks go to several people at Palgrave Macmillan: first to Eleanor Birne and Rebecca Mashayekh, present at the time of the book's commissioning; next to Emily Rosser, Paula Kennedy, and Chase Publishing Services who saw this project through. All were kind, helpful, and kept their sense of humor.

An editor of a volume of this kind must warmly thank his contributors for producing such fine chapters to work with – and for their patience during revisions and promptness in meeting deadlines. Particular gratitude goes to D.C. Rose for consultation on the Selected Bibliography, as well as his contribution of a thorough chronology. One must also acknowledge the entire thriving Wilde studies enterprise, which has given us, in the past 125 years, so much wonderful material to work with. For a book of this type, we should really thank (posthumously) a writer whose life and creations provoke such a degree of response. As the *Palgrave Advances* is published on the 150th anniversary of the author's birth, we look forward to a future of growth in Wilde studies. We are particularly indebted to the way that his grandson, author/editor Merlin Holland, continues to provide rich resources for his fellow scholars to cultivate.

As editor of this volume, I sincerely thank my teachers, colleagues, students, family, and friends for giving me so much to think about concerning Oscar Wilde, and for indulging my own Wildean appetites. Thank you for being there, and for your patience during the preparation of the *Palgrave Advances*. I appreciate now (as never before) the work of an editor.

notes on the contributors

Joseph Bristow is Professor of English at the University of California, Los Angeles. His recent books include *Wilde Writings: Contextual Conditions* (University of Toronto Press, 2003). His variorum edition of *The Picture of Dorian Gray* is forthcoming from Oxford University Press.

Francesca Coppa is Associate Professor of English at Muhlenberg College, where she teaches twentieth-century dramatic literature, sexuality theory, and performance studies. She has written and lectured widely on the playwright Joe Orton and the larger epigrammatic British comedy tradition. She is the editor of a three-volume collection of Orton's early works and *Joe Orton: A Casebook* (Routledge, 2003).

Anne Margaret Daniel teaches literature and history at Princeton and at the New School University. Her publications include essays on Yeats, Wilde, Kipling, Eliot, Woolf, Fitzgerald, and Auden. She is currently working on a book about cultural and literary representations of redheads.

Dennis Denisoff teaches at Ryerson University in Toronto. He is the author of *Sexual Parody and Aestheticism: 1840–1940* (Cambridge U P, 2001) and *Sexual Visuality from Literature to Film: 1850–1950* (Palgrave Macmillan, 2004). His second novel, *The Winter Gardeners*, was published in 2003 (Coach House Press).

Noreen Doody is a lecturer in Anglo-Irish Literature and Drama at University College Dublin, where she specializes in the literature and culture of the late nineteenth century and in contemporary Irish literature. Her recent articles include "'An Echo of Someone Else's Music': The Influence of Oscar Wilde on W.B. Yeats" (*The Importance of Reinventing*

Oscar: Versions of Wilde During the Last 100 Years; Rodopi, 2002) and "Oscar Wilde: Landscape, Memory, and Imagined Space" (*Irish Landscapes*; Universidad de Burgos, 2004). She is currently working on a critical study of the influence of Oscar Wilde on W.B. Yeats.

Richard A. Kaye is Associate Professor in the Department of English at Hunter College, City University of New York, and the author of *The Flirt's Tragedy: Desire Without End in Victorian and Edwardian Fiction* (Virginia, 2002) and *Voluptuous Immobility: St. Sebastian and the Decadent Imagination* (Columbia, forthcoming). He has edited the new Riverside edition of *The Portrait of Dorian Gray* (Houghton Mifflin) and, with the late Charles Bernheimer, a collection of essays entitled *The Queen of Decadence: Salome in Modern Culture* (Chicago, forthcoming).

Patrick R. O'Malley is Assistant Professor of English at Georgetown University. He is currently working on a book exploring the uses of gothic rhetoric and narrative in nineteenth-century British constructions of Catholicism and sexual difference.

Allison Pease is Associate Professor of English at John Jay College, City University of New York. She is the author of *Modernism, Mass Culture, and the Aesthetics of Obscenity* (Cambridge U P, 2000), and an assistant editor of the journal *Victorian Literature and Culture*.

Frederick S. Roden is Assistant Professor of English at University of Connecticut. He is the author of *Same-Sex Desire in Victorian Religious Culture* (Palgrave Macmillan, 2002). He is at work with Philip Healy on a translation/edition of Marc-André Raffalovich's 1896 *Uranisme et Unisexualité*.

D.C. Rose read Modern History at Magdalen College, Oxford and Arts Administration at University College Dublin. While attached to the Department of English at Goldsmiths College, London, he founded *The Oscholars* (June 2001) intended as a monthly newsletter to keep Wilde scholars in touch with one another. This has now expanded into an e-journal <http://homepages.gold.ac.uk/oscholars>, updated monthly, of Wilde and *fin-de-siècle* studies.

Philip Smith teaches in the English Department at the University of Pittsburgh. With Michael S. Helfand, he co-authored and co-edited *Oscar Wilde's Oxford Notebooks: A Portrait of Mind in the Making* (1989). He has also written articles on Wilde, Constance Naden, Robert Heinlein, Ursula LeGuin, Brian Aldiss, August Wilson, John Galsworthy, Charles Olson, and on issues of curriculum, staffing, and teaching in the profession of English studies. He is editor of the forthcoming *Approaches to Teaching the Works of Oscar Wilde* (Modern Language Association).

Margaret D. Stetz is Mae and Robert Carter Professor of Women's Studies at the University of Delaware. Her books include *British Women's Comic Fiction, 1890–1990* (2001), as well as *England in the 1890s: Literary Publishing at the Bodley Head* (1990) and *England in the 1880s: Old Guard and Avant-Garde* (1989), both co-authored with Mark Samuels Lasner, and the volume *Legacies of the Comfort Women of WWII* (2001), co-edited with Bonnie B.C. Oh. She has published more than fifty essays in academic journals and edited collections, including many on Wilde and his circle and on feminist writing. Since 1985, she has also been curator or co-curator of six major inter-disciplinary exhibitions on late-Victorian book history, art, literature, and culture, the most recent of which was "Gender and the London Theatre, 1880–1920" at Bryn Mawr College in 2003.

chronology

compiled by david rose

day	*month*	*year*	*event*
		1815	Birth of [Sir] William Robert Wilde at Castlerea, Co. Roscommon.
27	12	1821	Birth of Jane Elgee (Speranza, Lady Wilde).
09	10	1850	William Wilde appointed Assistant Census Commissioner.
12	11	1851	Wedding of Jane Elgee and William Wilde.
26	09	1852	Birth of William Charles Kingsbury Wilde (Willie).
16	10	1854	BIRTH OF OSCAR WILDE AT 21 WESTLAND ROW, DUBLIN.
		1855	The Wildes move to 1 Merrion Square.
26	04	1855	Wilde baptized at St. Mark's, Great Brunswick Street (now Pearse Street).
28	08	1855	Wedding of Horace Lloyd and Adelaide (Adele) Atkinson (parents of Constance Wilde).
02	04	1857	Birth of Isola Wilde.
	02	1861	The Wildes entertain Boucicault.
06	05	1863	Lady Wilde writes to Mary Travers.
28	01	1864	William Wilde knighted.
	02	1864	Wilde goes to Portora Royal School, Enniskillen [to 1871].
01	08	1864	The Wildes visit Bray [to 12 August].
12	12	1864	Travers v. Wilde opens [to 17 December].
23	02	1867	Death of Isola Wilde.
	08	1867	Wilde spends three weeks in Paris.
10	10	1871	Wilde goes up to Trinity College Dublin, with rooms at 18 Botany Bay [to 1874].

10	11	1871	Deaths of Emily and Mary Wilde.
26	11	1871	Wilde becomes a Queen's Scholar.
31	01	1872	Wilde placed third in Exam Honours.
29	04	1872	Wilde wins the Michaelmas Prize.
02	10	1872	Wilde gives *Selected Poems of Matthew Arnold* to Helena Sickert with accompanying letter.
09	06	1873	Wilde elected to a Foundation Scholarship.
19	11	1873	Wilde elected to the "Hist" at Trinity.
11	06	1874	Wilde's Magdalen demyship gazetted.
	08	1874	J.E.C. Bodley meets Wilde in Dublin during Horse Show Week.
17	09	1874	Wilde matriculates at Oxford.
17	10	1874	Wilde goes up to Magdalen College, Oxford.
19	01	1875	J.E.C. Bodley encounters Oscar Wilde with Willie at the Victoria Music Hall, Oxford.
23	02	1875	Wilde received into the Oxford University Freemasons, Apollo Lodge.
	03	1875	Willie Wilde called to the Bar.
22	04	1875	Wilde let off progging fine.
24	04	1875	Wilde raised to second degree Mason.
14	05	1875	Wilde on the Cher with Bodley and Goldsmidt. Wilde and Bodley dine at the Mitre.
25	05	1875	Wilde raised to Master Mason.
25	05	1875	Wilde and Bodley dine together. Lodge meeting: William Grenfell, Prince Leopold, Wilde, Bodley.
15	06	1875	Wilde in Florence.
15	06	1875	Wilde writes "San Miniato."
16–20	06	1875	Wilde visits Venice.
16–20	06	1875	Wilde visits Padua.
22	06	1875	Wilde in Milan with Mahaffy.
23	06	1875	Wilde in Milan.
24	06	1875	Wilde in Milan.
26	06	1875	Wilde arrives in Lausanne.
31	10	1875	Wilde and Bodley breakfast at the Mitre and go on to Wilde's rooms.
23	11	1875	Wilde at the dedication by Cardinal Manning of S. Aloysisus, Oxford.
03	12	1875	Bodley calls on Wilde.
19	04	1876	Death of Sir William Wilde.
22	04	1876	Funeral of Sir William Wilde.

05	07	1876	Wilde takes First in Mods.
	08	1876	Wilde at Moytura with Frank Miles.
14	12	1876	Wilde at the Albert Hall for a performance of Haydn's "Creation."
15	12	1876	Wilde and David Hunter Blair see Ellen Terry in "New Men and Old Acres" at the Court Theatre.
16	12	1876	Wilde goes to see Henry Irving in *Macbeth* with Arthur Dampier May.
17	12	1876	Wilde leaves for Ireland.
	02	1877	Wilde is elected to the St. Stephen's Club, London.
	03	1877	Wilde visits Greece with Mahaffy, returning via Rome in April.
03	03	1877	Wilde visits the Royal Academy.
05	03	1877	Wilde enters for the "Ireland" Scholarship.
14 c	03	1877	Wilde has tea with Frank Miles to meet Lord Ronald Gower and Constance Duchess of Westminster (d.1880).
31	03	1877	Wilde in Ravenna.
	04	1877	Wilde returns from Greece with Mahaffy via Rome.
01	04	1877	Wilde leaves Brindisi.
28	04	1877	Wilde rusticated from Magdalen.
30	04	1877	Wilde at inaugural reception of the Grosvenor Gallery, wearing a coat that from behind resembled a 'cello.
01	05	1877	Wilde at the official opening of the Grosvenor Gallery.
15	05	1877	Mr. Gladstone writes to Wilde.
09	06	1877	Wilde dines with Henry Wilson.
13	06	1877	Death of Henry Wilson (Wilde), aet. 39, of pneumonia.
	07	1877	Publication of Wilde's "The Tomb of Keats" in *The Irish Monthly*.
	08	1877	Wilde goes to Clonfin House, Granard to shoot.
29	10	1877	Mr. Gladstone writes to Lady Wilde.
29	12	1877	Publication of Wilde's article on Henry O'Neill anonymously in *Saunders Newsletter*, Dublin (but see 29.12.1878 as alternative).

01	05	1878	Wilde as Prince Rupert at Mrs. George Morrell's fancy dress ball, Headington Hall.
10	06	1878	Wilde wins the Newdigate Prize with *Ravenna*.
26	06	1878	Wilde recites *Ravenna* in the Sheldonian.
15	07	1878	Wilde's *Ravenna* published by Thos Shrimpton.
19	07	1878	Wilde takes a First in Greats.
	09	1878	Publication of Augustus Moore's "To Oscar Wilde, author of Ravenna" in *The Irish Monthly*.
28	11	1878	Wilde takes his B.A. at Oxford.
29	12	1878	Publication of Wilde's article on Henry O'Neill in *Saunders Newsletter*, Dublin (but see 29.12.1877 as alternative).
12	01	1879	Publication of Wilde's article on Henry O'Neill in *The Nation*, Dublin.
07	05	1879	Lady Wilde gives up 1 Merrion Square.
	06	1879	Publication of Wilde's poem "Easter Day" in *Waifs and Strays* no. 1 (Oxford, ed. by Harold Bolton).
02	06	1879	Wilde present at the opening of the Comédie Française London season at the Gaiety Theatre (to 12 July) ("Misanthrope" and "Les Précieuses Ridicules"). Act II of *Phèdre* (Sarah Bernhardt) as an entr'acte.
11	06	1879	Wilde publishes "To Sarah Bernhardt" in *The World*.
	07	1879	Wilde in Belgium with Rennell Rodd.
16	07	1879	Wilde publishes "Queen Henrietta Maria" in *The World*.
	08	1879	Wilde visits the Sickert family in Dieppe.
	10	1879	Wilde visits Oscar Browning in Cambridge.
Autumn		1879	Wilde takes rooms with Frank Miles at 13 Salisbury Street, Strand.
		1880	Wilde attends afternoon parties at Combe Bank.
04	01	1880	Publication of Wilde's sonnet "Portia" in *The World*.
04	02	1880	First cartoon of Wilde by George du Maurier appears in *Punch*.
04	02	1880	Wilde one of 350 guests (all men) at Irving's party at the Lyceum.
	03	1880	Publication of Wilde's poem "Impression de Voyage" in *Waifs and Strays* 3.

	08	1880	Wilde moves with Frank Miles to Keats House, Tite Street, Chelsea.
25	08	1880	Publication of Wilde's sonnet "Ave Imperatrix" in *The World*.
	09	1880	Wilde's "Vera" published by Ranken & Co.
25	09	1880	Wilde's "Pan, A Villanelle" published in *Pan*.
10	11	1880	Publication of Wilde's "Libertatis Sacra Fames" in *The New York World*.
28 c	02	1881	Gosse meets Wilde at a masked party at Alma-Tadema's, Wilde not masked.
	03	1881	Lillie Langtry stays with Sir George & Lady Lewis at Walton-on-Thames. Wilde and the Comyns Carrs visit.
02	03	1881	Wilde's "Impression du matin" published in *The World*.
23	04	1881	Wilde at first night of "Patience" at the Opéra Comique.
23	04	1881	Wilde's "Impressions" published in *Pan*.
25	04	1881	Wilde at the first night of the revival of Sheridan Knowles's *Virginius*, Theatre Royal, Drury Lane.
29	04	1881	Wilde at the General Private View for the Royal Academy Summer Exhibition.
02	05	1881	Wilde at first night of *Othello*.
17	05	1881	Wilde signs the contract with David Bogue for the publication of his poems.
30	06	1881	Publication of Wilde's *Poems*.
26	07	1881	Mr. Gladstone writes to Wilde.
03	08	1881	Mr. Gladstone encounters Wilde at the studio of Burne-Jones.
30	09	1881	Wilde receives telegram from Colonel Morse suggesting the U.S. lecture tour.
01	10	1881	Wilde sends telegram to Colonel Morse accepting the U.S. lecture tour.
30	11	1881	Wilde withdraws *Vera* from production.
	12	1881	Wilde dines at "one of the taverns of Bohemia" with Whistler and Rennell Rodd "just before" leaving for America.
17	12	1881	Wilde's *Vera* due, but fails, to open at the Adelphi Theatre with Mrs. Bernard Beere in the title role.
24	12	1881	Wilde embarks for America on the Guion Line's *Arizona*.

		1882	Death of the Revd. Ralph Wilde.
	01	1882	Wilde meets Boucicault in New York.
02	01	1882	Wilde arrives in New York.
03	01	1882	Wilde clears U.S. Customs with nothing to declare but his genius.
06	01	1882	Wilde attends a performance of *Patience* in New York.
08	01	1882	Wilde meets Louisa May Alcott at a reception.
09	01	1882	Wilde lectures on "The English Renaissance of Art" at the Chickering Hall, New York.
17	01	1882	Wilde lectures at the Horticultural Hall, Philadelphia.
18	01	1882	Wilde visits Walt Whitman.
19	01	1882	Wilde misses a party in his honor in Baltimore.
27	01	1882	Wilde lectures at Albany, NY.
29	01	1882	Wilde visits Longfellow.
31	01	1882	Wilde lectures at the Boston Music Hall and is mocked by Harvard undergraduates.
01	02	1882	Wilde lectures at Peck's Opera House, New Haven and is mocked by Yale undergraduates.
02	02	1882	Wilde lectures at Hartford Opera House.
03	02	1882	Wilde lectures at the Boston Academy of Music.
05	02	1882	Wilde lectures at the City Opera House, Utica, NY.
07	02	1882	Wilde lectures at Rochester, NY and is mocked by ruffians.
08	02	1882	Wilde lectures at Buffalo, NY.
09	02	1882	Wilde visits Niagara Falls.
10	02	1882	Wilde arrives in Chicago.
13	02	1882	Wilde lectures at the Central Music Hall, Chicago.
16	02	1882	Wilde lectures at the Old Academy, Fort Wayne, Indiana.
17	02	1882	Wilde lectures at the Music Hall, Detroit.
18	02	1882	Wilde lectures at the Case Hall, Cleveland, Ohio.
20	02	1882	Wilde lectures at Columbus, Ohio.
	03	1882	Wilde gives an interview to a San Francisco newspaper.
01	03	1882	Wilde lectures at Dubuque, Iowa.
02	03	1882	Wilde lectures at Rockford, Illinois.

03	03	1882	Wilde lectures at Aurora, Illinois.
04	03	1882	Wilde lectures at Racine, Wisconsin.
05	03	1882	Wilde lectures at the Grand Opera House, Milwaukee, Wisconsin.
06	03	1882	Wilde lectures at Joliet, Illinois.
07	03	1882	Wilde lectures at Jacksonville, Illinois.
08	03	1882	Wilde lectures at Decatur, Illinois.
09	03	1882	Wilde lectures at Peoria, Illinois.
10	03	1882	Wilde lectures at Bloomington, Illinois.
11	03	1882	Wilde lectures at the Central Music Hall, Chicago.
15	03	1882	Wilde lectures at the Academy of Music, Minneapolis.
16	03	1882	Wilde lectures at the Opera House, St. Paul, Minnesota.
17	03	1882	Wilde gives St. Patrick's Day speech at St. Paul, Minnesota.
20	03	1882	Wilde lectures at the Academy of Music, Sioux City.
21	03	1882	Wilde lectures at Boyd's Opera House, Omaha.
27	03	1882	Wilde lectures at Platt's Hall, San Francisco.
28	03	1882	Wilde lectures at the Light Cavalry Armory, Oakland, California.
29	03	1882	Wilde lectures at San Francisco.
30	03	1882	Wilde lectures at San Jose, California.
31	03	1882	Wilde lectures at Sacramento, California.
	04	1882	Publication of *Rose Leaf and Apple Leaf* by Rennell Rodd with an Introduction by Oscar Wilde. London: J.M. Stoddart & Co.
01	04	1882	Wilde lectures at Platt's Hall, San Francisco.
03	04	1882	Wilde in San Jose.
05	04	1882	Wilde lectures at Platt's Hall, San Francisco.
10	04	1882	Wilde at Salt Lake City.
11	04	1882	Wilde lectures at Salt Lake City.
12	04	1882	Wilde lectures at Denver, Colorado.
13	04	1882	Wilde lectures at the Tabor Grand Opera House, Leadville, Colorado.
14	04	1882	Wilde lectures at Colorado Springs.
14	04	1882	Wilde lectures at Denver, Colorado.
17	04	1882	Wilde lectures at The Coates Opera House, Kansas City, Missouri.

18	04	1882	Wilde lectures at St. Joseph, Missouri.
20	04	1882	Wilde lectures at Topeka, Kansas.
21	04	1882	Wilde lectures at Lawrence, Kansas.
26	04	1882	Wilde lectures at Des Moines, Iowa.
27	04	1882	Wilde lectures at the Iowa City Opera House.
28	04	1882	Wilde lectures at Cedar Rapids, Iowa.
02	05	1882	Wilde lectures at Dayton, Ohio.
03	05	1882	Wilde lectures at the Comstock Opera House, Columbus, Ohio.
11	05	1882	Wilde lectures on "The Practical Application of the Principles of Aesthetic Theory to Exterior and Interior House Decoration."
11	05	1882	Wilde lectures on "Decorative Art in America."
12	05	1882	Wilde lectures at Montréal.
13	05	1882	Wilde lectures at Ottawa.
15	05	1882	Wilde lectures at Toronto.
02	06	1882	Wilde lectures at the Globe Theatre, Boston.
11	06	1882	Wilde lectures at the Grand Opera House, Cincinnati, Ohio.
12	06	1882	Wilde lectures at Leubrie's Theatre, Memphis, Tennessee.
12	06	1882	Wilde lectures at Leubrie's Theatre, Memphis, Tennessee.
14	06	1882	Wilde at Vicksburg.
16	06	1882	Wilde lectures at The Grand Opera House, New Orleans.
19	06	1882	Wilde lectures at The Pavilion, Galveston, Texas.
21	06	1882	Wilde lectures at San Antonio, Texas.
24	06	1882	Wilde lectures at New Orleans.
26	06	1882	Wilde lectures at Spanish Fort, Louisiana.
27	06	1882	Wilde visits Jefferson Davis at Beauvoir.
28	06	1882	Wilde lectures at the Amusement Park, Mobile, Alabama.
30	06	1882	Wilde lectures at Columbus, Georgia.
22	10	1882	Wilde gives an interview to *The New York World*.
	11 ?	1882	Wilde begins *The Duchess of Padua*.
06	11	1882	Wilde at first night of Tom Taylor's *An Unequal Match*, Wallack's Theatre, New York.

07	11	1882	Publication of Wilde's "Mrs Langtry as Hester Grazebrook" in *The New York World*.
27	11	1882	Wilde leaves America on the S.S. *Bothnia* from New York.
04	12	1882	First mention of Wilde in Sweden, in *The Göteborg Newspaper*.
		1883	Maurice Barrès arranges a dinner in Wilde's honor at the Restaurant Voisin, rue St. Honoré.
	01	1883	Wilde in Paris, first at the Hôtel Continental and then (March) at the Hôtel Voltaire [till ?May] and is visited by Sickert.
	02	1883	Sickert meets Wilde.
01	02	1883	Wilde lectures on "Personal Impressions of America," The Winter Gardens, Southport.
	03	1883	Wilde finishes *The Duchess of Padua*.
15	03	1883	Wilde sends MS of *The Duchess of Padua* to Mary Anderson.
	04	1883	Wilde meets Robert Sherard "at the house of a Greek lady."
	04	1883	Wilde meets Robert Sherard "at a dinner-party at which I was also first introduced to Paul Bourget and John Sargent."
21	04	1883	Wilde meets Edmond de Goncourt.
	05	1883	Sickert a guest of Wilde at the Hôtel Voltaire.
05	05	1883	Wilde dines with Edmond de Goncourt and Giuseppe de Nittis.
20	06	1883	Wilde at a poetry recital in London.
30	06	1883	Wilde lectures to the Royal Academy arts students at their club in Golden Square, Westminster.
	07	1883	Wilde moves into rooms at 9 Charles Street, Berkeley Square.
	07	1883	Wilde lectures on America at the Prince's Hall, Piccadilly.
10	07	1883	Wilde lectures on "Personal Impressions of America," Prince's Hall, London.
20	07	1883	Wilde at a poetry recital. Also present Lady Wilde, Matthew Arnold, Robert Browning, Mary Endicott.
02	08	1883	Wilde sails for New York on board R.M.S. *Britannia*.
11	08	1883	Wilde arrives in New York.

20	08	1883	Wilde at production of *Vera* (Union Square Theatre, New York).
24	09	1883	Wilde begins lecture tour in England, lasting on and off all year.
11	10	1883	Wilde among those who see Irving and Ellen Terry off to the U.S.A. on the *Britannic* for their first American tour.
	11	1883	Wilde's last visit to Ireland. Stays in Dublin at the Shelbourne.
20	11	1883	Wilde gives a lecture on poetry in Dublin.
22	11	1883	Wilde lectures on "The House Beautiful" and "Personal Impressions of America" in Dublin.
26	11	1883	Wilde and Constance become engaged.
10	12	1883	Wilde lectures at the Claughton Music Hall, Birkenhead; Richard Le Gallienne in the audience.
23	12	1883	Whistler gives a breakfast party for Wilde and Constance; Lord and Lady Garmoyle present. Joyce Bentley dates this to 1884.
		1884	Publication of Lady Wilde's *Driftwood from Scandinavia*.
04 ?	03	1884	Wilde lectures on "The House Beautiful," Bijou Theatre, St. Leonard's.
29	05	1884	WEDDING OF OSCAR WILDE AND CONSTANCE LLOYD at St. James's, Sussex Gardens, London.
29	05	1884	The Wildes honeymoon at the Hôtel Wagram, rue de Rivoli, and in Dieppe [to 24 June].
04	06	1884	Wilde and Constance give a dinner party.
09	06	1884	Wilde gives an interview to the *Morning News* in which he discusses Sarah Bernhardt's *Macbeth*.
24	06	1884	The Wildes return from honeymoon.
25	06	1884	Wilde and Constance go to the theatre with Mme Gabrielli.
19	07	1884	Wilde and Constance at first night of *Twelfth Night* (Irving, Ellen Terry, Rose Leclercq).
14	10	1884	Publication of Wilde's "Woman's Dress" in the *Pall Mall Gazette*.
	11 ?	1884	Wilde and Constance visit Oscar Browning in Cambridge.
	01	1885	Morris meets Wilde at the Richmonds.
01	01	1885	The Wildes move to 16 Tite Street, Chelsea.

08	01	1885	Wilde probably present at Sidney Webb's lecture, Kelmscott House, on "The Irish National Movement and Its Bearing on Socialism."
20	02	1885	Wilde attends Whistler's Ten O'Clock Lecture at Prince's Hall.
21	02	1885	Publication of Wilde's "Mr Whistler's Ten O'Clock" in the *Pall Mall Gazette*.
28	02	1885	Publication of Wilde's "The Relation of Dress to Art" in the *Pall Mall Gazette*.
07	03	1885	Publication of Wilde's "Dinners and Dishes" in the *Pall Mall Gazette*.
14	03	1885	Publication of Wilde's "Shakespeare on Scenery" in *The Dramatic Review*.
15	03	1885	Adrian Hope lunches with the Wildes.
	05	1885	The Wildes at a party of Sir Morell Mackenzie.
09	05	1885	Publication of Wilde's "Hamlet at the Lyceum" in *The Dramatic Review*.
23	05	1885	Publication of Wilde's "Henry IV at Oxford" in *The Dramatic Review*.
	06	1885	Publication of Wilde's poem "Roses and Rue" in *Society*.
05	06	1885	Birth of Cyril Wilde.
18	11	1885	Publication of Wilde's "A Handbook to Marriage" in the *Pall Mall Gazette*.
16	12	1885	Publication of Wilde's "Aristotle at Afternoon Tea" in the *Pall Mall Gazette*.
		1886	Wilde meets Robert Ross.
	03	1886	Wilde and Constance dine with Mr. and Mrs. Charles Hancock.
28	04	1886	Wilde and Constance at a political conversazione at the Hancocks'.
	05	1886	Publication of Wilde's review "A Fire at Sea (from the French of Ivan Tougenieff)," *Macmillan's Magazine*.
	07	1886	Publication of Wilde's "Keats's 'Sonnet on Blue'" in the *Century Guild Hobby Horse*.
13	09	1886	Publication of Wilde's "Balzac in English" in the *Pall Mall Gazette*.
14	09	1886	Wilde meets Bernard Shaw at J.F. Molloy's house, Red Lion Square, London.

20	09	1886	Publication of Wilde's "Ben Jonson" in the *Pall Mall Gazette.*
03	11	1886	Birth of Vyvyan Oscar Beresford Wilde.
18	11	1886	Publication of Wilde's "A 'Jolly' Art Critic" in the *Pall Mall Gazette.*
24	11	1886	Wilde lectures on Chatterton at Birkbeck College, London.
		1887	Sometime this year Wilde lunches with the Frank Harrises, at 34 Park Lane, with Sidney Low, Arthur Bourchier, Charles Wyndham, Mary Moore and others.
23	03	1887	Publication of Wilde's "The American Invasion" in *Court & Society Review.*
28	03	1887	Publication of Wilde's "Great Writers by Little Men" in the *Pall Mall Gazette.*
13	04	1887	Wilde proposes meeting Alsagar Vian for dinner at Pagani's the following Friday.
18	04	1887	Publication of Wilde's "A Cheap Edition of a Great Man" in the *Pall Mall Gazette.*
02	05	1887	Publication of Wilde's "Injury & Insult" in the *Pall Mall Gazette.*
18	05	1887	Wilde begins editorship of *Woman's World.*
30	05	1887	Publication of Wilde's "From the Poets' Corner" in the *Pall Mall Gazette.*
11	06	1887	Publication of Wilde's "Mr Pater's Imaginary Portraits" in the *Pall Mall Gazette.*
13	07	1887	Wilde and Constance give a party at Tite Street.
17	07	1887	Wilde elected a Fellow of the Society of Authors.
23	07	1887	Wilde and Constance at the Irving benefit, Lyceum Theatre.
27	09	1887	Publication of Wilde's "Two Biographies of Keats" in the *Pall Mall Gazette.*
14	11	1887	Wilde attends magistrate's court hearing of Cunninghame Graham and John Burns, arrested on Bloody Sunday. Haldane, Asquith and Mrs. Pankhurst also present.
	12	1887	Gissing attends a lecture on art by Wilde.
		1888	Wilde at garden party given by Lady Archie Campbell.

		1888	Constance Wilde acts in John Todhunter's *Helena in Troas*.
		1888	Wilde attends the inaugural meeting of the British Association for the Advancement of Art in Relation to Industry at Grosvenor House.
20	01	1888	Publication of Wilde's "From the Poets' Corner" in the *Pall Mall Gazette*.
15	02	1888	Publication of Wilde's "From the Poets' Corner" in the *Pall Mall Gazette*.
	03	1888	Wilde lectures on Chatterton.
	04	1888	Wilde visited at *Woman's World* offices by Edith Somerville.
09	06	1888	Theatrical Dinner at the Garrick Club – possible attendance by Wilde?
14	07	1888	Mr. Gladstone writes to Wilde.
21	07	1888	Death of Mary Atkinson, née Hemphill, grandmother of Constance Wilde.
25	07	1888	Wilde at the Society of Authors' Dinner for visiting American writers, Criterion Restaurant. He sits next to Lady Colin Campbell, and this was not a successful placement.
25	07	1888	Yeats visits Lady Wilde for the first time.
	09	1888	Yeats meets Wilde at the house of W.E. Henley.
	10	1888	Wilde proposed but not accepted for the Savile Club.
	11	1888	Ill-mannered exchange between Whistler and Wilde in *The World*.
01	11	1888	Mr. Gladstone writes to Wilde.
06	11	1888	Wilde lectures at the Somerville Club for the Rational Dress Society.
08	12	1888	Publication of Wilde's "English Poetesses" in *Queen*.
11	12	1888	Publication of Wilde's "Sir Edwin Arnold's Last Volume" in the *Pall Mall Gazette*.
25	12	1888	Yeats keeps Christmas with the Wildes.
		1889	Wilde pays a brief visit to Kreuznach.
		1889	Wilde stays with the Tennants at Glen.
	01	1889	Wilde meets Lady Blanche Hozier.
	01	1889	Publication of Wilde's "London Models" in *The English Illustrated Magazine*.

	01	1889	Wilde and Constance at first night of *Macbeth* (Irving, Ellen Terry).
26	01	1889	Publication of Wilde's "The New President" in the *Pall Mall Gazette*.
	02	1889	Publication of Wilde's "Some Literary Notes" in *Woman's World* [Yeats].
03	02	1889	Dowson has suggested to Jean Thorel that he send Wilde a copy of *La Complainte Humaine*.
05	02	1889	Wilde present at Shaw's lecture to the Church & Stage Guild on "Acting, by one who does not believe in it."
	03	1889	Publication of Wilde's "Further Literary Notes" in *Woman's World*.
30	03	1889	Publication of Wilde's "The Birthday of the Infanta" as "The Birthday of the Little Princess" in French and English in *Paris Illustré*.
27 ?	05	1889	Wilde at a reception given by the Attorney-General, Sir Charles Russell QC (later Lord Russell of Killowen).
31	07	1889	Wilde at an Eighty Club reception.
	08	1889	Ricketts & Shannon publish *The Dial* and send a complimentary copy to Wilde.
27	09	1889	Wilde attends Wilkie Collins's funeral.
	10	1889	Wilde gives up the editorship of *Woman's World*.
	10	1889	Publication of Constance Wilde's *There Was Once*, a book for children.
16	11	1889	Yeats visits Lady Wilde.
	12	1889	Wilde attends the thought reading session of Dr. Onofroff.
	12	1889	Conversation between Yeats and Wilde.
17	12	1889	Wilde attends inaugural dinner for *The Speaker*, a new weekly.
19	12	1889	First night of Benson's "Midsummer Night's Dream," Wilde "a frequent visitor."
08	02	1890	Publication of Wilde's review of "Chuang Tzu: Mystic, Moralist and Social Reformer" in *The Speaker*.
12	03	1890	Publication of Wilde's "Mr Pater's Appreciations" in *The Speaker*.

24	05	1890	Lady Wilde awarded a civil list pension of £70/-/- a year.
20	06	1890	Publication of Wilde's *The Picture of Dorian Gray* in *Lippincott's Magazine*.
	07	1890	Wilde calls at the *Gazette* offices and protests to Jeyes about his review.
	07	1890	Wilde calls at the Whitefriars Club and has long talk about *Dorian Gray* with Sidney Low.
08	07	1890	Society of Authors Annual Dinner, Criterion Restaurant: Wilde present.
21	07	1890	Wilde at an "At Home" of Mrs. Chandler Moulton; Michael Field and George Moore also present.
		1891	Publication of Lady Wilde's "Notes on 'Men, Women and Books.'"
		1891	Wilde visits Rothenstein at his studio in the rue Fontaine with its bookshelf containing *The Picture of Dorian Gray, Intentions, Marius the Epicurean*, Huysmans's *Là-Bas* and Barbey d'Aurevilly's "Du dandyisme."
	01	1891	Wilde meets Lord Alfred Douglas for the first time.
	01	1891	Rhymers' Poetry reading at Herbert Horne's. Wilde there with John Gray.
	01	1891	Sherard sees "much" of Wilde in London.
02	02	1891	Wilde at a party of Herbert Horne's.
early	02	1891	Wilde at a meeting of the Rhymers' Club at 20 Fitzroy Street (Herbert Horne's).
24	02	1891	Wilde's first meeting with Mallarmé.
24	02	1891	First visit by Wilde to a Mallarmé "Mardi."
03	03	1891	Wilde visits Mallarmé.
11	03	1891	Wilde in Paris to meet Zola.
	04	1891	Publication of Wilde's *The Picture of Dorian Gray* in book form.
24	04	1891	Wilde sees "Hedda Gabler" at the Vaudeville Theatre, 2.30.
10	05	1891	Wilde, Constance Wilde and Edward and Georgiana Burne-Jones dine with the Ranee of Sarawak.
04	07	1891	Wilde at the Crabbet Club.
05	07	1891	Wilde at the Crabbet Club.

09	10	1891	Wilde at first night of Zola's *Thérèse Raquin* at the Royalty Theatre.
16	10	1891	Wilde lunches with William Heinemann.
27	10	1891	Wilde breakfasts with Wilfrid Blunt, George Curzon and Willy Peel in Paris.
	11	1891	Wilde in Paris (19 bvd des Capucines), writing Salomé.
	11	1891	Wilde visits Lord Lytton several times at the British Embassy.
02	11	1891	Wilde lunches at the British Embassy.
03	11	1891	Visit by Wilde to a Mallarmé "Mardi."
26	11	1891	First meeting of Wilde and Gide?
28	11	1891	Second meeting of Wilde and Gide chez Hérédia.
29	11	1891	Third meeting of Wilde and Gide.
29	11	1891	First meeting between Wilde and Pierre Loüys. Third meeting of Wilde and Gide.
30	11	1891	Fourth meeting of Wilde and Gide.
02	12	1891	Fifth meeting of Wilde and Gide. Dinner at Stuart Merrill's.
03	12	1891	Sixth meeting of Wilde and Gide. Dinner at Aristide Bruant's with Marcel Schwob.
06	12	1891	Seventh meeting of Wilde and Gide chez Princess Ouroussof.
07	12	1891	Eighth meeting of Wilde and Gide. Dinner at Marcel Schwob's.
08	12	1891	Ninth meeting of Wilde and Gide. Dinner at Aristide Bruant's.
11	12	1891	Tenth meeting of Wilde and Gide.
12	12	1891	Eleventh meeting of Wilde and Gide.
13	12	1891	Twelfth meeting of Wilde and Gide chez Princess Ouroussof, with Henri Régnier.
15	12	1891	Thirteenth meeting of Wilde and Gide plus Marcel Schwob.
17	12	1891	Wilde writes to Margot Asquith, saying he had dedicated "The Star Child" to her.
17	12	1891	Wilde, Mendès, Goncourt, Swinburne.
17	12	1891	Article on Wilde by Sherard (with contributions by Wilde!) appears in *Le Gaulois*.
		1892	Publication of Constance Wilde's *A Long Time Ago*, a book for children.

		1892	"Melmoth the Wanderer" reprinted with a biographical introduction acknowledging the help of Speranza and Oscar Wilde.
		1892	Wilde invited to a house party at Wilton, but the party is canceled.
	02	1892	Wilde chairs a public meeting.
07	02	1892	Wilde chairs a meeting of the Playgoers' Club.
19	02	1892	Wilde meets Graham Robertson.
20	02	1892	Wilde offends with Edward Shelley.
21	02	1892	Wilde calls on Coulson Kernahan, a.m. (possibly the 22nd).
24	02	1892	Wilde goes to dinner party at Philip Currie's.
04	03	1892	Wilde at first night of the triple bill *Le Baiser* (Banville, tr. John Gray), *A Visit* (Brandes), *A Modern Idyll* (adapted by Arthur Symons from the novel by Frank Harris).
07	04	1892	Wilde lunches at a Paris restaurant.
	05	1892	Wilde meets Richard Le Gallienne in Piccadilly, day after Osgood's death.
17	05	1892	Wilde has tea with Elizabeth Robins.
19	05	1892	First night of Brookfield's satire on Wilde, *The Poet & the Puppets*, at the Comedy Theatre. It runs for 40 performances.
20	05	1892	Wilde moves back to his mother's house.
26	05	1892	Wilde speaks at meeting of the Royal General Theatrical Fund.
31	05	1892	Society of Authors Annual Dinner, Holborn Restaurant: Wilde present.
30	06	1892	Wilde at the Lyric Club with George Ives.
03	07	1892	Wilde takes the cure at Homburg, staying at 51 Kaiser-Friedrich Promenade.
31	07	1892	Last night of Brookfield's satire on Wilde, *The Poet & the Puppets*, Comedy Theatre.
	08	1892	Wilde writes *A Woman of No Importance* at Grove Farm, Felbrigg, near Cromer, Norfolk [to September].
	09	1892	Wilde at a house party given by Mrs. Walter Palmer.
	11	1892	The Wildes rent Babbacombe Cliff, near Torquay.

18	11	1892	Wilde first offends with Frederick Atkins in Paris.
		1893	Publication of Lady Wilde's Notes on "Social Studies."
		1893	Death of Constance Wilde's Aunt Caroline, who leaves Constance £5,500.
		1893	Rothenstein visits Wilde in Tite Street; meets Wilde at a party "where Meredith was lion of honour"; and is introduced by Wilde to Ricketts and Shannon at the Vale, where he also meets Roger Fry, Walter Sickert and R.C. Trevelyan.
	02	1893	Wilde at a dinner party chez George Louis.
	02	1893	Wilde meets Debussy.
23	02	1893	Wilde sends Shaw a copy of *Salomé*.
05	03	1893	The Wildes leave Babbacombe.
13	03	1893	First night of *The Notorious Mrs Ebbsmith*. Alfred Taylor introduces Wilde to the Parkers. Wilde offends with Charles Parker at the Savoy Hotel.
2 ?	03	1893	Dowson sends Wilde a copy of *The Pierrot of the Minute*.
03	04	1893	First night of Brookfield's satire on Wilde *The Poet & the Puppets* at the Garden Theatre, New York.
20	04	1893	Wilde dines at the Albemarle Club with Lord Alfred Douglas, Max Beerbohm and Herbert Tree.
	05	1893	Wilde in Oxford.
14	05	1893	Wilde dines in Oxford with Max Beerbohm, Lord Encombe, Lord Basil Blackwood, Lord Kerry, Denis Browne and Lord Alfred Douglas.
25	05	1893	Wilde and Pierre Loüys quarrel.
	06	1893	Wilde at The Cottage, Goring-on-Thames.
02	06	1893	Society of Authors Dinner: Wilde present.
16	08	1893	Wilde at last night of *A Woman of No Importance*.
20	09	1893	First night of Henry Arthur Jones's *The Tempter*, but Wilde at the Alhambra with Lord Alfred Douglas "dancing attendance on Zola's attendants."
	10	1893	Wilde takes rooms at 10 and 11 St. James's Place and writes *An Ideal Husband*.
15	10	1893	Wilde dines at the Savoy with George Ives and (perhaps) Raffalovich and Sir Egbert Sebright.

19	10	1893	Wilde and Lord Alfred Douglas are guests of George Ives.
	12	1893	Wilde and Queensberry meet at the Café Royal.
13	12	1893	Wilde and Lord Alfred Douglas dine with George Ives at the Albemarle Club.
23	12	1893	Wilde dines with George Ives at the New Travellers Club.
		1893	Publication of a new edition of Lady Wilde's *Sidonia the Sorceress* by Reeves and Turner.
13	01	1894	Constance Wilde opens a fancy bazaar for the Ferdinand Place Mission Schoolroom, Chalk Farm.
	04	1894	Wilde takes Vyvyan to see *Once upon a Time* at the Theatre Royal, Haymarket.
01	04	1894	Wilde and Douglas lunch at the Café Royal and are seen there by Queensberry. Queensberry writes threatening letter to Lord Alfred Douglas, provoking the response "What a very funny little man you are."
21	04	1894	Wilde at first night of Shaw's *The Arms and the Man*.
27	04	1894	Wilde in Paris at the Hôtel des Deux Mondes with Bosie.
28 c	04	1894	Wilde meets Marcel Proust.
	05	1894	Wilde in Florence with Douglas. Meets Mary Costello (Berenson) several times.
	05	1894	Vyvyan Wilde goes to Hildersham House School, Broadstairs.
	05	1894	Fourteenth meeting of Wilde and Gide in Florence.
06	05	1894	Wilde writes to Rothenstein from the Hôtel des Deux Mondes.
26	05	1894	Wilde taken by Mary Costello to have tea with Eugene Lee Hamilton and Vernon Lee.
26 c	05	1894	Wilde has tea with Walpurga Lady Paget in Florence.
02	06	1894	Goncourt discusses Wilde with Baronne Deslandes.
18	06	1894	Wilde at the wedding of Violet Maxse and Lord Edward Cecil.
17	07	1894	Wilde lunches at the Asquiths'.

27	07	1894	Meeting between Wilde and George Ives.
	08	1894	Wilde begins writing *The Importance of Being Earnest* at Worthing, and is joined by Lord Alfred Douglas.
	08	1894	Wilde writes the scenario for *Mr & Mrs Daventry* at Worthing.
07	08	1894	Wilde lunches at the Café Royal with Lord Alfred Douglas and Max Beerbohm.
	09	1894	Wilde finishes *The Importance of Being Earnest.*
	10	1894	Wilde at Brighton with Lord Alfred Douglas.
	12	1894	Publication of Wilde's "Phrases & Philosophies for the Use of the Young" in *The Chameleon.*
25	12	1894	Wilde attends rehearsal of *An Ideal Husband.*
	01	1895	Wilde and Carson meet in The Strand.
04	01	1895	Gilbert Burgess interviews Wilde for *The Sketch.*
17	01	1895	Wilde visits Algiers with Lord Alfred Douglas.
30	01	1895	Fifteenth meeting of Wilde and Gide, in Algiers.
31	01	1895	Wilde returns from Algiers.
28	02	1895	Wilde calls on Charles Ricketts and goes on to the Albemarle Club where he is handed Queensberry's card.
01	03	1895	Wilde obtains warrant for Queensberry's arrest.
07	03	1895	Wilde at *The Importance* with Lord Alfred Douglas and Constance; Constance returns alone to Tite Street.
13	03	1895	Wilde and Lord Alfred Douglas go to Monte Carlo for a week.
25	03	1895	Wilde visits the fortune teller Mrs. Robinson.
01	04	1895	Wilde at *The Importance* with Lord Alfred Douglas and Constance, after dining together.
01	04	1895	The Café Royal meeting between Wilde, Douglas, Frank Harris and Shaw.
05	04	1895	Acquittal of Queensberry; Wilde consults Sir George Lewis; Wilde and Douglas lunch at the Holborn Viaduct Hotel, where George Wyndham tries unsuccessfully to see them; then go to the Cadogan Hotel, stopping en route at a bank where Wilde draws "a considerable sum of money."
05	04	1895	Wilde arrested at the Cadogan Hotel.

06	04	1895	Wilde charged at Bow Street and refused bail; imprisoned at Holloway [till 26 April].
14	04	1895	News of Wilde's plight discussed in Paris.
16	04	1895	Wilde writes to Sherard from Holloway.
24	04	1895	Lord Alfred Douglas goes abroad, not returning until November 1898.
24	04	1895	Selling up of Wilde's possessions at Tite Street.
26	04	1895	Wilde's first trial opens before Mr. Justice Charles.
	05	1895	The Wildes move to Nervi, near Margaret Brooke, Ranee of Sarawak.
04	05	1895	Frank Harris visits Wilde in Holloway.
07	05	1895	Wilde released on bail of £5,000.
08	05	1895	Wilde moves into his mother's house where he is visited by R.H. Sherard and Ernest Dowson.
(between) 08–19	05	1895	Wilde meets Robert Cunninghame Graham in Rotten Row.
(between) 08–19	05	1895	Wilde moves to the Leversons' house in Courtfield Gardens.
15	05	1895	Toulouse-Lautrec's drawing of Wilde appears in the *Revue Blanche*.
22	05	1895	Wilde's second trial opens before Mr. Justice Wills (Sir Alfred Wills). Lord Queensberry and Lord Percy of Hawick bound over to keep the peace.
25	05	1895	Wilde sentenced to two years' hard labor and imprisoned at Pentonville. Announcement of a knighthood for Henry Irving.
28	05	1895	Daudet brings to Paris news of Wilde from Sherard.
	06	1895	The Wildes move to Bevais, nr Neuchâtel and stay with Otho Lloyd. Here they change their names to Holland.
05	06	1895	Article in the *Daily Chronicle* suggesting Wilde is suffering a mental breakdown. This is read by Asquith who orders an investigation.
12	06	1895	Wilde visited by Haldane in Pentonville (miscalled Holloway in Haldane's *Autobiography*).

21	06	1895	Queensberry petitions for Wilde's bankruptcy.
04	07	1895	Wilde is transferred to Wandsworth.
06	07	1895	Mirbeau compares Wilde and Huysmans.
11	07	1895	Birth of Dorothy Ierne Wilde.
26	08	1895	Sherard visits Wilde in Wandsworth.
	09	1895	The Wildes move to Sori, nr Bogliasco.
21	09	1895	Constance visits Wilde in Wandsworth.
24	09	1895	Wilde's first examination in bankruptcy.
12	11	1895	Wilde's second examination in bankruptcy.
20	11	1895	Wilde transferred to Reading Gaol. The Clapham Junction incident.
03	02	1896	Death of Lady Wilde.
12	02	1896	Constance visits Wilde.
10	05	1896	Ricketts visits Wilde.
13	06	1896	Frank Harris visits Wilde in Reading Gaol.
02	07	1896	Wilde's petition for clemency forwarded to the Home Secretary.
10	07	1896	Report of the visiting medical commission on Wilde.
15	07	1896	Sir Eveleyn Ruggles-Brise suggests a new medical inquiry into Wilde's health should be undertaken.
21	11	1896	Alleged visit by Frank Harris to Wilde in Reading Gaol.
	01	1897	Wilde begins *De Profundis*.
	01	1897	Wilde is allowed to let his hair grow.
28	01	1897	More Adey visits Wilde in Reading Gaol.
	03	1897	Wilde finishes *De Profundis*.
17	04	1897	Frank Harris visits Wilde in Reading Gaol.
15	05	1897	Charles Ricketts, Robert Ross and More Adey visit Wilde.
18	05	1897	Wilde transferred to Pentonville.
19	05	1897	Wilde is released and goes to Stewart Headlam's house, 31 Upper Bedford Place, Bloomsbury, where he is visited by Ada Leverson.
19	05	1897	Wilde sails from Newhaven by the night boat, the *Tamise* Publication of *Dracula*.
20	05	1897	04.30. Wilde lands at Dieppe and stays at the Hôtel Sandwich.

26	05	1897	Wilde moves from Dieppe to the Hôtel de la Plage, Berneval-sur-Mer.
27	05	1897	Wilde is visited by Lugné-Poë.
	06	1897	Charles Wyndham visits Wilde at Berneval in the hope of persuading him to adapt Eugène Sue's play *Le Verre d'Eau*. Wilde turns the idea down in September.
16	06	1897	Wilde and Dowson together.
17	06	1897	Wilde and Dowson together.
20	06	1897	Sixteenth meeting of Wilde and Gide, in Berneval. Weather terrible.
20	06	1897	Wilde lunches with the Thaulows.
21	06	1897	Publication of Wilde's first letter to the *Daily Chronicle*.
	07	1897	Whistler visits Dieppe and is seen passing by, but does not see, Wilde.
24	07	1897	Wilde and Beardsley meet.
28	08	1897	Or perhaps 29th. Wilde gives a children's party at Berneval.
	09	1897	Wilde interviewed in Dieppe by Gideon Spilett for *Gil Blas*.
	09	1897	Wilde has suggested that Dowson should translate Loüys' *Aphrodite*.
04	09	1897	Wilde spends a week with Lord Alfred Douglas in Rouen (till the 11th); Douglas is staying at the Hôtel de la Poste.
15	09	1897	Wilde in Rouen.
20	09	1897	Wilde leaves Dieppe for Paris, staying in a hotel in the rue de Helder.
25 c	09	1897	Wilde arrives at Naples and stays with Douglas at the Hôtel Royal des Etrangers.
27	09	1897	Wilde stays at the Villa Giudice, Posillipo [37 via Posillipo].
15	10	1897	Wilde visits Capri with Lord Alfred Douglas.
18	10	1897	Wilde leaves Capri.
06	11	1897	The Academy prints a list of 40 possible members of a British Academy of Letters. Shaw and H.G. Wells suggest Wilde (13, 20 11 1897).
	12	1897	Wilde visits Sicily with Lord Alfred Douglas.
	12	1897	Wilde meets J. Joseph Renaud at lunch.

	01	1898	Wilde moves to 31 Santa Lucia, Naples.
13 ?	02	1898	Wilde moves to Hôtel de Nice, rue des Beaux-Arts, Paris.
13	02	1898	Publication of "The Ballad of Reading Gaol"; Wilde sends inscribed copies to William Archer, R.B. Haldane, Ada Leverson.
09	03	1898	Wilde meets George Ives in Paris.
13	03	1898	Wilde meets Carlos Blacker in Paris.
16	03	1898	Publication of Wilde's second letter to the *Daily Chronicle.*
27 ?	03	1898	Wilde moves to the Hôtel d'Alsace, 13 rue des Beaux-Arts.
28	03	1898	Wilde has an accident in a fiacre and cuts his lip badly.
	04	1898	Wilde dines at Pousset's with Henry and Aline Harland.
07	04	1898	Death of Constance Wilde in Genoa.
13	04	1898	Carlos Blacker visits Wilde, Ross also there.
14	04	1898	Wilde introduces Davray to Frank Harris at Foyot's.
	05	1898	Wilde meets and dines with Diaghilev.
26 ?	05	1898	Wilde goes to the Salon with Lord Alfred Douglas and Maurice Gilbert; then meets Sherard in Campbell's Bar and goes on to dine with the Vicomte d'Humières.
	06	1898	Wilde at Nogent-sur-Marne till July with Lord Alfred Douglas, who goes to Paris every day.
07	06	1898	Carlos Blacker visits Wilde at Nogent-sur-Marne.
	07	1898	Wilde leaves Nogent-sur-Marne.
05	07	1898	Wilfred Chesson calls on Wilde at Nogent.
	08	1898	Wilde at Chennevières-sur-Marne.
	11	1898	Frank Harris in Paris and gives Wilde dinner at Durand's.
	12	1898	Laurence Housman sends Wilde "All-Fellows."
	12	1898	A.E. Housman sends Wilde "A Shropshire Lad."
15	12	1898	Wilde leaves for La Napoule, near Cannes.
	02	1899	Publication of *The Importance of Being Earnest.* Wilde sends inscribed copy to William Archer.
	02	1899	Wilde visits Constance's grave.
	02	1899	Wilde leaves La Napoule for Nice.

25	02	1899	Wilde leaves Nice for Gland, just outside Geneva, to stay with Harold Mellor.
	04	1899	Wilde returns to Paris, Hôtel de la Neva, till May.
01	04	1899	Wilde leaves Gland for Santa Margherita.
13	04	1899	Death of Willie Wilde.
	05	1899	Wilde moves to the Hôtel Marsollier.
	05	1899	Wilde at Marlotte, near Fontainebleau.
	06	1899	Wilde dines with Stuart Merrill, meets André Hérold.
02 c	06	1899	Wilde meets Ada Rehan and Mr. & Mrs. Augustin Daly in a Paris restaurant.
11	06	1899	Wilde meets Ernest Dowson.
23	06	1899	Wilde at Trouville and Le Havre.
26	06	1899	Wilde leaves Trouville and Le Havre.
	07	1899	Wilde at Chennevières-sur-Marne.
	08	1899	Wilde moves back to the Hôtel d'Alsace.
	09	1899	Wilde meets Laurence Housman with Robbie Ross and Davray.
26	12	1899	Conversation between Yeats and Wilde.
02	04	1900	Wilde visits Palermo.
10	04	1900	Wilde leaves Palermo.
12	04	1900	Wilde in Rome [till 15 May].
15 ?	04	1900	Wilde leaves Rome.
	05	1900	Wilde spends ten days in Gland.
	07	1900	Wilde visits the Rodin Pavilion at the Exposition Universelle.
09 ?	08	1900	Wilde and Lord Alfred Douglas dine at the Grand Café.
08	09	1900	George Ives sends Wilde £5/-/-.
10	10	1900	Wilde's operation.
17	10	1900	Robert Ross arrives in Paris and visits Wilde.
20	10	1900	Wedding of Lily Wilde and Alexander Texeira de Mattos.
25	10	1900	First night of *Mr & Mrs Daventry*, Alec Ross and Lily Texeira de Mattos visit Wilde.
12	11	1900	Robert Ross visits Wilde at the Hotel d'Alsace. This is the last time he sees him alive.
28	11	1900	Carlos Blacker goes to Paris from Freiburg, but delays going to see Wilde.
30	11	1900	Death of Oscar Wilde.

03	12	1900	Wilde's funeral at Bagneux.
08	12	1900	Short piece on Wilde by Max Beerbohm in *The Saturday Review*.
		1902	Publication of *Oscar Wilde: The Story of an Unhappy Friendship* by R.H. Sherard.
03	07	1903	Wilde's creditors paid 13/4d in the £.
09	09	1904	Stuart Mason finishes his translation of André Gide: *Oscar Wilde, A Study from the French*. Oxford: Holywell Press, 1905.
		1906	Publication of *The Life of Oscar Wilde* by R.H. Sherard.
12	01	1906	Charles Hemphill, great uncle of Constance Wilde, raised to the peerage.
12	01	1906	First performance of Wilde's *Florentine Tragedy* in Berlin, directed by Max Reinhardt.
28	05	1906	Wilde estate declared solvent after all debtors are paid at 20/- in the £ + 4%.
	05	1907	Wilde's *A Florentine Tragedy* produced at the Théâtre de l'Oeuvre.
06	08	1907	Vyvyan Wilde meets Robbie Ross for the first time.
20	07	1909	Re-interment of Oscar Wilde at Père Lachaise.

1900	Wilde's [illegible].
1901	[illegible] Wilde's [illegible] in the [illegible] Review.
1902	[illegible] Oscar Wilde [illegible] by R. H. Sherard.
1905	Wilde's [illegible] published.
1905	Stuart Mason publishes his translation of André Gide's Oscar Wilde: [illegible] from the French, Oxford: Holywell Press, 1905.
1906	Publication of The Life of Oscar Wilde by R. H. Sherard.
1906	[illegible] the great [illegible] paid to the creditors.
1906	First performance of Wilde's [illegible] in Berlin, directed by Max Reinhardt.
1906	Wilde's estate is declared solvent; all creditors are paid at 20s. in the £.
1907	Wilde's A Florentine Tragedy produced at the Théâtre de l'Œuvre.
1908	[illegible] Wilde's [illegible] for the first time.
1909	Re-interment of Oscar Wilde in Père Lachaise.

introduction

frederick s. roden

The centenary of Wilde's death (or martyrdom?) has since passed and we are now looking at the 150 years since his birth. New critical approaches and theoretical trends in the academy have shifted the points of emphasis – only to strongly encourage still other approaches. We could begin this volume stating that Wilde stands apart from other writers for any number of reasons – the contemporary relevance of changing *mores* and laws with respect to sexuality; the use of the writer as a test-case in developing practical criticism reflecting current interest in Irish studies, material culture, feminism, and so forth. But how does that make Wilde any different from a whole array of authors whose lives and works have been re-evaluated in terms of changing strategies put forward by the guiding light of scholarly inquiry? *Why* does Wilde continue to offer the reader, the viewer, even the mystic such a suitable starting-point for that indescribable project of study?

Oscar Wilde challenges us to be more of our selves. As he writes in *The Soul of Man Under Socialism*, it is the realization of the self that serves as the true fulfillment of life's aim – and, in fact, art's aim as well. Wilde wakes us up. His works make us laugh; his poignant *vita* – however much mythologized for a range of social purposes, from gay liberation to Irish nationalism – provides us with high drama for self-identification. If *De Profundis* is Wilde's own *imitatio Christi* – a self-stylization by an artist of his martyrdom – it is also a work that invites the reader to experience death and potential resurrection for her- or himself.

I will make no apologies here for suggesting such a moral Wilde. Wilde serves as teacher to us. Perhaps no other writer offers such a literary and biographical example of Pater's call, in *The Renaissance*, to live in the moment, for the moment, and by the moment. At the same time, when we tease out the more than 100 years of construction of Wilde's life as we know it – through his works and their reception and criticism, and the many improvisations on the author – it is clear that we have the burden of trying to explain and understand a writer – for the nineteenth, twentieth, and now twenty-first centuries. *Who is Oscar Wilde?* Where can we find him – in the midst of his *opera* of posing, his hagiography by biographers, and his reduction by critics? Perhaps it is impossible, unfair, or irrelevant to ask the real Oscar Wilde to stand up. It may be that we can and should be content with his resonances, which continue to inspire new works of art, further scholarly inquiries, and, one assumes, many more new readers to re-think their lives.

This introduction is intended neither to be sentimental nor to further immortalize the writer and his works. It does, however, seek to depict the real fascination with Wilde that has been pervasive in our culture for the past 100 years. Contrary to some critical assertions, Wilde and his works really never fell out of favor or interest. Given the degree of scholarly and artistic productivity that the name *Oscar Wilde* has induced in the century since his death, it is clear that we simply cannot get away from this author. As the contributors to this volume will demonstrate, there are many reasons for the Wilde phenomenon. Nearly every chapter makes at least a brief mention of Wilde in popular culture. It is unnecessary and would in fact be redundant to provide a separate study of that approach to the writer. To chronicle books, plays, productions, films – throughout the twentieth century – might fail to capture the differing motives that provoked each of these individual creative works. At the same time, it is the aim of each chapter in this book to give some context for the variety of practical criticism that Wilde studies has engendered – and, by extension, to thus offer some commentary on the vast array of popular works that these approaches have inflected.

Wilde's breadth invites such a variety of critical forms. In editing this volume, I have argued that the author is ideally suited to produce an inquiry into the range of theoretical paradigms that populate the current academy. I do not argue that Wilde provides a model for our contemporary performance theory, or for postmodern notions of identity, or for gay liberationist politics, or whatever claim one might want to make. I will assert, though, that the Wildean *opera* and *vita* provide an abundance of modes for literary criticism. Each contributor to this volume has endeavored to produce, through analysis of Wildean criticism, some new reflections on the critical *modus operandi* itself. That is to say, for example: what does materialist criticism on Wilde teach us and tell us about the project of materialist criticism itself? This volume seeks to do more than simply provide a "state of the field" with respect to a diverse collection of contemporary critical approaches to Wilde. Our aim is to provide the reader with some reconsiderations of theoretical modes and operations themselves. We argue that Wilde is an ideal writer to employ for proceeding with such a project, engaging both theory and praxis.

This book is organized into discrete chapters that can be read individually; but of course the arguments also speak to one another. Joseph Bristow opens the discussion by looking into the Wildean biography and biographical approaches to Wilde, as well as other writers. This template should serve as a window into how we might proceed here provoking the reader to consider the place of the critic in the process of praxis as it has evolved since observers first began commenting on the public Wilde in the 1880s. Bristow's chapter is followed by an analysis of the writer's world offered by Anne Margaret Daniel. Daniel's chapter provides a matrix for the intertextual Wilde – as well as a context for reading and re-reading the author whose words so often seem to plagiarize themselves, not to mention others. Francesca Coppa's chapter on performance theory defines that contemporary critical approach, within which she locates Wilde as an ideal writer and performer for the project of such inquiry.

These chapters lead to a section on Wilde's thought, as understood in terms of Aestheticism, material culture, philosophy, and religion. Allison Pease documents the crucial place the author holds in the history of Aestheticism. Dennis Denisoff's chapter on the material Wilde complements Pease's arguments by offering further contextualization of commodity culture in the understanding of the author. Philip Smith goes deeper into the intellectual life and education of Wilde, as understood with respect to his philosophical thought. Smith evaluates how that area of study has been constructed. Patrick O'Malley provides a state-of-the-field analysis of religion in Wilde studies, demonstrating how this area has evolved, while also giving insight into the author's theological contexts.

The final section of this book brings us to the most familiar aspects of the popular Wilde: interrogating him with respect to sexuality, gender, and Irishness. Richard Kaye's chapter on gay studies and queer theory demonstrates the range of different approaches to questions of sexuality in the author. Kaye chronicles and critiques the Wilde homosexual phenomenon in the century since his death. Margaret Stetz's chapter complements Kaye's analysis by querying feminist responses to and readings of the author. Noreen Doody closes the volume with a thorough evaluation of the history of Irish studies approaches to Wilde and suggests the place of postcolonial theory in that project.

D.C. Rose, editor of *The Oscholars*, an online journal of Wilde studies, provides a rich chronology of Wilde's life. In the selected bibliography to this volume, perhaps the most important items listed are the reference works. It is clear that the grand size of contemporary Wilde studies prohibits an exhaustive evaluation in a volume of this type. The bibliography is the most important part of this guidebook because it acknowledges our debt, as we re-read the Wilde phenomenon, to so many scholars who have created and enriched this field.

Each reader and critic of Wilde may offer a different reason why s/he is drawn to the life and works of the writer. It is my hope that this volume, however much it amply provokes us to re-think theory and practice in Wilde studies and beyond, may also pointedly engage the reader to interrogate the passion for this author. Without that fire – Pater's gem-like flame – there would be no justification for this book nor works or critics to cite in it.

It is worth offering a bit of advice on how to read this book. If one goes straight through, the reader will find that certain works – by Wilde and others – recur in different chapters. I have chosen to let these arguments speak for themselves and to one another without commentary. I find their treatments to be complementary rather than mutually exclusive. As editor, I have cross-referenced arguments where appropriate. I draw the reader's attention to the fact that several contributors respond to Ian Small's question about how different approaches to Wilde might co-exist. It is the goal of this volume to demonstrate examples of various modes of practical criticism and assorted methodological orientations, which I believe to be illustrative of the rich *copia* found in Wilde studies today. Writers have taken a range of approaches to their topics. Some, such as Pease, Coppa, and Denisoff, have thoroughly interrogated the critical apparatus behind their theoretical frame. In their chapters, readers will find guides for practical criticism and histories. Others, such as Kaye, provide the reader with an abundance of resources for thinking about Wilde in relation to the chapter topic. Still others, especially Doody, offer rich literature reviews of work in an area. Certain fields are quite new – such as O'Malley's interrogation of queerness and religion – while other applications, including Bristow's iconoclastic approach to Wilde's biography, provide a glimpse into how we might re-gild the lily. Smith's take on philosophical subjects speaks to Pease's and Denisoff's; Kaye and Bristow use the Wildean biography much differently. Both Stetz and Daniel locate Wildean texts within a particular literary tradition that enters the twentieth century. In short, this book offers many different ways of looking at the Wilde *opera* and *vita*. Readers are encouraged to peruse at their leisure and risk. Unlike *Dorian Gray*, this is not a dangerous book – except in the good way.

One note about texts: unless otherwise indicated, the *Collins Centenary* complete works of Wilde and the Hart-Davis/Holland letters are the standards used.[1]

note

1. *Complete Works of Oscar Wilde*. Centenary Edition, ed. Merlin Holland. Glasgow: HarperCollins, 1999. Page numbers referred to parenthetically within the text. *The Complete Letters of Oscar Wilde*. Eds. Merlin Holland and Rupert Hart-Davis. London: Fourth Estate, 2000. Referred to in the Notes as *Complete Letters*.

1
biographies: oscar wilde – the man, the life, the legend[1]

Joseph Bristow

> I was so typical a child of my age that in my perversity, and for that perversity's sake, I turned the good things of my life to evil, and the evil things of my life to good.
>
> Oscar Wilde, *De Profundis* (732–733)[2]

I

By any account, Oscar Wilde experienced – one might say endured – a legendary life. Countless biographies, memoirs, and critical books have for more than a century sustained a good deal of mythmaking about his literary success and his scandalous sexuality. The legend continues to capture the imaginations of thousands of general readers, theatergoers, movie-buffs, university students, and college professors. Nowadays it would not be unfair to imagine that any reasonably educated person with an interest in the arts had heard some of the more absorbing stories about how and why Wilde commanded the attention of an adoring audience only to transmogrify into its most contemptible pariah. The considerable reputation that Wilde earned through his four witty Society Comedies, abruptly followed by the ignominy he suffered through three badly orchestrated trials in 1895, has left a lasting impression on cultural memory. But these two closely connected events have been recorded in an unstable manner that continues to distort our understanding of a writer whose career proved uneven in its achievements, whose behavior suffered from marked inconsistencies, and whose legacy for many years remained subject to tireless wrangling among a colorful cast of disreputable enthusiasts and censorious onlookers.

Wilde's earliest biographers, whose publications began to roll off the presses from 1902 onward,[3] did much to fuel the public's mounting interest many years before his works would be taken with any measure of seriousness in academic institutions. Despite the fact that Wilde suffered such brutal humiliation after he was sentenced to two years' imprisonment for committing acts of "gross indecency" with other men, and regardless of the fact that he died in poverty from meningitis at the early age of 46, his name – even if it remained unmentionable in certain polite circles – hardly passed into obscurity at the turn of the twentieth century. To be sure, it was not just the accounts of his legendary life that kept his identity in the public eye. Although he published the earliest editions of "The Ballad of Reading Gaol" (1898) under the pseudonym of "C.3.3." (the number of his prison cell), this fine poem – the last substantial work he wrote – sold 7,000 copies in the 20 months leading up to his death, since countless readers wanted to read about his suffering. By 1901 his Society Comedies returned to the London stage, and they have remained part of repertory theatre ever since.[4] Yet, just as theatre audiences would continue to enlarge their appreciation for his dramas throughout the twentieth century, the concurrent fascination with his rise and fall during the 1890s reached astounding proportions by the 1980s and 1990s. By 1987 Richard Ellmann's *Oscar Wilde* would become one of the best-selling literary biographies of all time, amplifying the author's status as a household name. Ellmann's research – which counts as the leading, though not entirely reliable, biography to date – has formed the basis of numerous screenplays, dramas, and fictional works that correspondingly extend the almost limitless market for yet more depictions of a mesmerizing life led by a truly exceptional man. In addition, Ellmann's enthusiastic biography did much to lend academic respectability to an author whose works had not always been taken very seriously in departments of English literature. But such respectability came at a price. The more glaring errors in Ellmann's scholarship spurred some university professors into unsuspecting meditations on such topics as Wilde's apparent interest in cross-dressing in the guise of his protagonist Salomé.[5]

As the by-now somewhat infamous example of Ellmann's readable study reveals, Wilde's life has always proved to be an unusually perilous subject for critical interpretation because there has long remained the suspicion that the man's perversities knew no bounds. In the following discussion, I explore how and why some of the biographies of Wilde – which remain pitted with errors that are repeated from one untrustworthy source to another – have at times found it hard to believe that he was anything but larger than life. Admittedly, biography comprises a literary genre that tends to reflect the biases, investments, and perspectives of the biographer as much as those of the subject whose life is put under scrutiny. But in Wilde's case the problem of gaining a reasonably clear view of his personal and professional achievements has been persistently misconstrued, for reasons that require some explanation.

The earliest biographies of course went on sale in a culture that, officially at least, proved mainly inhospitable toward a literary man whose erotic predilections had been vilified more intensely than any other figure at the time. It is perhaps only to be predicted that a once-lauded writer who underwent such harsh public condemnation for homosexual behavior that was proscribed in law would excite a great deal of prurient attention, as well as embarrassment, for his supposed perversity. When he stood trial in the 1890s, a decade when sensationalizing journalism had become a staple part of everyday life on both sides of the Atlantic, a man who enjoyed success as a playwright unwittingly transformed into an icon around which a cluster of social fears and sexual fantasies would quickly circulate. Like most subjects of scandal, his homosexual criminality would magnetize many troubled – but nonetheless overexcited – thoughts about types of artistic masculinity whose erotic preference, cultural taste, and personal style presented challenges to a nation whose moralistic double standards and imperialist arrogance his incisive wit had never ceased to mock. Problematically, the newspapers' penchant for depicting Wilde negatively as a degenerate or exotic being would be compounded by several old or ex-friends who sought to throw at least some positive light upon his career. Robert Harborough Sherard and Frank Harris, to give two notable examples, counted among Wilde's pals who had their own motivations for spinning some suspect stories. Their erratic tale-telling, which led to some ugly squabbles and even legal clashes, was in part the result of their wish to produce an engaging read. Meanwhile, Alfred Douglas maintained idiosyncratic reasons for distorting or repressing the facts in the 1910s and beyond – for the simple reason that this Roman Catholic convert's former intimacy with such a stigmatized personage as Wilde threatened to contaminate him.[6]

To this day there is still some danger in our being misled by Sherard's and Harris' mythmaking (Ellmann feeds readers one or two disreputable tales from these sources, just as he advances unreliable views held by Wilde's literary executor Robert Ross),[7] and some of these taller stories have gone a long way to ensure that readers maintain a somewhat implausible image of a literary man who has at times been portrayed as a homosexual martyr, revolutionary thinker, and original genius. While I applaud the fact that Wilde now enjoys greater respect as a literary author than ever before, I have some reservations about the tendency in the various biographical spin-offs – as well as the growing bulk of academic scholarship on him – to distort what he accomplished and what he stood for. Surely, at this point in history, we need to ask why our culture has grown so deeply attached to Wilde the man, his life, and his legend. Why does there seem to be no limit to the immense quantity of scholarly and popular attention that his life and works receive? Why has the film industry managed to put on general release no less than three star-studded adaptations of Wilde's life and works in a matter of five years?[8] Why has Oxford University Press decided to launch a variorum edition of Wilde's complete works long after the *oeuvres* of most canonical writers have received such painstaking attention? Why do students these days need a guide such as the present one to help them navigate through a varied canon of work that seldom featured prominently on the curriculum before the 1970s? Why, in other words, have mass culture and higher education come to appreciate Wilde with ever-increasing amounts of zeal in recent years?

The answers to these various but not unrelated inquiries would seem to be pretty self-evident. Whether consumed in the classroom, on the screen, or on the stage, the multiplicity of writings either about or by Wilde helps to bolster the largely unchallenged reputation of an author whose career not only provides us with an inexhaustible source of entertainment but also reminds us of our welcome liberation from what we might imagine were the worst aspects of late-nineteenth-century moralism. In 1967, after all, the punitive 1885 law under which Wilde was tried would be partially repealed in England and Wales.[9] It therefore appears to make sense that Wilde's career makes sense to us, in so far as we are expected to take pleasure in reading, studying, and watching stories about him, particularly the ones that recall the terrible injustice done to his mind and body as he underwent solitary confinement with hard labor. If Wilde's sexuality no longer seems strangely perverse in our eyes, then all the more reason for us to feel free to delight in his deliciously irreverent wit – a wit that made some of his contemporaries writhe with displeasure. From Ellmann's perspective, "Wilde is one of us" – contemporary, unorthodox, inimitable, fun.[10]

Ellmann, for all the pitfalls of his expansive biography, captures the cheering spirit in which the 1980s and 1990s would embrace this figurehead of flamboyant aestheticism and insubordinate Decadence: a progenitor, it seems, of what we moderns have become, or what – perhaps more accurately – we have come to tolerate. "Oscar Wilde," Ellmann declares, "we have only to hear the great name to anticipate that what will be quoted as his will surprise and delight us."[11] "His wit," he adds decisively, "is an agent of renewal."[12] But while he records at length the innumerable legends, as well as the unsavory rumors, that sprang up around Wilde, Ellmann may well be weaving one or two tall stories of his own. It might seem a mite churlish to respond to Ellmann's research by stating that some (though by no means all) of Wilde's wittiest aphorisms were hardly original or innovative. A number of them were adaptations of well-timed pieces of dialogue in French drama or familiar phrases from Ouida's clever potboilers.[13] Likewise, it might seem tedious to point out, as some of Wilde's contemporaries did, that one of the funniest scenes in *The Importance of Being Earnest* (1895) was lifted from a far less distinguished comedy by W.S. Gilbert (the play is called *Engaged*, and it premiered in 1877).

Is Wilde's wit, then, really such a source of inventive renewal, in the sense that it regenerates, energizes, and springs afresh from the worst kinds of complacency that we sometimes attribute to his moralistic peers who sent him to jail? Is his apparent brilliance so deserving of the modern biographer's praise? To some of his more skeptical critics in the 1890s, Wilde's effervescent maxims sounded more like tiresome repetition than bold invention. Having witnessed the premiere of *An Ideal Husband*, the conservative Clement Scott – an influential critic who rarely hesitated to recoil in horror from the seeming outrages of London stage – immediately noticed not only the derivative nature of Wilde's borrowings but also the formulaic nature of his epigrams:

> The similarity between Mr. Oscar Wilde's *Ideal Husband* and Sardou's *Dora* is too marked not to be noticed . . . It is quite clear to me that the mere fact that Mr. Oscar Wilde's play suggests something else does not in the least interfere with its success – a success that is naturally increased by the author's method and trick of talk. In fact, Oscar Wilde is the fashion. His catch and whimsicality of dialogue tickle the public. Just now the whole of society is engaged in inventing Oscar Wildeisms, just as a few months ago they were employed in discovering the missing word in competitions. It is the easiest thing in the world. All you have to do is to form an obvious untruth into a false epigram.[14]

Scott of course was accurate in detecting the implicitly tacky source: Sardou's celebrity in England stemmed from the popularity of what were nicknamed "cup-and-saucer" melodramas that traded in scenes of predictable, though titillating, sexual intrigue.

Scott hardly remained alone is making such sharp criticisms. Where Scott diminished Wilde's wit to the level of tabloid crosswords and quizzes, A.B. Walkley – another well-informed but more open-minded critic of the stage – expressed some satisfaction that the "wilful paradoxes" that "pullalte[d]" in Wilde's plays were less numerous in *An Ideal Husband*.[15] "These inverted commonplaces," Walkley observed, "are Mr. Wilde's distinctive mark."[16] "I do not know," he continued, "if Mr. Wilde claims the credit – if credit is the right word – for the invention of this topsy-turvy process, but it is certain that he has been anticipated by M. Paul Bourget."[17] To prove his point, Walkley proceeds to quote a speech made by Casal in Bourget's *Physiologie de l'amour* (1890). Thus Walkley concludes that "what we in London have learnt to call Oscarisms may long ago have been known in France may be known as Casalisms."[18]

Does it matter that Wilde ransacked English and French literature for epigrams that continue to provoke much laughter in our own time? I scarcely think that we need to condemn him outright for such brazen appropriations of other writers' works. Even if current disputes about intellectual property can be traced to the heated debates about copyright that raged when Wilde rose to short-lived fame, it remains moot if his literary pilfering was a criminal act. Was he, as the American painter James Whistler took pains to point out, a downright plagiarist – one whom Whistler felt had stolen some of his most well-honed phrases?[19] Can his abundant appropriations be categorized as theft? At what point do we stop asserting Wilde's seemingly energizing originality whose achievements can look avant-garde and start picturing him as a derivative writer whose recycled phrases belong to a larger pattern of borrowed plots? Such questions, I think, barely lessen the value of his writings. Instead, they point in various ways to significant aspects of his methods of composition, his insubordinate perception of artistic ownership, and his means of emphasizing his affiliation with specific literary traditions.

In any case, Wilde had some characteristically clever responses to make to those interlocutors who laid accusations of plagiarism at his door. To the young Max Beerbohm, whose brother Herbert Beerbohm Tree directed *A Woman of No Importance* (1893), the tales he gleaned about Wilde's impenitent attitude made entertaining gossip. On 15 April 1893, Beerbohm joked with Reggie Turner about Wilde's unabashed interjection into a conversation that prompted the author to defend his tendency to filch other people's *bon mots*:

> Speaking of plagiarism the other day, Oscar said: "Of course I plagiarise. It is the privilege of the appreciative man. I never read [Gustave]

> Flaubert's *Tentation de St. Antoine* without signing my name at the end of it. *Que voulez-vous*? All the Best Hundred Books bear my signature in this manner."[20]

True to form, Wilde flatly refused to apologize for having pocketed someone else's verbiage. Rather than repudiate the charge, he embraced it. Manipulating hyperbole, he deftly reversed the terms upon which the allegation against him had been laid. Here he ingeniously revealed that as a discerning reader he signed all the books in his cabinet library. Who, after all, owns a book? Is it the author or the purchaser? In Wilde's view, the answer was both. Here he provocatively contended that his signature on the endpapers carried as much weight as the author's name on the title page. And, his overstatement aside, Wilde – in a sense – was perfectly right.

But Wilde's ingenuity, given his penchant for exaggeration, also reveals his tendency to distort – to the point of making almost unrecognizable – what was plainly wrong in the eyes of his contemporaries. His unwillingness to acknowledge his peers' best turns of phrase threatened to mar a reputation that proved far more precarious than either he or his most avid followers would like us to believe. The point is that Wilde's mocking wit is not always as unique as we might care to imagine. But, then, the growing tradition of biographical interest in Wilde has frequently preferred to maintain a somewhat unrealistic standpoint on how radical, subversive, and even transgressive he was supposed to have been. Such accounts remain by turns inaccurate, misrepresentative, if not somewhat slanted, not least by the liveliness of the kind of tittle-tattle that Beerbohm amusingly records.

Undoubtedly, we can readily find much in Wilde's career that reveals his welcome attacks on received wisdom, humbug, and hypocrisy, especially in those epigrams that were the product of his own hand. "Public opinion exists," he observed astutely, "only when there are no ideas" (1243). "Only the shallow know themselves," he contended, adroitly turning commonsense upside down (1244). But it can come as a blow to learn that Wilde betrayed the closest supporters of the imprisoned Alfred Dreyfus in one of the worst anti-Semitic scandals of the time.[21] In drawing attention toward Wilde's lack of sympathy toward the Dreyfus cause, I am neither pointing the finger of blame nor seeking to undermine Wilde's undeniable commitment to feminism and socialism – which are evident in his editing of the magazine titled *The Woman's World* (1887–89) and in his polemical essay, "The Soul of Man under Socialism" (1891), respectively. It is simply that the affirmative claims that recent critics have been eager to stake on

Wilde's volatile career (e.g. he was "one of us") have at times proved as uncritical as some of their less reputable predecessors'.

In the remainder of this chapter, I want to clarify how and why biographical approaches to Wilde have always involved certain hazards. From a very early stage in his livelihood, Wilde's career was subject to a remarkable amount of well-publicized fables constructed on some rather shaky facts. In what follows I explore a number of crucial moments in Wilde's compelling life story – his American lecture tour, his trials, and his imprisonment – which provide a fairly representative sample of the striking ways in which the Wilde legend, both in his lifetime and our own, has been elaborated. In the process we also learn that Wilde himself made a significant contribution to some of the taller biographical tales that incautious readers might feel tempted to tell about him.

II

If we go back to the period when the 25-year-old Wilde strove to make his mark in fashionable London circles, then we witness the start of a pattern that would affect many subsequent accounts of his career. To put it bluntly, from the moment his name went into circulation Wilde was generally better known for what he did than what he wrote. In 1880, even though he had been working hard to establish a literary reputation (he had won a prestigious prize at Oxford for his long poem *Ravenna*, finished the draft of his play *Vera*, and had placed over 30 poems in magazines), Wilde was scarcely recognized as an author of any note. The earliest published account of his life, which appeared in *The Biograph and Review*, grasped this point when it stated: "he may be considered to have his career still before him."[22] Yet the writer of this unsigned article went on to observe that Wilde had "already attained eminence as one of the elect in a certain modern school of which he is held to be to the least of the apostles." "He is," the commentator observed, "a believer in the religion of beauty, a marked figure among the newest group of aesthetics."[23] At this juncture, the young Wilde was already gaining notoriety as a proponent of "art for art's sake" – a doctrine, central to the cultural movement known in Britain as aestheticism, which derived its principal ideas from such sources as the critical essays of French author Théophile Gautier and English writer Walter Pater.

But when one turns to the three poems by Wilde that accompany the summary of this "dweller in the high places of feeling," one is hardly amazed to find that the rival journal *Fact* scorned what it called *The Biograph and Review*'s "bio-eulogy" – adding that it was a "wretched blunder in taste."[24] The three flatly written sonnets barely suggest that Wilde possessed much literary potential. "How vain and dull this common world must seem / To such a One as thou," Wilde's speaker feebly declares to the famous French actress Sarah Bernhardt, whose appearance in Racine's *Phèdre* impressed audiences at London's Comedy Theatre in 1879 (835). "O Hair of Gold!" Wilde apostrophizes in another of these poems, "O Crimson Lips! O Face / Made for the luring and the love of man!" (835). These exclamations seek to communicate his excitement at seeing the great actress Ellen Terry in a revival of W.G. Wills's *Charles I* (1872). To *Fact* it was doubtless hard to reconcile Wilde's creaking rhetoric with his supposed position as a "marked figure" in one of the "newest" movements of the day.

Not surprisingly, when Wilde's volume simply titled *Poems* appeared the following year it met with a good deal of mockery.[25] But if by 1881 his literary ambitions remained unfulfilled, they failed to prevent a growing readership from wanting to know more about him, since his image – rather than his writings – enjoyed increasing familiarity throughout the culture. Wilde's habit of donning *outré* buttonholes and eye-catching attire prompted a number of cartoonists to caricature him. By this time, W.S. Gilbert and Arthur Sullivan had completed *Patience, or Bunthorne's Bride*, a light-hearted opera, which won favor in London and which, in part, satirized Wilde's aestheticism. The following year the theatre manager Richard D'Oyly Carte contracted Wilde to embark on a 12-month lecture tour of North America. By employing Wilde to pronounce on aesthetic topics, Carte aimed at boosting the publicity for the American production of *Patience*. Thus by early 1882 Wilde could be found at assorted venues straddling the nation repeating the following, somewhat banal, wisdom: "Art can never have any other claim but her perfection."[26] In order to impress his passion for beauty, Wilde agreed to adopt an "aesthetic" look, famously recorded in a set of fine photographs taken at Napoleon Sarony's studio in New York City. With flowing locks, silk stockings, tilted fedora, and fur coat, Wilde struck a number of memorable poses that made it plain that his style flew in the face of conventional masculinity. With such fanfare, he became a fad. In the United States, countless advertisements, as well as fun-poking illustrations, capitalized on his flamboyant presence, lauding and defaming him in equal measure.

Advance publicity of Wilde's impending arrival at New York City was so successful that an unofficial biography titled *Ye Soul Agonies in Ye Life of Oscar Wilde* went quickly into circulation. Equipped with a number of striking illustrations, this pamphlet proves instructive because it reveals how the young Wilde had already become a rather exotic figure around which some eccentric fantasies might be embellished. Much of *Ye Soul Agonies* draws its preposterous image of Wilde from Gilbert and Sullivan's operetta, where the young aesthete Bunthorne sings: "if you walk down Piccadilly with a poppy or a lily in your mediaeval hand. / And every one will say, / As you walk your flowery way, / . . . what a most peculiarly pure young man this our young man must be."[27] Wilde of course was hardly known for carrying such flowers in his hand. Nor did he embrace what *Patience* calls "mediaevalism's affectation," which accounts for the archaic title of the 1882 pamphlet.[28] But *Patience* is nonetheless right to acknowledge that the lilies and sunflowers that sometimes graced Wilde's lapels had become his stock-in-trade.

Ye Soul Agonies begins by picturing Wilde in the manner of Bunthorne. "The infant Oscar," we learn, "was no ordinary infant. Rejecting the toys of commerce, he loved to close his mottled fist upon a sunflower or a lily." Yet this description departs from Gilbert's libretto when it starts concentrating on Wilde's distinctive Irish heritage. "He would struggle from arms of his nurse, a lusty and buxom Connemara colleen."[29] To impress his Irish upbringing, the illustrator provides a most uncomplimentary picture of a young nursemaid with the kinds of simian characteristics that were common in American stereotypes of Hibernian men and women (Figure 1). While it remains the case that this pamphlet fails to give Wilde the apish physiognomy that cartoonists frequently attributed to Irish people, we need to remember – as Curtis Marez points out – that during "his American tour . . . Wilde was constantly represented with simian features."[30] But that is not to argue that *Ye Soul Agonies* refused to suggest that Wilde the Irish aesthete constituted a racial type. Charles Kendrick, the illustrator, sought to meld Wilde's racial difference with his outlandish aestheticism in a picture titled "A Symphony in Colour" (Figure 2). Affecting the pose of a dreamy lover of beauty, Wilde almost waltzes abstractedly in front a group of entranced black housemaids, one of whom holds a sunflower, while another looks longingly at a lily. The illustration, which is not the only one from this time to link Wilde with ethnic stereotypes, plainly connects Wilde with demeaning views of racial inferiority and mindless femininity.[31]

At the same time, however, *Ye Soul Agonies* makes it plain that Wilde's presence in the United States cannot be wholly dismissed out of hand, since his arrival as the apostle of a newfangled doctrine was supposed to have at least some cultural significance. Then again, the anonymous writer of this pamphlet is wholly skeptical of the overblown press coverage that greeted Wilde when he stepped off the S.S. *Arizona* at New York City on 2 January 1882. Most probably drawing on *The Biograph and Review*,

Figure 1: "Ye Rising son-flower," from *Ye Soul Agonies of Ye Life of Oscar Wilde*

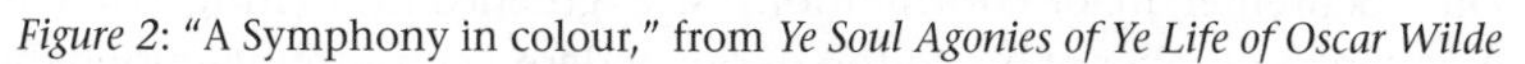

Figure 2: "A Symphony in colour," from *Ye Soul Agonies of Ye Life of Oscar Wilde*

the anonymous writer traces Wilde's history with some accuracy from the time of his birth to his years of study at Trinity College, Dublin and Magdalen College, Oxford in the 1870s. But the moment when the biography turns to Wilde's literary reputation, the story takes considerable pleasure in magically transforming the hopeless reception of *Poems* into an account of how his writing intimidated the most esteemed poets of the day:

> Alfred Tennyson, on hearing of Oscar's arrival, fled to the Isle of Wight and set to work on a poem on the Zulu War, which he named the "Charge of the Dark Brigade," in contradistinction to his "Charge of the *Light* Brigade." Browning commenced reading Johnson's Dictionary upside down, with a view to coining words, and Rossetti bought a job lot of goose-quill pens and some paper that had been injured by water at a fire. And for the minor poets, they borrowed "fivers" [i.e. £5 notes] where they could and went out of the country.[32]

The very idea that Alfred Tennyson, Robert Browning, and Dante Gabriel Rossetti feared for their reputations when the upstart Wilde landed on the literary scene embroiders the truth in order to deflate the rather puffed-up reputation that Carte and his workforce had tried to manufacture for him.

The buildup surrounding Wilde's American tour sustained him for several years afterward. When he returned to England, he managed to maintain his reputation as a public lecturer until 1884. His literary standing, however, remained low. Certainly, he published more poems, not that many of which have much distinction. But he had little fortune with the American production of *Vera*, his melodramatic play on Russian nihilism, in 1883. He nonetheless earned a modest income from reviews for popular papers such as the *Pall Mall Gazette*. For much of the 1880s he worked as a jobbing journalist, producing a phenomenal number of short articles in magazines as diverse as *The Dramatic Review* and *The Saturday Review*. His direction changed somewhat in 1888 with the publication of *The Happy Prince and Other Tales*; this beautifully printed volume of fairy stories was his first book to emerge from a respected publisher since 1881. Moreover, his two-year stint editing *The Woman's World* (a journal to which some of the most gifted women writers of the day, such as Olive Schreiner, made contributions) strengthened his footing as a man of letters; a number of his editorials on modern poetry count among the finest of the decade. More important, he had placed several distinguished essays – including an early version of "The Truth of Masks" (1885, revised

1891) and his witty "The Decay of Lying" (1889, revised 1891) – in such well-regarded periodicals as *The Nineteenth Century*.

Yet by the time Wilde clinched a deal with Joseph Marshall Stoddart of the J.B. Lippincott Company at Philadelphia for the temporary rights to *The Picture of Dorian Gray*, his longest work of fiction, he was still more or less an unknown literary quantity. Stoddart commissioned the story from Wilde in order to present to a largely American audience the brightest up-and-coming writers based in London. Thus when *Dorian Gray* appeared in *Lippincott's Monthly Magazine* in June 1890, the position set forth by *The Biograph and Review* some ten years earlier still held true. Even if his flamboyancy during the early 1880s remained vivid in popular memory, he could "be considered to have his career still before him."

III

In April 1890 when Wilde's somewhat delayed literary career began in earnest it created a hullabaloo. No sooner had *Dorian Gray* appeared than it caused ructions in some quarters of the British press, with the imperialist *Scots Observer* declaring that it was fit only "for none but outlawed noblemen and perverted telegraph boys" (a thinly veiled allusion to a recent homosexual scandal in London).[33] One newspaper rudely described the story as "ordure," while another believed that it displayed "effeminate frivolity."[34] These reviewers no doubt realized that the story's interest in the "new Hedonism" that Lord Henry Wotton advocates,[35] and which leads his acolyte Dorian Gray into an underworld of opium addiction and unspoken transgressions, had some implicit connection with homosexual activity. In any case, the allusions to works such as Suetonius' *History of the Caesars* would have alerted classically educated readers to Dorian Gray's knowledge of sodomy (108–109). Notably, there were supportive reviews that saw the story as a modern-day Faustian legend in which the dissolute protagonist must forfeit his physical beauty for taking sensual pleasures to extremes. But it would seem that the hostile notices of *Dorian Gray* exerted greatest influence on public opinion. At any rate, W.H. Smith, the country's largest booksellers, withdrew copies from circulation. The story therefore could hardly be regarded as a resounding success – at least in Britain.[36]

In the face of such a hostile reception, Wilde – who had long been a seasoned hand at dealing with adverse publicity – kept his name in the public eye by publishing eloquent letters of protest in each of the newspapers that had trounced him. At the same time, he sought to gain further attention by expanding *Dorian Gray* into a full-length novel. Even though he struck a deal for a book-length edition featuring six additional chapters, the handsomely bound volume that appeared from Ward, Lock & Co. in London in 1891 mustered poor sales; reviews of this edition, too, were disappointing. Thus it would be difficult to claim that the revised 1891 edition of *Dorian Gray* – a work that since the late 1980s has enjoyed widespread popularity on college campuses[37] – dazzled Wilde's contemporaries. It turned out that during Wilde's lifetime *Dorian Gray* would only gain further attention when it was upheld, not as testimony of his literary genius, but as evidence of his reprehensible homosexuality.

At this point, we need to look at the messy series of events that culminated in Wilde's prison sentence. The literary career, after the noticeably false start of *Dorian Gray*, would quickly flourish. His first Society Comedy, *Lady Windermere's Fan*, played for 260 performances, earning Wilde in the first year somewhere in the region of £1,200.[38] Almost instantaneously, he rivaled established playwrights such as Arthur Wing Pinero for supremacy on the London stage. Undeniably, as we have seen, reviewers expressed misgivings about his questionable borrowings from well-known sources and his habit of reusing ingenious axioms. But, in spite of some negative notices from the likes of Scott and Walkley, audiences remained eager to see the shows.

In order to reveal what led Wilde to jail amid this short-lived period of literary fame, I need to repeat some familiar bits and pieces of information that oftentimes mark the crescendo of the biographies. In the spring of 1895, the 40-year-old Wilde stood at the peak of his career, with two of his Society Comedies – *An Ideal Husband* and *The Importance of Being Earnest* – playing at prestigious theatres in the West End. In both dramas, his elegant dandies poke brilliant fun at the kinds of late-nineteenth-century social conservatism that championed moral abstinence and hard work. "I love talking about nothing," says Lord Goring to his father in *An Ideal Husband*. "It is the only thing I know nothing about." "You seem," says his father, "to be living entirely for pleasure." "What else is there to live for, father?" Lord Goring replies (523). In the same spirit, another stylish man of leisure named Algernon asks the equally wealthy Jack in *Earnest*: "What brings you up to town?" "Oh, pleasure, pleasure! What else should bring one anywhere?" Jack replies (358). Such spirited repartee certainly gives the impression, as Wilde puts it in "Phrases and Philosophies," that "Industry is the root of all ugliness" (1245). Further, such rhetorical brio goes some way to explain that Wilde, even when his axioms proved highly entertaining, remained a controversial phrasemaker to be reckoned with.

Almost overnight, the delight that Wilde aroused in the theatre would transform into disgust at the courtroom. Shortly after these two terrific Society Comedies opened he embarked on his perilous libel suit against his male lover Alfred Douglas' father, the notoriously headstrong Marquess of Queensberry. Wilde took this unwise action because the belligerent aristocrat left an offensive visiting-card at his club on 18 February. Queensberry had impertinently scrawled that the author was posing as a sodomite. This amounted to the deepest of the various insults that the Marquess had made at Wilde's expense for the best part of a year. Inflamed, Wilde – partly on the advice of his close friend Ross – put the matter into the hands of C.O. Humphreys, an experienced solicitor who would not have pursued the action unless he believed that Wilde, a married man with two sons, was in the right.

On 3 April that year, when Wilde began his prosecution at the Old Bailey, "Phrases and Philosophies" was discussed not for the pleasure it excited. Instead, his epigrams were cited as evidence of his immorality. In his plea of justification, the Marquess claimed that both *Dorian Gray* and "Phrases and Philosophies" "were calculated to subvert morality and to encourage unnatural vice."[39] According to the defense, Wilde's droll "Phrases and Philosophies" looked culpable because they appeared in an Oxford undergraduate magazine whose contents supported homosexual love. Published in *The Chameleon*, "Phrases and Philosophies" stood alongside two rather fine poems by Douglas. Moreover, *The Chameleon* contained a sacrilegious short story, also featuring desire between men, titled "The Priest and the Acolyte" by John Francis Bloxam. Early in the trial, Wilde's counsel, Edward Clarke, defied the defense to "suggest from these contributions" to the journal "anything hostile to Mr. Wilde." Clarke contended that Wilde's "Phrases and Philosophies" were "epigrammatical statements such as those which many of us have enjoyed when being interchanged in dialogue by the characters of such as *A Woman of No Importance* [1893]" – a play, we might note in passing, that recycles some of the cleverest dialogue in the 1891 edition of *Dorian Gray*.[40] Wilde's impudent turns of phrase, Clarke maintained, provided not only "brilliancy and effect to dialogue" but also "wisdom in a witty form."[41] Clarke's thoughtful comments certainly prompt us to ask how it could be that Wilde's sparkling wit was a source of instructive amusement in one context and proof of his shameful depravity in another.

Edward Carson, on Queensberry's behalf, rose to Clarke's challenge. With his shrewd lawyer's mind, Carson would quote an apothegm and then ask for Wilde's response to whether it was "moral or immoral."[42] "Religions die when they are proved to be true" (1244), Carson cited. "Do you think that was a safe axiom to put forward as a 'Phrase and Philosophy for the Use of the Young?'" he queried Wilde, insinuating that the author set out to corrupt unsuspecting youth. In response, Wilde claimed that such epigrams were "Most stimulating to thought."[43] "Pleasure is the only thing one should live for. Nothing ages like happiness" (1244), Carson quoted Wilde again, this time in an inquiring tone. "I think," Wilde answered, "that self-realisation – realisation of one's self – is the primal aim of life."[44] For the most part, Wilde's thoughtful replies refused to engage with the view that he propounded a dubious philosophy. His answers were generally consistent with the artistic principles that he had espoused in his lectures to American audiences many years before. Wilde would state his aestheticism succinctly in the "Preface" that he added to the 1891 edition of *Dorian Gray*. "There is no such thing as a moral or an immoral book," he declared (17). Carson's quick mind alighted on this statement. "That expresses your view?" he asked Wilde. "My view on art," the author affirmed.[45]

But as the cross-examination continued Wilde discovered that it would prove especially difficult to disentangle his published work from all of the other evidence that Queensberry had garnered (much of it through devious means). Once he dispensed with the "Preface," Carson asked the blunt question – one not reported in the press at the time – about *Dorian Gray*: "Is that open to interpretation as a sodomitical book?"[46] In order to pursue this inquiry, which understandably tested Wilde's patience, Carson shifted attention to the 1890 edition of *Dorian Gray*, which Wilde took some care to revise for the book-length version that appeared ten months later. The press's hostility to the shorter work he published in *Lippincott's Magazine* may have encouraged him to think better of maintaining the dialogue where the painter Basil Hallward declares to the protagonist: "I have adored you extravagantly."[47] Wilde eliminated the sentence from the 1891 edition, which Carson claimed had been "modified and purged a good deal."[48] Later, as he unearthed what he felt sure would serve as yet more literary evidence of Wilde's "sodomitical" perversion, Carson concentrated on Wilde's effusive love-letters to Douglas. "[T]hat those red, rose-leaf lips of yours should be made no less for music than for madness of kissing," Carson quoted.[49] (The letter, though this was not discussed in court, happened to be stolen property.)

From this point onward, the cross-examination lurched from bad to worse, taking directions that Wilde could hardly have foreseen. Wilde was quizzed about his relations with Alfred Wood (a homosexual blackmailer), Edward Shelley (an office-boy who worked for one of Wilde's publishers), Alphonso Conway (a teenager whom Wilde befriended on vacation),

Alfred Taylor (a procurer of male prostitutes), and a number of other young, mostly working-class men with whom he had become intimate. Faced with this barrage of unexpected questions, Wilde's wit began to falter. When Carson enquired if Wilde ever kissed Walter Grainger, a young servant at a house in Oxford, Wilde exclaimed: "Oh, no, never in my life; he was a peculiarly plain boy."[50] Such flippancy regrettably admitted the charge that it sought to deflect. As a result, Clarke appealed to the judge to withdraw his prosecution, finally conceding that the plea of justification was right to refer to the publication of both *Dorian Gray* and "Phrases and Philosophies." Thus, on 5 April, the court pronounced the Marquess of Queensberry "Not Guilty."

In usual circumstances, the case would have rested there, with the court awarding costs to the defense. But an extraordinary turn of events drove Wilde's predicament toward an unanticipated end. Wilde had to face consequences far more serious than defraying the substantial sum of £677. On the evening when Wilde lost his suit, the Director of Public Prosecutions (acting on behalf of the Crown) issued a warrant for his arrest. At Bow Street Magistrates' Court, Wilde was charged on two counts. First, he was accused of committing acts of gross indecency. Second, Wilde was impugned as a procurer of such acts. Refused bail, Wilde languished in jail for three weeks until the second, more extended trial opened. Meanwhile, the Marquess forced a bankruptcy sale of Wilde's possessions (at the time Wilde's debts, in addition to the legal costs, were considerable). In these dreadful circumstances, the press remained for the most part unforgiving. In the *National Observer*, the essayist and poet W.E. Henley expressed his gratitude to the Marquess for exposing the "obscene impostor" whose prominence remained a source of "social outrage" since Wilde departed from Dublin for Oxford in 1874.[51] Besides condemning Wilde as a dirty Irishman, Henley relished how the trial destroyed a man who had become "the High Priest of the Decadents." By this time, the epithet "Decadent," associated with French avant-garde writers whose works expressed an interest in sexual dissidence, had become a byword for corruption. While this furor raged in the press, Wilde's name was removed from the playbills advertising the two comedies that were running at the Haymarket and St. James's theatres. (Not long after, the plays would close down altogether.) Apart from letters and visits from loyal friends, the only succor Wilde could take came from Clarke, who said that he would defend the author for no fee.

In the two trials that ensued, the Crown prosecuted Wilde together with Alfred Taylor, and its representatives readily drew on the questionable evidence supplied by the Marquess's lackeys (one of whom, the actor

Charles Brookfield, was performing in *An Ideal Husband*).[52] On the first day, the blackmailer Charlie Parker confirmed that Wilde sodomized him at the Savoy Hotel, while landladies who had let rooms to this lowlife claimed that Wilde counted among Parker's visitors. There followed a parade of young men to whom Wilde had performed favors, sometimes in the form of cigarette cases, fancy dinners, fine clothes, and even a visit to Paris. But when Wilde was finally called as a witness the Crown prosecution turned not to his intimate liaisons with the likes of Parker but focused instead upon his involvement with *The Chameleon*.

Provocatively, Charles Gill interrogated Wilde's thoughts on Douglas's two contributions: a sonnet, titled "In Praise of Shame," and a longer, narrative work, called "Two Loves." While Gill failed to extract the coded homosexual meaning of "shame" from Douglas's sonnet, he received a very full account of the famous line that appears in "Two Loves." In this intriguing poem, which explores distinctions between same- and other-sex eroticism, a figure decried as "shame" states boldly: "I am the Love that dare not speak its name."[53] What, Gill wanted to know, was meant by such words? In phrasing that recalls a passage in *Dorian Gray*, Wilde rose to the occasion by declaring that such love was a "great affection of an elder for a younger man as there was between David and Jonathan." Moreover, "Plato made [it] the very basis of his philosophy," while Michelangelo and Shakespeare represented it in their works.[54] (He had said as much in *Dorian Gray*.[55]) "There is nothing unnatural about it," Wilde boldly maintained. But nonetheless the "world mocks at it and sometimes puts one in the pillory for it." Having uttered these noble sentiments, the courtroom broke into applause, although Wilde's detractors started hissing. Not to be outdone, Gill moved – just as Carson did – to question the florid locutions that featured in Wilde's correspondence with Douglas. "I am never ashamed of the style of my writings," Wilde remarked unapologetically.[56] But, by this stage, his effusive praise of Douglas's "red, rose-leaf lips" remained inextricably linked to the "alleged improper behaviour" with all the young men that Gill previously questioned. In the end, Wilde's intrepid exclamation "I am a lover of youth!" looked less like a defense of innocent affection than an avowal of downright pederasty.[57]

Even though the second trial foundered because the jury could not agree on two of the four counts (all of which concerned the committing or procuring of indecent acts), the case was more or less sealed. A retrial was ordered, and on this occasion the magistrate permitted Wilde bail of £5,000. Supporters provided sureties, as well as refuge. The stage was set for Wilde to flee to the Continent as a fugitive. But, for reasons that remain open to speculation, he went to meet his fate. He had no hope of acquittal. It was a sign of the Liberal government's determination to imprison Wilde that the Solicitor-General, Sir Frank Lockwood, led the prosecution. The highest attorney in the land did little more than rehash the evidence that had been scrutinized before, though he asked Wilde if the love-letter that described Douglas's "slim gilt soul" and praised the young man as "Hyacinthus, whom Apollo loved so madly" meant "love between men."[58] In his summing-up, Justice Wills asserted: "It is the worst case I have ever tried."[59]

It is telling to witness how the 1890s press interpreted Wilde's sentence as the culmination of a career that had long aroused suspicion. The popular *News of the World* expressed with relief: "The aesthetic cult, in the nasty form, is over."[60] The conservative *Daily Telegraph* drew a similar conclusion. "The man," it observed, "has now suffered the penalties of his career, and may well be allowed to pass from that platform of publicity which he loved into that limbo of disrepute and forgetfulness which is his due." In particular, the *Telegraph* deplored Wilde's "foolish ostentation, his empty paradoxes, his insufferable posturing, his incurable vanity." Advising clean living, sobriety, and respect for the law, the newspaper contended that to be cultured like Wilde "was not necessarily to be in perpetual revolt." More to the point, it felt that Wilde's aestheticism threatened to entrance the young generation through the "apish genius of paradox": the form of axiomatic wit that on this account expressed not just immorality but, more specifically, sexual perversion. On this view, Wilde's abbreviated literary career – the one thing he worked so hard to forge – only confirmed long-held suspicions that he had commanded unearned praise.

But if the press reports, which were frequently accompanied by grotesque illustrations of Wilde's physical appearance, could not have done enough to make the trials into an event that aroused considerable voyeurism, then it would be left to Wilde's biographers to make his exit from the Old Bailey into an even more mesmerizing spectacle, and it is here that the habitual distortions of his life become most visible. According to numerous accounts, on the afternoon of Saturday, 25 May 1895, when prison officers escorted Wilde out of the courtroom female prostitutes danced in the street. Take, for example, how H. Montgomery Hyde depicts this vivid scene in his widely read *The Trials of Oscar Wilde*:

> [I]n the streets outside the Old Bailey the verdict was received with sundry remarks of popular approval. A few people literally danced with joy, and some prostitutes were seen to kick up their skirts with

> glee at the news. "'E'll have 'is 'air cut regular *now*!" shouted one of them. This sally provoked a loud chorus of laughter from others on the pavement.[61]

In part, this anecdote derives from various newspaper reports that Hyde consulted when preparing his rather unreliable compilation of the proceedings which resulted in Wilde's sentence.[62] The *Sun* observed that "one of the most singular features of this scene" outside the Old Bailey "was that a number of flashily dressed women shouted and danced on the pavement outside."[63] There were, however, other less dependable sources which informed Hyde's arresting description of this chilling scene.

Repeated by other commentators, such as Irish poet W.B. Yeats,[64] certain details about this episode would seem to originate in Harris' *Oscar Wilde: His Life and Confessions* (1916), whose title makes it pretty obvious that his purported biography provides exposés of Wilde's otherwise shameful secrets. Harris – an American journalist whose editorial work on London journals provided Wilde with occasions to publish such works as "The Soul of Man under Socialism" – tells his readers that the "whole scene" inside the courtroom "sickened" him. Worse was to come when he stepped out onto the streets:

> We had not left the court when the cheering broke out in the streets, and when we came outside there were troops of the lowest women of the town dancing together and kicking up their legs in hideous abandonment, while the surrounding crowd of policemen and spectators guffawed with delight.[65]

Unfortunately, this is a lie. Harris' memory was clearly suffering some aberration when he penned these words in 1910 or thereabouts. As Wilde's devoted, tireless but ultimately dishonest biographer Sherard would point out in 1937: "Harris was not in the Court at all at any time during the fatal afternoon of May 25th, 1895, and certainly did not witness the scene in the Old Bailey which he borrowed from me."[66]

But that is not to say that Sherard is any less dependable because he was an eye-witness. In his 1902 biography, Sherard recalls the "fatal afternoon" at some length. When he and Ernest Dowson (the distinguished Decadent poet who, like a number of Wilde's acquaintances, belonged to the early-1890s Rhymers' Club) arrived at the Old Bailey that day, they were greeted by jeers from a crowd execrating them as "some more aristocrats."[67] The crowd was obviously mistaken, since neither Sherard nor Dowson had blood ties to the Crown. Sherard recalls saying to Dowson that the jeering represented "class hatred." Later, when the two men departed from the gallery after Wilde was escorted under guard to Pentonville Prison, they encountered the following spectacle:

> men and women joined hands and danced an ungainly farandole, where ragged petticoats and yawning boots flung up the London mud in *feu de joie*, and the hideous faces were distorted with savage triumph. I stood and watched this dance of death for a few minutes, regretting that [Russian painter Vasily] Veretschagin was not by my side.[68]

In many respects, it remains hard to figure out if this anecdote – which Sherard clearly saw as his personal property – is any more worthy of serious attention than Harris' plagiarism. In such a frightful tableau, it almost feels as if the grim reaper were about to spring from this grisly company into Sherard and Dowson's midst.

I am scarcely the first reader of these early biographies to question their boldly Gothic depictions of scornful prostitutes and depraved proletarians stamping around in the gutter. In *The Untold Life of Oscar Wilde* (1972), Rupert Croft-Cooke makes repeated warnings against Sherard's "Hogarthian description" along with other exaggerated pieces of reportage.[69] Croft-Cooke prefaces his otherwise disappointing biography with an instructive chapter on "The Biographers and the Legends" that undertakes to demythologize many of the seedier stories and fanciful tales that fill out Sherard's and Harris' respective recollections of Wilde. It is therefore disappointing to discover that Ellmann, as Merlin Holland has observed, reproduces a number of the myths that Sherard in particular created in order to make good copy.[70] But, as it turned out, it was not just Wilde's early biographers who developed a marked tendency to pervert his life story. Wilde himself indulged in a little autobiographical mythmaking of his own when he tried his best to bear up to his appalling prison sentence.

IV

The ruthlessness of prison certainly threatened to terminate Wilde's hard-won literary career. For many months the dreadful conditions – including hours of thankless repetitive labor, which involved sewing postal sacks and picking oakum – almost drove him insane. At first, the authorities prevented him from reading anything apart from the Bible and *Pilgrim's Progress*; the privilege of writing extended only to a restricted number of letters. Fed a far from nutritious prison diet, his weight dropped drastically. By 18 September 1895, when he had been moved at politician Richard Haldane's bidding from Pentonville to Wandsworth, he had shed 22 pounds. Haldane, it would seem, suggested that a further move – on this occasion to Reading Gaol – might ease Wilde's predicament. But under the strict governorship of the ex-military Major Isaacson, Wilde's life from mid-November 1895 onward fared not much better. Desperate for reading materials, he seized on his right to request from the Home Secretary privileges that would end his isolation from the great writings that helped to shape his literary sensibility. On 2 July 1896 he submitted a 2,000-word document that sought to justify his need for a greater supply than the two books per week that he had been allowed at Reading. Hoping to persuade the authorities to take pity on his condition, Wilde claimed that his "monstrous sexual perversion" could be explained through "the works of eminent men of science such as [Cesare] Lombroso and Max Nordau" which had identified "the intimate connection between madness and the literary and aesthetic temperament."[71] There was, he claims, a direct correspondence between his flourishing literary success and what he called, after Nordau, his "Degenerescence":

> The Petitioner is now keenly conscious of the fact that while the three years preceding his arrest were from the intellectual point of view the most brilliant years of his life . . . still that during that entire time he was suffering from the most horrible form of erotomania, which made him forget his wife and children, his high social position in London and Paris, his European distinction as an artist, the honour and name of his family, and left him the helpless prey of the most revolting passions.[72]

What should we make of this statement? Are we to accept that Wilde honestly believed Max Nordau's pseudo-scientific theory that artistic temperaments were more prone than others to immoral behavior because they were the result of a heritable condition that was known in English as "degeneration"? Did Wilde truly think that Nordau's study, which first appeared in Germany in 1892 and which gained attention in Britain in 1895, provided a plausible account of his literary success and his sexual behavior? By way of an answer, it may well be that the only reasonable approach to understanding this petition is to read it as a strategic document – in other words, as a work that makes a show of appealing to "degeneration" in order to obtain what he wanted: pen and ink, together with all of the literary books that would enable him to sustain his literary identity. Perhaps this was a convenient tale for Wilde to tell at the time.

Yet it becomes clear that in his other prison writings Wilde would form equally distorted impressions of his personal history, as we can see in the document that in 1905 Ross would name, after Psalm 130, *De Profundis* (Wilde's own title, after Horace, was "Epistola: In Carcere et Vinculis": "Letter: In Prison and in Chains"). Wilde was at last able to compose this remarkable document perhaps six months (maybe earlier) after the Home Secretary turned down his petition.[73] In the end, he obtained the pen and paper that he required from the benign Major Nelson, who replaced Isaacson as governor in the summer of 1896. Written on pale-blue prison foolscap, this 30,000-word work was in principle written as a recriminatory letter to Douglas, whom Wilde – quite mistakenly – believed had ignored him in prison out of characteristically fickle behavior. (Douglas, as it turned out, failed to contact Wilde on the advice of a prison governor.) *De Profundis*, however – as Small has pointed out – cannot be characterized solely as a lengthy epistle.[74] Part letter to a former lover, part autobiographical reflection, and part contemplation of pain and suffering, the document is also a retrospective on Wilde's career. In particular, two paragraphs crystallize Wilde's assessment of the brief period in which his literary productions attracted considerable public attention:

> I was a man who stood in symbolic relations to the art and culture of my age. I had realised this for myself at the very dawn of my manhood, and had forced my age to realize it afterwards. Few men hold such a position in their own lifetime and have it so acknowledged. It is usually discerned, if discerned at all, by the historian, or the critic, long after both the man and his age have passed away. With me it was different. I felt it myself, and made others feel it. Byron was a symbolic figure, but his relations were to the passion of his age and its weariness of passion. Mine were to something more noble, more permanent, of more vital issue, of larger scope.
>
> The gods had given me everything, I had genius, a distinguished name, high social position, brilliancy, intellectual daring: I made art a philosophy, and philosophy an art: I altered the minds of men and the colours of things: there was nothing I said or did that did not make people wonder: I took the drama, the most objective form known to art, and made it as personal a mode of expression as the lyric or the sonnet, at the same time as I widened its range and characterisation: drama,

novel, poem in rhyme, poem in prose, subtle or fantastic dialogue, whatever I touched I made beautiful in a new mode of beauty. (729)

The high caliber of Wilde's prose may well tempt us to take him at his word. Without doubt, the fine cadences of these exquisitely written sentences display the skill of a craftsman whose powers remain admirably undiminished in the face of the oppressive conditions of a jail cell that was nine feet long and six feet wide. Yet, on closer inspection, Wilde's comparison between himself and the undoubtedly eminent but sexually controversial poet George Gordon Byron, whose *Childe Harold's Pilgrimage* (1812–18) and *Don Juan* (1819–24) enjoyed unrivaled sales in their time, is nothing less than extravagant. Did Wilde really believe that in stature he superseded Byron – certainly one of the most legendary, if not widely read, literary men of the nineteenth century – because this great Romantic precursor appeared limited by the "passion of his age and its weariness of passion"? What exactly was the "more noble" quality, the "more permanent" characteristic that gave Wilde's relations to his age their "larger scope"? In reply, it would not be unjust to say that his claims at times somewhat exceed the bare facts, and his belief that he attained stratospheric heights is not by any account accurate, as the rather mixed reviews of his works show. In any case, as Vincent O'Sullivan was among the first critics to note, "Wilde made little or no money by his [published] writings"; the most he earned from any one of his numerous books was probably £200.[75] Thus in the prison document it seems that much of Wilde's embittered remembrance of things past shapes a career that he would have loved to have accomplished: an appealing legend about a great but fallen idol to which "the gods had given . . . almost everything."

In *De Profundis*, Wilde presents a number of alluring myths about his professional prowess and his fated intimacy with Douglas. His suave tale-telling, if not put under scrutiny, can certainly sway modern readers toward a rather distorted interpretation of his life. "I was typical a child of my age in my perversity," he writes, "and for that perversity's sake, I turned the good things of my life to evil, and the evil things of my life to good" (*Complete Letters*, 722–723). Once again, this reads like a seductive formulation; it possesses a neat symmetry, like a chiasmus, that is rhetorically satisfying. But it remains an open question if his life conformed to the smooth contours of his undoubted literary skill. Was Wilde really so typical of the era he inhabited? Was he truly the representative man of the historical moment that he inhabited? Given the immense enthusiasm that currently exists for Wilde, it is not too presumptuous to assert that many scholars, students, and theatregoers would have little or no objection in responding to both queries in the affirmative. But, as I hope to have suggested, in our encounters with Wilde we need to gain some perspective on such legend-making claims in order to focus on why the inflated stories that have come to surround an extraordinarily gifted literary man continue to matter so much to us today.

notes

1. My thanks go to the staffs of the William Andrews Clark Memorial Library, University of California, Los Angeles, where much of the research for this chapter was carried out.
2. When quoting from the prison document known as *De Profundis*, I refer to the annotated edition presented in the *Complete Letters* (683–780), where it is published as a letter addressed "To Lord Alfred Douglas." *De Profundis* also appears in the Collins *Complete Works*, 980–1059. As I explain later in this chapter, the title of *De Profundis* was given to this document by Robert Ross in 1905; in that year, Ross published a carefully abridged version that excluded those passages that seek to inculpate Wilde's lover, Alfred Douglas, for encouraging the libel suit that began the series of legal events that resulted in Wilde's imprisonment. In 1913 Douglas instigated a libel suit against Arthur Ransome and his publisher for issuing a study of Oscar Wilde in 1912 which alluded to those sections of *De Profundis* that calumniated Douglas. Ransome had access to the unpublished parts of *De Profundis* through Ross. Douglas lost his case against Ransome. Since this document proved to be a source of such contentious wrangling, the complete text did not appear until 1949, some four years after Douglas's demise; an authoritative, annotated edition of the work appeared in the *Collected Letters of Oscar Wilde*, edited by Rupert Hart-Davis, in 1962. The variorum edition has been edited by Ian Small (Oxford: Oxford University Press, 2004).
3. Arguably, the first developed biographical exploration of Wilde's career is Robert Sherard's *Oscar Wilde: The Story of an Unhappy Friendship* (London: Hermes, 1902), though Sherard would later make a point of stating this work was "in no sense of the word a biography" (*The Real Oscar Wilde: To be Used as a Supplement to, and an Illustration of "The Life of Oscar Wilde"* (London: T. Werner Laurie, 1915), viii); Sherard would proceed to write more sustained – if highly contradictory – accounts of Wilde's achievements: *The Life of Oscar Wilde* (London: T. Werner Laurie, 1906); *Oscar Wilde Twice Defended from Andre Gide's Wicked Lies and Frank Harris' Cruel Libels to Which is Added a Reply to George Bernard Shaw, A Refutation of Dr. G.J. Renier's Statements, A Letter to the Author from Lord Alfred Douglas, an Interview with Bernard Shaw by Hugh Kingsmill* (Chicago: The Argus Bookshop, 1934); *Bernard Shaw, Frank Harris, and Oscar Wilde* (London: T. Werner Laurie, 1937). Sherard's 1934 and 1937 studies are largely devoted to repudiating presumed errors in other biographers' works, when in fact his own work is riddled with mistakes. As this chapter shows, an 1880 article in *The Biograph and Review* provides the earliest biographical outline of Wilde.

4. Tanitch notes that in 1901 *Lady Windermere's Fan* played at the Coronet Theatre ("No author's name appeared on the program"), *A Woman of No Importance* returned to the stage at the Empire Theatre, Balham, and *The Importance of Being Earnest* enjoyed a run at the Coronet Theatre (Robert Tanitch, *Oscar Wilde on Stage and Screen* (London: Methuen, 1999) 103, 201, and 261). *An Ideal Husband* was revived at the St. James's Theatre in 1914. Tanitch, op. cit., 227.
5. When Ellmann's substantial biography appeared in the spring of 1987, it was greeted with considerable acclaim in the British press. But seasoned Wilde scholars were quick to identify a number of errors in Ellmann's research. In 1989 Horst Schroeder issued an 80-page inventory of errors in Ellmann's work; more recently, Horst Schroeder has revealed the full extent of the unreliable nature of Ellmann's references (*Additions and Corrections to Richard Ellmann's Oscar Wilde*, 2nd ed. (Braunschweig: Privately printed, 2002). For reasons best known to Ellmann, he chose at times to rely on Harris' undependable 1916 biography. He also printed a photograph subtitled "Oscar Wilde as Salomé" which happens to feature the Hungarian singer, Alice Guszalewicz, in an early-twentieth-century production of Richard Strauss's opera, *Salomé* (which is based on Wilde's drama of that name). This photograph in Ellmann's 1987 study prompted both Elaine Showalter and Marjorie Garber (*Vested Interests* (New York: Routledge, 1992)) to elaborate thoughts on Wilde's supposed cross-dressing. This and other errors in Ellmann's research have been discussed not only in Schroeder but also in Merlin Holland, "Biography and the Art of Lying," *The Cambridge Companion to Oscar Wilde* (Cambridge: Cambridge University Press, 1997), 3–17; and Senelick. [Compare Bristow's treatment of Ellmann here with Kaye's in Chapter 8 – ed.]
6. I do not wish to repeat in detail what I have said elsewhere about Alfred Douglas's notorious repudiation of Wilde in *Oscar Wilde and Myself* (London: John Long, 1914), a book – mostly written by T.W.H. Crosland – that served to attack Wilde in light of the libel suit that Douglas lost against Arthur Ransome. Before 1913 Douglas remained loyal to Wilde's memory. But the allusions that Ransome made in his 1912 study to the unpublished parts of *De Profundis* – which appeared in an abridged form in 1905 (see Note 2) – prompted Douglas to sue Ransome for libel. Hereafter, Douglas engaged in a series of legal battles against Ross. Later, after Ross's death in 1918, Douglas would recant what he said in his 1914 book; see also Douglas, *Without Apology* (London: Martin Secker, 1938) and *Oscar Wilde: A Summing-Up* (London: Duckworth, 1940).
7. Ellmann's belief that Wilde's death was "syphilitic in origin" (Richard Ellmann, *Oscar Wilde* (New York: Random House, 1988), 579) has its basis in Arthur Ransome's 1912 *Oscar Wilde: A Critical Study* (London: Martin Secker), 199, and it would be repeated in Harris' 1916 biography (see Frank Harris, *Oscar Wilde: His Life and Confessions* (New York: Privately printed, 1918), II.539). Harris would repeat another anecdote that can be traced to Ross – namely, the idea that Wilde's corpse exploded after he expired (II.539). As Holland (op. cit., 12) has noted, at one point Sherard stated that he never saw in Wilde "the slightest sign of a malady which has a very distinct way of announcing its existence" (Sherard, *Real*, op. cit., 385). Yet later Sherard would change his tack by stating that "Wilde was doubly the victim of syphilis . . . [H]e undoubtedly

had inherited the diathesis from his libertine father" (Sherard, *Shaw*, op. cit., 10). In any case, Sherard had already spun some fanciful thoughts about the forces that drove Wilde to an early grave: e.g. "Oscar paid in his innocent person the toll that nature exacted for centuries of Hibernian conviviality of rollicking ancestors" (Sherard, *Life*, op. cit., 336). Other examples could be cited from all of Sherard's biographies, which bundle together assorted ideas about Wilde's supposedly "feminine soul" from a number of early-twentieth-century sexological sources (see Sherard, *Real*, op. cit., 96).

8. The films are *Wilde* (Dir. Brian Gilbert, 1997); *An Ideal Husband* (Dir. Oliver Parker, 1999); and *The Importance of Being Earnest* (Dir. Oliver Parker, 2002). (Dates are for first British releases.)
9. Wilde was convicted under the eleventh section of the Criminal Law Amendment Act (1885), which banned acts of "gross indecency" between males in private. The Sexual Offences Act (1967) repealed this provision, making the age of consent for sexual intimacy between men 21, while the age for heterosexual intimacy was 18. The 1967 act excluded members of the armed forces, and it covered only England and Wales. Similar legislation was passed for Scotland in 1980 and – in light of a ruling in the European Court – Northern Ireland in 1981 (see Stephen Jeffery-Poulter, *Peers, Queers, and Commons: The Struggle for Gay Law Reform from 1950 to the Present* (London: Routledge, 1991), 142–154).
10. Ellmann, op. cit., xvii.
11. Ibid., xv.
12. Ibid., xvii.
13. Talia Schaffer, "Wilde, Ouida, and the Origins of the Aesthetic Novel," in *Oscar Wilde: Contextual Conditions*, ed. Joseph Bristow (Toronto: University of Toronto Press, 2003).
14. Karl Beckson, ed. *Oscar Wilde: The Critical Heritage* (London: Routledge and Kegan Paul, 1970), 178–179.
15. Ibid., 180.
16. Ibid., 180.
17. Ibid., 180.
18. Ibid., 181.
19. On 2 January 1890 Whistler wrote to the scandal-mongering *Truth* that Wilde's essay, "The Decay of Lying" (which appeared in *The Nineteenth Century* in 1889), "deliberately and incautiously incorporated . . . a portion of a well-remembered letter in which" he "acknowledge[d] that 'Oscar has the courage of the opinions – of others!'" (*Complete Letters*, 419). One or two of the ideas in Wilde's critical essays can be traced to Whistler's "Ten o'Clock Lecture" (1885; published 1888), which Wilde reviewed (see Oscar Wilde, *The Collected Works*, ed. Robert Ross (London: Methuen, 1908), XIV.64–65).
20. Max Beerbohm, *Letters to Reggie Turner*, ed. Rupert Hart-Davis (London: Rupert Hart-Davis, 1964), p. 36.
21. See Mark Hichens, *Oscar Wilde's Last Chance* (Edinburgh: Pentland Press, 1999).
22. Anon., "Oscar Wilde," *The Biograph and Review*, 4(1880), 130.
23. Ibid., 130.
24. Anon., *Fact*, 21 August 1880, 8.
25. Beckson, op. cit., 37, 42–47, 50–52.
26. Wilde, *Collected Works*, op. cit., XIV.263.

27. W.S. Gilbert and Arthur Sullivan, *The Complete Annotated Gilbert and Sullivan*, ed. Ian Bradley (Oxford: Oxford University Press, 1996), 293.
28. Ibid., 293.
29. Anon., *Ye Soul Agonies*, illus. Charles Kendrick (New York: NP, 1882), 1–2.
30. Curtis Marez, "The Other Addict: Reflections on Colonialism and Oscar Wilde's Opium Smoke Screen," *ELH* 64(1997), 266.
31. Mary Blanchard, *Oscar Wilde's America: Counterculture in the Gilded Age* (New Haven: Yale University Press, 1998), 32–33.
32. *Ye Soul Agonies*, op. cit., 11.
33. Beckson, op. cit., 75.
34. Ibid., 68, 72.
35. The Collins *Complete Works* reprints the 20-chapter 1891 edition of *Dorian Gray*. In the shorter, 13-chapter 1890 edition, reprinted in *The Picture of Dorian Gray*, ed. Donald L. Lawler (New York: W.W. Norton, 1987) and *The Picture of Dorian Gray: The 1890 and 1891 Editions*, ed. Joseph Bristow (Oxford: Oxford University Press, 2004), Lord Henry's remark refers to the "new hedonism."
36. *Lippincott's Monthly Magazine* counted among the prestigious American monthlies whose sales in the United States ran into thousands. Precise circulation figures for this journal, however, were never disclosed by the J.B. Lippincott Company. Then again, the sales were likely to have been considerably less than the rival *Century Illustrated Monthly Magazine*, which sold 222,000 copies in the early 1880s, and *Harper's New Monthly Magazine*, which sold 200,000 copies during this period. For further information about the publication of the 1890 and 1891 editions of *Dorian Gray*, see Bristow, ed., op. cit.
37. In the United States the appearance of Donald L. Lawler's edition of *The Picture of Dorian Gray* (op. cit.) brought Wilde's longest work of fiction to a much broader student audience than before.
38. Josephine M. Guy and Ian Small, *Oscar Wilde's Profession: Writing and the Culture Industry in the Late Nineteenth Century* (Oxford: Oxford University Press, 2000), 109.
39. Merlin Holland, *Irish Peacock and Scarlet Marquess: The Real Trial of Oscar Wilde* (London: Fourth Estate, 2003), 291.
40. Ibid., 40.
41. Ibid., 40.
42. Ibid., 75.
43. Ibid., 75.
44. Ibid., 75.
45. Ibid., 80.
46. Ibid., 81.
47. Lawler, ed., op. cit., 232.
48. Holland, *Peacock*, op. cit., 78.
49. Ibid., 105; *Complete Letters*, 544.
50. Holland, *Peacock*, op. cit., 207.
51. W.E. Henley, Notes *National Observer*; even though these 'Notes' are unsigned, they have been traditionally attributed to Henley. 6 April 1895, 547.
52. It is worth noting that Brookfield had earlier co-authored (with James Glover) a burlesque of *Lady Windermere's Fan* titled *The Poet and the Puppets*, which drew attention to Wilde's borrowings from other dramas; this burlesque is reprinted, with commentary, in Richard W. Schoch, ed. *Victorian Theatrical Burlesques* (Aldershot: Ashgate, 2003), 209–246.

53. H. Montgomery Hyde, *The Trials of Oscar Wilde*, 2nd ed. (New York: Dover, 1962), 200.
54. Ibid., 201.
55. See chapter VIII of the 1890 edition and chapter X of the 1891 edition; Wilde's sentiments, in part, derived from his attentive reading of Walter Pater's *Studies in the History of the Renaissance* (1873), known as *The Renaissance* from its second edition of 1877.
56. Hyde, op. cit., 201.
57. Ibid., 202.
58. Ibid., 245; *Complete Letters*, 544.
59. Hyde, op. cit., 272.
60. "News Cuttings of Three Trials" (1895–1914). Wilde Uncatalogued Rare. Bound Boxed. Clark Library.
61. Hyde, op. cit., 273.
62. Hyde's *The Trials of Oscar Wilde*, which first appeared in 1948 and was revised in 1962; it is still the most widely available account of the trials, and it is arguably the least reliable. Much of Hyde's book is based on Stuart Mason [Christopher Sclater Millard], *Oscar Wilde: Three Times Tried* (London: Ferrestone Press, 1912). Holland's *Irish Peacock* provides, for the first time, a reliable account of the first trial; Holland has transcribed a record made in legal shorthand.
63. "News Cuttings," op. cit., f.143.
64. W.B. Yeats tells the tale of the prostitutes dancing in the streets after Wilde left the Old Bailey in "The Tragic Generation" (1922), which was collected in *Autobiographies* (1926) (see *Autobiographies*, ed. William H. O'Donnell and Douglas N. Archibald (New York: Scribner, 1999), 227). This anecdote would be repeated by Arthur Symons in his *A Study of Oscar Wilde* (London: C.J. Sawyer, 1930), 66.
65. Harris, op. cit., I.319–320.
66. Sherard, *Shaw*, Op. cit., 40.
67. Sherard, *Oscar Wilde*, op. cit., 200.
68. Ibid., 200.
69. Rupert Croft-Cooke, *The Untold Life of Oscar Wilde* (London: W.H. Allen, 1972), 16.
70. Holland, "Lying," op. cit., 10–14. Merlin Holland remains impressed by Harris' biography, noting that its "outspoken approach" to Douglas's intimacy with Wilde infuriated Douglas ("Lying," 6). Wilde's former lover threatened legal action if Harris' biography appeared in Britain.
71. H. Montgomery Hyde, *Oscar Wilde: The Aftermath* (New York: Farrar, Straus, 1963), 71; *Complete Letters*, 656–657.
72. Hyde, *Aftermath*, op. cit, 71; *Complete Letters*, 657.
73. For information about the dates when Wilde composed *De Profundis*, see Ian Small's variorum edition, op. cit.
74. Ian Small, "Identity and Value in *De Profundis*," in *Oscar Wilde: Contextual Conditions*, op. cit.
75. In all probability, this is the sum that Wilde received from Stoddart for the 1890 edition of *The Picture of Dorian Gray* (see *Letters*, 416). On Wilde's earnings from his plays and publications, see Guy and Small, *Oscar Wilde's Profession*, op. cit.

2
wilde the writer

Anne Margaret Daniel

> "Quack, quack, quack," [the Duck] said. "What a curious shape you are! May I ask were you born like that, or is it a result of an accident?"
>
> "It is quite evident that you have always lived in the country," answered the Rocket, "otherwise you would know who I am. However, I excuse your ignorance. It would be unfair to expect other people to be as remarkable as oneself. You will no doubt be surprised to hear that I can fly up into the sky, and come down as a shower of golden rain."
>
> Oscar Wilde, *The Remarkable Rocket*

> He makes me tired.
>
> Ambrose Bierce, *The San Francisco Wasp*, 1882

> If the British public will stand this, they can stand anything.
>
> John Addington Symonds on *Dorian Gray*, 1890

Oscar Wilde did everything there is to be done with words. He spoke them, his contemporaries tell us, like no one else. He wrote plays in which the dialogue mirrored his own spoken ability and agility, plays that have remained popular and perpetually performed – even during the years of what everyone at the time, including Wilde, referred to as his "downfall" and disgrace. He strung them together in poems, from long historical tributes to art to sonnets, songs, and ballads. He used them for fictions, from short fairy tales and *fabliaux* to one full-length novel that still dazzles, confounds, and upsets. He crafted criticism, from literary reviews to opinion pieces about art to public letters to social critiques. He edited the work of others, most notably for the publication he renamed *The Woman's World* – as he found its former title, *The Lady's World*, insulting to the progressive readers he hoped to attract. And he was usually doing all of these varied things with words, in any and all of these genres and modes of expression, simultaneously.

What did his contemporaries make of Wilde, knowing his work first, and only, as it appeared, unfortunately – or mercifully – without our Epimethean capabilities to look back at Wilde from the here and now, with our knowledge of him as it is? In order to understand Wilde as a writer, it is essential to know what he read in the papers as his works emerged, and what advice he clearly took, and what he ignored, as he went on creating his fictions and himself. And in looking at Wilde in this manner, we can also come to know the transgressive and truly radical, and radically self-incriminating and self-punishing, trajectories of some of his best-known and most popular, now-canonical, writings.

wilde's published prose: every text an art

Wilde's published prose is either criticism or fiction. His largest prose output, the letters, might go along with criticism – or, now and again, with fiction; Wilde's prose texts are never easy to categorize. But in the criticism is much fiction, and vice versa.

Storytelling was Wilde's forte and first love; he was a born teller of tales. All his works hold this quality, bound up in the Celtic tradition of the bard, the singer of songs for princes. Like the Scots Robert Louis Stevenson, who was "Tuisitala," teller of tales, in Samoa, Wilde awed his friends, acquaintances, and enemies with what he had to say, and how he spun it – a man who "made of his life a fable and lived by its recitation" – a less generous view is, of course, that his fables, poems in prose, and fairy-tales are all "those of a born liar."[1] As was the case with the lectures he gave in America and Britain in the 1880s, Wilde did not bother to write down most of his stories; others, like Andre Gide and Frank Harris, told, and sold, some after his death. But his first prose book publication was *The Happy Prince and Other Tales* (May 1888), a collection of fables he had made up for Cyril and Vyvyan. They were popular, and moderately well-received critically.

Walter Pater, to Wilde's delight, liked them, particularly *The Remarkable Rocket* and *The Selfish Giant* – in his review for the *Athenaeum*, Pater said, "There is a piquant touch of contemporary satire which differentiates Mr. Wilde from the teller of pure fairy tales; but it is so delicately introduced that the illusion is not destroyed and a child would delight in the tales without being worried or troubled by their application, while children of larger growth will enjoy them and profit by them."[2] All the tales are extended inversions, indeed paradoxes, upon simple and memorable themes, and many involve an ultimate sacrifice on the part of one character: the golden prince who literally gives himself away for his people, only to render himself disposable in their eyes; the nightingale who gives her heart's blood for a rose, only to have the love-token tossed aside by both the spoiled girl who demanded it and the conceited student who offered it; poor Hans, who dies so the Miller might serve as his chief mourner. The only tale centering around (a specifically middle-class) condemnation and punishment is, perhaps not surprisingly, Pater's favorite, *The Remarkable Rocket.*

When the Grosvenor Gallery opened in 1877, Whistler's *Nocturne in Black and Gold* (*The Falling Rocket*) was the painting that caused Ruskin to comment caustically on Whistler's "art," and Whistler to sue him for libel, successfully but unlucratively. Ruskin had written, in a review: "'I have seen and heard much of Cockney impudence by now, but never expected to hear a coxcomb ask two hundred guineas for flinging a pot of paint in the public's face.'"[3] Wilde doubtless meant a witty dig at Whistler (with whom he had not yet had his public falling-out) by writing about a rocket, but the title character is more Wildean than anything, or anyone, else. The Rocket is terribly proud of his heritage as the son of "the most celebrated Catherine Wheel of her day" and a high-flying father "of French Extraction," who "flew so high that people were afraid he would never come down again. He did, though . . . and he made a most brilliant descent in a shower of golden rain. The newspapers wrote about his performance in very flattering terms."[4] The other fireworks, priding themselves in turn on their lack of prejudice, are rude and insulting to the Rocket; they do not understand what they see as his affectation, and his deep friendship for the fair-haired, violet-eyed Prince he has never even met – yet another amazingly predictory instance, in Wilde's writings, of his having imagined Lord Alfred Douglas before meeting him (something Wilde himself immediately recognized). It is "a very dangerous thing to know one's friends," the Rocket admits, as he spoils himself by beginning to cry. The other fireworks, all "extremely practical," mock him with shouts of "'Humbug!'" and, soaked with tears, he fails to go off. Thrown into the mud, and further tormented by the "decidedly middle-class mind" of a passing Duck, the Rocket, pondering "the loneliness of genius," is taken up by two little boys who toss him on a fire. He explodes alone – no one hears him, no one sees him – and falls back to earth gasping and content that he has "create[d] a great sensation."[5]

The harsh judgment of his peers, and their failure to understand him, have ruined the Rocket, but he remains remarkable all the same. More Hans Christian Andersen than brothers Grimm, without Aesop's violence but with a well-buried, personalized edge, these "safe" fables would be the only book of his father's Vyvyan Holland could find, or remember seeing during his youth, upon his return to England – "But I had a great shock when I saw that the name Oscar Wilde had been scratched off the cover and that a piece of stamp-paper had been pasted over the title-page."[6]

Lord Arthur Savile's Crime and Other Stories (1891) is notable for introducing crime, and criminal behavior, into Wilde's world. The title story is about a "crime" that Wilde, at first, contrives to excuse as no crime at all. Assuming the title story to be farce, the *Graphic* maintained in its review that nobody "with the slightest sense of humour, or, for that matter, nobody with the strongest, can fail to enjoy the story of a man to whom murder presented itself in the light of a simple duty."[7] This entirely misses the point of Savile's severe punishment: the "simple duty" that is his sentence is marriage to Sibyl Merton in the end. All his attempted crimes have been frantic attempts to buy time, to stave off his real fate. Savile is punished – by enforced normality – in the end.

W.B. Yeats, writing for *United Ireland*, found the stories to be "an extravagant Celtic crusade against Anglo-Saxon stupidity," engineered by a man "who does not care what strange opinions he defends or what time-honoured virtue he makes laughter of, provided he does it cleverly."[8] Young Arthur Savile, his first name that of England's mythic king, his last that of the place where gentlemen get dressed – all nobility and nice clothing, and little more – is told that he will be a murderer. Out in London at night, Savile is excited by a city perilous, with "its fierce fiery-coloured joys, and its horrible hunger"; similarly, he is very excited by the thought of his own "shameful memory" of being a murderer well before he is one. When poisoning – "It was safe, sure, and quiet, and did away with any necessity for painful scenes" – fails him, Savile, having run away to languish in his brother's company in Venice, returns home "to blow up his uncle, the Dean of Chichester."[9] But he is a lord, not a revolutionary. This, too, fails. It is only when Savile, quite by happenstance, and in flippantly described fashion, tosses the cheiromantist Podgers into the Thames that the "curse" Podgers himself had read is lifted. It is no murder, in the end, but a sort of eye-for-an-eye. Podgers spoiled Savile's life with a sentence; Savile replied in kind, and society, believing Podgers a suicide (and, therefore, a moral criminal himself) does not punish Savile in an obvious way. He is punished, though, and too subtly for his sunny, simple, upper-class nature to see – Wilde sentences him to the "normal." No more forays into London at night for Lord Arthur Savile; it is two children, the country house, and a worshipping, perfect wife 24 hours a day.

The Portrait of Mr. W.H. was deemed unprintable in book form even by Wilde's progressive publishers at John Lane/The Bodley Head, known familiarly in *Punch* as "The Sodley Bed."[10] Wilde extensively, compulsively revised the manuscript until it was stolen during the sack of his home in April 1895 (it resurfaced in New York in 1921), but his first version of this story appeared in July 1889. Like "Pen, Pencil and Poison," "Mr. W.H." is about forgery. Unlike anything else Wilde had published, it is undebatably and obviously about an older male genius's deep affection for, and poetic creation for, a younger man. That the older man is Shakespeare, and the youth the mysterious inspiration for Wilde's favorite sonnets (and, Wilde opines, also the actor who played Shakespeare's great female leads – after they were written specifically with him in mind), ruffled the reading public.

The legal question, and argument, in Wilde's text is related to that of "Pen, Pencil and Poison." Is forgery, a severely punished crime against the state and the Treasury, a crime if it is perpetrated to prove a literary and artistic theory? If it is "merely the result of an artistic desire for perfect representation"?[11] The answer is yes, and yes again. Edward Merton's work itself is a real painting; it is Cyril Graham's verbal representation of it that opens the portrait to definition as a "forgery." A dedicatee indicated as "Mr. W.H." – if Shakespeare even wrote the dedication and envoi – was the "onlie begetter" of Shakespeare's sonnets; the name Willie Hughes or Hews is a forgery, and the portrait is, too. It is an idealized version, in fact, of Cyril Graham, who was "always cast for the girl's parts" and made "the only perfect Rosalind" – who is never seen in the story, for he is dead as Erskine tells it. When Erskine insisted, in a rage, that the portrait was a forgery, Graham left a letter confessing to the forgery, despite the "truth" of his theory, and shot himself. "I daresay I was unjust," Erskine reminisces, but justice has indeed been done.[12] Graham, and Wilde, know the penalty for forgery. They execute. And, when Erskine himself writes a false letter to the young narrator, threatening suicide, this too is a forgery of sorts. He has no intention of committing suicide. He is dying anyway. The realization of this as just deserts for espousing Mr. W.H. as the original, or authentic, when he is no more than symbol, keeps the young narrator from pursuing the theory further.

How can any original work of art be a forgery? It is a beautiful painting of a beautiful person, or personality, as Wilde would say. There is a fascinating double sense, though, in which "forgery" also means creation. James Joyce would use this idea to show Stephen Dedalus's great expectations, and to also mock the grandiosity and falsity of them, in the conclusion of his novel with the Wildean title, *A Portrait of the Artist as a Young Man.*[13] To forge is at once to counterfeit – coin, signatures – and this is, historically, one of the most violently punished crimes against property in English law. Forgery is also what is done in a smithy; the blacksmith's forge a strong societal (and literary, as in the case of Dickens's Joe Gargery) symbol of reliable, honest labor crucial to human transportation and commerce. Is "forging," then, a crime or an accomplishment? Both. Had "Mr. W.H." been read more widely, its destabilizing threat to English legal definition, as well as to the complacent canon of English Literature, might have provoked as much of an outcry as *Dorian Gray* soon would.[14] Yet even it shares with *Dorian*, and with Wilde's other work, a strong commitment to transgression punished. There is, and perhaps was, no Mr. W.H. Those who believed in him die. Those who admire his exterior, and the idea of him, but without commitment, live.

Those essays collected in *Intentions* (1891) were ones Wilde had composed, revised, and published in journals and reviews in the late 1880s. During this time (from November 1887 to October 1889), Wilde was editing *The Woman's World* and contributing book and art reviews to, chiefly, W.T. Stead's the *Pall Mall Gazette. The Woman's World* was called *The Lady's World* until Wilde renamed it – a change both timely and universalizing (there are New Women, but no New Ladies, of the 1890s), and also artistically superior. Wilde's title change focused upon gender, and not class, as an important nod to women not ladies but now capable of, and interested in, reading – and writing for – such a publication; and *Woman's World* is more lyrical, more memorably alliterative, something for which Wilde, though like Yeats famously tone deaf and not an aficionado of music, had a spectacular ear. *Woman's World* bore Wilde's status as editor prominently on its title page (which also features, as the magazine's logo, a bare-breasted Amazon clad in leopardskin, bow in hand, wrapped by a banner reading "La Belle Sauvage" – an interesting choice to illustrate woman and her world). Contributors included Ouida, Violet Fane, Ella Hepworth Dixon, Amy Levy, Olive Schreiner, Lady Wilde, and Constance Wilde; topics ranged from lacemaking in Ireland and colleges for women to Japanese art wares and biographies of famous women. Sonnets and art by both women and men (including Arthur Symons and Charles Ricketts) filled out the magazine; apart from some sparse "Literary Notes," in which he provides some mild criticism and, at one point, offers the opinion that "Charlotte Bronte's [style was] too exaggerated," the editor himself was not a contributor.[15]

Now, what were Wilde's intentions in *Intentions*? As Lawrence Danson recalls, Wilde's literary intentions "had always been suspect, from the time of *Poems* (1881), when the word 'plagiarism' was first pronounced against him, to *The Picture of Dorian Gray*, when the word was 'sodomitical.'"[16] "The Decay of Lying" and "Pen, Pencil and Poison" were both published in January 1889, the former in *The Nineteenth Century* and the latter in Frank Harris' *The Fortnightly Review*.[17] In these essays it is simple to see the effect of Pater – a "Pater-familias," the *Pall Mall Gazette* called Wilde, finding *Intentions* nevertheless "a fascinating, stimulating book, with more common sense in it than he would perhaps care to be accused of."[18] Arthur Symons praised the volume for its "paradoxical truths" and "perverted common sense," though he did not like "Pen, Pencil, and Poison," "which suffers from the lack of intrinsic interest in its subject. A pretentious, affected writer does not become interesting merely because he commits a murder."[19] Crime, even a major one successfully committed, cannot redeem bad art.

"The Decay of Lying," a "Dialogue" between two young men sharing names with Wilde's sons, is a close analysis of this fading "art" – the demise, during the late 1800s, of "the true liar, with his frank, fearless statements, his superb irresponsibility, his healthy, natural disdain of proof of any kind."[20] Frank, fearless, hearty, natural – all those *echt* English adjectives to describe a liar? Wilde's writerly intention is, as it often is, inversion.

Vivian purports to set art apart, most specifically, from issues of punishment, criticizing Charles Reade for his "foolish attempt to be modern" by spending the rest of his life trying "to draw public attention to the state of our convict prisons, and the management of our private lunatic asylums," after "one beautiful book," *The Cloister and the Hearth*. "Dickens," Vivian sniffs, "was depressing enough" in this vein, but the thought of Reade, "a man with a true sense of beauty, raging and roaring over the abuses of contemporary life like a common pamphleteer or a sensational journalist, is really a sight for the angels to weep over."[21] The chief form of punishment for Wilde's era, the massive Victorian prison, is glossed over and tossed into the catchall category of "abuses of contemporary life," a fit arena over which pamphleteers and journalists may engender and express concern, but not one with which artists should enter. Why, then, is such a passage even in Vivian's argument? If Reade's was such a foolish attempt, why does it merit so much notice? And why, when it comes to finding an example for his ruling proposition that "Life is Art's best, Art's only pupil," does Wilde have Vivian use one of modern literature's most powerful texts of hidden life, hidden evil, violent crime, and ultimate punishment, Stevenson's *Jekyll and Hyde*? When the essay's "final revelation is that Lying, the telling of beautiful untrue things, is the proper aim of Art,"[22] then it follows directly that Life, as Art's best and only pupil, must have the same aim. This is a heavy weight for paradox to bear: what is untrue is not only beautiful, but proper. The equations of both Keats and Mrs. Grundy are upset herein; and Wilde leaves, hanging unspoken, a dangerous possibility for Life's coupling of ugly and improper truths.

James MacNeill Whistler, enraged that Wilde, in "The Decay of Lying," had plundered his well-known "Ten O'Clock Lecture" (advocating art that did not imitate nature), made just such a coupling when the essay first appeared. He attacked Wilde in strikingly sexually specific terms in a letter to *Truth* in January 1890: "I learn, by the way, that in America he may, under the Law of '84, be criminally prosecuted, incarcerated, and made to pick oakum." For America read "at the Old Bailey," for '84 read *Truth* editor Labouchere's own amendment of 1885, and this is what would happen in 1895. And, in a note he sent Wilde and made public as the end of this letter, Whistler bastardized a phrase of Molière's as Wilde would render it: "You, Oscar, can go further, and with fresh effrontery, that will bring you the envy of all criminal confreres, unblushingly boast, 'Moi, je prends son bien la ou je le trouve!'"[23] Oscar goes further. His criminal brothers-in-arms envy him for his ability to do so.

To this smashing charge Wilde responded strictly in terms of plagiarism: Whistler's assertions were "as deliberately untrue as they [were] deliberately offensive," and, besides, Whistler's own ideas about art were completely unoriginal – how can one copy a copy? This clarifies Wilde on forgery; a copy of a copy is indeed art. The final lines of the letter, however, reveal the attitude that would lead Wilde to court in five years: "It is a trouble for a gentleman to have to notice the lucubrations of so ill-bred and ignorant a person as Mr. Whistler, but your publication of his insolent letter left me no option in the matter." The rantings of the well-born but ill-bred Queensberry were a trouble for the son of Sir William and Lady Wilde to have to notice, until the publication of an insolent card at the gentleman's ultimate refuge, one of Wilde's private clubs, made him feel as if he had no option but to sue for libel. Whistler fired one more salvo and then was content; in this last letter he imagines Wilde "in the dock, bas[ing] his innocence upon" a master-disciple relationship with an older man – Whistler himself – and describes Wilde being "entrusted with the materials for his crime" across a supper table.[24]

The thought of Wilde's impassioned speech in his first trial, testifying on his own behalf, and after the prosecution's sordid case against him had already been made, about his belief in the love that "is such a great affection of an elder for a younger man," and of the suppers he gave at London's finest restaurants as preludes to the "criminal" acts of which he would stand accused, makes Whistler's letter all the more vicious for its exposed knowledge. Wilde's plagiarism, or "play-giarism," might be viewed "less [as] a crime committed than a commitment to crime, a new paradigm of authorship"[25] today, but this was not the case when he was writing. Parody, or imitation as translation exercise or satire, was appropriate. Other forms of using others' work, from copied ideas to sonnets based on "poems-in-prose" letters, would keep Wilde in trouble from the time he published his highly derivative *Poems* in 1881. The pastiche, mosaic textual notions of modernism had not yet legitimized lifting a line or an idea from an earlier writer to "make it new," and it is interesting that even a 1990s critic sympathetic to Wilde refers to his authorship, or editorship, as crime.[26]

"Pen, Pencil and Poison: A Study in Green" is a story about art and crime – the art of crime, and the crimes of art. Wilde would return to this decadent, philosophical coupling again, at great length, in *Dorian Gray*, and it was a *fin-de-siècle* commonplace in English literature, thanks to him, by 1895. It would be no accident that Wilde's prosecutors, the popular press, and popular criminology all "linked crime and art – thereby conditioning middle-class suspicion of art and encouraging their divorce; and today it is impossible to know who took the vocabulary of disease, degeneration and genius from whom."[27] "Pen, Pencil and Poison" is a weird celebration of Thomas Griffiths Wainewright, friend of the essayists, Shakespeareans, and respectively apologist and murdereress Charles and Mary Lamb. He is "not merely a poet and a painter, an art-critic, an antiquarian, and a writer of prose, an amateur of beautiful things, and a dilettante of things delightful, but also a forger of no mean or ordinary capabilities, and as subtle and secret [a] poisoner almost without rival in this or any age." Though painting is the art that fascinates him first, Wainewright soon graduates to pen, and poison – linked as professional arts. Yet Wilde pointblank refuses to call Wainewright a criminal. The most he has committed is a moral, and not a criminal, act – a "sin."[28]

But in England, forgery and poisoning were historically two of the most vigorously prosecuted and severely punished (public spectacle ending in death) crimes.[29] Wilde himself maintains this tradition, as he unravels in his purported defense of Wainewright. His language begins to harden, as he finds excuses for Wainewright to displease him – Wainewright's greed, harassment, artistic incompetence – and therefore permit condemnation. Wainewright greedily sues an insurance company for money due him on one of his victims' lives. Wainewright foolishly follows a woman who does not love him to England, and is arrested. Wainewright's forgeries, so easily seen to be such, cannot be great art after all. Wilde's pose is to shock the reader – who would find poisoning alone quite enough – so Wilde must rationalize his own condemnation of Wainewright on artistic grounds: the artist does not fumble in a greasy till for cash; the artist does not give over his freedoms to societal constraint for rejected love – of a woman, at least. Finally, Wilde is forced to equate crime and sin – no longer using the Biblical, moralizing word, but the contemporary, legal one: "His crimes seem to have had an important effect on his art. They gave a strong personality to his style, a quality that his early work certainly lacked . . . one can fancy an intense personality being created out of sin."[30] This language attempting to differentiate a person from a personality would resound uncannily in Wilde's trials, where he – again unsuccessfully – sought to ignore or deny the former, and beautify the latter as an artful abstraction.

Having given in to admitting Wainewright is indeed a criminal, Wilde then trails off into weak and generalized defenses. He makes strained and feeble couplings, like "there is no essential incongruity between crime and culture," and argues that, when criminals are far removed from us and our English society – criminals like Tiberius, or the Borgias – we actually like reading about them. He ignores, though he certainly registers, the fact he leaves out: without culture, there is no crime. And if criminals of the past "are not in immediate relation to us," and "[w]e have nothing to fear from them,"[31] what reason, then, for their impassioned defense? What have they to fear from us? It is certainly far, far simpler to put a criminal in a large prison outside "our" comfortable, late-Victorian world and forget him, or enjoy reading about him in the tabloid press as we wish, than it is to consider, abstractly, what Cesare Borgia did one evening in Venice. Wilde might, snidely, dismiss his own critics as "the reporters of the police-court of literature, the chroniclers of the doings of the habitual criminals of art,"[32] but he knew, full well, that when art and literature are lopped off, these phrases still stand to apply in life. Wainewright deserved to die for poisoning others, and "we" like reading about his punishment for it in contemporary reports even more than we like reading about the Borgias.

As the essays of *Intentions* were typeset as a book, Wilde's longest, and most important, prose work was being read in magazines. *The Picture of Dorian Gray* is a critique of aestheticism, "which is shown to bring Dorian to ruin; yet readers have been won by Dorian's beauty and regretful, rather than horrified, at his waste of it, so that he has something of the glamor of a Faust rather than the foulness of a murderer and drug addict."[33] This apt synopsis of the seductive trouble caused by *Dorian*, and Dorian, does not add "the foulness of an unspeakable sexual indecency," which was included in contemporary minds at the time. In Jeff Nunokawa's words, "The love that dare not speak its name has never been less at a loss for words than it is in *The Picture of Dorian Gray*, whose sybaritic expanses form a virtual theme park for passions." All the familiars – the guyconography, if you will – of this unspeakable love are present: "Paterian sentiments, ecclesiastical vestments, anthems to Hellenism, the extremities of aestheticism, a passion for interior decoration, glimpses of cross-dressing, dubious meetings on the waterfront, 'the terrible pleasures of double life,' and the threat of blackmail that never ceases to darken it."[34]

The best-known contemporary review appeared anonymously in the *St. James's Gazette*, and is patently confused by the novel, but knew something was rotten in it. The review is a mass of qualifications, attack, and defense. Beginning what looks to be a very harsh review of this work "which Messrs. Ward, Lock & Co. have not been ashamed to circulate in Great Britain," the reviewer scrambles for ground high enough to permit condescension:

> Not being curious in ordure, and not wishing to offend the nostrils of decent persons, we do not propose to analyse *The Picture of Dorian Gray*: that would be to advertise the development of an esoteric prurience. Whether the Treasury or the Vigilance Society will think it worth while to prosecute Mr. Oscar Wilde [or his publisher] we do not know; but on the whole we hope they will not.[35]

This beginning is a strange statement of negation. A prominent publisher is avowedly not ashamed to publish Wilde's book. Incense for some may be ordure to others; but the very idea of ordure conjures up unavoidably Wilde's Anglo-Irish predecessor Dean Swift and popular novelists of the eighteenth century, solidly canonical despite purported Victorian squeamishness and dislike for earthy humor and commentary. We are curious in, and about, ordure (and wickedness, and scandal, and the rich and languid). Far from not analyzing *Dorian Gray*, and Dorian

Gray, the review subjects both work and character to deep scrutiny. And, having made the sweeping intimation that some sort of decency prosecution might be considered, the reviewer immediately backpedals to erase this proposition: "we do not know . . . we hope they will not." Why has Wilde, "a young man of decent parts," put his name to this? "Let nobody read it in the hope of finding witty paradox or racy wickedness." With the name Wilde upon it, everybody will read it expecting witty paradox and, perhaps, what they can term racy wickedness. If Rider Haggard's "chaste delight" in "gore and gashes" is truly more acceptable to this reviewer, more natural to the "cultivated palate" than *Dorian*'s "mere licentiousness," why the dripping, sexually analogized terms for Haggard's work, and such a flat description of what *Dorian* appears to espouse?[36]

In finding, ultimately, that Wilde's purpose for the story is "Not to give pleasure to his reader," the *St. James's* reviewer protests too much one last time – he has found pleasure in reading, and reviewing, the book, more pleasure than he can say. When, in conclusion, he insists that *Dorian Gray* should "be chucked into the fire. Not so much because [it is] dangerous and corrupt . . . as because [it] is incurably silly" – it is palpably clear that this book must be consigned to flames not for its silliness, but for the dangerous and corrupt effect it has had upon someone who has tried hard to deny it, but who cannot, even in struggling to dismiss *Dorian* as "silly," keep from the sickly, decadent vocabulary that has infected his prose, tagging on the adjective "incurably."[37]

The *Daily Chronicle* also tried, and failed, to trivialize *Dorian* as a sort of oddity, like a gypsy entertainer, "unclean, though undeniably amusing." The *Chronicle* got the point of connecting it with French literature, and took full advantage, as English journals did and will, of a chance to condemn all that was rotten across the Channel:

> It is a tale spawned from the leprous literature of the French Decadents – a poisonous book, the atmosphere of which is heavy with the mephitic odours of moral and spiritual putrefaction – a gloating study of the mental and physical corruption of a fresh, fair and golden youth, which might be horrible and fascinating but for its effeminate frivolity, its studied insincerity, its theatrical cynicism, its tawdry mysticism, its flippant philosophisings, and the contaminating trail of garish vulgarity.

They peg the ancient world for what it means here: Dorian's face, "rosy with the loveliness that endeared youth of his odious type to the paralytic patricians of the Lower Empire."[38] Shades of Tiberius and his minnows.

The *Scots Observer* got Dorian's sexual points most unequivocally. "The world is fair, and the proportion of healthy-minded men and honest women to those that are foul, fallen, or unnatural is great." Though the fair-and-foul twist is appropriately allusive, the reviewer might have recalled that, in *Macbeth*, fair is foul, and vice versa, and fair faces often mask foul or false souls beneath – rather supporting Wilde's "false art" as true. But the review's conclusion contains the memorable lines so often quoted after Wilde's trials:

> The story – which deals with matters only fitted for the Criminal Investigation Department or a hearing in camera is discreditable alike to author and editor. Mr. Wilde has brains, and art, and style; but if he can write for none but outlawed noblemen and perverted telegraph boys, the sooner he takes to tailoring (or some other decent trade) the better for his own reputation and the public morals.[39]

Punch did not pull its punches in a review Wilde himself particularly remembered for its "'offensive tone and horridness.'" Dorian is "beautiful and Ganymede-like" – not just a beauty, but Zeus's own beauty, given a name always, and only, applied to young male objects of older male desire.[40] "'[W]e artists'," sniffed *Punch*, in more stock sexual allusion – this time that of pistolry – "do not always hit what we aim at, and despite his confident claim to unerring artistic marksmanship, one must hazard the opinion, that in this case Mr. Wilde has 'shot wide.'" Shot wide – he has missed the "normal" mark; or perhaps been aiming for another mark entirely, not what we aim at, but what he chooses to. This is exactly, though unspokenly, "the unsavoury suggestiveness which lurks in [the novel's] spirit."[41]

Other "literary evidence" would include the models for *Dorian*, and Dorian – none of them "healthy" or "normal," by Carson's definitions. "Dorian Gray," with the odd Christian name and the Americanized spelling of "grey," merits parsing, given the importance Wilde always attached to names and naming. Stanley Weintraub notes the basic Dorian–Doric connection[42] – add to it "doron," or "gift of God," to complete the Greek-love trifecta. As to the gray, it is a particularly English, and yet aesthetic, color, suitable for damp London fogs, mouse-grey gloves and (as Jane knows in Gilbert and Sullivan's *Patience*) English officers' uniforms: "there is a cobwebby grey velvet, with a tender bloom like cold gravy."[43]

French decadents and American writers of horror rub shoulders, here, with the Earl of Beaconsfield; certainly J-K. Huysmans's *A Rebours* (1884), Edward Heron-Allen's *Ashes of the Future: The Suicide of Sylvester Gray* (1888), the stories of Hawthorne and Poe, the novels of Wilde's ancestor Charles Robert Maturin, Goethe's *Faust*, Stevenson's *Jekyll and Hyde*, and Disraeli's *Vivian Grey* (1825) rate mention. When Wilde first began classes at Oxford, Disraeli was Prime Minister: an ennobled "foreigner" (created an earl and raised in the Church of England, Disraeli was of Jewish heritage), a wit, a dandy, a maker of epigrams, and a name known throughout England and the world. *Vivian Grey* is not simply a satire on English politics, but has a healthy, or rather unhealthy, dose of Gothic, from spectacular outdoor supernatural events (generally in the Alps) to portraits with eyes that move. When, in Disraeli's novel, Max Rodenstein is slain, hundreds of miles away from the hall where it hangs, the expression that suddenly crosses the painted face of his portrait sends another (female) character into a swoon. And in Disraeli's less well known *Venetia* (1837), the title character and heroine suffers an artist father, Marmion Herbert, whose portrait is kept locked away by her mother.[44] After the mother – behaving rather like Meleager's, a classical connection that would have appealed to Wilde – stabs and shreds the canvas one day, Herbert dies.

Dorian Gray opens in an artist's studio and ends before a portrait. It is an "extraordinary romance" of "artistic idolatry,"[45] but also, and more so in the revised version, a catalog of crime. However, the unnatural laws presiding over *Dorian* are largely laws of inaction. Lord Henry Wotton may murmur in Dorian's ear of "day-dreams and sleeping dreams whose mere memory might stain your cheek with shame," dreams that purportedly spring from Hellenic ideals,[46] but Wotton is a talker, not a doer. In more than one letter Wilde reflects on his own willingness to talk and dislike for action, commenting later that he found *Dorian Gray* "rather like my own life – all conversation and no action."[47]

Wotton, without lifting a single lethargic finger, engages constantly, obsessively, in what Byron so vividly condemned Keats for, "a sort of mental masturbation – he is always frigging his *Imagination*."[48] The man who talks such a good game, whose one act is to send Dorian the mysterious poisonous yellow book (Wilde originally had named it as "Le Secret de Raoul, by Catulle Sarrazin"),[49] Wotton might be a suspect, but he is no criminal. Out of the company of his male friends, he is a rather dull man married to a woman with a supremely irritating laugh. Alan

Sinfield perfectly analyzes the sexuality of Wilde's dandy characters, both beautiful and effete youths and beautiful Graecophilosophizing older (but not *too* old) men when he says that they "passed, we might now say, not by playing down what we call camp behaviour, but by manifesting it exuberantly" – and also by chasing women; Wotton, who is too lethargic to chase an actress, but has an eye for them and loves to talk about them, is the prime example of the Wildean dandy.[50]

Basil Hallward is more problematic.[51] He, too, appears to be a talker and not a doer. But there is one impulse, one "bad" impulse, upon which he does act. He admittedly worships Dorian Gray, and in a rich and strange way: "I knew that I had come face to face with some one whose mere personality was so fascinating that, if I allowed it to do so, it would absorb my whole nature, my whole soul." Not only the nature and soul are involved; it is Dorian's face and body, too, he worships: "The merely visible presence of this lad . . . defines for me . . . all the perfection of the spirit that is Greek. The harmony of soul and body – how much that is!" As Basil concludes his introductory paean on Dorian, his first "scene" in the novel, Wotton murmurs anticlimactically and obviously, "What you have told me is quite a romance."[52]

To enact this romance with Dorian in physical terms, in real life, would have meant jail time for Basil since 1885. And he does enact it in physical terms. He "takes" Dorian, not his likeness, and sets him into his own canvas. As Hallward signs the "vermilion" name at the end he has literally put his life's blood into the work, and Dorian has breathed his life into it – the two are combined, in the consummation Hallward devoutly wishes, in the portrait. The picture of Dorian Gray is a possessed, cross-gendered, inversion of the Pygmalion and Galatea myth. Basil uses his art to bring what he loves beneath his touch, living and breathing, aging and changing. "[B]iting the end of one of his huge brushes" as he looks from the finished portrait to Dorian and back again, Basil finally feels his triumph, and brands his Dorian by giving him, like a married woman, his own "name in long vermilion letters." Dorian realizes what has been done to him, albeit with his own knowledge and semi-acquiescence, and begins to weep; consent is no defense to Basil's possession. When Dorian leaves the studio that day, it is as an ivory automaton, called "Dorian" and capable of the inhuman, for "the real Dorian" stays with Basil.[53] And this is why Basil receives a death sentence. He takes the boy, in an utterly physical fashion; therefore his Galatea steps from the frame and murders him.

When the two Dorians are united under one roof, horror ensues for both. In proximity, capable now of mirroring, the painting and the painted function like the two human halves of "The Fisherman and His Soul," which Wilde was also writing at, roughly, the same time. Sibyl Vane, in her "prison of passion," loses her ability to be Shakespeare's heroines because of her "Prince Charming! Prince of life!", and for her mistake suffers under Dorian's pronouncement, "You have killed my love."[54] Literally, she does kill his love – herself – immediately. And, in an appropriate punishment, this action kills Dorian's true love as well. The portrait he has stared at for hours, and kissed "in boyish mockery of Narcissus," and heartfelt attraction too, immediately begins to bear the visible penalties for Dorian's acts.[55] It is no longer kissable. It is not even fit to be seen. It will be put away, alone, like Bertha Mason Rochester in her attic, or a felon in a cell.

Dorian's actions from the time of Sibyl's death are reported as rumors, and generally in the passive voice. Wilde's use of the passive is endemic in his prose; it allows a speaker or narrator to be noncommital, to depersonalize a situation. *De Profundis*, with hardly an active verb except "force" in the text, bears a particular sense of something having been done to, rather than by, Wilde. Similarly, Dorian's agency is removed, and doubt cast on his actions, by the passive. Was he really "brawling with foreign sailors in a low den in the distant parts of Whitechapel"? Does he "consor[t] with thieves and coiners and kn[o]w the mystery of their trade"? What does he do during those "extraordinary absences," and what makes them "notorious"? Why do his intimates, particularly women, come to shun him, and "grow pallid with shame or horror if Dorian Gray entered the room"? These "whispered scandals," societal creations and conjectures all, he does nothing to quell, and they simply add to "his strange and dangerous charm."[56] Why strange? Wherefore dangerous? Is it thinking alone that makes them so?

Yes, until Dorian murders Basil. This scene of action shows two things: first, the portrait bearing witness to the truth of the whispered scandals and dirty rumors; and second, Dorian committing a horrible crime in vivid language and in plain view. The last thing Basil sees before he dies, and we see it through his eyes, is the "hideous face on the canvas," "Dorian Gray's own face," with the thinning gold hair, the sensual mouth, sodden blue eyes all pale and terrible reminders of "that marvellous beauty" he had worshipped. It is no forgery, no "foul parody, some infamous, ignoble satire" but his own work, his own brushstrokes, his own idol, and Basil cannot endure this. He does not embrace the sobbing man he once loved, or offer him comfort, but collapses into sanctimony and Biblical quotation, urging Dorian to pray, and chastising him for having "done enough evil in [his] life." Coming from the artist who wished most to make himself master of Dorian's youth and beauty, this is too much hypocrisy; the "grinning lips" of the canvas suggest it, and the beautiful Dorian does it – Basil Hallward dies horribly, and downright naturalistically:

> He rushed at him, and dug the knife into the great vein that is behind the ear, crushing the man's head down on the table, and stabbing again and again. There was a stifled groan, and the horrible sound of some one choking with blood. Three times the outstretched arms shot up convulsively, waving grotesque stiff-fingered hands in the air. He stabbed him twice more, but the man did not move. Something began to trickle on the floor.[57]

Wilde's command of yet another developing genre of fiction peculiarly and phenomenally popular in England, the detective/thriller, is already presaging the later Arthur Conan Doyle, Dorothy Sayers, and Agatha Christie.[58]

Pacing his lovely drawing-room "like a beautiful caged thing," Dorian is let out of prison by Alan Campbell, the Scots chemist whose life he has already touched, and chilled, once. Dorian confesses the murder to him, and, in response to Campbell's horrified refusal to help and the comment that "Nobody ever commits a crime without doing something stupid,"[59] silently hands Campbell a note that obviously shows Dorian's intent to commit a further crime: blackmailing Campbell. Campbell destroys the body. Does Dorian follow through on this intent anyway? Is that why Alan Campbell's suicide is soon the talk of the town? Is that why Dorian is so desperate to buy oblivion at the opium dens that his next trip there is not just a rumored one, but one on which Wilde permits us to come along?

The death of James Vane frees Dorian from the last threat of exposure and punishment at the hands of any other character. Lord Henry, "Prince Paradox," laughs off Dorian's confession of killing Basil with the dismissive – and, as we and Dorian see, blind – comment that this is just "posing" on Dorian's part: "All crime is vulgar, just as all vulgarity is crime. It is not in you, Dorian, to commit a murder. . . . Crime belongs exclusively to the lower orders." Wotton refuses to see Dorian as an actor, because he himself is not, and because "Art has no influence upon action."[60] But Dorian Gray has committed criminal acts, and, in the end, he dies for them. Wilde executes the beautiful boy, and resurrects in his stead the work of art, a painting utterly incapable of action and capable only of golden perfection.

In February 1891 an essay Wilde did not collect, and always referred to as "The Soul of Man," was published in *The Fortnightly Review*.[61] Art and crime do, indeed, connect in real life, whether on an individual or societal level. Insisting, as always, that "What is true about Art is true about Life," Wilde characterizes Art as "this intense form of Individualism" that will paradoxically, if fostered and shared by all, lead to true socialism and happiness.[62] Stepping dangerously upon the most strongly protected area of English law, Wilde argues that, "When private property is abolished there will be no necessity for crime, no demand for it; it will cease to exist." But Wilde immediately veers away from this stock socialistic point back into Art – our modern-day criminals "are, as a class, so absolutely uninteresting" because "Starvation, and not sin, is the parent of modern crime." Wilde would give up all private property in a trice for one "marvellous Macbeth" or "terrible Vautrin."[63] The posturing admiration of famous past criminals, though, recognizes that the same societal condemnation Shakespeare's audiences felt for the Scots hell-kite still applies to paler modern malefactors.

His view of crime in this essay differs only from that in "Pen, Pencil and Poison" in that Wilde addresses the issue of punishment with such specificity, noting that, "in the original authorities of each time, one is absolutely sickened, not by the crimes that the wicked have committed, but by the punishments that the good have inflicted."[64] However, Wilde clearly realizes that he lives within such a time. He knows the law and its power. And I believe this accounts for his violent attack, in summation, upon the press – viewed by so many as a democratic, equalizing, leveling force, but which Wilde abhors, or, more accurately, fears: "In the old days men had the rack. Now they have the Press."[65]

Presciently, powerfully, Wilde analogizes the relation between publication and punishment: "In centuries before ours the public nailed the ears of journalists to the pump. That was quite hideous. In this century journalists have nailed their own ears to the keyhole. That is much worse. . . .The private lives of men and women should not be told to the public. The public have nothing to do with them at all."[66] What Wilde elides is the fact that it is the public, still, who have nailed journalists' ears, and eyes, to the keyholes of such semi-public spaces as hotel-room doors and rented rooms not one's home. The society that jealously guards itself will have the "truth" told to it, and Fleet Street will keep it in the know – and its own coffers healthy.

From his best-known work of fiction, *Dorian Gray*, through the fairy tales he wrote for his sons, [67] through the essays, which, in their style and form, are fictional, Wilde consistently condemns even the most beautiful of bad actors. They are charming, often eloquent, highly artistic – but all of these Wildean leading characteristics cannot save them in the end. In the glittering world of his plays, Wilde's most popular writings of all, will matters be different? No.

wilde's plays

> One name can make my pulses bound,
>   No peer it owns, nor parallel,
> By it is Vivian's sweetness drowned,
>   And Roland, full as organ-swell;
>   Though Frank may ring like silver bell,
> And Cecil softer music claim,
>   They cannot work the miracle –
> 'Tis Ernest sets my heart a-flame.
>
> John Gambril Nicholson, "Of Boys' Names," *Love in Earnest* (1892)

> Scandals used to lend charm, or at least interest, to a man – now they crush him. And yours is a very nasty scandal. You couldn't survive it.
>
> *An Ideal Husband* (1895)

> Crushed again!
>
> Reginald Bunthorne's last line, *Patience* (1881)

Wilde's most popular works were, and are, his plays – an outgrowth, I think, of the grand public performances he first gave as a young man straight out of Magdalen ten years before. Like Shakespeare, Wilde did not officially, at least initially, set down the texts of what he first provided as public performance. During the early 1880s he lectured on dress, art, literature, history, and criticism in America and throughout Britain, but, apart from what he set down as part of his comparatively few published essays, or what was reported in contemporary news accounts, Wilde's words on these matters lived only for their hearers at the time. He had attempted writing down performances for others at this time, but his efforts were flops or short runs not even staged in London (*Vera*, New York, 1883; *Guido Ferranti*, New York, 1891) or unproduced plays (*The Duchess of Padua*, a variation of *Guido Ferranti*; and the unfinished *La Sainte Courtesane* and *A Florentine Tragedy*).

In 1891, after marked success and fame – as well as condemnation – for his prose, Wilde tried drama again. He wrote *Lady Windermere's Fan: A Play About a Good Woman* during the summer of 1891, beginning it (and continuing his personal tradition, which had started by felicitous chance with his Newdigate poem *Ravenna*, of using place names where he had visited or lived as names in his works) at a friend's Lake Country home.[68] Wilde was working on *Salomé* that fall as he revised *Lady Windermere*, began *A Woman of No Importance* in July of 1892 after his bitter disappointment when *Salomé* was deemed unproduceable by the Lord Chamberlain, and, as soon as *A Woman of No Importance* had been staged, started *An Ideal Husband* at the summer house he and Bosie had taken for the 1893 season at Goring-on-Thames. With *An Ideal Husband* in rehearsals, Wilde, first with his family, and then with Bosie, at the seaside at Worthing, wrote *The Importance of Being Earnest* within weeks. *Earnest* opened at the St. James's on Valentine's Day, 1895, with the first-nighters arriving in a rare London blizzard, barely a month after *An Ideal Husband* had gone up at the Haymarket. The speed and ease with which he completed his plays, and their sequential flow, is unmatched by anything in Wilde's prose work but his constant, conversational letters; and Wilde's career as a dramatist seemed both unchangeable in terms of genre, and unbreakable in terms of success, in the early spring of 1895.

The plays, written over such a brief time period as to match the for-profit output of Wilde's beloved Renaissance masters like Shakespeare, Marlowe, and Webster, all deal with critical treatment of crime and punishment – to a script, to an act, and very nearly to a scene. At a time when blackmail (and the threat of what it might uncover if left unpaid), improbable and imprisonable debt, and lying to the extent of self-perjury were issues in Wilde's life, they lace his plays and, in ironic fact, hold them together.

Sexual transgression is the offense held up for analysis in the first play. Lady Windermere, the serious young wife who confesses freely, and rather proudly, to having "something of the Puritan in me," allows of "no compromise" between "what is right and what is wrong."[69] She immediately qualifies herself by delivering these lines to Lord Darlington, the first of Wilde's dramatic characters, like Lord Henry Wotton in *Dorian*, to be popularly and critically associated with Wilde himself. Lord Darlington, condemned by the Duchess of Berwick as "thoroughly depraved," maintains that "to be intelligible is to be found out" and, most famously, that he can "resist everything but temptation." As a butler bearing the surname of the two brothers who would testify against Wilde, Parker, pops in and out, Darlington entertains Lady Windermere's tea guests, then exits just before the "real" and yet sublimely unimportant scandal of the play, Lord Windermere's connection to Mrs. Erlynne, is revealed in Act I. It is Lady Windermere herself who turns the private public by cutting the covers of her husband's secret bankbook, proclaiming (before an audience) that she feels "degraded," "utterly stained," and "tainted" by what she believes to be his affair with Mrs. Erlynne, and speaks of the horror that her husband "should pass from the love that is given to the love that is bought." Windermere chastises her for her spying and "unjust" condemnation – and asks that she invite Mrs. Erlynne into their home. She will not; it is left to Parker to deliver the invitation. The audience is given a clue immediately as to "who this woman really is," though Windermere cannot tell his wife as "the shame would kill her"[70] – a shame not daring to speak, here, the name of "Mother."

Lord Darlington immediately urges a divorce on most Wildean grounds – "there are moments when one has to choose between living one's own life, fully, entirely, completely, or dragging out some false, shallow, degrading existence that the world in its hypocrisy demands" – and invites Lady Windermere to leave England with him.[71] She intends to, but by interception of her letter, her mother saves her from "the brink of a hideous precipice" with a staggering, and staggeringly correct, speech on the wages of societally perceived sin in England, circa 1890:[72]

> You don't know what it is to fall into the pit, to be despised, mocked, abandoned, sneered at – to be an outcast! to find the door shut against one, to have to creep in hideous byways, afraid every moment lest the mask should be stripped from one's face, and all the while to hear the laughter, the horrible laughter of the world, a thing more tragic than all the tears the world has ever shed. You don't know what it is. One pays for one's sin, and then one pays again, and all one's life one pays.

Laughter in a theatre pays the bills. "The horrible laughter of the world" is another matter. When Mrs. Erlynne's "wonderful act of self-sacrifice" in claiming the fan saves Lady Windermere from the same charges she has leveled at her husband, she is redeemed – but only technically, not morally. Wilde makes it clear that it is for the money, and the convenience and pleasure of living abroad as Lady Lorton, that she will marry the foolish Augustus. And Darlington disappears entirely from Act IV, after his cruel surprise, at the "unmasking" end of Act III, to find that the woman concealed in his room is not the one he believed to be there, but her older, cleverer, predecessor – a woman more fitting for his character, more fitting to accompany him to the Continent and partake of its charms, but not the younger, fresher model he wants.

A Woman of No Importance has a sexual secret, too, and a more tangled one. Lord Illingworth, this play's poser of paradoxes, double entendres, and quips, has fathered a son whom he has never known, but whom he wishes to engage as his private secretary. Two young men Wilde knew worked, or had worked, as private secretaries. Both had ceased to do so under extremely suspect, unspokenly sexual circumstances. Francis Douglas, Lord Drumlanrig, was Bosie's oldest brother, and personal secretary to Prime Minister Rosebery, who had created Francis an English peer, Lord Kelhead. Francis would be found dead in the fall of 1894, just prior to his marriage, on his estates in Scotland, a gun beside him. He may have died accidentally, but it was immediately rumored, and believed by his father, that Francis killed himself over being blackmailed because of his affair with his boss. And Bosie himself was dismissed as Lord Cromer's personal secretary in Cairo over muddy but avowedly unpleasant circumstances just after a trip Bosie took up the Nile with E.F. Benson and other friends, and just before his return to England to live with Wilde as he wrote this play.[73]

Not his mother's objections, nor the tale of Lord Illingworth's despoiling someone Gerald immediately feels couldn't have been "a really nice girl," can stop the relationship. But Illingworth's completely meaningless attempt to kiss Hester does. Gerald takes on all the American girl's prudishness with her; he insists that his father and mother marry, until Hester, unbending, absolves Mrs. Arbuthnot with the promise of "other countries over the sea, better, wiser, and less unjust lands."[74] Illingworth, the self-proclaimed "*fin-de-siècle* person," "The Puritan," is left out of the family circle for the triple transgression of the engendering of Gerald, the attempt to take Gerald from his mother, and the attempt to take Hester from Gerald.

An Ideal Husband is a black comedy about blackmail. The characters are stock, by now – Mabel Chiltern with her "apple-blossom" English prettiness; the red-headed, heliotrope-wearing Mrs. Cheveley (note that for Wilde only women prefaced with "Mrs.," and never "Lady," are the fallen ones); a successful Lord and Lady – but their actions are entirely unpredictable in this most nervous, most jittery, most uncomfortable of all Wilde's plays. Consider the stage directions as, particularly, the male leads make their first entrances: Sir Robert Chiltern, "A personality of mark . . . . A nervous temperament, with a tired look . . . . There is nervousness in the nostrils, and in the pale, thin, pointed hands"; and Lord Goring, the Wildean/dandy figure, who "plays with life," and "is fond of being misunderstood." Mrs. Cheveley's blackmailing of Chiltern – over a letter written when he was in his personal-secretary days – shatters his false propriety in a heartbeat. First he offers her money for the letter, and, when she refuses, immediately caves in with an "I consent." Lady Chiltern, insisting that "One's past is what one is," questions him violently about any "shame" he might be concealing with an incantational repetition of the word, and the reiteration, like Mrs. Erlynne's, of the idea of having to pay for one's societally judged sins: "I know that there are men with horrible secrets in their lives – men who have done some shameful thing, and who in some critical moment have to pay for it, by doing some other act of shame – Oh! don't tell me you are such as they are!" He is "such as they," but she precludes him from speaking it – "don't tell me" – and insists that he do the right thing, which will destroy him publicly, by challenging and denying Mrs. Cheveley in writing.[75]

Chiltern then proceeds, on the advice of Lord Goring but without any prompting, to do very much the wrong thing by hoisting Mrs. Cheveley on her own petard. It is not, he insists, fair at all "that the folly, the sin of one's youth, if men choose to call it a sin [and they certainly do], should wreck a life like mine, should place me in the pillory, should shatter all that I have worked for, all that I have built up." Chiltern's response is to probe for Mrs. Cheveley's past follies, sins of youth, and try to blackmail her back. He is inept, she tells his secret to his wife, and Lady Chiltern is devastated; her response is in physical, sexual terms, and based in the shock of a purposefully hidden and sordid truth suddenly revealed in an unexpected and public fashion: "Don't come near me. Don't touch me. I feel as though you had soiled me for ever. Oh! what a mask you have been wearing all these years! A horrible painted mask! You sold yourself for money! Oh, a common thief were better! You put yourself up for sale to the highest bidder! You were bought in the market! You lied to the whole world."[76]

It is up to Lord Goring to commit a bad act himself to save his friends, and their marriage – to blackmail Mrs. Cheveley by threatening to reveal her as "a common thief" and, perhaps inadvertently, to knock Lady Chiltern off her pedestal by letting Mrs. Cheveley, deprived of one letter, make off with another. But a letter without an envelope or addressee is always a safe one – Chiltern mistakes his wife's missive to Goring for one to him. There is no more danger of revelation; Mrs. Cheveley is a conveniently forgotten part of the past; Chiltern accepts his Cabinet seat; and Goring, such a good friend to both Chilterns, accepts their beautiful young daughter as his thanks.

The Importance of Being Earnest, Wilde's most popular work, is a story set in the unreal space where illusion and reality can cohabit in bliss in the end. "Bunburying" means only one thing to critics today: Wilde's blatant construction of a stage facsimile of the two worlds he lived in by Valentine's Day, 1895, one with his wife and sons when he was in residence at home in Chelsea, and the other with Douglas, his friends, and hired rent boys down the river at the Savoy Hotel.[77] Did contemporary critics pick up on Wilde's clear allusions at the time? George Alexander, the theatre manager who starred as Algernon in the first production, would not permit Wilde to include most of the Bunburying, chiefly that involving Jack's legal complications and threatened arrest because of outstanding bills from the Savoy and a string of West End restaurants. A whole act was cut; on opening night, Wilde, "his large face smiling," told Alexander, "'do you know, from time to time I was reminded of a play I once wrote myself, called *The Importance of Being Earnest.*'"[78]

Bunburying is quite simply what Shakespeare would call a lie direct. "Bunbury" is not a real person, but the made-up story of a sickly old friend, who has Algernon perpetually on call whenever Algernon wants an excuse not to do something – usually a social obligation – he ought, or is expected, to undertake. On the pretext of going to visit poor Bunbury in the country, Algy can now remain in London and see his young male friends – as long as the circles in which he moves do not intersect, thereby blowing his cover. As Algy explains to Jack, "If it wasn't for Bunbury's extraordinary bad health for instance, I wouldn't be able to dine with you at the Savoy to-night, for I have really been engaged to Aunt Augusta for more than a week." Well, what happens when the worlds collide? What happens when someone who frequents the Savoy's private dining-rooms, and bedrooms, turns up for supper at Aunt Augusta's home? On stage, one cannot "be imprisoned in the suburbs for having dined in the West End! It is perfectly ridiculous!"[79] Off stage, or, rather, in everyday life – if either of these expressions can rightly be applied to Wilde, who was a constant performer and would certainly have argued that his life was *never* "everyday" – one certainly *can* be imprisoned for dining and then spending the night, in a public hotel or private room, with someone of the same sex.

The time for the play Wilde specifies as not an abstract, safely distancing past, but the "Present." Confirmed bachelor Algy opens the first scene concerned as ever about his appetites (ostensibly for champagne and cucumber sandwiches) and advising strongly that Jack not marry Gwendolen ("If ever I get married, I'll certainly try to forget the fact"). The cigarette case, infamously Wilde's standard gift to the young men he met through Alfred Taylor, reveals a better reason than Algy's advice for putting off the marriage: the same man is "Ernest in town and Jack in the country," leading a double life as "a confirmed and secret Bunburyist."[80]

The Savoy Hotel is, specifically, the place that has Ernest in legal trouble. Although Jack is wealthy, "Ernest is one of those chaps who never pay a bill. He gets writted about once a week." He owes the Savoy over £700, and when Algy decides to Bunbury as Ernest in the country as the best way to meet Cecily, he is confronted with this. The whisper of this most dangerous subplot remains in the play as premiered; in the suppressed section, a solicitor, Mr. Gribsby, of the firm of Parker and Gribsby (Parker, again, was the name of one of the chief witnesses against Wilde), arrives with a writ of attachment on behalf of the Savoy, and a resultant "order for the committal of your person." An "officer of the Court whose function it is to seize the person of the debtor is waiting in the fly outside. He has considerable experience in these matters." Algy, as a gentleman, protests that "No gentleman ever has any money," and the solicitor responds gravely, and pointedly, "My experience is that it is usually relations who pay!" Algy will do anything to get out of the looming trip to Holloway Gaol except tell the truth – to reveal himself as Algy, not Ernest – and Jack sides with the voices of Victorian rectitude, Chasuble and Prism, insisting "that incarceration would do [Algy] a great deal of good." Only when Cecily threatens to intervene and keep "Ernest" out of jail with her own money does Jack pull out his checkbook, and Algy rudely dismisses his would-be captor with "No gentleman cares much about knowing a solicitor who wants to imprison one in the suburbs."[81]

With the threat of jail removed, the play sparkles on: Bunbury is "quite exploded"; the handbag (with handles to it) left at Victoria Station, the Brighton line, is recovered; Jack is indeed Algy's brother after all; and their father's Christian name is discovered to be Ernest. But the disturbing subtext – so prominent in the original play as to be text, not subtext – lingers. And, as the reviewer for *The Speaker* said of the play, one can so readily, too readily, see

> that the conduct of the people in itself is rational enough; it is exquisitely irrational in the circumstances. Their motives, too, are quite rational in themselves; they are only irrational as being fitted to the wrong set of actions. And the result is that you have something like real life in detail, yet, in sum, absolutely unlike it; the familiar

materials of life shaken up, as it were, and rearranged in a strange, unreal pattern.[82]

H.G. Wells, reviewing the play on opening night for the *Pall Mall Gazette*, wrote one line about *Earnest* intended to compliment the play and, rightly, set it apart from anything else on the London stage at the time. The Marquess of Queensberry simply must have seen, and taken violently to heart, this sentence in Wells's review: "Most of the [new plays today], after the fashion of Mr. John Worthing, J.P, last night, have simply been the old comedies posing as their own imaginary youngest brothers."[83] Queensberry would echo this loaded verb, obsessed by the idea of an older man, posing with and beside his young son, when, two days later, he scribbled a note to "Oscar Wilde, posing [as] somdomite." *The Importance of Being Earnest*, his most popular and beloved play, was in a horrible irony the writing that led directly to Wilde's trials, downfall, and premature death.

Contemporary events of allegedly criminal behavior, of the sort of which, after the premiere of *Earnest*, Queensberry finally accused Wilde must have made Wilde feel as if no harm could come to him by prosecuting Queensberry for libel. The Cleveland Street male-brothel scandal, which broke in July 1889, had also been based in a libel action – but one against a newspaper, which was won by the prosecutor, Lord Euston. The sexual misconduct and crimes alleged to have taken place in the house of Cleveland Street were unmentionable, unprintable corollaries to the libel action brought against the editor of the *North London Press*, Ernest Parke, by Euston, who was rumored in the paper to be a Cleveland Street patron. Parke was given a year in jail, while Lord Euston was not prosecuted for the newly criminalized "gross indecency" or for anything else.[84] As in Wilde's plays, and as in the Wilde trials, aristocrats suffer only the passing punishments of publicity and a brief snubbing, solved by a little time on the Continent. The untitled characters – the mere misters and mistresses – suffer the full approbation of society; the stars never do.

Likewise, when 18 men were arrested at a private house at 46 Fitzroy Street on 12 August 1894, only the two working-class boys wearing women's clothing were held for any length of time. The rest, including a gentleman of good background and independent fortune named Alfred Waterhouse Somerset Taylor and those young men he had brought with him to the party, were released without being charged. Wilde's condolence letter after the arrest to the man Alfred Taylor lived with and called his "wife," was considerate, and utterly frank: "My dear Charlie, I was very sorry to read in the paper about poor Alfred. . . . It is a dreadful piece of bad luck." After wishing he could help Taylor out financially, and apologizing for not being able to do so at the present, Wilde signs off blithely, "Let me know . . . how you yourself are going on in your married life."[85]

In the Fitzroy Street scandal, the gentlemen headed home to continue their lives, whatever those lives were. In the Cleveland Street scandal, a lord alleged to have committed gross indecencies sued a literary man for libel and won. But the next, and biggest sexual scandal of Queen Victoria's century would not bear the name of the place where it happened, but that of the literary man, self-styled "lord of the language" but not nobility in any other sense, who sued a Marquess for libel and lost.[86]

*

> to the Irishman . . . there is nothing in the world quite so exquisitely comic as an Englishman's seriousness. It becomes tragic, perhaps, when the Englishman acts on it . . .
>
> G.B. Shaw, reviewing *An Ideal Husband*, 1895

As he sentenced Oscar Wilde to two years' hard labor for acts of "gross indecency," Mr. Justice Wills, Wilde's neighbor on Tite Street, struggled to find words. Like Herman Melville's Bartleby, Wills would prefer not to use the language he had to hand to express both the verdict and his own sentiments. "It is no use for me to address you. People who do these things must be dead to all sense of shame, and one cannot hope to produce an effect on them." But Wills continued his address to Wilde, and his co-defendant Taylor – perhaps to produce an effect anyway, or perhaps to convince himself that these two Oxbridge gentlemen were not, indeed, dead to all sense of shame? "It is the worst case I have ever tried," insisted Wills, and to have to pass only "the severest sentence that the law allows" was a constraint upon him. "In my judgment [two years] is totally inadequate for such a case as this. The sentence of the Court is that each of you be imprisoned and kept to hard labour for two years."[87] It was 25 May 1895 – Queen Victoria's birthday.

Oscar Wilde came on flawlessly, beautifully, in all his writings – criticism, epigraphs, essays, fictions, plays – about the verisimilitude, the interchangeability, of art and life. He knew of bad, but never of immoral, art – and life was the same. A poisoner, a criminal who does it beautifully, is an artist. Yet in the end, Wilde the writer always punished these artful criminals. The forger who tries to pass off "Mr. W.H.," Dorian Gray, the fisherman and his soul, the blackmailers, the slippery debtors – none go unscathed, through their art or artifice. Whether their punishments entail death, disgrace, or – perhaps worst of all – marrying a nice girl and finding themselves constrained into upper-middle-class English society, they all suffer thought-provoking and unbeautiful fates at Wilde's hand. Wilde the writer joined in his culture's own harsh and final condemnations of such perpetrators.

*

> I . . . wish we could meet to talk over the many prisons of life – prisons of stone, prisons of passion, prisons of intellect, prisons of morality, and the rest. All limitations, external or internal, are prison-walls, and life is a limitation.
>
> Oscar Wilde, February 1898

Living and working in a society troubled, and excited, by the shock of the new, Wilde the writer was subjected to conservative attempts to regulate culture and its definitions, to voices of tradition near-hysterical in their need to maintain control. From the critical reviews condemning his sensation-laden *Poems* (1881) to the wildly hyperbolic language of Mr. Justice Wills, condemning Wilde himself, the frantic note of convention deeply threatened, and determined to rule at any cost, sounds against Wilde's art and life.

Wilde's conviction, the end of his literary output, and his death did not lessen this reactionary reaction. Wilde's work and his self were always inseparable – to others, and to him. *An Ideal Husband* was written by a husband who was not. *Dorian Gray* "became" Alfred Douglas, or, alternately, Wilde's dream of himself as the beautiful decadent able to live two lives in the same place, among the same people, and evade society's punishments. Even in a more symbolic, historically remote work like *Salomé*, Bosie is the spoiled, sexed princess, and Wilde the prophet in his cell awaiting death because of her.[88]

What critics have elided, or ignored, is the fact that, wherever "Wilde" is present in his work, he punishes his "self" for that character's transgressions. Wilde put punishment into his work, for Dorian and Wotton, Illingworth and the Selfish Giant alike, just as he would let it into his life with his testimony. That Wilde punished his own characters in his fiction with severe, traditional punishments and subtle harshness for their crimes is true. That he condemned himself in his own trials with what he said – even under a statute he thought unjust – is plain in the transcripts. That he acquiesced to English society's continued punishment after his ostensible release from jail is evident in the spirit of his writings, his voluntary removal from the London culture that had been his life before 1895, and his own unnaming.

Max Nordau, surprised enough by the events of spring 1895 to term Wilde's arrest and conviction "the shocking fate," managed an uncannily prescient comment in his 1896 edition of *Degeneration*:[89]

> But although he was sentenced to hard labour, [and] the English may have banned his plays from their theatres and his books from their bookshops, it is not so easy to erase his name from the social history of our time. Oscar Wilde remains the most informative embodiment of a mentality [Denkweise] which has played a part in modern spiritual life and which is still embraced by no small number of degenerates and their imitators. Consequently it seemed impossible to pass him by in silence and with averted gaze.

Impossible, indeed. Just as Mr. Justice Wills had wished for, Wilde got far more than a simple sentence of two years' hard labor. When the sentence was finished, the prisoner's debt to society was discharged, and he was to be freed from continued punishment and admitted into that society once more. But not one part of *this* sentence is true, in the case of Oscar Wilde. He was not freed, and neither was his good name. "Oscar Wilde" became an unspoken, unspeakable term, not a writer's name.

Yet the idea of "Oscar Wilde" as the embodiment of a mentality – England's, and his own – is righter, even, than Nordau might have intended: Wilde's flashing mind as an intellect housed within the (actor's; indulgent; corrupt) body was the genesis of his genius and (self-)destruction. The satisfactions of a mentality embodied called for both mind and body to be punished.

Nordau's language, veering from modern spiritual life to the degenerate embrace, and the classically Greek idea of learning through imitation – parody, copying, forgery – is violently, indisputably Wildean. And concluding with "consequently" is something Wilde always does. Consequences are what actions always have – whether Wainewright the artist, Arthur Savile the dilettante, Dorian the explorer of sensation, or Wilde the stylist are engaged in them. The silence and averted gaze of men, confined to hard labor and marching around the prison-yard, followed his progress as Wilde stepped back outside on 19 May 1897 – yet there is an impossibility in continuing this aspect of punishment without the convict's assent and complicity. And Wilde acquiesced, helping to make the world his panopticon.

The Victorian thought that hiding punishment – making it "humane" by pretending, from the bench, that there are limits to a sentence and that jail is good for the criminal – fails. Wilde was for a few brief years living proof of this. The pillory was kinder in the eighteenth century – it was a fixed thing, into which the condemned was fitted and left to be mocked, or maimed, or killed as the crowd saw fit, and every jury handing down a verdict and judge passing sentence knew this to be the case. The permanent pillory that made and defined what Englishmen and women saw when they looked at Oscar Wilde did not fall away from him, or his works, after Pentonville, after Reading. It was not shed in Dieppe, or Naples, or Paris. "All trials are for one's life," he said in *De Profundis*, and Wilde got a life sentence indeed. It did not stop when he left Reading Gaol. Mr. Justice Wills wished that he could have given Wilde a longer sentence, and the English public obliged, ending Wilde's life among them in May 1895 and giving him a portable prison for his private life, in exile, until his death.

Wilde's life sentence was – violently and ironically – what he had always wanted, and created, for the erring characters in his own work. It was an archaic English, even Biblical, spectac-ular, eye-for-an-eye sentence, because Wilde's whole life was to be regarded, to be heard and seen. The true outcome of the Wilde trials was, after his long stint in the courtroom spotlights, to keep him from ever being heard from, or seen as, Oscar Wilde during his lifetime, and even thereafter. But he was still seen, watched, judged, punished. Oscar Wilde the celebrated wit and playwright? No. Sebastian Melmoth the exiled, unproductive, perverted drunk? Yes, this was fine, a fine spectacle.

Silent incarceration and the other trappings of hard labor, Victorian constructions, give way, even today, to the eighteenth century and before: spectacle as punishment and cultural celebration at once. Upon his release from prison, and after death, despite his own promotion of the "disappearance" of "Oscar Wilde," the spectacle goes on. There is, as Nordau said in 1896, a sheer impossibility in passing – in the sense of passing for, passing as – Wilde by, or off, as anything but Oscar. Further punishment is inherent as the spectacle continues: a man walks along the beach at Berneval or up the road to the villa at Posillipo, tries out a bicycle, rides in a motorcar in Switzerland, learns to use a camera in Italy (where he immediately has himself photographed, with Douglas, amidst the commemorations – and rubble – of antique Rome), sits at a café in Paris, looking different to every different pair of eyes. Even modern criticism differs – how else? – wildly. Was Wilde down-at-heels and shabby in Paris, or clean, reserved, neatly dressed? Was he constantly drunk, and publicly, on absinthe, falling into gutters and walking out in front of cabs, staggering towards some criminal destination with a French flower-boy in hand, or did he confine his drinking to what little he could afford, and generally in the evenings, alone in his room at the Alsace? No one could take their eyes off him, critical and wondering eyes, while he lived; and no one can stop looking, and wondering, today.

*

In the recent flush of the "Wilde Centennial," the hundredth anniversaries, mind you, of his trials and his death – Wilde has been fully resurgent in many, many ways. He has starred in plays from David Hare's *The Judas Kiss* to Moises Kaufman's *Gross Indecency* and in the film *Wilde*, thanks to Stephen Fry's sensitive and generous portrayal. Several of his plays have been filmed with all-star casts, two of them featuring the gay actor Rupert Everett in the leading Wildean-dandy roles. Two statues of Wilde were dedicated in his two home cities, Dublin and London. The statue in Merrion Square, of Wilde rendered in porcelain, quartz, and bronze, and lounging on a granite pedestal, was unveiled first, in 1997, and immediately dubbed "the fag on the crag" in the local tradition of naming all Dublin statues in rhyme. The statue in Adelaide Street, London, of Wilde's tormented bronze bust (complete with green lapel carnation) and hands (complete with cigarette) rising from a polished stone tomb, has been both damned and praised.[90] And last, but most importantly for purposes of this chapter, a creative writing competition, in honor of Wilde's release, was held at Reading Gaol during the week of 18 May 1997. Governor William Payne, of what is today Her Majesty's Young Offender Institution and Remand Centre Reading, said proudly, "'I think Oscar would be surprised . . . that we have an education department that helps people with poor numeracy and literacy skills and encourages those with greater ability.'"[91]

Wilde did, and self-consciously stood for, something new in his own critical and creative writings, and in his life. What that "something" was or is varied at the time, depending on the critic constructing an argument around Wilde, and still varies, from critical eye to critical eye. Ought we to focus upon aestheticism; decadence; the whole rich tapestry of ideas, art, and attitudes contained in the phrase *fin de siècle*; defining elements of (male) "homosexuality"; the end of Victorianism; the object lesson that Victorianism had not, in fact, ended? Wilde evokes an immensely passionate critical response, from blind support for his prose style and personal lifestyle to intense reaction against what is condemned as his radical, or unnatural, life and literature. The power of his art as a writer can have no greater testament than the simple fact that Wilde made people feel – and he still does.

notes

1. Richard Pine, *The Thief of Reason: Oscar Wilde and Modern Ireland* (Dublin: Gill and Macmillan, 1995), 161, 150.
2. Karl Beckson, ed., *Oscar Wilde: The Critical Heritage* (London: Routledge and Kegan Paul, 1970), 60. Hereafter *CH*.
3. See Lisa A. Golmitz, "The Artist's Studio," in *Reading Wilde, Querying Spaces: An Exhibition Commemorating the 100th Anniversary of the Trials of Oscar Wilde* (New York: Fales Library/New York University, 1995), 43–51, 45–46.
4. Oscar Wilde, *Complete Works of Oscar Wilde* (Glasgow: HarperCollins, 1994), 296. All further citations to Wilde's works will be from this volume (*CW*) unless otherwise indicated.
5. *CW*, 297, 301.
6. Vyvyan Holland, *Son of Oscar Wilde* (1954; Oxford: Oxford University Press, 1987), 136.
7. Beckson, *CH*, 107.
8. Ibid., 110–111.
9. *CW*, 168–169, 171, 175.
10. Alison Hennegan, "Personalities and Principles: Aspects of Literature and Life in *Fin-de-Siecle* England," in Mikulas Teich and Roy Porter, eds., *Fin de Siecle and its Legacy* (Cambridge: Cambridge University Press, 1990), 170–215: 195.
11. *CW*, 302.
12. Ibid., 305, 311.
13. Zack Bowen, "Wilde about Joyce," in R.B. Kershner, ed., *Joyce and Popular Culture* (Gainesville: University Press of Florida, 1996), 105–115.
14. Hennegan, op. cit., 205.
15. Oscar Wilde, "Some Literary Notes," in *The Woman's World* (1889); rprt. Source Book Press, 1970, 3 vols., 2:164.
16. Lawrence Danson, *Wilde's Intentions: The Artist in his Criticism* (Oxford: Clarendon, 1997), 13.
17. Richard Ellmann, *Oscar* Wilde (New York: Alfred A. Knopf, 1988), 299.
18. Beckson, *CH*, 91–92.
19. Ibid., 94–95.
20. *CW*, 1072.
21. Ibid., 1077.
22. Ibid., 1091–1092.
23. Beckson, *CH*, 63, 64. Translation: "[As for] Me, I take mine wherever I find it" – or, with the French masculine in effect, the sentence *could* as well translate, more dangerously, "I take mine wherever I find *him*."
24. Ibid., 65, 66.

25. Corinna Sundararajan Rohse, "The Sphinx Goes Wild(e): Ada Leverson, Oscar Wilde, and the Gender Equipollence of Parody," in Gail Finney, ed., *Look Who's Laughing: Gender and Comedy* (Langhorne, PA: Gordon and Breach, 1994), 119–136; 129. The expression "play-giarism" for what Wilde commits is, according to Rohse, Linda Hutcheon's.
26. Said Douglas of *Intentions*, "When it is good it is not Wilde's [but Whistler's], and when it is bad it is horrid, and not necessarily Wilde's at that." Alfred Douglas, *Oscar Wilde and Myself* (New York: Duffield, 1914), 215.
27. Regenia Gagnier, ed., *Critical Essays on Oscar Wilde* (New York: G. K. Hall, 1991), 30.
28. *CW*, 1093, 1103.
29. Leon Radzinowicz, ed., *A History of English Criminal Law and Its Administration From 1750*, Vol. 1, *The Movement for Reform, 1750–1833* (New York: Macmillan, 1948), 4, 8–9, 592–594.
30. *CW*, 1106.
31. Ibid., 1106–1107.
32. Ibid., 1120.
33. Richard Ellmann, *Four Dubliners: Wilde, Yeats, Joyce, and Beckett* (New York: Braziller, 1987), 36.
34. Jeff Nunokawa, "The Disappearance of the Homosexual in *The Picture of Dorian Gray*," in George Haggerty and Bonnie Zimmerman, eds., *Professions of Desire: Lesbian and Gay Studies in Literature* (New York: The Modern Language Association of America, 1995), 183–190; 183.
35. Beckson, *CH*, 69.
36. Ibid., 69–70.
37. Ibid., 70–71.
38. Ibid., 72, 73.
39. Ibid., 75.
40. See, e.g., the sodomy scene in *Fanny Hill* that so shocks the unshockable Fanny, where the "sweet pretty" blond "Ganymede" arranges himself "obsequiously" over a chair for the "attack" of his older lover. John Cleland, *Memoirs of a Woman of Pleasure* (1749; Oxford University Press/World's Classics, 1985), 158–159.
41. Beckson, *CH*, 77.
42. Stanley Weintraub, "Disraeli and Wilde's Dorian Gray," *Cahiers Victoriens et Edouardiens*, 36, October 1992, 19–27; 20–22.
43. W.S. Gilbert, *Patience; or, Bunthorne's Bride* (New York: Doubleday Page, 1902), 21.
44. Weintraub, op. cit., 25–26.
45. Oscar Wilde, *The Picture of Dorian Gray*, *Lippincott's Monthly Magazine*, July 1890 1–100; 7. *Dorian Gray* came out in England and America in *Lippincott's*, and was published as a book, with some important deletions and some new chapters, in 1891. Major publishing houses had objected to the book as it first appeared; Alexander Macmillan found "something in the power which Dorian Gray gets over [Campbell], and one or two other things, which is rather repelling." Quoted in Warwick Gould, "The Crucifixion of the Outcasts: Yeats and Wilde in the Nineties," in C. George Sandulescu, ed., *Rediscovering Oscar Wilde* (Gerrards Cross, Bucks.: Colin Smythe/Princess Grace Irish Library, 1994), 167–192; 184. For more on the revisions of *Dorian*, see Donald Lawler,

An Inquiry into Oscar Wilde's Revisions of The Picture of Dorian Gray (New York: Garland, 1988). Further citations in this chapter to *Dorian*, unless otherwise noted, are from *CW.*

46. *CW*, 28–29.
47. Quoted in Pine, op. cit., 162.
48. George Gordon, Lord Byron, in Leslie A. Marchand, ed., *Lord Byron: Selected Letters and Journals* (Cambridge: Harvard University Press/Belknap, 1982), 346.
49. Oscar Wilde, *The Picture of Dorian Gray*, ed. Donald L. Lawler (New York: W.W. Norton, 1988), 68–69.
50. Alan Sinfield, *The Wilde Century: Effeminacy, Oscar Wilde, and the Queer Moment* (London: Cassell, 1994), 3–4.
51. There was no "actual" Basil Ward, portrait painter, in London in 1890, as too many Wilde biographies from Hesketh Pearson's on insist – at least none who has been found. Basil Ward is an invention from a pirated 1904 version of *Dorian Gray*, picked up by Boris Brasol in 1938, and then by Hesketh Pearson in his critical biography of Wilde (Kerry Powell, "Who Was Basil Hallward?", *English Language Notes*, 24:1 (September 1986), 84–91; 84–85). There was a man named Frank Holl, dead in 1888, who was a celebrated portraitist and whose work was common in the Grosvenor Gallery, "whose exhibitions Wilde twice reviewed and whose Pre-Raphaelite atmosphere he much preferred to that of the Royal Academy" (Powell, op. cit., 86). Wilde reviewed art critic Harry Quilter's *Sententiae Artis* for the *Pall Mall Gazette* (18 November 1886), and might have read therein the arresting description of Holl's work: "I have seen portraits (and fine portraits too) by him, of most estimable people – deans, and masters of colleges, &c. – who never had a wrong thought in their lives, but to whom Mr. Holl has given such a don't-meet-me-on-a-dark-night kind of look that one almost felt that he must, in the course of his painting, have discovered some dreadful secret in those apparently blameless breasts, such 'damnable faces' have his sitters shown" (quoted in Powell, op. cit., 87).
52. *CW*, 21, 24, 25.
53. Ibid., 32, 34.
54. Ibid., 71, 72.
55. Ibid., 84. Steven Bruhm quotes Havelock Ellis, in *Studies in the Pathology of Sex* (Vol. 1, 1897), for the contemporary belief that Narcissism was at the core of taking a same-sex lover, "more . . . amour propre than sexual desire" (quoted in Steven Bruhm, "Taking One to Know One: Oscar Wilde and Narcissism," *English Studies in Canada*, 21: 2 (June 1995), 170–188; 171).
56. *CW*, 106–107.
57. Ibid., 115, 117.
58. David Rose is currently at work on Wilde's influence upon the stories of Arthur Conan Doyle. Conversation, David Rose, New York City, 18 November 2003.
59. *CW*,122, 124.
60. Ibid., 140, 152, 156.
61. Alfred Douglas, years later, said that socialism was of no lasting importance to Wilde. It "attracted" Wilde at the time, he said, "because it was odd and [George Bernard] Shaw was Irish." Douglas, op. cit., 61.
62. *CW*, 1194, 1184.

63. Ibid., 1178, 1182.
64. Ibid., 1182.
65. Ibid., 1188.
66. Ibid., 1189.
67. For some readings of the fairy tales as coming-out idylls, see Gary Schmidgall, *The Stranger Wilde: Interpreting Oscar* (Harmondsworth: Dutton/Penguin, 1994), 145–168.
68. Ellmann, *Wilde,* op. cit., 333.
69. *CW*, 422.
70. Ibid., 425, 422, 424, 429, 432.
71. Ibid., 439–440.
72. Ibid., 447–448.
73. What "prevented [Bosie] from tormenting Oscar from the outset was that he was in North Africa with Lord Cromer, to whom he acted as personal secretary. A sharp dispute with Lord Cromer brought Bosie back to England and left him unexpectedly at a loose end," and this is why Anne Clark Amor believes he took up with Wilde. Anne Clark Amor, *Mrs. Oscar Wilde: A Woman of Some Importance* (London: Sidgwick and Jackson, 1983), 111. For more on the Rosebery subplot to the Wilde trials, see Michael S. Foldy, *The Trials of Oscar Wilde: Deviance, Morality, and Late-Victorian Society* (New Haven: Yale University Press, 1997).
74. *CW*, 509.
75. Ibid., 518, 521, 529, 532–534.
76. Ibid., 536, 552.
77. See, e.g., Elaine Showalter, *Sexual Anarchy: Gender and Culture at the Fin de Siecle* (Harmondsworth: Penguin Books, 1990), 106.
78. Ruth Berggren, ed., *The Definitive Four-Act Version of The Importance of Being Earnest: A Trivial Comedy for Serious People,* by Oscar Wilde (New York: The Vanguard Press, 1987), 33.
79. *CW*, 362, 386.
80. Ibid., 357, 359, 361.
81. Ibid., 362, 385, 387.
82. Beckson, *CH*, 199.
83. Ibid., *CH*, 187.
84. Ed Cohen, *Talk on the Wilde Side: Toward a Genealogy of a Discourse on Male Sexualities* (New York and London: Routledge, 1993), 103–104, 122–123.
85. Oscar Wilde, *The Letters of Oscar Wilde*, ed., Rupert Hart-Davis (New York: Harcourt, Brace, 1962), 363–364.
86. Merlin Holland, *The Wilde Album* (New York: Henry Holt, 1997), 164.
87. H. Montgomery Hyde, *The Trials of Oscar Wilde* (London: William Hodge, 1948; rprt. New York: Dover, 1962), 339, 341 *et seq.* A shorthand transcript for the first Wilde trial, to which Hyde, I believe, had some sort of access even if limited, recently surfaced in London and is published in Merlin Holland, ed., *The Real Trial of Oscar Wilde: The First Uncensored Transcript of the Trial of Oscar Wilde vs. John Douglas (Marquess of Queensberry), 1895* (New York: HarperCollins/Fourth Estate, 2003). Jonathan Goodman's exhaustive effort, in *The Oscar Wilde File,* to compile the relevant contemporary reports and opinions on the trial is still invaluable. Jonathan Goodman, ed., *The Oscar Wilde File* (London: Allison & Busby, 1988).

88. It is for many critics simply "impossible to disentangle [Wilde's work] today from our knowledge of its author's trials and imprisonment," Joel H. Kaplan, "Wilde in the Gorbals: Society Drama and Citizens' Theatre," in C. George Sandelescu, ed., *Rediscovering Oscar Wilde* (Gerrards Cross: Colin Smythe/ Princess Grace Irish Library, 1994), 214–223; 218. And, in support of her Wilde-as-John-the-Baptist reading of *Salomé*, Melissa Knox offers: "In *De Profundis* . . . Wilde summed up his own weakness in yielding to the influence of Lord Alfred with this significant statement: 'I lost my head.'" Melissa Knox, "Losing One's Head: Wilde's Confession in *Salome*," in *Rediscovering*, op. cit., 232–243, 237. See also Knox's book, *Oscar Wilde: A Long and Lovely Suicide* (New Haven: Yale University Press, 1994).
89. Max Nordau, *Degeneration* (1895; rprt. New York: Howard Fertig, 1968), 317–318.
90. There is now a window honoring Wilde in Westminster Abbey as well. The London sculpture was unveiled by Wilde's great-grandson Lucian Holland in December 1998. *New York Times*, Arts section, 2 December 1998 (B1).
91. Claire Garner, "My dear boys: Reading inmates write for Wilde; Oscar was locked up 100 years ago. Prisoners at his old jail are putting pen to paper," *Independent*, 18 May 1997: 6.

3
performance theory and performativity

francesca coppa

> Most people are other people. Their thoughts are someone else's opinions, their lives a mimicry, their passions a quotation.
>
> Oscar Wilde, *De Profundis*

introduction

Oscar Wilde has variously been given credit for inventing postmodernity, celebrity culture (including, of course, the celebrity scandal and subsequent trial), queer theory, fashion journalism, and camp. Strangely, the claims only get grander from here. Wilde himself took credit for inventing Aubrey Beardsley, Tom Stoppard recently implied that Wilde invented Love, and in the 18 May 1998 issue of *The New Yorker*, Adam Gopnik claimed that Wilde "invented the talk show guest before there was a talk show to welcome him."[1]

But all of these "inventions" can, in fact, be seen to stem from Wilde's first and foremost invention: the performed persona of "Oscar Wilde." If there is one thing that makes us feel that Wilde, dead for over one hundred years now, is our contemporary, a man who would be perfectly at home in the world of Andy Warhol and Madonna, David Bowie, Baz Lurhmann, and The Osbournes, it is his understanding of the self as performance. In fact, in both his life and his art, Wilde not only anticipates and illustrates but actually embodies many of the suppositions of performance studies, not least of which is the blurring of the boundaries between "life" and "art," "body" and "text."

In the theatre, texts are literally embodied; scripts are put into production and become three-dimensional performances in which human behavior is seen to be loaded with meaning and history. Performance studies, a field at the crossroads of theatre and anthropology, takes this idea a step forward by refusing to distinguish sharply between staged and lived behavior. All human behavior is enmeshed in history and infused with meaning, and performance studies puts behavior on a continuum, so that the actor playing Hamlet, the bride at a wedding, the man hailing a taxi, the woman angling for a promotion, the boy playing stickball, and the man walking up Piccadilly with a lily in his hand can all be seen to be doing essentially the same thing: *performing*. Richard Schechner, one of the pioneers of performance studies, defines performance as "restored" or "twice-behaved" behavior. These restored behaviors "consist largely of routines, habits, and rituals; and the recombination of already behaved behaviors,"[2] or what Diana Taylor calls "rehearsed, or conventional or event-appropriate" actions.[3] These "rehearsed" behaviors include not only those associated with specific and discrete theatrical or ritual events – which is to say, events bracketed in some ways *as* performances – but *all* behaviors precisely to the extent to which all human behavior is taught (or at the very least, *learned*), and then put on some sort of display.

Schechner calls this display "showing doing," which is to say, "pointing to, underlying, and displaying doing."[4] Performance, therefore, is behavior on display, but this display is not limited to theatrical productions or ritual events. The man hailing a taxi has learned a series of gestures that communicate meaning; in performing the script of "I want a cab," he is not merely doing but "showing doing." So too the boy playing stickball, who is probably not only performing his role in the game but attempting to show his friends precisely how well he performs as an athlete. The woman seeking promotion at work is probably keenly aware that her job performance is being evaluated; she may, in fact, have had a "performance review" of some sort, and she will be aware that it is not enough simply to be *doing* her job, but that she must be *showing* her doing of it. Furthermore, her behavior must be not only reliable (which is to say, repeatable) but also recognizable; her gestures must convey meaning – in this case, "successful work" – to others. Performance studies therefore recognizes that behavior, as well as speech, is a language that has rules and is structured by a grammar, and, as with any other language, comprehension depends on recognition, which is to say, re-cognition, or knowing something again when we see it.

Both the pleasures of Wilde's work and the problems of Wilde's life can be understood in precisely these performative terms. The pleasures of Wilde's writing are tied up in (insider) knowledge and recognition of a variety of (theatrical, comedic, aristocratic, linguistic) behaviors; in particular, Wilde offers us the chance to take pleasure in recognizing the displayed rituals of leisured English culture, and to appreciate the utter constructedness of "modern" human beings and their behaviors. Similarly, the problems of Wilde's life stemmed from society's sudden recognition, and swift repudiation, of the decadent philosophies embodied in the public performance of "Oscar Wilde."

wilde in performance

Performance studies is explicitly *not* an approach to "literary" texts – in fact, some practitioners resent the idea of even categorizing performances as "texts," with that word's historical connection to the literary.[5] Rather, performance studies takes as its subject not the word but the *body* – its position in space, how it's costumed, what it's projecting, representing, and/or symbolizing within a particular frame – and therefore privileges live-ness, present-ness, and three-dimensionality.

Consequently, performance studies generally addresses itself to specific theatrical productions, examining the behaviors embodied by particular performers as directed by particular directors. However, there are, of course, certain behaviors and actions already scripted into most dramatic literature, and Wilde's plays are no exception, despite the fact that they are often discussed as if they consisted only of their famous dialogue – though this, too, is significant from a performance point of view. The successful delivery of Wilde's dialogue all but *requires* the actor's performance of aristocratic languor (or straight-backed hauteur, in the case of women. As an actress friend of mine, a former Gwendolyn in *The Importance of Being Earnest*, wryly remarked to me when I discussed this with her, "Social mores come and go, but posture comes from *boning*. You try being languorous in a corset"). Actors in Wilde *perform* a kind of physical stillness which is not only characterological (though of course it is, as none of Wilde's characters are much inclined to exertion), but also practical in terms of delivering the Wildean epigram with maximum impact.

In an interview I did with John Alderton for my *Casebook on Joe Orton*, Alderton compared performing Orton's and Wilde's plays, which are similar in many respects, particularly in their witticisms, paradoxes, and epigrams. Both writers' works, Alderton noted, required "pretty heavy comedic expertise in order to hit the back of the stalls with the epigrams, because they [the audience] have to hear ... every word."

> John Alderton: And the trick of Wilde? It is the actual words, not anything else really. It's quite often just the beauty of the way the words are created and the rhythms within the sentences, which are

very very special – tremendously beautifully put together as a ball of words, as something to play with. [Orton's play *What The Butler Saw*] needs all the requirements of Wilde, which is a great requirement in order to get the style, but you also have to do runabout trousers-down farce at the same time. So you're doing two things.

Francesca Coppa: Right, so in Wilde, they're posing, they're still –

J.A.: Posing, speaking beautifully, and nobody runs anywhere. You stand and speak. Then these lovely words roll off your [tongue] ... but with Joe, you've got to do that, and run at 90 miles per hour, and lose your trousers at the same time.[6]

Similarly, actor Kenneth Williams once spoke of the performance technique he used for Orton's epigrams, which also "goes for Wilde":

> "You've got to breathe. If you're going to say lines like, 'The Vatican would never grant an annulment. Not unless he'd produced a hybrid' you've got to gather it up, otherwise it's lost. If you're going to stop in the middle, the whole impact is destroyed. This is in the tradition of classic English comic writing. It goes for Wilde, the same construction, the same intake of breath. It occurs also in Coward. Shaw uses the construction again and again."[7]

Actors speak of a particular kind of breathing necessary to speak an epigram (which can be quite long) with sufficient *authority*. (The epigram, with its pronouncing tone, is all about authority, e.g. "The truth is rarely pure and never simple. Modern life would be very tedious if it were either, and modern literature a complete impossibility," or "In matters of grave importance, style, not sincerity, is the important thing".) It is necessary to have the breath to deliver an epigram in one authoritative swoop, to root oneself to the spot and properly *pronounce*.

However, despite the importance of epigrams to Wilde's work, it is important to remember that the biggest laugh in *The Importance of Being Earnest* traditionally comes not from any witticism or epigram but from Jack's slow, stately entrance in Act II, "dressed in the deepest mourning, with crepe hatband and black gloves" (380). Wilde highlights Jack's performance of grief by having Jack mourn a fictional brother who for all intents and purposes is sitting in the dining room behind him, thereby removing any cause of grief which might appear to naturalize Jack's behavior. Thus we are keenly made aware that Jack is *demonstrating* his grief through performance (slow gait, black hat and gloves, crepe, tortured expression, tragic manner), and we are forced to acknowledge that even something as apparently heartfelt as grief is, in fact, ritualized and performative.[8]

The fact that the "action scenes" in Wilde's plays – the often-farcical routines, plots, and behaviors – tend not to be addressed in "literary" criticism results from a two-fold bias in literary studies: 1) for dialogue over direction/action, 2) for the "original" over the "derivative," and, as Kerry Powell has shown in his still-seminal 1990 book, *Oscar Wilde and the Theatre of the 1890s*, it is in his stage actions that we see Wilde as most a part of (and most indebted to) the theatre of his day. As Powell says:

> Algernon Moncrieff's gluttonizing of muffins and cucumber sandwiches in Wilde's play is reminiscent generally of the ritual food gags of Victorian farce – from pouring tea in a hat in *Charley's Aunt* to throwing bacon and chops out the window in *Box and Cox* ... Labiche and Delacour's *Celimare le bien aimé* anticipates the "Bunburying" motif in *Earnest* by presenting an imaginary invalid whose feigned illness is used to escape certain social responsibilities. In Musset's *Il ne faut jurer de rien* ... an ingenue named Cécile – rather than Cécily, as in Wilde's play – is the reluctant pupil of her clerical tutor and falls in love with a young man pretending to be someone else. In W.S. Gilbert's *Engaged* two young women turn from gushing friendship to hostility when they discover one may have inadvertently married the other's fiancé, anticipating a similar development between Cecily Cardew and Gwendolyn Moncrieff in *Earnest*. And like Jack Worthing in Wilde's play, one of the characters in *Engaged* comes to stage dressed in deep mourning for what turns out to be only an imaginary death. But this device had already been used by John Maddison Morton, whose *A Husband to Order* has a character enter "in a black costume," disguised as his own brother, mourning his own make-believe death.[9]

Powell demonstrates that the behaviors and actions in Wilde's plays are drawn from the larger Victorian theatre, but to dismiss those actions as therefore "derivative" is to miss the point. Richard Schechner's definition of performance as "twice-behaved behavior" underscores the extent to which "uniqueness" and "originality" are not the appropriate standards; behaviors are *meant* to be repeated, recognized, and repeated again. Instead, the question becomes, "What meanings are carried by the reiteration of particular behaviors?" and in Wilde's case, the performance of these Victorian tropes both connects him to and separates him from the theatre of his time. Wilde not only *uses* the clichés, but he *displays* his use of them, and that second performative level of *showing-doing* frequently allows Wilde to complicate, undercut, or even contradict their primary meanings by adding a level of self-consciousness or artificiality not present in earlier iterations of the action. However, it would be a mistake to see this as only or merely subversive, because Wilde's iteration of these actions and behaviors also shows his love of them, much as Wilde's epigrams help to preserve, as well as undercut, the common wisdom upon which they are based.[10] In that way, too, Wilde is our contemporary – simultaneously highbrow and pop culture junkie, artist and entertainer. Wilde's breadth of appeal didn't hurt his bottom line, either.

wilde *as* performance

I implied above that literary critics often give short shrift to the bodies, behaviors, and actions in Wilde's plays, perhaps following W.H. Auden's famous description of *The Importance of Being Earnest* as "pure verbal opera" – a body-banishing statement if there ever was one. But there *is* of course a body, a set of behaviors and actions, at the center of the discussion of all of Wilde's works – Oscar Wilde.

Overtly or covertly, Wilde's body is central to all literary, theatrical and biographical Wilde criticism. The American reporters who met Wilde's boat in New York were surprised at his physical size and height, having been prepared for a considerably slighter figure by the depiction of the aesthete in Gilbert's *Patience*; English society during the trials would be in a hysteria over the crimes of Wilde's sexualized body; once convicted, Wilde's body would be dressed in prison garb, subjected to public view (Wilde claims that he was spit upon whilst waiting for the train that would take him to prison) and physically confined to a cell. Even in death, as Joseph Bristow points out in "Memorialising Wilde: An Explosive History," Wilde's body continued to act: not only was his moment of death literally narrated by Frank Harris as explosive ("there was a loud explosion: mucus poured out of Oscar's mouth and nose") but eight years after Wilde's death, "The Los Angeles Examiner ... carried a full-page feature that declared – on the authority of a worker at the Alsace – that the dying Wilde had been secretly whisked out of the hotel for medical treatment that saved him at the last minute." Bristow notes that, like "Elvis Presley, Wilde's disease-ridden body enjoyed a phantasmatic afterlife," and wryly welcomes what he calls the recent shift in critical attention from "Wilde's actual body to his textual corpus."[11]

But Wilde's person(a) was always central to his corpus; in fact, the idea is central to Wilde's dictum that nature imitates art. Certainly, Wilde's persona at Oxford was the direct product of a body of literature: classical and Catholic texts filtered through the lens of Walter Pater's *History of the Renaissance*. This Oxford persona, as represented in numerous journalistic accounts and satirical cartoons, would in turn provide inspiration for the behaviors of such theatrical creations as Lambert Stryke in F.C. Burnard's 1881 play *The Colonel* and the aesthetes Reginald Bunthorne and Archibald Grosvenor in Gilbert and Sullivan's *Patience* the same year, the success of the latter work creating the demand for a real-life aesthete to tour America. And who better than Wilde to be cast in that role? Later, Wilde would use his experience as "Professor of Aesthetics" to create the character of Lord Henry Wotton in *The Picture of Dorian Gray*, and Merlin Holland has claimed that Wilde all but conjured up the real Lord Alfred Douglas through his creation of the fictional Dorian Gray.[12] As David Foster has put it, by the time of *Dorian Gray*, Wilde had created "a rich intertext of posing: the early stories, newspaper and magazine articles and photos, *Punch* caricatures, and word of mouth, all contribut[ing] to the complex public persona."[13]

This complex intertext would, in some ways, prove Wilde's undoing: during the trials, the words and actions of Wilde's fictional characters would be held against Wilde as if they were his own, *which of course they were*. Similarly, the drama critics had not failed to notice that the characters in Wilde's plays acted and sounded rather a lot like Wilde himself. Henry James, for example, dismissed *Lady Windermere's Fan* by noting that, "'There is of course absolutely no characterization and all the people talk equally strained Oscar,'"[14] and an anonymous reviewer, possibly Wilde's own brother Willie, noted that "'the author peoples his play with male and female editions of himself.'"[15] Sitting in the dock, Wilde embodied all of this and more, and ultimately, in *De Profundis*, he would cast the experience as a classical tragedy with precisely the same Hellenistic flair that had brought him to Oxford in the first place.

Wilde's presence looms so large within literary works that W.H. Auden's description begins to seem a deliberate attempt to banish the corrupt Wildean body and leave the "pure" words floating in the air over the stage, utterly disembodied. But Wilde's body refuses to leave the stage. Joseph Bristow has noted how many different stories have been "plausibly woven around [Wilde's] body"[16] over the years, and our understanding of the plays is dependent on unpacking these many stories and their accumulative meanings.

Performance studies, with its focus on the body and the complex behaviors of the body in space, is ideal as a lens for this sort of analysis. Much recent criticism has been devoted to documenting the myths, legends and histories that have accrued around Wilde and his corpus, but for the purposes of this discussion, I am going to limit myself to the multiple and often contradictory *sexual* narratives embodied in Wilde's public persona, showing both how they are performative as well as analyzing them "as," or in terms of, performance. Each of these sexual narratives has a separate and specific performance *history*, even though they may share some of the same visible *behaviors*; in other words, the same behaviors may *mean* differently in different narratives. In particular, Wilde can be seen to be *performing effeminacy*, *posing sodomite*, and *personifying homosexuality*, and each of these simultaneously shares certain performative qualities and is quite distinct.

performing effeminacy

Alan Sinfield has done much of the pivotal recent work on effeminacy, particularly as it pertains to Wilde; Sinfield's *The Wilde Century: Effeminacy, Oscar Wilde and the Queer Moment* remains the key resource in this area. Sinfield argues that a number of the performative behaviors that Wilde and his male characters exhibited ("They are effete, camp, leisured or aspiring to be, aesthetic, amoral, witty, insouciant, charming, spiteful, dandified") which have since come to form "the mid-twentieth century stereotype of the queer man," could not have been simply read at the time as "homosexual," since Wilde was a well-known public figure and many sophisticated people were surprised when he was accused and convicted.[17] Instead, Sinfield demonstrates that a number of these behaviors fell into the category of "effeminacy," a term that, up until Wilde, meant not being womanish, and consequently desiring men (what Foucault calls "hermaphrodism of the soul"[18]), but rather, spending too much time *on* and *with* women, and consequently not being sufficiently occupied with proper manly pursuits.

The barest skimming of Wilde's biography shows behaviors that validate this interpretation. In his very public adoration of women like Lilly Langtree and Sarah Bernhardt, in his public obsession with fashion and interior design, in his editorship of *The Woman's World*, Wilde was not only effeminate but displaying that effeminacy in ways potentially threatening to the larger culture.

First of all, in the feminist 1890s, a close alliance to women was, in itself, suspect. In her article, "The Bi-Social Oscar Wilde and 'Modern' Women," Margaret Diane Stetz describes Wilde as "bisocial," pointing out that while most Victorian men could, and in fact did, spend all their time in the all-male environments of university, office, and club, Wilde moved easily among both men and women. Furthermore, Wilde was comfortable with women both in the traditional (female, effeminate) drawing-room setting and within the workplace; in fact, Stetz emphasizes that Wilde particularly "befriended women who worked – especially women who worked in the arts," and that these women "were creatures to be viewed with suspicion, if not hostility" by other men of the time. Wilde, however, was publicly recognized as someone who not only shared women's interests, but was also supportive of women's ambitions.[19]

Even more threateningly, Wilde openly associated with "bad" or "fallen" women, a category which described many, if not most, of the actresses with whom Wilde hobnobbed. As Kerry Powell describes in *Oscar Wilde and the Theatre of the 1890s*, a key question of late Victorian culture was whether to resolve the sexual double standard by having women adopt the less stringent, traditionally male, norms, or if men should raise themselves to the higher standards of behavior set for women. On this issue, Wilde voted with both mind and body, as a man and as an artist; he openly associated with glamorous but socially problematic women (Sarah Bernhardt, Ellen Terry) in his life, and also caused such women to be gorgeously and triumphantly depicted on the stage (Mrs. Erlynne, Mrs. Cheveley – even Lady Bracknell, who of course married above her station even as she's chiding Jack about his; these wonderful Wildean women get away with murder, by Victorian standards). Stetz argues that Wilde was in this way a "social rebel – almost a traitor to his gender" for "*demonstrating* how comfortable he was inhabiting [women's] sitting rooms or going with them to their dressmakers, while also *publicizing* the pleasure he took in doing so." The italics are mine, but it is in the demonstrating and publicizing that the performance lies. Wilde was not simply *being* bisocial; he was showing-doing his effeminacy.

But Wilde's performance of effeminacy wasn't merely a vote for a certain kind of feminism; it could also be construed as a threat, or at the very least, a critique, of imperial British masculinity. Joseph Bristow suggests, in his book *Effeminate England: Homoerotic Writing After 1885*, the subversive power of performed effeminacy: both Wilde and his most Wildean characters are at pains to underline their aversion to work, or indeed to physical activity of any kind, particularly the "proper" "manly" pursuits of the late Victorian gentleman.[20] (Imagine the affront to the sportsman Queensberry.) These languid souls do not seem to demonstrate the spirit that forged an Empire. However, recent critical work further complicates the relationship between effeminacy and empire. In "The Soul of Man Under Imperialism," Ian Fletcher complains that:

> It seems that we have advanced very little since Ashis Nandy established a relationship between effeminacy and empire by suggesting that Wilde and his successors, notably Bloomsbury, represented an indirect, aestheticized revolt against the demands imperialism placed on its metropolitan male subjects ... "Literary" scholarship needs to catch up with "historical" scholarship on the imperial discourses and practices of masculinity and sexuality.

Instead, Fletcher argues for a more nuanced examination of "Wilde's distinctly uneven engagement with race and empire," that takes into account more problematic issues connected to Wilde's effeminacy such as servitude, slavery, and sexual tourism.[21]

posing sodomite

Or should I say, "*somdomite*"?[22] In an article in the *New Statesman*, David Jays notes that Wilde is "less a sod than a 'somd', his own category of unique slippage."[23] It is only appropriate that there is a malapropism at the center of the Wilde trials; if, as Foucault says, modern sexuality is characterized by a discursive explosion, it is tempting to read Queensberry's slip of the tongue as a performative speech act, the accidental *abracadabra* that brought "the homosexual" as a type into being. Foucault mentions "all those minor perverts whom nineteenth century psychiatrists entomologized by giving them strange baptismal names: zoophiles and zooerasts, auto-monosexualists, mixoverts, gynecomasts, presbophyles, sexoesthetic inverts, dyspareunist women"[24] – why not, among this strange collection, that rare creature, the *somdomite*?

Queensberry mis-spoke (or more accurately, mis-wrote), but his mistake was indicative of something larger, as was the additional hedge of "posing." To pose as somdomite was neither to be effeminate (since a fascination with women traditionally implied heterosexuality), nor to actually *be* a sodomite (because, in Queensberry's words, "to pose as a thing is as bad as to be it,"[25] therefore the act itself doesn't matter) – but some new slippage between the two. Previously, as Foucault notes, sodomy had been "a category of forbidden acts," but modern homosexuality would be defined "less by a type of sexual relations than by a certain quality of sexual sensibility."[26] In this way, Queensberry's odd remark indicates a shift from the *performance of particular sexual acts* to the *performance of particular social behaviors*, many of them the "queer" behaviors that Alan Sinfield listed as associated with Wilde ("effete, camp, leisured or aspiring to be, aesthetic, amoral, witty, insouciant, charming, spiteful, dandified").[27] Furthermore, as Edward Cohen notes in his seminal volume on the trials, *Talk on the Wilde Side*, this switch from act to person(a) served the interests of the theatre of journalism by allowing the unnameable act (sodomy) to be referenced by the name of the actor (the homosexual, Oscar Wilde).[28]

In his essay, "Redressing Oscar: Performance and the Trials of Oscar Wilde," David Schulz, following Cohen, claims that:

> The gesture – sodomy – entered into a more complete discourse through displacement onto a larger character – the homosexual. In other words, the character signified the act. Ironically, Victorian sexual repression incited a discourse of a homosexual identity and lifestyle in order to avoid invoking (or provoking) the body in action.[29]

As Schulz notes, this situation becomes even more ironic if Frank Harris was being truthful about Wilde's assertion of innocence regarding sodomy. Wilde supposedly told Harris that the stained sheets from the Savoy Hotel, brought up as evidence against him at trial, were not in fact his, but Douglas's. According to Harris, Wilde insisted, "I was never bold enough."[30] Schulz succinctly summarizes the potential consequences: "If Harris is correct, then Wilde remained posing as a sodomite throughout all three trials. Even to the point of judgment, Wilde was performing."[31] Schulz, however, then quotes Wilde's apparent admission in the same conversation, "Oh, Frank ... you talk with passion and conviction, as if I were innocent."[32] Wilde seems to believe he is guilty, but that only begs the question: guilty of *what?*

The answer can't be sodomy; sodomy was, arguably, the least of Wilde's crimes, if even it was his crime at all. After all, as Schulz notes, "Wilde was never technically on trial for sodomizing boys; because of the phrasing of the law he was tried for violations against the male sex."[33] Wilde's violations, as rehearsed at trial, were not primarily physical; Wilde's crime was, in this way, "*somdomy*," which is to say the slippage itself of sodomy into both effeminate (female) and homosocial (male) cultures. (While these may now seem like natural bedfellows, they had previously been oppositional cultures, which is why current discourse about sexuality remains confused.) This slippage put Victorian society into a state of crisis that could only be resolved by what anthropologist and performance studies pioneer Victor Turner calls "social drama." Turner's social drama develops in four phases: (1) a cultural breach creates (2) a public crisis, which is contained by (3) the performance of a redressive action, usually a public ritual, which is sometimes an informal affair and sometimes involves bringing all the social and legal machinery of a culture to bear on a situation, as in the case of the Wilde trials. The final phase (4) "consists either of the reintegration of the disturbed social group or of the social recognition and legitimization of an inseparable schism between contesting parties."[34]

Schulz describes the particular social drama of the Wilde trials as "an all male performance for an all male audience," since only men were allowed in the courtroom, and since the drama was set against a background of "clubs, educational institutions, and cultured street life that in late Victorian society were almost exclusively dominated by men."[35] In other words, Wilde was queering the Victorian male's homosocial world, a situation that required what Schulz, following Turner's model of social drama, calls, "the massive mobilization of cultural performance," i.e. the trials and the media circus around them, and ultimately the identification, scapegoating and expulsion of Oscar Wilde from the larger society.[36]

But women were equally threatened and infuriated by Wilde's behavior. First and foremost, as Stetz notes, Wilde had publicly betrayed his wife; many women at the time identified and empathized with Constance, who would now have to bear the weight of her husband's scandal and disgrace. But possibly more threatening, to quote Stetz: "did any lady who spent the summer in the country really know where her husband went when he said that he had to run up to town on business?"[37] Women knew that their husbands lived in an almost entirely homosocial world and had deep emotional and intellectual attachments to their men friends, but Wilde's behavior suddenly cast doubt upon those previously normal social behaviors, casting them in a different and damaging light. The fact that the traitor was *Oscar Wilde* must have come as a particular shock, because, as noted earlier, Wilde was publicly understood to be a man who particularly *liked* women, who moved comfortably in their world and shared their interests and pursuits. Wilde's effeminacy would have, in this context, made him a *less* likely rather than a *more* likely homosexual, and the shocking question could therefore be phrased thus: if even this most effeminate of men could be homosexual, what to make of all those men who didn't seem to like women much at all?

As a result, various threatened groups participated in the social drama that was the Wilde trials. Wilde's crime was not the private act of sodomy, but his public performances, the complex acts of public signification that Queensberry called "posing somdomite" and Moe Meyer, in "Under the Sign of Wilde: An Archaeology of Posing," calls "an embodied homoeroticism" composed of a number of "signifying practices that included dress, speech, gesture, and even a mode of text production."[38]

personifying homosexuality

"The homosexual" as type or species, "homosexual sensibility," "the gay subject" – whatever you want to call it, it seems in many ways to have emerged, or at least crystallized, during the social drama that was the Wilde trials. At the center, the man who had been *posing somdomite* was now to personify homosexuality for his Victorian audience, which was ironic, since Wilde was, to quote David Schulz, only "marginally representative"[39] of homosexual culture at the time. Schulz uses a performance model to question what he calls the queer "character" that emerged from the Wilde trials, and he asks the provocative question: "Just what have they [gay men] been playing out, and who wrote the script?"[40]

As with any theatrical creation, the answer seems to be that it was a thoroughly collaborative enterprise: part script, part improvisation (though of course, improvisational behavior requires vast amounts of skill and practice; nothing requires more preparation than the appearance of spontaneity). Certainly, the basic dramatic structure was the trial itself, which organized the kind of performances that were possible, or at least authorized; the various judges frequently rebuked the gallery for laughing or clapping, for instance. Schulz describes, with reason, Edward Carson's cross-examination of Wilde during the libel trial as "the most famous cross-examination scenes of any trial,"[41] and, as we learned from Moises Kaufman's documentary play *Gross Indecency: The Three Trials of Oscar Wilde*, these scenes still make for great theatre. Wilde replied to Carson's questions with the wit and skill developed over endless hours of repartee in the drawing room and at the dinner table; Wilde was, in this way, well rehearsed, and, at least initially, he had a number of rhetorical moves at his disposal.

In *Who Was That Man? A Present for Mr. Oscar Wilde*, Neil Bartlett demonstrates Wilde's reluctance ever to waste an epigram (some appear in three or more of his works), and goes so far as to claim, with some affection, that Wilde "was a plagiarist, like us, like me. He was especially good at plagiarizing himself."[42] Bartlett goes on to describe how even Wilde's famous answer to Carson's question, "What is 'The Love That Dare Not Speak Its Name,'" was a self-quotation: "He was combining, from memory, two unconnected passages from *Dorian Gray*."[43] In her article, "Oscar Wilde's Speech from the Dock," Lucy McDiarmid complicates the genealogy of Wilde's speech by noting an additional level of intertext:

> Wilde ... was quoting what he himself had said in a previous improvisational moment. He had given the speech, or something close to it, in 1891 as part of the curious hazing ritual of Wilfrid Blunt's Crabbet Club, a "convivial association" of forty-five men who met annually at Blunt's family estate in Crabbet Park. Each new member, before his election, had to have a devil's advocate, and Wilde's was George Curzon. In the presence of all the other members of the club, Curzon (recorded Blunt) played "with astonishing audacity and skill upon [Wilde's] reputation for sodomy." As Wilde stood up to reply, Blunt felt sorry for him, but Wilde soon "pulled himself together ... and gradually warmed into an amusing and excellent speech." Four years later, during the second trial, "'Oscar's line of defence'(wrote Blunt)" "'was precisely the same as that made in his impromptu speech that evening at Crabbet.'"[44]

McDiarmid concludes by reminding us that this earlier speech wasn't off-the-cuff, either, that Wilde had used similar words in *Dorian Gray*. Clearly, Wilde had been preparing his thoughts on the subject, which allowed him, at the moment of "improvisation," to step forward and define, with some passion, what could still not, at that point, even be named.

> "The love that dare not speak its name" in this century is such a great affection of an elder for a younger man as there was between David and Jonathan, such as Plato made the very basis of his philosophy, and such as you find in the sonnets of Michelangelo and Shakespeare. It is that deep, spiritual affection that is as pure as it is perfect. It dictates and pervades great works of art like those of Shakespeare and Michelangelo, and those two letters of mine, such as they are. It is in this century misunderstood, so much misunderstood that it may be described as "the love that dare not speak its name," and on account of it I am placed where I am now. It is beautiful, it is fine, it is the noblest form of affection. There is nothing unnatural about it. It is intellectual and it repeatedly exists between an elder and a younger man, when the elder has intellect, and the younger man has all the joys, hope, and glamour of his life before him. That it should be so, the world does not understand. The world mocks at it, and sometimes puts one in the pillory for it!

"Well that too is a quotation," Bartlett grumbles after citing the speech. "At the moment of extreme emotion, with all the attendant mannerisms of honesty, he was quoting himself."[45] I'm surprised at the attitude

Bartlett takes toward quotation, which strikes me as unbecoming of a man of the theatre, and churlish besides: one could say the same of any Shakespearean soliloquy, any Wagnerian aria. Bartlett observes, rather tetchily, that

> for one who attributed such importance to individuality, to the personal and unrepeatable arts of lifestyle and conversation, to the exquisite, to the limited edition, Wilde seems to have shown remarkably little interest in being original. His life was *fashionable*, if fashion is the art and industry of making an imitation look like a novelty.[46]

I'd take Bartlett's definition of "fashion" and blur it with that of *theatrical production*: both are concerned with making something new out of something that already exists in the world. In theatrical production, a previously existing text is embodied anew; when scripts are put into production, they become, as I noted above, three-dimensional performances in which human behavior is seen to be loaded with meaning and history. From a performance studies view, *all* behavior is restored behavior, all action a production, and Wilde's performance of the above speech *was* an original creation which did something *entirely* new (more about which later) despite being an "imitation."

In fact, the performance model complicates Bartlett's binary terms "imitation" and "novelty" (which is why I'm surprised he would resort to this easy opposition as a theatre practitioner). In theatre, it's difficult to point to any kind of definitive artistic "original." In "Theatrical Performance: Illustration, Translation, Fulfillment, or Supplement?" Marvin Carlson tests out each of these terms (performance as *illustration* of the text, as *translation* of the text, as *fulfillment*, etc.) before arguing in favor of the Derridian supplement as a model for the script–performance relationship, since the supplement denies that either script or performance is ever complete in itself. In this paradigm, the literary text is not some kind of true "original" of which every theatrical production is a mere copy, quotation, or novelty. Rather, a production, in supplementing the script, demonstrates meanings not apparent in the written text, revealing it as incomplete; simultaneously it "reveals also a potentially infinite series of future performances providing further supplementation."[47] Or, in other words, a production illustrates not only that "not all that this play has to say has been said" but also that "other different but equally rich experiences with it are always possible",[48] so that a production simultaneously denies the completeness of the extant text, declares its own uniqueness, and prophesizes further performative interpretations and innovations.

Wilde's sense of "originality" has always implied this kind of performance model; there is a way in which Wilde's epigram, "The one duty we owe to history is to rewrite it," can be understood as "The one duty we owe a script is to produce it." All of Wilde's life was a "production" in these terms – since a production takes the textual past and makes it mean anew, makes it newly relevant to *us*, makes it speak to *us*, in our terms.[49] Alan Sinfield describes this process in terms of the production of Shakespeare's plays: "The inventiveness of directors and the subtleties of critics are designed, precisely, to bridge the historical gap. Shakespeare keeps going because these strategies keep him going; he is relevant because he is purposely interfered with."[50] The language Sinfield uses here strikes me as suggestive, and Wilde, tried for violations against the male sex, can actually be seen to be tried for interfering with *texts* in this way – which is to say *producing* them, which in theatre is always *reproducing* them – with meanings and contexts of which the larger culture disapproved.

In that way, the Wilde trials can be read as an elaborately-staged negative review. A powerful strand within Victorian culture rejected Wilde's (re)productions of the classical works of antiquity; of David, Jonathan and Salomé; of Shakespeare, Sidney, Donne, Byron, Morris, Swinburne, and "sixty more";[51] of Ruskin and Pater; of *A Rebours*, *East Lynne*, and all the other stage melodramas he stole from; of proverbs and other common wisdom.[52]

But Oscar Wilde continued to operate in precisely this way throughout the trials, and while none of the elements were precisely original (the effeminate behavior, the epigrammatic wit, the thrice-given speech defending sodomy), the resulting performance put something new into the world: it was the first mainstream, public personification of homosexuality. This simply hadn't been done before; as Lucy McDiarmid argues, in her article, "Oscar Wilde's Speech from the Dock," Wilde's Love-that-dare-not-speak-its-name speech cannot be considered a speech in the "Irish rebel paradigm" as some recent scholars have claimed, precisely because *what Wilde was doing had no precedent.* McDiarmid explains that

> the whole point of an Irish patriot's speech from the dock is its intertextuality. The textual tradition links the patriots across the years, and the continuing series of linked speeches serves as an accumulating collective memory of political resistance and confirms the tradition.

> The 1867 publication of the Sullivan brothers' book *Speeches from the Dock* persevered and enshrined the tradition, thereby assuring its continuity.[53]

Wilde, she points out, had no such continuity to work with:

> If in fact there had been collective memory of earlier eighteenth and nineteenth century male homosexual scandals; if Wilde had alluded in his testimony to the 1870 Boulton-Park case, in which two young men were "arrested for dressing as women" and later tried for "conspiring to commit sodomy"; and if Wilde had given a speech openly and unapologetically acknowledging his homosexual activities and invoking as a genealogy all the previous defendants in such trials – then he would be the gay martyr Eagleton and Paulin turn him into. But there was no such collective memory.[54]

The speech from the dock was designed to remind the assembled that there was a long line of patriots ready to die for the cause of freedom, that the speaker was one of them, and that he would surely not be the last. Wilde, not having a line of homosexual martyrs to draw upon, instead drew upon what McDiarmid calls "iconic figures of Western culture, men who had died of natural causes, unpunished for any homoerotic passions: David and Jonathan, Plato, Michelangelo, Shakespeare."[55] Actually, I'd amend this to argue that Wilde didn't so much evoke the men as much as their *texts*: not so much David and Jonathan as the Bible itself; not so much Plato but the *Symposium* and the *Phaedrus*; not so much Shakespeare-the-man but Shakespeare-the-body-of-work, and Michelangelo the still-living artist. In perhaps the ultimate blurring between life and art, Wilde called a series of dead artists and living texts to bear witness for him at trial.

In *Who Was That Man*, Neil Bartlett observes that Wilde and his generation had "found their peers not in other men, but in other texts,"[56] and wonders where the actual men were. After all, there had been other trials, other scandals, before Wilde's: why weren't they known? Having nobody else's defense of homosexuality to hand, Oscar Wilde stood in the dock and quoted himself. But McDiarmid is right to point out that Wilde's speech actually denies his sexuality and consequently protests his innocence, since his definition of homosexual love is entirely cultural-intellectual and explicitly not physical, which is to say, explicitly not criminal. In this way, it was hardly the speech of a martyr, and McDiarmid obviously resents the comparison of Wilde with "the Irish patriots

[who] accepted the higher criminality of their militant nationalism."[57] But paradoxically, Wilde's act of denial was simultaneously an act of creation, just as his triple self-quotation produced something unique and original. Wilde articulated modern homosexual subjectivity as a defense against sodomy; his defense can be seen to be, essentially, "I didn't *do* it; I *am* it." Wilde apparently thought it safer to identify himself with, and therefore to stand as the embodiment of, two thousand years of scripted homosexual sensibility rather than to be an apparently isolated Victorian body having committed a specific, illegal act. Wilde's performed "quotation" thus becomes the foundation of a tradition; typical of the performance as supplement, Wilde's speech not only reveals a prior lack (the lack of a political movement around homosexuality, which itself lacked even a name!) but prophesizes further productions, future action, further performances of this newly articulated sensibility.

The twentieth century was to fulfill this prophesy in spades – not only with the (re)production of trial after trial (the sheer number of them leading directly to decriminalization of homosexuality in Britain[58]); not only with marches, demonstrations, and spectacularly performative riots; but particularly with the productions and reproductions of Wilde himself over the century: all the men who defined themselves, like E.M. Forster's Maurice, as being "of the Oscar Wilde sort" and all the biographical plays, screenplays and other reproductions of Oscar Wilde himself.[59]

wilde in production: *velvet goldmine*

Wilde was the first to perform "Oscar Wilde," but he wouldn't be the last. The 1998 Todd Haynes film *Velvet Goldmine* features two kinds of Wildean reproduction: the character of "Oscar Wilde" (as played by young actor Luke Morgan Oliver), as well as a number of other male characters who are "of the Oscar Wilde sort," or in some way playing out a Wildean script.[60]

This tale of early 1970s glam rockers begins with a fairy-tale introduction in which the infant Wilde is brought to earth on a glittering spaceship that moves like a shooting star. The child is left on the Wilde family doorstep in what the caption tells us is "Dublin, 1854," a large glowing green brooch pinned to his swaddling clothes. Cut to a line of Victorian schoolboys, each announcing in turn what they want to be when they grow up. "I want to be a doctor," "I want to be a barrister" and then the young Wilde stands and declares: "I want to be a pop idol." The film then jumps a hundred years to where another young British schoolboy is being beaten up on a playground. Left bloodied and face down in the dirt, the boy finds Wilde's green brooch half buried beneath his scrabbling fingertips. The boy is Jack Fairy – he is, in the film's mythology, homosexuality incarnate – and the voiceover informs us that his finding of the brooch represents the "mysterious day when Jack would discover that somewhere there were others like him, singled out for a great gift." Wilde's brooch is eventually stolen from Jack Fairy by the David Bowie-inspired glam rocker, Brian Slade, who subsequently passes it on to his lover, until eventually it passes into the hands of a young journalist whose sexuality was formed through and around Brian Slade's albums and the larger glam rock movement. This journalist is told explicitly that the gem he holds used to belong to Oscar Wilde; he is thus explicitly connected to a tradition that the film figures as having begun with Wilde. As if to confirm this, the film ends with the journalist and his lover naked on a rooftop, while the shooting star/spaceship associated with Wilde's arrival on earth arcs gracefully through the sky overhead.

Thus Wilde appears in *Velvet Goldmine* not only as a particular historical character but as the embodiment of a set of "alien" attitudes (signified by the green brooch) that circulate throughout the culture. Cheeky young Wilde, wearing the brooch on his velvet collar, wants to be a pop idol; willowy Jack Fairy, in a full length gown and wearing the brooch as an earring, embodies the newly-visible homosexuality of the 1960s which made glam rock possible; the outrageous and self-interested Brian Slade, brooch pinned to the aviator's scarf wrapped around his neck, becomes the world's first bisexual superstar; Curt Wild, brooch tacked to the collar of his beat-up leather jacket, brings his raw (homo)sexuality and rage to the rock stage – they are all of them, in their way, incarnations – or should we say productions – of the alien sensibility that first fell to earth with Wilde. (It's important to note that Wilde is not, even here, figured as the *originator* of this sensibility but only as the first earthly *messenger* of it; the child Wilde, like the young Superman, simply drops from the sky with his bit of green rock, a representative of an alien culture. The question of "originality" is therefore neatly evaded – displaced offworld, rendered inaccessible and incomprehensible.)

Brian Slade, in particular, is seen as a contemporary embodiment of Wilde. Slade – like Wilde, like Bowie, Warhol, Madonna, Baz Lurhmann and sixty others – is a thief, a magpie, a plagiarist, which is to say, a great artist who steals. Slade holds long conversations composed entirely of Wildean epigrams (in fact, Wilde wrote so much of the film's dialogue that he ought to have been given credit as a screenwriter) and the film's plot turns, as in *The Importance of Being Earnest*, on a form of Bunburying which is chronological rather than geographical. Here, it's not a matter of being Jack in the country and Ernest in the city; rather, we are given a man who is "Brian Slade" in the 1970s and "Tommy Steele" in the 1980s. "Brian Slade" is a socially subversive glam rocker, whereas "Tommy Steele" is a commercial, corporate act, which rehearses not only the two sides of Jack (man about town, respectable country gentleman) but the two sides of Wilde (highbrow artist and commercial success; man of society, social deviant). Slade, like Jack, like Wilde, is deeply invested in keeping his two lives separate, and attempts to frustrate the journalist who tries to prove that Tommy Steele used to be glam rocker Brian Slade.

Like Jack, Brian attempts to "explode" his "Brian Slade" personality by staging his own assassination during a concert. But performance *is* reality, and while Slade's graphic death-by-shooting may be a performance, it does in fact destroy him. Slade's fans, outraged by the deception, turn against him, effectively driving him from public life (and into the socially acceptable persona of heterosexual Tommy Steele, the film's Jack in the country). Slade's ex-wife, questioned late in the film about the fake shooting, wryly adds, in a paradox worthy of Wilde, "And what a fake it was – tricking us all in the end with such an authentic demise."

The Wilde trials are also re-produced toward the end of the film, staged as part trial, part media circus. Slade, wearing a shiny gold top hat and tails, is cross-examined by a series of reporters/prosecutors, and he answers entirely in Wildean quotations. (To be sure that the film's audience *knows* that they're quotations, they're written out on cue-cards.)

Q: Maxwell Demon is the story of a space creature who becomes a rock and roll messiah, only to be destroyed by his own success. Are you saying this is *your* destiny? Are *you* Maxwell Demon?

Slade: Man is least himself when he talks in his own person. Give him a mask and he'll tell you the truth.

Q: Is it your belief that all dandies are homosexual?

Slade: Ha! – nothing makes one so vain as to be told one is a sinner.

Wilde's words turn up unexpectedly in characters' mouths just as the alien green brooch has a habit of turning up on unexpected collars. The performance of Oscar Wilde – words, gestures, behaviors, costumes – is still circulating meaningfully throughout the culture, as is Wilde's methodology of making art. Wilde is, after all, positioned in the film as the first pop-idol, and the film encourages *everyone* to become one – or to at least dress like one, which amounts to much the same thing.

Velvet Goldmine therefore sees Wilde not only as a famously influential historical figure to be represented, but as a role that any of us (properly costumed, directed and rehearsed, of course) might successfully perform and make our own.

notes

1. Adam Gopnik, "The Invention of Oscar Wilde," *The New Yorker* 18 May 1998, 78–88.
2. Richard Schechner, *Performance Studies: An Introduction* (New York: Routledge, 2002), 28.
3. Diana Taylor, "Translating Performance," in *Profession, 2002* (New York: The Modern Language Association of America, 2002), 45.
4. Schechner, op. cit., 22.
5. Catherine Soussloff and Mark Franko, *Social Text* 20.4 (2002) 29–46.
6. Francesca Coppa, "A Conversation with John Alderton and Leonie Orton," in *Joe Orton: A Casebook*, edited and introduced by Francesca Coppa. *Casebooks On Modern Dramatists* (New York: Routledge, 2002), 162.
7. John Lahr, *Prick Up Your Ears: The Biography of Joe Orton* (New York: Vintage, 1987), 278.
8. At the risk of perpetrating an inferior epigram, it's very difficult to grieve "originally." It's not simply the upper-class rituals of mourning that are performative; everyone now "knows" what grief looks like. The entire spectrum, from dead-eyed, stiff-backed silence to convulsive, throw-yourself-on-the-coffin type shrieks, has been "done." Similarly, it is at times of great shock when we tend to most rely on our social scripts, saying "the things people say," at times of sorrow and "going through the motions" of usual behavior.
9. Kerry Powell, *Oscar Wilde and the Theatre of the 1890s* (Cambridge: Cambridge University Press, 1990), 109.
10. An epigram is typically an elaboration on a proverb; the proverb is the first, oral articulation of an idea, the short and memorable codification of "common wisdom." In contrast, the epigram is typically a later, written, variation on the idea which often contests, argues with, or renegotiates the meaning of the original comment; in this way, an epigram articulates an "uncommon" wisdom. Consider Wilde's epigram: "History never repeats itself. The historians repeat each other," or, more recently, Roseanne Barr's joke: "The fastest way to a man's heart is through his chest." See Francesca Coppa, "Oscar Wilde and the Theatre of Epigram," in *Reading Wilde: Querying Spaces*. eds. Carolyn Dever and Marvin Taylor (New York: New York University Press, Fales Library, 1995).
11. Joseph Bristow, "Memorialising Wilde: An Explosive History," *Journal of Victorian Culture*, Autumn 2000, Vol. 5 Issue 2, p311, 12p. Ebscohost. Trexler Library, Muhlenberg College. 9 February 2003 <http://www.epnet.com>.
12. Merlin Holland, *The Wilde Album* (New York: Henry Holt and Company, 1997), 138.
13. David Foster, "Oscar Wilde, *De Profundis*, and the Rhetoric of Agency," *Papers on Language and Literature*, Winter 2001, Vol. 37, Issue 1, p85, 26p. Ebscohost.

Trexler Library, Muhlenberg College. 9 February 2003 <http://www.epnet.com>.

14. Jonathan L. Freedman, *Professions of Taste: Henry James, British Aestheticism, and Commodity Culture* (Stanford: Stanford University Press, 1990), 173.
15. Richard Ellmann, *Oscar Wilde* (New York: Vintage Books, 1988), 369.
16. Bristow, op. cit.
17. Alan Sinfield, *The Wilde Century: Effeminacy, Oscar Wilde and the Queer Moment* (London: Cassell, 1994), vi.
18. Michel Foucault, *The History of Sexuality: Volume I: An Introduction* (New York: Vintage, 1980), 43.
19. Margaret Diane Stetz, "The Bi-Social Oscar Wilde and 'Modern' Women," *Nineteenth Century Literature* (March 2001), Vol. 55, Issue 4, p515, 23p. Ebscohost. Trexler Library, Muhlenberg College. 9 February 2003 <http://www.epnet.com>.
20. Joseph Bristow, *Effeminate England: Homoerotic Writing After 1885* (New York: Columbia University Press, 1995).
21. Ian Christopher Fletcher, "The Soul of Man Under Imperialism: Oscar Wilde, Race, and Empire," *Journal of Victorian Culture*, Autumn 2000, Vol. 5, Issue 2, p334, 8p. Ebscohost. Trexler Library, Muhlenberg College. 9 February 2003. <http://www.epnet.com>.
22. On 18 February 1895, the Marquess of Queensberry, Lord Alfred Douglas's father, left a card for Wilde at his club that read, "Oscar Wilde, posing [as] somdomite [sic]." On the basis of this accusation, Wilde sued Queensberry for criminal libel. Upon losing this case, Wilde was himself arrested, tried, and convicted of gross indecency. He was sentenced to two years' hard labor.
23. David Jays, "Wilde Disappointment," *New Statesman*, 25 September 2000, Vol. 129, Issue 4505, p61, 3p. Ebscohost. Trexler Library, Muhlenberg College. 9 February 2003. <http://www.epnet.com>.
24. Foucault, op. cit., 43.
25. Quoted in Ellmann, op. cit., 417.
26. Foucault, op. cit., 43.
27. Sinfield, op. cit., vi.
28. Ed Cohen, *Talk on the Wilde Side* (New York: Routledge, 1993), 145.
29. David Schulz, "Redressing Oscar: Performance and the Trials of Oscar Wilde," *The Drama Review* 40, 2, (T150), Summer 1996, 46.
30. Frank Harris, *Oscar Wilde* (New York: Carroll & Graf, 1992), 166.
31. Schulz, op. cit., 58. Schulz also cites Xavier Mayne; Mayne, writing about homosexuality in 1908, is eager to differentiate Wilde from other "Uranians." He notes that Wilde repudiated "the morality of the homosexual instinct" and calls Wilde a "shrewd and superficial poseur, to the very last." Schulz, op. cit., 37.
32. Harris, op. cit., 167.
33. Schulz, op. cit., 47.
34. Victor Turner, *Dramas, Fields, and Metaphors* (Ithaca: Cornell University Press, 1974), 37–41.
35. Schulz, op. cit., 47.
36. Ibid.
37. Stetz, Op. cit.

38. Moe Meyer, "Under the Sign of Wilde: An Archaeology of Posing," in *The Politics and Poetics of Camp*, ed. Moe Meyer (London: Routledge, 1994), 97.
39. Schulz, op. cit., 38.
40. Ibid., 39.
41. Ibid.
42. Neil Bartlett, *Who Was That Man? A Present for Mr. Oscar Wilde* (London: Penguin, 1993), 202.
43. Ibid., 204.
44. Lucy McDiarmid, "Oscar Wilde's Speech from the Dock," *Textual Practice* 15.3 (2001), 454.
45. Bartlett, op. cit., 204.
46. Ibid., 201.
47. Marvin Carlson, "Theatrical Performance: Illustration, Translation, Fulfillment, or Supplement?" *Theatre Journal* 37 (March 1985), 10.
48. Ibid., 11.
49. It is worth noting that the continued "relevance" bestowed upon theatrical works by new productions is not uncritically a good thing. Brecht, in particular, has claimed that the constant re(production) of older plays sends the false (and politically conservative) message that nothing changes, that human nature remains the same, that any attempt at progressivism or revolution is essentially futile. Every generation may have its Hamlet, but the world has changed a great deal since *Hamlet*, a fact which may not be fully appreciated by the audience of a traditional theatrical production of Hamlet or any other play since the goal of such a production is typically to evoke empathy in the audience, not critical distance. Hence, Brecht's advocacy of the "alienation effect" in the *Short Organum for the Theatre* and anti-empathetic stance in "Theatre for Pleasure or Theatre for Instruction." Both pieces can be found in *Brecht on Theatre*, edited by John Willett, (New York: Hill and Wang or London: Methuen, 1978).
50. Alan Sinfield, *Cultural Politics – Queer Reading* (Philadelphia: University of Pennsylvania Press, 1994), 4–5.
51. The Oxford Union in 1881 rejected the gift of Wilde's first collection of poems. Oliver Elton, speaking for the majority, claimed that the poems were "for the most part not by their putative father at all, but by a number of better-known and more deservedly reputed authors. They are in fact by William Shakespeare, by Philip Sidney, by John Donne, by Lord Byron, by William Morris, by Algernon Swinburne, and by sixty more." Ellmann, op. cit., 146.
52. Again, see Francesca Coppa, "Oscar Wilde and the Theatre of Epigram," op. cit., for more about Wilde's use of proverbs and epigrams.
53. McDiarmid, op. cit., 448.
54. Ibid., 453.
55. Ibid., 456.
56. Bartlett, op. cit., 199.
57. McDiarmid, op. cit., 457.
58. In "A Perfectly Developed Playwright: Joe Orton and Homosexual Reform," I discuss the ways in which the legalization of homosexuality in 1967 was an attempt to re-legitimize the moral authority of British law in the wake of the widespread chain arrests and entrapment of homosexuals in the 1940s and 1950s. The sheer number of arrests produced by these law-enforcement

strategies during those years had demonstrated quite effectively that homosexuality was too widespread to be combated by prosecution. To quote Ian Gilmour, Member for Norfolk, during the Commons Sexual Offenses debate of 1967: "It [the current law] is unenforceable because there are too many of these people to enable the law to be enforced. We do not know how many there are but, if there are half a million and we were able to catch them, we would not have any idea of what to do with them." See Francesca Coppa, "A Perfectly Developed Playwright: Joe Orton and Homosexual Reform," in *The Queer Sixties*, ed. Patricia Juliana Smith (New York: Routledge, 1999).

59. Plays about or featuring Wilde include Leslie and Sewell Stokes' *Oscar Wilde: A Play*; Terry Eagleton's *St. Oscar*; Moises Kaufman's *Gross Indecency*; David Hare's *The Judas Kiss*; Tom Stoppard's *The Invention of Love*; Neil Bartlett's *In Extremis*; Michael Mac Liammoir's one man show *The Importance of Being Oscar*; Bernard Mouffe's *Le Proces d'Oscar Wilde*; Robert Badinter's *C.33*; Ulick O'Connor's *A Trinity of Two*. Films include *Oscar Wilde* (1960) starring Robert Morley, *The Trials of Oscar Wilde* (USA: *The Man With the Green Carnation*) (1960) starring Peter Finch, and the 1997 film *Wilde* starring Stephen Fry. For further discussion of works featuring Wilde, see John Bull, "'What the Butler Did See': Joe Orton and Oscar Wilde," in *Joe Orton: A Casebook*, edited and introduced by Francesca Coppa. *Casebooks On Modern Dramatists* (New York: Routledge, 2002).
60. Compare Coppa's discussion here with that of Kaye, Chapter 8 – ed.

4
aestheticism and aesthetic theory

allison pease

Oscar Wilde believed that the self is multiple. One testament to the multiplicity of Oscar Wildes can be found in critical opinion of his aesthetics. To some he is an idealist who saw the mind as the focal point of all aesthetic interactions. To others he is a materialist concerned with "extreme sensuousness."[1] Evidence and combined critical opinion suggest that Wilde's aesthetics are both idealist and materialist. Wilde, an eager student of Hegel at Oxford, paraphrased the philosopher's ideas in his Commonplace Book, writing that "Every philosophy must be both idealist and realist: for without realism a philosophy would be void of substance, and matter without idealism would be void of form and truth . . . In the rhythm of both the line of dialectic finds its true course of progress."[2] Wilde, always a straddler of two worlds at once, is no different in his aesthetics.

Though Wilde's ideas about aesthetics are so much a part of his oeuvre that scholars have had to contend with them all along, the 1990s enjoyed a proliferation of studies investigating them. This scholarship followed in the wake of a renewed interest in aesthetic theory arising from academic debates about aesthetic value in the 1980s and 1990s that forced theorists to explain aesthetic value, either from a materialist or idealist perspective.[3] To understand Aestheticism and Wilde's aesthetics, it is useful to have a sense of how they fit into a broader body of aesthetic ideas that began to be articulated in the eighteenth century.

the philosophical roots of aestheticism

Modern aesthetics have their roots in eighteenth-century theories of taste in England and aesthetic philosophy as first articulated by Kant in Germany in the 1790s. Thinkers like Shaftesbury, Hutcheson, Kames,

Hume, and Burke, along with Kant, Hegel, Schopenhauer, and Schiller, though they represented aesthetic experience diversely in its particulars, attempted to find a universal agreement, or "standard" of taste wherein true aesthetic experience could be said to take place. All assert a subject's disinterested pleasure in apprehending an object of beauty; locate aesthetic pleasure in the rational and reflective rather than sensual faculties; emphasize the importance of form in producing beauty; and find objects of beauty autonomous and irreducible to utility.[4] Almost all conceived of the aesthetic as that which formed a middle term between sense and cognition. One can find the roots of Wilde's aesthetic ideas on form, autonomy, utility, the relations between spirit and sense, and the premier role of the "spectator" of art in these thinkers. Though "apartness from the praxis of life . . . had always constituted the institutional status of art" as articulated in the eighteenth century, the impetus for the rise of aesthetic ideas was, in England, distinctly social.[5]

Expressions of taste in eighteenth-century England were written partly in response to, and in order to educate, the rising middle classes. Displays of taste demonstrated one's right to join the polite society of gentlemen by indicating one's leisure had been rigorously and morally applied toward rational reflection upon the secular arts. In Wilde's time 150 years later, espousing aesthetic ideas and living aesthetically were still signs of upward mobility and a claim to an elite realm not based on birth or inheritance.

As opposed to the popular, and exaggerated, portrayal of Aestheticism as a hedonistic cult of individual sensibility, however, eighteenth-century aesthetics were understood as an implicit social contract between what Kant saw as "on the one hand, the universal feeling of sympathy, and, on the other, the faculty of being able to communicate universally one's inmost self – properties constituting in conjunction the befitting social spirit of mankind, in contradistinction to the narrow life of the lower animals."[6] Both subjective and universal, eighteenth-century aesthetics fostered a turning outward of what could be experienced only subjectively, a movement away from the individual, sensuous, and particular to the general and abstract, what could be communicated between men. By turning men's minds outward, expressions of taste were intended to contribute to the making of a rational public sphere.

aestheticism in france and england

Aestheticism was in part a continuation of, and in part a rejection of, eighteenth-century aesthetics. As an extension of aesthetics in the tradition of Shaftesbury and Kant, Aestheticism continued, and even foregrounded, the claim of art's autonomy, its value apart from morality, utility, and pleasure. As a departure from aesthetics in the tradition of Shaftesbury and Kant, Aestheticism lost faith in the possibility of a rational public sphere and shifted importance away from a subjectively universal response toward a private response that could not be universally communicated.

French Aesthetes Théophile Gautier (whose professor, Victor Cousin, lectured on Kant and coined the phrase "*l'art pour l'art*") and Charles Baudelaire perpetuated and radicalized aesthetics in the tradition of Shaftesbury and Kant by calling for art's complete autonomy from moral, social, or practical purpose. In an article tracing the French history of *l'art pour l'art*, John Wilcox claims that the rise of this French rubric stems from a "fantastically careless and incompetent misreading" of Kantian aesthetic theory before it was translated into French in 1846.[7] This reading ignored German idealism's subtly stated understanding of the sense of beauty as a sensuous grounding for morality and sociability, and instead used Kantian aesthetic autonomy as a way to challenge the moral and political order of a tumultuous France.[8]

As in France, English Aestheticism has been defined as a reaction against a number of forces in industrial, nineteenth-century England: utility, rationality, scientific factuality, technical progress, middle-class conformity, industrial capitalism, democratic leveling, athleticism, sexual mores and oppressive moralism.[9] Wilde has long been celebrated as the figurehead of English Aestheticism, the loosely based movement whose positive conviction, as R.V. Johnson states in his classic account, is that "the enjoyment of beauty can by itself give value and meaning to life."[10] Aestheticism manifested itself in multiple aspects of late nineteenth-century life. In its more rarified, ideal form, Aestheticism is the concern with developing a heightened awareness and responsiveness to life and art. In its popular, material forms, Aestheticism is bound with the idea of making conscious, individual consumer choices in homage to the beautiful.

Though John Ruskin is largely credited with setting the tone for Aestheticism in his call for beautifying everyday life, Pre-Raphaelite artists, including Dante Gabriel Rossetti, Edward Burne-Jones, and Algernon Charles Swinburne, among others, exemplified it in expressing a sensuous yearning for ideal beauty. Aestheticism's most complete articulation is traditionally found in the writings of Pater and Wilde in the 1870s, 1880s and 1890s.[11] Roughly, Aestheticism tends to place a high value on the following: artistic form, a heightened consciousness that is alert to both physical and spiritual experience (spirituality often deriving from physicality), art's ability to create sympathy, art's ability to recreate the individual beholder through a process of conscious self-transcendence (this may also be called "self-culture"), and the individual's need for self-expression in spite of, or at the expense of, social norms.

In nineteenth-century England, a large and socially fragmented reading public made the eighteenth-century ideal of a "rational" public sphere seemingly impossible. Wilde's dependence on, and yet disdain for, the "fatal development of the habit of reading amongst the middle and lower classes of" England demonstrates a new relationship between artist and audience in which the artist only knows the audience as a consuming, capricious mass. ("Critic as Artist," 1115). One reaction to this new relationship is to focus on the individual, private response to art. As Linda Dowling notes, Walter Pater's formulation in the preface to *The Renaissance* "what is this song . . . to *me*?" is an attack against aesthetics in the tradition of Shaftesbury and Kant, which sought to universalize individual judgments of taste.[12] Like Pater, Wilde privileges the individually specific aesthetic experience. In his 1882 lecture "The English Renaissance of Art" he eschews "any abstract definition of beauty – any such universal formula for it as was sought for by the philosophy of the eighteenth century," choosing instead to privilege the specific, the concrete, and the material.[13]

The turn toward the subjective and the particular, what cannot be generalized, can be explained through Wilde's fascination with moods. Wilde says in a letter to H.C. Marillier dated 12 December 1885, "Only one thing remains fascinating to me, the mystery of moods. To be master of these moods is exquisite, to be mastered by them more exquisite still."[14] It is the mystery of moods, their incommunicability that distinguishes them for Wilde (and consequently, along with their irrationality, what marks them as distinctly anti-Kantian). As he comments in "The Critic as Artist": "Art is a passion, and, in matters of art, Thought is inevitably coloured by emotion, and so is fluid rather than fixed, and, depending upon fine moods and exquisite moments, cannot be narrowed into the rigidity of a scientific formula or a theological dogma" (1144). The aesthetic process is for Wilde irrational, personal, and time-bound, relative not universal. From Kant to Wilde, one can see an Enlightenment faith in a universal human subjectivity yielding to a modernist/postmodernist focus on the unique, the individual not as governed by reason but by time, emotion, or random circumstance.

wilde's aestheticism

Wilde was not the first to insist on art's autonomy, more popularly known as "art for art's sake," but he has frequently been seen as championing the idea. Critical opinion is divided, however, on what that idea meant to him. Does art for art's sake really mean a divorce from the social sphere? Or does it suggest a separate sphere for art that, in being separate, acts as a socially redemptive sphere of being? Wilde scholarship has remained divided on this topic, with earlier twentieth-century accounts more consistently favoring the Wilde of "Decay of Lying" who claims "Art never expresses anything but itself. It has an independent life, just as Thought has, and develops purely on its own lines" (1091), and critics of the 1990s more consistently favoring the Wilde of "The English Renaissance of Art" who sees art as the expression of its national culture, noting "It is for the critic to create for art the social aim, too, by teaching the people the spirit in which they are to approach all artistic work, the love they are to give it, the lesson they are to draw from it" (17). Wilde consistently stressed that it was the critic's job to find social and political meaning in art, stating later in "The Critic as Artist" that "It is only by the cultivation of the habit of intellectual criticism that we shall be able to rise superior to race-prejudices" (1153).

For the scholars who take the claims of art's autonomy as meaning a complete separation from the social sphere, it is the individual and particular nature of Aestheticist experiences of art that makes them apolitical. This view has been expounded by Ian Small where he says that

> until the middle decades of the nineteenth century it was a commonplace that art was capable of embodying a form of knowledge about the world, and principally a form of moral knowledge. A change began in the late 1860s. . . . For the Aesthete of the 1870s and 1880s, art and literature, with all the rich social, institutional, political, and moral values which traditionally had been held to be expressed by them, had become reduced to a set of individual aesthetic experiences: and so they had, in nearly all significant respects, become merely private matters.[15]

Early critiques of Wilde corroborate this argument. An unsigned review of Wilde's *Poems* said in the *Spectator* that Wilde "abjures the world he is so dissatisfied with, and devotes himself to what he calls the world of Art, really, in his case, a world of fragments of coloured glass, hardly even arranged, as the child's kaleidoscope arranges them, into something like harmonious form."[16] More enthusiastically, Agnes Reppelier, writing for the *North American Review* in 1892 said that the "Decay of Lying" outlines a "great truth . . . the absolute independence of art."[17] For evidence of this attitude one need look no further than Wilde's creations. Lord Henry Wotton says in *Dorian Gray*, "Art has no influence upon action. It annihilates the desire to act" (156). Anne Varty has characterized Wotton's statement as delineating a "Kantian mental state of disinterested contemplation," and indeed Kant's purpose in demarcating the aesthetic as a sphere devoid of interest was to evacuate the political from the realm of aesthetics in order, paradoxically, to improve the social sphere.[18]

The idea that Wilde's aesthetics were strictly apolitical was countered frequently in the 1990s in the wake of expanded scholarship in aesthetic theory. Thus Jonathan Freedman claims "When aestheticist writers like Swinburne or Pater deployed the slogan of 'art for art,' they did so as part of a larger argument or dialectic that is trivialized when compacted into so simple and rigid a notion."[19] Freedman, among others, views Wilde as a dialectician along the lines of Hegel, a view that has been largely supported by the scholarship of Phillip E. Smith and Michael S. Helfand's annotations to Wilde's Oxford notebooks. In this view, Wilde seeks in art a utopian model through which reality can be better conceived. Wilde says in "The English Renaissance of Art," "Art never harms itself by keeping aloof from the social problems of the day: Rather, by so doing, it more completely realizes for us that which we desire. For to most of us the real life is the life we do not lead" (12). Regenia Gagnier, in a cagier construction, suggests that Wilde's work "typically consisted of thought experiments on the social limits of aesthetic autonomy."[20] Lawrence Danson claims that "In both 'The Critic as Artist' and 'The Soul of Man under Socialism,' aesthetic concerns are inescapably also political concerns, and explicitly they involve questions of real power. Who will judge the artists and who will control their products?"[21] The central argument of Julia Prewitt Brown's *Cosmopolitan Criticism: Oscar Wilde's Philosophy of Art* is that Wilde's aesthetic is tied to a political vision, seeing Wilde's ideas as informed by classical Greek literature, where the political and the aesthetic are intertwined.[22] Guy Willoughby argues that "Wilde's powerfully imaginative Jesus embodies a commitment to the community at large, and to an expanded view of self and society that derives from aesthetic appreciation, rather than moral instinct."[23] Though these critics agree in finding Wilde's aesthetics as politically and socially engaged, most would likely also agree with Smith and Helfand that, according to Wilde, art's social function can only be indirect and utopian, not didactic.[24]

However politically progressive Aestheticism's ambitions, Freedman has observed in his well-regarded account of the movement, they were dulled by the co-optive nature of a thriving commercial culture: "the politically progressive ambitions of aestheticism were continually thwarted not by the hostility of the press or the public . . . but rather by the eager adoption of its central tenets by the commercial press, the advertising industry, and by the manufacturers and vendors of 'new' aesthetic commodities."[25] British Aestheticism was complicit with, even while it rejected, consumer culture, and no one was more aware of this tenuous stance than Wilde himself.

Wilde's impact as a public figure and an Aesthete were felt in ways that are difficult to measure. Walter Hamilton devoted an entire chapter to Wilde in his 1882 book, *The Aesthetic Movement in England*, *Punch* featured Wilde-like caricatures in its pages throughout the early 1880s, and Oscar Browning reviewed Wilde's *Poems* in 1881 as "representing the newest development of academical aestheticism."[26] Yet Danson claims that by the early 1880s Aestheticism was no longer news. Wilde was a second-generation aesthete, having been preceded by Ruskin, Dante Gabriel Rossetti, Burne-Jones, Morris, and Pater. Further, Danson sees Wilde's assertion of Aestheticist ideas in the 1890s as retrograde: "*Intentions* [1891] is an attempt to forge a forward-looking theoretical position by deploying older attitudes to oppose a theoretical position – realism or naturalism – which at that moment was laying strong claims to being more politically progressive."[27] To some, Wilde was an embarrassing after-effect of more original Aestheticist thinkers.

There has been in Wilde studies a persistent Romantic bias, indeed a sense of embarrassment, that Wilde so candidly echoed, some say plagiarized, his mentors and Aestheticist forebears. Wilde's contemporaries openly disdained these echoes. Reviews of *Poems* accuse his poetry of resembling an anthology of plagiarism.[28] Arthur Symons's biting review of his *Collected Works* in 1908 states that Wilde's

> expression of what he conceived by beauty is developed from many models, and has no new ideas in it; one can trace it, almost verbally, to Pater, Flaubert, Gautier, Baudelaire, and other writers from whom he drew sustenance. . . . Of the writer's names, all but the last had their own sense of beauty, their own imaginative world where they were at home, and could speak its language naturally. Wilde's style is constantly changing, as made things do when one alters them, and it is only at intervals that it ceases to be artificial, imitative, or pretentious.[29]

In 1914 Ernst Bendz's study of the influence of Arnold and Pater, though scholarly and appreciative, outlined paragraph-by-paragraph similarities in idea and language between Wilde, Pater, and Arnold. Wilde struck a similar tone to Pater, and often paraphrases the lush prose of *The Renaissance* ("that book which has had such a strange influence over my life" Wilde wrote in *De Profundis*, 1022) in his own writing, most notably in "The English Renaissance of Art" and *The Picture of Dorian Gray*. Wilde was, like Pater, focused on the responsiveness of the individual mind to the art object.

Recent critics, however, have worked hard to establish ties to Ruskin and Arnold, writers who were more engaged politically. Brown, for instance, argues for a revision of the long-established tie between Wilde and Pater, suggesting that Pater's materialism was superseded by Wilde's truly idealist bent. Instead, Brown claims, Arnold was a more important figure in shaping Wilde's aesthetics: "Like Arnold, Wilde understood the importance of viewing culture as a whole, as an integral rather than an aggregate."[30] Smith and Helfand, who argue that Hegel was a formative influence on Wilde's thought, also claim that "Some of Ruskin's critical interests and assumptions decisively influenced Wilde's development. He shared with Ruskin an idealist perspective and consequently an antimaterialist and antiutilitarian position in culture and politics."[31] With recent critics, the idealist strain in Wilde's thought is in the ascendant.

Though Wilde was the butt of many cartoon jokes of the 1880s and 1890s, and his efforts on behalf of English art and Aestheticism thus appear popular, ephemeral, and perhaps merely entertaining, at the time of Wilde's death in 1900 his efforts on behalf of Aestheticism were viewed as having left a lasting impact on British culture. An unsigned obituary notice in the *Pall Mall Gazette*, the magazine for which he did a good deal of writing in the 1880s, said "Mr. Wilde led a movement in the eighties, which, in spite of its absurdities, killed much vulgar Philistinism."[32] A 1908 review notes that

> Through his personality and poses he did more than any one to spread abroad the not too abstruse elements of the aesthetic doctrines excogitated by wiser and more silent men than himself, and to give the minds and men of middle class something, at least, of the benefit of a movement which we have not so completely absorbed into our daily lives that we forget what our culture owes to it.[33]

These notices serve as a useful reminder that Aestheticism was something that was both lived materially in England, an idea Gagnier's *Idylls of the Marketplace* has done much to establish, as well as conceived ideally. It was both high and mass cultural.

Wilde was effective at communicating to both elite and popular publics. Dowling, whose book, *The Vulgarization of Art: The Victorians and Aesthetic Democracy*, focuses most exclusively on these issues, sees Wilde as leaning on an aristocratic tradition while affirming "the democratic scope of and generous utopian dimension of art."[34] "To see how often Wilde is compelled to speak as though to an aristocracy of scattered spirits raised by art and timeless beauty above the swarming vulgarity of the age," Dowling notes, "is inescapably and simultaneously to see that such an elite, like an earlier European aristocracy based on birth and privilege, was very likely a remnant on its way to extinction."[35] Similarly, Gagnier writes that "the standardizing effects of the public schools, the rise of the new journalism facilitated by the expansion of advertising, and academic specialization had divided the market and was effectively silencing the former man of letters."[36]

Wilde has often been seen as the last, and most diminutive, in a line of Victorian sages following Carlyle, Ruskin, Arnold and Pater. But he had to contend with market forces and increasing professional specialization that made the role, or perhaps the audience, of the man of letters more difficult to find.[37] Though Wilde rebelled against the specialization and consequent marginalization of art – "Art does not address herself to the specialist. Her claim is that she is universal" – the "generality" or "universality" to which he addressed himself is debatable ("Critic as Artist," 1149–1150). As editor of *Woman's World* and a regular contributor to the *Pall Mall Gazette* under sensationalist W.T. Stead's editorship, his writing certainly reached a large mass-market audience. As a contributor to *Court and Society Review*, *Queen*, and *The Speaker* he wrote for a middle-class audience with pretensions to the upper-middle class or aristocracy. Over the course of his career, his numerous letters to the editors of the *Scots Observer*, the *Daily Telegraph*, the *St. James Gazette*, and the *Pall Mall Gazette*, among others, suggest that he actively courted the ears of not just a rarified collection of gentlemen readers, but a mass market. Wilde published the essays that later appeared in *Intentions* in up-market, widely distributed liberal monthly magazines, *The Fortnightly Review* and *The Nineteenth Century* (which had a circulation of 20,000 according to Danson).[38] He first published *The Picture of Dorian Gray* in *Lippincott's* magazine. His audience was as middle-class as he was, and the breadth of these magazines and newspapers demonstrates Aestheticism's rise in conjunction with the organization and growth of the mass-circulation press in the 1880s and 1890s. As Guy and Small say in their book *Oscar Wilde's Profession: Writing and the Culture Industry in the Late Nineteenth Century*, "It is difficult to imagine a part of the publishing industry more mired in British bourgeois values than the bubble economy of the popular periodical press in the 1880s."[39] Wilde's journalism would seem to confirm Bashford's claim that rather than an elitist, Wilde was a populist, striving "to help persons participate in the aesthetic realm . . . to humanize them in the sense of enabling them to do what only human beings do."[40]

wilde's aesthetics

What were Wilde's specific beliefs about art and how did they function in his own works? I now turn to an examination of these ideas and to the critical commentary about them.

form

Modern aesthetics since the eighteenth century has argued that form distinguishes true art from what is merely agreeable or useful. In Kant, what raises an object from the agreeable to the beautiful is a finality of form that allows the mind in its free play with that form to achieve a disinterested delight that is universally communicable. Shaftesbury similarly argues that the value of beauty lies in what it reveals in the realm of form. These definitions exclude emotional or sensuous response from the realm of pure form so that the art-object becomes an independent object of aesthetic contemplation.

Aestheticism, especially as espoused by Swinburne, Pater, and Wilde, further privileged form as art's primary signifier. Form both defined art and became its subject: the real artist, Gilbert says in "The Critic as Artist," "gains his inspiration from form, and from form purely, as an artist should" (1148). At the same time, "Forms are required by Wilde's principle for expression to realize itself."[41] Dorian's musings in *The Picture of Dorian Gray* where he says "Words. . . . They seemed to be able to give a plastic form to formless things. . . . Was there anything so real as words?" (29) are a homage to form, and the power of form to shape consciousness. In a typically Wildean paradox – one that reveals his dialectic bent – Wilde viewed form as a marker *of* consciousness, or of the conscious will, which in turn shaped the work of art.

Wilde made the role of form as an expression of the artist's will one of the focal points of his aesthetic philosophy in the late 1880s as he crafted for publication in *The Nineteenth Century* "The Critic as Artist" (titled "The True Function and Value of Criticism: with some remarks on the Importance of Doing Nothing" in its original published form) and "The Decay of Lying." In a December 1888 review of English poetesses in *Queen*, Wilde wrote of Elizabeth Barrett Browning that she disliked "facile smoothness and artificial polish. In her very rejection of art she was an artist. She intended to produce a certain effect by certain means, and she succeeded."[42] Notably, he recycled this phrase in praise of Walt Whitman in the *Pall Mall Gazette* a month later in January 1889, saying "For in his very rejection of art Walt Whitman is an artist. He tried to produce a certain effect by certain means and he succeeded."[43] Wilde's insistent repetition of these phrases suggests that he had hit upon a formula that worked for him: the artist as conscious shaper, and form, or the determined lack of it, as the sign of the artist's conscious shaping. Neil Sammells, in his book *Wilde Style: The Plays and Prose of Oscar Wilde*, argues that "style" is the term Wilde, along with Poe and Baudelaire, uses to describe this process. Willoughby likewise affirms the centrality of conscious aesthetic shaping in Wilde's work: "Wilde's work *in toto* celebrates the human power to imagine and impose order, however fleetingly, on experience."[44]

Wilde's two most famous critical essays, "The Decay of Lying" and "The Critic as Artist," are full expressions of the centrality of form in, and form as the signifier of conscious limitation to, art. In "The Decay of Lying" Vivian, speaking for Wilde, says that "selection . . . is the very spirit of art" (1079). In "The Critic as Artist" Gilbert explains that it is "not merely in art that the body is the soul. In every sphere of life Form is the beginning of things. . . . it is Form that creates not merely the critical temperament, but also the aesthetic instinct, that unerring instinct that reveals to one all things under the conditions of beauty" (1148–1149). Wilde exacts form in these two essays as that which secures the landscape of the imagination and wrests its content from bleak, unconscious Nature: "What Art really reveals to us is Nature's lack of design, her curious crudities, her extraordinary monotony, her absolutely unfinished condition" (1071). Wilde was nothing if not a stylist. For to him style, a signifier of consciousness, was truth, as he indicated in "The Decay of Lying."

In his own art Wilde experimented most freely with form in his plays, daringly applying his anti-naturalistic premises in *Salomé*.[45] Reviews by Lord Alfred Douglas, who collaborated with Wilde on the play, and William Archer both herald the play as approaching music, a claim that echoes Pater's declaration in *The Renaissance* that "all art aspires to the condition of music."[46] *The Importance of Being Earnest*, as Archer argues, "imitates nothing, represents nothing, means nothing, is nothing, except a sort of rondo capriccioso, in which the artist's fingers run with crisp irresponsibility up and down the keyboard of life."[47] Avoiding naturalistic representation as much as possible, *Earnest* "approaches pure form as nearly as words have ever been able to do."[48]

This emphasis on form, the decorative aspect of his works, was criticized by a number of Wilde's contemporaries. *Poems*'s reviewers attacked its "studied artificiality" and Richard Le Gallienne complained of *Intentions* that Wilde "seems to lay over-much stress on the sensuous side of art, a side which is, after all, external and impossible without an informing, formative soul."[49] Of *Dorian Gray*, an unsigned review suggested that "A truer art would have avoided both the glittering conceits, which bedeck the body of the story, and the unsavory suggestiveness which lurks in its spirit."[50] Wilde's contemporary reviewers based their criticism on a definition of art as a blending of body and soul, or spirit. The separation of form from content, body from soul, was a source of concern.

Perhaps surprisingly, Wilde shares this concern in "The Soul of Man under Socialism" and *De Profundis*. In these two works, writing in the tradition of the "Victorian sage" who values the social body over art, Wilde seeks the union of soul and body. The union serves a greater social purpose: ideas (soul) are vital to informing the (body) public. In "The Soul of Man under Socialism" Wilde states that "form and substance cannot be separated in a work of art" (1187). This same claim is made in *De Profundis*: "What the artist is always looking for is that mode of existence in which soul and body are one and indivisible: in which the outward is expressive of the inward: in which Form reveals" (1024). Although these claims are not markedly different from those in "The Decay of Lying" and "The Critic as Artist," the subtle difference is the emphasis on both form and content, body *and* soul. Where in "The Critic as Artist" the body *is* the soul, in these two works body and soul are separate, interdependent components, one meant to reveal the other.

egotism, will, and self-expression

Preferring the particular over the general, Wilde, like Pater, saw art not as the expression of a universal truth, but personal truth. Thus, as Pater says, art "in any way imitative or reproductive of fact – form, or colour, or incident – is the representation of such fact as connected with soul, or a specific personality, in its preferences, its volition and power."[51] Wilde's awareness of the individual, volitional consciousness that shapes form is central to his aesthetics. Art, as Gilbert says in "The Critic as Artist," "springs from personality" (1131). Wilde throughout his career emphasized the idea that art is the expression of the individual ego: that is, the conscious or thinking self. Consciousness and will, what the human thinks and how he shapes those thoughts, are so crucial to

Wilde's aesthetics that it is impossible to overstate their importance. As Wilde said in a letter to Lord Alfred Douglas in 1897 "The egoistic note is, of course, and always has been to me, the primal and ultimate note of modern art."[52] A year later he complained to a family friend, "*la joie de vivre* is gone, and that, with will-power, is the basis of art."[53] In an 1889 article about the new president of the Royal Society of British Artists Wilde explains that "Art deals with appearances, and the eye of the man who looks at Nature, the vision in fact of the artist, is far more important to us than what he looks at."[54]

The reason that art does not hold up the mirror to nature in Wilde's aesthetics is that the prism of the mind is too absorbing, too interesting, not to become the central focus of art itself. Furthermore, the history of art is the history of consciousness in contact with its environment, including other art. In one of the more famous passages from "The Decay of Lying" Vivian exclaims:

> For what is Nature? Nature is no great mother who has borne us. She is our creation. It is in our brain that she quickens to life. Things are because we see them, and what we see, and how we see it, depends on the Arts that have influenced us. To look at a thing is very different from seeing a thing. One does not see anything until one sees its beauty. Then, and then only does it come into existence. At present, people see fogs, not only because there are fogs, but because poets and painters have taught them the loveliness of such effects. (1086)

In all aesthetic endeavor consciousness and self-consciousness are the foundation, "For there is no art where there is no style, and no style where there is no unity, and unity is of the individual" (1119). As the individual is of such importance to art's creations, so self-realization becomes the goal of both artist and spectator alike. Jesus is for Wilde the prototype of the ideal artist because he advocates developing one's own personality (1181).

Under this aesthetic, the artist's special burden is that the quality of his work "depends on the intensification of personality" (981). Personality is for Wilde never essential, but potential and multiple. Wilde believed, as Bashford says, "that the self is plural and that it develops through being the many disparate selves it contains."[55] This multiplicity is shown most clearly in "The Portrait of Mr. W.H." when the narrator asserts that "all Art . . . [is] to a certain degree a mode of acting, an attempt to realise one's own personality on some imaginative plane out of reach of the trammeling accidents and limitations of real life" (302). Both artist and spectator are implicated in this process: through witnessing the self-realization of the artist as expressed through the art object, the spectator of art realizes him or herself, at least partially.[56] Self-realization, or intensification, is the goal not only of the artist and his audience, but also of the art critic: "it is only by intensifying his own personality that the critic can interpret the personality and work of others, and the more strongly this personality enters into the interpretation, the more real the interpretation becomes, the more satisfying, the more convincing, the more true" (1131).

the role of art's audience

In "The Critic as Artist" Gilbert claims that "the highest criticism deals with art, not as expressive, but as impressive purely" (1130). By focusing on art's impressive rather than expressive power, Wilde, again, locates art in consciousness, this time more centrally in the consciousness of the viewer, reader, or spectator of art. And again it is the power of that consciousness to transform itself in and through art – to be impressed – that comprises the aesthetic process. Art is not so much the object as it is the process of aesthetic apprehension and, in turn, self-realization:

> for the meaning of any beautiful created thing is, at least, as much in the soul of him who looks at it as it was in his soul who wrought it. Nay, it is rather the beholder who lends to the beautiful thing its myriad meanings, and makes it marvellous for us, and sets it in some new relation to the age, so that it becomes a vital portion of our lives. (1029)

Wilde practices this form of criticism himself in "The Portrait of Mr. W.H.," creating a new artwork out of the impressions of another. The dialectical nature of this exchange between artist, art-object, and audience – the essence of Wilde's aesthetics – confirms Smith and Helfand's claim that Wilde's aestheticism was based on "a carefully reasoned philosophical and political stance, a synthesis of Hegelian idealism and Spencerian evolutionary theory."[57]

If Wilde was influenced in his views by a long history of philosophical thought, he may also have been influenced, as Small has argued, by contemporary thought in the newly burgeoning science of psychology. Psychology in late-Victorian England attempted to describe physiological and affective response, and several of those interested in its findings, including Grant Allen and Vernon Lee, wrote aesthetic treatises examining the role of the spectator's body and emotions in aesthetic response. Wilde's fascination with the aesthetic response, like Pater's, may have been stimulated by this pioneering work in psychology.[58]

Along with the concern for individual aesthetic response, Wilde expressed a distinct and unprecedented awareness of audience.[59] As Gagnier has suggested, the greater part of *Intentions* "is devoted to the public and journalism – in fact, to the creation of an audience for art and life."[60] In a review of the *Collected Works* in 1909, G.K. Chesterton noted that for all his scorn of the bourgeoisie, Wilde wrote for his audience:

> Wilde and his school professed to stand as solitary artistic souls apart from the public. They professed to scorn the middle class, and declared that the artist must not work for the bourgeois. The truth is that no artist so really great ever worked so much for the bourgeois as Oscar Wilde. No man, so capable of thinking about truth and beauty, ever thought so constantly about his own effect on the middle classes.[61]

Wilde's awareness of the ideal role of the critic/reader/spectator, coupled with his own material concerns for making money through his journalism and his art, forced him into an attentiveness to audience response that both frustrated and amused him. Perhaps out of an awareness of the limitations of audience, Wilde sought to show how art could and should act as a catalyst to individual development, often at the expense of middle-class conventions.

individual invention against convention

"The Soul of Man under Socialism" is Wilde's fullest statement of his belief in art as the means by which the individual protests the status quo and reshapes reality as it should be. "Art is Individualism," Wilde says, "and Individualism is a disturbing and disintegrating force. . . . what it seeks to disturb is monotony of type, slavery of custom, tyranny of habit, and the reduction of man to the level of a machine" (1186). This refrain echoes even in Wilde's earliest work. In his Oxford commonplace book Wilde wrote "Progress in thought is the assertion of individualism against authority."[62] Rodney Shewan has argued that the theme of "The Rise of Historical Criticism" is the gradual emancipation from primitive, inhibiting cultural traditions by means of the cultivation of the critical instinct.[63] In his introduction to Wilde's critical work, Richard Ellmann characterizes Wilde's thought as claiming that, "criticism is self-consciousness; it enables us to put our most recent phase at a distance and so go on to another. It disengages us so we may reengage ourselves in a new way."[64] Similarly Danson says, "the critic must 'see the object as in itself it really is not,' in order to escape the prison of the already constructed, to be creative instead of imitative. The Wildean critic neither knows nor feels the world, but makes it."[65] Art is never for art's sake alone, but for the individual so that he may find a better voice through which to rebel against received reality.

art's spiritual versus didactic purpose

Though Pater said of Wilde that more than any other writer he carried on the "brilliant critical work of Matthew Arnold," and some recent critics have labored to show that Wilde shared Arnold's view of culture as an integral whole, Wilde did reject the Arnoldian dictum that the artist must "see the object as in itself it really is, "arguing instead against objectivity, against ignoring the claims of individual consciousness in the aesthetic process.[66] Wilde's progressive aesthetics also attack Arnold's conservative notion of a national program to study "the best that is known and thought in the world": as Wilde notes in "The Soul of Man under Socialism," "the public make use of the classics of a country as a means of checking the progress of Art. They degrade classics into authorities. They use them as bludgeons for preventing the free expression of Beauty in new forms" (1186). Art cannot become the center of cultural authority, as Arnold urged, because its benefits are transmitted too subtly.[67] Instead art must act as example, the influence of which makes one better. Varty has suggested that *The Picture of Dorian Gray* does just this: "The final version of the novel is an extraordinary anthology of styles, dovetailed to express the central ethical idea that art, serving as a repository for the conscience of a culture, extends or constrains the perceptual range of humanity."[68]

Rejecting Arnold's didacticism, but not his concern for the renovation of culture, Wilde maintains that "The good we get from art is not what we learn from it; it is what we become through it" ("English Renaissance of Art," 25). Culture for Wilde is a process of *individual* development. "For the development of the race depends on the development of the individual," and "where self-culture has ceased to be the ideal, the intellectual standard is instantly lowered, and, often, ultimately lost" (1140). Thus individuals can be inspired, but not instructed. This is precisely "the charm about Christ. . . . He doesn't really teach one anything, but by being brought into his presence one becomes something" (1037).

Throughout his career Wilde maintained that the spheres of ethics and art were distinct and separate.[69] More than that, Wilde went further than any other Victorian Aestheticist thinker in claiming "Aesthetics are higher than ethics. They belong to a more spiritual sphere. To discern the beauty of a thing is the finest point to which we can arrive" (1154). Brown argues that this line of thought is again part of his progressive aesthetics, for "Without the aesthetic . . . there can be no 'higher ethics,' because it is from the aesthetic that the power to *progress* derives."[70] Progress is its own good, and because "the demand of the intellect is simply to feel itself alive," "the contemplative life, the life that has for its aim not *doing* but *being*, and not *being* merely, but becoming" is Wilde's ideal ("Critic as Artist," 1149, 1138–1139).

Wilde's ethics center around the idea that the imagination *is* sympathy, and that the individual imagination fosters compassion for others. These ideas are expressed most clearly in "The Soul of Man under Socialism," *De Profundis*, and Wilde's post-Reading Gaol letters.[71] In the spring of 1897 after leaving Reading Gaol, Wilde complained bitterly to Robert Ross of the artist Charles Ricketts who offended him by remarking that time must move quickly in prison. Wilde characterized Ricketts's remark as "a singularly unimaginative opinion, and one showing an entirely inartistic lack of sympathetic instinct."[72] In the same letter he goaded Ross, "You and my other friends have so little imagination, so little sympathy, so little power of appreciating what was beautiful, noble, lovely, and of good report."[73] Two weeks later he wrote to Ross that he feared seeing Lord Alfred Douglas: "I have a real terror now of that unfortunate ungrateful young man with his unimaginative selfishness and his entire lack of sensitiveness to what is in others."[74] In these letters, a feisty, wounded Wilde links the imagination to sympathy as he had before, though never so clearly.

De Profundis, written not long before the letters mentioned above, attacks Douglas for his lack of imagination, and by implication, his aesthetic defects. In "The Critic as Artist" Gilbert says "if you wish to understand others you must intensify your own individualism" because, he says later, "it is the imagination that enables us to live these countless lives" (1131, 1138). In "The Soul of Man under Socialism" Wilde opines that "When man has realised Individualism, he will also realise sympathy and exercise it freely and spontaneously" (1195). Ethics, then, in Wilde, are bound up in the idea of individual becoming, a process that is dependent on aesthetic consciousness. To be aesthetically conscious, to contemplate, is to act ethically.[75]

wilde's aesthetics after wilde

In trying to assess the impact of Wilde's aesthetic theories on artists who followed him, critics have often looked to see if his thought was in itself consistent. Wilde rejected the idea of consistency: "Who wants to be consistent? The dullard and the doctrinaire, the tedious people who carry out their principles to the bitter end of action, to the reductio ad absurdum of practice. Not I. Like Emerson, I write over the door of my library the word 'Whim'" says Vivian in "The Decay of Lying" (1072). Despite this, many critics claim to read the statement in "The Truth of Masks" that "A Truth in art is that whose contradictory is also true" as in itself the grounds of a consistent aesthetic program. Critics such as Behrendt, Brown, R.J. Green, Sammells, Shewan, Smith and Helfand, and Willoughby find Wilde's aesthetics consistent, typically through his focus on individual self-development and conscious will.[76] Others such as Bashford, Danson and Lucas agree with Gagnier that "his opinions on aesthetics were capricious enough to belie a coherent program."[77]

Whether Wilde's ideas are consistent or not, many critics have argued that his legacy can be traced through modernism to postmodernism, cubism to postimpressionism. R.J. Green sees *Intentions* as an early example of a revolutionary Modernism that climaxed in 1914.[78] Danson likewise sees Wilde in dialogue with the Modernists. Hilda Schiff says that Wilde contributes to, or at least anticipates, a shift in modern criticism to the conception and evaluation of literature as organized images and symbols.[79] Reading Wilde as an early modernist, Small says "Wilde's *oeuvre* suggests that early modernists well knew that pictorial or literary art could embody interpretative 'openness' and thus invite questions about their functions as representation; but that they also knew that these features in themselves did not prevent art objects from being assigned specific social value or being used within a specific social function."[80] Alice I. Perry Wood argues that Wilde's ideas anticipate postimpressionism and cubism in art and symbolist literature.[81] Ellmann claims Wilde laid the basis for a number of critical positions of the twentieth century, including those of Northrop Frye and Roland Barthes.[82] Gagnier says that Wilde anticipated Bakhtin's dialogism.[83] Varty sees Wilde as the inspiration for a number of critical ideas of the twentieth century, "from Wimsatt's argument about the 'intentional fallacy' and the importance of this for the principles of 'practical criticism' developed by I. A. Richards, to Barthes' account of 'the death of the author' and the significance of this argument for the schools of deconstruction and post-structuralism."[84] Behrendt notes that scholars have long found *The*

Importance of Being Earnest a precursor to the theatre of the Absurd. Danson notes that Wilde's elevation of criticism into a "creative and independent" activity makes his work the precursor of ideas that reappear, still controversially, in modern and postmodern theory.[85] Like later theorists for whom he prepared the way, Wilde's critic as artist inhabits a realm where words construct the world, and society is a text to be rewritten.[86] Freedman sees in Aestheticism a link to postmodernism, suggesting that postmodernism embraces the contradictions that Aestheticism explored and Modernism tried to efface.[87] In the 1980s many critics claimed that deconstructionist criticism was as elite and aloof as Aestheticism was purported to be. Jonathan Loesberg takes up this claim and counters that Aestheticism and modern deconstruction both produce philosophical knowledge and political effect through persistent self-questioning or "self-resistance" to conventional truths, once again supporting the recent critical shift away from viewing "art for art's sake" as in any way reflecting an apolitical stance.[88]

Can there be an "aesthetic" approach to Wilde? Is there any approach that is *not* aesthetic? Wilde would tell us that even our recent attempts to historicize aesthetics, and therefore gain objectivity, are but more rigorous forms of subjectivity: "Time and space, succession and extension, are merely accidental conditions of Thought. The Imagination can transcend them, and move in a free sphere of ideal existences. Things, also, are in their essence what we choose to make them. A thing *is*, according to the mode in which one looks at it" (1059).

notes

1. Quoted in Karl Beckson, ed. *Oscar Wilde: The Critical Heritage* (New York: Routledge, 1970), 206.
2. Philip E. Smith and Michael S. Helfand, *Oscar Wilde's Notebooks: A Portrait of a Mind in the Making* (New York: Oxford University Press, 1989), 127.
3. Debate about what comprises "the canon" was the impetus for dozens of books in the late 1980s and 1990s, all of which cannot be documented here. For an example of a materialist approach to the canon, see John Guillory, *Cultural Capital: The Problem of Literary Canon Formation* (Chicago: University of Chicago Press, 1993). For an example of an idealist approach to the canon, see Harold Bloom, *The Western Canon: The Books and Schools of the Ages* (New York: Riverhead Books, 1995). Though it wasn't the first to articulate aesthetics as historically and politically rooted, Terry Eagleton's *The Ideology of the Aesthetic* (Oxford: Basil Blackwell, 1990) was a trailblazing text in its materialist approach to aesthetic philosophy.
4. See Allison Pease, *Modernism, Mass Culture, and the Aesthetics of Obscenity* (Cambridge: Cambridge University Press, 2000), 1–34.

5. Peter Burger, *The Theory of the Avant-Garde*, trans. Michael Shaw (Minneapolis: University of Minnesota Press, 1984), 27. For social histories of taste and aesthetic philosophy, see John Barrell, *The Birth of Pandora and the Division of Knowledge* (Philadelphia: University of Pennsylvania Press, 1992); Howard Caygill, *Art of Judgment* (Oxford: Basil Blackwell, 1989); Linda Dowling, *The Vulgarization of Art: The Victorians and Aesthetic Democracy* (Charlottesville: University of Virginia Press, 1996); Lawrence E. Klein, *Shaftesbury and the Culture of Politeness* (Cambridge: Cambridge University Press, 1994); Preben Mortensen, *Art in the Social Order: The Making of the Modern Conception of Art* (Albany: State University Press of New York, 1997); Pease, op. cit.; and Martha Woodmansee, *The Author, Art, and the Market* (New York: Columbia University Press, 1994).
6. Immanuel Kant, *The Critique of Judgment*, trans. James Creed Meredith (Oxford: Clarendon Press, 1991), 226.
7. John Wilcox, "The Beginnings of *l'art pour art*," *Journal of Aesthetics and Art Criticism* 2 (June 1953), 361.
8. See Gene H. Bell-Villada, *Art For Art's Sake and Literary Life: How Politics and Markets Helped Shape the Ideology and Culture of Aestheticism 1790–1990* (Lincoln: University of Nebraska Press, 1996), 1–91.
9. See Bell-Villada, op. cit., 9; Jonathan Freedman, *Professions of Taste: Henry James, British Aestheticism, and Commodity Culture* (Stanford: Stanford University Press, 1990), 2; Regenia Gagnier, *Idylls of the Marketplace: Oscar Wilde and the Victorian Public* (Stanford: Stanford University Press, 1986), 3; Carl Woodring, *Nature into Art: Cultural Transformations in Nineteenth-Century Britain* (Cambridge: Harvard University Press, 1989), 229.
10. R.V. Johnson, *Aestheticism* (London: Methuen, 1969), 10.
11. Who or what comprised Aestheticism is an ongoing debate. In traditional accounts of Aestheticism, men have been at its center. Talia Schaffer's *The Forgotten Female Aesthetes: Literary Culture in Late Victorian England* (Charlottesville: University of Virginia Press, 2000) takes aim at traditional accounts because "the tacit definitions on which most aestheticist critics seem to agree are self-fulfilling; that is, they are predicated on the work of recognized aesthetes (Wilde, Beerbohm, Dowson, Johnson, Yeats) and therefore admit only those aesthetes" (3). Instead she claims that by starting from the magazine Wilde once edited, *Woman's World*, one can see a different kind of aestheticism than has been the account of Wilde's coterie, one centered upon women. This account of Aestheticism, described by Schaffer and Kathy Alexis Psomiades in their coedited volume *Women and British Aestheticism* (Charlottesville: University Press of Virginia, 1999) as a set of concerns and ways of writing literature from 1850 to 1930, invites new scholarship on female writers, especially novel writers, who have heretofore received little attention.
12. Walter Pater, *Selected Writings of Walter Pater*, ed. Harold Bloom (New York: Columbia University Press, 1984), 17; Dowling, op. cit., 82.
13. *Aristotle at Afternoon Tea: The Rare Oscar Wilde*, ed. John Wyse Jackson (London: Fourth Estate, 1991), 3.
14. *Complete Letters*, 272.
15. Ian Small and Josephine Guy, *Conditions for Criticism: Authority, Knowledge, and Literature in the Late Nineteenth Century* (Oxford: Clarendon Press, 1991), 7–8.

16. Quoted in Beckson, op. cit., 43.
17. Ibid., 104.
18. Anne Varty, *A Preface to Oscar Wilde* (Harlow: Addison Wesley Longman, 1998), 112–113.
19. Freedman, op. cit., 9.
20. Regenia Gagnier, "Wilde and the Victorians," in *The Cambridge Companion to Oscar Wilde*, ed. Peter Raby (Cambridge: Cambridge University Press, 1997), 31.
21. Lawrence Danson, *Wilde's Intentions: The Artist and His Criticism* (Oxford: Clarendon Press, 1997), 129.
22. Julia Prewitt Brown, *Cosmopolitan Criticism: Oscar Wilde's Philosophy of Art* (Charlottesville: University Press of Virginia, 1997), 4.
23. Guy Willoughby, *Art and Christhood: The Aesthetics of Oscar Wilde* (Rutherford, NJ: Associated University Presses, 1993).
24. Smith and Helfand, op. cit., 47–50.
25. Freedman, op. cit., 13.
26. Quoted in Beckson, op. cit., 38.
27. Danson, op. cit., 27.
28. See Beckson, op. cit., 37–54.
29. Quoted in Beckson, op. cit., 298.
30. Brown, op. cit., 49.
31. Smith and Helfand, op. cit., 13.
32. Quoted in Beckson, op. cit., 229.
33. Ibid., 302.
34. Dowling, op. cit., 90.
35. Ibid., 97.
36. Gagnier, *Idylls*, op. cit., 26.
37. See Small and Guy, op. cit.
38. Danson, op. cit., 21.
39. Ian Small and Josephine M. Guy, *Oscar Wilde's Profession: Writing and the Culture Industry in the Late Nineteenth Century* (Oxford: Oxford University Press, 2000), 19.
40. Bruce Bashford, *Oscar Wilde: The Critic As Humanist* (Madison: Associated University Presses), 142–143.
41. Bashford, op. cit., 30.
42. Quoted in *The Artist as Critic*, ed. Richard Ellmann (Chicago: University of Chicago Press, 1969), 102.
43. Ibid., 122.
44. Willoughby, op. cit., 18.
45. See Neil Sammells, *Wilde Style: The Plays and Prose of Oscar Wilde* (New York: Longman, 2000).
46. Quoted in Beckson, op. cit., 139–142; Pater, op. cit., 55.
47. Quoted in Beckson, op. cit., 190.
48. Woodring, op. cit., 262.
49. Quoted in Beckson, op. cit., 101.
50. Ibid., 77.
51. Pater, op. cit., 106.
52. *Complete Letters*, 874.
53. Ibid., 1035.

54. Quoted in Ellmann, op cit., 127.
55. Bashford, op. cit., 14.
56. See "The Soul of Man under Socialism."
57. Smith and Helfand, op. cit., vii.
58. Small and Guy, *Conditions*, op. cit., 58–87.
59. For a greater account of the intersection between the commodification of literary culture and Wilde's role as a professional writer, see Small and Guy, *Oscar Wilde's Profession*, op. cit.
60. Gagnier, *Idylls*, op. cit., 20.
61. Quoted in Beckson, op. cit., 312.
62. Quoted in Smith and Helfand, op. cit., 121.
63. Rodney Shewan, *Oscar Wilde: Art and Egotism* (London: Macmillan, 1977), 22.
64. Ellmann, op. cit., xxii.
65. Danson, op. cit., 140.
66. Quoted in Beckson, op. cit., 83; Brown, op. cit., 49; Matthew Arnold, "The Function of Criticism at the Present Time," in *Poetry and Criticism of Matthew Arnold*, ed. A. Dwight Culler (Boston: Houghton Mifflin, 1961), 237.
67. See Brown, op. cit., 50.
68. Varty, op. cit., 115.
69. See "The Critic as Artist," 1039, 1042, 1048, 1058; Wilde's letters to various editors after the publication of *The Picture of Dorian Gray* (in *Complete Letters*).
70. Brown, op. cit., 55.
71. Willoughby has suggested that in *The Happy Prince* and *A House of Pomegranates* only those with compassion have the aesthetic instinct (op. cit., 33); indeed, Swallow from *The Happy Prince* and Nightingale in *The Nightingale and the Rose* are practical, if masochistic, embodiments of the romantic imagination: both birds are so imaginatively sympathetic that their compassion kills them.
72. *Complete Letters*, 816.
73. Ibid., 818.
74. Ibid., 858.
75. For a discussion of the origins of this idea in Aristotle's *Ethics*, see Smith and Helfand, op. cit., 13–16.
76. Patricia Flanagan Behrendt, *Oscar Wilde: Eros and Aesthetics* (New York: St. Martin's Press, 1991); Brown, op. cit.; R.J. Green, "Oscar Wilde's *Intentions*: An Early Modernist Manifesto," *British Journal of Aesthetics* 13.4 (Autumn 1973): 397–404; Sammells, Shewan, Smith and Helfand, Willoughby, op. cit.
77. For Lucas' opinions, see Beckson, op. cit., 246.
78. Green, op. cit.
79. Hilda Schiff, "Nature and Art in Oscar Wilde's 'The Decay of Lying,'" in *Essays and Studies*, Vol. 18, ed. Sybil Rosenfeld (London: John Murray, 1965), 83–102.
80. Ian Small, "Semiotics and Oscar Wilde's Accounts of Art," *British Journal of Aesthetics* 25.1 (Winter 1985): 50–56.
81. Alice I. Perry Wood, "Oscar Wilde as a Critic," *North American Review* 202 (July–December 1915): 899–909.
82. Ellmann, op. cit.
83. Gagnier, *Idylls*, op. cit.

84. Varty, op. cit., 58.
85. Danson, op. cit.
86. Lawrence Danson, "Wilde as Critic and Theorist," in *The Cambridge Companion to Oscar Wilde*, op. cit., 81.
87. Freedman, op. cit., 25.
88. Jonathan Loesberg, *Aestheticism and Deconstruction* (Princeton: Princeton University Press, 1991).

5
oscar wilde, commodity, culture

dennis denisoff

Victorians would rarely have mentioned the terms "commodity" and "culture" in the same breath. Nevertheless, the last three decades have seen both subjects become key issues in the study of aestheticism and, in particular, Oscar Wilde. Such a development would not be that peculiar save for the fact that the values articulated for roughly the past 150 years under the concept of culture have often been regarded as standing in stark contrast to those associated with commodification. And yet their convergence in Wilde studies is perhaps appropriate, seeing as how paradox itself has become something of a cornerstone of scholarship on his texts, views, and life.

The traditional depiction of the dandy-aesthete is of a man utterly dedicated to image and art, with no interest in consumerism or the mass market. Such things appeared wholly anathema to the refined sensibilities of the fashionable young things who, so devoted were they to beauty, could attain sufficient sustenance at luncheon by simply admiring a lily. Or at least that was the persona depicted in the innumerable *Punch* cartoons that Victorian society consumed like so many cigarettes. And an extremely popular image it was, in large part because Wilde and other key participants in the Aesthetic Movement were themselves spreading a notion of high culture as something beyond the materiality of consumerism. They were, in short, selling an image of the cultured as *not for sale*. This paradoxical linkage of commodity and culture has become a principal paradigm through which we now understand many of the other contradictions and ironies that characterise Wilde's work and life.

"You don't suppose I have got any money?" says Algernon, in *The Importance of Being Earnest*; "How perfectly silly you are. No gentleman ever has any money" (385). Cash – including the elitist image of not needing any – was a mainstay of Victorian literature. In the popular fiction of the era we have Lady Audley prepared to kill for dollars; Dracula scooping up coins even as he dodges his would-be murderers; and highwaymen, cut-throats, and pirates oozing from not only the Penny Dreadfuls but also the more respectable three-decker novels. At least as far as the fiction was concerned, Victorian Britain *was* a Treasure Island. At the same time that literature about money-obsessed villains was flooding a seemingly insatiable market for such stuff, we find a respected artist like John Everett Millais taking a commission to paint *Bubbles* (1886) as an advertisement for Pears soap; William Morris popularizing socialist economics in the domestic sphere; and the still unestablished poet Wilde being hired to dress in a dandy costume and sell aestheticism to North Americans.

It appears that, for mass society during the second half of the century, the culture of consumption was actually more than entertainment; it was part of the lifeblood of the economy, the symbolic discourse of the public sphere, and the image many members of British society had of themselves as a prosperous yet refined, civilized nation.[1] As the association of artists with business became more common, however, so too did literary and artistic depictions emphasizing anxieties about the impact of commodity culture.[2] It was in Wilde's time that the concepts of art and culture became inseparable from issues of consumption, with the connoisseur building a career as culture critic, the consumer becoming a popular subject of art and literature, and shopping becoming a creative talent. As Richard D'Oyly Carte realized when he sent Wilde off to North America dressed in "aesthetic" clothes to lecture to the masses on "The Beautiful," culture had become a lucrative resource. And for many Victorians, as well as many critics today, Wilde was the embodiment of the industry. This chapter begins by offering scholars new to this area of study a summary of views that helped shape the concepts of culture and commodity in late-Victorian England and up to the time before the scholarship on Wilde and consumerism first took off in the 1960s. It then considers more closely the more recent analyses of Wilde's relationship to the subject.

victorian "culture" and commodification

Prior to the Industrial Revolution, culture in Western Europe was seen to exist primarily in two forms – as the pleasures of the wealthy and as the less exclusionary entertainments now known as folk culture. With industrialization, urbanization, and increased education and literacy, however, new sources and forms of entertainment developed that disturbed the previous distinctions. In articulating his concerns about these shifts, Matthew Arnold formulated what has remained a principal view of what constitutes culture. In *Culture and Anarchy* (1869), he asserts that culture "consists in becoming something rather than in having something, in an inward condition of the mind and spirit, not in an outward set of circumstances."[3] It is one's moral aspiration toward an improved self, and not an investment in material or social concerns such as entertainment or the pleasure derived from ownership. Collectively, this moral development will then help maintain civil order in the face of industrial change and dangerous shifts in class-based power dynamics.

In Arnold's view, the aristocrats had become superficial in their values and the working class lacked adequate self-control. It was the lifestyles and perceptions of working-class people, as well as their growing infiltration into bourgeois employment and politics, that constituted the principal challenge to culture – namely, anarchy. "Long lain half hidden amidst its poverty and squalor," Arnold warned, the working class "is now issuing from its hiding-place to assert an Englishman's heaven-born privilege of doing as he likes, and is beginning to perplex us by marching where it likes, meeting where it likes, bawling what it likes, breaking what it likes."[4] While culture fosters the development of civilization, anarchy brings about its degeneration and Arnold believed that, in order to safeguard against this threat, his society required a strong social order that would ensure a unified cultural identity. And who would spearhead the new order? "The mass of mankind will never have any ardent zeal for seeing things as they are; very inadequate ideas will always satisfy them. . . . whoever sets himself to see things as they are will find himself one of a very small circle; but it is only by this small circle resolutely doing its own work that adequate ideas will ever get current at all."[5] This select group charged with developing and spreading culture would arise, Arnold felt, from the middle class to which he himself belonged.

Although seeing control as inevitably remaining in the hands of a clear-sighted minority, Arnold also proposes the ameliorative strategy of educating the masses in the best ideas that have been thought:

> The sweetness and light of the few must be imperfect until the raw and unkindled masses of humanity are touched with sweetness and light. . . . Again and again I have insisted how those are the happy moments of humanity, . . . how those are the flowering times for literature and art and all the creative power of genius, . . . when the whole of society is in the fullest measure permeated by thought, sensible to beauty, intelligent and alive.[6]

The most effective means of such education is through developing the mass's literacy and taste for poetry. Because of poetry's inherent aspiration toward beauty and harmony (which also characterize the moral ideal toward which humans should aspire), it is the art form that possesses the greatest capacity for testing the worth of human values.

The literacy campaign was well underway when *Culture and Anarchy* made its pitch for poetry. However, so was a growing anxiety that the members of the working class were in fact becoming all the more dangerous precisely because so many of them could now read. A decade before *Culture and Anarchy*, the novelist Margaret Oliphant conjectured that, "if reading of itself were a virtuous and improving exercise, as innocent people once considered it, we too might echo the exultation with which a superficial sentiment regards the extending bulk of literature; but when we regard the matter with eyes less arbitrary, we are obliged to confess that it impresses us with a very doubtful satisfaction."[7] Oliphant goes on to observe that the members of the working class, having been taught to read, have gone off to consume materials that did not support the values and ideals toward which the wealthier members of society had hoped they would aspire. Rather, they favored literature that focused on narratives of sensationalism, violence, crime, and adventure, with no particular interest in the quality of writing or the presence of a moral.

Wilde's response to Arnoldian aesthetics was complex. In *The Vulgarization of Art*, Linda Dowling notes that Wilde, building on positions held by John Ruskin and Walter Pater, supported a relativist notion of human taste that can be seen as anti-Arnoldian.[8] This view encouraged a democratization of aesthetics and an acceptance of diversity (which harmonized with Wilde's sympathy for other forms of difference such as the sexual). That said, in part due to his own engagement with mass culture, Wilde was also sensitive to the aesthetic vulgarity of the middle class. In his effort to establish some standard of quality, Dowling argues, Wilde reverted to an exclusive, aristocratic aesthetics of the kind associated with the third Earl of Shaftesbury in the early eighteenth century. Yet another reason Wilde would have felt encouraged to retain a notion of aesthetic exclusiveness was his desire to continue to have a product of his own to sell; if no single aesthetic view could be seen as superior to others, then the value of his wares would diminish. Although there is much to be admired in aesthetic democracy, Wilde felt it risked championing a low, populist notion of culture that would remove the authority he required to sell his views. While to an extent distancing himself from Arnold, Wilde's interests in self-marketing encouraged him to maintain a notion of culture that in reality was in accord with many of the ideas put forward in *Culture and Anarchy*.[9]

In this, his most influential work, Arnold depicts the working class as a burdensome rabble that could nevertheless be educated by a middle-class elite and thus could help raise all of society to a more full experience of culture. Writing at roughly the same time, Karl Marx envisioned the working class itself as the source of a revolution that would allow an equitable distribution of pleasure and comfort. Viewing society as an economic structure characterized by exploitation, Marx argued that "the class which has the means of material production at its disposal, has control at the same time over the means of mental production. . . . Consequently their ideas are the ruling ideas of the age."[10] It is only due to historical conditions that humans have not yet realized their full potential. The base of a society, for Marx, consists of the forces of production – such as raw materials, tools, workers, and skills – and the relations of the people involved in production. A society's mode of production – the way it is organized to produce necessities such as food and shelter – influences its social structure and thereby establishes the society's character, culture, politics, and so on.[11] The base dictates the shape of what Marx refers to as a society's "superstructure," its ideologies and institutions, such as those of culture, politics and law. Even though social change can arise from within the superstructure itself, it primarily only reflects and implicitly legitimizes the base and current class-based exploitation.[12]

Marx felt, however, that capitalism had reached a stage that could end such inequality so that the dreams constructed by the dominant institutions as other-worldly could actually be fulfilled in real life. But what members of society had begun to worship, through the act of "commodity fetishism," were the products of their own labor: "the relation of the producers to the sum total of their own labour is presented to them as a social relation, existing not between themselves, but between the products of their labour. Through this transference the products of labour become commodities, social things."[13] Commodity fetishism is, in other words, the reification of labor in an idealized image of the commodity. The site of identification for the members of society had shifted from the act of production to the product itself.

The loss of respect for the act of labor had already been heavily criticised by John Ruskin, whose views had become well-known before Wilde studied under him at Oxford. In the first volume of *Modern Painters* (1843), Ruskin states that "perfect taste is the faculty of receiving the greatest possible pleasure from those material sources which are attractive to our moral nature in its purity and perfection."[14] As Ruskin's displeasure with the products of Victorian capitalism grew, his morality-based aesthetics gained a stronger socialist edge. In the lecture "Modern Manufacture and Design" that he delivered to the Mechanics Institute in Bradford, England in 1859, he proposes that "beautiful art can only be produced by people who have beautiful things about them, and leisure to look at them; and unless you provide some elements of beauty for your workmen to be surrounded by, you will find that no elements of beauty can be invented by them."[15] Ruskin goes on to argue that, to date, the high arts have been supported by the upper class without any consideration for the toil and discomfort of the masses. Historically, a civilization at its pinnacle of artistic success has also been one at the stage of decadence that marks its inevitable decline.[16]

William Morris similarly argued for a "democracy of the arts" where there would no longer be a sense of the high arts' superiority over the "decorative." This split, he believed, arose due to class segregation that was exacerbated by economic developments and a shift in attention among the arts to commercial concerns. "All art, even the highest," he proclaims, "is influenced by the conditions of labour of the mass of mankind, and . . . any pretensions which may be made for even the highest intellectual art to be independent of these general conditions are futile and vain. . . . ART IS MAN'S EXPRESSION OF HIS JOY IN LABOUR."[17] When decorative artists present themselves as intellectuals, their products are, in Morris's view, "of little value to the world, though there is a thriving market for it, and their position is neither dignified nor wholesome . . . They are, in fact, good decorative workmen spoiled by a system which compels them to ambitious individualist effort."[18] Too many individuals were fighting for the limited monetary rewards offered to intellectual artists, fostering overall a predominantly business-minded approach to beauty. According to Morris, people should focus their admiration on those qualities of an object that reflect the worker's skill. Aesthetics itself needed to shift from celebrating exclusive genres and objects to a greater appreciation for the beautiful of daily life and labor as exemplified within the middle-class home.[19]

Despite notable differences, Arnold, Ruskin, and Morris all voiced a disrespect for those individuals whose artistic production is inspired by monetary goals. As George Du Maurier's extremely popular novel *Trilby* (1894) makes clear, this position was a familiar one in Victorian society. Today, the novel is known only for its infamous character Svengali, the money-grubbing, mesmerizing artist. An outstanding musician, his obsession with recognition and fame is couched within a monetary discourse that enhances its image of dangerous deviancy. Thus even true intellectual talent – to use Morris's language – can be destroyed by a desire for fame and wealth. In his novel, Du Maurier contrasts Svengali with the character of Little Billee, a middle-class British painter whose talent and moral rectitude keep him clean of both filthy lucre and bohemian pestilence. The hero's two closest colleagues never prove as promising as Little Billee but, in accord with Morris's recommendation, Du Maurier has the narrator praise them for their unembittered recognition of their own mediocrity. As he says of one of them, Taffy: "He is a far better sportsman than he will ever be a painter; and if he doesn't sell his pictures, it is not because they are too good for the public taste: indeed, he has no illusions on that score himself, even if his wife has! He is quite the least conceited art-duffer I ever met." "Would only that I might kill off his cousin Sir Oscar," the narrator goes on to speculate in a sudden sinister turn, "and Sir Oscar's five sons . . . that stand between Taffy and the baronetcy, and whatever property goes with it." The knowingly mediocre artist becomes, in Du Maurier's eyes, an ideal gentleman whose predominant traits are humility and honesty: "He looks as if he could be trusted down to the ground . . . Taffy is a 'gentleman', inside and out, up and down."[20] Taking into account the fact that Du Maurier was the most popular comic caricaturist of Wilde at the time, the narrator's willingness to single-handedly kill off all the Oscars suggests that, for the author, Wilde stood in stark contrast to Taffy as somebody who was vain, dishonest, and unwilling to accept his own mediocrity.

Max Nordau would take Du Maurier's conflation of the unhealthy with commodification and commerce to an infamous extreme. A mix of science, ethics, and cultural theory, Nordau's 1895 study of social progress and natural morality, *Degeneration*, argues that Western Europe had become sick from the decadence of a small group of "rich educated people" and "fanatics" who have an intense influence on modern notions of beauty:

> The former give the *ton* to all the snobs, the fools, and the blockheads; the latter make an impression upon the weak and dependent, and intimidate the nervous. All snobs affect to have the same taste as the select and exclusive minority, who pass by everything that once was considered beautiful with an air of the greatest contempt.[21]

Nordau is describing here an aesthetic elitism rooted in the desire for attention more than actual reactions to beauty. Elsewhere, he argues that "the present rage for collecting, the piling up, in dwellings, of aimless bric-à-brac" is "a stigma of degeneration," an illness called "oniomania" or "buying craze," reflecting one's sense that the goods one owns define one's "greatness."[22] Nordau's claim was that aesthetics had become something to possess and display for the sole purpose of directing attention onto the individual who possesses it.

Echoing Arnold's dictum that the aim of the critic is "to see the object as it really is," Nordau attacks the men found at fashionable European "watering-places" because they "try to present something that they are not."[23] For Nordau, this degeneracy is embodied in Wilde, who

> dresses in queer costumes which recall partly the fashions of the Middle Ages, partly the rococo modes. He pretends to have abandoned the dress of the present time because it offends his sense of the beautiful; but this is only a pretext in which probably he himself does not believe. What really determines his actions is the hysterical craving to be noticed.

And he goes on: "When, therefore, an Oscar Wilde goes about in 'aesthetic costume' among gazing Philistines, exciting either their ridicule or their wrath, it is no indication of independence of character, but rather from a purely anti-socialistic, ego-maniacal recklessness and hysterical longing to make a sensation."[24] Marx's notion of "commodity fetishism" describes an act of veneration by which social relations and notions of self are embodied in the products of labor. In Nordau's analysis, beauty has been commodified such that its signifiers have been distorted into symbols of individuality and genius. The fetishization of commodities in which more and more people are participating, Nordau laments, reflects a spreading degeneracy in which being recognized as a consumer has become more important than the objects consumed.

Theodor Adorno takes Marx's argument even further, arguing that in fact consumers do not fetishize the commodity but the money they have paid to consume it. His reading, which he developed with Max Horkheimer, diverges from Marx's notion of the fetishism of objects in a capitalist society to consider the worship of culture itself. In *Aesthetic Theory* (which first appeared in German in 1970), Adorno argues that the commodification of art and taste attains its greatest clarity through aestheticism and the notion popularized by Wilde and others that the object's valuation has no connection to use. He notes, for example, that in *The Picture of Dorian Gray*, "the interiors of a chic aestheticism resemble smart antique shops and auction halls and thus the commercial world Wilde ostensibly disdained."[25] As a number of more recent theorists have demonstrated, this extension marks a late-Victorian shift from an economy based on production to one based on consumption. Moreover, it fostered a society that placed increasingly greater value on individuals' *signification* of their consumption potential, a move that reinforces the dominant economic order. The idealized notion of culture put forward by Arnold did foreshadow British aestheticism's view that art objects should be valued only by aesthetic criteria. However, the successful campaign for this focus on beauty and pleasure over use fostered a broader social emphasis on the fulfillment of personal desires that did not ultimately require Arnoldian moral idealism. As Jonathan Freedman has argued, however, Adorno's Marxist critique of aestheticism for wallowing in commodity culture (despite its pretensions to superiority) exposes the elitist aim of his own theoretical project and his own conception of aesthetics as indeed above politics.[26]

Marx suggests that the cultural phenomena that become popular are material manifestations of the dominant ideology. This is a standard synopsis of classical Marxism and its determinist character. Marx himself noted, however, that the control of the dominant stratum of society is limited and often obscure. There seem to always be counter-active if not original movements arising from subordinate groups. With the work of the Frankfurt School – Adorno, Horkheimer, Walter Benjamin, Herbert Marcuse, and others – the focus shifted further to the means by which mass culture is produced, what Horkheimer and Adorno, in their 1947 study *Dialectic of Enlightenment*, dubbed "the culture industry."[27] For them, the industry of mainstream film, radio, and literature submerges the working class and middle class within a single ideological model that reinforces the status quo. This proscription then limits the political potential of the masses. Acts of rebellion may succeed as subversions of certain values but only *within* the dominant model; that model itself remains virtually unchallenged. The only means by which their society can escape from the "prison house of mass culture" is through high culture – or, as Marcuse calls it, "affirmative culture." Because high culture is not based on the ideals of capitalism and consumerism, it offers a realm of possibility beyond the ideological bubble that the masses generally see as the limit of what they can conceive. To some degree in accord with Arnold, Marcuse argues that high culture fulfills a quasi-religious function by revealing a realm of beauty and virtue beyond the world in which one operates on a daily basis. It offers both a taste of a more pleasurable existence and hope for future, longer experiences of such a life. In this way, high culture implicitly undermines the dominant system. For Marcuse, twentieth-century popular culture threatened to usurp the promises of high culture by bombarding the masses with a celebration of the present as a completely satisfying experience that, in fact, marks the fulfillment of what high culture had once promised. "Desire" is now replaced by "fulfillment." One is lulled by the mass production of culture into accepting capitalism as appropriate and chosen, when in fact it simply sustains a biased model that oppresses the majority of people by blinding them to the forced labor in which they participate.

It is Walter Benjamin's famous essay "The Work of Art in the Age of Mechanical Reproduction" (1935) that most succinctly counters the pessimism of Marcuse's argument.[28] A marginal member of the Frankfurt School, Benjamin suggests that high culture has relied on tradition and a fixed notion of an ideal aesthetic realm, a view of art epitomized by the "art for art's sake" position of which Wilde was often a proponent. For Benjamin, however, this unattainable promise does less to inspire individuals than to foster a general social sense of stagnation and malaise. This view accords with that of writers such as Du Maurier and Nordau; later Modernists; and scholars who supported an image of Modernism as a vibrant radical change. They all recognized such a sense of stagnation in the Victorian *fin de siècle*.[29] Benjamin argues, however, that the malaise can be addressed through technology, with the mechanical duplication of high culture objects idolized for their authenticity releasing society from the constraints of a single tradition. The art object becomes available for innumerable interpretations, all of which hold the possibility of ideological subversion. Capitalist mass production, in other words, fosters the encounter between an object and numerous consumers, allowing the masses greater agency in the construction of aesthetics, culture, and value.

Benjamin's depiction of mass production as a democratizing of art and culture has been challenged as over-celebratory. The main concern of F.R. Leavis, the major twentieth-century proponent of an Arnoldian approach to culture, was that the commercialism and dehumanization of the mass culture arising from the Industrial Revolution had resulted in the corruption of a craft-based social system. While not utterly opposed to mass production, Leavis was anxious that it would encourage society's loss of tradition. He therefore emphasized the need to educate the masses to ensure that culture would continue to benefit from and adapt the best material manifestations of human values – the "'picked experiences of ages' regarding the finer issues of life," as he and Denys Thompson described them in *Culture and Environment*.[30] It was up to a small group of culture critics to ensure that these finer issues were kept in the foreground of society: "Upon the minority depends our power of profiting by the finest human experience of the past; they keep alive the subtlest and most perishable parts of tradition. Upon them depend the implicit standards that order the finer living of an age."[31] Leavis claims that the shift from a craft-based economy in which individuals take pride in the fruits of their work to factory labor which – albeit of some use – was destroying the sense of personal worth and tradition. Meanwhile, such commodified goods as popular literature gutted language of its inspirational potential by subordinating such values to sales: "this debasement of language is not merely a matter of words; it is a debasement of emotional life, and the quality of living."[32] Here, Leavis extends Arnold's notion of high culture's ameliorative role and civilizing reward in a new direction. Literature that is created by those with an eye on profit does not just numb the human experience of culture; it alters life itself. The implication is that culture constructs reality (or at least reality as far as one can understand it), a notion with important correlations to the historical materialist approach to culture that was built on Marxism.

It is with the work of Raymond Williams, the scholar who initiated the cultural materialist approach to literature, that theoretical models invested in economics began being used intensely to analyze literature, art, and culture. By exploring correlations between cultural elitism and the individualism arising from class-based segregation and consumerist mentality, Williams and other mid-twentieth-century Marxist scholars offered economic explanations for the central paradox of aestheticism – the aesthetes' simultaneous investment in and apparent disdain for mass consumption and popular culture. In *Marxism and Literature* (1977), Williams argued for a historical emphasis in the study of literature and culture because of the strong influence that material goods have on cultural value.[33] He proposes that culture – including the production of meanings and values through discourse – impacts on our perception and construction of the economic structure. The materialism that developed from Williams's insights therefore addresses cultural texts as "historical processes" rather than as static representations of such processes. The relationship between popular and high culture during the second half of the nineteenth century, for example, is regarded by these materialists as not just a reflection of cultural developments such as increased literacy, cheaper printing techniques and material, and increased disposable income. The relationship was itself a catalyst for these changes, creating a demand that stimulated the invention of cheaper production methods, for example, and genres of literature that reflected the interests and analytical capabilities of a growing readership among the working class and the young. Moreover, high and low culture during the Victorian era

– and especially the image of their class-based segregation – was not as distinct as is often assumed. Historical analyses have demonstrated that it is difficult to distinguish the actual consumers of works that might have been categorized as "pulp" or "low brow."

oscar wilde, consumed by scholars

Beginning in the 1960s, considerations of commodity culture and economics in relation to Wilde moved from using the author as an example to prove a broader social claim to primarily two other approaches. Some scholars focused on Wilde as a major participant in the rise of commodity culture. Others were more interested in the author himself, with his relationship to consumerism being presented as one facet of his work and character. Williams's *Culture and Society* (1958) introduced the first wave of work on the relationship between economic and aesthetic developments during the latter half of the nineteenth century by contending that aestheticism was a reaction against the influence of consumerism and its desire to please the masses.[34] Susan Sontag, however, writing her essay "Notes on 'Camp'" in the Warholian 1960s, explored the aesthetics of commodification itself in relation to Wilde. Although scholars have critiqued Sontag's argument that camp is apolitical, the essay has had its own renaissance during the past 15 years, primarily through queer theorizations of the topic.[35] Dedicating the piece to Wilde, Sontag defines camp as a matter of taste, a concept that she then quickly expands to include virtually all mental functioning: "To patronize the faculty of taste is to patronize oneself. For taste governs every free – as opposed to rote – human response. Nothing is more decisive. There is taste in people, visual taste, taste in emotion – and there is taste in acts, taste in morality. Intelligence, as well, is really a kind of taste: taste in ideas."[36] For Sontag, camp is primarily an aesthetic way of seeing the world, but rather than doing so in terms of beauty, one does so in terms of artifice and stylization. It is the packaging that becomes important – the excess of style that points to the construction of the artifact itself, whether it be a painting, a piece of furniture, or a persona. It is this perspective on camp and Wilde's aesthetics that fosters Sontag's reference to it as apolitical, an argument that Adorno would make against aestheticism in general in his 1970 study *Aesthetic Theory*. For Adorno, the shift to an object's formal qualities constructs art as autonomous from praxis. Such art's uselessness makes it politically irrelevant and socially ineffectual. The result, Adorno concludes, is an art that is self-centered and severed from the everyday life of the bourgeoisie.[37]

While Sontag does not explicitly articulate the position, her essay tracks a socialist nerve in Wilde that can also be found in Ruskin and Morris. Recognizing Wilde's admiration for a past elitist dandyism, she also finds an equalizing effect in an aesthetic perspective that has Wilde trying to "live up to" his dishes (as he put it), or comparing a doorknob to a painting.[38] The doorknob's mass production does not diminish its aesthetic value. Sontag argues that Wilde's democratic approach to the experience of beauty formulates taste as a mode of enjoyment rather than judgment. With his help, western society developed a notion of value as pleasure-based, as rooted in the act of individual consumption rather than production. Individuals simply cheat themselves of pleasures if they only delve into high culture and avoid "the coarsest, commonest pleasures, in the arts of the masses."[39]

Sontag's essay suggests that she believes that individual consumption is more important than expert evaluation. This argument accords with the famous rewordings of Arnold's claim that the aim of criticism is "to see the object as in itself it really is." A few years after Arnold's summation, Walter Pater revised the assertion to shift emphasis away from the object and to the perceiver; the aim was now first "to know one's impression as it really is."[40] Almost two decades later, Wilde, building on the aesthetic arguments of both Pater and Ruskin, came along to propose that the aim of the critic was "to see the object as in itself it really is not" (1128). Wilde's revision has been interpreted in various ways, but the general sense is that he was saying that the critic has no responsibility to the object under review, let alone its creator; rather, critics should see themselves as creative forces. As the character Gilbert proclaims in "The Critic as Artist" – in which Wilde often uses Arnold as a foundation on which to build his own arguments – "an age that has no criticism is either an age in which art is immobile, hieratic, and confined to the reproduction of formal types, or an age that possesses no art at all" (1119). For Wilde, the critical eye thus stands in opposition to mass reproduction and the homogenization of cultural taste.

The claim is complicated by the fact that, in "The Soul of Man under Socialism," Wilde seems to celebrate an imposition of taste as long as the right people are in control. The language of a specialized group imposing their aesthetic values on the ignorant masses echoes that of Arnold. Notably, Wilde explains this process as rooted in the sensitivity of the workers: "The craftsmen of things so appreciated the pleasure of making what was beautiful, and woke to such a vivid consciousness of the hideousness and vulgarity of what the public had previously wanted, that they simply starved the public out. . . . However they may object to it, people must nowadays have something charming in their surroundings" (1192). The concept and language are taken from Ruskin and Morris. Wilde uses the argument to establish that "all authority in such things is bad" (1192) but, as Rachel Bowlby points out, "ironically, in welcoming what he perceives as a return to authentic, artisanal forms of production, [Wilde] valorises the workings of the large-scale marketing system he is implicitly opposing. . . . He effectively congratulates the craftsmen for having succeeded in establishing a uniform monopoly."[41] The contradiction is especially notable because it appears in an essay in which Wilde uses a discourse of consumerism to value individualism above all else.

In the 1980s one of the most interesting claims to be made in Wilde scholarship was that he was not simply a man devoted either to the aesthete image or the politics of his works, but was also a strategist who aimed at cashing in on the Aesthetic Movement. In other words, he invited his construction as a product for mass consumption. This process began early in his career. Consider the trip he took to Canada and the United States in the early 1880s. Notwithstanding the fact that Wilde propounded on aestheticism and the "House Beautiful," he was not himself the refined, famous, highly respected philosopher that took the stage. At the time of the tour, he had managed to make himself seen at the fashionable galleries, but he had only published one book of poetry (not too well received) and was in fact probably best known as one of the inspirations for the aesthetic character of Bunthorne (a not-too-French French bean) in Gilbert and Sullivan's comic opera *Patience*. The costumes he wore on his tour, it turns out, were chosen for him, and the talks he gave are now virtually ignored by scholars. Once he had been fashioned by managers, critics, and other writers as the embodiment of the Aesthetic Movement, it appears he was eager to take on the mantle even if he had not actually done much to deserve it.[42]

In this guise Wilde presented what Sontag describes as a principal characteristic of camp – a surface without substance. As Freedman explains in 1996, Wilde's career was circumscribed by

> knowledge-producing and consuming institutions both within and without the mass market economy: the university; the booming mass magazines and their auxiliary, advertising . . .; and the publishing industry . . . . Indeed, Wilde learned (at first giddily, thereafter tragically) that within such a world, one's very being could be transformed into a marketable good – a piece of information, an object of publicity, gossip, and revilement, all in the interests of selling more papers.[43]

This process is inseparable from the dandy-aesthete's own efforts to market his expertise in culture and taste. In his 1990 study *Professions of Taste*, Freedman analyzes this dual movement as "the rise of aesthetic professionalism" and the commodification of culture itself.[44] By encouraging the incorporation of the critic into a mass market economy, Wilde gained value but at the same time made a notable sacrifice of his own public persona to the machinations and fickleness of the system.

In *The Vulgarization of Art* (1996), Linda Dowling argues that Wilde should be seen less as working the system or even choosing to sacrifice himself to its machinations than as an individual unable, because of his financial situation, to work against it:

> Thrust out of the Eden of Oxford, living by his wits as a writer and critic . . ., Wilde found himself implicated in and economically determined by the aesthetic preferences of a vast new democratic audience, its numbers swollen by working classes newly educated into "Board School ignorance" and newly endowed with leisure and money undreamt of by their predecessors. Invited by an exponentially increasing array of consumer products and impelled by the stimulus of disposable income, these audiences were now in a position forcibly to impress their aesthetic preferences on the material realm.[45]

Regardless of this dependence on the tastes of the masses, Wilde, Dowling demonstrates, never lost his greater social vision. In *Wilde's Intentions* (1997), Lawrence Danson categorizes the product that Wilde became as the "commodified" personality that "depends for its existence upon the perceptions of the less personified consuming others."[46] Danson notes the subordination of one's "self" in the act of self-commodification or the allowing of one's commodification by others. Just as a critic sees the object as it is not, so too do consumers see another's personality as a reflection of their own tastes, values, and desires. "It is the spectator, and not life, that art really mirrors," writes Wilde (17). However, as Danson makes clear through his discussion of Wilde's multiple personalities, it is possible for the man to sustain his self-image as consumer/critic even as he fulfills the role of a personality for others.

In "The Soul of Man under Socialism," Wilde marks individual personality as the ultimate reward of a cultured society:

> Nobody will waste his life in accumulating things, and the symbols for things. One will live. . . . It will be a marvellous thing – the true personality of man – when we see it. . . . It will have wisdom. Its value

> will not be measured by material things. It will have nothing. And yet it will have everything, and whatever one takes from it, it will still have, so rich will it be. It will not be always meddling with others, or asking them to be like itself. It will love them because they will be different. (1178–1179)

Through an anti-materialist socialism, the individual personality becomes the ultimate commodity of a consumerist society.[47] In *Dorian Gray*, Wilde has Lord Henry declare that "a cigarette is the perfect type of a perfect pleasure. It is exquisite, and it leaves one unsatisfied" (67). "The Soul of Man under Socialism," published in February of the same year, offers a different item as the potential ideal – personality itself. It differs from the cigarette in that it fulfills desire and maintains its use-value not because it is habitual or addictive but because of its unending supply of new sources of pleasure. A similar argument can be found in tales by Wilde such as "The Young King" and "The Happy Prince."[48] This view of personality as the ideal commodity also suggests an explanation for why, as Stephen Calloway points out, the author does not appear to have approached his home's interior or its objects with the degree of refined concern one might have expected of a dandy-aesthete.[49]

In her 1987 essay "Promoting Dorian Gray," Rachel Bowlby explores the late-Victorian move from an economy of needs to one of desires, and demonstrates that Lord Henry's hedonistic emphasis on gratification reflects a broader shift in cultural focus from accumulation to expenditure.[50] This change accords both with Pater's emphasis, in *The Renaissance*, on maximizing each of one's momentary experiences of passion as well as with Wilde's anti-materialist celebration of "personality" in "The Soul of Man." It does not fit comfortably, however, with Wilde's discussion in the same essay of the craftsmen's monopoly and the forced taste of interior design and "the House Beautiful." Moreover, as Jeff Nunokawa has argued, the reciprocal borrowings between market capitalism and the late-Victorian dandy-aesthete in *Dorian Gray* that Bowlby explores can be usefully extrapolated onto a plane of economic analysis: "Lord Henry's promotion of desire is not merely '*like* an advertisement,' it *is* an advertisement, albeit for every commodity, rather than any commodity in particular. The universal desire he seeks to inculcate is less a homology for consumer demand, than a totality that comprehends it."[51] Not just a salesperson of pleasures, Wilde's character becomes a spokesperson for commodity culture itself. Just as such a culture sustains demand and desire by creating a sense of boredom with the familiar, so too does Wilde's text sustain our interest by offering only fleeting passions and shifting love for its plot, politics, and wit. Nunokawa concludes by noting that the image of eternal male–male love idealized by Wilde and others suggests a passion that functions outside of this logic of market capitalism. But here as well there is an eventual sense of dissatisfaction. In this case it is not the moments of loss that follow each fleeting moment of satisfaction, but the dwindling of pleasure as one sees the wasting away of the youthful beauty that first sparked desire.

In *Idylls of the Marketplace* (1985), the first book-length study of Wilde in relation to commodity culture, Regenia Gagnier also complicates the passive image of the personality as commodity. Building on Guy Debord's theories of spectacle in post-industrial society and Michel Foucault's articulation of the relations among power, language, and ideology, Gagnier considers Wilde's work, persona, and career as not only representative of his society, but responsive to it. She argues that the man's public personality was not simply something upon which others saw the reflection of their own desires, but equally, if not more so, an oppositional gesture – "an engaged protest against Victorian utility, rationality, scientific factuality, and technological progress – in fact against the whole middle-class drive to conform – but the emphasis is on engaged."[52] Gagnier's demonstration of Wilde's performative oppositionality undermines Sontag's suggestion that Wilde's style – as camp – was apolitical. It also counters Williams's depiction of participants in the Aesthetic Movement as supporting an elitist separation of themselves from mass culture. Gagnier goes on to argue that the only way to really understand the contradictions within Wilde and his work is to recognize the diverse audiences toward which his material is directed. That is to say, Wilde's protestations were selective and strategic; his self-fashioning and his representations of commodity culture arose from a combination of political motives and the aim to satisfy his customers.

Joseph Donohue has argued that Gagnier's work does not accurately reflect the class composition of Wilde's consumers, but the qualification stands less as a critique than as a suggestion for an area in which Gagnier's insights could be developed.[53] Gagnier does demonstrate that, for Wilde and other members of his society, socialist theory did not stand in contradiction to publicity or self-commodification: "The late-Victorian socialist propaganda and the management of advertising in the last decades of the century used similar techniques of dissemination – for example, the engaging of the lower classes – and a similar rhetoric of 'free choice,' 'promise,' and 'the goal of a better life.'"[54] Aestheticism's image of apolitical "art for art's sake" was not only a minority's attempt at bourgeois bating, but a reflection of the broader social shift to a consumptionist ethos. Similarly, Wilde's interest in image and spectacle was, in fact, part of a development within the middle class itself as it shifted to a market society.

Gagnier's work over the next 15 years following the publication of *Idylls* on aesthetics and economics appeared collectively as *The Insatiability of Human Wants*. Giving greater emphasis to the logic and rhetoric of economic and marketing theory than she had in *Idylls*, Gagnier argues in the later text that not only Wilde, but Ruskin, Morris, Rossetti, and Pater, indeed "virtually all the aesthetes were only too conscious of their own implication within consumer, or commodity, culture."[55] Pater's *Renaissance*, she points out, emphasizes economics and the scarcity of goods as fundamental elements of his aesthetic. Thus his encouragement that we "get as many pulsations as possible into the given time" reflects an economics of pleasure, in which a maximizing of sensations becomes paramount.[56] This is exactly what Dorian attempts to fulfill in his conspicuous consumption of various perfumes, music, tapestries, and so on.[57]

Gagnier argues that essays such as "The Soul of Man under Socialism" and "The Portrait of Mr. W.H." should be understood as Wilde's attempts to be heard among the journalists' and critics' voices that heavily influenced the dominant views of mass society. Emphasizing the mediatory role that journalists and critics played between producers and consumers of art and aesthetic taste, Gagnier observes that taste had become increasingly important to members of a bourgeois Victorian society who, now seeing its basic needs as satisfied, turned to fulfilling its desires. Gagnier refers to this appetite as "the insatiability of human wants." Wilde was himself sensitive to this public dynamic and worked to maintain agency throughout the economic process. He frequently changes his position as an artist, a critic, and a consumer. As Gagnier argues, noting the diverse aesthetico-economic positions of works such as *Salomé*, *Dorian Gray*, and "The Soul of Man under Socialism", "aesthetics were, for Wilde, a performance that altered in kind with his audience and location."[58]

Ian Small has commented that Gagnier's later work relies heavily on economic ideological models that do not necessarily offer an accurate reflection of the actual market conditions in which Wilde operated. Both Small, in "The Economies of Taste," and Small and Josephine Guy, in their jointly authored *Oscar Wilde's Profession*, encourage an approach that, while theoretical and aware of conceptual economic models, is committed to close empirical study of the kind that is generally associated with bibliographers and textual scholars.[59] D.F. McKenzie has called this latter approach "the sociology of texts."[60] In such scholarship, the focus is on discovering and historicizing material conditions and interactions between writers, readers, publishers, and others who would have influenced an author's production.[61] Such a traditional historicist approach, Guy and Small argue, reveals that Wilde was not an astute reader and strategic manipulator of the new consumerist culture. The notable number of his literary failures – from a sales standpoint – reflects his difficulties in forecasting or working the system. Their most forceful claim is that there has been what can perhaps even be seen as a "fetishization" of Wilde's life in readings of him as an Irish, gay, or ur-postmodernist author, when the clearest understanding of the narrative of his literary production arises from focusing on monetary motivations. For Guy and Small, Wilde was an opportunist so intent on deriving a satisfactory income from his writings that he allowed his persona to be constructed and sold, in large part, by others.[62]

Guy and Small are misleading in their suggestion that scholars who analyze Wilde from a nationalist, sexual, or other perspective have, like themselves, been attempting to establish the single greatest influence on Wilde. As they acknowledge, any reading that emphasizes one particular issue or paradigm in the man's career does so at the expense of others.[63] An empirical cataloguing and summation of his participation in the culture industry does reflect a desire for financial success, but this does not obviate other reasons he had for writing. It would be inadequate to conclude, for example, that Wilde's work is not gay because there is no archival support for such a claim, because the cultural moment would have deterred the production and safe-keeping of such material; one must turn elsewhere than archives for an exploration of his sexuality. There is a risk, in other words, of over-emphasizing the "sociology of texts" at the expense of the sociology of the author. That said, Guy and Small's research into and narration of the minutiae of Wilde's career add restraint and complexity to the broader theoretical approaches to late-Victorian commodity culture. In light of the limited agency the author had in large part due to financial concerns and the need to accommodate the demands of the publishing institutions as well as specific players in those systems, his ability to insinuate personal, often unaccepted views into his work is all the more intriguing.

Throughout their study, Guy and Small propose that Wilde was not only complicit with the culture industry but that he was used by it more than he used it. In accord with Dowling's observations, they claim that his rebellions were circumscribed by his being "in a position of weakness in relation to the demands of publishing and theatrical institutions."[64] As a number of scholars have noted, the dandy-aesthete persona that he often performed in public and its aura of indifference to the tastes and demands of consumers was a façade, an early product of the star system. Although Guy and Small do not pursue this line of analysis, Wilde's subordinate position within the culture industry itself suggests yet another way in which the man would have been reminded of his exclusion from a central position in his society. The socialist economics found in "The Soul of Man under Socialism," the tales, and elsewhere – which have been read as a defense of cultural and sexual diversity – can also be read as a reflection of his own personal sense of financial dependence.

wilde, the perfect pleasure

From Arnold through the Leavises and on to the present day, it has been a common rhetorical strategy to refer to mainstream cultural artifacts such as popular literature as addictive products that leave one drugged into complacency and craving more. As cheap as cigarettes, they were equally as habit forming. But as both Arnold and Marx would have recognized, the appeal of such material could also be used to popularize other, less easily digested views. Wilde would have suggested that literature sensitive to its market should operate much like a cigarette – being a perfect pleasure that nevertheless always leaves one unsatisfied. Bowlby offers an especially insightful discussion of Wilde's cigarette relatively early in the study of his relation to commodity culture. She puts forward the argument that the aesthete is the "perfect type" of new consumer. Lord Henry's epigram on the cigarette, she argues, reads less like an elitist claim to refined taste than a bit of advertising. The tobacco's limited satisfaction makes it an ideal product because consumers will continue to demand more. This, Bowlby argues, is exactly what Wilde's aphorisms do – with the momentary pleasure of their wit soon being replaced with a sense of non-satisfaction arising from what ultimately remains an ambiguous paradox.[65] As my consideration of theoretical approaches to Wilde's relation to commodity culture suggests, the paradoxical nature of his work and career as a commentator on culture have made the author himself a similarly perfect pleasure. It offers an explanation not only for the decades of insightful paradoxes that characterize Wilde studies, but also for our own on-going scholarly consumption of the man and his work.

notes

1. Although scholars generally agree that national notions of popular culture grounded in consumption arose at the end of the nineteenth century, earlier

eras did have popular entertainment that carried nationalist connotations. Folk culture or "bread and circuses," for example, is seen to have fostered the development of nationalist identities. In *Popular Culture in Early Modern Europe* (London: Temple Smith, 1978), P. Burke recognizes a rise of nationalist cultures in late eighteenth-century Europe that have a more politicized intent, with poets consciously developing this image. On popular consumer culture of Wilde's era in relation to the literary market, see, for example, Norman Feltes's *Literary Capital and the Late Victorian Novel* (London: University of Wisconsin Press, 1993).

2. On the commercialized image of the artist during the Victorian era, see Julie F. Codell's "The Public Image of the Victorian Artist: Family Biographies," *The Journal of Pre-Raphaelite Studies* 4 (Fall 1996), 5–34; and Dianne Sachko Macleod's *Art and the Victorian Middle Class* (Cambridge: Cambridge University Press, 1996).
3. Matthew Arnold, *Culture and Anarchy* (New York: Macmillan, 1936), 45.
4. Ibid., 103.
5. Matthew Arnold, "The Function of Criticism at the Present Time," in *Essays in Criticism* (London: Macmillan, 1865), 25.
6. *Culture and Anarchy*, op. cit., 66.
7. Margaret Oliphant, "The ByWays of Literature: Reading for the Million," *Blackwood's Edinburgh Magazine* 84 (August 1858), 202.
8. Linda Dowling, *The Vulgarization of Art: The Victorians and Aesthetic Democracy* (Charlottesville: University of Virginia Press, 1995).
9. The conflicting support for and disagreement with Arnold's model of a cultured society is one of Wilde's many paradoxes, just as his support for diversity must be placed against his defense of same-sex male desires as an ideal beyond the barbs of a brutish consumer society. On the subject, see Jeff Nunokawa, "The Importance of Being Bored: The Dividends of Ennui in *The Picture of Dorian Gray*," *Studies in the Novel* 28.3 (Fall 1996), 357–371. On Wilde's conflicted vacillation between Arnoldian and consumerist interests, also see Jonathan Freedman's *Professions of Taste: Henry James, British Aestheticism, and Commodity Culture* (Stanford: Stanford University Press, 1990), 47–55, and Regenia Gagnier's *The Insatiability of Human Wants: Economics and Aesthetics in Market Society* (Chicago: University of Chicago Press, 2000), 114.
10. Karl Marx, *Selected Writings in Sociology and Social Philosophy*, eds. T. Bottomore and M. Rubel (Harmondsworth: Penguin, 1963), 93.
11. Karl Marx, *A Contribution to the Critique of Political Economy* (London: Lawrence and Wishart, 1971).
12. For an extensive consideration of the methods by which an ideology dominates a social system, see Antonio Gramsci's articulation of the notion of "hegemony" in *Selections from Prison Notebooks* and R. Simon, *Gramsci's Political Thought: An Introduction* (London: Lawrence and Wishart, 1982). Although not a direct response to Gramsci, Mikhail Bakhtin's work on the carnivalesque offers a useful exploration of folk culture's destabilization of hegemonic order.
13. Marx, *Selected Writings*, op. cit., 183.
14. John Ruskin, *Modern Painters*, Vol. 1 (London: George Allen, 1900), 30.
15. John Ruskin, "Modern Manufacture and Design," in *The Two Paths* (London: Cassell, 1907), 92.

16. Ibid., 96.
17. William Morris, "Art under Plutocracy," in *Art in Theory: 1815–1900,* eds. Charles Harrison and Paul Wood (Oxford: Blackwell, 1998), 763.
18. William Morris, *Art and Society: Lectures and Essays by William Morris*, ed. Gary Zabel (Boston: George's Hill, 1993), 21.
19. For a related anti-commercial argument, see Dante Gabriel Rossetti's "Hand and Soul," *The Germ* 1 (January 1850), 23–32.
20. George Du Maurier, *Trilby* (Oxford: Oxford University Press, 1998), 288–289, 289, 286.
21. Max Nordau, *Degeneration* (Lincoln: University of Nebraska Press, 1968), 7.
22. Ibid., 27.
23. Arnold, "Function," op. cit., 1.
24. Nordau, op. cit., 9–10, 317, 319.
25. Theodor Adorno, *Aesthetic Theory*, trans. Robert Hullot-Kentor (Minneapolis: University of Minnesota Press, 1997), 239, 16.
26. Freedman, *Professions*, op. cit., xxi–xxii.
27. Theodor Adorno and Max Horkheimer, *Dialectic of Englightenment* (New York: Herder and Herder, 1972).
28. Walter Benjamin, "The Work of Art in the Age of Mechanical Reproduction," in *Illuminations* (London: Fontana, 1973).
29. Some readings of the late-Victorian period as showing the utter decay of western society include R.V. Johnson's *Aestheticism* (London: Methuen, 1954), Graham Hough's *The Last Romantics* (London: Duckworth, 1949), and Peter Bürger's *Theory of the Avant-Garde*, trans. Michael Shaw (Minneapolis: University of Minnesota Press, 1984). Conversely, F.R. Leavis has famously argued that the early twentieth century was even more desperately dehumanizing than the late-Victorian period: *Mass Civilization and Minority Culture* (Cambridge: Minority, 1930). Indeed every era faces this sort of commentary, but the *fin de siècle* stands out for the number and intensity of the criticism. The fact that Victorians had themselves succeeded in commodifying ennui and decadence points to their sensitivity to the connection.
30. F.R. Leavis and Denys Thompson, *Culture and Environment* (London: Chatto and Windus, 1933), 81.
31. Leavis, *Mass Civilization*, op. cit., 2.
32. Leavis and Thompson, *Culture and Environment*, op. cit., 4.
33. Raymond Williams, *Marxism and Literature* (Oxford: Oxford University Press, 1977).
34. Raymond Williams, *Culture and Society* (London: Chatto and Windus, 1958).
35. The two essay collections that first gave camp academic credibility are David Bergman, ed. *Camp Grounds: Style and Homosexuality* (Amherst: University of Massachusetts Press, 1993) and Moe Meyer, ed. *The Politics and Poetics of Camp* (London: Routledge, 1994).
36. Susan Sontag, "Notes on 'Camp,'" 1964, rpt. in Jonathan Freedman, ed. *Oscar Wilde: A Collection of Critical Essays* (Saddle River, NJ: Prentice Hall, 1996), 10.
37. In *Theory of the Avant-Garde* (op. cit), Peter Bürger builds on Adorno's argument in order to construct works from the first half of the twentieth century as vital, politicized, and productive.

38. Sontag, op. cit., 19.
39. Ibid., 19.
40. Walter Pater, *The Renaissance*, 1873 (Oxford: Oxford University Press, 1990), xxix.
41. Rachel Bowlby, "Promoting Dorian Gray," *The Oxford Literary Review* 9 (1987), 157–158.
42. In *Oscar Wilde's Profession: Writing and the Culture Industry in the Late Nineteenth Century* (New York: Oxford University Press, 2000), Josephine M. Guy and Ian Small offer a useful contextualization of Wilde's North American tour, demonstrating the control that the producer Richard D'Oyly Carte had on the dandy image that was sold. Jonathan Freedman also notes, however, that North American audiences produced their own svelte image of the man before he even arrived.
43. Jonathan Freedman, "Introduction: On Oscar Wildes," in *Oscar Wilde: A Collection of Critical Essays*, op. cit., 4–5.
44. Freedman, *Professions of Taste*, op. cit., xii.
45. Dowling, *The Vulgarization of Art*, op. cit., 91.
46. Lawrence Danson, *Wilde's Intentions: The Artist in His Criticism* (Oxford: Clarendon, 1997), 87.
47. On the relation between individualism and socialism in Wilde, see also Terry Eagleton, *Saint Oscar* (Lawrence Hill, Derry: Field Day, 1989).
48. In *Wilde's Intentions* (op. cit.), Danson offers a brief discussion of these two tales in relation to "The Soul of Man under Socialism" (148–150).
49. Stephen Calloway, "Wilde and the Dandyism of the Senses," in *The Cambridge Companion to Oscar Wilde*, ed. Pete Raby (Cambridge: Cambridge University Press, 1997), 34–54.
50. Bowlby, op. cit., 152.
51. Nunokawa, op. cit., 366.
52. Regenia Gagnier, *Idylls of the Marketplace: Oscar Wilde and the Victorian Public* (Stanford: Stanford University Press, 1985), 3.
53. Joseph Donohue, "Recent Studies of Oscar Wilde," *Nineteenth Century Theatre* 16.2 (1988), 126–136.
54. Gagnier, *Idylls*, op. cit., 52.
55. Gagnier, *Insatiability*, op. cit., 53.
56. Pater, op. cit., 153.
57. Scholars have frequently noted that the images of Dorian's collecting strongly echo the actions of Joris-Karl Huysmans's hero Des Esseintes in *A Rebours*. A central text in the Decadent movement (which had its greatest influence and developments in France), Huysmans's novel has proven crucial for scholars' association of Decadence with mass consumption, theorizations that offer useful insights for a consideration of Wilde and commodity culture. See, for example, the essays in Liz Constable, Dennis Denisoff, and Matt Potolsky, eds., *Perennial Decay: On the Aesthetics and Politics of Decadence* (Philadelphia: University of Pennsylvania Press, 1999).
58. Gagnier, *Idylls*, op. cit., 157.
59. Ian Small, "The Economies of Taste: Literary Markets and Literary Value in the Late Nineteenth Century," *ELT* 39.1 (1996), 7–18; Guy and Small, *Oscar Wilde's Profession*, op. cit.

60. D.F. McKenzie, *Bibliography and the Sociology of Texts* (London: The British Library, 1986).
61. Small, "Economies," op. cit., 12–13.
62. Guy and Small, *Oscar Wilde's Profession*, op. cit., 221, 13.
63. Ibid., 9.
64. Ibid., 21.
65. Bowlby, op. cit., 147–148.

6

philosophical approaches to interpretation of oscar wilde

philip smith

Nineteenth-century readers of Wilde appreciated and sometimes condemned aspects of the philosophical thought in his creative and critical work. However, the notoriety of Wilde's life and trial in the 1890s created a public image which overshadowed the philosophical references, allusions, and subtleties in his writing. In the first decades of the twentieth century, homophobia and cultural pudency obscured serious attention to Wilde by scholars and critics. By the middle of the century, Wilde's thought attracted the attention of formalist critics who suggested the coherence of its philosophical foundations for aestheticism. With the explosion of new approaches to Wilde in the last two decades of the twentieth century and the turn of the twenty-first, novel and sometimes contentious interpretations have emerged, for example, those which have emphasized queer theory, the Irishness of Wilde, as celebrity or performer for commodity culture, Wilde and psychoanalysis, and so on. There has never been as much critically various and astute reception of Wilde's work as at present and among the important recent approaches is the revaluation of Wilde as an intellectual with serious philosophical interests. I will review some of the major moments in the recent construction of a philosophical Wilde, focusing on longer considerations of significant work by J.E. Chamberlin and Rodney Shewan in the 1970s and by Julia Prewitt Brown and Bruce Bashford in the 1990s.

Philosophical approaches to literary analysis and interpretation include several traditional and powerful models of extrinsic investigation into the constitutive contexts and intertexts of literary texts, such as biographical, historical, source-study, and history-of-ideas approaches. Contemporary theorized critical approaches with affinities to traditional philosophical approaches include discourse analysis, deconstruction, phenomenological analysis, sociological and Marxian criticism, and dialogics. I take a "philosophical" approach to Wilde as one from a theoretically or philosophically grounded perspective which also attends to Wilde's education, use of philosophy, or construction of a philosophical theory of life, society, and aesthetics. Philosophical approaches to Wilde attend to one or more of the following: Wilde's considerable knowledge and textual references to or quotations from philosophy in his published writing, letters, and notebooks; his own philosophical approach to constructing critical theory, which has been variously understood by critics as monological or as pluralistic; and, finally, to the constitutive rationale in philosophy of the approach itself. Obviously, the breadth of possibility for philosophical interpretations is large; practicers of many critical approaches might seek to interpret Wilde's writings from philosophical literary-theoretical positions. I will focus here on critics who attempt to understand Wilde's foundational and operative principles rather than those who focus narrowly on a topical or explicative approach.

nineteenth- and twentieth-century anticipations

The philosophical foundations of Wilde's critical theory were the stuff of English and Irish university curricula in the 1870s and 1880s. As his notebooks reveal, Wilde's studies in classics at Trinity College, Dublin and his academic work for his first-class honors B.A. degree in the *Literae Humaniores* (Greats) program at Oxford, as well as the preparation and writing of his first major essay, "The Rise of Historical Criticism," which was submitted for the Chancellor's English Essay Prize of 1879, all told, gave him the equivalent of a contemporary postgraduate education in classical and modern philosophy, history, sociology, literature, religion, art, political economy, philology, anthropology, linguistics, and natural science.[1] A contemporary of Wilde's at Oxford, Lewis R. Farnell, recalled in his memoirs that "In the 'Greats'-circle, Philosophy was our mistress that claimed most of our devotion, roused most of our ardour, and decided our fate in the schools."[2] Wilde's philosophical studies at Oxford reflect the shaping influence of the Oxford Hegelians, especially Benjamin Jowett and William Wallace, whose writings he copied and annotated in his Commonplace Book. Wallace's "Prolegomena" to *The Logic of Hegel* (1874) and Jowett's Hegelian interpretations of Plato in his introductions to the second edition of *The Dialogues of Plato* (1875) were particularly important in shaping Wilde's philosophical position. As the careers of Wilde, Walter

Pater, John A. Symonds, and Lord Alfred Douglas amply demonstrate, an Oxford education in philosophy and classics, particularly one which immersed an all-male student population in the works of Plato, also posed philosophical and personal questions concerning the homosocial and homosexual inclinations of these students and their dons.[3]

In our edition and commentary, Michael Helfand and I argue that Wilde created a philosophical position which brought his Hegelian philosophical idealism into synthesis with the Darwinist developmental theories of materialist evolutionary scientists and philosophers like Darwin, Herbert Spencer, Thomas H. Huxley, William K. Clifford, and John Tyndall.[4] We contend that Wilde's philosophical synthesis provides the intellectual foundation for his developing aesthetic and critical theory as it informs his lectures in America, *Intentions*, *The Picture of Dorian Gray*, and his essays, reviews, and stories such as "The Soul of Man under Socialism," "A Chinese Sage," and "The Portrait of Mr. W.H."

Wilde's philosophical basis for creative and critical writing was at least partly understood by a few of his contemporary readers. One of them, Ernest Newman, who published "Oscar Wilde: A Literary Appreciation" in the *Free Review* in June 1895, only a week after Wilde's sentencing, said of Wilde that "his is one of the clearest and soundest intellects in England to-day" and that "there is material enough in his scattered essays to make an excellent treatise on aesthetic [sic]."[5] Writing in appreciation of Wilde's doctrine of art for art's sake, Newman identifies its philosophical basis as Hedonism:

> Wilde, holding ideas like these on art, is a Hedonist in the fullest sense of the word. There are still, I believe, sombre people in the world afflicted with Nonconformist consciences and knowing it not, who look upon the Hedonist as a rather immoral creature, and preach to us, in season and out of season, the doctrine of self-sacrifice and duty. That doctrine is well enough in its way, but I think that Hedonism is better. It is not the philosophy of pleasure that is truly selfish, but the philosophy of sacrifice. The easiest form of sympathy, as Mr. Wilde has said, is sympathy with pain: the higher form of sympathy with others' joy is infinitely harder to attain to. And it is easier to sympathise with suffering, he says, than to sympathise with thought.[6]

Newman's appreciation of Wilde's doctrine of art for art's sake goes on to connect his aesthetics with his socialism, anticipating another of the foci for twentieth-century critics who have seen the relationships among Wilde's philosophical idealism, aesthetics, and political utopianism.

Another who appreciated the philosophical turn in Wilde, ironically, was Max Nordau, the author of *Degeneration* (1892; 1895 English translation), a physician and journalist whose conservative cultural critique made him a major opponent of Wilde and other members of the European artistic and philosophical avant-garde. Nordau included Wilde among other "degenerates" like Henrik Ibsen, Friedrich Nietzsche, Richard Wagner, Leo Tolstoy, Walt Whitman, and Emile Zola as writers who violated the canons of morality and self-restraint and whose works were likely to encourage humans to deviate from the positive and normative development of culture. In particular, Nordau compared Wilde to Nietzsche, whom he classed as an egomaniacal individualist who had willfully distorted Hegelian idealism. Nordau also noted correspondences between Nietzschean thought and Wildean ideas on art and their expression in aphorisms:

> The passage in *Zur Genealogie der Moral* (p. 171) in which he glorifies art, because "in it the lie sanctifies itself, and the will to deceive has a quiet conscience on its side," might be in the chapter in Wilde's *Intentions* on "The Decay of Lying," as, conversely, Wilde's aphorisms: "There is no sin except stupidity." "An idea that is not dangerous is unworthy of being called an idea at all." And his praises of Wainwright, the poisoner, are in exact agreement with Nietzsche's "morality of assassins," and the latter's remarks that crime is calumniated, and that the defender of the criminal is "oftenest not artist enough to turn the beautiful terribleness of the crime to the advantage of the doer." . . . The similarity, or rather identity, is not explained by plagiarism; it is explained by the identity of mental qualities in Nietzsche and the other egomaniacal degenerates.[7]

Nordau's moralistic objections to Wilde and Nietzsche should not obscure the attention that Nordau paid to the philosophical foundations of the writers he dismisses. His criticisms represent the very bourgeois and Philistine mentalities which Wilde and Nietzsche opposed, but his perspicacity in recognizing their similarities anticipates the judgments of twentieth-century critics. Richard Ellmann suggested Wilde's importance to modernist literature and criticism this way:

> Wilde sounds like an ancestral Northrop Frye or Roland Barthes. These portentous comparisons do indeed claim virtue by association, and such claims may be broadened. André Gide found Nietzsche less exciting because he had read Wilde, and Thomas Mann in one of his

last essays remarks almost with chagrin on how many of Nietzsche's aphorisms might have been expressed by Wilde and many of Wilde's by Nietzsche. What I think can be urged for Wilde then, is that for his own reasons and in his own way he laid the basis for many critical positions which are still debated in much the same terms and which we like to attribute to more ponderous names.[8]

Modern arbiters of critical opinion did not elevate Wilde into the top rank of canonized literary figures. However, as Michael Helfand and I have pointed out, Wilde's *Intentions* was recognized by William Wimsatt and Cleanth Brooks as well as by René Welleck as a theoretically important document of the art-for-art's-sake movement and as a work of idealist aestheticism which showed the influence of Hegelianism.[9] This mid-twentieth-century literary-historical classification meant that Wilde's cultural significance was trivial compared to the major Victorian novelists, poets, and prose writers.

late twentieth-century philosophical approaches to wilde

As Ian Small points out in *Oscar Wilde Revalued*, since the 1970s scholarly research and criticism have constructed new views of Wilde and have produced significant enrichment and change in the variety and kinds of interpretation: "The 'new' Wilde is preoccupied with issues such as authority, gender, identity, and prison reform; he is seen as thoroughly and seriously engaged with some of the most contentious intellectual issues of his day." This revaluation of Wilde has occurred within the discipline-wide reassessment of literary historical and critical theories over the last three decades of the century.[10]

Small's review of recent scholarship and criticism led him to a set of expectations and judgments about the use of evidence in literary research which are important to the value and reception of philosophical approaches to Wilde. He observes that literary studies, unlike other disciplines, does not have the kinds of paradigm shifts which invalidate or replace ways of knowing; instead, he deplores a critical Tower of Babel:

> Today it is easy to find critics writing of Wilde the Irish nationalist, Wilde the homosexual, Wilde the craftsman-writer, as well as Wilde the plagiarist. Rarely is there a sense that these different interpretations are not easily compatible with each other: or, rather, an acknowledgment of the simple truth that Wilde cannot be *all* of these things at the same time.[11]

Small suggests that this situation results from the distrust of empirical evidence characteristic of some varieties of critical theory which emerged in the 1980s; it is a situation which prompts difficult questions:

> At a practical level, how is the account of the "Irish Wilde" compatible with the "gay" Wilde; and how are either of these compatible with the Wilde who had to learn [sic] his living entirely by his pen? A useful project for future studies of Wilde might be an attempt to reconcile the insights generated by critical theory with the attention to secure evidence associated with traditional empiricist historiography.[12]

The most substantial recent challenge to philosophical interpretation of Wilde comes from two scholars who have jointly studied the material practices of publishing. In *Oscar Wilde's Profession: Writing and the Culture Industry in the Late Nineteenth Century*, Josephine Guy and Ian Small document Wilde's efforts to make a living as a journalist, novelist, and playwright in an intensively competitive culture of commercial publishing. In their view, Wilde is best understood as "a writer who saw no real disjunction between making and selling his work, between art and its market, despite his frequently expressed contempt for the public's tastes."[13]

Philosophical approaches can be nonreductive and can argue for comprehensive and coherent views of the subject, even a subject like Wilde who writes and behaves in contradictory ways. Such approaches, therefore, have the power and critical authority to present, for example, a rationale for how Wilde could be understood as a gay, Protestant Irishman with Catholic tendencies and feminist sympathies, living from the earnings of his writing and at the same time intellectually aware of and responsive to social, political, aesthetic, and philosophical issues which inform his work. A comprehensive philosophical understanding should be based on several kinds of evidence, for example, textual interpretation of Wilde's own published and unpublished writing, letters, and notebooks, biographical accounts and supporting records such as business records, other official documents, news stories, and personal reminiscences and other relevant evidence. However, the central assumption of such an approach would be one of nuanced explanatory coherence based on a principled approach and a relational understanding of philosophical and material reasons for valuing evidence. That is, a philosophical approach should address questions such as: how should a critic weigh competing explanations, for example, which would explain Wilde's motives for writing the essays later collected in *Intentions*? Do the material causes (e.g., financial profit and public recognition) outweigh or contradict or complement what might be called the philosophical causes (e.g., amusing expression of serious ideas, participation in a critical debate, and persuasive education of readers)?

Philosophical approaches to texts usually assert intellectual continuities in thought and privilege interpretations which reveal such continuities within or among texts, perhaps as an essentially "Wildean" quality of thought. My focus in the remainder of this chapter, then, will be to assess the explanatory merit of some of them. Particularly, with a writer influenced by European idealist philosophy, such ideas could be called "essentialist" and might be exemplified in Wilde, for example, as the Hegelian idea of World Spirit mentioned in "The Critic as Artist" (1154). As I will show, philosophical interpretations usually privilege such continuities: Bashford, for example, sees individual works like "The Critic as Artist" or "The Soul of Man under Socialism" as exhibiting both continuities and differences as examples of subjectivist criticism. However, Bashford accommodates the differences among Wilde's texts as when they are addressed under the more general rubric of Wilde's humanism, which is the focusing essential quality of Wilde's critical discourse. Brown privileges an essential "ethical aestheticism" characteristic of the texts she classifies as "cosmopolitan criticism." Smith and Helfand see Wilde as one who reflected in the thematics of most of his major works a synthesis of Hegelian idealism and nineteenth-century evolutionary theories.

Two important books which helped to set the standards and to suggest new resources for late twentieth-century philosophical approaches appeared in 1977: J.E. Chamberlin's *Ripe Was the Drowsy Hour: The Age of Oscar Wilde* and Rodney Shewan's *Oscar Wilde: Art and Egotism*. Both scholars did significant research in the Wilde archives, inspecting hitherto ignored manuscripts and notebooks, and broadened the scope of reference for understanding Wilde's intellectual and cultural contexts.

Chamberlin's approach incorporates the methodology of the history of ideas; his aim in showing the intellectual contexts for Wilde is based on establishing interpretive coherence, a premise of most philosophical approaches. Chamberlin posits "the coherence that we invent or discover" not as an essential quality inherent in his materials, but as an interpretive conclusion, one in keeping with Wilde's own approach:

> Wilde used to insist that our sense of the coherence of an age depends upon the way in which we perceive its abstract and ideal qualities, and I think his instinct was sound in that respect. Furthermore, and in any event, the ways in which such coherence is derived are more than

historical curiosities, for they are to a considerable extent continuous with the ways in which we still derive a sense of our own culture, our own age.[14]

Chamberlin's allusive and wide-ranging chapter on "The Age of Oscar Wilde" sketches many of the intellectual contexts for Wilde's philosophical and aesthetic commitments to individualism and socialism. Chamberlin observes: "The point that was fairly universally accepted was that individual self-consciousness and self-respect could hardly flourish if their very existence depended upon structures and relationships which were not organically continuous with their sustaining energies, as the structures and relationships of capitalist society appeared not to be."[15] Thus, he argues, when Wilde contends in "The Soul of Man under Socialism" that socialism can be understood as a higher form of individualism, he participates in helping to define a principle of culture in which "the unification of the self and the realization of the personality is the aim of cultural development, and this development is a creative accomplishment whose validity depends upon our understanding of the nature of cultural coherence."[16] In Chamberlin's approach, then, Wilde's ideas about politics and culture are seen as coherent with his commitment to art and individualism.

Chamberlin argues that Wilde's aesthetics, his rejection of the bourgeois or Philistine standards of art and society and his preference for the elevation of artifice, led him to value drama as his "most personal form of expression."[17] The dramatic forms of tragedy and comedy presented a paradoxical estrangement from and involvement with life, allowing audiences simultaneously to be "escaping from it in aesthetic awareness only to return to it more comprehensively through the aesthetic experience."[18] This paradox enables Chamberlin to compare Wilde's aesthetic of life perceived as art to similar ideas in Pater, in the English Romantic poets, and in James Joyce. He refers to Thomas Mann's attempt to show that Nietzsche was an aesthete by comparing Wilde and Nietzsche as aphorists – a proposition Chamberlin rejects. However, he urges his readers to understand than Mann's comparison illuminates Wilde's "firm conviction that life and art are both structures of experience; that art is the expression of life, though not its routine imitator. . . ."[19]

Extending this interpretation in his fourth chapter, Chamberlin argues for an important distinction in the genealogy of Wilde's aestheticism: after he places Wilde in contextual relation to classical and romantic ideas of beauty as well as to Paterian impressionism and French symbolism, he develops the consequences of Wilde's awareness of the tensions and contradictions, creative and destructive, of the imagination. He argues that Wilde adopted a Hegelian philosophical solution to accommodate the dilemmas, contradictions, and dichotomies which arose from his development of a complex and unorthodox aesthetics. Chamberlin, in common with most critics who take a philosophical approach, focuses on Wilde's Hegelian conclusion to "The Truth of Masks," his famous statement that only in art-criticism can the Platonic theory of ideas and the Hegelian system of contraries be realized (1173):

> Hegel's "system of contraries" was a system of progressive revelation of the truth (and the beauty) which inhered in the imaginative fusion of opposites, the opposites which defined human experience and perception. In perpetual flux there is coherence and order; the subjective and objective depend upon each other for their definition; form and matter are separable yet inextricably and inexplicably linked in an indissoluble union; music combines unity and variety and, when we contemplate the ideal "music of the spheres," we possess the ultimate conception of a single harmonious order and the infinite variety of the cosmos – these are only some of the themes which a consideration of Hegel had brought into a focus. But this focus was sharpened by a contemporaneous adaptation of Hegelian dialectic to Platonic dialogue, and even to the Darwinian struggle for survival, especially when it was further suggested (by Benjamin Jowett among others) that "the struggle for existence is not confined to the animals, but appears in the kingdom of thought."[20]

Chamberlin's connection of Hegelian and Darwinian ideas as a crucial philosophical and cultural basis for an understanding of Wilde's critical theory has ample warrant in the evidence he presents, that is, Wilde's citation of Hegel in "The Truth of Masks" and the presence of entries regarding evolutionary theory and Hegelian philosophy in Wilde's notebooks. Chamberlin's reading of the notebooks was fruitful for his argument but, as Michael Helfand and I have argued in the commentary accompanying our edition, considerably more evidence exists for Wilde's synthesis of Hegelian and Darwinian thought. To cite only one example, on page 204 of his Commonplace Book, Wilde noted William Wallace's remark that "Hegelian dialectic is the natural selection produced by a struggle for existence in world of thought [sic]" next to remarks drawn from Jowett concerning Plato's anticipation in his concept of *eros* of the evolutionist theories of Aristotle.[21]

For Wilde, in the notebooks and also later in his published writing, *eros* becomes not only love but also the dialectical energy of thought which Chamberlin, in his concluding chapter, considers under the figure of Pan or Marsyas. Here Chamberlin indulges his own thoughtful energy by posing a succession of mythological and dramatic figures as significant for an understanding of both the culture of the late nineteenth century and of Wilde as a writer who partially reveals the truths of himself complexly behind masks. The intertextual complications of these referential loci offer Chamberlin the interpretive foundation to bring Wilde's celebrations of Christ, Dionysus, Persephone, and Marsyas into readings of *De Profundis*, and *Salomé*. Chamberlin takes Wilde's conception of Christ back to his reading (also recorded in the notebooks) of Renan's *Vie de Jesus* but shows how Wilde also mixed in the figures of Narcissus and the androgyne and was led to the compelling figure of Salomé (whose story is also told by Renan). Finally, writing with audacious allusiveness, Chamberlin also connects Pierrot and Ossian to Wilde and suggests that his power as a dramatist on stage and in life may be seen through these figures:

> the images which especially appeal to the artists of the time – of Pan and Persephone and Pierrot, of Dionysus and Salomé and Narcissus, of androgynous figures and paradoxical dilemmas – these bear witness to the ambiguous relationships between art and life, and among the categories of each, which fascinated the age of Wilde.[22]

Chamberlin's intertextual approach relies upon his careful research into Wilde's education, allusions, and connections or similarities to other figures in "the age of Oscar Wilde." It is, therefore, not a work of textual explication but, instead, a philosophical approach which suggests, often provocatively, connections and coherences among texts which inform the intellectual and artistic life and work of Wilde.

Rodney Shewan published *Oscar Wilde: Art and Egotism* in the same year as Chamberlin's *Ripe Was the Drowsy Hour*; like Chamberlin, Shewan bases his analysis on evidence from the published texts and unpublished manuscripts, letters, biographies, cultural contexts, and he includes a far larger sample of the critical response to Wilde. As his title suggests, Shewan thematizes as "egotism" what he calls "patterns of self-projection and self-objectification through Wilde's career" manifested through the development of Wilde's writing.[23] Because he focuses on illuminating Wilde's aims and ideas and attends to philosophical backgrounds, Shewan's approach can be thought of as philosophical; however, his method for explicating texts is more conventionally literary-historical than Chamberlin's.

Shewan traces Wilde's 30-year development as a writer associated with *fin-de-siècle* decadence but he argues that Wilde remained "rooted in the earlier humanist tradition," celebrated aestheticism as a potential rebirth of humanism, and wrote as "an eminent, though reluctant, Victorian."[24] Shewan claims that the "working principle" of aesthetic formalism in Wilde's career was set in his early lecture in America, "The English Renaissance" (1882) when he "united classical and Romantic by treating the momentary and exceptional under the conditions of serene and dispassionate form."[25] Shewan argues that "Wilde remained a Romantic, according to his own definition, throughout his life, devoted to the moment and convinced that he was exceptional."[26] This exceptionalist egoism led Wilde to experiment with varieties of attitudes, to choose inconsistency as a virtue, and to develop the paradox as his most characteristic form of expression in a writerly development of "gradual change from Romantic posturing in verse and tragedy to social sparring in prose, eventually in stage comedy dominated by the dandy."[27]

These are Shewan's most general principles for analysis, intended to support his overall psychological interpretation of Wilde and egoism; however, at the level of specific analysis, his approach includes the attribution of philosophical coherence which he observes in Wilde's critical and creative work over the length of his career. Having inspected the Commonplace Book, Shewan acknowledges the importance for Wilde of Hegelian idealist philosophy and Darwinism. Shewan sees a continuity in the development of Wilde's essentially Romantic concept of New Hellenism, which ranges from his earliest lectures and essays to the major critical texts of the 1890s: "it is the Hegelian prose tradition rather than the tradition of the English or German poet-prophet that stands behind Wilde's new sublime."[28] In particular, Shewan points out that Wilde's concept of "soul," as promulgated in "The English Renaissance of Art" and revisited in later works, notably *The Picture of Dorian Gray*, "combines both intellectual and spiritual qualities" and that it "affords a further point of comparison with the protagonists of Hegel's *Phenomenology of Spirit* of the 'spirit' or 'mind.'"[29] Finally, among the coherent connective ideas Shewan notes is that "the redemptive, reintegrating power of criticism projected at the end of 'The Critic as Artist' and in 'The Soul of Man Under Socialism' is anticipated by Wilde's concluding sentence" to "The Rise of Historical Criticism," which was composed for the Chancellor's English Essay Prize of 1879.[30]

Shewan continues to note the philosophical coherences and interpretive connections as he makes his way, story by story, through Wilde's fiction. He points out the connections among the ideas of experience, knowledge and self-knowledge in *Dorian Gray, A House of Pomegranates*, and

> "The Critic as Artist" where the image of the Romantic *peregrinatio*, the journey towards complete knowledge and final reintegration of the fragmented personality, is combined with the evolutionary metaphor of social Darwinism. Heredity makes possible the idea of "concentrated race experience," and the true critic is he who will reach through fastidious self-culture that state which Schelling, Schiller and Hegel variously posited as the goal of philosophic endeavour.[31]

Shewan's explications of Wilde's critical essays remain useful readings which show the relations of Wilde's theories to previous literary criticism as well as to Hegelian idealism and Darwinian evolutionary theory, both of which undergird Wilde's use of the dialogue form and his utopian socialism. Shewan carefully and closely reads Wilde's society dramas, where he finds echoes and continuities among the plays as well as references to the fiction and criticism, especially around the figure of the dandy. Closing with readings of *De Profundis* and "The Ballad of Reading Gaol," Shewan sees in the former a rejection of the dandy and critic in favor of "the fulfillment of the committed Romantic individualist. Christ's personality replaces Hegel's philosophic principle as the best expression of all-inclusiveness."[32]

Shewan's and Chamberlin's serious revaluations of Wilde were followed in the 1980s by publications like Richard Ellmann's biography (1987) and the edition of Wilde's notebooks I edited with Michael Helfand (1989).[33] The publication of such extensive new information about Wilde's life and intellectual formation gave great impetus to critical revaluations. In addition, as literary-critical and homophobic prejudices eroded and as the institution of literary criticism challenged traditional views of canonical literature, so the application of literary theories produced new interpretive approaches focused around cultural, ethnic, material, and gender studies. Among the emergent critical books, three deserve mention and two from the 1990s merit more extended consideration as philosophical approaches. Regenia Gagnier's *Idylls of the Marketplace: Oscar Wilde and the Victorian Public* (1986) thoughtfully deployed modern critical theory to analyze Wilde's aesthetics in terms of spectacle and the location of discourse in a market economy.[34] Ian Small's *Conditions for Criticism: Authority, Knowledge, and Literature in the Late Nineteenth Century* (1991) provided a précis of the development of *fin-de-siècle* academic professionalism in the social sciences, philosophical aesthetics, and literary criticism.[35] Small argued that these contexts shaped the debates over intellectual authority in which Wilde and Pater participated. Michael Patrick Gillespie's *Oscar Wilde and the Poetics of Ambiguity* (1996) used a reader-response approach to catalog and evaluate the multiplicity of meanings and interpretations of Wilde's texts.[36] All three of these books usefully broadened the scope of study and interpretation which philosophical approaches usually attempt to span. However, two other books from the 1990s presented more substantial and important philosophical interpretations of Wilde.

Julia Prewitt Brown's *Cosmopolitan Criticism: Oscar Wilde's Philosophy of Art* (1997) adds significantly to the critical conversation about the relationship of philosophy to Wilde's writings because it proposes similarities between them and significant texts in continental philosophy and criticism. Responding to the recent burgeoning of interpretations, especially by materialist critics of Wilde, Brown notes their characteristic "general neglect of his philosophy of criticism and art."[37] Brown objects that, "current trends in 'materialist' criticism are not often attuned to the manifestly idealist bent of Wilde's thought; it would seem that his spiritual pleasures offend contemporary pieties scarcely less than his bodily pleasure offended the Victorians."[38]

Brown's approach emphasizes the intellectual primacy of Wilde's idealist thought and its analogues and influences in continental philosophy. She acknowledges the importance of Wilde's philosophical formation as revealed in the Oxford notebooks and credits the Smith/Helfand interpretation for "illuminating the original philosophical orientation and context of Wilde's thought."[39] The consistent focus of her study centers on Wilde's criticism as an "ethical aesthetic," which she describes as Wilde's conviction "that the experience of art is the only viable means in the contemporary world of countering the commercial spirit, or of arriving at that critical understanding of the past and present that is essential to a safe future."[40] Although there is no evidence for any influence of Nietzsche upon Wilde or vice-versa, Brown, reflecting a late twentieth-century appreciation of the German philosopher in the genealogy of both existentialism and post-structuralism, emphasizes the similarities between the two thinkers.

Brown notes Wilde's ethical commitment to socialism as the political system which would enable the fullest development of individualism but also suggests that he saw "the aesthetic limitations of the socialist vision, its tendency to bypass the question of art" at the same time that he sought "a solution that would satisfy both ethical and aesthetic imperatives."[41]

Brown argues that Wilde's "ethical aesthetic" also led him to embrace "what he called 'cosmopolitan criticism,'" and with it the cultures of other nations. Importantly, for Brown, "Wilde's cosmopolitanism was therefore dialectical in nature, in a sense which Wilde, as a reader of Hegel, would most likely appreciate, even though he himself did not take up this term."[42] In fact, Wilde did use the terms "dialectic" and "dialectical" extensively in his Commonplace Book, and he mentions "dialectics" and "Dialectic" in "The Rise of Historical Criticism" (1199, 1225) but it is not a major term in his later critical essays. His famous reference is instead to Hegel's "system of contraries" in "The Truth of Masks" (1078).

While Brown acknowledges Wilde's Hegelian formation, she emphasizes a different tradition of German and continental philosophical influence from Kant and Schiller to Kierkegaard and Nietzsche, one that, she argues, connects Wildean thought with "the preeminent cosmopolitan artist-critics of this century, Benjamin and Adorno."[43] There is only scant evidence that Wilde could have been influenced by Schiller; for example, one passing reference to him in the Commonplace Book, in regard to Euripides, who, Wilde says, "occupied great poets as Shelley, Schiller, Browning with the task of translating him."[44] Brown has no evidence for her claim that Wilde read Schiller's *Letters on Aesthetic Education*.[45] Her argument, then, often relies upon comparison and insightful assertion of similarities between Wilde and another writer in regard to "ethical aestheticism." For example, conceding that Wilde could not have read Kierkegaard's *Either/Or*, Brown nevertheless suggests that "it speaks to his predicament more than almost any other work" because it poses the problem of reconciling ethics and aesthetics in the sense of "how to give one's 'life' the meaning of 'art.'"[46]

Brown has some warrant for claiming the influence of other nineteenth-century writers upon the formation of Wilde's cosmopolitanism. She credits Kant's "rational ideal of self development" for helping shape Wilde's utopian idea of a fulfilled individualism under socialism.[47] There is evidence in the college notebooks and in other remarks that Wilde had read Kant, but nothing which conclusively shows he knew Kant's *Critique of Pure Reason* or the other essays which, Brown argues, contain ideas which Wilde later parallels or repeats. Brown also sees influential ideas in the writings of Baudelaire, Carlyle, Mill, Arnold, Newman, Ruskin, and Pater, to whom Wilde refers in several places. Her concern in acknowledging these influences is to build the case for Wilde's ethical aestheticism and she is quite selective in her choice of moments from these writers to point out similarities or differences. Further, while she acknowledges the references to Kant in the notebooks, she does not point out that Wilde noted several of them from indirect sources such as William Wallace's "Prolegomena" to *The Logic of Hegel* and that Wilde's notes from Wallace demonstrate Hegel's philosophical advances over Kant.

When she addresses the similarities and differences between Wilde's and Nietzsche's positions, Brown argues from insights produced by comparison rather than from textual evidence of influence. She asserts that:

> Wilde and Nietzsche inherited the same situation in philosophy: what earlier in the century Engels had called the "despair of reason," its confessed inability to solve the contradictions with which it is ultimately faced. The flaunting of paradox in each writer (what Nietzsche early characterized as a consequence of "logic's biting its own tail") is a function of this despair as well as a bid to master it, just as their shared deployment of aphorism may be seen as a sign of resistance to enter any system.[48]

Brown's comparisons are sometimes compelling, especially when she points out the crucial divergences in initially parallel ideas, such as the ways in which Wilde and Nietzsche similarly but differently attack the utilitarianism and herd morality of the English bourgeoisie: Wilde insists, she says, on an intellectual response to the ethical and material corruption of Victorian society. In the development of a contemplative ethical position for the cosmopolitan critic, she reintegrates Arnold into the genealogy of argument as she shows how Wilde's refinement of Arnold's "disinterestedness" conforms to the cosmopolitan goals of influencing and advancing civilization. Brown cites Arnold's "entire conception of culture as one in which art and criticism are intimately connected to our experiences of life, and in fact determine its quality," as "a crucial precedent" for both Wilde's and Walter Benjamin's ideas of the responsibility of the "artist-critic" for renewing the past in the present.[49]

Brown's readings of some of Wilde's major works briefly but suggestively elucidate her philosophical approach to Wilde's "ethical aesthetic" and its similarities to other approaches. For example, she finds *The Picture of Dorian Gray* to have triple significance, first, as a fulfillment of the Romantic idea of criticism in that it enacts Friedrich Schlegel's demand for a work of criticism to become "an autonomous work of art"; second, as a realization of Wilde's own intentions from "The Decay of Lying" and "The Portrait of Mr. W.H.,"; finally, as an anticipatory exploration of "the modern 'destructive' relation to art such as Benjamin would invoke."[50]

In her short account of the novel there are some sharp observations and applications of both Benjamin's and T.S. Eliot's perceptions, but these insights remain confined within the ethical/aesthetic thematic. There are similarly brief appreciations of "The Soul of Man under Socialism," *Salomé*, *A Woman of No Importance*, *An Ideal Husband*, and *The Importance of Being Earnest* in which the telling comparisons reach forward to the twentieth century, as in her observation that the "vibrating linguistic universe" in the text of *Earnest* "playfully anticipates Benjamin's philosophy of language."[51]

Brown concludes her consideration of Wilde's philosophy of art with a substantial analysis of *De Profundis* which asserts that it is much more than a love letter or a guilty meditation on the figure of Christ: "We shall see that even the more personal utterances in the letter are part of a larger philosophical pattern of recurrence and overcoming."[52] For Brown, the power of this text has to do with the transformational affect of art operating together with the aesthetically receptive and shaping mind of the critic. Here Brown powerfully compares Wilde's ideas to others in the European idealist philosophical tradition in an explication of Wilde's creative understanding of Christ:

> In Wilde, as in Kant (who emphasizes the faculty of "building" or *Bilden*), there is no consciousness of any kind that is purely passive. But neither is the mind simply assertive, arbitrarily imposing its modes of perception onto the subject. These modes are suspended in true creation, as Schiller keeps suggesting in the *Aesthetic Letters*. In the aesthetic state, one is essentially vibrating between activity and passivity; the antitheses as such are suspended. One becomes. One receives *in order* to become; one does not receive in order to consume or simply to mirror.[53]

Therefore, for Wilde as well as Nietzsche, there is no transcendental redemption of the soul through Christ but instead an absorption for individuals of a Christ-like practice of immersion in the material world accompanied by an acceptance of fate, what Nietzsche called *amor fati*, love of fate.

Brown juxtaposes passages from Nietzsche and Wilde to show that for both writers, "To love one's fate is to realize the ultimate interconnectedness of all things, the inconspicuous logic by which the most difficult, harmful and questionable of experiences do not detract from but *complete* the whole."[54] For Wilde, Brown asserts, *De Profundis* signifies a "retrieved personal redemption" and the achievement of his art-in-life itself becomes, in Wilde's language, "a symbol."[55] Seizing upon Wilde's phrase, "What lies before me is my past," Brown meditatively asserts her interpretation of Wilde's philosophical self-realization: that is, Wilde has passed

> beyond what Nietzsche describes as the "profound superficiality" of the Apollonian stance, beyond the world with which Wilde is sometimes associated. . . . Whereas in the comparatively flat Apollonian perspective one willfully becomes what one is not, *amor fati* makes it possible, through entry into a new dynamically interwoven temporality, to "become what one is."[56]

Brown asserts that Wilde's "exalted state of mind" after prison enabled him to understand and identify with the immanent spirit of language, and she argues that such an existential position perhaps helped him deal with the struggle to maintain his artistic identity.[57] Her insistence on understanding Wilde's last years as manifesting a state of redemption causes her to claim, in spite of all Wilde's letters begging for money from his friends, that he scorned any note of pity or self-pity until his death.

In sum, Brown's method of philosophical analysis assertively reads Wilde's life and works and compares him to other thinkers based on similarities among ideas. With "ethical aestheticism" as her central concept, she sees the existential development of cosmopolitan criticism in Wilde as an analogue to Nietzschean thought and as an anticipation of Benjamin. Brown's claims for interpretive coherence in this account of Wilde are sustained by an argument which, while it occasionally mentions divergent or alternate views, does not try to account for them by incorporation or argument to the contrary. Nevertheless, Brown sustains an enlightening comparative interpretation which provides some striking insights.

In contrast, Bruce Bashford's style of exposition and argument in *Oscar Wilde: The Critic as Humanist* carefully includes and weighs evidence and arguments for and against his claims about Wilde as a subjectivist critic who assumes that "meanings are always *someone's*, are always attached to or embodied in a person."[58] He explains and deploys both rhetorical and critical theories which he uses in close and substantial readings of "The Decay of Lying," "The Critic as Artist," "The Portrait of Mr. W.H.," "The Rise of Historical Criticism," and *De Profundis*. His narrow focus enhances the depth of his engagement with the critical issues of his philosophical approach to Wilde. His purpose is to exhibit

Wilde's capacity and agility as a thinker and writer of texts which set forth theories; he proposes a definition of humanism that shows how Wilde "reconciles the traditional tenets of humanism with intellectual commitments not obviously compatible with those tenets."[59]

On the controversy over Wilde's consistency of thought, Bashford argues that "though Wilde's critical writings do share common concerns and nearly all have a common starting point, they explore these concerns in ways which must finally be distinguished."[60] Bashford has carefully studied the Oxford notebooks, Wilde's major and minor texts, and other philosophical approaches to the criticism. He does not agree with the Smith/Helfand proposal for a Hegelian-Darwinian synthesis but his interpretation of Wilde's critical theory as subjectivism sustains a claim for consistency: "In my view the sign that Wilde does think consistently within single works is that one *can* reconstruct the theories implicit in these works."[61]

Bashford's overture to Wilde as critic is a short chapter on "Interpretation and the Self in 'The Portrait of Mr. W.H.'" which introduces a version of hermeneutic theory important to Wilde's criticism. In the story of an explanation for the composition of Shakespeare's sonnets:

> each time someone is convinced of the theory, he believes that there is evidence that would support it. . . . But the story insists that inspiration is fundamental to persuasion by implying that being in an inspired state is a prerequisite for recognizing the strength of evidence.[62]

Since the source of interpretive inspiration in the story is the soul, which has an existence independent of the mind, it raises the question of the relationship, especially for a critic, between the conscious deliberations of the mind and the subconscious (and, in the story, controllingly powerful) inspirations of the soul, especially if it is someone else's soul. Bashford poses the question of the soul's authority versus the mind's as a challenge to subjectivist criticism and also as a way of encountering the issue of creative works as criticism in themselves.

In the following chapter on the critical dialogues, Bashford elucidates the roles of culture and judgment in the fashioning of Wilde's subjectivist critical position, showing Wilde's focus upon the relationship between the formal qualities of an artwork and the possibilities for a critic's own expressive potentialities. This explanation leads him to distinguish significantly between the influence of the soul over a critic's interpretation in the theory in "The Portrait of Mr. W.H." and the powerful influence of inherited racial experience over the critic in the dialogues. Bashford shows how Wilde, speaking through his interlocutor, Gilbert, carefully places the experience of the soul, the transmission of racial experience, in conversation with the faculty of judgment in the conscious mind:

> The imagination as Gilbert conceives it, then, plays a role in the theory of the dialogues both important and limited: important in that its link to our shared race experience provides an entry into the works of others and limited in that it is preparatory to the full exercise of the critical faculty. By giving the imagination this role, Wilde has found a way to turn the plurality of the experiences that the imagination carries from a danger to an asset: rather than threatening the critic's self-possession, this variety now insures that she will have the maximal opportunity to use the expressions of others as occasions for her own self-realization.[63]

Bashford turns next to *De Profundis*, where he shows that Gilbert's reconciliation of soul and judgment in the dialogue is called into question by the letter's revisions of the earlier theory. Bashford points out that "for the Wilde of the dialogues, the process of taking on form contains a push toward pure intelligibility, and his theory as a whole traces how the reflexive action of his basic principle becomes in the ideal critic a godlike self-awareness of her own activity."[64] However, in *De Profundis*, the soul as carrier of experience becomes much more enigmatic: "Wilde's revision of his thought in *De Profundis* makes it difficult even to set forth a position to be questioned. He decides – or feels forced – to move his principle further within the individual."[65] Therefore, Bashford argues, the subjectivist theory in the letter has some unsettling similarities to that presented in "Mr. W.H." since "in both works the determinant of a person's identity is the soul, a soul encountered in a region below that of the artistic or cultural forms."[66] For Bashford, then, the letter marks a third important variant of Wilde's subjectivist theory. Bashford argues effectively that all three are coherent in themselves and are also related expressions of the same general theory.

Wilde's coherence as a thinker also appears in the means and modes of presentation he employs. Bashford approaches the rhetorical purpose of paradoxes in Wilde's critical dialogues using Chaim Perelman's rhetorical theory of philosophical pairs in reversal arguments in comparison with Jonathan Dollimore's analysis of ideological binaries. He shows that Perelman's more formal analysis is a better mode to demonstrate the rationality of Wilde's arguments than Dollimore's ideology critique. In doing so, Bashford proposes an important revision to critical understanding of the Hegelian coda to "The Truth of Masks." Critics, including Smith and Helfand, have used the term "dialectical" to describe Wilde's thought, and have referred to this passage as one of a number of substantiating instances. As Bashford notes, "the mention of the dialecticians Plato and Hegel here might suggest that Wilde's habits as a thinker, especially his interest in contradictions and paradoxes, derive from a special theory of logic, one with a metaphysical ground."[67] Bashford insists that close attention must be paid to Wilde's limiting phrase:

> while this passage is often cited as expressing Wilde's general view of thought, a closer look shows that it is actually making a more limited point: "*only in art criticism*" is the contradictory of a truth also true. . . . Rather than deriving critical discourse from a special, metaphysically grounded logic, Wilde's addendum actually says that it is the realm of art and criticism that gives Plato's theory of forms and Hegel's system of contraries whatever application they have[68] (emphasis in original).

Wilde may be a dialectician, Bashford concedes, but he is a rhetorical rather than a metaphysical one who capably presents, in "The Decay of Lying," an argument focused around opposing philosophical pairs which is organized in a rhetorically dialectical manner.

Having established Wilde as subjectivist critic and rhetorical dialectician, Bashford turns in the second half of his book to consider Oscar Wilde as a humanist, beginning with the difficult task of defining the term heuristically. For Bashford, the salient characteristics are the humanist ideas which are often identified and sometimes dismissed as "rhetorical commonplaces": "In fact, I think they are a kind of commonplace yet to be identified as a distinct type and one way to develop my suggestion for defining humanism is to explore the likenesses and differences between rhetorical and humanist commonplaces."[69] Bashford concedes that humanist commonplaces do not constitute a philosophy because they could be developed in different ways with different emphases, that is to say, "humanism is a potential *source* of a philosophy" (emphasis in original) and its commonplaces can be worked and reinterpreted to have value for humanists of different stripes.[70]

Bashford bases his argument for Wilde as a humanist on the differences between modes of argument and explanation in Wilde's "The Rise of Historical Criticism" (1879) and "The Critic as Artist" (1891). He shows that "The Rise" presents a strong case for the power of historical criticism as an activity related to the discourses of Enlightenment rationality and natural science which themselves "stress the cognitive rigor of this power.

. . . Again, what he is describing there is the imagination as a source of explanatory concepts, its role in a total act of mind that is directed toward verifiable truth."[71] Bashford contends that Wilde's view in this early essay assigns such power to the regularity of the laws governing historical development that human capacity for free will, choice, and action are compromised. In contrast, Bashford reasons, "The Critic as Artist" and "The Decay of Lying" present a fundamentally different interpretation of the individual power of the critic: "To put this line of conjecture in wiser terms, these differences between 'The Rise' and the dialogues indicate that in the latter Wilde turns in a different direction at what I called . . . a nodal point, a point where he has to make a basic choice concerning his version of humanism."[72]

In his analysis of "The Critic as Artist," Bashford explains the crucial difference it makes for Wilde to have Gilbert claim that the critic is creative and that no artist is as creative as the critic: the humanist critic, empowered by the faculty of judgment, becomes independent of the power of the primary work and, in creating an interpretation, the humanist critic adds the moods, passions, and imagination which, in Wilde's famous formulation, turn criticism into "the only civilised form of autobiography" (1125). Further, Bashford connects ideas from the Oxford notebooks concerning poetic versatility to the demonstrable power of the versatile humanist critic to appreciate and interpret newly from artistic objects of a complex modern culture: "The critic, who does not do but judges, and who is versatile enough to appreciate everything, clearly occupies the position of the humanist."[73]

Bashford's approach to Wilde depends upon an encyclopedic knowledge of the critical positions adopted by the interlocutors of the dialogues and "Mr. W.H." as well as those argued in the essays. His analysis also brings rhetorical theory to bear in illuminating ways to help discriminate among crucial differences in interpretation such as the much-debated Hegelian coda of "The Truth of Masks." Finally, his analysis helps to shine a different light upon Wilde's critical positions by recasting them in terms of the commonplaces of humanism and by showing Wilde's considerable sophistication as a critical theorist.

The promise of further serious work on Wilde from philosophical approaches seems strong, especially since several of the major strands of Wildean interpretation, which have produced the Irish Wilde, the gay Wilde, and the materialist Wilde as writer for profit, have yet to be significantly connected to the Wilde who read Hegel, Darwin, Kant and a host of other philosophers and thinkers and who imagined a critical theory, or theories, which included a system of contraries and a creative role for the critic.

My critical position remains committed to the philosophical approach. It is based upon my understanding of Wilde's texts and of their intertexts, especially those connected to his education and later reading, as well as upon biographical evidence. I recognize that Wilde valued the rewards of remuneration and public notoriety and that he sought them through writing as well as the public performance of his several personae. However, I contend that his reasons for writing and the evidence in his texts also show that he wrote out of an intellectual commitment to philosophical and scientific positions, social convictions, and ethical and aesthetic beliefs which developed over the course of his education and career as a writer and which are expressed in many, if not most, of the major texts in his *oeuvre*. As I have shown, other critics and scholars have shared this philosophical approach since the first publication of Wilde's writing; their contributions over the history of Wildean interpretation continue to yield important insights.

notes

1. The edition of Wilde's notebooks which Michael Helfand and I edited contains an extensive commentary on Wilde's education and its influence on his life and works to which this brief summary is indebted. Philip E. Smith II and Michael S. Helfand, *Oscar Wilde's Oxford Notebooks: A Portrait of Mind in the Making* (New York: Oxford University Press, 1989). Additional information on the shaping importance of philology and philosophy in late Victorian education and poetics may be found in Linda Dowling's *Language and Decadence in the Victorian Fin de Siecle* (Princeton: Princeton University Press, 1986).
2. Lewis R. Farnell, *An Oxonian Looks Back* (London: Martin Hopkinson, 1934), 43.
3. See Linda Dowling, *Hellenism and Homosexuality in Victorian Oxford* (Ithaca and London: Cornell University Press, 1994); Richard Jenkyns, *The Victorians and Ancient Greece* (Cambridge, MA: Harvard University Press, 1980); and Frank M. Turner, *The Greek Heritage in Victorian Britain* (New Haven, CT: Yale University Press, 1981).
4. Smith and Helfand, op. cit., 33–34 and *passim.*
5. Karl Beckson, ed. *Oscar Wilde: The Critical Heritage* (London: Routledge & Kegan Paul, 1970), 206–207.
6. Ibid., 208–209.
7. Max Nordau, *Degeneration* (Lincoln: University of Nebraska Press, 1993), 443–444.
8. Richard Ellmann, ed., *The Artist as Critic: Critical Writings of Oscar Wilde* (New York: Vintage, 1970), x.
9. Smith and Helfand, op. cit., 53.

10. Ian Small, *Oscar Wilde Revalued: An Essay on New Materials & Methods of Research* (Greensboro, North Carolina: ELT Press, 1993), 3. Ian Small's useful guide and its supplement, along with Melissa Knox's guide and Thomas Mikolyzk's bibliography are all indispensable tools for research; each has its idiosyncrasies and shortcomings but altogether they help scholars and critics to locate and assess critical articles and books as well as manuscript materials: Small, *Oscar Wilde Revalued,* op. cit. and *Oscar Wilde: Recent Research, a Supplement to "Oscar Wilde Revalued"* (Greensboro, NC: ELT Press, 2000); Melissa Knox, *Oscar Wilde in the 1990s: The Critic as Creator* (Rochester, NY: Camden House, 2001); and Thomas A. Mikolyzk, comp. *Oscar Wilde: An Annotated Bibliography* (Westport, CT and London: Greenwood Press, 1993).
11. Small, *Supplement,* op. cit., 12.
12. Ibid., 13.
13. Josephine Guy and Ian Small, *Oscar Wilde's Profession: Writing and the Culture Industry in the Late Nineteenth Century* (Oxford: Oxford University Press, 2000), 12.
14. J.E. Chamberlin, *Ripe Was the Drowsy Hour: The Age of Oscar Wilde* (New York: The Seabury Press, 1977), xii–xiii.
15. Ibid., 78.
16. Ibid., 79.
17. Ibid., 109.
18. Ibid., 109.
19. Ibid., 115.
20. Ibid., 151.
21. Smith and Helfand, op. cit., 149.
22. Chamberlin, op. cit., 184–185.
23. Rodney Shewan, *Oscar Wilde: Art and Egotism* (New York: Barnes & Noble, 1977), 6.
24. Ibid., 3.
25. Ibid., 3.
26. Ibid., 3.
27. Ibid., 5.
28. Ibid., 19.
29. Ibid., 22.
30. Ibid., 24.
31. Ibid., 52.
32. Ibid., 197.
33. Richard Ellmann, *Oscar Wilde* (London: Hamish Hamilton, 1987).
34. Regenia Gagnier, *Idylls of the Marketplace: Oscar Wilde and the Victorian Public* (Stanford, California: Stanford University Press, 1986).
35. Ian Small, *Conditions for Criticism: Authority, Knowledge, and Literature in the Late Nineteenth Century* (Oxford: Clarendon Press of Oxford University Press, 1991).
36. Michael Patrick Gillespie, *Oscar Wilde and the Poetics of Ambiguity* (Gainesville, FL: University Press of Florida, 1996).
37. Julia Prewitt Brown, *Cosmopolitan Criticism: Oscar Wilde's Philosophy of Art* (Charlottesville and London: University Press of Virginia, 1997), xiv.
38. Ibid., xv.
39. Ibid., xv.

40. Ibid., 51.
41. Ibid., xiii–xiv.
42. Ibid., xiii–xiv.
43. Ibid., xviii.
44. Smith and Helfand, op. cit., 132.
45. Brown, op. cit., 17.
46. Ibid., 18.
47. Ibid., 32.
48. Ibid., 58.
49. Ibid., 74.
50. Ibid., 77.
51. Ibid., 89.
52. Ibid., 95.
53. Ibid., 98.
54. Ibid., 102–103.
55. Ibid., 103.
56. Ibid., 104.
57. Ibid., 105.
58. Bruce Bashford, *Oscar Wilde: The Critic as Humanist* (Madison, NJ and London: Fairleigh Dickinson University Press and Associated University Presses, 1999), 11.
59. Ibid., 11.
60. Ibid., 11.
61. Ibid., 12.
62. Ibid., 24–25.
63. Ibid., 44.
64. Ibid., 52.
65. Ibid., 52.
66. Ibid., 52–53.
67. Ibid., 66.
68. Ibid., 66.
69. Ibid., 81.
70. Ibid., 84.
71. Ibid., 93.
72. Ibid., 102.
73. Ibid., 123.

7
religion

patrick r. o'malley

> "But we preach Christ crucified, unto the Jews a stumbling-block, and unto the Greeks foolishness."
>
> 1 Corinthians 1.23

In a life perhaps still more famous for its scandals than for its works, Wilde's deepest scandal – as perhaps it has ever been – is the scandal of the Cross. Indeed, Wilde's obsession with religion throughout his life reminds us that by far the earliest uses of the English word "scandal" refer to religion rather than sexuality; the *Oxford English Dictionary* does not cite the term's modern implication of "damage to reputation" until the late sixteenth century, but it does note that as early as the thirteenth century, "scandal" did suggest the "conduct, on the part of a religious person, which brings discredit on religion. Also, perplexity of conscience occasioned by the conduct of one who is looked up to as an example." Wilde's scandalous religious yearnings are both: they challenge religious orthodoxy even as they serve as stumbling-block to those who would read Wilde as the prophet of a gleefully atheistic queerness.

That religion is a specter haunting Wilde criticism seems clear simply from glancing at the titles of the various literary biographies that the past century has produced. There is Frank Harris' 1916 *Oscar Wilde: His Life and Confessions*; there is Boris Brasol's 1938 *Oscar Wilde: The Man, the Artist, the Martyr*; there is John Stokes' 1996 *Oscar Wilde: Myths, Miracles, and Imitations*. Yet just as clear is the way in which that specter vanishes, in which the titles usually represent a rhetorical provocation that the texts themselves rarely develop. While interest in Wilde's religion will speak its name, it typically has nothing else to say. This avoidance of sustained analysis of religion in Wilde's life and work seems all the more strange for the recurrent – and overt – obsession with the fundamental questions of theology and scriptural representation present in all the genres that Wilde produced, including the short story ("The Fisherman and His Soul," for example), drama (*Salomé* and the unfinished *Cardinal of Avignon* and *La Sainte Courtesane*), poetry ("E Tenebris," "Ave Maria Gratia Plena," "On Hearing the *Dies Irae* Sung in the Sistine Chapel," to name only a few), longer narrative (*The Picture of Dorian Gray*), and essay ("The Soul of Man under Socialism," *De Profundis*). Wilde flaunts religion even more consistently than he does sexuality or Irishness, but criticism – like a Victorian society through a distorting looking glass – has apparently registered its disapproval largely by choosing to overlook it.[1]

The outlines of Wilde's religious biography are relatively straightforward, if marked by the same ambivalences and ironies that touched the other parts of his life. Both of his mother's grandfathers were Anglican clergymen, and she was related to Charles Maturin who, although now primarily known as the author of *Melmoth the Wanderer*, also held the more respectable profession of curate of St. Peter's in Dublin. Both of Oscar Wilde's uncles on his father's side were also clergymen in the Church of Ireland. William Wilde's nationalistic inclinations did not comprehend Papism, but Speranza's did, and despite her solid Church of Ireland roots, her flair for the dramatic seems to have attracted her to Roman Catholicism;[2] the biographer Richard Ellmann relates that Oscar and his brother Willie were baptized into the Church of Ireland but baptized again (in an unregistered ceremony) by the Roman Catholic priest Father L.C. Prideaux Fox when Oscar was a boy, a rechristening that Ellmann sees as suggesting those planned in *The Importance of Being Earnest*.[3] Immediately upon his release from prison, Wilde contacted the Jesuit community in London, asking to spend a six-month retreat with them, a request which was denied on the grounds that he had not spent a full year of discernment before taking this step.[4] And at the end, after a lifelong series of flirtations with Roman Catholicism, Wilde (who had asserted that "Catholicism is the only religion to die in"[5]) converted to Rome, receiving the Sacraments of Baptism, Extreme Unction, and Absolution at the hands of Father Cuthbert Dunne, a priest native to Dublin but living in Paris and serving at the Passionate Church of St. Joseph.[6]

For Ellmann, this final conversion is of dubious religious value: "The application of sacred oils to his hands and feet may have been a ritualized pardon for his omissions or commissions, or may have been like putting a green carnation in his buttonhole."[7] Significantly, neither of Ellmann's options leaves open the possibility of sincerity; both read Wilde's religion solely as *style*, whether the stylized forms of ritual or the stylized forms of aesthetic dandyism. A conversion that is a "ritualized pardon for his omissions or commissions" leaves Wilde's own subjectivity entirely out of the equation, focusing instead on the decision of the Church to bind or loose. And indeed, Ellmann emphasizes that Wilde may have *had* no volition in this final conversion. He thus cites Robert Ross's later uncertainty about Wilde's awareness of his surroundings ("He was never able to speak and we do not know whether he was altogether conscious"[8]) rather than Father Dunne's more definitive account ("Indeed I was fully satisfied that he understood me when told that I was about to receive him into the Catholic Church and give him the Last Sacraments. From the signs he gave as well as from his attempted words, I was satisfied as to his full consent"[9]) or even Ross's own second-guessing description immediately following Wilde's death, a description that stresses that Wilde had asked for a priest considerably before his death: "You know I had always promised to bring a priest to Oscar when he was dying, and I felt rather guilty that I had so often dissuaded him from becoming a Catholic, but you know my reasons for doing so."[10]

The tendency to downplay or even erase the significance of religion in Wilde's life is most evident in analyses that read Wilde first and foremost as a forerunner of modern homosexuality; religious readings of Wilde similarly tend to consider his sexuality almost allegorically. There is, of course, no necessary reason why a critical essay of a particular methodology should have to address all possible other angles; analyses of Wildean irony, for example, are not in all cases obliged to consider sexuality or nation.[11] Yet since virtually all of the texts that take Wilde's religion as a central question focus most intensely on *De Profundis*, there is an element of the perverse not to consider perversity itself, especially since it was Wilde's trial on the charges of "acts of gross indecency with another male person" that landed him in prison in the first place and thus provided the impetus for the composition of that monumental essay-letter. The blindness in the other direction – toward religion by critics interested first and foremost in sexuality – is more justifiable, although it necessitates that those critics gloss over large parts of the Wildean *oeuvre*. It is also, I think, a misguided oversight, as I will argue, since it necessarily distorts the complexity of Wilde's notion of sexuality often in the interests of an ideological purity which wants to read Wilde's work (at least the best of Wilde's work) as fundamentally progressive and religion (particularly Catholicism) as incompatibly and irredeemably reactionary.

Among the queer-theoretical works that actually address Wilde's relationship to religion, there are two major and largely contradictory trends. There is, on the one hand, an understanding of Roman Catholicism as structurally aligned with (albeit theologically opposed to) homoerotics through its establishment of an all-male, at least nominally celibate priesthood, which in practice provided cover for men who did not desire to marry women. On the other hand, there is a different, even opposing strand of criticism which (in stressing theology) comprehends Catholicism as fundamentally opposed to the interests of homoerotically-inclined men such as Wilde. Joseph Bristow's book, *Effeminate England: Homoerotic Writing after 1885*, is an important example of the first of these trends. It dedicates some pages to Ronald Firbank's appreciation of the perversity of Catholic ritual and refers to John Henry Newman and John Francis Bloxam as forebears in developing a notion of Ritualist Anglicanism or Roman Catholicism as particularly attractive to "men with homoerotic interests," but Wilde's implication in this same combination of attractions remains unanalyzed.[12] James Eli Adams brings a similar reading of Anglo and Roman Catholicism to an analysis of Wilde himself; for Adams, Wilde's interest in the Oxford Movement and Newman's own conversion to Catholicism is as much "structural" as it is theological:

> The Tractarians offered the model of an elite brotherhood that defined itself through the possession of arcane (and presumably unorthodox) wisdom or values. That same structure helps to explain the popularity of later Tractarianism, or "ritualism," among gay men. . . . It was not just theology that led Wilde to repeatedly request the works of Newman for his reading material in prison: the structure of Tractarian reserve parallels in remarkable detail Wilde's preoccupation with the double life, another extremely exacting mode of masculine discipline.[13]

Later, Adams observes that "The appeal of social exclusivity joined with the energetic consciousness of danger certainly helps to explain Wilde's fascination with various forms of secret societies, including the Catholicism with which he flirted throughout his life."[14]

Adams's suggestion that it is "not just theology" that guides Wilde's reading in prison implies that the motivation is at least in part theological, but Adams's book focuses almost exclusively *on* structure rather than theology (even unorthodox theology). Eve Kosofsky Sedgwick, in *Epistemology of the Closet*, likewise provides a compelling reading of Roman Catholicism's relationship to nineteenth- (and twentieth-) century structures of gay desire primarily by reading Catholicism as image largely divorced from theology:

> Catholicism in particular is famous for giving countless gay and proto-gay children the shock of the possibility of adults who don't marry, of men in dresses, of passionate theatre, of introspective investment, of lives filled with what could, ideally without diminution, be called the work of the fetish. . . . And presiding over all are the images of Jesus. These have, indeed, a unique position in modern culture as images of the unclothed or unclothable male body, often in extremis and/or in ecstasy, prescriptively meant to be gazed at and adored.[15]

This is undoubtedly true and it usefully condenses what is rather mystified in such early accounts of the relationship of (Anglo-) Catholicism to homoerotics as David Hilliard's "Unenglish and Unmanly: Anglo-Catholicism and Homosexuality."[16] Nonetheless it still constructs Catholicism primarily as *pretext* for homosexuality; we are thrilled by the spectacular body of Christ first and foremost because it *is* a male body. Religion and sexuality here largely collapse into *one* phenomenon, the phenomenon of sexuality.

In contrast, by explicitly *opposing* Catholicism to same-sex desire, Jonathan Dollimore provides a strongly articulated version of the second of the trends that I have identified in analyses of the queer Wilde.[17] In *Sexual Dissidence: Augustine to Wilde, Freud to Foucault*, Dollimore argues that Wilde's *De Profundis* provides the quintessential example of a retreat from potentially progressive politics into reaction: "written in prison, [*De Profundis*] involves a conscious renunciation of his transgressive aesthetic and a reaffirmation of tradition as focused in the depth model of identity."[18] Dollimore continues:

> This may be seen as that suffering into truth, that redemptive knowledge pointing to the transcendent realization of self beyond the social, so cherished within idealist culture. Those who see *De Profundis* as Wilde's most mature work, and equate maturity with renunciation and expiation, often interpret it thus. It can be regarded differently, as a containment, a tragic defeat of the kind which only ideological coercion, reinforced by overt brutality, can effect.[19]

For Dollimore, it is not the focus on Christ *per se* that marks *De Profundis* as deeply reactionary, but its renunciation of perverse surfaces for an ideology of depth, of self-constructed identity for an appeal to essence: "It leads me to speculate that had Wilde escaped incarceration and turned his transgressive aesthetic on Christianity, and created his oppositional

Christ, it might just have been not the supreme instance of containment, not a fatal 'essentialist' complicity, but his most radical work."[20]

Dollimore is not explicit in naming those critics who read *De Profundis* as a happy triumph over perversity rather than a retreat in the face of ideological oppression, but that reading is still probably the dominant strain among those critics who take religion, rather than sexuality or nation or rhetorical style, as the principal term of Wilde's literary production. Philip K. Cohen, for instance, manifests the privileging of redemptive suffering that Dollimore sees in conservative criticism:

> The chaos of conflicting views present in the play [*The Importance of Being Earnest*] and scenarios [*Love is Law* and *The Cardinal of Avignon*] of 1894 amply documents the state of inner dissonance and fragmentation in which Wilde entered the trials and prison. But he left Reading Gaol on May 19, 1897, with a thoroughly integrated vision of God, self, and society. . . . [I]n *De Profundis* he reveals his discovery of authenticity as the only viable basis for identity and states his intention to re-create himself.[21]

For Cohen's reading, as for Dollimore's later analysis, a type of orthodoxy in religion trumps "perversity," although that term has here a radically different valuation. For Cohen, homosexuality represents not the potentially radical glories of self-construction but the depths of depravity: "the result of Wilde's relationship with Douglas can be viewed as the issue of perverse sexuality, or the weak-willed artist's surrender to life's lure," although Cohen also (strangely) sees it as a compassionate sacrifice on Wilde's part to Douglas's "sins."[22] Wilde's suffering is, in Cohen's account, absolutely necessary for his redemption.[23] And, as Dollimore rightly notes, this suffering depends upon a new model of identity based both on depth and on a fundamentally reactionary acceptance of "tradition" as a good in itself: "Wilde's ideal of saintly individualism through the imitation of Christ supplied simultaneously a selfhood generated from within, a typological identity endorsed by tradition, and a social identity."[24] It is a rejection of Wilde's own past, a past that saw identity as the product of shifting surfaces: "the term *mask*, which recurs throughout *De Profundis*," Cohen asserts, "always bears connotations of falsity and deception."[25]

Continuing this essentialist religious (and fundamentally homophobic) reading of Wilde, Guy Willoughby, in *Art and Christhood: The Aesthetics of Oscar Wilde*, published 15 years after Cohen's study, consistently euphemizes Wilde's sexuality, transforming it into merely one more vague occasion for an approach to Christ. In *De Profundis*, Willoughby claims,

"Wilde is suggesting that, by accepting all his punishing experience with full humility, he will attain the complex perfection that only Christ, and his most imaginative and selfless followers, have ever achieved."[26] Willoughby notes Wilde's residence at Reading Gaol only as the opportunity of writing *De Profundis*, as though it were a sort of religious retreat sought out for its spiritual amenities; the circumstances of his imprisonment, the ideological violence against male–male sexuality that motivated both Queensberry's vicious attacks on Wilde and the Court's ultimate imprisonment of him, vanish completely. Douglas – after all, the addressee of *De Profundis* – hardly appears at all in Willoughby's reading, and when he does, it is either as typologically representative of sinners generally ("Like Jesus, the writer has been faced with 'the hard Hedonists ... those who waste their freedom in becoming slaves to things,' as vividly personified in the person of Lord Alfred Douglas"[27]) or – weirdly – as a trope of nineteenth-century religious controversy ("His traumatic relationship with Alfred Douglas has become, like Charles Kingsley's accusations of Dr. Newman, the occasion for a new definition of the Christlike self"[28]). Like Cohen, however, Willoughby sees in *De Profundis* the culmination of a life's work that comes ever closer to a redemptive understanding both of the role of suffering in the world and of true identity as deeply essential:

> Not only do the subjects of Christ and the "Artistic life" combine in *De Profundis* itself, but the stories, dramas, and parables examined in this study presage these more explicit formulations. Under different species of plot, genre, and setting, each fable confirms that individual realization depends, ultimately, on a full and unabashed knowledge of the intrinsic pain and reversal of human existence; that true beauty or completeness of self begins in the denial of the superficial attractions that the world may offer in place of human involvement; and that Christ is the archetype for this acknowledgment and the mode of life that flows from it.[29]

Similarly, in an essay published the year after Willoughby's, Ronald Schuchard reads Wilde's conversion as a repudiation of the "devouring sin" of lust.[30] Schuchard, however, situates this conversion not in the years of Reading Gaol but as early as the 1880s: "Though Wilde was to convert his own religious inversions into the stuff of his art, he kept his aesthetic mask marvelously intact, however bankrupt and destructive he now knew aestheticism, as a philosophy, to be."[31] Schuchard is more forthright than Willoughby about the "sins" he sees represented – and repudiated – in Wilde's work, including *Salomé*'s "veritable cauldron of unholy loves – homoerotic, promiscuous, incestuous, lustful."[32] But to Schuchard, this decadence itself is, for Wilde, a mask hiding the artist's authentic religious convictions that would, despite the temptations of his "distasteful public homosexuality,"[33] find their telos (as they do also in Willoughby's analysis) in the expiatory suffering of imprisonment. In Schuchard's account, the true tragedy is not Wilde's brutal punishment or the homophobic culture that supported it, but the fact that Wilde had so convincingly played the *part* of the aesthete that his friends could not immediately recognize "his desperate cries for faith."[34]

It should be observed that Dollimore's analysis, like that of the critics he opposes, reads Wilde's life and work as a type of trajectory with *De Profundis* its telos. From one perspective, religion (as manifested in *De Profundis*) represents a maturation into the "truth" of redemption; from the other, it is the containment of a deliciously transgressive constructivism. Neither position really allows for the possibility of the sort of strategic essentialism articulated by Diana Fuss in *Essentially Speaking*, two years before the publication of *Sexual Dissidence*:[35] "One of the main contentions of this book," Fuss asserts there, "is that essentialism, when held most under suspicion by constructionists, is often effectively doing its work elsewhere, under other guises, and sometimes laying the groundwork for its own critique."[36]

Wilde himself insists, in *De Profundis*, that the letter constitutes neither a radical break from his past nor the teleological culmination of a life increasingly dedicated to Christ through suffering. Yes, he argues that "Suffering – curious as it may sound to you – is the means by which we exist, because it is the only means by which we become conscious of existing" (884), but he *doesn't* here suggest that suffering *changes* existence; on the contrary, because it is the most intense of aesthetic experiences, it is the very condition of *all* existence. In the move from suffering as "the means by which we exist" to "the only means by which we become conscious of existing," Wilde continues to insist that existence – that identity – is constructed out of sensations. Indeed, suffering is necessarily non-teleological, since it arrests time: "Suffering is one long moment. We cannot divide it by seasons. We can only record its moods, and chronicle their return. With us time itself does not progress. It revolves" (904). This is not only the case for suffering, but – Wilde asserts – for life itself: "At every single moment of one's life one is what one is going to be no less than what one has been. Art is a symbol, because man is a symbol" (922). Human existence – like art itself – is a "symbol": timeless, fundamentally anti-teleological. This is why Wilde does not, in this section of *De Profundis*, argue that his works have progressed to deeper and deeper understanding but rather that they all – from the very beginning – manifest the same concerns, even if he himself was not always fully conscious of that. "Of course," he claims, as if pointing out the obvious,

> all this is foreshadowed and prefigured in my art. Some of it is in "The Happy Prince": some of it in "The Young King," notably in the passage where the Bishop says to the kneeling boy, "Is not He who made misery wiser than thou art?" a phrase which when I wrote it seemed to me little more than a phrase: a great deal of it is hidden away in the note of Doom that like a purple thread runs through the gold cloth of *Dorian Gray*: in "The Critic as Artist" it is set forth in many colours: in *The Soul of Man* it is written down simply and in letters too easy to read: it is one of the refrains whose recurring *motifs* make *Salome* so like a piece of music and bind it together as a ballad: in the prose-poem of the man who from the bronze image of the "Pleasure that liveth for a Moment" has to make the image of the "Sorrow that abideth for Ever" it is incarnate. (922)

In the claim of prefiguration, Wilde constructs his entire literary production as a seamless text, indeed a Scripture always continuous and coherent even if we have occasionally seen it only through a glass darkly.

This is also why, despite some appearances to the contrary, Wilde avers that he is *not* in fact renouncing his life, its desires, or its pleasures: "I don't regret for a single moment having lived for pleasure. I did it to the full, as one should do everything that one does to the full. There was no pleasure I did not experience. . . . But to have continued the same life would have been wrong because it would have been limiting. I had to pass on. The other half of the garden had its secrets for me also" (922). Suffering is one more exquisite experience; *De Profundis* approaches it not as the antitype of Wilde's decadent ethic but as part of its necessary completion. As Frederick S. Roden has compellingly demonstrated, "'The Soul of Man' and *De Profundis* operate as complementary works. They are successive only in chronology."[37] It was, after all, not Douglas but Robert Ross who orchestrated Wilde's deathbed conversion to Catholicism; it was also Ross who, according to Ellmann, introduced Wilde as well to homosexual activity,[38] a convergence that should give pause to critics who see the conversion as the necessary renunciation of the sex.

This is something that some of the best readers of *De Profundis* right after its publication in 1905 themselves observed, although the fact that Ross expurgated the letter to remove direct references to Douglas may certainly have prejudiced the readings.[39] The *Times Literary Supplement* observed of the analysis of Christ in the letter not that it breaks radically from Wilde's past work but that it explicitly continues it: "It bears every trace of his old gift of whimsical invention and embroidery. The rest of the book is studied and overstudied; but this is fresh and spontaneous."[40] George Bernard Shaw read *De Profundis* not as tragic renunciation of Wilde's past but as the triumphant fulfillment of the Wildean comic aesthetic. To Ross, he wrote that

> I am half tempted to cut into the *Saturday Review* correspondence with a letter giving the *comedic* view of *De Profundis*. It is really an extraordinary book, quite exhilarating and amusing as to Wilde himself, and quite disgraceful and shameful to his stupid tormentors. There is pain in it, inconvenience, annoyance, but no real tragedy, all comedy. . . . It annoys me to have people degrading the whole affair to the level of sentimental tragedy. . . . The British press is as completely beaten by him *de profundis* as it was *in excelsis*. . . .[41]

Max Beerbohm, in a remarkably insightful review in *Vanity Fair*, specifically took on the "*De Profundis* is radically different" reading of Wilde: "Some of the critics, wishing to reconcile present enthusiasm with past indifference . . . have been suggesting that *De Profundis* is quite unlike any previous work of Oscar Wilde – a quite sudden and unrelated phenomenon. Oscar Wilde, according to them, was gloriously transformed by incarceration. Their theory comprises two fallacies." The first, claims Beerbohm, is that a passion for "wit" rather than for "beauty" and "thought" was the characteristic element of Wilde's earlier work; the second misreading, he points out, is that *De Profundis* represents a new move to sincerity, what Dollimore reads as its relinquishment of surfaces for depths: "In *De Profundis* was he, at length, expressing something that he really and truly felt? Is the book indeed a heartcry? It is pronounced so by the aforesaid critics. There we have the second fallacy."[42] Beerbohm continues: "Nothing seemed more likely than that Oscar Wilde, smitten down from his rosy-clouded pinnacle, and dragged through the mire, and cast among the flints, would be *diablement changé en route*. Yet lo! he was unchanged. He was still precisely himself. He was still playing with ideas, playing with emotions."[43] This is for Beerbohm the greatness of the letter: "Oscar Wilde was immutable. The fineness of the book as a personal document is in the revelation of a character so strong that no force of circumstance could change it, or even modify it."[44] In describing the effect of *De Profundis* as "revelation," Beerbohm constructs it – in its very *adherence* to the principles of Wilde's aestheticism – as a type of religious experience. And indeed in describing the "humility" of *De Profundis*, Beerbohm himself invokes the Catholic hierarchy in this review, not as the model for the renunciation of the cult of sensational experience but as the very quintessence of that cult:

> And about humility [Wilde] writes many beautiful and true things. And, doubtless, while he wrote them, he had the sensation of humility. . . . The attitude was struck, and the heart pulsated to it. Perhaps a Cardinal Archbishop, when he kneels to wash the feet of the beggars, is filled with humility, and revels in the experience. Such was Oscar Wilde's humility. It was the luxurious complement of pride.[45]

In its reference to critics who construct a gap between the early works and *De Profundis* in the interest of "reconcil[ing] present enthusiasm with past indifference," Beerbohm's reading compellingly identifies the root of the difficulties that have dogged analyses of Wilde's representation of religion: a fundamental discomfort with paradox. For many critics who read Wilde first and foremost as the herald of sexual liberation, his interest in religion – specifically in Catholicism – is embarrassing. For many of those who read him as fundamentally a religiously orthodox man, his homosexuality is a scandal. We want to imagine that those authors whose work we like would agree with our cultural politics – particularly in terms of sex and religion – and the untidy paradoxes of history and biography then have to give way to critical narratives that produce that happy amity.

It is hard for us to believe that Wilde may very well have had attractions simultaneously to Catholicism and to other men, both sincere and both subject to irony. As James Winchell has powerfully argued of Wilde's self-presentation in *De Profundis*, "these two 'opposites' do not oppose each other: the expiatory legend – as scapegoat and redeemer – precisely elaborates the problem of the public life of the self-referential dandy."[46] Winchell's reading of *De Profundis* rejects the binary between religious and sexual experience, pointing out that "the synthesis, for Wilde, will be accomplished by his own substitution for his imprisoned equivalent of excruciated yet autonomous Eros, highly visible, pleasurably crucified, and eternally impervious."[47] For Winchell, this represents a prototype of the "literary schizophrenia of modernity itself: erotic love of desire and ascetic hatred of desire."[48] But Wilde's own letters suggest that Catholicism and sexual transgression are not, for him, necessarily opposed poles fighting over his soul but often surprisingly similar articulations of his resistance to socially-prescribed norms. Thus in 1876, he writes that he is "more than ever in the toils of the Scarlet Woman,"[49] situating the attraction of Roman Catholicism precisely in its figuration as the Whore of Babylon (a rhetorical trope that he used again in 1877[50]). Also in 1876, he writes of attending a Mass by Henry Manning in the language of "fascination": "Yesterday I heard the Cardinal at the Pro-Cathedral preach a charity sermon. He is more fascinating than ever."[51] It is language remarkably prescient of that which, almost 15 years later, Basil Hallward will use for Dorian Gray: "I knew that I had come face to face with some one whose mere personality was so fascinating that, if I allowed it to do so, it would absorb my whole nature, my whole soul, my very art itself" (21). Even when Wilde suggests a disinclination toward Romanism, he frames it as "fascination," as though it were a lover whose embraces he cannot give up: "Still I get so wretched and low and troubled that in some desperate mood I will seek the shelter of a Church which simply enthrals [sic] me by its fascination. . . . *Do* be touched by it, *feel* the awful fascination of the Church, its extreme beauty and sentiment, and let every part of your nature have play and room."[52]

For David Alderson, this conflation of Catholicism and erotics is a matter of the appeal of alterity, of Wilde's resistance to his own Protestantism and attraction to the exotic otherness of Romanism. Alderson quotes another of Wilde's 1876 letters: "I ride sometimes after six, but don't do much but bathe, and although always feeling slightly immortal when in the sea, feel sometimes slightly heretical when good Roman Catholic boys enter the water with little amulets and crosses round their necks and arms that the good S. Christopher may hold them up."[53] Alderson argues that

> Wilde – from a Protestant, Anglo-Irish background, and a student from Oxford who suppressed the signs of his Irishness – finds the alterior appeal of these boys in their apparent freedom and naïve faith. . . . Moreover, the religion and the desire are conflated – Wilde feels "sometimes slightly heretical" in the boys' presence – so that the attractions of sexual and religious "perversion" are collapsed. In this way the sexual desirability of these boys is clearly bound up with their cultural otherness; indeed, this very fact seems to enable the desire.[54]

In Alderson's essay, Wilde's conflation of deviant sexuality and Catholicism is primarily symptomatic of a more fundamental resistance to bourgeois English norms, what Alderson calls "his dissident relations to the dominant culture."[55] Catholicism, in this account, is merely an expendable pretext for a broader cultural critique: "Wilde was attracted to Catholicism only for so long as it seemed to offer the possibility of an alternative to the supposedly rational and unmistakable unaesthetic, deeply conscientious world of Protestantism. . . . Primarily, Catholicism and, by extension, Catholic subjects were symbolically opposed to the constraining world of English puritanism, however wide of the mark this might seem to us."[56]

It is true that Wilde's letters do not – until after his conviction – continue to demonstrate the obsession with an eroticized and deviant Church of Rome that marks those of the late 1870s. But an increasingly complicated understanding of a relationship between Catholicism and sexuality shifts instead to Wilde's literary production, into the space of imaginative fantasy and art itself. As Ellis Hanson has compellingly argued in *Decadence and Catholicism*, Catholicism offered Wilde not the erasure of his homoerotics but its very enactment: "For his dandyism and his aestheticism, there was beautiful ritual and passionate faith. For his taste for scandal, there was a discourse of sin. And for his aesthetic and sexual martyrdom, there was the language of penitence and hagiography."[57] Hanson is one of the few critics of Wilde who have rightly seen in his work a truly productive dialectic between sexuality and religion, and not only in the empty forms of Catholic ritual but in its fully-engaged fulfillment of authentic theology and practice. "[I]f Wilde were simply a 'pagan,' why did he consider conversion so often?" Hanson asks. "Why did he attend Catholic services so often? Why did he return again and again to Christian themes in his work? How could he have written about Christ as sensitively as he did in his prison letter to Douglas? . . . There is ample evidence for Wilde's religious sincerity and Christian faith, just as, to his credit, there is ample evidence for his doubt."[58] Hanson does not, however, like so many critics who take Wilde's religion seriously, read it as fundamentally oppositional to his homosexuality: "Wilde often spoke of Christ and the Church in the same way he spoke of beautiful objects and beautiful boys – in the language of fascination and seduction."[59] If "Faith for Wilde is a passion that concerns itself with the beauty of a religion, not the truth of its doctrines,"[60] that does not make him any less passionate, or indeed, any less engaged with the question of authentic faith. It simply means that his art works through the *question* of faith and authenticity rather than taking it for granted.

This is certainly true in *De Profundis*, but it is also true in *Salomé* (1893) and *The Picture of Dorian Gray* (1890) as well. It is not only the biblical setting of *Salomé* that marks its engagement with the question of religion; were that the case, criticism would certainly be justified in reading religion in this play simply as background, as pretext for a more significant development of erotics. Yet in fact, *Salomé* consistently produces those erotics *as* deeply intertwined with an analysis of religion itself and for its own sake.[61] Sacramental and incarnational religion is not simply the context for a play about sexuality here; sexuality only exists in this play as it emerges precisely *from* a crypto-Catholic religious iconography. Salomé is, in Jokanaan's words, "daughter of Babylon" and "daughter of Sodom" (559), simultaneously the Scarlet Woman of Rome that Wilde wrote of in his letters and the image of deviant sexuality itself. Richard Dellamora has read Salomé's kissing of the head of Jokanaan as symbolic of perverse desire, and that reading is surely correct.[62] But this kiss simultaneously writes that desire *as* Catholicism; we can certainly (as in Sedgwick's interpretation of Catholicism) read the head as fetish, but we can also read it as relic, the only important distinction between these two terms lying in the question of whether there is something "real" behind the curtain of faith.

I would argue that in *Salomé* at least, Wilde proposes that there is, or at least that faith is as real as erotics. The scene where Salomé kisses Jokanaan's head is instructive. Right before she is killed by the soldiers, Salomé muses about the taste of "love" and the taste of blood: "I have kissed thy mouth, Jokanaan, I have kissed thy mouth. There was a bitter taste on my lips. Was it the taste of blood? . . . Nay; but perchance it was the taste of love. . . . They say that love hath a bitter taste . . . But what matter? What matter? I have kissed thy mouth" (575; ellipses in original). It is her last line of the play, followed only by Herod's command that she be killed. Here, the "bitter taste" suggestive of blood evokes again the Whore of Babylon, herself (as Revelations tells us) "drunk with their blood." It further, however, echoes Catholic Eucharistic sacramentalism, where God's love literally embodies itself in Christ's bloody sacrifice, a sacrifice re-enacted in the theatricality of Mass. That the bitterness of "love" might taste like blood in a play that continually evokes the bloody cup of Babylon's abominations suggests that, even in this final moment of the play, Catholicism and sexual transgression mirror each other as variations of perversion and variations of desire.

That same mirror enriches and troubles *Dorian Gray*, which first appeared in *Lippincott's Monthly Magazine* in 1890 and which Wilde revised for publication in book form in 1891. In Wilde's first trial, Edward Carson read a passage describing Basil Hallward's relationship to the portrait: "But, as I worked at it, every flake and film of colour seemed to me to reveal my secret. I grew afraid that the world would know of my idolatry."[63] Carson suggests here that "idolatry," that is, religious transgression and particularly (from the perspective of Protestant iconoclasm) Catholic blasphemy, is relevant to legal proceedings dedicated to the question of whether Wilde was "posing [as a] Somdomite," as the Marquess of Queensberry had suggested. In fact, Carson's rhetorical slippage from sexuality to religion turns out to have its own analog in *Dorian Gray*, where the term "idolatry" itself becomes a sort of *Doppelgänger*, a Dorian Gray from which the scars of darker passions have been displaced. In the novel version, Basil tells Lord Henry of the portrait that "I have put into it some expression of all this curious artistic idolatry, of which, of course, I have never cared to speak to him" (13), but the original *Lippincott* version puts the emphasis on the erotic rather than the sectarian deviance: "Because I have put into it all the extraordinary romance of which, of course, I have never dared to speak to him." In the whitewashing move from magazine to book, the romance that dares not speak its name has become the idolatry that cares not to speak its name. Homoerotics and Catholicism, in Wilde's text, seem to be simply more and less scandalous versions of the same trope, of the same "romance."[64] Dorian, like Basil and Salomé and Wilde himself, has difficulty keeping the rhetorics of religion and erotics separate; after Sybil Vane's death, the narrator, in free indirect discourse, notes that "love would always be a sacrament to him now" (87).

This conflation of sex and religion reaches its climax in the stunning reversal at the end of the novel, which enacts in almost allegorical form the allusions to the Christological Passion already troped in the details of the ecclesiastic robes in Dorian's chests.[65] As Dorian gazes upon the portrait for the last time before he attacks it with his knife, he focuses with increased emphasis upon the blood that has come to stain it:

> The thing was still loathsome – more loathsome, if possible, than before – and the scarlet dew that spotted the hand seemed brighter, and more like blood newly spilt. Then he trembled. Had it been merely vanity that had made him do his own good deed? Or the desire for a new sensation, as Lord Henry had hinted, with his mocking laugh? Or that passion to act a part that sometimes makes us do things finer than we are ourselves? Or, perhaps, all these? And why was the red stain larger than it had been? It seemed to have crept like a horrible disease over the wrinkled fingers. There was blood on the painted feet,

> as though the thing had dripped – blood even on the hand that had not held the knife. (166)

The specifics of the blood stains are significant here: both hands, both feet, precisely the locations of the nails of the Crucifixion. Transformed as if by a disease of blood, the portrait is simultaneously transfigured into the Christ of the *Ecce Homo*, displaying the stigmata upon hands and feet. It is an image subtly prefigured by the key Christological and erotic term "passion" for the impulse "to act a part that sometimes makes us do things finer than we are ourselves." And finally, Dorian's attack on his image with the knife promises to provide the last wound of the stigmata, the bleeding side of Christ, penetrated by the spear of the centurion. Dorian's image becomes that of Christ himself, his body splayed on the wall in the corrupted reliquary of portraiture. It is no accident that Basil cries out "Christ!" when he sees the transfigured portrait of the object of his idolatry (122); as Isobel Murray has pointed out, it is the one instance in the whole manuscript where the novel version of *Dorian Gray* returns to the manuscript's text explicitly overriding editor J.M. Stoddard's alterations in *Lippincott's*.[66] The degraded object of Basil's homoerotic affection can only be named in the language of Christian blasphemy.

The completion of the wounds of Christ's own Passion, enacted against the portrait, produces (it seems) Dorian's own death. The end of the novel has typically been read, with surprising consistency, as an allegory pitting aestheticism against the "truth" of the soul. Ellmann, for instance, reads a straightforward moral into the book: "The text: Drift beautifully on the surface, and you will die unbeautifully in the depths."[67] And variants of this same claim appear – more surprisingly – in explicitly queer-theoretical work. In discussing Dorian's collection of Catholic liturgical vestments, for example, Hanson observes that "Wilde is signaling to us that Dorian has missed the point."[68] Roden claims that "Holy union requires the wedding of flesh to spirit, and Dorian lacks the latter. He is all body."[69] These readings corroborate Wilde's own assertions in his defense of the novel (as it appeared in *Lippincott's*) to the *St. James Gazette*:

> The painter, Basil Hallward, worshipping physical beauty far too much, as most painters do, dies by the hand of one in whose soul he has created a monstrous and absurd vanity. Dorian Gray, having led a life of mere sensation and pleasure, tries to kill conscience, and at that moment kills himself. Lord Henry Wotton seeks to be merely the spectator of life. He finds that those who reject the battle are more deeply wounded than those who take part in it.[70]

Three representations of aestheticism, three men who have sorely "missed the point": the case would seem to be closed.

By why should we – especially those of us inspired by the queerness of this novel's erotics – necessarily take Wilde's explicitly defensive word for it? After all, he would later make a very different claim about the relevance of *Dorian Gray* to desire: "Basil Hallward is what I think I am: Lord Henry what the world thinks me: Dorian what I would like to be – in other ages, perhaps."[71] There is no suggestion of the self-destructiveness of aestheticism here. And this assertion is by now so familiar that it is easy to forget that it is part of an attempt at epistolary seduction. Written to a Ralph Payne of 50 Ennismore Gardens, London, it is immediately followed by a less than coy proposition: "Will you come and see me? . . . Your handwriting fascinates me, your praise charms me." For Wilde, it seems, the "moral" of *Dorian Gray* is driven by expedience: it can be a renunciation of aestheticism or an aesthetically erotic enticement. The preface appended to the novel version of *Dorian Gray* explicitly rejects the very "moralism" that Wilde had located in his text in the letter to the *St. James Gazette*: "The moral life of man forms part of the subject-matter of the artists, but the morality of art consists in the perfect use of an imperfect medium. No artist desires to prove anything" (17). Again, there is certainly no need to take Wilde's text at its word here, but the aphorism counters what might look like earnestness in the letters to the *Gazette*.

What we do have is the text of *Dorian Gray* itself, and the end of the novel is not in fact nearly as straightforward as might be assumed from the general agreement in the critical literature. After Dorian stabs the portrait, the narrative shifts abruptly to a different point of view; the last paragraph of the novel, which seems to "reveal" what has occurred, follows three servants: "When they entered they found, hanging upon the wall, a splendid portrait of their master as they had last seen him, in all the wonder of his exquisite youth and beauty. Lying on the floor was a dead man, in evening dress, with a knife in his heart. He was withered, wrinkled, and loathsome of visage. It was not till they had examined the rings that they recognized who it was" (167). The delayed recognition here echoes the response of Christ's disciples on the road to Emmaus, the rings (with, as Hanson points out, their "intimation of an effete aestheticism"[72]) slyly taking the place of the sacramental breaking of bread.[73] We are clearly in the realm of the fantastic, even of the Christian fantastic, but it is not clear whether the logic of this final moment is the logic of Christian moralism or of Christian typology. The moral logic, which is the dominant although unanalyzed assumption of the critical literature, would insist that Dorian must be punished for his "sins," that he has, in Ellmann's words, drifted too beautifully on the surface and so must die unbeautifully in the depths. But given that the ending is explicitly fantastic, why must we assume that it is the "real" picture back in its frame and the "real" Dorian dead on the floor? Why must we assume, that is, that the requirements of morality necessarily enact a containment of the novel's delightful perversities? Dorian has put his soul in the balance for the bargain through which *he* can "be always young, and the picture . . . grow old" (34). If we take the Christian typology seriously, we might imagine that that prayer has worked. Dorian – like Christ – has been transfigured by the violence of "death," freed from the constraints of the flesh and raised in iconographic splendor into the fulfillment of his desire. It could, then, be *Dorian* in the frame, immortal and forever young, and the *picture* dead and withered on the floor. He would, then, have become, as in Winchell's description of Wilde's self-representation in *De Profundis*, "eternally impervious." The end of the novel, in that case, would not pit aestheticism against Christian typology but would produce them – as Wilde would do in *Salomé* and *De Profundis* – as mutually constructive. Salvation – not punishment – is enacted through the transubstantiation of flesh into symbol; Christian theology, no less "real" for this, is revealed to be first and foremost aestheticism itself.

The novel does not insist upon this reading, but neither – the critical near-consensus notwithstanding – does it insist upon a "moral" reading that opposes "religion" to erotics and to aesthetics. We can interpret the ending as the punishment of a sinner, or we can see Dorian's erotic and other "sins" as the necessary preconditions of a strikingly literal ascension. That would mean that we would have to embrace the seeming paradox of a man who explored in his literature and life simultaneously the aestheticized pleasures of religion and the aestheticized pleasures of male–male sex. It would mean that we could blur what might look like clear dichotomies of sacred and sexual representation in Wilde's work, reading *De Profundis*, for example, as *both* an assertion of redemptive power *and* a reaffirmation (as Max Beerbohm saw) of an oppositional erotics. Queer theory would have to take religion seriously, and not only as reactive oppression; and religious studies of Wilde would have to give up the assumptions that religious experience necessitates the rejection of homosexual pleasures. The radical ambiguity of the end of *Dorian Gray* suggests indeed a radical ambiguity between the phenomena of religion and aesthetic sexuality that can provide a new framework for reading

Wilde's lifelong interest in both of these spheres of human experience. Or, even for the transgressive Wilde, would that be too scandalous?

notes

1. Ian Small's *Oscar Wilde: Recent Research* (Greensboro, North Carolina: ELT Press, 2000) includes in its "New Paradigms in Literary and Cultural History" the rubrics "The Gay Wilde," "The Irish Wilde," and "Wilde and Consumerism," but not (except as it is related to Irishness) anything resembling "Wilde and Religion." [See also Doody, Chapter 10, on Wilde's Catholic Irishness – ed.]
   Alan Sinfield, at the opening of his wonderful book *The Wilde Century*, makes the crucial observation that "the place of homosexuality in [Wilde's] plays is by no means plain. Many commentators assume that queerness, like murder, *will out*, so there must be a gay scenario lurking somewhere in the depths of *The Importance of Being Earnest*. But it doesn't really work" (Sinfield, *The Wilde Century: Effeminacy, Oscar Wilde and the Queer Moment* (New York: Columbia University Press, 1994), vi; emphasis in original). There are, however, two at least mock religious conversion scenarios in that very play (and it is one of the least obsessed with religion of any of Wilde's works): the planning for the re-christening of Algernon and Jack, and Canon Chasuble's ultimate renunciation of his early declaration that "The precept as well as the practice of the Primitive Church was distinctly against matrimony" for marriage to Miss Prism (380). Whereas there have been a series of excellent queer readings of this play, there have been fewer analyses of religion in it, although those readings would seem more obviously to "work," in Sinfield's terms.
2. See Richard Ellmann, *Oscar Wilde* (New York: Vintage Books, 1988), 34.
3. See ibid., 19–20.
4. Ibid., 527–528.
5. See ibid., 583.
6. For Dunne's account of Wilde's conversion, see *Complete Letters*, 1223.
7. Ellmann, op. cit., 584.
8. See ibid., 584.
9. *Complete Letters*, 1224.
10. Ibid., 1220.
11. In the critical literature on Wilde, discussions of Catholicism frequently open what are in fact analyses of Wilde's *Irishness*. While Roman Catholicism and Irishness are certainly importantly related topics at the end of the nineteenth century, particularly given Lady Wilde's nationalistic conflation of the two, I do want here to consider religion (to the extent that it is possible) *separately* from questions of nationality, in part because there have been very good readings of Wilde's Irishness and in part because Wilde himself seemed often to consider the two as separable. Certainly, neither *Salomé* nor *The Picture of Dorian Gray*, both of which engage deeply with Catholicism, makes Irishness central to that particular analysis. As Frederick S. Roden has pointed out, "Despite his Irishness, Wilde's Catholicism was that of the male, homosocial Oxford Movement – not the cultural Roman Catholicism of his ethnic heritage" (Frederick S. Roden, *Same-Sex Desire in Victorian Religious Culture* (New York: Palgrave Macmillan, 2003), 155). Wilde himself claimed in a late

letter, "My position is curious: I am not a Catholic: I am simply a violent Papist" (*Complete Letters*, 1184). With this assertion, Wilde insists upon a radical Ultramontanism that divorces Romanism from Irish Catholicism (and even from the strongly national Roman Catholicism of John Henry Newman, who opposed, for example, the declaration of Papal Infallibility).

12. Joseph Bristow, *Effeminate England: Homoerotic Writing after 1885* (New York: Columbia University Press, 1995), 117–119.
13. James Eli Adams, *Dandies and Desert Saints: Styles of Victorian Manhood* (Ithaca and London: Cornell University Press, 1995), 98.
14. Ibid., 208–209n. See also Richard Dellamora's claim about Wilde's *Salomé* that "Although men committed to sexual and emotional ties with other men did in fact gather in particular religious communities and parishes from the late 1860s until the end of the century, the 'practical step' to which *Salomé* tends is not, as in the case of Newman, towards the church but towards Wilde's declaration of himself as a lover of men in all senses of the word" (Dellamora, "Traversing the Feminine in Oscar Wilde's *Salomé*," in *Victorian Sages and Cultural Discourse: Renegotiating Gender and Power*, ed. Thaïs E. Morgan (New Brunswick and London: Rutgers University Press, 1990), 246).
15. Eve Kosofsky Sedgwick, *Epistemology of the Closet* (Berkeley and Los Angeles: University of California Press, 1990), 140.
16. In *Victorian Studies* 25 (1982): 181–210.
17. See also Christopher Craft's *Another Kind of Love: Male Homosexual Desire in English Discourse, 1850–1920* (Berkeley and Los Angeles: University of California Press, 1994). For Craft, the Catholic Church's implication in that "other kind of love" is solely theological and oppositional; it is the inspiration for the later (secular) juridical condemnation of sodomy (Craft, *Another Kind of Love*, 8), and the context for Thomas Aquinas's *Summa Theologiae*, which provides the basis for that condemnation (ibid., 13).
18. Jonathan Dollimore, *Sexual Dissidence: Augustine to Wilde, Freud to Foucault* (Oxford and New York: Oxford University Press, 1991), 95.
19. Ibid., 95.
20. Ibid., 98. A striking instance of this sort of understanding of the fundamentally antagonistic relationship of Catholicism to Wildean homoerotics occurs not in the criticism proper but in Moises Kaufman's remarkable drama *Gross Indecency: The Three Trials of Oscar Wilde* (which itself functions as a sort of critique, not only of Wilde but also of Wilde studies). At the end of the play, one of the several narrators relates that "After Wilde's death Lord Alfred Douglas married and had two children. He became a Catholic, and eventually a Nazi sympathizer" (Kaufman, *Gross Indecency: The Three Trials of Oscar Wilde* (New York: Vintage Books, 1998), 130). Here the renunciation of homoerotic desire and the entry into apparently inevitably reproductive heterosexuality flow seamlessly both into fascist reaction and Catholicism (which themselves seem synonymous in Kaufman's formulation). See also Ellmann, op. cit., 587, for a similar description of Douglas.
21. Philip K. Cohen, *The Moral Vision of Oscar Wilde* (London and Cranbury, New Jersey: Associated University Presses, 1978), 235.
22. Ibid., 244.
23. See ibid., 246–247.
24. Ibid., 258.

25. Ibid., 251.
26. Guy Willoughby, *Art and Christhood: The Aesthetics of Oscar Wilde* (London and Cranbury, New Jersey: Associated University Presses, 1993), 114.
27. Ibid., 113.
28. Ibid., 118.
29. Ibid., 115. A similar pattern emerges in John Albert's "The Christ of Oscar Wilde," which urges its readers to consider Wilde's works "material for the monastic exercise of *lectio* that leads to meditation, prayer and contemplation" (John Albert, O.C.S.O., "The Christ of Oscar Wilde," in *Critical Essays on Oscar Wilde*, ed. Reginia Gagnier (New York: G.K. Hall and Company, and Don Mills, Ontario: Maxwell Macmillan Canada, Inc., 1991), 241). Albert supports that usage largely by quoting long sections of Wilde's poetry and prose, interspersed with a sort of homiletic interpretation. For Albert, *De Profundis* and "The Ballad of Reading Gaol" are "the fullest sources of Wilde's doctrine of Christ" (ibid., 241). He hardly mentions homosexuality at all, except euphemistically as the cause of Wilde's "tragedy," and once in a pathologizing gesture that suggests that Wilde's homosexual activity was the result of poor self-esteem (ibid., 245).
30. Ronald Schuchard, "Wilde's Dark Angel and the Spell of Decadent Catholicism," in *Rediscovering Oscar Wilde*, ed. C. George Sandulescu, *The Princess Grace Irish Library Series*, Vol. 8 (Gerrards Cross, Buckinghamshire: Colin Smythe, 1994), 385.
31. Ibid., 382.
32. Ibid., 385.
33. Ibid., 387.
34. Ibid., 388.
35. Dollimore does in fact cite Fuss but without relinquishing his claim that essentialism in Wilde (to some extent as opposed to essentialism in Gide) is necessarily reactionary.
36. Diana Fuss, *Essentially Speaking: Feminism, Nature and Difference* (New York and London: Routledge, 1989), 1.
37. Roden, op. cit., 148. See also Ellis Hanson, *Decadence and Catholicism* (Cambridge, Massachusetts and London: Harvard University Press, 1997), 294.
38. See Ellmann, op. cit., 275–276.
39. Although he directed the letter to Douglas, Wilde gave the manuscript to Ross after his release from prison. Ross published extracts of it in 1905 as *De Profundis* (Wilde's title had been *Epistola: In Carcere et Vinculis*, derived – explicitly in the pattern of Papal bulls – from the first words of the letter). In the 1905 edition, Ross edited out all explicit references to Douglas, but after Douglas sued Arthur Ransom (who had written a book on Wilde) for libel in 1912, the whole letter was read in court. Shortly thereafter, Ross published a very limited (and faulty) edition of the entire manuscript in order to maintain copyright; Douglas blocked wider publication until after his death in 1945. See Vyvyan Holland's 1949 Introduction to *De Profundis*, reprinted in *De Profundis and Other Writings*, by Oscar Wilde (New York and London: Penguin Books, 1954), 91–95.

40. Edward Verral Lucas (unsigned), review in *Times Literary Supplement*, 24 February 1905; reprinted in *Oscar Wilde: The Critical Heritage*, ed. Karl Beckson (New York: Barnes and Noble, Inc., 1970), 247.
41. G.B. Shaw, letter to Robert Ross, 13 March 1905; reprinted in *Oscar Wilde: The Critical Heritage*, 244.
42. Max Beerbohm, "A Lord of Language," *Vanity Fair*, 2 March 1905; reprinted in *Oscar Wilde: The Critical Heritage*, 249.
43. Ibid., 249–250.
44. Ibid., 251.
45. Ibid., 250.
46. James Winchell, "Wilde and Huysmans: Autonomy, Reference, and the Myth of Expiation," in *Critical Essays*, 237.
47. Ibid., 237.
48. Ibid., 237.
49. *Complete Letters*, 15.
50. Ibid., 39.
51. Ibid., 20.
52. *Complete Letters*, 39.
53. Ibid., 27; quoted in David Alderson, "Momentary Pleasures: Wilde and English Verse," in *Sex, Nation, and Dissent in Irish Writing*, ed. Éibhear Walshe (New York: St. Martin's Press, 1997), 43.
54. Alderson, op. cit., 43.
55. Ibid., 56.
56. Ibid., 44.
57. Hanson, op. cit., 231.
58. Ibid., 231–232.
59. Ibid., 233.
60. Ibid., 234.
61. See also Hanson's reading of the play, ibid., 271–279.
62. For this, and for a reading of Aubrey Beardsley's drawings of this kiss, a reading that emphasizes the multiple sexual implications of the scene, see Dellamora, op. cit., esp. 252–256.
63. See H. Montgomery Hyde, *The Trials of Oscar Wilde* (New York: Dover Publications, 1962), 113; quoting Wilde, *Complete Works*, 94.
64. For a reading of Wilde's similar rewriting of the homoerotic poem "Wasted Days" as the Marian "Madonna Mia," see Roden, op. cit., 133–134.
65. For one reading of the vestments, see Hanson, op. cit., 250–251.
66. See Isobel Murray, "Textual Notes," *The Picture of Dorian Gray* by Oscar Wilde, ed. Murray (Oxford: Oxford University Press, 1974), 230.
67. Ellmann, op. cit., 315.
68. Hanson, op. cit., 250.
69. Roden, op. cit., 144.
70. *Complete Letters*, 430.
71. Ibid., 585.
72. Hanson, op. cit., 286.
73. See Luke 24.13–35.

8

gay studies / queer theory and oscar wilde

richard a. kaye

"One man opposing a society
If properly misunderstood becomes a myth."
Wallace Stevens[1]

If there is an author who seems to evoke today's complex and shifting sexual *Zeitgeist*, animating contemporary fantasies, anxieties, and obsessions, it is surely Oscar Wilde. As I write this in New York City, Wilde the erotic dissident and decadent artist (the two roles, as we shall see, are today entangled) is everywhere in evidence: recently a new production of Strauss's *Salomé* ran at the New York City Opera, the set for which – a court of Herod dominated by a huge, glittering staircase – borrowed winkingly from the Billy Wilder Hollywood movie *Sunset Boulevard*. On Broadway, a musical version of the film *A Man of No Importance*, adapted to the stage by the playwright Terrence McNally, depicted as its protagonist a Wilde-obsessed homosexual bus-driver. A new production of *The Importance of Being Earnest* at the Jean Cocteau Repertory Company closed several months ago, only to be followed by another production by the Aquila Theater Company set in contemporary times that recently opened on off-Broadway. A "reading" of *Salomé* has migrated from Brooklyn to Broadway, starring Al Pacino, Aiden Quinn, Diane Wiest, and Jennifer Jason Leigh (a role then assumed by Marisa Tomei), with Pacino recapitulating his Broadway role of Herod from the 1980s. So pervasive is Wilde's influence on the contemporary stage that *The New York Times* chief theatre critic Ben Brantley recently claimed that in his new Broadway play about romantic relations between women, *Boston Marriage*, David Mamet, celebrated for his tough-guy theatrical idiom, "takes on Oscar Wilde and Ronald Firbank at their own epicene, epigrammatic games."[2] The newest screen version of *The Importance of*

Being Earnest, featuring Rupert Everett, received fervent reviews, while the British novelist Will Self has just published *Dorian: An Imitation*, a rewriting of Wilde's novel set in the gay coteries of London in the early 1980s and featuring a psychopathic Dorian Gray, a bisexual Lord Henry, and a video artist, Basil Hallward, whose film of Dorian decomposes. Wilde's influence can be detected everywhere in the culture. An article on the Spring 2002 Paris ready-to-wear shows in *The New York Times* reported that some of the "most influential fashion editors on the planet converged on the Oscar Wilde Room at L'Hotel," where Wilde died, but noted that whereas the hotel had once become a "mecca for sensitive young men and wizened literary types," the newest pilgrims had made the trek "to view a collection of recycled T-shirts stitched together by a sewing circle of women in Alabama and featuring embroideries of drawings" by the photographer Lola Schnabel.[3]

This widespread fascination with Oscar Wilde often encompasses some extravagantly personal responses. A friend who this year visited Wilde's grave at Paris's Père Lachaise cemetery was astonished to behold the Jacob Epstein tomb covered in lipstick-stained kisses – evidence of worship, given the nature of Wilde's appeal, among either men or women or both. This obsessive attention to the modern era's first literary superstar coincides with intensified scholarly interest, evidenced in biographies of major and minor figures in the writer's life (two studies of Robert Ross, biographies of Ada Leverson, Wilde's mother, and Wilde's niece Dolly, as well as a revisionist account of the life of Bosie). Collections of letters, new editions of Wilde's texts, and a proliferation of gift volumes with titles like *The Wit and Wisdom of Oscar Wilde* show no signs of stopping. Wilde has replaced other Victorian writers – Dickens and the Brontës come to mind – who once commanded a widespread public readership. Beyond explicit invocations of his name, the "decadent" Wilde permeates contemporary cultural reporting, so that one can detect the traces of *Yellow Book* sensibility in the gushing debauchery of a film reviewer in *New York* magazine, writing of Brian De Palma's 2002 film *Femme Fatale*, claiming that the movie is a "pure (guilty) pleasure trip ... dirty, twisted, voyeuristic, a vast glissando of amorality."[4] Even those who share her cultural and political values might question the self-assurance with which the neo-conservative historian Gertrude Himmelfarb declared, in her polemical *The Demoralization of Society: From Victorian Virtues to Modern Values*, that the "movement known as the *fin de siècle* was well-named; it did not survive the siecle."[5] Himmelfarb's prognosis is reminiscent of Arnold Bennett's rash 1927 estimation of Wilde as an "outmoded" writer whose "style lacked the elements of permanence," and that Wilde's plays had failed to achieve the popularity of those by Somerset Maugham and Frederick Lonsdale.[6]

Not surprisingly, Gay Studies and Queer Theory have been at the forefront of the renewed interest in Wilde. Summarizing developments in Wilde Studies over the last decade, Ian Small identifies three primary areas of new scholarship: the Gay Wilde, the Irish Wilde, and the Wilde who represents Consumption.[7] It is unquestionably the first of these three Wildes that has dominated popular and scholarly concern in the last decade. In terms of male writers within a British literary tradition, Wilde continues to be *the* literary figure around whom Gay Studies and Queer Theory in Britain and the United States have defined themselves as academic fields, a scholarly interest that overshadows such figures as Christopher Marlowe and Lord Byron, both of whom also end "controversial" lives and who arguably deserve to be analyzed with the tools of Gay Studies and Queer Theory as much as any author. But the events of Wilde's trial intersected with historically pivotal developments in modern sexuality and with homosexual desire in particular in a way that continues to harbor a broad current resonance. Twenty-first century British and American readers, audiences, and scholars may have trouble identifying with Marlowe's risky atheism or Byron's sexual adventurism and passion for Greek independence, but Wilde's troubles with Lord Queensberry and Edward Carson continue to reverberate in a period that has witnessed the humiliation and sometimes downfall of renowned public figures because of their sexual imbroglios. Yet despite the frequency with which Wilde is invoked in explorations of modern sexuality, his precise place in literary history is still very much a matter of debate. As Andrew Hewitt has observed, "Although a canonical figure in the reconstruction of a homosexual literary history, Wilde's position within the broader literary canon is rather less clear: the aesthetic of artifice he represents has been identified as both decadent and modern."[8] Indeed, Wilde's "aesthetic of artifice" became the very terms for a politically freighted reaction against his anti-realist art and the brazen sexuality such art denotes. In Saul Bellow's novel *The Dean's December* (1982), the protagonist Albert Corde, a college administrator who battles radical students and spineless liberal colleagues, comes upon a collection of Wilde's writings published by "some British reader's society in red cardboard, faded to weeping pink," and recalls his adolescent fondness for Wilde's "The Harlot's House" and its detailing of the "scandals of Greek love, the agonies of young men who had done so well in school but who woke up besides their murdered mistresses." At first amused to find a familiar passage (the "earth reeling underfoot, and the weary sunflowers ..."), Corde casts aside the "not-so-amusing book. He found the street more interesting."[9] The mature realist must turn away from Wilde, whose case illustrates youth's blindness to the intractable actualities of life. (Had Corde wanted to encounter he might have read Wilde's "The Ballad of Reading Gaol," an attack on capital punishment.)

In the following pages I want to focus on several important impasses that have divided Gay Studies scholars and Queer Theory critics in their encounter with Wilde, touching, as well, on some rifts within Queer Theory itself as it has encountered Wilde's legacy. Those rifts were recently signaled in Moises Kaufman's play *Gross Indecency* (1998) which mocks current Queer academic conceptions of Wilde, presenting a Gender Studies professor who mouths academic jargon as the play itself portrays Wilde in Manichean terms as a victim of a punitive Victorian culture. Although Kaufman's play did not offer an especially original conception of the playwright, *Gross Indecency* signaled the value of the Wilde-as-Gay-Martyr myth to gay liberationists. For in some ways Wilde, whose trial rendered him as public a homosexual as was possible in a Victorian context, represents a more fitting subject for a strictly Gay Studies approach, with its stress on explicit scenarios of "coming out." While I will be focusing largely on Wilde as the subject of Queer Theory inquiries, in fact it is Wilde's contemporary Henry James who has generated the most sustained critical attention from Queer-Theory critics and who, with his seemingly impenetrable private life and the formal opacities that define his fiction, most invites a theoretical model highlighting identity-postponing refusals of naming. My own preference for a Queer-Theory critical framework should be apparent. As Wilde once noted of matters of taste in the judgement of works of art, only an auctioneer is able to be equally appreciative of all artistic works; the same might be said of a critic examining an array of differing critical approaches.

While the Gay Studies/Queer Theory division has been acrimonious, it ultimately has proven itself a creative dialectical rupture, one that helped to determine a wider and more rigorous comprehension of Wilde and his epoch. As we shall see, Queer Theory at least initially defined itself in reaction to what it perceived as the triumphalist position of Gay Studies, focusing its critique on, among other issues, the reductive momentum of "literary biography" so fundamental to Gay-Studies critics, the role of differing forms of psychoanalysis in the interpretation of Wilde's life and writing, and the problem in seeing Wilde as an individual actor challenging Victorian norms as opposed to viewing him as cultural "object" or "product." This last aspect of Queer-Theory approaches to Wilde undermines Small's too-schematic distinction between a "Gay" Studies Wilde and a perspective focusing on "Consumption." For although Foucault is clearly the single most important theoretical influence for Queer Theorists dealing with Wilde, Pierre Bourdieu has had a nearly as influential role in shaping the perception of a writer who frequently is described as the modern era's most self-conscious marketer of his own image. Like most Queer Theorists, Bourdieu de-emphasizes the biographical, focusing instead on social systems and the institutional foundations for literary movements and reputations. In his work on Flaubert especially, Bourdieu explained the market forces that shaped the philosophy of "art for art's sake" and demonstrated that even the most avowedly anti-utilitarian artistic movements, such as Symbolism and Decadence, were deeply embedded in a social system. Most Queer Theorists working on Wilde have drawn a great deal of theoretical sustenance from such claims – and indeed, Cultural Studies is often a fundamental aspect of the Queer-Theory approach to Wilde.

forbidden love in commodity culture: gay studies vs. queer theory

Although scholars writing outside Gay Studies and Queer Theory usually consider these fields as harboring indistinguishable concerns and methodologies, there are fundamental differences between the focuses, assumptions, and methods of each of these critical enterprises, nowhere more so than in scholarship devoted to Wilde. Most obviously, Gay-Studies scholars traditionally have invested considerable energy in establishing a "gay canon," a project in which Wilde invariably ranks very high. Queer Theorists, on the other hand, are far more skeptical concerning canon-formation, viewing such projects as inevitably complicit with hegemonic cultural values. By definition, Queer Theory accentuates not only the marginal aspects of literary history, but the ways in which canonically-oriented critics define certain experiences and writers as peripheral. Attempting to situate Wilde at the "center" of gay culture, this critique goes, only legitimizes the rigidities of hierarchical, arbitrary literary and cultural principles, which are always historically contingent. Furthermore, while Gay-Studies criticism insists on the salutary nature of writing by self-identified homosexuals, Queer Theorists perceive in such tendencies a naive rapprochement with normative social and psychological values.

Historically, such tensions were inevitable, since the Oscar Wilde celebrated by Gay Liberationists in every avenue from New York City's

Oscar Wilde Memorial Bookshop to the Dorian Society of Seattle often was built on a sentimental narrative of the playwright as at once a "victim" of an oppressive social order and a "martyr" for the cause of Gay Liberation. This highly functional mythology, seeing Wilde as a positive example for a "gay community," the Great Gay writer as mascot for a "forbidden love," was critiqued by many postmodern theorists in the 1980s and 1990s as a highly limited and even reactionary formulation. Eschewing a transcendent Wilde or a Wilde who can be made to fit into a literary canon, Queer Theorists found in such neglected and once-disreputable forms as Hollywood films, dime-store novels, camp theatre, comic books, and pornography an important avenue for the exploration of same-sex desires, one that lay far outside the elitist cultural "heritage" to whose ranks so many wished to consign Wilde. In 1980, writing in the London Gay Left Collective's anthology *Homosexuality: Power and Politics*, Stephen Gee asserted that once "Gayness might be suggested by use of camp in Oscar Wilde, or in the dark fatalistic metaphors of horror films," but added that "Our reclaimed gay culture is now using the correct pronouns and transforming innuendo and suggestion into affirmation."[10]

Today, however, Queer Theorists are far more receptive to coded forms of camp artifice, seeing such cultural formations as complex, politically freighted gestures. Yet a thorough-going social positivism and movement triumphalism continues to inform even the best works of Gay Studies, such as Byrne Fone's *A Road to Stonewall: Homosexuality and Homophobia in British and American Literature, 1750–1969* (1995), whose teleological notion of "gay history" as progressing forwards to an enlightened liberationist present is implicit in its title. For Fone, "there can be no doubt that by writing about who they were," the writers he explored, Wilde chief among them, had "courageously contributed to who we are becoming."[11] Contrastingly, Queer Theory depended for its professional legitimacy on non-essentialist notions of identity, a desentimentalized understanding of Wilde as well as other writers, an emphasis on erotic "desire" as opposed to romantic "love," and a view of history that privileged neither the past nor the present in calibrating periods of advanced sexual consciousness.

Given the pressure on academic critics to work within a theoretically rigorous and precisely historicizing framework, Queer Theory has seen its insights concerning the contingent nature of sexual identity become the received wisdom of humanistic scholarship. Perhaps the greatest rift today facing Gender Studies, then, is not so much one between Queer Theorists and academics working within a Gay-Studies framework but between academically-oriented critics won over to Queer Theory and literary and cultural journalists writing on gay and lesbian subjects. In his recent *Love in a Dark Time, and Other Explorations of Gay Lives and Literature* (2002), a collection of essays on Wilde and other writers that first appeared in *The London Review of Books*, the novelist and critic Colm Tóibín declared that:

> Some of the greatest writers of our age were fully alert to their own homosexuality. In their work they might write in code yet they also managed, once or twice, despite their own reticence and the dangers involved, to tell the truth in their fiction, to reveal the explicit drama of being themselves.[12]

The presentist and essentialist assumptions implicit in these seemingly simple statements (in which there is a homosexual "truth" to be revealed), the naive aesthetic premise (whereby all writing is reducibly autobiographical), and the gesture towards a rousing universalism (the phrase "our age" invoking an imaginary shared history) all run diametrically counter to the viewpoint offered by Queer Theorists. The kind of sentimental attachment to Wilde typified by Tóibín's portraiture invites a counterattack that inadvertently duplicates the very same dehistoricized terms of a maudlin understanding of Wilde; thus, in a recent issue of *The Atlantic Monthly*, the critic Geoffrey Wheatcroft mocks efforts to construe Wilde as a "gay martyr" (by which Wheatcroft means a heroically activist homosexual), since Wilde, according to Wheatcroft, implicitly denied his homosexuality when he sued Queensberry for insinuating that the playwright was "posing [as] somdomite" and then later when Wilde offered "spiritual" justifications in court for his sexual activities. As in Tóibín's account, Wilde (who during his trials strenuously had refused to submit to the characterizations of his personal life offered by the prosecutor Carson) is appraised by the standards of today, a measurement which judges him a disappointing Gay Liberationist and perhaps a coward.[13]

As we shall see, it is around the claims of humanist biography and positivist histories of sexuality (exemplified in the historian Peter Gay's *Bourgeois Experience* trilogy) that the rifts in Gay Studies and Queer Theory have become most pronounced. In their insistence on seeing subjects in either heroic or anti-heroic terms, as either repressed Victorians or daring militants on behalf of a liberating sexual ethos, and in stressing a conventional, universalist, anecdotal biographical framework as a tool for understanding Wilde, Gay-Studies critics made themselves especially vulnerable to a Queer-Theory critique. For even scholarship that saw itself as advancing Wilde's cause as that of a major but hitherto neglected author unwittingly borrowed, as several Queer critics have insisted, from normative assumptions of a conservative tradition in Wilde scholarship. That critical legacy, which invariably saw Wilde as a dangerous experimenter who willed his own fate by deliberately crossing societal and legal boundaries, is attached to a conception of Wilde as a martyr with a death wish. Conversely, Queer Theory offers a critique of such assumptions as heteronormative, especially as they inform psychoanalysis. In place of such outmoded psychoanalytic paradigms, Queer Theory points to, among other issues, the political dimension in the history of psychoanalysis, the didactic structure of standard humanist biography, the role of the artist as cultural "product" in a nineteenth-century marketplace saturated in image-production, and the subversive dimension of Decadent Art throughout the 1890s.

Additionally, in distinguishing itself from the more celebratory, canon-creating tactics of Gay Studies, Queer Theorists have placed a much greater stress on Wilde as historical figure and cultural commodity rather than on his achievements as a writer. To be sure, many Queer Theorists have offered meticulous exegeses of Wilde's texts, offering readings as "close" as those provided by any New Critic. But such interpretations are always informed by a sense of Wilde not simply as motivated by "private" impulses but as functioning within a historical framework, a writer whose achievements are determined by what was allowable within the restrictions, aspirations, and expectations of the Victorian literary and theatrical marketplace. In the works of such critics as Ed Cohen and Alan Sinfield, for example, Wilde is as much a player in a narrative of history as an accomplished playwright – indeed, Wilde the writer disappears altogether in the work of a number of Queer Theorists attending to Wilde as cultural myth and product. Thus Ed Cohen's *Talk on the Wilde Side: Towards a Genealogy of Discourse on Male Sexualities* (1993), a seminal study of the playwright's trials that scrupulously explores how press accounts of the case determined the modern conceptualization of the homosexual, did not include a single discussion of any aspect of Wilde's *oeuvre*. Rather, in Cohen's study Wilde represents a kind of mutating signifier, an especially colorful agent in the ongoing process whereby the modern homosexual subject is "invented," a procedure that Foucault had theorized so influentially in *The History of Sexuality*.[14] (However, Cohen's earlier essay "Writing Gone Wilde: Homoerotic Desire in the Closet of Representation" (1987), had been one of the first Queer-Theory readings of *The Picture of Dorian Gray*, exploring in detail Wilde's "displacement of the erotic onto the aesthetic," its disembodiment of homoerotic desire, and the first theoretically sophisticated article to explore the contrastingly "embodied" *Teleny*, the pornographic text that Wilde may have had a hand in authoring."[15])

While Gay Studies is keenly girded in invocations of Wilde and Queer Theory has found much in Wilde for its theoretical propositions, some Queer Theorists have dispensed with Wilde altogether. Leo Bersani, for example, builds a radical Queer ideological stance out of a literary triumvirate of Proust, Gide, and Genet – all of whom, Bersani contends, share a refusal to think in terms of a socially "redemptive" homoerotics.[16] The impulse on the part of Queer Theorists to take a position against the celebration of Wilde as Great Gay Genius has led to some surprising demythologizing strategies. One critic, writing in a collection of essays edited by Eve Kosofsky Sedgwick devoted to Queer readings of novels, declared that *The Picture of Dorian Gray* is, "Let's face it ... boring" and "unbelievably uninteresting," a judgment that inadvertently accorded with that of several decades of literary critics hostile to Wilde out of allegiance to Leavisite standards of a Great Tradition.[17] Such critiques aside, throughout the 1980s and 1990s *The Picture of Dorian Gray* emerged as a paradigmatic text of late-Victorian British literature and Wilde's fortunes in the academy increased exponentially, as the writer came to define the *fin* of two centuries.

the new queer *fin-de-sièclists*

Adding to the enduring Queer Studies absorption in Wilde is an intensified interest in the *fin de siècle* itself, a field that has proven remarkably viable in the last two decades. One might have expected that throughout the 1940s and 1950s that New Criticism, with the high premium it placed on aesthetic works as necessarily sequestered from strictly mimetic functions, could have gained considerable sustenance from Wilde's philosophically-oriented essays such as "The Decay of Lying." By and large, however, New Critics eschewed Wilde's writing, and even critics of more expansive and anti-New Critical tendencies, such as Edmund Wilson, ignored Wilde. In *Axel's Castle: A Study of the Imaginative Literature of 1870–1930* (1931), a volume that cried out for a consideration of Wilde's aesthetic perspective given its focus on European experimental forms, gave two passing references to Wilde. Elsewhere, as in his 1946 review of Hesketh Pearson's study of Wilde, Wilson could be a cogent critic of Wilde, whom Wilson sought to depict in hyper-masculine terms by characterizing him (along with Yeats) as a "man of action" and not, as popular conception would have it, "soft and wilting."[18] Similarly, the so-called New York Intellectuals centered around *Partisan Review* in the

1940s and 1950s, with their distillation of socialist principles in politics and modernist sympathies in art, largely disregarded Wilde. Thus Mary McCarthy's debunking of a 1947 New York production of *The Importance of Being Earnest* in the *Partisan Review*, in which she hazarded that "there was something *outré* in all of Wilde's work that makes one sympathize to a degree with the Marquess of Queensberry," was memorably hostile.[19] It was not until the 1950s and early 1960s in the favorable estimate of writers such as W.H. Auden, Eric Bentley, Louis Kronenberger, Cyril Connolly, and Kingsley Amis (most of whom were, significantly, non-academic critics, poets, and novelists) that Wilde was discussed as a major literary figure. Auden and Bentley, moreover, discussed Wilde in terms of details of his private life, a topic that many of those seeking to burnish the playwright's legacy tactfully downplayed.

To be sure, several wide-ranging scholarly accounts of Victorian culture such as Jerome Buckley's *The Victorian Temper* (1951) included sections such as "The Aesthetic Eighties" and "The Decadence and After" which dealt with what was called "Turn-of-the-Century" literature, although Buckley dismissed the Decadent as displaying a "passive gallantry" that was "precious, effeminate, effete" and who could never "face the social realities of his time."[20] That view already had been tacitly rebutted in Edouard Roditi's brilliant study *Oscar Wilde* (1947), which included a chapter on "The Politics of the Dandy" that gave full measure to Wilde as a serious dialectical thinker, a socialist-utopian visionary in the tradition of Proudhon. (Revising his text in 1986, Roditi added three new chapters that partly explored homosexual themes – for example, the question of Wilde's possible authorship of the pornographic *Teleny*.[21]) Rupert Croft-Cooke's *Feasting with Panthers: New Considerations of Some Late-Victorian Writers* (1967) signaled something of a breakthrough in its frank exploration of the sexual tastes of Wilde and members of his circle, in a rum account of such neglected *fin-de-siècle* figures as Lionel Johnson and Count Stenbock. In his gossipy introduction, Croft-Cooke claimed he would treat his subjects as "neither monsters nor villains," although his attitude towards much of Wilde's work could be both tepid and quarrelsome, as when he calls Dorian Gray a "phony diabolist" and suggested that Salomé was a glorified "streetwalker."[22] Such studies typically perceived the Decadent Nineties as a cultural blip or insignificant intermezzo, beguiling but ultimately irrelevant (an idea that endures in John Updike's recent reference to "Romanticism's final *fin-de-siècle* flicker" and "its rather mauve" afterlife in modernist writing[23]). Echoing Max Nordau's notorious denunciation of Wilde in *Degeneration*, the Marxist critic Ernst Fischer in *Art Against Ideology* (1967) derided the depiction of "hysteria as a substitute for passion" in Wilde's *Salomé* (although Fischer allowed that "'Decadence,' fascinated by ugliness, cleared the way for a realistic, as opposed to idealizing, portrayal of proletarian life and unrest"[24]).

Such perspectives either avoided a discussion of homoerotic issues altogether or nervously touched upon them. The critic Karl Beckson, in his useful anthology of out-of-print, turn-of-the-century texts, *Aesthetes and Decadents of the 1890s* (1966), offered the following dedication to the volume: "To my sons, who are neither aesthetes nor decadents," a comment that would seem to express more paternal panic than affection for the writers gathered in the volume.[25] Cautious evasion was *de rigueur*, sometimes via a determined effort to see Decadence as a purely language-oriented enterprise. In 1969, Bernard Bergonzi noted that "The word 'Decadence' has a broader application, but suffers from its ambiguity; some of the time it suggests a combination of physical lassitude and psychological and moral perversity ... although more properly it should refer only to language."[26] Similarly, Richard Gilman's essay *Decadence: The Strange Life of an Epithet* sought to empty the word of its sexual-political implications since, for Gilman, decadence was sheer idea, with no actual historical corollary.[27] As late as 1979 an entire volume devoted to "Decadence and the 1890s" included only a handful of references to the subject of sexuality, including an essay that declared that *De Profundis* is a "failed autobiography" that reveals "an individual no longer capable of distinguishing self from false self" and a "failed development manifested in the denial of growth ..."[28] Otherwise discerning works such as Jean Pierrot's *The Decadent Imagination, 1880–1900* (1981) and David Weir's *Decadence and the Making of Modernism* (1995) largely sidestep a discussion of same-sex desire, what Pierrot coyly calls the "hidden love of Sodom."[29] Outside of passing references to *The Picture of Dorian Gray* and Gide's *L'Immoraliste*, Weir confines his study to formal issues – specifically, Decadence's stylistic determination of modernist writing.

What once merited only passing references today demand book-length studies, while the epoch now known as the *fin de siècle* requires its own theoretical paradigms and theories. One of the key works in making homoerotic eros and its attendant sexual politics central to an exploration of *fin-de-siècle* culture was Elaine Showalter's *Sexual Anarchy: Gender and Culture at the Fin de Siècle* (1990), in which Wilde's works are a focal point of British cultural life.[30] Showalter's study was also vital in drawing links between Feminist Theory and the then-embryonic field of Queer Studies, in the process inaugurating a critical alliance between feminist concerns and Queer Studies that has continued until today, although not without its dissenters within Queer Theory and Feminist Theory. In very few other areas of Anglo-American literary criticism has there been such a fruitful interpenetration of the preoccupations of Feminist Criticism and those of Queer Theory as there has been in scholarship related to the *fin de siècle*. Richard Dellamora's much-cited *Masculine Desire* is another key text, as are Sedgwick's *Between Men* and *Epistemology of the Closet*, although these studies are not devoted to an estimation of the *fin de siècle* per se.

Subsequent critical works such as Kathy Alexis Psomiades's *Beauty's Body: Femininity and Representation in British Aestheticism* (1997) and Talia Schaffer's *The Forgotten Female Aesthetes* (2000) solidified and expanded on the insights of Showalter's and Dellamora's studies by presenting the *fin de siècle* as a time of shifting cultural ferment.[31] These works demonstrated that *fin-de-siècle* culture had been a boon for innovative women's thought and writing, as homosexually-identified men inspired as well as fomented distress – along with new creative aspirations – in the period's women writers, whose own writing (as Schaffer meticulously demonstrates) was sometimes the inspiration for more well-known male-authored texts of the period. Psomiades, meanwhile, examined how the aestheticist use of androgyny and hermaphroditism as figures of male–male desire located "femininity" at the center of the Victorian discourse of homoeroticism. In Dennis Denisoff's inquiry into parodic modes in *fin-de-siècle* literary culture, *Aestheticism and Sexual Parody, 1840–1940* (2000), parodies – even when seemingly most hostile to Wildean aestheticism – emerge as richly constitutive of multiple homosexual identities during and after Wilde's lifetime. Denisoff discovers a complex dialectic among differing discourses on same-sex erotics, from Robert Hichens's parodic novel on Wildean aestheticism, *The Green Carnation*, to Beerbohm and Coward.[32] The best of these studies demonstrated the relevance of factionalized *fin-de-siècle* debates to postmodern theory, in which such topics as the political dimension in camp artistry, the role of women in aestheticism, and the significance of satire in the formation of sexual identity took center stage.

richard ellmann's *oscar wilde*: humanist biography and its queer discontents

In many respects this new era of scholarship was generated by Richard Ellmann's 1988 biography of Wilde; indeed, it is impossible to overestimate the impact of Ellmann's work, especially for those interested in exploring the subject of same-sex eros in Wilde's life and writing. Although it has become customary for scholars to note Ellmann's factual errors, Ellmann's study was in fact a work of meticulous, original research that shaped (through the marshaling of biographical detail) a new epoch in the critical estimation of Wilde. Whereas Ellmann had once rashly declared in an essay, "The Uses of Decadence," that Aestheticism had never spawned a "movement" in Britain, his biography of Wilde implied that this was precisely what Wilde had helped inspire. Because of the high repute of Ellmann's reputation (as one of the few biographers to command respect among academic literary critics for his biographies of Yeats and Joyce), his attention to Wilde itself gave the writer new legitimacy as a subject for scholarly inquiry. Not least important, Ellmann's willingness to re-imagine Wilde's romance with Bosie not only as tragic cautionary fable but as compelling narrative, a love story equal in importance to that between Joyce and Nora, put an end to an earlier era of Wilde Studies given over to evasive demurrals. That period included several moralizing accounts of the writer's life, a largely psycho-biographical approach that informed editions of Wilde's works, anthologies of *fin-de-siècle* texts, and even textual editions. Indeed, the uneasiness of Wilde scholars when confronted with the details of his private pleasures and travails was everywhere in evidence in Wilde Studies in the first half of the twentieth century. Surprisingly popular for a scholarly biography with numerous asides reflecting on details of intellectual history, Ellmann's book made the case for Wilde as a major figure in British literature. With an uncanny ability to identify with his subject, Ellmann presented Wilde as a writer of gnarled and expansive passions, profuse sympathies, and (still an open question for many critics in 1988) of canonical importance. For Ellmann, Wilde's encounter with Bosie, like Joyce's meeting with Nora in Ellmann's earlier biography, signifies *the* turning point in Wilde's life, in a configuration, typical of humanistic biography, in which a narrative of love trumps questions of history.

Yet more politically-minded critics, biographers, and Queer Theorists as varied in their perspectives as Gore Vidal, Gary Schmidgall, Ed Cohen, and Alan Sinfield explicitly and implicitly critiqued Ellmann's work as diminishing Wilde as a historic and political agent. Ellmann's biography, went the argument, harbored a naively essentialist view of homosexual acts and a blindly ahistorical notion of sexuality. Reviewing *Oscar Wilde* in the *Times Literary Supplement*, Vidal declared that Ellmann was "our time's best academic biographer" but that Wilde "does not quite suit his schema or subject." In "Thatcherite Britain" (and by implication, Reaganite America), Vidal explained, it "is now necessary to trot out an Oscar Wilde suitable for our anxious plague-ridden times." Vidal found the entire narrative informed by an "obligatory Freudianism," a narrative that was altogether too familiar a story of decline and fall – one that, Vidal opined, "may suit altogether too well the AIDsy Eighties."[33]

Against Ellmann's claim that "Wilde belongs to our world more than to Victoria's," Queer Theorists insisted on Wilde's contiguous relation to Victorian culture and, simultaneously and somewhat paradoxically, on his political and sexual deviations from its norms.[34] For Cohen, Ellmann's intense identification with Wilde was precisely the problem structuring his biography, since, as Cohen saw it, Ellmann universalized Wilde in order to fit him into a "'great male' tradition that [Wilde] himself sought to interrupt." In directing readers "away from the social and historical stage upon which Wilde acted," Cohen maintained, Ellmann "fails to comprehend the ways in which Wilde's behavior was an explicit challenge to the hegemony of late Victorian middle class."[35] Along with Cohen, Alan Sinfield in his important study, *The Wilde Century: Effeminacy, Oscar Wilde, and the Queer Moment* (1994), questions Ellmann's contention that Wilde's male relationships were "always, from the start, somehow already homosexual," since given the "mobility of sexualities in our cultures and the pressures against same-sex practices, it is a mistake to read anyone as 'really homosexual' from the start."[36] More broadly, Sinfield documents why one must distinguish between a mid-nineteenth-century aestheticism that Victorians associated with an aristocratic effeminacy and the insinuations of homosexual activity that Wilde accrues during his headline-grabbing trials.

Beyond such questions in the history of sexuality, Ellmann never addressed the ways in which Wilde functioned as a political figure in his own time as well as posthumously; his Wilde is delivered to an amorphous, discriminating "us." One would never know from Ellmann's strictly literary biography, for example, that in the years immediately after Wilde's death his legacy proved salutary to, for example, the Anarchist Movement in America seeking rights for individuals of same-sex preferences (*De Profundis* was excerpted in Emma Goldman's radical newspaper *Mother Earth* in 1906). Additionally, Wilde represented a figure of significance for late-twentieth-century radicals on behalf of "homosexual liberation," a point that becomes difficult to grasp within Ellmann's universalizing framework, in which Wilde's struggle seems largely to involve his (delayed) acceptance into a British literary canon.

Yet there are blind spots in a strictly Foucauldian approach to Wilde, in which the author's works represent a refraction or residue of history because literary texts are simply another discourse. Thus Cohen's *Talk on the Wilde Side* amply privileges legal and medical discourse over aesthetic modes or intellectual history. Yet one of the most powerful features of

Ellmann's work is the way in which it lends Wilde's thinking concerning same-sex eros a deeply-grained genealogy in British and even European thought. Aestheticism itself harbored a sexual politics, as Ellmann often made implicit in tracing Wilde's intellectual trajectory as it was shaped by Pater's and Ruskin's writings and public reputations:

> An atmosphere of suppressed invitation runs through Pater's work, just as an atmosphere of suppressed refusal runs through Ruskin's work. As to homosexuality, Ruskin refused to allow that it was sanctified because practiced in Athens, arguing that "the partial corruption of feeling" for women and the excessive "admiration for male physical beauty" had conduced to the fall of Greece. But Ruskin's own obsession with the child Rose La Touche made it difficult to take his pronouncements about normal sexuality seriously. Pater's blandishments were more persuasive. Something of the extraordinary effect of the *Studies* upon Wilde came from their being exercises in the seduction of young men by the wiles of culture. As against the resolute "noli me tangere" of Ruskin, Pater drew from the Renaissance the subversive lesson that we must continue it, hand in male hand.[37]

This comprises a brilliant synthesis of biographical portraiture and nineteenth-century intellectual history, deepening a sense of Wilde as formed by his "readings" of his predecessors' writings as much as by their public acts and reputations. (Ellmann might have added Hazlitt to his inventory of nineteenth-century critics whose calumnious private lives would have struck a chord in Wilde; the playwright who generated scandal by taking on a young lover doubtless would have been aware of Hazlitt's obsessive infatuation with his landlady's daughter, recorded in Hazlitt's extensive 1823 correspondence, first published in an 1893 edition entitled *Liber Amoris* that included an introduction by Richard Le Gallienne.) Whatever its limitations as a history of sexuality, Ellmann's *Oscar Wilde* powerfully conveyed how Wilde, drawing on Victorian "sages," sought to make same-sex erotics a paramount issue within European culture. Elsewhere, in his 1984 essay "The Uses of Decadence," Ellmann offered original readings of Wilde's texts. "In *Salome* the pageboy loves the Syrian soldier, but this is only one of the erotic relationships suggested," he noted. "For the Syrian, like Herod, loves Salome, Salome loves John the Baptist, John the Baptist loves Jesus. All love appears as deviation, and no deviation is superior to any other. All bring their tragic consequences."[38] This account, emphasizing a variety of illicit desires, arguably stood as the first "Queer reading" of Wilde's play.

Not all the critiques of Ellmann took an especially anti-biographical or theoretical stance, however. Schmidgall's *The Stranger Wilde* (1994) observes the traditional forms of humanist biographical narrative (even referring affectionately to Wilde throughout as "Oscar"). But Schmidgall stressed Wilde as political protagonist as much as a literary figure, insisting, too, on the writer's contemporary value for modern-day gay-identified men. In his chapter "Why He Stayed," Schmidgall offers several reasons for Wilde's refusal to flee England once he was "caught in the judicial vise" and suggests that Wilde hoped to create a *cause célèbre*. "Did he," asks Schmidgall, "perhaps recall a speech he had written three years earlier for the Oscarian character in 'Lady Windemere's Fan'?: 'There are moments when one has to choose between living one's own life, fully, entirely, completely – or dragging out some false, shallow, degrading existence that the world in its hypocrisy demands.'"[39] For other critics, the answer to Schmidgall's question was related to a problem of psychic disorder.

martyr complex: psychoanalysis in and out of history

One of the most useful critiques offered by Queer Theory addresses an enduring view of Wilde, pervasive among psychoanalytically-oriented critics of a conservative stripe, that comprehends the playwright as self-destructive in a pathological way. Ever-present but today more theoretically vulnerable, this reductionist conception of the playwright sees him as a self-destructive "martyr" whose narrative signifies a cautionary tale of sexuality run amok, a "pathological" case who trespassed on civilization's precepts. From this perspective, Wilde is not so much a rebel in Victorian society as an object lesson of what is taken to be the wisdom of the "mature" Sigmund Freud of *Civilization and Its Discontents*. The "martyr" for homosexual emancipation that many Gay Liberationist critics embrace is adapted for other purposes: Wilde becomes a "martyr" as in "martyr complex," a negative historical exemplum denoting a masochism that seeks out its final destruction in transparently perilous (not to be confused with politically bold or even significant) causes.

No doubt because of Wilde's life-long self-identification with a martyred saint – specifically, as the Roman soldier-turned-Catholic-symbol St. Sebastian – the idea of the playwright as death-courting masochist has assumed an enduring resonance. However, Wilde's eagerness to see himself as the object of martyrdom had more to do with Sebastian's complex associations of divine beauty under siege than Wilde's sense of himself as self-destroying psychological case. Particularly towards the end of his life, Wilde developed a deepening sense of his larger role in history, claiming, most famously in *De Profundis*, that "I am a man who stood in symbolic relations to the art and culture of my age." What is usually neglected are the lines immediately following this sentence, in which Wilde adds, "I had realized this for myself at the very dawn of my manhood, and had forced my age to realise it afterward" (1017). This key elaboration allows Wilde to present himself as a figure whose manhood commences when he assumes the role of actor, one who forces his contemporaries into historical consciousness, in a process that might otherwise render him an inert figure in history, a mere refracting "symbol." For Wilde, as for many other Decadents, it is St. Sebastian who represented an ideal symbol for an opprobrium that is simultaneously a political, sexual, and aesthetic attack. (One hardly requires better evidence of the collapse of such distinctions than that the *Lippincott's* edition of *The Picture of Dorian Gray* was quoted as incriminating evidence at one of Wilde's trials.) In a 1983 letter by Robertson Davies to fellow Canadian novelist Margaret Atwood, Davies highlighted this all-important difference between Wilde as political agent and self-willed martyr and took a stand for the latter. Noting that Wilde "has haunted me all my university days, grad students love him, and some of them are subsumed in his persona," Davies commented:

> I have a high regard for him, but stop several yards this side of idolatry ... To me, the saddest remark in the whole silly mess was Ross's "If Oscar had stayed with me, none of this would have happened." But Oscar was doom-eager, as our ancestors said, and was hog-wild for martyrdom – martyrdom, the ultimate in sensational publicity. I sigh when I hear him brought forward in evidence by the fiercely political gays of our time. ... But it delights me that Canada had a good big finger in that scandalous pie; it decreases our image as a nation of stick-in-the-muds.[40]

Davies prefers to envision his Oscar as a self-immolating martyr, a very different kind of figure, indeed, from that invoked by those "fiercely political" gays.

This attitude finds its roots in the received wisdom of conservative psychoanalytic critique as well as popular works drawing on prevalent psychological paradigms of the 1950s and 1960s. Perhaps because of his evident avowal of what convention-bound psychologists continue to call "Abnormal Psychology," Wilde has always been a favorite subject for psychoanalytic study, particularly in the United States since the 1950s. Contemporary works of fiction and pop-psychology texts saw in Wilde at worst an implicitly homoerotic venality or at best a cautionary case of individualist appetites gone amok. Meyer Levin's novel *Compulsion* (1956), based on the 1920s Leopold and Loeb case, explained its subjects' propensity to murder by drawing on references to *The Picture of Dorian Gray* – as when, for example, Leopold's stand-in, Judd, imagines addressing his friend Artie, a comely young man based on Loeb, as "Dorian."[41] With a similar sense of homosexuality as arising from youthful disorder but with a charming reliance on hokey causalities, Marvin Miller's *The Gay Geniuses: Psychiatric and Literary Studies of Famous Homosexuals* (1965) bluntly argued that Wilde's "fond but tactless mother's upbringing of him as a little girl, his shock at the perfidy of women when his father was ruined, and his classical education under Walter Pater ... acting together, made Wilde the most famous homosexual in the Western World."[42] The sociologist Philip Rieff, whose *Freud: The Mind of the Moralist*, had insisted on a Freud of cautious opprobriums, saw in Wilde a great wit and genius but also an abject lesson in the value of not crossing over civilization's necessary boundaries. In a 1970 introduction to an anthology of Wilde's writings, Rieff declared that "Nothing is more contemporary than Wilde's imagination" – something less than tribute since, for Rieff, Wilde's heirs were the "young revolutionaries in advanced industrial orders" who "conceive of themselves more artists than proletarians." To Rieff, Wilde "was less than a martyr and more than a victim." With the grim assurance of a timorous high-school guidance counselor, Rieff insisted that "Wilde's attack on authority is too easy" and "True individuality must involve the capacity to say no..."[43] In 1995, the leading academic expert on narcissism, Christopher Lasch, indulged a similar worry, warning that Wilde was the prophet for an overreaching, narcissistic counterculture, calling his "religion of art" the "most durable" and "most insidious of the nineteenth-century's secular religions," a faith adopted by elitist "revolutionary students" in the 1960s who adopted slogans much closer to Wilde than to Marx.[44] In "The Book of Ephraim" (1976), the American poet James Merrill caricatured this convention-hobbled psychoanalytic approach to Wilde in depicting a psychiatrist (distressed by the poet and his lover David Jackson's fondness for Wilde's remark that "Given a mask, we'll tell the truth") declaring: "Harmless; but can you find no simpler ways/To sound each other's depths of spirit/Than taking literally that epigram/Of Wilde's I'm getting damn/Tired of hearing my best patients parrot?" For Merrill, Wilde had become a curious ally of the gay analytic subject, whose love of artiface is maddeningly resistant to depth-psychology.[45]

Updating Lasch's neo-conservative critique in an all-out 1993 condemnation in *The Hudson Review*, Harold Fromm linked Wilde to Foucault as a fellow intellectual fabricator of a debased, polymorphously perverse culture. For Fromm, the lust for his stepdaughter expressed by Herod in Wilde's *Salomé* would be off-limits in a politically correct culture, just as Salomé would be a cultural heroine for her perverse female desires: "Today, for his lecherous sexism [Wilde's] Herod would be crushed under the shields of ACT UP, and Salome, having the courage of her kinks and the spunk of telling society to go screw itself, would probably wander off with her girlfriend to enjoy some Foucaultian limit experience."[46] This alarmist attitude coalesced at the *fin de siècle* in Roger Shattuck's polemical *Candor and Perversion: Education, Literature and the Arts* (1999), in which Shattuck quotes Wilde's "The Critic as Artist" on the value of aesthetics over ethics as the "extreme point of an antinomian, decadent aestheticism" that led, according to Shattuck, directly to the twentieth-century fascism of Germany and Italy.[47]

Less shrilly, Harold Bloom and Melissa Knox have sought to depict Wilde as psychologically curtailed, a "genius" but also a paradigmatic homosexual "case" of self-destructive impulses, a man with a martyr complex who unconsciously sought out his own destruction. In these accounts, Wilde's arrogant temptation of the powers-that-be obliquely refer to the modern male homosexual as Faustian explorer, willing to risk everything – friends, family, public respectability, overtly articulated goals – in the pursuit of underground, unconsciously-derived pleasures. In Bloom's *Genius: A Mosaic of One Hundred Exemplary Creative Minds* (2002), it is not surprising to find Wilde making Bloom's cut, but there is the following startling assessment of Wilde the man:

> Wilde exemplifies the two major senses of genius, an innate fathering-and-mothering force, and an other self, looking for and finding destruction in what is innate. A century later, when homosexuality cannot provide social immolation, Wilde would have to find an alternate way down and out, something beyond imagining.[48]

If I read Bloom correctly, he is arguing that Wilde had an essential ("innate") self, defined here in implicitly Jungian terms as maternal and paternal, that sought out its own destruction in "social immolation." This defining aspect of Wilde's personality meant that Wilde needed, innately, to destroy himself in some cause, any cause, so long as it satisfied his impulses. Homosexuality, this logic runs, is not so much a self-destructive erotics as a historically convenient means of destroying the self. But such views fail to see that Wilde's so-called "self-destruction" had a creative function, just as they neglect to note that in his last trial Wilde came very close to a polemical defense of same-sex eros, generating applause and tears in audience members (many of whom were Oxford acolytes who had come down to London to lend their support).

Knox's *Oscar Wilde: A Long and Lovely Suicide* (1994) presents itself as the first "psychoanalytic biography" of Wilde and in her introduction Knox brashly asserts that "To ignore the unconscious conflicts beneath [Wilde's] show of self-assured bravado is to miss an opportunity to understand not just Wilde's personality but some of the deepest influences on the development of his many literary styles."[49] Much of this grates: a "show of self-assured bravado" would seem to suggest bravado as a mask for some deeper conflict, a fallacy of critical understanding that Wilde mocked in his essay "The Truth of Masks." Wilde's self-assurance arose from his awareness of his own "genius" as well as from his knowledge that he was finding growing public admiration. Knox's ahistorical version of psychoanalysis (which is undeterred by the difficulty of gaining access to anyone's unconscious domain) creates "problems" to be unraveled. One need not seek an "explanation" in an unconscious dynamic for Wilde's pleasure in his public success, or for his bold, proto-political statements at his trial, any more than one needs to find an unconscious motivation in Proust's exuberant socializing – and in his eventual eremetical retreat into a cork-lined room when he became disgusted with the Dreyfus trials. One of the limitations of Knox's approach is its impulse to view risk-taking ventures into the public sphere (and as Schmidgall notes, politically loaded ones) as indicative of a self-destructive psychic impulse, a norm-privileging paradigm in which social conformity registers as a state of healthy psychic stasis.

Knox adopts her book's title from a letter, postmarked 12 December 1885, that Wilde wrote H.C. Marillier (although Knox inexplicably dates it as "ca. Early 1886"):

> Our most fiery moments of ecstasy are merely shadows of what somewhere else we have felt, or of what we long some day to feel. So at least it seems to me. And, strangely enough, what comes of all this is a curious mixture of ardour and indifference. I myself would sacrifice everything for a new experience, and I know there is no such thing as a new experience at all. I think I would more readily die for what I believe in than for what I hold to be true. I would go to the stake for a sensation and be a skeptic to the last! Only one thing remains infinitely fascinating to me, the mystery of moods. To be master of these moods is exquisite, to be mastered by them more exquisite still. Sometimes I think that the artistic life is a long and lovely suicide, and am not sorry that it is so.[50]

Knox interprets this beautifully paradoxical passage (at once a defense of and a detachment from ecstatic experience) as a transparent declaration of Wilde's will to die, when it is apparent that Wilde means nothing so blunt. With a yearning for new experience coupled with an awareness that there "is no such thing as a new experience," Wilde lends an ironic gloss to the insights of his mentor Pater. But his comment that the artistic life is a "long and lovely suicide" should not be read as an actual hankering for self-destruction, although that is precisely what Knox does. She maintains that Wilde's inability to grasp the full future implications of his action against Queensberry is not just a failure of foresight but a desire to sabotage his position as family man. Writes Knox: "It is impossible to believe that he was completely unaware of the dangers caused by his flamboyant, public homosexual conduct ... Something drove him to put himself in a position that would destroy his career, his family, and himself."[51] In Knox's account, the multifarious circumstances determining Wilde's refusal to leave England are reduced to an unconscious death-wish.

Missing from Knox's analysis is any awareness of the legal and social traps set by Labouchère or the intricacies of the trials themselves. Significantly, the name of the prosecutor Edward Carson appears only once in Knox's book – in a footnote – and the Labouchère Amendment, under whose broad rubric Wilde was prosecuted, not at all. Moreover, as A.N. Wilson recently points out in *The Victorians* (2002), there were many reasonable bases for Wilde's decision to remain in England, the most likely of which is that he was in thrall to Bosie and so followed his lover's wishes.[52] Knox's approach signals a psychoanalysis cut off from history, driven by the most normative of assumptions, and uncognizant of the sophisticated range of non-mechanistic approaches within current psychoanalytic theory. In Knox's reading, Wilde's texts are all reducibly autobiographical, an impulse that leads her to make many claims based on dubious evidence, heavy speculation, and banal psychologizing. "Like Wilde, Jokanaan feels no attraction to women," is a characteristic observation; at another point Knox insists that Wilde reveals in his children's tales "fears about the health of his own young family, particularly his two sons, Cyril and Vyvyan: he seems to have worried about what sort of children he as a syphilitic would produce and how they might blame him for making them ill."[53] (That Wilde contracted syphilis was an idea initially advanced by Arthur Ransome, a theory that has been forcefully challenged by, among others, Wilde's grandson, Merlin Holland.)

A number of more historically-conscious perspectives on Wilde also construe him in moralizing terms as a self-dooming martyr; in the case of the Marxist critic Terry Eagleton, on behalf of his decadent class if not his sexuality. "One can feel in Wilde's too-brilliant career, the gathering hubris of a man who is riding too high, hanging on by his wits," admonishes Eagleton, "and who seems at times to be perversely courting disaster ... Just like his own profligate class in Ireland, finally pulling down the roof upon his own head ..."[54] Such approaches tap into, when they do not help to shape, the reductionism of the popular culture in their depictions of Wilde's life. A 2002–03 exhibition of photographs at the Metropolitan Museum of Art included one of the much-reproduced Sarony photographs of Wilde with a caption that priggishly began, "In this image Wilde, exhibiting none of the effects of self-indulgence and high-living of his later years, leans towards the viewer ...." Similarly, a recent review of the 2002 film version of *The Importance of Being Earnest* in *Rolling Stone* magazine began "For a playwright imprisoned for two years for 'gross indecency,' Oscar Wilde was a pretty funny guy." In such a way does Wilde's fate as a "tragic" figure get read back into his life so that it serves as totalizing, life-defining myth.[55]

Paradoxically, such prescriptive simplifications were aired at a time when many Queer Theorists were finding in psychoanalysis the terms for a radical understanding of the homosexual subject. Gay Studies, like Women's Studies before and contiguous with it, had begun with a repudiation of Freud, especially the Freud that took hold in the United States in the post-World War II years. More recently, however, Queer Theorists, much like Feminist Theorists, have come to dispense with an anti-Freudian line in exploring issues of same-sex erotics. In *Sexual Dissidence: Augustine to Wilde, Freud to Foucault* (1991), for example, Jonathan Dollimore conceives of both Freud and Wilde as united in their implicitly liberationist insights, with Wilde the multiple purveyor of masks representing a fluidly postmodern conception of sexuality in opposition to Gide's earnestly essentialist self-conception.[56] In *The Ruling Passion: British Colonial Allegory and the Paradox of Homosexual Desire*, Christopher Lane shrewdly offers a largely psychoanalytic engagement with Wilde's work on behalf of a Queer critique, in which, for example, Freud's analogy between "the Unconscious and the Mystic Writing-Pad (1924), in which impressions appear on second, hidden sheet," are similar to the way in which Dorian Gray's portrait "unfailingly records the *vanishing* of desire."[57] Drawing on Lacanian models of subjective desire, William Cohen's "Willie and Wilde: Reading 'The Portrait of Mr. W.H.'" deals with Wilde's tale of two men who harbor a theory of Shakespeare's sonnets in which the beloved recipient of Shakespeare's attentions is a young boy actor. Cohen argues that Wilde's story demonstrates that belief in the theory "constitutes the subjectivity of the one who possessed it." For Wilde, then, Oedipal myths are replaced by a myth of Narcissus.[58] In "Traversing the Feminine in Oscar Wilde's *Salome*" (1990), Richard Dellamora critiqued Ellmann's "Overtures to *Salomé*" (1973) for imposing an orthodox Freudian model on the play. In Dellamora's Queer-psychoanalytic account, Salomé's kissing of the Baptist's severed head evokes perverse female desire and homoerotic perversion, both of which were historically linked in the 1880s and 1890s.[59] It is a mark of the richness of the Queer-Studies approach to Wilde that recent Freudian conceptions of Wilde now function in tandem with approaches once deemed incompatible with psychoanalysis. For the writer some of the most invigorating debates over Wilde in the 1980s and 1990s concerned something as contentious as desire: History, a topic that once escaped the attention of psychoanalytically oriented critics.

queering wilde, dissenting over queer history

The most innovative work of Queer-Theory criticism devoted to Wilde is Neil Bartlett's *Who Was That Man? A Present for Mr. Oscar Wilde* (1988), a volume that mixes genres – literary criticism, autobiographical reflection, social history, political manifesto, urban exploration, history of sexuality – as it seeks to tackle an amorphous Wilde. In contrast to the humanist universalism of orthodox Wilde scholarship, Bartlett proffered a series of personal meditations often directly addressed to Wilde.[60] If Queer Theory sometimes has a reputation for chilly rigor, skeptical of the sentimental attachment that many Gay-Studies writers felt before their saintly Oscar, Bartlett's emotionally rich responsiveness to Wilde and his legacy suggested an alternative approach within Queer Theory. Other works providing provocative historically informed analyses include the chapter on *De Profundis* in Oliver S. Buckton's *Secret Selves: Confession and Same-Sex Desire in Victorian Autobiography* (1998), in which, contesting Gay-Studies received wisdom, Buckton sees Wilde's last major work not as unmediated confession but as a work of complex formal strategies.[61] Kevin Kopelson's *Love's Litany: The Writing of Modern Homoerotics* (1996), includes a chapter on Wilde's "love deaths" as part of an investigation of the role played by romantic love in the construction, not of sexuality *per se*, but of homosexuality. Without explicitly endorsing a "gay canon" but reclaiming a subject that Queer Theorists typically relegated to the mushy realm of Gay-Studies scholarship, Kopelson examines a number of erotic texts by Wilde, Gide, Woolf, Stein, Yourcenar, Renault, and Barthes, to elucidate works that "rewrite, and unwrite" heterosexual romantic love scenarios and serve to "script" modern gay and lesbian sexuality.[62]

Another notable contribution to a history-cognizant Queer-Studies approaches to Wilde is Michael S. Foldy's *The Trials of Oscar Wilde: Deviance, Morality, and Late-Victorian Society* (1997), a study that astutely builds on the work of Ed Cohen but makes an original contribution to a comprehension of late-Victorian sexual dissidence.[63] Employing an impressive command of social theory in the writing of Bourdieu and Georg Simmel, as well as of details of the Wilde trials, Foldy depicts Wilde as caught in a dilemma in which his aestheticist philosophy competed with the erotic "utilitarianism" of his relations with working-class young men and the aims of a punitive British state. (Foldy speculates that Lord Rosebery, prime minister during the trials, may have sought to target Wilde in order to prevent revelations about his own homosexual past.) Taking full measure of the contradictions in Wilde's philosophy of art, Foldy shows how Wilde's bold, highly spiritualized philosophy of Greek love as articulated in the courtroom contradicted Wilde's emotional and erotic habits, which centered on relations involving the exchange of money for "favors" with proletarian youths.

A number of other works in Wilde Studies complicated an understanding of their subject by broadening the range of discourses beyond the literary contexts of most Gay Studies critics as well as the legal and journalistic terms in which critics such as Cohen had framed his study. Ellis Hanson's *Decadence and Catholicism* (1997) and Frederick Roden's more authoritative *Same-Sex Desire in Victorian Religious Culture* (2003) both broke new ground in seeing forms of nineteenth-century religious belief as entangled in issues of same-sex erotics, a new configuration in which Wilde held a key role. Although Ellmann had claimed that Wilde was "fascinated by the *forms* of Catholicism rather than its content," both of these studies contest such neat distinctions.[64] Other valuable studies that expanded the focus on Wilde to include the writer's posthumous influence and broader cultural effect include Joseph Bristow's *Effeminate England: Homoerotic Writing After 1885* (1995), which demonstrates how effeminate behavior, invariably associated with homosexual acts, manifested itself in the writings of Forster, Symonds, and Quentin Crisp.[65] With an analogous focus on Wilde's posthumous cultural authority, John Stokes' *Oscar Wilde: Myths, Miracles, and Imitations* (1996), while not an explicitly Queer-Studies work, provided an impressive countermyth to the conception of Wilde as self-lacerating martyr. Stokes refuses to see Wilde in terms of a narrative of cultural rise and fall – as a man whose humiliation and death put an end to Nineties' achievements, a view that, as we have seen, remains one of the most troublingly pervasive "myths" in Wilde Studies. (Refreshingly, Stokes eschews the term "martyr," preferring to think of Wilde as a "secular prophet."[66]) In a further demonstration of the contiguous bonds between Wildean aestheticism and Victorian cultural belief, critics recently have elucidated Wilde's debt to Darwinian thought.[67]

Queer Theory as practiced today is impossible to imagine without the theoretical contributions of Eve Kosofsky Sedgwick, who has offered several analyses of *The Picture of Dorian Gray*. *Dorian Gray* is unquestionably the text by Wilde that has earned the most sustained and sophisticated attention from Gay-Studies scholars and Queer Theory-oriented critics, a work that seemed to invite more historically informed readings than, say, *Salomé* (a play that, although a favorite subject for theatrical directors, has earned surprisingly few readings by Queer Theorists). In *Epistemology of the Closet*, Sedgwick had focused her discussion of Wilde on this novel, largely relying on her much-reiterated model of the "homosocial." To be sure, Wilde did represent *The Picture of Dorian Gray* as a homosocial universe – in the opening chapters of the text, preeminently, but even here the scenario is scarcely the homosocial (and fundamentally unconsciously eroticized) realm that Sedgwick had so forcefully explored in her seminal study, *Between Men*. In the model that Sedgwick adopts from René Girard's work on triangular desire, males, unaware of the implications of their triangulating actions, erotically mediate over a female. Yet is it possible to argue that Wilde's text not only depicts that scenario but up-ends it? And although Sedgwick grasps the historical significance of *The Picture of Dorian Gray* as "enabling a European community of gay mutual recognition and self-constitution," she holds a curious conception of Wilde's novel as constituting a "sentimental" text (because of its powers of "vicariousness") as well as a work of "paranoia" (a term that has perhaps over-determined Queer readings of the late-Victorian novel).[68] Wilde's novel resists Sedgwick's framework precisely because *The Picture of Dorian Gray*, unlike such mid-Victorian works as Dickens' *Edwin Drood* that Sedgwick had dazzlingly taxonomized in *Between Men*, so knowingly hides and represents the homosexual subculture of the 1890s. The binary of sexuality that seems to so perfectly fit the doubled set-up of *Dorian Gray* in fact oversimplifies the erotic cross-currents of that text.

In the related arguments on *Dorian Gray* in *Between Men* and *Epistemology of the Closet*, Sedgwick contends that the triangular relationship linking Basil, Lord Henry, and Dorian makes sense only in homosexual terms and that in this relationship one witnesses the collapse of prevailing nineteenth-century models of homoerotic desire, based on Greek paederastic paradigms, as Dorian turns to the mirroring image of his own decaying portrait. Thus the "suppression of the original defining differences between Dorian and his male admirers" shifts "in favor of the problematic of Dorian's similarity to the painted male image," as a new modernist mimetic constellation emerges.[69] The reason that the author declined to render *The Picture of Dorian Gray* as an openly homoerotic text, according to Sedgwick, was that

> For Wilde, in 1891 a young man with a very great deal to lose who was trying to embody his own talents and desires in a self-contradictory male-homosocial terrain where too much was not enough but, at the same time, anything at all might be too much, the collapse of the homo/hetero with self/other must also have been attractive for the protective/expressive camouflage it offered to distinctly gay content. Not everyone has a lover of their own sex but everyone, after all, has a self of their own sex.[70]

This deftly captures the success of homosexual camouflaging in *Dorian Gray*. However, Sedgwick tends to collapse the novel into a range of earlier texts of mid-Victorian homosexual "panic," even though the 1890s are culturally radical precisely because the Aestheticist and Decadent movements complicated an on-going, more rigid discussion of same-sex eros. To be sure, that contribution was enacted in coded terms, but in a way that would have been off-limits in pre-1890s decades. As Richard Dellamora argues, while *The Picture of Dorian Gray* "exists between a heterosexual framework which demands that desire between men be negated, had Wilde written *Dorian Gray* in 1865 instead of 1890, he likely would have resolved the male triangle by arranging a marriage between Dorian and a strong young woman." Wilde, writes Dellamora, "parodies the improbable yet normalizing conclusion in Dorian's attraction" to Sibyl Vane.[71] In another critique of Sedgwick's reading of *Dorian Gray*, Andrew Hewitt maintains, against Sedgwick's characterization of modernist modes as eclipsing nineteenth-century forms of depiction of same-sex erotics, that avant-garde aesthetics supplies an alternative to evasive modernist ambiguities. For Hewitt, the "homotextual may be identified neither with representationalism, nor with its rejection," in what Hewitt calls the "figural."[72]

A conspicuous strain in Queer-Studies readings of *Dorian Gray* situated Wilde's text within a much wider temporal lens, connecting (as Showalter had done in *Sexual Anarchy*) the 1890s with the 1990s, as fears about syphilis and "New Women" were replaced by fears of AIDS and "marriage-postponing" women. Jeff Nunokawa's essay "All the Sad Young Men: AIDS and the Work of Mourning" (1990), for example, located in Wilde's novel an influential conception of homosexuality as linked to an early death-doomed homosexual youth – in a morbid configuration that was eerily duplicated in the 1990s by the representation of young gay men brought down by HIV infection. For Nunokawa, Wilde's text inadvertently participated in "heteronormative" assumptions of same-sex desire that proved surprisingly resilient in another *fin de siècle*.[73] (Elsewhere, Nunokawa noted the ironies adhering to Wilde's novel, in which the "love that dare not speak its name has never been less at a loss for words" but in which "the expression of homosexual desires cancels, rather than clarifies the definition of the character through whom it is conducted."[74]) In a suggestive synthesis of the insights of Queer Theory and Reader-Reception Theory, Wayne Koestenbaum argued that, with the dissemination of Wilde's major texts, one witnessed the "birth" of a self-consciously gay reading public.[75] Laurel Brake has situated the evolution of this "gay reading public" between 1880 and 1892 in the publication history of the journal *The Artist and Journal of Home Culture*, which, under the editorship of Charles Kains-Jackson, produced a thinly-coded homosexual discourse through the writings of John Gray, André Raffalovich, John Addington Symonds, and Lord Alfred Douglas, until Kains-Jackson was fired in the wake of the 1889 Cleveland Street scandal.[76]

A breach within Queer Studies over exactly when Victorians denoted same-sex desire as a distinct category generated one of the more illuminating critical scuffles of the 1990s, this time centering on varying conceptions of "queer history" as articulated in *The Importance of Being Earnest*. Christopher Craft sees the play as parading a series of punning references to an actual Victorian homosexual subculture, most obviously in the ongoing reference to the naughty activity of "bunburying."[77] In his essay "'A Complex Multiform Creature': Wilde's Sexual Identities," Joseph Bristow rebuked Craft's reading of Wilde's play, claiming that Craft molds Wilde's drama "into a play with a fully developed homosexual undercurrent, one that would comply with our post-Stonewall comprehension of not only what it meant to be *homosexual*, but also what it means to be gay." For Bristow, only in the years of the *fin de siècle* (that is, in the period contemporaneous with the Wilde trials) did psychology, social science, and medicine make "cardinal distinctions" between homosexuals and heterosexuals.[78] Such disputes gave Queer-Theory readings of Wilde's works an enhanced sensitivity to the differences between decades and dates, as debates about the diverse *mentalités* of an epoch once loosely labeled "late Victorian" took on an impressive historicizing precision. A similar historical exactness animated the representation of Wilde in popular culture, where Wilde emerged both as an actor in a historical drama and as a history-transcending icon.

selfish giants, glam rockers, and other shirt-lifters

The rupture dividing Gay Studies and Queer Theory may seem like an esoteric academic dispute, but that rift played itself out in two works of popular culture drawing on Wilde's life. The differing uses to which Wilde is put in a pair of widely distributed films produced within a two-year period – Brian Gilbert's *Wilde* (1997) and Todd Haynes' *Velvet Goldmine* (1998) – vividly exemplify the divergences between a "gay-friendly" biographical approach, relying on the narrative devices of cinematic realism, and a more historically cognizant "queer aesthetic" that eschewed realist models. Gilbert's film is based on Ellmann's biography and follows the terms of that account, although with some of its own emphases. The stress in Gilbert's film falls on Wilde (played by Stephen Fry) as a good-hearted but deluded romantic who allows his family to implode out of a slavish love for Bosie. In a welcome if limited conceit, it is not *The Picture of Dorian Gray* that is the talismanic text for an understanding of a divided Wilde, but rather, Wilde's 1888 children's fable "The Selfish Giant," in which a blundering colossus bars children from trespassing on his garden and then, as a perpetual winter sets in, comes to regret banning them, especially one boy. We see Wilde reading the yarn to his adoring children and then, as a beautiful, bewildered Constance confusedly looks on, rushing off to London to cavort with Bosie in the London whirl. (In the film's only inclusion of what some viewers might deem shocking scenes, we see the pair participating in sexual three-somes.)

The allusions to "The Selfish Giant" add a much-needed poetic dimension to the relentlessly realist proceedings that otherwise dominate Gilbert's film. Even with these sequences the movie fails to explore the full metaphorical implications of Wilde's fable, perhaps because the conclusion of Wilde's tale suggests not so much a sugar-coated children's story as a provocative Christian allegory of male–male, cross-generational devotion, in which the giant, transformed into an ardent friend of his child-friends, at last finds his favorite boy but sees that he is pierced on his hands and feet ("They are the wounds of love," the boy explains.) In Gilbert's earnest conception of Wilde's life, the playwright is not a contemptible cad but poignantly foolish, a big, befuddled, cuddly giant – a Disney Oscar Wilde. The Selfish Giant allows himself to be degraded by Bosie, a petulant brute (played by Jude Law), as the movie intimates that Wilde would have been better served by level-headedly embracing an "adult" relationship with the kindly Robbie Ross. The steadfast realist terms of Gilbert's directorial style sometimes offer genuine emotional punch. Unlike earlier directors focusing on Wilde's life (Robert Morley's

1960 penny-dreadful portrayal, Peter Finch's heroically defiant version, also released in 1960), Gilbert's film allows us to see the newly successful playwright enjoying his privileges as a star of the London stage. With its depiction of the playwright sipping champagne at opening-night performances, the film illustrates Yeats' observation that Wilde, disliking bohemia, preferred to associate with salon sophisticates, theatrical *précieuses*, and well-heeled literati. Still, the reliance on the conventions of standard Hollywood bio-pics for an account of Wilde's life seems misguided for an artist whose success was as much a matter of formal as erotic deviation.[79]

With a view of outer space and a flying object descending to earth in the opening shots of *Velvet Goldmine*, we know that the tropes of realism are being ostentatiously discarded. A woman's voice-over tells us that "Histories, like ancient ruins, are the fictions of empires. While everything forgotten hangs in dark dreams of the past, ever-threatening to return." The camera zooms in on the doorstep of a house, where we see a maid lifting a baby, a green brooch pinned to its blanket, that has been deposited on the stoop and a caption reads: "Dublin, 1854, Birthplace of Oscar Wilde." (For Haynes, Wilde's genius is so otherworldly it could *only* be extraterrestrial.) Swooping over the heads of boys in Victorian garb tormenting a schoolmate, the camera focuses on the child, knocked to the ground, as he searches for – and then finds – his missing brooch. In the next shot, a classroom of children announces to the camera what they want to be when they grow up; Oscar declares that he wants to be a "pop idol." Jumping to 1982 and then backwards to the late 1960s and early 1970s, the rest of Haynes' film traces the fortunes of the Glam Rock star Curt Wild, the androgynous spiritual embodiment of Wilde, as well as the fellow maverick musicians Jack Fairy and Brian Slade (Jonathan Rhys Meyers). It is Slade who is the focus of the film and who serves as a stand-in for the real-life British rock sensation, David Bowie.

In the movie's conception, Slade embodies a new, glittery era of erotic experimentation as well as the music of such actual British rock groups as Roxy Music and T-Rex. (In the United States, Glam Rock took on a slightly different form in Lou Reed's Velvet Underground and Iggy Pop's The Stooges.) *Velvet Goldmine* is narrated retrospectively in a dreary, post-revolutionary present. A rock reporter Arthur Stuart (Christian Bale), seated in drab New York after his encounter with Slade, establishes a sense of this vanished period. Stuart's own youth had been transformed by Slade's music as well as by the spirit of Wilde. (Before he flees his oppressive home in the provinces, he looks on spell-bound as a teacher reads a stirring passage from *The Picture of Dorian Gray*.) Standard histories of the counter-culture tend to collapse all strains of the period's varying rebellions, but *Velvet Goldmine* insists on a sharp shift from the spirit of the 1960s to what it takes to be the more daring, mascara-saturated aims of Glam Rock (which in actuality probably had a short span from about 1969 to 1973). As a camera glides over the heads of hippies in peasant clothes sitting on patch-work quilts – and then along the silky purple dress that the androgynous Slade has donned for an open-air concert – Slade's former agent recalls in voice-over: "He despised the hypocrisy of the peace-and-love generation. *His* revolution, he said, would be a sexual one." (Haynes' aerial camera-gliding lends his film a sense of uncontrollable freedom.) We watch as Slade plays a song on his guitar which, in another, this time oblique tribute to Wilde, contains the refrain, "They Called Me Sebastian." An audience sits listening in the sun, and although it is difficult to imagine how anyone could resist the pull of Slade's lyrically evocative tune, there are dissenters. "Who is this idiot?" grumbles one listener to another, to which his acquaintance replies, "Some shirt-lifter from Birmingham." It's only a matter of time before the reporter Arthur finds himself enjoying the bisexual pleasures that Glam Rock-culture allows. Slade, meanwhile, has become the lover of an American rock star (Ewan McGregor), a blond-haired composite of the 1980s music sensations Iggy Pop and Kurt Cobain. Giddily in love with stylish excess, *Velvet Goldmine* never lets go of the spirit of Wilde; in one scene, the rock-nova couple evade reporters' prying questions about their sexual identities by shooting back a volley of Wildean paradoxes. (The film also reprimands the medical establishment's treatment of "shirt-lifters," as in a sequence in which an adolescent Curt Wild is tied down in a hospital and subjected to electro-shock therapy.)

Haynes, a 1980s graduate of Brown University's Semiotics Program, was explicit about his debt to the ideas that later coalesced under the rubric of "Queer Theory." As he explained in an interview after the release of his film, "Because glam rock would challenge with style and wit, any leaning towards 'the natural' in society, drawing heavily as it does from underground gay culture, this film commemorates Oscar Wilde as the original glam rocker, the one who knew to speak the truth only through the most exquisite of lies."[80] Haynes, whose 2003 movie *Far From Heaven* also narrated a tale of same-sex longing in the extravagant manner of another epoch (the film director Douglas Sirk's visually lush, politically restrained 1950s), may be the contemporary cinema's most flamboyant aesthete, but he is an aesthete with an almost Marxian sense of struggle. He sees historical styles as playing a crucial role in the skirmishes of cultural and sexual history. But if Haynes views the so-called excesses of the counter-culture as anarchic, salutary, visionary, and enduring, he is no sentimentalist of Glam Rock or erotic upheavals. Like Gilbert's *Wilde*, the film concedes that women sometimes lose out in sexual revolutions: years after the collapse of her marriage to Brian, we see his ex-wife in a darkened bar as she is interviewed by another "survivor," Arthur. She seems subdued, foggy about her ex-husband's whereabouts and about what he meant to her. (She is sweetly flirtatious with her interviewer.) In this movie about instant transformations, sexual and metaphysical, Slade has disappeared and may have assumed the identity of another rock star. But the spirit of Slade and Wilde maintains a posthumous life, fictive and actual. Dispensing with the literal tropes of biographical film narrative and its attendant reductive psychology, *Velvet Goldmine* is a supernatural tribute to the ghost of an ever-mutating, "unnatural" Oscar Wilde. (Glam Rock gives off a vibrant twenty-first century after-glow; at a 2003 New York City protest march against the imminent United States invasion of Iraq, members of a group called GlamAmericans carried colorfully fringed placards with such Wildean slogans as "Peace Is the New Black" and "War is SO Twentieth-Century.")

In a culture increasingly indifferent to the strictly literary, a writer such as Wilde, whose work translates so smoothly into non-literary modes, has a promising future. Moreover, with his fascination with questions of truth and artifice in the presentation of social selves, he seems to have anticipated the concerns of many Gender-Studies critics. For Gay-Studies and Queer critics alike, there are still sizable parts of Wilde's life, *oeuvre*, and reputation that cry out for new interpretations. That *The Picture of Dorian Gray* and *The Importance of Being Earnest* have received renewed attention is welcome, but one still awaits further critical interest in Wilde's other work – the children's tales, short fiction, poetry, "minor" plays such as *An Ideal Husband*, and, especially needed given Queer Theory's penchant for non-canonical texts, the pornographic novel *Teleny*, whose authorship and cultural implications remain largely unresolved critical issues. Welcome, as well, would be a full exploration of Wilde's correspondence, arguably as complex and multi-textured an autobiography as *De Profundis*. Valuable, too, would be a fuller account of Wilde's journeys in America in terms of the multiple "queer personae" he deployed there. For those scholars, critics, and artists committed to the idea of Wilde as a key figure in the history of sexual representation, the twenty-first century promises to be an abundantly contentious epoch.

notes

I would like to thank David Kurnick for his acute comments on this essay and Terrance Kissack for sharing with me his research on Wilde and the Anarchists Movement.

1. Wallace Stevens, "Lytton Strachey, Also, Enters Into Heaven," in *Opus Posthumous: Poems, Plays, Prose*, ed. Samuel French Morse (New York, Vintage, [1957] 1982), 38.
2. Ben Brantley, *The New York Times*, 21 November 2002, 36.
3. Horacio Silva, "Whatever Lola Wants," *The New York Times*, Fashion of the Times Supplement (18 August 2002), 104.
4. Peter Rainer, Review, *New York* magazine (11 November 2002), 105.
5. Gertrude Himmelfarb, *The Demoralization of Society: From Victorian Virtues to Modern Values* (New York: Alfred Knopf, 1995), 232, 213.
6. Arnold Bennett, "Books and Persons," *Evening Standard* (30 June 1927), reprinted in *Oscar Wilde: The Critical Heritage*, ed. Karl Beckson (New York: Barnes and Noble, 1970), 417–418.
7. Ian Small, *Oscar Wilde: Recent Research* (Greensboro: ELT Press, 2000).
8. Andrew Hewitt, *Political Inversions* (Stanford, CA: Stanford University Press, 1996), 214.
9. Saul Bellow, *The Dean's December* (New York: Pocket Books, 1982), 51.
10. Stephen Gee, "Gay Activism," in *Homosexuality: Power and Politics*, ed. Gay Left Collective (London: Allison and Busby, 1980), 203.
11. Byrne Fone, *A Road to Stonewall: Homosexuality and Homophobia in British and American Literature, 1750–1969* (New York: Twayne, 1995), xix.
12. Colm Tóibín, *Love in a Dark Time, and Other Explorations of Gay Lives and Literature* (New York: Scribner, 2002), 6.
13. Geoffrey Wheatcroft, "Not Green, Nor Red Nor Pink," *The Atlantic Monthly* (May 2003): 125–131. Wheatcroft also debunks recent arguments that Wilde was an Irish Nationalist and a socialist.
14. Ed Cohen, *Talk on the Wilde Side: Towards a Genealogy of Discourse on Male Sexualities* (New York: Routledge, 1993).
15. Ed Cohen, "Writing Gone Wilde: Homoerotic Desire in the Closet of Representation," *PMLA* 102 (1987): 810–813.
16. Leo Bersani, *Homos* (Cambridge, MA: Harvard University Press, 1995). That Bersani is a scholar of French literature only partially accounts for his choices; in an earlier study, *A Future for Astyanax*, he devoted a chapter to D.H. Lawrence.
17. Jeff Nunokawa, "Being Bored in *The Picture of Dorian Gray*: The Vicissitudes of Ennui," in *Novel Gazing: Queer Readings*, ed. Eve Kosofsky Sedgwick (Durham: Duke University Press, 1997), 151.
18. Edmund Wilson, "Oscar Wilde: One Must Always Seek What is Most Tragic," in *Classics and Contemporaries: A Literary Chronicle of the Forties* (New York: Farrar, Straus, and Co., 1950), 331–342.
19. Mary McCarthy, "The Unimportance of Being Oscar" (1947), in *Theater Chronicles: 1937–1962* (New York: Farrar Straus and Giroux, 1963).
20. Jerome Hamilton Buckley, *The Victorian Temper: A Study in Literary Culture* (New York: Random House, 1951), 236.

21. Edouard Roditi, *Oscar Wilde* (New York: New Directions [1947] 1986).
22. Rupert Croft-Cooke, *Feasting with Panthers: A New Consideration of Some Late-Victorian Writers* (New York: Holt Rinehart, and Winston, 1967), x, 45.
23. John Updike, *More Matter* (New York: Alfred Knopf, 1999), 636.
24. Ernst Fischer, *Art Against Ideology*, trans. Anna Bostock (London: Allen Lane/ Penguin, 1969 [1967]), 156, 149.
25. Karl Beckson, *Aesthetes and Decadents of the 1890s* (New York: Vintage, 1966).
26. Bernard Bergonzi, "Aspects of the *Fin de Siècle*," in *The Penguin History of Literature: The Victorians*, ed. Arthur Pollard (New York: Viking, 1969; 1993), 463.
27. Richard Gilman, *Decadence: The Strange Life of an Epithet* (New York: Farrar Straus and Giroux, 1979).
28. Jan B. Gordon, "'Decadent Spaces': Notes for a Phenomenology of the *Fin De Siècle*," in *Decadence and the 1890s* (New York: Holmes and Meier, 1979), 53.
29. Jean Pierrot, *The Decadent Imagination, 1880–1900* (Chicago: University of Chicago Press, 1981); David Weir, *Decadence and the Making of Modernism* (Amherst: University of Massachusetts Press, 1995).
30. Elaine Showalter, *Sexual Anarchy: Gender and Culture at the Fin de Siècle* (New York: Viking, 1990).
31. Kathy Alexis Psomiades, *Beauty's Body: Femininity and Representation in British Aestheticism* (Stanford: Stanford University Press, 1997); Talia Schaffer, *The Forgotten Female Aesthetes: Literary Culture in Late-Victorian England* (Charlottesville: University of Virginia Press, 2000).
32. Dennis Denisoff, *Aestheticism and Sexual Parody, 1840–1940* (London: Cambridge University Press, 2000).
33. Gore Vidal, "Oscar Wilde: On the Skids Again," in *United States: Essays, 1952–1992* (New York: Random House, 1993), 215–221.
34. Richard Ellmann, *Oscar Wilde* (New York: Alfred Knopf, 1988), 589. [Compare Kaye's treatment of Ellmann here with Bristow's in Chapter 1 – ed.]
35. Ed Cohen, "Nothing Wilde," *The Nation* (13 February 1988), 203–206.
36. Alan Sinfield, *The Wilde Century: Effeminacy, Oscar Wilde, and the Queer Moment* (New York: Columbia University Press, 1994), 5–6.
37. Ellmann, *Oscar Wilde*, 51.
38. Richard Ellmann, "The Uses of Decadence" (1984), reprinted in *a long the river run* (New York: Vintage Books, 1990), 7–8.
39. Gary Schmidgall, *The Stranger Wilde: Interpreting Oscar* (New York: Dutton, 1994), 253.
40. Robertson Davies, *For Your Eyes Alone: Letters*, ed. Judith Skelton Grant (New York: Penguin, 1999), 104–105.
41. Meyer Levin, *Compulsion* (New York: Carrol and Graf [1956] 1996).
42. Marvin Miller, *The Gay Geniuses: Psychiatric and Literary Studies of Famous Homosexuals* (Glendale, CA: Miller Press, 1965), 200.
43. Philip Rieff, "Introduction: The Impossible Culture: Wilde as Modern Prophet," in *The Soul of Man Under Socialism and Other Essays* (New York: Harper and Row), xxxvii. Reprinted in "Homosexuality: Sacrilege, Visions, Politics," *Salmagundi* (Fall 1982/Winter 1983).
44. Christopher Lasch, *Revolt of the Elites and the Betrayal of Democracy* (New York: Norton, 1995), 234.

45. James Merrill, "The Book of Ephraim" (1976), in *The Changing Light of Sandover* (New York: Alfred Knopf, 1992), 30.
46. Harold Fromm, "Foucault's Woodnotes Wilde," *The Hudson Review* (Autumn 1993), 525.
47. Roger Shattuck, *Candor and Perversion: Education, Literature and the Arts* (New York: W.W. Norton, 1999), 278.
48. Harold Bloom, *Genius: A Mosaic of One Hundred Exemplary Creative Minds* (New York: Warner Books, 2002), 246.
49. Melissa Knox, *Oscar Wilde: A Long and Lovely Suicide* (New Haven: Yale University Press, 1994), xii–xiii.
50. *Complete Letters*, 272.
51. Knox, *Oscar Wilde*, xii.
52. A.N. Wilson, *The Victorians* (New York: W.W. Norton, 2002).
53. Knox, *Oscar Wilde*, xvi, 66. In a caustic review of Knox in the *Times Literary Supplement*, Wilde's grandson Merlin Holland adumbrated several factual mistakes and misquotations in Knox's text.
54. Terry Eagleton, *Heathcliff and the Great Hunger* (London: Verso, 1995), 128.
55. Anonymous review, *Rolling Stone* (6 June 2002), 84.
56. Jonathan Dollimore, *Sexual Dissidence: Augustine to Wilde, Freud to Foucault* (Oxford: Oxford University Press, 1991).
57. Christopher Lane, *The Ruling Passion: British Colonial Allegory and the Paradox of Homosexual Desire* (Durham: Duke University Press, 1995), 86.
58. William Cohen, "Willie and Wilde: Reading 'The Portrait of Mr. W.H.'" in *Displacing Homophobia: Gay Male Perspectives in Literature and Culture*, eds. Ronald R. Butters, John M. Clum, and Michael Moon (Durham: Duke University Press, 1989).
59. Richard Dellamora, "Traversing the Feminine in Oscar Wilde's *Salome*," in Thais E. Morgan, ed. *Victorian Sages and Cultural Discourse: Renegotiating Gender and Power* (New Brunswick: Rutgers University Press, 1990).
60. Neil Bartlett, *Who Was That Man? A Present for Mr. Oscar Wilde* (London: Serpent's Tail, 1988).
61. Oliver S. Buckton, *Secret Selves: Confession and Same-Sex Desire in Victorian Autobiography* (Chapel Hill: University of North Carolina Press, 1998).
62. Kevin Kopelson, *Love's Litany: The Writing of Modern Homoerotics* (Stanford: Stanford University Press, 1996).
63. Michael S. Foldy, *The Trials of Oscar Wilde: Deviance, Morality, and Late-Victorian Society* (New Haven: Yale University Press, 1997).
64. Ellmann, *Oscar Wilde*, 34. Ellis Hanson, *Decadence and Catholicism* (Cambridge, MA: Harvard University Press, 1997); Frederick S. Roden, *Same-Sex Desire in Victorian Religious Culture* (New York: Palgrave Macmillan, 2003).
65. Joseph Bristow, *Effeminate England: Homoerotic Writing After 1885* (New York: Columbia University Press, 1995).
66. John Stokes, *Oscar Wilde: Myth, Miracles, and Imitations* (Cambridge: Cambridge University Press, 1996).
67. See "Queer Darwin," in Richard A. Kaye, *The Flirt's Tragedy: Desire Without End in Victorian and Edwardian Fiction* (Charlottesville: University of Virginia Press, 2002).
68. Eve Kosofsky Sedgwick, *Epistemology of the Closet* (Berkeley: University of California Press, 1990), 148.

69. Ibid., 160.
70. Ibid., 160–161.
71. Richard Dellamora, "Representation and Homophobia in *The Picture of Dorian Gray*," *Victorian Newsletter* (Spring 1988), 28–31.
72. Hewitt, *Political Inversions*, 221.
73. Jeff Nunokawa, "All the Sad Young Men: AIDS and the Work of Mourning," in *Inside/Outside: Lesbian Theories/Gay Theories*, ed. Diana Fuss (New York: Routledge, 1990).
74. Jeff Nunokawa, "Homosexual Desire and the Effacement of the Self in *The Picture of Dorian Gray*," *American Imago* 48.3 (1992), 311, 313.
75. Wayne Koestenbaum, "Wilde's Hard Labor and the Birth of Gay Reading," in Jonathan Freedman, ed. *Oscar Wilde: A Collection of Critical Essays* (Upper Saddle River, NJ: Prentice-Hall, 1996), 234–247.
76. Laurel Brake, "Gay Space: *The Artist and Journal of Home Culture*," in *Print in Transition, Studies in Media and Book History* (London: Palgrave, 2001).
77. Christopher Craft, "Alias Bunbury: Desire and Termination in 'The Importance of Being Earnest,'" in *Another Kind of Love: Male Homosexual Desire in English Discourse, 1850–1920* (Berkeley: University of California Press, 1994).
78. Joseph Bristow, "A Complex, Multiform Creature: Wilde's Sexual Identities," in Peter Raby, ed. *The Cambridge Companion to Oscar Wilde* (Cambridge: Cambridge University Press, 1997), 197–198.
79. For a review of other recent film and theatrical versions of Wilde's life, including David Hare's *The Judas Kiss* and Tom Stoppard's *The Invention of Love*, see Richard A. Kaye, "The Wilde Moment," *Victorian Literature and Culture* (2002): 347–352.
80. Quotation from Haynes appears on a website devoted to *Velvet Goldmine* at <http://members.tripod.com/monlettevelvet.html.> [See also Coppa's treatment of this work in Chapter 3 – ed.]

9
oscar wilde and feminist criticism

margaret diane stetz

If feminist criticism only came around to embracing Oscar Wilde late, very late in the twentieth century, we can lay at least some of the blame for that at the feet of Virginia Woolf. From the turn-of-the-century through the late-1930s, she spoke both to and from the heart of modernist circles. Her opinions of books and authors were delivered authoritatively and took on the weight of authority, whether issued anonymously in the *Times Literary Supplement* or through her two series of the *Common Reader* in 1925 and 1932. And of Wilde she consistently said little, neither engaging with his work nor addressing the significance of his life. It was clear from such silence that she did not consider him a subject of importance – just the opposite of the view that might have been expected. After all, she herself was a sexual dissident, her dearest Bloomsbury friends were gay men, and she was opposed both politically and morally to repressive institutional forces of the kind that had contrived to prosecute Wilde, as she demonstrated through her sympathetic portrait of the persecuted Septimus Smith in *Mrs Dalloway* (1925).

Whether a matter of neglect or of deliberate avoidance, the absence of attention to Wilde in her critical writing is puzzling. It is doubly so, when we consider that, as a public figure, he was a presence throughout the first 18 years of her life. Born in 1882, she certainly was old enough to have been aware of such highly publicized events as Wilde's death in 1900 and to have heard stories about his career either before or afterwards. (How strange it is, too, to consider that she would have been exactly the same age as some of the young men with whom Wilde consorted in France and Italy, after his release from prison.) She was undoubtedly aware of Wilde's status as an Irish outsider – and, moreover, as a gay outlaw – and thus as a figure apart from the Great Victorian Men whom she identified with her father and consequently regarded with hostility.

Yet Woolf seems never to have distinguished Wilde from the immediate English male predecessors she rejected. When dismissing the Victorians, she never bothered to exempt Wilde by name from her scorn.

Her published comments on him were brief and few. Unlike Gissing, Hardy, Meredith, and others among his contemporaries, he was favored with no separate essay devoted to his reputation. She treated him as a minor phenomenon and relegated him to a place on a list of past oddities. Reviewing Richard Le Gallienne's 1926 volume of memoirs, *The Romantic '90s*, for the *Nation & Athenaeum*, she wrote:

> Mr le Gallienne [sic] is a profound believer in the importance, to art and letters at least, of the 'nineties. "Generally speaking, all our present-day developments amount to little more than pale and exaggerated copying of the 'nineties. The amount of creative revolutionary energy packed into that amazing decade is almost bewildering in its variety," he writes. To most of us this will seem a curious over-statement. The figures of Dowson, Oscar Wilde, Arthur Symons, Aubrey Beardsley, and John Davidson scarcely seem to call for such epithets.[1]

One year later, in "Poetry, Fiction and the Future," an essay published in the *New York Herald Tribune* and based on a paper she had delivered to the Oxford University English Club, she declared:

> There is a candour, an honesty in modern writing which is salutary if not supremely delightful. Modern literature, which had grown a little sultry and scented with Oscar Wilde and Walter Pater, revived instantly from her nineteenth century languor when Samuel Butler and Bernard Shaw began to burn their feathers and apply their salts to her nose. She awoke; she sat up; she sneezed.[2]

The gendered personification was no accidental image. In Woolf's eyes, the figure of modern literature, like the real-life woman of the period, had little for which to thank Wilde. Woolf did not see him as a liberator or a champion. On the contrary, she associated his notions of style and his ideals of femininity alike with enervation and stagnation; she charged Wilde with confining both literature and women to mere decorative roles.

Her private comments upon Wilde's works were scarcely more admiring than her public dismissals. In her voluminous and detailed diary, she again had little to say about them, even about a masterpiece such as *The Importance of Being Earnest*. After attending a staging of that play at the Globe Theatre – a production famous for Edith Evans's performance as Lady Bracknell – Woolf devoted one sentence to it in the entry for 19 January 1940: "And last night The Importance of Being Earnest, a thinnish play, but a work of art; I mean, its bubble don't [sic] break."[3] Hers was faint praise indeed, with a grudging acknowledgment of success balanced by the damning adjective.

Yet these critical evaluations of Wilde as seemingly irrelevant to the progress both of modern literature and of modern women were belied by her repeated, unacknowledged borrowings from him. Consciously unimpressed, Woolf nonetheless showed the impress of Wilde's writings on her own style. The same diary passage that recorded her very modified rapture over *Earnest* also contained a recognizably Wildean epigrammatic summary of Hugh Walpole's appearance: "Hugh is rather like the winter sun – his ruddy edges slightly blurred."[4] From one decade to the next, Woolf employed such epigrams frequently in her prose, whether for private or public consumption, just as she drew upon the comic timing that Wilde had perfected.

Her most conspicuous achievement in feminist theory, *A Room of One's Own* (1929), was dependent upon that timing. Even as she argued, in chapter 4, that a female prose writer could learn nothing from her male counterparts, and that it is "useless" for a woman "to go to the great men writers for help, however much one may go to them for pleasure," the rhythms of her own polemic suggested the opposite.[5] Sentence upon sentence of *A Room* borrowed shamelessly from Wildean comic irony, while paragraphs built lengthy strings of detail toward the short, deflating climaxes familiar from Wilde's work:

> Few women even now have been graded at the universities; the great trials of the professions, army and navy, trade, politics and diplomacy have hardly tested them. They remain even at this moment almost unclassified. But if I want to know all that a human being can tell me about Sir Hawley Butts, for instance, I have only to open Burke or Debrett and I shall find that he took such and such a degree; owns a hall; has an heir; was Secretary to a Board; represented Great Britain in Canada; and has received a certain number of degrees, offices, medals and other distinctions by which his merits are stamped upon him indelibly. Only Providence can know more about Sir Hawley Butts than that.[6]

Who could read that closing zinger and not hear an echo in the distance of Lady Bracknell proclaiming, "That's all that can be said about land"?

What Woolf's style owed to Wildean rhetoric, her fictional imagination also owed to Wildean inventions, particularly when it came to the realm of the fantastic. *Orlando* (1928), with its beautiful, aristocratic youth who will not die or age (and who will not remain staunchly fixed in any single sexual identity), would have been impossible, but for the ageless and androgynous Dorian Gray, who threw himself passionately into the consumption of texts, much as did Woolf's book-worshiping protagonist.

Thus, there is a major disjunction between the fact of Wilde's non-appearance as a topic in Woolf's criticism and the presence of this apparitional Wilde, who haunts Woolf's writing with the persistence of the Canterville Ghost. We may liken such a situation to what Ann L. Ardis demonstrated in *New Women, New Novels: Feminism and Early Modernism* (1990) about the work of Woolf's high modernist male contemporaries, who learned "decentered subjectivity and disrupted linearity" from narratives by feminist novelists of the 1890s, then erased that debt to women, in order to "establish the authority of their work."[7]

But the absence of studies affirming Virginia Woolf's reliance upon Oscar Wilde meant that the feminist Second Wave, which crested in the 1970s and 1980s, did not immediately rediscover or recover Wilde, when it began to celebrate Woolf. For anyone who did not experience personally that revolutionary moment in literary studies, it is difficult now to appreciate how central Woolf was, both as figurehead and as guide. When Alice Walker, the African American novelist and essayist, published "Saving the Life That Is Your Own: The Importance of Models in the Artist's Life" in her influential *In Search of Our Mothers' Gardens*, the 1983 volume that also offered her groundbreaking definition of "womanism" as an alternative to "feminism," she placed Virginia Woolf alongside Zora Neale Hurston as one of the inspirations both for her writing and for her resolve not to succumb to suicidal impulses. Walker's list of the models whose courage helped to keep her alive included male artists and writers, such as Vincent Van Gogh and Jean Toomer. Yet she did not mention Oscar Wilde, whose example as a radical thinker, a daring artist, and a social martyr might well have been expected to win him a place there. Did the fact that his name was missing from Woolf's own critical works help to determine this neglect, which was hardly confined to feminist/womanist reappraisals of literature found in Walker alone?

Yet surely Woolf cannot bear sole responsibility for the slowness of late-twentieth-century feminism to look back to Wilde or to do so favorably. The major boom in Virginia Woolf studies throughout the 1970s and 1980s was accompanied by a minor renaissance for another female modernist novelist and literary critic, Dame Rebecca West. Unlike Woolf, Rebecca West (who died in 1983) was still alive to enjoy the first stirrings of this revival, which was particularly strong in England and which returned to print, via the London-based feminist press Virago, most of her major publications. But like Woolf, Rebecca West too had been oddly silent on the subject of Wilde.

Known originally (and then known once again) for her early suffragist activities, the forthright declaration of her feminist principles before and after World War I, and her defense of high modernist male pathbreakers, such as James Joyce, in *The Strange Necessity: Essays and Reviews* (1928) and *Ending in Earnest: A Literary Log* (1931), West ostensibly saw no greater value to women in Oscar Wilde or his *oeuvre* than had Woolf. To the Second Wave generations of feminist critics, she had little or nothing to say in his favor, devoting no essays to him (though in 1916 she produced one of the first monographs on his contemporary, Henry James). In her capacity as a professional reviewer, moreover, she chose not to write notices of any of the numerous books about him that appeared in her lifetime. These included H. Montgomery Hyde's several studies and biographies from the 1950s through the 1970s, Rupert Hart-Davis's 1962 edition of Wilde's letters, and Vyvyan Holland's 1954 memoir, *Son of Oscar Wilde*.

Her private expressions of opinion of Wilde, as revealed in Bonnie Kime Scott's edition of *Selected Letters of Rebecca West*, ran more toward disparagement or occasional grudging compliments than praise. Early in West's career, a gift to her by George Bernard Shaw of Frank Harris's *Oscar Wilde: His Life and Confessions* (1916) prompted outpourings of abuse. Thanking Shaw in a letter from 1917–18, she went on to loose a torrent of invective against the hapless subject of Harris's book, saying "I can never make out why there is all this fuss about Wilde," asserting that "the figure of Wilde does not amuse me," and characterizing him as "no more a subject for art than a congenital cripple is for a picture." In his arrogance and "condescension" toward art, his "horrible snobbery," his "appalling lovelessness of soul," and his careless ruining of the life of the woman he married, Wilde seemed to her the awful double of her own father, although "My father was a more imaginative and fastidious man and instead of indulging in abnormalities (so that we never had the satisfaction of seeing him go to prison) he used to go on exploring expeditions in Africa, where he behaved with most splendid courage and dash . . . while my mother and sisters and I starved at home."[8] Only half a century later, in the early 1960s, could she bring herself to utter a kind word about Wilde, after reading the published volume of his letters. "He was a sweet and delightful person and the letters show it," she announced, while also noting that "He no longer, for one thing, appears as primarily a homosexual. . . . Indeed, the letters surprised me . . . by their revelation how little he was of a homosexual," as though that explained why she could now look upon him more favorably and not revile him as a villain, particularly to the women in his life. At the same time, absolving Wilde of his supposed sins did not lead to any greater admiration for his art: "All the plays have gone except *The Importance of Being Earnest,* the poetry is unfashionable, the essays have been rendered unappreciable," she concluded.[9]

As with Woolf, however, there was another side to this apparent lack of engagement between Wilde and high-profile, twentieth-century British feminists. To look at Rebecca West's own life was to see a deep, personal involvement with the members of Wilde's immediate circle. She enjoyed a friendship for many years with one of Oscar Wilde's own dear boys, Reggie Turner (a middle-aged man when she first met him); as Victoria Glendinning says, he "became Rebecca's 'dearest Uncle Reggie', with whom she subsequently corresponded regularly."[10] And the links to Wilde could not have been closer than through her long intimacy with Vyvyan Holland, Wilde's surviving son – a romantic affair that metamorphosed into a non-sexual relationship which extended across the decades until Holland's death in 1967. (The connection could also be said to have continued through West's friendship, up to the end of her own life, with Wilde's grandson, Merlin Holland, whose education West had subsidized in the 1950s.[11])

Wilde was important to West, too, in other ways. Just as Virginia Woolf made Wilde's style part of the new "woman's sentence" that she fashioned and proudly offered up for inspection in her feminist classic, *A Room of One's Own,* then covered up the traces of that influence, so West turned to Wilde as her unacknowledged mentor for *Sunflower.* In this unfinished novel, written in the mid-1920s and only published posthumously in 1986, West voiced her feminist protest against men's mistreatment of women. Her vehicle was a narrative about a heroine who embodied Wildean aesthetic principles and wore the 1920s equivalent of aesthetic dress. Like Sibyl Vane, the beautiful innocent destroyed by Dorian Gray, West's Sunflower (whose offstage name was also "Sybil") was a noble-spirited actress, but the victim of corrupt and powerful men. Like Wilde himself, she was the target of Philistine scorn, for "she had noticed that good clothes, like any other form of fine art, were always greeted with ridicule when they were brought out into the open among ordinary people." A tragic figure, she was denied sympathy and subject to mockery by the public, which rejected "the beauty of tragedy, and the beauty of good clothes, which is one and the same beauty."[12]

What feminist criticism of the later twentieth century inherited, therefore, was a tradition of surface inattention to Wilde and his writings, accompanied by uncredited dependence upon both his life story and his work. But the lack of open acknowledgment by Woolf or West of his importance to their texts meant that neither the widespread revival of Woolf nor the more limited one of West led to any immediate feminist revaluations of Wilde. (This remained true despite the fact that texts by other rediscovered women authors did pay explicit tribute to him, however briefly. The University of Illinois Press's 1984 reissue of *Dust Tracks on a Road*, for instance, made visible Zora Neale Hurston's bow to "The Ballad of Reading Gaol" as a formative part of her literary education.[13])

Still, feminist critics would not have been so long in taking up Wilde as a topic had there not been other forces at play. It is shocking that there is to this day no equivalent of Margaret R. Higonnet's edited collection of essays, *The Sense of Sex: Feminist Perspectives on Hardy* (1993), nothing that brings together in this way some of the scattered evaluations of Wilde. It is even more shocking that the evaluations are not greater in number. How should we account for this?

Certainly it did not help that some gay male critics proved reluctant in the 1970s to embrace the women's movement actively or to describe it as essential to their own liberation struggle. At the same time, some feminist writers – including important lesbian feminist theorists – asserted that they found little difference between the misogyny and the patriarchal privilege exercised by heterosexual men and by gay men, thereby furthering the creation of what I am tempted to call two "camps." The division between lesbian feminism and gay male history was never clearer in Second Wave criticism than in Adrienne Rich's groundbreaking 1980 essay for the journal *Signs*, "Compulsory Heterosexuality and Lesbian Existence." There, Rich labored consciously to bring lesbians out from under the shadow of male homosexuality, which she portrayed in unflattering terms, and to establish a *herstory* that owed nothing to gay men:

> Part of the history of lesbian existence is, obviously, to be found where lesbians, lacking a coherent female community, have shared a kind of social life and common cause with homosexual men. But this has to be seen against the difference: women's lack of economic and cultural privilege relative to men; qualitative differences in female and male relationships, for example, the prevalence of anonymous sex and the

justification of pederasty among male homosexuals, the pronounced ageism in male homosexual standards of sexual attractiveness, etc. In defining and describing lesbian existence I would hope to move toward a dissociation of lesbian from male homosexual values and allegiances. . . . [The] term "gay" serves the purpose of blurring the very outlines we need to discern, which are of crucial value for feminism and for the freedom of women as a group.[14]

Subsequent feminist scholars, influenced by Rich's perspective, were unlikely to devote their energies to re-examining and rehabilitating Oscar Wilde as an icon of male feminism and of support for women, whether lesbian or heterosexual ones, when they could spend the same time promoting silenced female voices of the past. They were given instead to categorizing Wilde as a figure outside their own interests, passing over the significance of his career and of his achievements and assuming that, as a man of his times and as a gay one at that, he must have looked upon women with distaste and women's writing with suspicion.

This point of view proved long lasting. Traces of it remain in Elaine Showalter's influential 1990 study of challenges to conventional masculinity and femininity in late-Victorian literature and art, *Sexual Anarchy: Gender and Culture at the Fin de Siècle*. For Showalter, Wilde's positive view of women was a mere surface matter: "In his personal life, Wilde might have been said to support the cause of the New Woman. As editor of the magazine *The Woman's World*, he had commissioned articles on feminism and women's suffrage." But beneath this superficial encouragement of late-Victorian women's causes lay a profound hostility to women's bodies and souls alike – an antagonism that surfaced, for Showalter, in *The Picture of Dorian Gray*:

This rationalization of homosexual desire as aesthetic experience has as its subtext an escalating contempt for women, whose bodies seem to stand in the way of philosophical beauty. The aristocratic dandy Lord Henry Wotton speaks the most misogynistic lines in the novel, a series of generalizations about the practicality, materiality, grossness, and immanence of women, who "represent the triumph of matter over mind."[15]

To Showalter, Lord Henry's views of women were unequivocally those of the novel's author, and the publication of *Dorian Gray* marked the promulgation of misogyny as an integral part of the new male homosexual discourse that Wilde was helping to shape.

Yet Second Wave feminist literary critics were by no means a monolithic group, even in their assessment of Wilde. Boldly and innovatively, Jane Marcus would use her book *Art and Anger: Reading Like a Woman* (1988), which appeared two years before Showalter's *Sexual Anarchy*, to argue for a different understanding of Wilde's relationship to women and to their struggle for equality and recognition. The volume's opening chapter, "Salomé: The Jewish Princess Was a New Woman," saw Marcus insisting that Wilde had been an unabashed feminist who wished to hold up the protagonist of his Biblical play as a heroine, if not as a role model, by presenting her as an artist, a voice for women's rights, an activist fighting both religious and state oppression, and a sexual dissident. Marcus praised Wilde for his endorsement of Salomé as a desiring subject. She went so far, moreover, as to claim that Wilde had written the play "from the lesbian position."[16] Such a practice on Wilde's part was, for Marcus, entirely consistent with his politics and his personal sympathies: "Oscar Wilde did not approach women with fear and loathing. He liked strong women. The son of Speranza, who called herself an eagle and thought of herself as Joan of Arc . . . was attracted by heroic women."[17]

Sharply in contrast to Marcus's reading of *Salomé* as an expression of Wilde's advocacy of both the demands of 1890s New Women and "the lesbian position" was Gail Finney's view of the play. One year later, in "The (Wo)Man in the Moon: Wilde's *Salomé*," the second chapter of *Women in Modern Drama: Freud, Feminism, and European Theater at the Turn of the Century* (1989), Finney would articulate her belief that Wilde's protagonist was only nominally a female figure at all: "Seen this way, Wilde's *Salomé* emerges less as a misogynistic denunciation of the femme fatale than as a masked depiction of one man's prohibited longing for another."[18] While conceding that "Wilde had feminist sympathies as well," Finney nonetheless asserted that Salomé spoke as a homosexual man of her otherwise unspeakable desire for the body of another man: "Wilde used a female character as a mask for a male homosexual."[19] In Finney's treatment, Salomé's poetic rhapsodies over Jokanaan became not the signs of Wilde's appreciation of the creative potential of a woman poet-figure, of female subjectivity, or of women's own sexual agency, but covert hymns to male homoeroticism.

Subsequent feminist critiques of *Salomé* seem often to have drawn upon (or drawn away from) Jane Marcus's and Gail Finney's arguments. Patricia Kellogg-Dennis's 1994 "Oscar Wilde's *Salome*: Symbolist Princess," for instance, invoked Marcus, if only to disagree with her. The conclusion of this later essay built toward a sweeping denial of Marcus's most controversial proposition. Far from creating a politically rebellious heroine for a revolutionary play, Wilde was, according to Kellogg-Dennis, merely "outmannering the Mannerist conventions of Symbolist/Decadent art and literature. What he gave us is a Salome who, like Strindberg's Miss Julie, probably had a death wish. . . . Oscar Wilde's Salome wasn't a New Woman; she is a paradigm of the symbolist *femme fatale*."[20] Kellogg-Dennis's essay indeed positioned itself as a rebuke to anyone who hoped to enlist Wilde posthumously into the ranks of literary men who wrote as feminists (or, in Marcus's terms, as lesbians):

> Feminist criticism should not attempt to rewrite what has been written; rather, it should attempt to understand what has been written. Oscar Wilde's *Salome* is clearly a product of male – in Wilde's case bisexual – attitudes about women. The fascination of Wilde's depiction of Salome lies in his synthesis of western – and many eastern – ways of stereotyping women.[21]

But Kellogg-Dennis did not, however, explain precisely in what ways Wilde's attitudes were "bisexual" ones or how those differed from either late-Victorian heterosexual or gay male ideas about women.

The rise in academic circles, throughout the 1990s, of queer criticism did much to bridge the political distance between feminism and Wilde Studies, just as it brought together supposedly discrete sexual identities and united literary explorations of gender in general. Eve Kosofsky Sedgwick's *Between Men: English Literature and Male Homosocial Desire* (1985) was an early and important entrant into this field. But it was Judith Butler's later questioning of gender itself as a stable category that proved most influential. Her theory of gender as "performative" rather than essential – as something that had to be performed and enacted continually in accordance with social codes – meshed beautifully with Oscar Wilde's notions, one hundred years earlier, of a performed self. When it came to interpreting Wildean attitudes toward women, "queer" readings emphasized contradiction and uncertainty, rather than the fixed judgments implicit in words such as "misogyny" or "stereotyping," and thus helped to rescue Wilde's works from their former place in a patriarchal canon, rendering them newly interesting for feminist analysis.

We can see the effects of this "queering" of Wilde in an essay such as Amanda Fernbach's 2001 "Wilde's *Salomé* and the Ambiguous Fetish." Fernbach's argument aligned "Decadent men such as Beardsley and Wilde" in a common project with "advocates of the New Woman and the many female novelists who, breaking convention, dared to depict women's sexuality"; yet it did not blur the political distinctions between these groups, as Marcus had done. Fernbach's essay, too, distinguished Wilde's perspective from that of the heterosexist male patriarchy, saying that "because of the fluidity of gender and sexualities within *Salomé,* its fetishistic imagery generates a plurality of erotic meanings and fantasies that are not limited to the framework of male heterosexual desire."[22] But Fernbach's reading of this "fluidity" did not concur with Finney's vision of Wilde as having limned a female character solely as a "mask" for male homoeroticism. For Fernbach, the possibility was there for Salomé to be imagined "as a male transvestite," particularly when "the body of a potentially male Salomé is eroticized through the sexually charged dance." Yet the dance could signify to an even greater degree the radical "undecidability" of gender, rather than any unitary identity.[23] "Part of the ambiguity of the fetishistic imagery in Wilde's play is due to its inclusion of feminized as well as phallic fetishes"; for Fernbach, it was this very ambiguity which helped to explain the continued attraction of Wilde's play for women, "both lesbian and heterosexual" (including performers such as Maud Allan and Alla Nazimova and their female-centered audiences). In making her argument, Fernbach reflected the shared tendency of recent queer studies of Wilde to highlight "the conjunction between" – though not the homogenization of – "feminist, lesbian, and male homosexual politics" in his work.[24]

A similar impulse to locate that conjunction retrospectively, at the turn of the last century, certainly animated Wilde-related biographical and cultural studies volumes of the past few years, such as Philip Hoare's *Oscar Wilde's Last Stand: Decadence, Conspiracy, and the Most Outrageous Trial of the Century* (1997), a book tying the legal persecution of Wilde in the 1890s to the later anti-lesbian and misogynist persecution through the English courts of Maud Allan. Joan Schenkar's controversial and not wholly well-received 2000 biography, *Truly Wilde: The Unsettling Story of Dolly Wilde, Oscar's Unusual Niece,* took further this exploration of Wilde's importance to a later lesbian (and sometimes feminist) community of women artists and intellectuals. Even artists producing queer visual work, such as the photographers María DeGuzmán and Jill Casid (who collaborated under the name "SPIR: Conceptual Photography"), have examined this link in their Dolly Wilde-inspired series of images titled "Oscaria/Oscar" from 1994, which has been exhibited at the CEPA Gallery in Buffalo, the Institute of Contempoary Art in Boston, and other venues.[25]

Lately, the search for sites of alliance between Wilde's life and texts and those of his female contemporaries and immediate successors has also been a prominent feature of more conventional collections of academic writing, such as *Women and British Aestheticism* (1999), edited by Talia Schaffer and Kathy Alexis Psomiades. Much of the scholarship represented in that volume of essays, especially by feminist critics, turned sympathetically to the question of connections between Wilde's work and the projects (feminist and otherwise) of female aesthetes. The same quest has also informed single-author scholarly studies, including Jody Price's 1996 *"A Map with Utopia": Oscar Wilde's Theory for Social Transformation*. There, Price provided new feminist readings of neglected Wilde texts, such as the poems "*Impression du Matin*" and "The Harlot's House," and found in them statements condemning "the oppression of women." For Price, Wilde's poetry about prostitution falls under the designation of "problem" literature; it defiantly "tears down the facade between the life of the prostitute and that of the middle-class woman" under the marriage system. In doing so, it indicts women's existence within "Victorian capitalism," points to "Wilde's emerging understanding of the ideology which oppressed and destroyed him," and "carries this into his empathy with women."[26] Price has portrayed Wilde as a social reformer who acknowledged and addressed the same "plight of the woman" as did his feminist contemporaries in the 1880s and 1890s.

One of the sticking-points, in fact, for earlier feminist critics had been the relationship of Wilde to Victorian marriage – specifically, the issue of Wilde's own conduct as a husband to Constance Lloyd. In the period leading up to 1895, with its scandals and trials, as well as its social and financial ruin for both Wildes and their children, had Oscar been fair in his treatment of his wife? Or had he in effect exercised the same arrogance and indifference toward one placed in the legal position of a dependent that his unenlightened heterosexual male contemporaries had shown toward the women they married? Was he guilty of the same sort of behavior that had inspired the protests of New Women against bourgeois late-nineteenth-century marriage and men? Unanswered questions about whether Constance might have been doubly victimized – most certainly by homophobic British social attitudes and by the laws underpinning them, but perhaps also by her husband's failure to deal honestly with her and thus empower her to seek her own freedom – were undoubtedly another factor in feminist critics' reluctance to reach out to Wilde, up until the very end of the twentieth century. A lingering uneasiness about how Wilde had managed what we might call his domestic affairs gave impetus, too, to the suggestions of Elaine Showalter and others that Lord Henry Wotton's speeches in *Dorian Gray* were reflections of the author's contempt for wives in general and for his own wife in particular. Literary criticism has never existed in isolation from the prevailing zeitgeist; the social mood that made a transatlantic hit in 1984 of *The Life and Loves of a She-Devil*, Fay Weldon's comic novel about a wronged wife's revenge upon the husband who took her for granted and discarded her in favor of a lover, also worked against favorable reconsiderations of Wilde.

During the period of Second Wave feminist approaches, therefore, some of the feminist attention that might otherwise have gone directly to Wilde went to him instead obliquely (and not always flatteringly), through studies championing the women in his family circle and his circle of friends. Notable among these were two biographies of Constance Lloyd Wilde which appeared almost simultaneously in 1983: Joyce Bentley's *The Importance of Being Constance* and Anne Clark Amor's *Mrs. Oscar Wilde: A Woman of Some Importance*. Both were, as the title of the first and the subtitle of the second imply, to some degree special pleadings – appeals for a new public regard for their subject, as though to counter retroactively her husband's private disregard. Amor called the chapter of her book focused on Wilde's marital conduct in 1894–95 "Deception" and used it to argue for Constance's selfless fortitude in the face of her husband's selfish recklessness:

> Still in ignorance of the nature of things, Constance continued to run their home and family life virtually unassisted, and even managed to find time to care for Speranza [Lady Wilde, Oscar's mother], of whom she was so deeply fond. That Constance could still be unaware of Oscar's activities seemed to many people impossible at the time; yet wives are usually the last to find out about their husbands' mistresses. How much more are they likely to remain unaware that their husband has taken a male lover. . . .
>
> Oscar's skill in covering his tracks was consummate. . . . His normal standards of fair dealing naturally predisposed Constance to trust him, and she did so without fear or hesitation. Perhaps it was naïve on her part; and yet trust has never been regarded as a vice.[27]

The slippage into the present tense ("yet wives are usually the last to find out") is telling. A universalizing impulse lay behind Amor's account, which became part of a larger body of 1970s and early-1980s literature of the plaints of middle-class women whose lives and homes had been shattered by their cheating husbands. Bentley's *The Importance of Being Constance*, which lacks the scholarly apparatus and academic bent of Amor's book, reinforced the same message – that Constance had been heartlessly sacrificed to her husband's pursuit of pleasure. Bentley added her own view of Constance as noble and as unjustly doomed to misery:

> Her protective instinct, already fostered by the championing of her father and grandfather, combined with the loyalty which her brother had recognized years earlier as being her chief characteristic, soon took over . . . She shed many tears of frustrated bewilderment that Oscar, who loved his children so much, should blatantly jeopardize not only his own brilliant future but the future of two innocent children who worshipped him. . . .
>
> There was no relief, for, lastly, she would feel herself deprived above all else, because of the very nature of her anxiety, of the most elementary consolation, that of having someone to confide in, to talk it over with, to advise her. Mrs Wilde was indeed the unhappiest woman in London.[28]

The circulation through popular writing of these portraits of Constance as a martyr had a chilling effect on feminist critical thinking about Wilde.

Late in the next decade, however, pop culture would intervene in a different way and alter both this notion of the Wilde marriage and the climate in which Wilde himself was received. The year 1997 saw the release of the film *Wilde*, in which Brian Gilbert, the director, and Julian Mitchell, the screenwriter, collaborated to create a picture of Wilde as a doting domestic figure, tormented by the deceit in which he was compelled to engage in order to fulfill the demands of his nature. The image of the actor Stephen Fry resting his pain-filled, puppy-dog eyes on Constance in a tortured gaze imprinted itself on all who saw this film. Indeed, the suggestion that Wilde derived little pleasure (beyond physical release) from his liaisons and that his suffering as the betrayer was even greater than his wife's as the betrayed became part of the new *mythos* – a change that encouraged subsequent women critics to let him off the very hook on which Amor and Bentley had hoisted him.

The result of this shift could be found three years afterward in Barbara Belford's *Oscar Wilde: A Certain Genius* (2000), the first major modern biography of him undertaken by a woman. There Belford presented Wilde as trapped by circumstances: "He missed Cyril and Vyvyan [their sons] but was weary of lying to his wife." Constance, meanwhile, was shown to be almost pathologically dedicated to her husband and determined to monopolize his affections:

> The positive attitude Constance maintained toward her marriage cannot be explained by traditional concepts of wifely love. Her devotion transcended the usual marital loyalties. During their engagement, she had pledged to love her husband with such devotion that he would never leave or love anyone else as long as she could love and comfort him. That she had done and in all likelihood would have continued; in her mind, loving the sinner was more important than the sinner's transgressions.[29]

Belford's account went so far as to imply that there was a toxic element of possessiveness in such love: "Constance wanted to worship her husband, but he eluded her." At the same time, Belford's book also made much of the consolation that Constance took in 1894 from the companionship of the bookseller Arthur Humphreys, hinting that their relationship reached the level of an affair: "Now Mrs. Oscar Wilde had her own intimate secret."[30]

Some feminist critics have grown more willing to engage positively with Wilde and his works as they have ceased to see Constance merely as her husband's wretched victim. Others have been swayed by the new status among the oppressed (or among those oppressed twice-over – once through sexuality and once through ethnicity) afforded him by Irish Studies. Volumes of essays such as *Wilde the Irishman* (1998), edited by Jerusha McCormack, have emphasized the Irish heritage that kept Wilde a permanent outsider to both the social and the patriarchal hierarchy of England, despite his class identity as a "gentleman." These studies have highlighted, too, the feminized position of the Irish vis-à-vis the English, in the nineteenth century, and the similarities between misogynist definitions of the Victorian woman and racist constructions of the Irish man as childlike, silly, superstitious, irrational, and in need of governance with a firm hand. Relabeled as the representative of a colonized culture who was patronized and later persecuted by his English rulers because of his Irishness, Oscar Wilde has become an icon with whom present-day feminists could more readily identify. As McCormack put the matter, "he was of the oppressed peoples which embodied all that was alien . . . [and which] in turn . . . rejected what Wilde called the 'inherited stupidity' of the master-race."[31]

Yet there are scholars who have continued to number Wilde with the oppressor classes, in light of his dismissal of some of his female contemporaries in life and of feminism in his texts. Kerry Powell, in particular, has proved adamant in his view of Wilde as a two-faced friend to actresses and as the purveyor of what can at best be called ambivalent sentiments towards women's issues in the major fiction and plays. Through several essays on Wilde's relations with Elizabeth Robins, Powell has made the case that Wilde ultimately failed this actress-author, promising her a degree of support for her theatrical projects that never materialized. Most recently in "Wilde and Two Women" (1994), Powell has stated that Robins's own sense of disappointment pervaded her unfinished memoir (now in the Fales Library of New York University), where her positive assessment of Wilde was undercut by "an underlying uneasiness, even a sense of estrangement from the man to whom these pages were written in homage."[32] In "A Verdict of Death: Oscar Wilde, Actresses and Victorian Women" (1997), Powell has read the figure of Sibyl Vane in *Dorian Gray* as an insult to the actresses of Wilde's acquaintance, finding in her fate a mere recapitulation of conventional prejudices:

> Sibyl is defined at last with the rhetoric of sickness and death that came so easily to Victorians who wrote about actresses and their difference from so-called "ordinary women." . . . Like so many actresses in so many Victorian texts, Sibyl Vane is written out of love and marriage, and, again like other actresses in other texts, written out of humanity too. . . . Despite its enthusiasm for a great actress, *The Picture of Dorian Gray* . . . followed the Victorian strategy of neutralising power when a woman held it, or rationalising a strong voice when it happened to be female and compelled men to silence.[33]

Powell has also described Wilde's plays as expressions of their author's hostility toward late-Victorian feminism. By the time that Wilde conceived his successful series of stage works, as Powell has asserted in *Oscar Wilde and the Theatre of the 1890s* (1990), Wilde had

> scrapped the position he took as editor of *Woman's World* . . . that society should empower women politically because to do so would infuse "the family ideal" into the state and bring about the "moralisation of politics." This yielding to domestic authority no longer attracts Wilde in *An Ideal Husband*; it is what he fears rather than hopes. To stop the feminization of man, he is prepared to embrace the Victorian idea of women as creatures of vast feeling, but scant intellect, properly confined to the domestic sphere and the expression of that womanly love which bonds marriages and families.[34]

Quite recently, Powell has reiterated his opposition to defining Wilde's attitudes as feminist-friendly, asserting in "Wilde Man: Masculinity,

Feminism, and *A Woman of No Importance*" (2003) that the latter play, too, demonstrated Wilde's antagonism to the late-Victorian women's movement and its so-called "puritanical morality."[35]

Kerry Powell's reading of these texts as signs of backsliding or of Wilde's competing interest in liberating masculinity from women's control has been countered since the late 1990s by other feminist critics. Sos Eltis, for instance, turned her *Revising Wilde: Society and Subversion in the Plays of Oscar Wilde* (1996) into a defense of Wilde as a political radical, whose vision included a progressive feminist stance. Even in the seemingly anti-feminist fate of Lady Chiltern in *An Ideal Husband*, Eltis found neither backlash nor a set of prescriptive pronouncements by Wilde about women and domesticity, but only a set of deliberate paradoxes:

> *An Ideal Husband* is thus as ambiguous and complex a play as its predecessors. Beneath the surface melodrama of society intrigue, political blackmail, and conventional definitions of sexual roles lies a more subtly contradictory play of social and political satire. *An Ideal Husband* is not a play of answers. Like its predecessor [*A Woman of No Importance*] it highlights the flaws in any absolute definition or social generalization.[36]

For Eltis, there was ultimately no disjuncture between Wilde's "complex" representation of female characters in his dramas and his "sympathy with the struggle of intelligent women to gain an equal footing in society" or with the feminism he displayed during "his editorship of the *Woman's World*."[37]

The issue of his editorial philosophy while at the helm of that periodical has also been the focus of a number of discussions of Wilde and the Woman Question in recent scholarship. Critics employing a feminist perspective have raised the profile of Wilde's work for the *Woman's World* and allowed readers to appreciate his journalistic practice as central to his literary career as a whole, rather than as a sidenote. Laurel Brake helped to pioneer this area of study with the publication in 1994 of *Subjugated Knowledges: Journalism, Gender and Literature in the Nineteenth Century*. Her analysis in the chapter titled "Oscar Wilde and the Woman's World," moreover, linked Wilde's interest in opening opportunities for women to be "serious" and to receive "education and acculturation" with his equal eagerness to enable men "to be trivial" and "useless," if they wished.[38]

Among the critics following Brake's lead in examining Wilde's editorship have been Anya Clayworth, Stephanie Green, and, most recently, Diana Maltz.[39] In her 2003 essay, "Wilde's *The Woman's World* and Aesthetic

Philanthropy," Maltz has gone further than the usual assumptions about Wilde's feminism as focused primarily upon middle-class women; she has highlighted Wilde's use of his editorship to print articles on "the struggles of poor needle-women, Irish weavers, French lace-makers, London dressmakers, and those temporary female laborers who took whatever work was seasonally available: makers of matchboxes, jam, and fans."[40] Linda Hughes, meanwhile, has weighed Wilde's editorial handling of content directed toward women against W.E. Henley's contemporary inclusion of a fashion column in his magazine, the *Scots Observer*.[41] In "Wilde the Journalist" (1997), John Stokes has looked beyond Wilde's achievements as an editor to consider his role, too, as a contributor to *Woman's World*, finding in his signed and unsigned writings there a critical assessment of women writers that was "consistently well informed: witty yet quite unpatronising."[42]

But my own 2001 article, "The New Woman and the Periodical Press of the 1890s," has placed Wilde's decisions about how to represent feminism in the *Woman's World*, both through verbal and visual images, within the wider context of late-Victorian business strategies. Seen in this light, Wilde's choices – like those of many male editors and publishers – appear to have been simultaneously supportive and exploitative of progressive women, who were often used as icons of modernity and as "harbingers of change" to advertise the cutting-edge nature of new (or newly revamped) magazines.[43] Wilde may indeed have featured New Women out of political loyalty to them; nonetheless, he also remained shrewdly aware of their commercial appeal to the public.

The rise of literary and historical studies centering upon the "New Woman" movement has brought with it fresh attention to Wilde's relationships with these figures. My own "The Bi-Social Oscar Wilde and 'Modern' Women" (2001) uncovered a consistent pattern of Wilde offering encouragement and assistance to unconventional women, though especially to those who were supporting themselves via careers in the arts – a pattern traceable to the influence of Lady Wilde, a professional poet throughout her years as a wife and mother.[44] At the same time, my article recorded the largely (if not wholly) favorable response to Wilde in writings by his female contemporaries from "Michael Field" and "George Egerton" to Katharine Tynan, along with their sympathetic outrage on his behalf occasioned by the 1895 trials and prison sentence. This sense of an important connection between Wilde and New Women – as well as between dandies and "effeminate" males in general and 1890s feminists – has been affirmed by two subsequent essays. Ann Heilmann's 2002 "Wilde's New Women: The New Woman on Wilde" has addressed both the alliances and the sometimes contentious disputes between Wilde and figures from the late-Victorian women's movement, while Lisa Hamilton's "Oscar Wilde, New Women, and the Rhetoric of Effeminacy" in the volume *Wilde Writings* (2003) has outlined the reasons for the New Woman writers' attraction toward, yet suspicion of, the "effeminate" type of male embodied by Wilde.[45]

Indeed, it seemingly has become impossible to study Wilde without considering him in relation to feminist politics, whether late-Victorian or current, just as it has become impossible to overlook his status either as a sexual dissident or as a product of Ireland. One sign of the pervasiveness of this assumption is a book such as John Sloan's *Oscar Wilde* (2003). Sloan's study appears in Oxford's "Authors in Context" series – a series which (as its advertising blurb proclaims) "examines the work of major writers in relation to their own time and to the present day[,] . . . provides detailed coverage of the values and debates that colour the writing of particular authors and considers their novels, plays, and poetry against this background."[46] The second chapter, "The Fabric of Society," contains a sub-section titled "Women's Rights" devoted to topics such as the "New Woman," but the volume as a whole also turns frequently to analyzing Wilde's texts in terms of their feminist content. Feminism certainly is not the focus of Sloan's volume, nor is it the principal methodology used, yet it is never far from the matter at hand.

Would Virginia Woolf have been pleased at this development? Or would she have turned up her nose (which looked nothing like the ugly prosthetic one attached to Nicole Kidman in the film, *The Hours*) at the idea that Wilde had anything to do with the political or literary progress of women, let alone that Oxford University Press had declared him a "major" writer? Would she perhaps have been happier to know that Ian Small's *Oscar Wilde: Recent Research* (2000) includes a chapter titled "New Paradigms in Literary and Cultural History," but identifies only three such "new paradigms" – "The Gay Wilde," "The Irish Wilde," and "Wilde & Consumerism" – and omits the feminist one? We cannot, of course, know how Woolf or her generation of early-twentieth-century feminist thinkers, who did so much to inspire later critics and historians, would have responded to the current identification of Wilde with women's issues.

But we can be sure that some of Wilde's contemporaries would have approved. One of the first books to "revalue" Wilde sympathetically after his death was by an American-born acquaintance, Anna, Comtesse de Brémont. Long before Woolf proposed her own theory about the truly creative mind as androgynous, the author of *Oscar Wilde and His Mother:*

A Memoir (1911) proferred her notion of the relationship between gender and genius: "The feminine soul in the masculine brain-building creates the genius of man." Oscar Wilde, she wrote, "possessed the feminine soul," which "endowed him with the supreme love and appreciation of beauty in every form . . . and the fine and delicate vision that created in him the instinct of the poet."[47] Perhaps we are merely revising a past perception, instead of inventing a new approach, when we say that if Wilde's was not a feminine soul, then it can at least be talked about as a feminist one.

notes

1. Virginia Woolf, "Romance and the 'Nineties," in *The Essays of Virginia Woolf, Volume IV, 1925–1928*, ed. Andrew McNeillie (London: Hogarth Press, 1994), 359–360.
2. Ibid., 434.
3. Virginia Woolf, *The Diary of Virginia Woolf, Volume V: 1936–1941*, ed. Anne Olivier Bell (London: Hogarth Press, 1984), 258.
4. Ibid., 258.
5. Virginia Woolf, *A Room of One's Own* (New York and London: Harcourt Brace Jovanovich, 1929; rpt. 1981), 76.
6. Ibid., 85–86.
7. Ann L. Ardis, *New Women, New Novels: Feminism and Early Modernism* (New Brunswick and London: Rutgers University Press, 1990), 170–171.
8. Rebecca West, *Selected Letters of Rebecca West*, ed. Bonnie Kime Scott (New Haven and London: Yale University Press, 2000), 37–39.
9. Ibid., 378.
10. Victoria Glendinning, *Rebecca West: A Life* (London: Weidenfeld and Nicolson, 1987), 73.
11. *Selected Letters of Rebecca West*, 286.
12. Rebecca West, *Sunflower* (London: Virago, 1986), 23.
13. Zora Neale Hurston, *Dust Tracks on a Road: An Autobiography* (Urbana and Chicago: University of Illinois Press, 1984), 149.
14. Adrienne Rich, "Compulsory Heterosexuality and Lesbian Existence," in *The Signs Reader: Women, Gender & Scholarship*, eds. Elizabeth Abel and Emily K. Abel (Chicago and London: University of Chicago Press, 1983), 157–158.
15. Elaine Showalter, *Sexual Anarchy: Gender and Culture at the Fin de Siècle* (New York: Viking, 1990), 175–176.
16. Jane Marcus, *Art and Anger: Reading Like a Woman* (Columbus, OH: Ohio State University Press, 1988), 17.
17. Ibid., 8.
18. Gail Finney, *Women in Modern Drama: Freud, Feminism, and European Theater at the Turn of the Century* (Ithaca, NY: Cornell University Press, 1989), 65.
19. Ibid., 67.
20. Patricia Kellogg-Dennis, "Oscar Wilde's *Salome*: Symbolist Princess," in *Rediscovering Oscar Wilde*, ed. C. George Sandulescu (Gerrards Cross, Buckinghamshire, UK: Colin Smythe, 1994), 230.

21. Ibid., 227.
22. Amanda Fernbach, "Wilde's *Salomé* and the Ambiguous Fetish," *Victorian Literature and Culture* 29.1 (2001), 196–197.
23. Ibid., 201.
24. Ibid., 210–211.
25. See the website of "SPIR: Conceptual Photography" at <http://home.earthlink.net/mdeguzman/>.
26. Jody Price, *"A Map with Utopia": Oscar Wilde's Theory for Social Transformation* (New York: Peter Lang, 1996), 32–33.
27. Anne Clark Amor, *Mrs. Oscar Wilde: A Woman of Some Importance* (London: Sidgwick & Jackson, 1983), 135.
28. Joyce Bentley, *The Importance of Being Constance* (New York: Beaufort Books, 1983), 103.
29. Barbara Belford, *Oscar Wilde: A Certain Genius* (New York: Random House, 2000), 241–242.
30. Ibid., 243.
31. Jerusha McCormack, "Introduction: The Irish Wilde," in *Wilde the Irishman*, ed. Jerusha McCormack (New Haven and London: Yale University Press, 1998), 2.
32. Kerry Powell, "Wilde and Two Women: Unpublished Accounts by Elizabeth Robins and Blanche Crackanthorpe," in Sandelescu ed. *Rediscovering Oscar Wilde*, 315.
33. Kerry Powell, "A Verdict of Death: Oscar Wilde, Actresses and Victorian Women," in *The Cambridge Companion to Oscar Wilde*, ed. Peter Raby (Cambridge: Cambridge University Press, 1997), 191–192.
34. Kerry Powell, *Oscar Wilde and the Theatre of the 1890s* (Cambridge: Cambridge University Press, 1990), 106–107.
35. Kerry Powell, "Wilde Man: Masculinity, Feminism, and *A Woman of No Importance*," in *Wilde Writings: Contextual Conditions*, ed. Joseph Bristow (Toronto: University of Toronto Press, 2003), 127.
36. Sos Eltis, *Revising Wilde: Society and Subversion in the Plays of Oscar Wilde* (Oxford: Clarendon Press, 1996), 169.
37. Ibid., 160.
38. Laurel Brake, *Subjugated Knowledges: Journalism, Gender and Literature in the Nineteenth Century* (New York: New York University Press, 1994), 142.
39. Anya Clayworth, "The Woman's World: Oscar Wilde as Editor," *Victorian Periodicals Review* 30.2 (1997), 84–101; Stephanie Green, "Oscar Wilde's The Woman's World," *Victorian Periodicals Review* 30.2 (1997), 102–120; Diana Maltz, "Wilde's *The Woman's World* and Aesthetic Philanthropy," in Bristow ed. *Wilde Writings*.
40. Maltz, "Wilde's *The Woman's World*," 186.
41. Linda Hughes, *Strange Bedfellows: W.E. Henley and Feminist Fashion History*. Occasional Series No. 3. (Arncott, Oxon, UK: Eighteen Nineties Society, 1997).
42. John Stokes, "Wilde the Journalist," in Raby ed. *The Cambridge Companion to Oscar Wilde*, 72.
43. Margaret Diane Stetz, "The New Woman and the British Periodical Press of the 1890s," *Journal of Victorian Culture* 6.2 (2001), 273.

44. Margaret Diane Stetz, "The Bi-Social Oscar Wilde and 'Modern' Women," *Nineteenth-Century Literature* 55.4, 515–537.
45. Ann Heilmann, "Wilde's New Women: The New Woman on Wilde," in *The Importance of Reinventing Oscar: Versions of Wilde During the Last 100 Years*, eds. Uwe Böker, Richard Corballis, and Julie Hibbard (Amsterdam and New York: Rodopi, 2002), 135–145.
46. John Sloan, *Oscar Wilde* (Oxford: Oxford University Press, 2003).
47. Brémont, Anna, Comtesse de, *Oscar Wilde and His Mother: A Memoir* (London: Everett & Co., 1911), 15–16.

10
oscar wilde: nation and empire

noreen doody

The significance of Oscar Wilde's nationality to his life and work is a relatively recent area of modern critical inquiry. In fact, up until the 1990s Wilde's claim to Irish identity was contested by some critics. In 1954, the writer, Flann O'Brien, strenuously opposed the notion of Wilde's Irishness, proclaiming that he was undoubtedly an English writer and Irish only by accident of birth. Maurice Harmon's and Roger McHugh's ambiguous attitude to Wilde's Irish nationality has been noted by various writers in the field of Irish Studies.[1] Writing in their *Short History of Anglo-Irish Literature*, these critics acknowledged Wilde's Irish origins but consigned him to the history of English theatre.[2]

In his book of essays on Irish authors, *Celtic Revivals* (1985), Seamus Deane not only excludes Wilde from a line-up that includes Yeats, Synge, Joyce and Beckett, but remarks that none of Wilde's works, with the exception of *De Profundis* and "The Ballad of Reading Gaol," are of lasting literary value.[3] Indeed, Wilde is described by Deane in this essay as "a minor nineteenth-century figure." More recently, in the *Field Day Anthology of Irish Writing*, Christopher Murray while acknowledging Wilde's subversive wit in its use against English hypocrisy accords no great political or cultural significance to his work.[4] Declan Kiberd, however, also writing in *Field Day*, counteracts this image of cultural and political impotence in situating Wilde at the epicenter of Irish literary and national history: he proclaims Wilde a "militant Irish Republican" and places him, alongside George Bernard Shaw, as "the godfather of the Irish renaissance."[5]

Kiberd's postcolonial and anthropological readings of Wilde contributed largely to the development of a newly focused critical approach to Wilde in the 1990s. This emergent dynamic in critical thinking during this decade along with new biographical documentation of Wilde's Irish upbringing and background (particularly Davis Coakley's *Oscar Wilde: The Importance of Being Irish*), led to a reassessment of Wilde's place within Irish Studies.[6] In the preceding decades the critical focus on Irish aspects of Wilde had been minimal. There were some allusions and references made to his Irish origins and a few critics, notably Richard Ellmann and Katharine Worth, recognized certain critical implications of his background for his writing.[7] Before that period, in the early years of the twentieth century and during the late 1890s critics looked on the critical significance of Wilde's nationality to his work as an obvious correlation. Yeats, Shaw and Joyce wrote of him in terms of nation and empire. In current critical research by Noreen Doody the significance of the nation-based criticism of Wilde's contemporaries and his own perception of his nationality is explored and elucidated.[8]

There are two main sections in the following chapter. In the first of these sections I will survey current critical work on Wilde in relation to his nationality and take a look at recent biographical work on Wilde. In the second section I will explore the nineteenth-century view of Wilde in relation to nation and empire and recent critical inquiry into this area.

I

criticism since the 1990s

The heightened awareness of Wilde's nationality and its relevance to his work which emerged in the 1990s produced exciting readings of his work and effective methods for understanding the writer. Access to postcolonial theory encouraged critics to examine work written by writers such as Wilde in the context of empire and colonization. Valuable and creative critical work has been carried out in relation to Wilde in this area, although a great deal more work remains to be done.

The most comprehensive study of Wilde in the context of nation and empire has been carried out by Declan Kiberd. Kiberd's penetrating critical vision offers a radical and insightful reading of Wilde. Kiberd's criticism is included in his books, *Inventing Ireland* and *Irish Classics* and also in various introductions, articles and essays.[9]

For the most part, critical writings concerning Wilde and his national context have tended to be in the form of essays, articles or a chapter in a larger work. *Wilde the Irishman*, edited by Jerusha McCormack, differs in format only in that the essays are collected in a book wholly devoted to aspects of Wilde's Irish identity.[10] The content of nation-based criticism varies from consciousness-raising and affirmation of Wilde's Irishness to theories arising from his cultural inheritance. These theories fall into two main categories, those based on Irish cultural tradition and those based on the relationship between colony and empire. Elements such as Wilde's use of language and his much lauded skill as a talker are seen as having their origin within Ireland's ancient oral tradition; his vivacity and sharp wit are acknowledged as belonging within the continuum of Gaelic and English-speaking Irish writers. Critical inquiry into England's perspective on nineteenth-century Ireland throws light on matters of religion, sexuality and identity as they relate to Wilde. Indeed, an understanding of Irish/English relations in the nineteenth century is crucially important to an understanding of Wilde's psychological profile.[11]

Wilde was born into a country that had been colonized by England over a period of 700 years. Ireland was governed from London; laws, educational edicts and social decrees were issued from London and administered by the Lord Lieutenant of Ireland and his officials in Dublin. Wilde was the recipient of a bicultural inheritance: while he was brought up speaking English in an English literary tradition, he belonged to a family who were deeply acquainted with ancient Irish culture, its folk tales, legends, history and archaeology. His father, Sir William Wilde, an eminent ophthalmic and aural surgeon, was also a talented amateur archeologist, a collector of Irish folklore and member of the Royal Irish Academy. His mother, Lady Wilde, was a Nationalist poet, famed throughout Ireland as "Speranza" of Nationalist Ireland's newspaper, *The Nation*. W.B. Yeats once observed that she had defied the Protestant upper middle class into which she was born in order to join her voice with the common people of Ireland.[12]

bicultural identity: mask and pose

Wilde's bicultural heritage has important implications for his sense of identity and patterns of thought. Declan Kiberd in *Inventing Ireland* draws attention to Wilde's hybridity.[13] He contrasts Wilde's upbringing in Dublin in the mid-nineteenth century with his manner of living in London in later years. He describes Wilde's home in Dublin as somewhat chaotic and colorful and finds his parents' eccentricities resemble in many respects characters from a stage Irish production. In England, Kiberd suggests, Wilde consciously reversed this image by means of the pose and constructed himself in the image of an elegant, ultra-English Englishman. Kiberd maintains that the Victorian propensity for seeing everything within a framework of binary opposition was exploited by Wilde who perceived that, far from excluding its opposite, a thing always partakes of the nature of its opposite. According to Kiberd, Wilde exploded Victorian binaries, recognizing that within every Irishman was the sensibility of an Englishman and vice versa, just as every man has feminine qualities and every woman the qualities supposedly exclusive to the male. Kiberd explains that in his mimicry of Englishness, Wilde reduced to an absurdity the perception of Ireland and England as totally opposing entities. He states that Wilde's pose has often been misinterpreted and taken as an abnegation of his Irish identity but was in fact parodic, a not-uncommon strategic response of colonized people to the colonial situation.[14]

Wilde both challenged and disarmed English prejudicial notions of the Irish and gained for himself an ease of movement behind the self-imposed mask of gentility in the capital of empire. Homi Bhabha writes of this strategy of mimicry often employed by colonized people in relation to the colonizer.[15] Fintan O'Toole also observes that performance, the exaggeration of characteristics, is often practiced by the exile in an effort to establish identity.[16]

However, there is a further element in Kiberd's criticism of Wilde which originates in Wilde's awareness of the double nature of his cultural identity. Kiberd maintains that in deconstructing the binaries, Wilde sought their reconciliation or underlying unity. He further suggests that in challenging difference and discerning a commonality between the peoples of both islands, England and Ireland, Wilde opens the way for cultural understanding, equal rights and resolution. Kiberd situates Wilde's philosophical viewpoint within an on-going Irish social and political discourse.[17]

Both Kiberd and Owen Dudley Edwards allude to Parnell as another Irishman who challenged English misconceptions of Ireland by his personal behavior in London.[18] Dudley Edwards states that Parnell's success in the political sphere furthered the acceptability of the Irish in England at this time. Both critics comment on Wilde's association with Parnell. W.J. McCormack pursues this line of inquiry in his essay, "Wilde and Parnell."[19]

imperialist image of ireland: individualism, doubleness and wilde

Terry Eagleton suggests that Wilde only acknowledged his Irish identity as it suited him.[20] Neil Sammells takes issue with Eagleton's assessment, contending that it undermines the importance which Wilde attached to his national identity.[21] Both Sammells and Richard Pine believe Wilde's negotiation of identity to be a more complicated issue and see his response to his position as outsider in London in the donning of a mask of Englishness.[22] Sammells sees Wilde's device as analogous to Algernon Moncrieff's use of Bunbury in *The Importance of Being Earnest*. In fact, he finds in Bunbury the Irish presence in England, a comic representation of

Wilde's dual identity. Kiberd goes further in suggesting that Bunbury and Algy mirror colonial treatment of Ireland by England.[23] Kiberd maintains that the colonial power projects its own fantasies, suspected failings and secret longings on to its subject thus preserving an image of its own respectability and relieving itself of all responsibility for that which it most fears in itself. The colony is turned, simultaneously, into an image of distaste and desire. In the same way, Kiberd suggests, Bunbury is the repository of the irresponsible Algy's misbegotten deeds.

Ireland in the nineteenth century, as Kiberd has pointed out, was seen by English authorities to be everything England was not. The Irish were seen to be dirty, lazy, childlike, ineffectual and morally and intellectually inferior to their neighbor. The illustrated journals of the period, such as "Punch" and "Judy", depict gross simian caricatures of the Irish which reflect this attitude.[24] Kiberd suggests that Wilde's insistence on the autonomy of the individual is a direct challenge to nineteenth-century England's espousal of Determinism because by Determinist reasoning the Anglo-Saxon view of the Irish becomes a fixed entity and refuses any possibility for enlightenment or change of mind.[25] Fintan O'Toole shows American awareness of Ireland's colonial image during Wilde's American tour in the 1880s: Wilde was caricatured in national newspapers and journals, sometimes as a simian-featured creature, sometimes as a negro, who like the Irish were considered by the imperialist mindset as an inferior type of being.[26] O'Toole explores the ambiguities of identity both projected by Wilde and applied to him within the American context. He shows how Irish identity was at once identified with the "savage" Indians and at the same time with the colonizers of America. Irish identity in America was ambivalent. Wilde's original lecture in America was on the English Renaissance and the promoter of his tour described him as an English poet. However, O'Toole explains, Wilde's Irish identity, with its connotations of barbarity, made it impossible for Americans to accept him as a civilizing voice.

anglo-irish identity

The uneasy position of Wilde as Irishman in imperial London was further complicated by his Anglo-Irish status at home.[27] This position is interrogated by Richard Pine who explains Wilde's sense of belonging and difference in terms of his Anglo-Irish identity.[28]

Anglo-Ireland's position within Irish society was complex. The majority of Ireland's population were peasant and Catholic. The Anglo-Irish were Protestant and as a class originated as English settlers. The Anglo-Irish had long enjoyed a privileged position in Ireland. They held positions of authority in the administrative and legal professions which were not available to Catholics and were often landowners. Anglo-Ireland saw itself as Irish but had close affiliations with England – many of its people had relations in the British army or in colonial positions throughout the empire, while some lived both in Ireland and England, having a network of friends and relatives in both countries. In the later stages of the nineteenth century Anglo-Ireland, which had enjoyed a hierarchical position in Ireland, was beginning to feel a foreboding sense of change as Ireland moved towards independence from England. Terry Eagleton reminds us that the demise of the Anglo-Irish as a ruling class exactly paralleled Oscar Wilde's life-span.[29]

Wilde was twice displaced: in Ireland, outside the majority culture of his fellow countrymen, in England an outsider by birth. Curtis Marez maintains that Wilde's construction of an English-type identity in London was an attempt to convert his uncertain status as middle-class Anglo-Irish into a position of strength.[30] Marez considers the complexities of Anglo-Irish identity and its diverse loyalties: to homeland, empire and home rule. He recognizes Wilde's pride in his Irishness but suggests that he was also patriotically English. Marez opposes Kiberd's contention that Wilde was an avid republican and rather sees Wilde attempting to displace his Irish otherness on to non-western ornaments and the people who made them. While Kiberd argued that Wilde exploded the myth of the polarity of Irish and English identity in adopting an English pose, Marez suggests that Wilde projected difference, the exotic and inferiority, on to non-Europeans in an attempt to rid himself of an inferior colonized identity and integrate his Irishness within Empire. Marez sees Wilde's endeavor as a failed enterprise, as in spite of his best efforts, both England and America persisted in designating him lowly Irish.

Marez's theory of Wilde's displacement of Irishness on to the East recalls Kiberd's theory of the behavior of the imperial power in relation to its subject as illustrated by Algy and Bunbury.[31]

utopia and resolution

Kiberd demonstrates Wilde's search for an ideal society in which a cultural exchange and eventual resolution between Ireland and England are possibilities. He indicates the similarity between Irish peasant and English aristocrat in Wilde's depiction of character: leisure loving; impervious to the constraints of time; sensitive to the possibility offered by language.[32] Kiberd promotes Oscar Wilde as an Irish Modernist incorporating within that stance social radicalism and cultural traditionalism. Whereas Kiberd perceives the duality of Wilde's identity and posits a belief in his egalitarian hopes for both England and Ireland, Curtis Marez sees Wilde in a more polarized position, battling unsuccessfully for parity with the colonizer.[33] Marez detects in Wilde's search for Utopia a quest to overcome inferior status by relocating a mutually dependent Ireland and England within an aesthetic empire. According to Richard Pine, in creating an aesthetic world, Wilde clears a space where it is possible for him to get beyond a problematic identity and enter into literary discourse.

the ludic, the lie and empowerment in wilde's use of language

In his essay, "Language Play: Brian Friel and Ireland's Verbal Theatre," Richard Kearney discusses Anglo-Ireland's response to its displacement within Irish culture as discernible in Anglo-Irish writers' playful use of language.[34] Seamus Deane takes up the issue of language in *Field Day*.[35] He contends that all the major Irish Writers from Beckett to Wilde have been anxious to exhibit their dexterity with language as it serves to illustrate their control and possession of a language which is not theirs by birthright. He implies that language is both their creation and their impetus towards creating. Terry Eagleton extends this point, describing language in the Irish context as a source of empowerment, an alternative to oppression.[36] Eagleton sees Wilde's use of language as having an Irish provenance: language enables the transformation of fact into fiction. In his "Introduction" to *Plays, Prose Writing and Poems* Eagleton states that language in the Irish creative context provides a freedom which was unavailable in the area of the actual. He contends that Wilde's privileging of wit and fantasy over reality reflects the colonized and constrained position of Ireland.[37]

Richard Kearney refers to Wilde's linguistic playfulness as belonging within the Irish literary tradition and acknowledges Wilde as a pre-eminent precursor of the Theatre of Language phenomenon in contemporary Ireland.[38] F.C. McGrath in his essay, "Brian Friel and the Irish Art of Lying," situates Wilde alongside Brian Friel and J.M. Synge within another Irish literary tradition, that of mendacity, the power of the lie to transform.[39] Both McGrath's and Kearney's essays, although not exclusively about Wilde, are important to Wilde Studies, in that they delineate two central features of the use of language in the Irish literary tradition: the ludic element and the displacement of reality into fiction.

One of the basic tenets of Wilde's philosophy is that the artist imagines reality and that life follows the images with which art presents it. This perception of Wilde is interpreted within the context of his colonial status by David Alderson in his essay, "Momentary Pleasures: Wilde and English Virtue."[40] He sees Wilde's acclamation of lying as an attempt to convert the

English notion of the underhand, duplicitous Irish into a more positive and praiseworthy image. Declan Kiberd, in a more comprehensive argument, also perceives the connections between Wilde's thoughts on lying and his political and historic context.[41] Kiberd concurs with Eagleton that in the colonial situation, language is often used by the disempowered as a weapon.[42] Within the context of colonization, dissimulation, ambiguity and deception were often employed by the colonized Irish in the interests of self-protection and survival. Kiberd indicates the many ways in which lying was endemic to the Irish situation. He cites the Penal Laws as an example of the disjunction between aspiration and practice in the Irish social system. The Penal Laws were a harsh code of anti-Catholic laws introduced into Ireland in the seventeenth century which had built into its system penalties for those Anglo-Irish magistrates who might refuse to implement its measures. Many magistrates did refuse to implement them and Kiberd makes the point that a law which had such doubts about the possibility of its own implementation from first appearing on the statute books was inherently ambiguous about its own actuality. He cites further examples of the ambiguity of actuality and reality in Irish society and concludes that it is from the state of disjunction between what is claimed to be and what actually is that the great Anglo-Irish writers, including Wilde, gained their "bi-focal vision."

Kiberd traces an association between the lie and the law in Ireland back to the early poets, the filí. It was the duty of these poets both to keep the records of the law and to tell magnificent lies or stories. There is, as Kiberd suggests, a certain cynicism in the overlap of these functions. This cultural inheritance, as Kiberd describes it, has distinct relevance for Wilde's dissertation on the decay of lying and his revolt against the age of realism. Kiberd shows that Wilde's philosophy had creative consequences for J.M. Synge and later Irish writers.

Writing in *Irish Writing: Exile and Subversion* Neil Sammells compares Synge's creative expansion of the English language to fit the rhythms and cadences of the Gaelic language, as tactically similar to Wilde's transformation of the English language.[43] Sammells observes the precision and ultra-elegance of Wilde's English and contends that Wilde in his exploitation of the language attempts to distance himself within it, thus paralleling his position as an Anglo-Irishman within empire. Declan Kiberd expresses a somewhat similar view in *Inventing Ireland*.[44] Terry Eagleton refers to the compromised and tragic position of language in Ireland: the loss of the Gaelic language in the nineteenth-century famine and the imposition of the English language. He recognizes nationality as a factor in Wilde's virtuosity and self-conscious regard for language.[45]

oral culture, folklore and celticism

Many critics have noted the connection between Wilde's use of language and his Irish cultural context. Richard Ellmann describes Wilde's style as the aristocratic version of the peasant oral tradition.[46] Deirdre Toomey expands on this notion in her essay, "The Story-Teller at Fault: Oscar Wilde and Irish Orality."[47] Toomey points out that many of Wilde's contemporaries preferred his oral storytelling and valued the spoken over the written versions of his stories. She ascribes the non-proprietorial stance which Wilde adopts towards his spoken stories to his origins within an oral culture. Sins of plagiarism, use of stereotype and cliché of which Wilde has often been accused Toomey explains as legitimate principles of creativity within the oral tradition. Alan Stanford in his essay, "Acting Wilde," notes that Wilde's belief in the magical quality of words is an attitude to be found in the oral tradition.[48]

Wilde's use of folklore is noted by Frank McGuinness and Owen Dudley Edwards in *Wilde the Irishman*; McGuinness instances *De Profundis* and Edwards refers to *The Picture of Dorian Gray* in this regard.[49] Wilde was making use of folklore within his own creativity long before it became a common practice in the Irish Literary Revival – another reason, perhaps, for Declan Kiberd's designation of him as godfather to that movement. Angela Bourke believes that *Dorian Gray* has particularly strong folkloric connections, a view taken by Davis Coakley in *Oscar Wilde: The Importance of Being Irish*.[50]

The notion of the Celt is discussed by Bernard O'Donoghue in his essay, "The Journey to Reading Gaol: Sacrifice and Scapegoat in Irish Literature."[51] O'Donoghue maintains that contrary to the popular image, Celtic thought and literature is pragmatic rather than insubstantial. He discusses the notion of sacrifice within Celtic literature and, placing Oscar Wilde within the cultural context of other Irish Writers, finds that they belong within a culture of shame rather than guilt. He applies this concept to a critical understanding of their work.

Richard Haslam also finds Wilde's Celticism at variance with that proposed by Matthew Arnold.[52] Haslam perceives Wilde's Celticism in his essay, "The Soul of Man under Socialism" and in his poem, "The Ballad of Reading Gaol," and identifies it with Wilde's "self-transforming" empathy with the suffering of others.

subversion: weapon of the colonized

Wilde's use of subversion within his work has often been noted and is well documented. However, his use of subversion as a tool of the colonized against imperialist domination is a relatively recent critical perspective in Wilde Studies. Davis Coakley in *Oscar Wilde: The Importance of Being Irish* explores this phenomenon.[53] Coakley cites the example of Wilde's play, *A Woman of No Importance*, which was attended on its first night by Arthur Balfour and Joseph Chamberlain. The play contained a strongly derogatory description of the state of England at the time and while the play was well-received, Wilde was booed by the audience after the performance. Whether or not the offensive description of England contributed to Wilde's poor reception, he later cut it from the scene. Sos Eltis in *Revising Wilde: Society and Subversion in the Plays of Oscar Wilde*, a book not particularly about Irish aspects of Wilde, attributes subversive writing to the outcast and revolutionary which in the context of Wilde's colonized background is apposite.[54] Jerusha McCormack in "The Wilde Irishman: Oscar Wilde Aesthete and Anarchist" concurs with this perspective.[55] Christopher Murray, writing in *Field Day*, while acknowledging subversion as a method of protest employed by Irish writers writing in colonial England, does not feel that politics entered into the equation until the writing of W.B. Yeats.[56] It is difficult to see how acts of subversion by colonized Irish writers were not political, if anarchically so. Terence Brown sees Wilde as a reformer of English society, his subversion an act of restoration; Declan Kiberd also holds this view.[57] According to Kiberd's perspective, Wilde holds up a mirror to a society emasculated by its own imperialist and hypocritical pretensions, a society in which imagination and progressive thought had been stifled. Richard Pine suggests that Wilde's position as an outsider paradoxically draws him into the center where he becomes involved in purloining material of mainstream concern. Richard Allen Cave is in agreement with Pine.[58] Writing in his "Introduction" to *Oscar Wilde: The Importance of Being Earnest and Other Plays*, Cave reiterates the dangerously central position from which Wilde critiques British society. Cave, like Kiberd, considers Wilde a prominent participant in the contemporary Irish cultural movement which sought to reinstate a distinct Irish voice, independent of and separate from the imperialist cultural position.

For David Alderson, Wilde's subversion of English Victorian society is manifest in his avowal of Celticism, Catholicism and in images of the dandy and laconic artist.[59] Alderson's reading of *De Profundis* uncovers Wilde's fundamental Irishness. He observes that Wilde's assertion of his own racial qualities are oppositional to those he proposes for Alfred Douglas and his family. Alderson observes that Wilde inverts the stereotype of the simian Irish in his description of the Marquess of Queensberry and infers a racial divide between the philistine image of empire and the aesthetic Celtic race. Alderson concludes that Wilde frames his own fate at the hands of empire within the larger context of colonial oppression of his country.

cultural heritage: religion, gender and race

Wilde's belief in racial heritage, his sexuality and interest in Catholicism are seen by Alderson as strategies by which he seeks to distance himself from the dominant culture. The belief that Wilde's interest in Catholicism had much to do with incense and ritual has long been proclaimed by critics, and Alderson seems to suggest something of this sort. However, this notion is challenged by Declan Kiberd and Jarlath Killeen who note something more robust in Wilde's Catholicism when this religion is understood in its Irish rather than English form.[60] Kiberd reminds us that Catholicism was the religion of the majority of Irish people who suffered extreme deprivation in protesting their right to its practice. He interprets Wilde's form of Catholicism as an act of solidarity with his countrymen. Kiberd makes the point that within the historic context of Ireland, Wilde's espousal of Catholicism constituted a revolutionary act.

Catholicism was viewed by the mainly Protestant Victorian English community as somewhat suspect, somewhat foreign and feminine. Within Victorian thinking the feminine was identified as weak and inferior. Ashis Nandy in "The Intimate Enemy" describes how colonialism replicated the nineteenth-century model of the sexual stereotype with its imputation of male superiority and approval of the dominance of male over female.[61] Kiberd makes the connection between feminized Catholicism, Wilde's sexuality and the colonial view of its subject country as feminine and therefore inferior. Jarlath Killeen in his essay, "Woman and Nation Revisited: Oscar Wilde's 'The Nightingale and the Rose,'" notes that it would have been impossible for a Catholic to have been seen as properly English in the nineteenth century. In his essay, Killeen critically applies Wilde's knowledge of Catholicism to a reading of his fairy tale, "The Nightingale and the Rose." Killeen details the iconography of Mary in Irish culture as both national and religious. He posits Wilde's use of the female image as implying both nation and Catholicism – a reading which shows Wilde's serious intent and commitment to both. Owen Dudley Edwards concurs with Killeen in an implicit relationship existing between nationalism and Catholicism in Ireland.[62]

Vicki Mahaffey's book, *States of Desire,* takes as one of its themes sexuality and nation in relation to Wilde. Although somewhat lacking in clarity, this book usefully explores the integrity of Wilde's nationality with respect to his views on youth, sexuality, individuality and criminality.[63]

She, like Neil Sammells, discerns shades of nationalism, homosexuality and youth in his use of the color green. Wilde's sexuality in relation to his Irishness is alluded to by Adrian Frazier in *Gender and Sexuality*, but is found to be marginal to the national narrative.[64] In *Sex, Nation and Dissent*, Éibhear Walshe aims to explore the homoerotic as an imaginative component in Irish writing.[65] Wilde is discussed in this context by David Alderson. In "'I see it is my name that terrifies': Wilde in the 20th Century," Alan Sinfield questions whether Oscar Wilde was ever accepted as gay by Irish critics and claims that it is typical of Nationalism to find sexual "irregularities" a trait of imperialism.[66] He contends that Wilde's homosexuality was associated with Englishness and that this may explain why even in Ireland, Wilde was often identified as an English writer. Sinfield suggests that the Irish persona shares much in common with gay style and argues that what are termed Wilde's Irish characteristics are commensurate with gay, camp style.

Lucy McDiarmid prefaces her essay, "Oscar Wilde's Speech from the Dock," by endorsing his nationalist convictions.[67] Her chief concern in this essay is to refute the conception of Wilde as either a gay or republican martyr. McDiarmid examines Wilde's situation within the Irish Republican tradition of speech-making from the dock and finds Wilde's position incompatible with that of his Republican predecessors. McDiarmid proves that Wilde did not consciously choose to be a martyr but she does not interrogate the concept of martyrdom: whether to be a martyr necessarily implies choice or is rather an attributed status. McDiarmid also fails to explore the more germane question as to whether Wilde's position as a colonized Irishman in the court of empire had any bearing on the trial proceedings; for instance, it is interesting that Sir Edward Lewis should refer to Wilde's nationality in his summing-up speech, his final attempt to exonerate Wilde, as though perhaps an appeal to the generally-accepted nineteenth-century view of the Irish as less responsible than their English "betters" might in some way help Wilde's case.

biography

Very little notice of Wilde's position as a colonized Irish writer was taken by his biographers until Davis Coakley's book, *Oscar Wilde: The Importance of Being Irish,* was published in 1994.[68] Richard Pine's short biography of Wilde, published some years earlier in 1983, was the first to stress the Irish aspects of Wilde's life.[69] More recently Pine has extended this biographical work to include a fuller exposition of Wilde's colonial status and its relevance to his writing.[70] Richard Ellmann situated Wilde among his countrymen, Yeats and Joyce, in *Eminent Domain* and detected an interplay of ideas and creative influence passing between them.[71] In grouping Wilde, Joyce and Yeats in this way, Ellmann acknowledged their common origins. However, in his biography of Oscar Wilde Ellmann repeats his observations on Wilde's influence on Yeats and details Wilde's childhood and adolescence in Ireland but is quick to accept that Wilde abandoned his Irish identity in Oxford. Ellmann's biography does not interrogate Wilde's behavior and position as Irishman in the nineteenth-century capital of empire.

Davis Coakley's biography, *Oscar Wilde: The Importance of Being Irish*, is a major act of recovery.[72] Coakley provides a detailed account of the cultural and historical context of Wilde's childhood and formative years. Coakley describes Wilde's family in Ireland, his upbringing and schooling. He shows the great learning and interest of Wilde's parents in Irish culture, folklore, archeology and literature and how Oscar, his sister and brother were brought up with a deep knowledge of their Irish cultural heritage. Coakley describes Wilde's familiarity with the Ireland of his youth: Dublin, Portora, the west. Coakley's biography firmly establishes Wilde within his cultural and historical context and shows the importance of Wilde's nationality to his creative work.

In an essay published in 2003, Coakley continues his discourse on Wilde's Irish background.[73] He focuses on Merrion Square, the neighborhood in which Wilde was reared. The denizens of the square are variously described by Coakley as learned, professional people renowned for their wit and conversation and flamboyant style of dress. In this essay Coakley depicts the milieu in which Wilde grew up and which nurtured his later literary and personal characteristics.

Although Joy Melville's book, *Mother of Oscar: The Life of Jane Francesca Wilde*, is primarily concerned with Wilde's mother's life, it is also useful in providing contextual material on Wilde's antecedents, family history, his childhood and cultural background in Ireland.[74] Perhaps its greatest strength, in the context of Wilde's nationality, is its depiction of the bond of friendship between Wilde and his mother, the Nationalist poet Speranza, and her immense influence on her son.

The updated version of Wilde's letters, *The Complete Letters of Oscar Wilde*, offers some interesting insights into Wilde's nationalist sympathies and Irish nationality. The letters include mentions of Charles Stewart Parnell, the Irish countryside and Portora Royal School.

A short book on Wilde's schooldays, *Forgotten Schooldays: Oscar Wilde at Portora Royal School*, by Heather White, examines the young Wilde's education from 1844 to 1871 at a Protestant boarding school in County Fermanagh.[75] Like Davis Coakley's essay on the Dublin environs of Wilde's youth, this book is useful in its insight into the social and educational aspects of his formative years in Ireland.

II

Although the critical connection between Wilde's Irishness and his writing may seem to have been shown by recent critical exploration, critics Ian Small and Josephine Guy are not convinced.[76] In their book, *Oscar Wilde's Profession*, they register reservations about the critical value of acknowledging Wilde's nationality and suggest that recent criticism overlooks the problematic areas of Wilde's national origins. In an earlier work *Oscar Wilde: Recent Research*, Small suggests that Wilde's nationalist feeling depends on whether or not he was involved with Irish Nationalists in his daily life – this betrays a distinct unfamiliarity with Irish culture, identity and history, which spills over into the more recent book, *Oscar Wilde's Profession*.[77] Although these critics are very thorough in their critical inquiry into Wilde as professional writer, they fail to apprehend the complexities of the Irish situation in the nineteenth century.

Wilde's Irish contemporaries in nineteenth-century London were under no doubt that one's national identity was integral to an understanding of one's personality and literary work. The position of Irish writers in London was different from that of their English counterparts: imperialism accorded an inferior status to its colonized subjects and while this hierarchical assumption was not always overtly expressed, it nevertheless remained the unquestioned underlying presumption of British social order. A history of 700 years of occupation marked the difference in outlook between both countries.

In his review of Wilde's book, *Lord Arthur Savile's Crime and Other Stories*, W.B. Yeats, Wilde's contemporary and younger countryman, contends that the English were mystified by Wilde's witty attacks on English society because they failed to comprehend the complexity of being Irish.[78] Yeats situates Wilde's subversive humor within the continuum of Gaelic writers whose work elicits profane and irreverent laughter. In her essay "Yeats, Wilde: Nation and Identity," Noreen Doody examines how Yeats's perception of Wilde is informed by his understanding of the colonized culture into which they were born: Yeats interprets Wilde's recklessness and extreme individualism as the result of dispossession from his country of birth necessitated by colonization and alienation from the imperial capital, his adoptive home.[79] The authority of the colonized is undermined in the one, and in the other lacks any right of birth. Yeats concludes that the social and political position of Ireland is a determining factor in Wilde's personality and literary works. Doody suggests that Yeats's cultural understanding of Wilde provided a sound basis for the growth of Wilde's literary influence on Yeats. In his essay, "The Crucifixion of the Outcasts," Warwick Gould illustrates the imaginative engagement between Wilde and Yeats.[80]

Yeats ascribed Wilde's overuse of the English language to his fascination with it as a foreigner from Ireland.[81] He interpreted Wilde's roleplay in England as a direct response to his upbringing in Ireland.[82]

George Bernard Shaw, another of Wilde's contemporaries, concurred with Yeats that Wilde's humor perplexed his English audience.[83] In keeping with the Victorian practice of discussing all matters in terms of opposing characteristics, Shaw finds that the basic difference between England and its colony is humor and the lack of it. In his review of Wilde's *An Ideal Husband*, Shaw states that the Irish find English seriousness an endless source of fun. He describes Wilde's method of confusing the English into laughing at themselves, and their frustration on discovering this. Shaw is actually describing what postcolonial critics identify as a tactical strategy used by the colonized writer in dealing with imperialist authority.

The power relations between imperial England and its colonized subject is again inferred by Shaw in his work, *The Matter with Ireland*. He interprets Wilde's last prose work, the letter written in Reading Gaol, *De Profundis*, as a triumph of Wilde's imaginative power in its ability to overturn official England's judgment of him as degraded outcast.[84]

In "Oscar Wilde: Poet of 'Salomé'" James Joyce also draws a clear distinction between the Irish and English situation.[85] He explains Wilde in terms of the mythology of his Irish names: Oscar, Fingal, O'Flahertie; and suggests the incongruity of Wilde's existence in English society: the dual nature of his life, his unequal status and eventual denunciation by that society. Joyce's assertion that Wilde's aesthetics have their basis in a very Catholic tradition – the commission of sin being a necessary concomitant of redemption – connects strongly with Wilde's national heritage. In her Introduction to *The Major Works of Oscar Wilde* Isobel Murray cites Shaw, Yeats and Joyce in arguing Wilde's critical awareness in his ironic assault on Victorian complacency.[86]

Neil Sammells observes that Wilde's nationality and its relationship to imperialism affected his total artistic endeavor: Wilde's exile was occasioned by the social and political situation at home; his subversive writing was a response to these circumstances.[87] Sammells discusses Wilde's use of humor as a political tool and comments upon Wilde's overt political writings in his critiques of J.A. Froude's book, *The Two Chiefs of*

Dunboy, and J.P. Mahaffey's book, *Greek Life and Thought: From the Age of Alexander to the Roman Conquest*.[88]

John Pentland Mahaffey, Wilde's tutor at Trinity College Dublin, was a staunch Unionist supporter whose book strongly reiterated his political views. In his review of the book Wilde betrays his own political affiliations in the vehemence with which he castigates Mahaffey's anti-nationalist stance and imperialist sympathies.

It is in his factual writings that Wilde directly addresses his nationalist feelings while in his creative writing he expresses these feelings through wit, subterfuge and subversion. Wilde's review of nineteenth-century historian, J.A. Froude's, novel, *The Two Chiefs of Dunboy*, is notable for the anger of its response. Wilde compares Froude's fiction with the official parliamentary *Blue Books on Ireland* and denounces England's treatment of its colony as shameful. Wilde subscribed to the nineteenth-century view of the Celt as imaginatively superior to the Anglo-Saxon and there are various references to this issue in his letters.

An insight into Wilde's involvement with his cultural heritage can be gained from an article written by him in 1877 and discussed by Owen Dudley Edwards in *The Irish Book*.[89] In his article, Wilde appeals to the Royal Irish Academy to make a bursary available to the Irish artist, Henry O'Neill, who had fallen on hard times. O'Neill's drawings of ancient Irish High Crosses are much praised by Wilde, whose knowledge in this area is impressive. Wilde's knowledge of early Christian art in Ireland is again demonstrated in an article of that name published in the *Pall Mall Gazette* in 1887, in which he discusses with scholarly assurance the ancient artefacts of Ireland.[90]

In "Oscar Wilde: landscape, memory and imagined space," Noreen Doody claims that Wilde's knowledge of Irish antiquities and Irish landscape derived from his childhood familiarity with the countryside of the West of Ireland and his father's intimate knowledge of its ancient historical sites and structures.[91] She suggests that this familiarity and knowledge is fundamental to Wilde's theory of cultural memory which he outlines in "The Critic as Artist." In this paper Doody states that the absence of an Irish landscape in Wilde's creative work is explained by his wish to by-pass the contentious political issues pertaining to the colonized landscape of Ireland and push the imagination beyond the present circumstance into a moment of boundless possibility. Declan Kiberd describes this situation in *Inventing Ireland* and further contends that such a cleared space allows for the possibility of cultural understanding and perhaps political resolution.[92]

The critical consideration given during the past decade to Wilde's political and cultural context has elucidated patterns in his work and behavior and offered new insights into his creativity: Wilde's art and life coincide in theories of dispossession, mask and other; language is politicized; religious expression becomes an act of rebellion and humor a strategy of empowerment. Wilde's cultural heritage is seen to inform his theories of imaginative experience and life's subservience to art; his theory of the reconciliation of opposites is seen to owe something to his cultural hybridity.

The 1990s and early twenty-first century have seen something of a revolution in Wilde Studies. Critical exploration of Wilde's nationality and the context of empire in which he lived have provided us with a powerful means of reading and understanding Wilde's work. One hundred years separate us from a comparable type of understanding of Wilde by the critics of his own time: W.B. Yeats, George Bernard Shaw and James Joyce. The rediscovery of this avenue of inquiry, revitalized as it is by postcolonial perspective, is of immense importance in achieving a full and accurate critical profile of the work of Oscar Wilde.

notes

1. Owen Dudley Edwards, "The Soul of Man under Hibernicism," in *Reviewing Ireland: Essays and Interviews from Irish Studies Review*, eds. Sarah Briggs, Paul Hyland and Neil Sammells (Bath: Salis Press, 1998), 105–114; "Impressions of an Irish Sphinx," in *Wilde the Irishman*, ed. Jerusha McCormack (New Haven: Yale University Press, 1998), 47–70.
2. Maurice Harmon and Roger McHugh, *Short History of Anglo-Irish Literature: From Its Origins to the Present Day* (London: Wolfhound, 1982).
3. Seamus Deane, *Celtic Revivals: Essays in Modern Literature 1880–1890* (London: Faber, 1985).
4. Christopher Murray, "Drama 1690–1800," in *The Field Day Anthology of Irish Writing*, Vol. 1, ed. Seamus Deane (Derry: Field Day and Cork University Press, 1991), 500–507.
5. Declan Kiberd, "The London Exiles: Wilde and Shaw," in *The Field Day Anthology of Irish Writing*. Vol. 11, op. cit., 372–376.
6. Davis Coakley, *Oscar Wilde: The Importance of Being Irish* (Dublin: Town House and Country House, 1994).
7. Richard Ellmann, *Oscar Wilde* (London: Hamish Hamilton, 1987); Katharine Worth, "Salomé and a Full Moon in March," in *The Irish Drama of Europe from Yeats to Beckett* (London: Athlone Press, 1978), 99–119.
8. Noreen Doody, "Wilde, Yeats: Nation and Identity," in *New Voices in Irish Criticism,* ed. P.J. Mathews (Dublin: Four Courts, 2000), 27–33.
9. Declan Kiberd, *Inventing Ireland* (London: Cape, 1995), 1–50; "Anarchist Attitudes: Oscar Wilde," in *Irish Classics* (London: Granta Books, 2000), 325–339.

10. McCormack, op. cit.
11. David Cairns and Shaun Richards, *Writing Ireland: Colonialism, Nationalism and Culture* (Manchester: Manchester University Press, 1988); Kiberd, *Inventing Ireland*, op. cit.; R.F. Foster, *Paddy and Mr. Punch: Connections in Irish and English History* (London: Penguin, 1993); David Lloyd, *Anomolous States: Irish Writing and the Post Colonial Moment* (Dublin: Lilliput, 1993); Joseph Theodoor Leerssen, *Remembrances and Imagination: Patterns in the Historical and Literary Representation of Ireland in the Nineteenth Century* (Cork: Cork University Press, 1996); Anne McClintock, *Imperial Leather: Race, Gender and Sexuality in the Colonial Context* (New York and London: Routledge, 1995).
12. W.B. Yeats, "Two Lectures for America (1903 and 1913)," Typescript 627 and Microfiche 30,627, Michael Yeats Collection, National Library of Ireland.
13. Kiberd, *Inventing Ireland*, op. cit.
14. Kiberd, "Wilde and the Belfast Agreement," in *Textual Practice*, 13.3, ed. Alan Sinfield (London: Methuen, 1999), 441–445.
15. Homi Bhabha, "Of Mimicry and Man: The Ambivalence of Colonial Discourse," in *The Location of Culture* (London: Routledge, 1994), 85–92.
16. Fintan O'Toole, "Venus in Blue Jeans: Oscar Wilde, Jesse James, Crime and Fame," in *Wilde the Irishman*, op. cit., 71–81.
17. Kiberd, "Wilde and the Belfast Agreement," op. cit.
18. Kiberd, "The London Exiles," op. cit.; Edwards, op. cit.
19. W.J. McCormack, "Wilde and Parnell," in *Wilde the Irishman*, op. cit., 95–102.
20. Terry Eagleton, *Saint Oscar* (Derry: Field Day, 1989).
21. Neil Sammells, "Oscar Wilde: Quite Another Thing," in *Irish Writing: Exile and Subversion*, eds. Paul Hyland and Neil Sammells (London: Macmillan, 1991), 116–125.
22. Richard Pine, *The Thief of Reason: Oscar Wilde and Modern Ireland* (New York: St. Martin's Press, 1995); Neil Sammells, "Rediscovering the Irish Wilde," in *Rediscovering Oscar Wilde*, ed. George Sandulescu (Gerrard's Cross: Colin Smythe, 1994), 362–370.
23. Kiberd, *Inventing Ireland*, op. cit.
24. L. Perry Curtis, *Apes and Angels: The Irishman in Victorian Caricature* (Newton Abbot: David and Charles, 1971).
25. Kiberd, "The London Exiles," op. cit.
26. O'Toole, op. cit.
27. Cairns and Richards, op. cit.; Edwards, op. cit.
28. Pine, op. cit.
29. Terry Eagleton, "Oscar and George," in *Heathcliff and the Great Hunger: Studies in Irish Culture* (London: Verso, 1995), 320–341.
30. Curtis Marez, "The Other Addict: Reflections on Colonialism and Oscar Wilde's Opium Smoke Screen," *English Literature in Transition*, 64.1 (1997), 257–287.
31. Kiberd, *Inventing Ireland*, op. cit.
32. Kiberd, "Anarchist Attitudes," op. cit.
33. Marez, op. cit.
34. Richard Kearney, "Language Play: Brian Friel and Ireland's Verbal Theatre," in *Brian Friel: A Casebook*, ed. William Kerwin (New York: Garland Publishing, 1997), 77–116.

35. *Field Day*, op. cit.
36. Eagleton, "Oscar and George," op. cit.
37. Terry Eagleton, "Introduction," in *Plays, Prose Writing and Poems*, Everyman's Library (London: Random Century, 1981), vii–xxiii.
38. Kearney, op. cit.
39. F.C. McGrath, "Brian Friel and the Irish Art of Lying," in *Brian Friel*, op. cit.
40. David Alderson, "Momentary Pleasures: Wilde and English Virtue," in *Sex, Nation and Dissent*, ed. Éibhear Walshe (Cork: Cork University Press, 1997), 43–59.
41. Declan Kiberd, "Oscar Wilde: The Resurgence of Lying," *The Cambridge Companion to Oscar Wilde*, ed. Peter Raby (Cambridge: Cambridge University Press, 1997), 276–294.
42. Eagleton, "Oscar and George," op. cit.
43. *Irish Writing*, op. cit.
44. *Inventing Ireland*, op. cit.
45. Eagleton, *Saint Oscar*, op. cit.
46. Richard Ellmann, *Eminent Domain* (New York: Oxford University Press, 1967).
47. Deirdre Toomey, "The Story-Teller at Fault: Oscar Wilde and Irish Orality," in *Wilde the Irishman*, op. cit., 24–35.
48. Alan Stanford, "Acting Wilde," in *Wilde the Irishman*, op. cit., 152–157.
49. Frank McGuinness, "The Spirit of Play in *De Profundis*," in *Wilde the Irishman*, op. cit., 140–145; Edwards, op. cit.
50. Angela Bourke, "Hunting Out the Fairies: E.F. Benson, Oscar Wilde and the Burning of Bridget Clery," in *Wilde the Irishman*, op. cit., 36–46; Coakley, op. cit.
51. Bernard O'Donoghue, "The Journey to Reading Gaol: Sacrifice and Scapegoat in Irish Literature," in *Wilde the Irishman*, op. cit., 103–112.
52. Richard Haslam, "Oscar Wilde and the Imagination of the Celt," *Irish Studies Review* 11 (Summer 1995), eds. Neil Sammells, Paul Hyland and Sarah Briggs (Bath: Bath College of Higher Education, 1995), 2–5.
53. Coakley, op. cit.
54. Sos Eltis, *Reviewing Wilde: Society and Subversion in the Plays of Oscar Wilde* (Oxford: Clarendon Press, 1996).
55. Jerusha McCormack, "The Wilde Irishman: Oscar as Aesthete and Anarchist," in *Wilde the Irishman*, op. cit., 82–94.
56. Murray, op. cit.
57. Terence Brown, "Introduction to the Plays," in *Complete Works of Oscar Wilde*, ed. Martin Holland (Glasgow: HarperCollins, 1999), 351–356; Kiberd, *Inventing Ireland*, op. cit.
58. Richard Allen Cave, "Introduction," in *The Importance of Being Earnest and Other Plays*, ed. R. Allen Cave (London: Penguin, 2000), vii–xxvi.
59. Alderson, op. cit.
60. Kiberd, "Anarchist Attitudes," "The London Exiles," op. cit.; Jarlath Killeen, "Woman and Nation Revisited: Oscar Wilde's 'The Nightingale and the Rose,'" in *Critical Ireland: New Essays in Literature and Culture*, eds. Allan A. Gillis and Aaron Kelly (Dublin: Four Courts, 2001), 141–147.

61. Ashis Nandy, "The Intimate Enemy: Loss and Recovery of Self under Colonialism," in *Exiled at Home* (Oxford: Oxford University Press, 1995), 1–121.
62. Edwards, op. cit. [See O'Malley, Chapter 7, for a lengthier discussion of Wilde and Catholicism – ed.]
63. Vicki Mahaffey, *States of Desire: Wilde, Yeats, Joyce and the Irish Experiment* (New York: Oxford University Press, 1998).
64. Adrian Frazier, "Queering the Irish Renaissance: the Masculinities of Moore, Martyn and Yeats," *Gender and Sexuality in Modern Ireland,* ed. Anthony Bradley and Maryanne Giulanella Valiulis (Amherst: University of Massachusetts Press, 1997), 8–38.
65. *Sex, Nation and Dissent,* op. cit.
66. Alan Sinfield, "'I see it is my name that terrifies': Wilde in the 20th Century," in *The Wilde Legacy,* ed. Eiléan NiChuileanain (Dublin: Four Courts, 2003), 136–142.
67. Lucy McDiarmid, "Oscar Wilde's Speech from the Dock," in *The Wilde Legacy,* op. cit., 113–135.
68. Coakley, op. cit.
69. Richard Pine, *Oscar Wilde* (Dublin: Gill and Macmillan, 1983).
70. Pine, *Thief of Reason,* op. cit.
71. Ellmann, *Eminent Domain,* op. cit.
72. Coakley, op. cit.
73. Davis Coakley, "Oscar Wilde and the Wildes of Merrion Square," in *The Wilde Legacy,* op. cit., 35–50.
74. Joy Melville, *Mother of Oscar: The Life of Jane Francesca Wilde* (London: John Murray, 1994).
75. Heather White, *Forgotten Schooldays: Oscar Wilde at Portora Royal School, Inniskillen, Co. Fermanagh, Ireland, 1864–1871* (Gortnaree, Co. Fermanagh: Principia Press, 2002).
76. Josephine M. Guy and Ian Small, "Wilde the Writer," in *Oscar Wilde's Profession: Writing and the Culture Industry in the Late Nineteenth Century* (Oxford: Oxford University Press, 2000), 1–13.
77. Ian Small, *Oscar Wilde: Recent Research Supplement to Oscar Wilde Revalued* (Gerrard's Cross: Colin Smythe, 2000).
78. W.B. Yeats, "Oscar Wilde's Last Book," in *Uncollected Prose by W.B. Yeats: First Reviews and Articles* 1886–1896, Vol. 1, ed. John P. Frayne (London: Macmillan, 1970), 202–205.
79. Doody, "Wilde, Yeats," op. cit.
80. Warwick Gould, "The Crucifixion of the Outcasts," in *Rediscovering Oscar Wilde,* op. cit., 167–192.
81. Yeats, "Oscar Wilde's Last Book," op. cit.
82. W.B. Yeats, *Autobiographies* (London: Papermac, 1980).
83. George Bernard Shaw, "Two New Plays," in *Dramatic Opinions and Essays with an Apology* (New York: Brentano's, 1916), 7–15.
84. George Bernard Shaw, "Oscar Wilde," in *The Matter with Ireland,* trans. Dr. Felix F. Strauss and Mr. Laurence (London: Hart-Davis, 1962), 28–32.
85. James Joyce, "Oscar Wilde: The Poet of 'Salomé,'" in *The Critical Writings of James Joyce,* eds. Mason Ellsworth and R. Ellmann (Ithaca: Cornell University Press, 1996), 201–205.

86. Isobel Murray, "Introduction," in *Oscar Wilde: The Major Works*, ed. Isobel Murray (Oxford: Oxford University Press, 2000), vii–xxix.
87. Sammells, "Oscar Wilde," op. cit.
88. Oscar Wilde, "Two Chiefs of Dunboy by J.A. Froude," *Pall Mall Gazette* (13 April 1889), *The Artist as Critic: Critical Writings of Oscar Wilde*, ed. Richard Ellmann (Chicago: University of Chicago Press, 1969), 136–140; "Greek Life and Thought: From the Age of Alexander to the Roman Conquest by John Pentland Mahaffey," *Pall Mall Gazette* (9 November 1887).
89. Owen Dudley Edwards, "Oscar Wilde and Henry O'Neill," *The Irish Book* 1.1 (Spring 1959), 11–18.
90. Oscar Wilde, "Early Christian Art in Ireland," *A Critic in Pall Mall: being extracts from reviews and miscellanies*, Vol. xiii, *Collected Works of Oscar Wilde*, ed. Robert Ross (London: Methuen, 1919), 81–85.
91. Noreen Doody, "Oscar Wilde: Landscape, Memory and Imagined Space," in *Irish Landscapes*, eds. José Francisco Fernández Sánchez and Maria Elena Jaime de Pablos (Almeria: University of Almeria, 2004).
92. Kiberd, *Inventing Ireland*, op. cit.

selected bibliography

wilde: works

Ellmann, Richard, ed. *The Artist as Critic: Critical Writings of Oscar Wilde*. Chicago: University of Chicago Press, 1969.

Wilde, Oscar. *Aristotle at Afternoon Tea: The Rare Oscar Wilde*. Ed. John Wyse Jackson. London: Fourth Estate, 1991.

——. *The Complete Letters of Oscar Wilde*. Eds. Merlin Holland and Rupert Hart-Davis. London: Fourth Estate, 2000.

——. *Complete Works of Oscar Wilde*. Centenary Edition, ed. Merlin Holland. Glasgow: HarperCollins, 1999.

——. *The Complete Works of Oscar Wilde*. Ian Small, series ed. Oxford English Texts. New York: Oxford University Press, 2000–. *Poems and Poems in Prose*, eds. Bobby Fong and Karl Beckson, 2000; *De Profundis*, ed. Ian Small, forthcoming; *The Picture of Dorian Gray*, ed. Joseph Bristow, forthcoming.

——. *De Profundis: A Facsimile Edition of the Original Manuscript*. Ed. Merlin Holland. London: The British Library Publishing, 2000.

——. *Oscar Wilde's The Importance of Being Earnest. A Reconstructive Critical Edition of the Text of the First Production, St. James's Theatre, London, 1895*. Eds. Joseph Donahue and Ruth Berggren. New York: Oxford University Press, 1996.

edited volumes of criticism (general)

Bloom, Harold, ed. *Oscar Wilde*. New York: Chelsea, 1985.

Bristow, Joseph, ed. *Wilde Writings: Contextual Conditions*. Toronto: University of Toronto Press, 2003.

Dever, Carolyn and Marvin Taylor, eds. *Reading Wilde, Querying Spaces*. New York: Fales Library, New York University, 1995.

Ellmann, Richard, ed. *Oscar Wilde: A Collection of Critical Essays*. Englewood Cliffs: Prentice, 1969.

Freedman, Jonathan, ed. *Oscar Wilde: A Collection of Critical Essays*. Upper Saddle River, NJ: Prentice Hall, 1996.

Gagnier, Regenia, ed. *Critical Essays on Oscar Wilde*. New York: G.K. Hall and Company, 1991.

NíChuilleanain, Eiléan, ed. *The Wilde Legacy*. Dublin: Four Courts, 2003.

"Oscar Wilde Special." *Irish Studies Review*, Volume 11 (Summer 1995), eds. Neil Sammells, Paul Hyland and Sarah Briggs. Bath: Bath College of Higher Education.

Raby, Peter, ed. *The Cambridge Companion to Oscar Wilde*. Cambridge: Cambridge University Press, 1997.

Sandulescu, C. George, ed. *Rediscovering Oscar Wilde*. Gerrards Cross, Buckinghamshire, UK: Colin Smythe, 1994.

Smith, Philip E. *Approaches to Teaching the Works of Oscar Wilde*. New York: Modern Language Association, forthcoming.

wildean thought: art and theory

Bashford, Bruce. *Oscar Wilde, the Critic as Humanist*. Madison, NJ and London: Fairleigh Dickinson University Press and Associated University Presses, 1999.

Behrendt, Patricia Flanagan. *Oscar Wilde: Eros and Aesthetics*. New York: St. Martin's Press, 1991.

Brown, Julia Prewitt. *Cosmopolitan Criticism: Oscar Wilde's Philosophy of Art*. Charlottesville and London: University Press of Virginia, 1997.

Chamberlin, J.E. *Ripe Was the Drowsy Hour: The Age of Oscar Wilde*. New York: The Seabury Press, 1977.

Cohen, Philip K. *The Moral Vision of Oscar Wilde*. London and Cranbury, NJ: Associated University Presses, 1978.

Danson, Lawrence. *Wilde's Intentions: The Artist in His Criticism*. Oxford: Clarendon Press, 1997.

Gillespie, Michael Patrick. *Oscar Wilde and the Poetics of Ambiguity*. Gainesville, FL: University Press of Florida, 1996.

Kohl, Nobert. *Oscar Wilde: The Works of a Conformist Rebel*. Trans. David Henry Wilson. Cambridge: Cambridge University Press, 1989.

Nassaar, Christopher S. *Into the Demon Universe: A Literary Exploration of Oscar Wilde*. New Haven: Yale University Press, 1974.

Price, Jody. *"A Map with Utopia": Oscar Wilde's Theory for Social Transformation*. New York: Peter Lang, 1996.

San Juan, Epifanio Jr. *The Art of Oscar Wilde*. Princeton: Princeton University Press, 1967.

Shewan, Rodney. *Oscar Wilde: Art & Egotism*. New York: Barnes & Noble, 1977.

Smith, Philip E. II, and Michael S. Helfand. *Oscar Wilde's Oxford Notebooks: A Portrait of Mind in the Making*. New York: Oxford University Press, 1989.

wildean praxis: culture and production

Blanchard, Mary Warner. *Oscar Wilde's America: Counterculture in the Gilded Age*. New Haven: Yale University Press, 1998.

Bowlby, Rachel. "Promoting Dorian Gray." *The Oxford Literary Review*. 9 (1987): 147–162.

Gagnier, Regenia. *Idylls of the Marketplace: Oscar Wilde and the Victorian Public*. Stanford: Stanford University Press, 1986.

Guy, Josephine M. and Ian Small. *Oscar Wilde's Profession: Writing and the Culture Industry in the Late Nineteenth Century*. Oxford: Oxford University Press, 2000.

Nunokawa, Jeff. "The Importance of Being Bored: The Dividends of Ennui in *The Picture of Dorian Gray*." *Studies in the Novel*. 28.3 (Fall 1996): 357–371.

Stetz, Margaret D. *Useful and Beautiful: British Books of the 1890s. An Exhibition at the National Gallery of Art Library*. Washington, DC: Board of Trustees, The National Gallery of Art, 1999.

Stetz, Margaret D. and Mark Samuels Lasner. *England in the 1880s: Old Guard and Avant-Garde*. Charlottesville: University Press of Virginia, 1989.

——. *England in the 1890s: Literary Publishing at the Bodley Head*. Washington, DC: Georgetown University Press, 1990.

wilde: desire and the text

Cohen, Ed. *Talk on the Wilde Side: Towards a Genealogy of Discourse on Male Sexualities*. New York: Routledge, 1993.

——. "Writing Gone Wilde: Homoerotic Desire in the Closet of Representation." *PMLA*. 102 (1987): 810–813.

Nunokawa, Jeff. *Tame Passions of Wilde: The Styles of Manageable Desire*. Princeton: Princeton University Press, 2003.

wilde and irish studies

Alderson, David. "Momentary Pleasures: Wilde and English Virtue." In *Sex, Nation and Dissent*. Ed. Éibhear Walshe. Cork: Cork University Press, 1997. 43–59.

Coakley, Davis. *Oscar Wilde: The Importance of Being Irish*. Dublin: Town House and Country House, 1994.

Eagleton, Terry. "Oscar and George." In *Heathcliff and the Great Hunger: Studies in Irish Culture*. London: Verso, 1995. 320–341.

Edwards, Owen Dudley. "The Soul of Man under Hibernicism." In *Reviewing Ireland: Essays and Interviews from Irish Studies Review*. Eds. Sarah Briggs, Paul Hyland and Neil Sammells. Bath: Salis Press, 1998. 105–114.

Kiberd, Declan. "Anarchist Attitudes: Oscar Wilde." In *Irish Classics*. London: Granta Books, 2000. 325–339.

—— "Wilde and the Belfast Agreement." *Textual Practice* 13.3, ed. Alan Sinfield. London: Methuen and Co., 1999. 441–445.

——. *Inventing Ireland*. London: Cape, 1995.

——. "The London Exiles: Wilde and Shaw." In *The Field Day Anthology of Irish Writing*. Vol. 11. Ed. Seamus Deane. Derry: Field Day and Cork University Press, 1991. 372–376.

——. "Anglo-Irish Attitudes." In *Ireland's Field Day*. Ed. Seamus Deane. London: Hutchinson, 1985. 83–105.

Mahaffey, Vicki. *States of Desire: Wilde, Yeats, Joyce and the Irish Experiment*. New York: Oxford University Press, 1998.

McCormack, Jerusha, ed. *Wilde the Irishman*. New Haven and London: Yale University Press, 1998.

Pine, Richard. *The Thief of Reason: Oscar Wilde and Modern Ireland*. New York: St. Martin's Press, 1995.

White, Heather. *Forgotten Schooldays: Oscar Wilde at Portora Royal School, Inniskillen, Co. Fermanagh, Ireland, 1864–1871*. Gortnaree, Co. Fermanagh: Principia Press, 2002.

wilde's women

Amor, Anne Clark. *Mrs. Oscar Wilde: A Woman of Some Importance*. London: Sidgwick & Jackson, 1983.
Bentley, Joyce. *The Importance of Being Constance*. New York: Beaufort Books, 1983.
Brémont, Anna, Comtesse de. *Oscar Wilde and His Mother: A Memoir*. London: Everett & Co., 1911.
Clayworth, Anya. "The Woman's World: Oscar Wilde as Editor." *Victorian Periodicals Review* 30, no. 2 (1997): 84–101.
Green, Stephanie. "Oscar Wilde's The Woman's World." *Victorian Periodicals Review* 30.2 (1997): 102–120.
Melville, Joy. *Mother of Oscar: The Life of Jane Francesca Wilde*. London: John Murray, 1994.
Stetz, Margaret Diane. "The Bi-Social Oscar Wilde and 'Modern' Women." *Nineteenth-Century Literature* 55.4: 515–537.
Wyndham, Horace. *Speranza: A Biography of Lady Wilde*. New York: Philosophical Library, 1951.

the douglas: bosie and company

Croft-Crooke, Rupert. *Bosie: The Story of Lord Alfred Douglas: His Friends and Enemies*. London: W.H. Allen, 1963.
Douglas, Lord Alfred. *My Friendship with Oscar Wilde*. New York: Coventry, 1932. First pub. as *The Autobiography of Lord Alfred Douglas*. London: Martin Secker, 1929.
——. *Oscar Wilde and Myself*. London: Long, 1914.
——. *A Summing Up*. London: Duckworth, 1940.
——. *Without Apology*. London: Richards, 1938.
Murray, Douglas. *Bosie*. New York: Hyperion, 2000.
Queensberry, Marquess of. *Oscar Wilde and the Black Douglas*. London: Hutchinson, 1949.

classic readers

Auden, W.H. "An Improbable Life." In *Forewords and Afterwords*. New York: Vintage, 1973. 302–324.
Gide, Andre. *Oscar Wilde*. Ed. Stuart Mason. Oxford: Holywell, 1905.
Joyce, James. "Oscar Wilde: The Poet of 'Salomé.'" In *The Critical Writings of James Joyce*. Eds. Mason Ellsworth and R. Ellmann. Ithaca: Cornell University Press, 1996. 201–205.
McCarthy, Mary. "The Unimportance of Being Oscar" (1947). In *Theater Chronicles: 1937–1962*. New York: Farrar Straus and Giroux, 1963.
Ricketts, Charles. *Recollections of Oscar Wilde*. London: Nonesuch, 1932.
Shaw, George Bernard. "Oscar Wilde." In *The Matter with Ireland*. Trans. Dr. Felix F. Strauss and Mr. Laurence. London: Hart-Davis, 1962. 28–32.
Symons, Arthur. *A Study of Oscar Wilde*. London: Charles J. Sawyer, 1930.

Vidal, Gore. "Oscar Wilde: On the Skids Again." In *United States: Essays, 1952–1992.* New York: Random House, 1993. 215–221.
Yeats, W.B. Review. "Oscar Wilde's Last Book." In *Uncollected Prose by W.B. Yeats: First Reviews and Articles 1886–1896*. Vol. 1, ed. John P. Frayne. London: Macmillan, 1970. 202–205.

early criticism

Beckson, Karl, ed. *Oscar Wilde: The Critical Heritage*. London: Routledge & Kegan Paul, 1970.
Birnbaum, Martin. *Oscar Wilde: Fragments and Memories*. London: 1914.
Brasol, Boris. *Oscar Wilde: The Man, the Artist, the Martyr.* New York: Scribner's, 1938.
Braybrook, Patrick. *Oscar Wilde: A Study.* London: Braithwaite, 1930.
Broad, Lewis. *The Friendships and Follies of Oscar Wilde.* New York: Crowell, 1955.
Ervine, St. John. *Oscar Wilde: A Present Time Appraisal*. London: Allen & Unwin, 1951.
Harris, Frank. *The Life and Confessions of Oscar Wilde.* New York: Duffield, 1914.
Ingleby, Leonard Cresswell [Cyril Arthur Gull]. *Oscar Wilde.* London: T. Werner Laurie, 1907.
——. *Oscar Wilde: Some Reminiscences*. London: T. Werner Laurie, 1912.
Mason, Stuart [Christopher Millard]. *Oscar Wilde: Art and Morality – A Defence of "The Picture of Dorian Gray."* London: J. Jacobs, 1908.
Pearson, Hesketh. *Oscar Wilde: His Life and Wit.* London: Methuen; NY: Harper, 1946.
Ransome, Arthur. *Oscar Wilde: A Critical Study*. London: Martin Secker, 1912.
Roditi, Edouard. *Oscar Wilde*. [1947] New York: New Directions, 1986.
Sherard, Robert. *The Life of Oscar Wilde*. London: Laurie, 1905.
——. *Oscar Wilde: The Story of an Unhappy Friendship*. London: Greening and Co., 1908.
Wilson, Edmund. "Oscar Wilde: One Must Always Seek What is Most Tragic." In *Classics and Contemporaries: A Literary Chronicle of the Forties*. New York: Farrar, Straus, and Co., 1950. 331–342.
Woodcock, George A. *The Paradox of Oscar Wilde*. London: T.V. Boardman, 1949.

crime and punishment

Foldy, Michael S. *The Trials of Oscar Wilde: Deviance, Morality, and Late-Victorian Society*. New Haven: Yale University Press, 1997.
Hyde, H. Montgomery. *The Trials of Oscar Wilde*. New York: Dover Publications, 1962.

wilde and the theatre

Dellamora, Richard. "Traversing the Feminine in Oscar Wilde's *Salomé*." In *Victorian Sages and Cultural Discourse: Renegotiating Gender and Power*. Ed. Thaïs E. Morgan. New Brunswick and London: Rutgers University Press, 1990. 246–264.

Eltis, Sos. *Revising Wilde: Society and Subversion in the Plays of Oscar Wilde*. Oxford: Clarendon Press, 1996.
Fernbach, Amanda. "Wilde's *Salomé* and the Ambiguous Fetish." *Victorian Literature and Culture* 29.1 (2001): 195–218.
Powell, Kerry. *Oscar Wilde and the Theatre of the 1890s*. Cambridge: Cambridge University Press, 1990.
Sammells, Neil. *Wilde Style: The Plays and Prose of Oscar Wilde*. New York: Longman, 2000.
Stetz, Margaret D. *Gender and the London Theatre, 1880–1920*. High Wycombe, UK: Rivendale Press in association with Bryn Mawr College Library, 2004.
Tanitch, Robert. *Oscar Wilde on Stage and Screen*. London: Methuen, 1999.
Worth, Katharine. "Salomé and a Full Moon in March." In *The Irish Drama of Europe from Yeats to Beckett*. London: Athlone Press, 1978. 99–119.

films

Asquith, Anthony, dir. *The Importance of Being Earnest* (1952; with Michael Redgrave, Michael Denison, Joan Greenwood, Dorothy Tutin, Edith Evans).
Dassin, Jules, dir. *The Canterville Ghost* (1944; with Charles Laughton, Robert Young, Margaret O'Brien, William Gargan, Reginald Owen).
Gilbert, Brian, dir., *Wilde* (1997; with Stephe Fry, Jude Law, Vanessa Redgrave, Jennifer Ehle, Gemma Jones).
Haynes, Todd, dir. *Velvet Goldmine* (1998; with Ewan McGregor, Jonathan Rhys-Meyers).
Hughes, Ken, dir. *The Trials of Oscar Wilde* (*The Green Carnation*, 1960; based on play by John Furnell; with Peter Finch, Yvonne Mitchell, James Mason, Lionel Jeffries, John Fraser).
Krishnamma, Suri, dir. *A Man of No Importance* (1994; with Albert Finney, Brenda Fricker, Michael Gambon, Tara Fitzgerald, Rufus Sewell; play by Terrence McNally, 2002).
Lewin, Albert, dir. *The Portrait of Dorian Gray* (1945; with Hurd Hatfield, George Sanders, Donna Reed, Angela Lansbury).
Parker, Oliver, dir. *The Importance of Being Earnest* (2002; with Colin Firth, Rupert Everett, Frances O'Connor, Reese Witherspoon, Judi Dench).
Parker, Oliver, dir. *An Ideal Husband* (1999; with Cate Blanchett, Minnie Driver, Julianne Moore, Rupert Everett, Jeremy Northam).
Preminger, Otto, dir. *Lady Windemere's Fan* (*The Fan*, 1949; screenplay, Dorothy Parker et al; with Jeanne Crain, Madeleine Carroll, George Sanders, Richard Greene).
Ratoff, Gregory. *Oscar Wilde* (*Forbidden Passion*, 1960; based on play by Leslie Stokes; with Robert Morley, Ralph Richardson, Phyllis Calvert, John Neville).
Russell, Ken, dir. *Salomé* (*Salomé's Last Dance*, 1988; with Glenda Jackson, Stratford Johns, Nickolas Grace, Douglas Hodge).

wilde in the twentieth century

Böker, Uwe, Richard Corballis, and Julie Hibbard, eds. *The Importance of Reinventing Oscar: Versions of Wilde During the Last 100 Years*. Amsterdam and New York: Rodopi, 2002.

Hoare, Philip. *Oscar Wilde's Last Stand: Decadence, Conspiracy, and the Most Outrageous Trial of the Century.* New York: Archade Publishing, 1997.
Schenkar, Joan. *Truly Wilde: The Unsettling Story of Dolly Wilde, Oscar's Unusual Niece.* London: Virago, 2000.
Sinfield, Alan. *The Wilde Century: Effeminacy, Oscar Wilde and the Queer Moment.* New York: Columbia University Press, 1994.

works inspired by wilde

Ackroyd, Peter. *The Last Testament of Oscar Wilde.* London: Hamish Hamilton, 1983.
Bartlett, Neil. *Who Was That Man? A Present for Mr. Oscar Wilde.* London: Serpent's Tail, 1988.
Eagleton, Terry. *Saint Oscar.* Derry: Field Day, 1989.
Hare, David. *The Judas Kiss.* New York: Grove, 1998.
Kaufman, Moises. *Gross Indecency: The Three Trials of Oscar Wilde.* New York: Vintage Books, 1998.

biographies and general studies

Belford, Barbara. *Oscar Wilde: A Certain Genius.* New York: Random House, 2000.
Byrne, Patrick. *The Wildes of Merrion Square.* London: Staples, 1953.
Croft-Cooke, Rupert. *The Unrecorded Life of Oscar Wilde.* London: Allen, 1972.
Ellmann, Richard. *Oscar Wilde.* London: Hamish Hamilton, 1987.
Goodman, Jonathan, comp. *The Oscar Wilde File.* London: Allison & Busby, 1988.
Holland, Merlin. *The Wilde Album.* New York: Holt, 1997.
Holland, Vyvyan. *Oscar Wilde and His World.* Revised ed. London: Thames and Hudson, 1966.
——. *Son of Oscar Wilde.* Oxford: Oxford University Press, 1954.
Hyde, H. Montgomery. *Oscar Wilde: A Biography.* New York: Farrar, 1975.
Jullian, Philippe, *Oscar Wilde.* Trans. Violet Wyndham. London: Constable, 1969.
Knox, Melissa. *Oscar Wilde: A Long and Lovely Suicide.* New Haven: Yale University Press, 1994.
Mckenna, Neil. *The Secret Life of Oscar Wilde.* London: Century, 2003.
Pine, Richard. *Oscar Wilde.* Dublin: Gill and Macmillan, 1983.
Raby, Peter. *Oscar Wilde.* Cambridge: Cambridge University Press, 1988.
Schmidgall, Gary. *The Stranger Wilde: Interpreting Oscar.* New York: Dutton, 1994.
Sloan, John. *Oscar Wilde.* Oxford: Oxford University Press, 2003.
Stokes, John. *Oscar Wilde: Myth, Miracles, and Imitations.* Cambridge: Cambridge University Press, 1996.
Sullivan, Kevin. *Oscar Wilde.* New York: Columbia University Press, 1972.
Symons, Arthur. *A Study of Oscar Wilde.* London: Sawyer, 1930.
Varty, Anne. *A Preface to Oscar Wilde.* Harlow: Addison Wesley Longman, 1998.
Winwar, Francis. *Oscar Wilde and the Yellow Nineties.* New York: Harper, 1940.
Worth, Katharine. *Oscar Wilde.* New York: Grove, 1983.

guides to research

Beckson, Karl. *The Oscar Wilde Encyclopedia.* New York: AMS Press, 1998.

Fletcher, Ian and John Stokes. "Oscar Wilde." In *Anglo-Irish Literature: A Review of Research.* Ed. Richard Finneran. New York: 1976. 48–137.

——. "Oscar Wilde." In *Recent Research in Anglo-Irish Writers.* Ed. Richard Finneran. New York: 1983. 21–47.

Knox, Melissa. *Oscar Wilde in the 1990s: The Critic as Creator.* Rochester, NY: Camden House, 2001.

Mason, Stuart. *Bibliography of Oscar Wilde.* London: 1914.

Mikhail, E.H. *Oscar Wilde: An Annotated Bibliography of Criticism.* London: Macmillan, 1978.

Mikolyzk, Thomas A., comp. *Oscar Wilde: An Annotated Bibliography.* Westport, CT and London: Greenwood Press, 1993.

Page, Norman. *An Oscar Wilde Chronology.* London: Macmillan, 1991.

Schroeder, Horst. *Additions and Corrections to Ellmann's Oscar Wilde.* Braunschweig, 1989.

Small, Ian. *Oscar Wilde: Recent Research: A Supplement to "Oscar Wilde Revalued."* Greensboro, NC: ELT Press, 2000.

——. *Oscar Wilde Revalued: An Essay on New Materials & Methods of Research.* Greensboro, NC: ELT Press, 1993.

online resources

The Oscholars. Monthly journal of Wilde studies. Archived. <http://homepages.gold.ac.uk/oscholars>.

The Princess Grace Library of Irish Studies. Online Wilde bibliography found at: <http://www.pgil.eirdata.org/html/pgildatasets/authors/w/Wilde,O/crit.htm>.

index

compiled by frederick s. roden

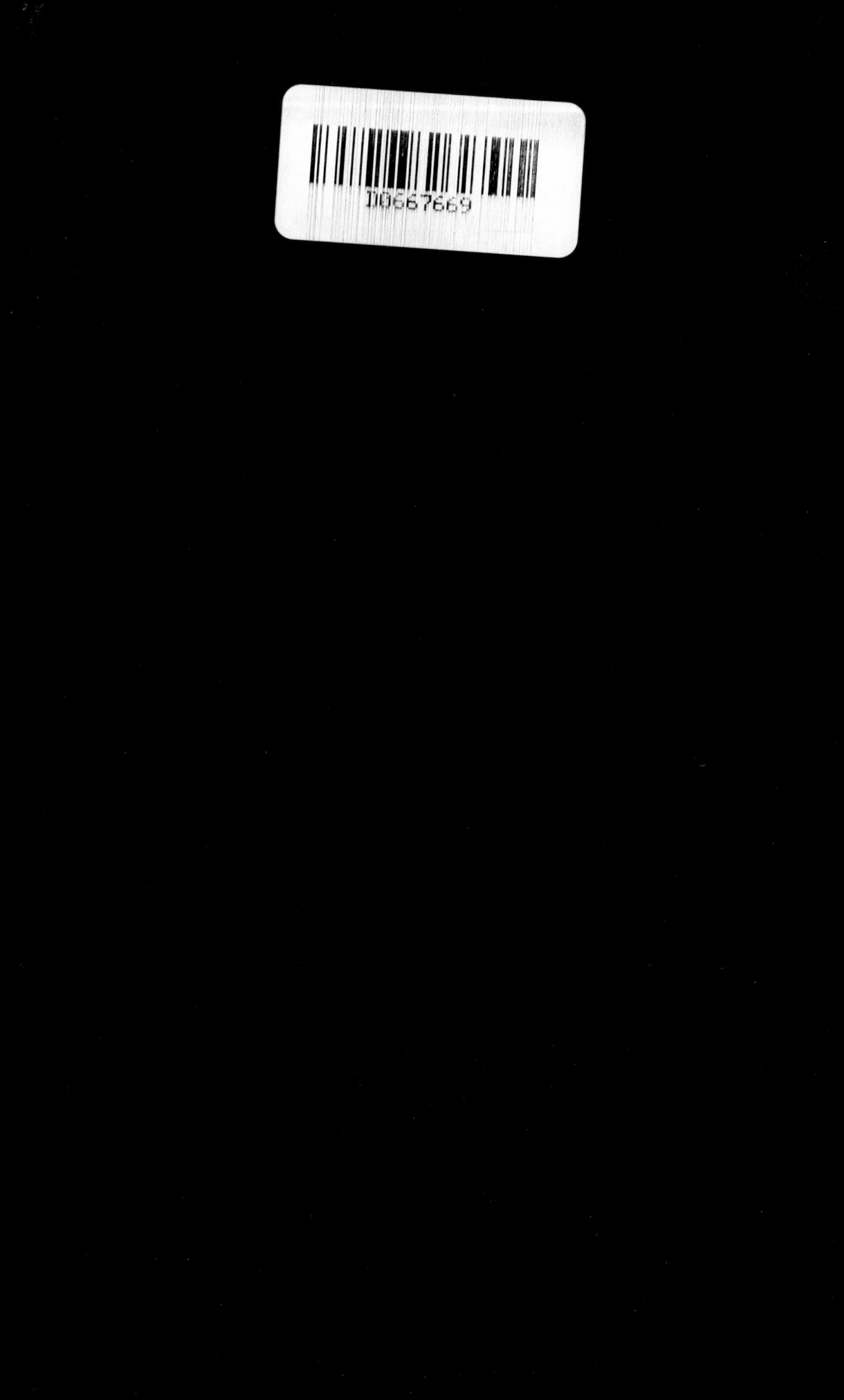

D0667669

Psych Yourself Rich

Psych Yourself Rich

Get the Mindset and Discipline You Need to Build Your Financial Life

Farnoosh Torabi

Vice President, Publisher: Tim Moore
Associate Publisher and Director of Marketing: Amy Neidlinger
Executive Editor: Jeanne Glasser
Editorial Assistant: Pamela Boland
Development Editor: Russ Hall
Operations Manager: Gina Kanouse
Senior Marketing Manager: Julie Phifer
Publicity Manager: Laura Czaja
Assistant Marketing Manager: Megan Colvin
Cover Designer: Alan Clements
Managing Editor: Kristy Hart
Project Editor: Betsy Harris
Copy Editor: Keith Cline
Proofreader: Water Crest Publishing
Indexer: Lisa Stumpf
Interior Designer: Gloria Schurick
Senior Compositor: Gloria Schurick
Manufacturing Buyer: Dan Uhrig

Published by Pearson Education, Inc.
Publishing as FT Press
Upper Saddle River, New Jersey 07458

Printed in the United States of America

Second Printing October 2010

ISBN-10: 0-13-707927-3
ISBN-13: 978-0-13-707927-8

Pearson Education LTD.
Pearson Education Australia PTY, Limited.
Pearson Education Singapore, Pte. Ltd.
Pearson Education North Asia, Ltd.
Pearson Education Canada, Ltd.
Pearson Educatión de Mexico, S.A. de C.V.
Pearson Education—Japan
Pearson Education Malaysia, Pte. Ltd.

Library of Congress Cataloging-in-Publication Data

Torabi, Farnoosh.

Psych yourself rich : get the mindset and discipline you need to build your financial life / Farnoosh Torabi.

p. cm.

ISBN-13: 978-0-13-707927-8 (hardcover : alk. paper)

ISBN-10: 0-13-707927-3

1. Finance, Personal—Psychological aspects. 2. Money—Psychological aspects. I. Title.

HG179.T593 2011

332.024'01—dc22

2010016381

For my family

Contents

PART II Psych It Up

PART III Raise the Bar

Acknowledgments

I have the great fortune of knowing encouraging and inspiring individuals who've made my career and life an absolute joy, in addition to having helped spring my ideas and this book to life.

Thank you to my superb agent, Adam Kirschner, who pushed for this project, just as I was about to give up hope. Thank you to the very supportive and talented Pearson team: Jeanne Glasser, Tim Moore, and Julie Phifer. Thank you all for rallying behind me and reminding me to always think big. Boom!

This book could not have been possible without the generosity and brilliance of behavioral experts, teachers, and economists who shared with me their perspectives, theories, and thoughts. Thank you especially to the great Dan Ariely, Jay Ritter, Terri Ciochetti, and Joseph Brusuelas.

I am enormously grateful to the television producers who have allowed me to share my perspectives on their airwaves. First and foremost, Patricia Luchsinger, a magnificent producer at the NBC *Today Show*, who was the first person to take a serious chance on me and put me on live, national TV at a young age. Thanks for the big break and for inviting me back. Thank you to the excellent Katherine Billman, also from the *Today Show*. Thank you to all the brave and inspiring participants on *Bank of Mom & Dad*. And of course, monstrous thanks to my *Bank of Mom & Dad* family at ABC Daytime and BBC America who helped bring this very important program to life: Ann Miller, Lillian Lim, Marianne Fleschman, Allison Wallach, Bob Kirsh, Shirley Escott, Jerry Kolber, and Tracey Finley.

My deepest gratitude to all the individuals with whom I've had the opportunity to collaborate in the past year, who've helped me extend my reach in educating everyday people about money. I'm especially thankful for Christine Schirmer, Jen Garcia, Jen Fellner, Scott Gulbransen, Chelsea Marti, Kathryn Zambito, Courtney Leddy, Chris Lee, Kathleen McGraw, Katie Grafer, Denise Vitola, Kristen Ronan, Colleen McCarthy, and Naomi Borno.

I have wonderful friends who keep me brave: Kate Dailey, Bethany and Tim McGee, Ariel Gornizky, Kathryn Ricker, Tim Chan, Kafi Drexel, Margie Fox, Brian Maloney, David Dapko, Annika, Michael, Luke, and Blake O'Looney, Susan, Michael, Allison, and Amanda Beacham, Kathy Braddock, Kelly and Eric Tiedeken, Christine and Mike Rzasa, Tim Hedden, Kristin Bentz, Susie Banikarim, and Dan Arnall. Thanks to all of you for your unconditional friendship and support.

Thank you to Dean Jim Thomas and Joyce Matthews and the entire Smeal College of Business at Pennsylvania State University, my alma mater.

A great thank you to my Lancaster, PA family for their love and support: Eileen and Phil Jaquith; Kate Dussinger; and Doug, Jean, and Bradley Dussinger.

Speaking of family, much love and a great big thank you to Aunt Sheren, Uncle Nasser, and my AZ cousins Alex and Allen.

Thank you to Adam and Sheila Torabi, my amazing parents—to whom I owe pretty much my entire life. The greatest gift they ever gave me—besides guidance, unconditional love, and trust—was my brother Todd back in 1991. With Todd, there is inspiration and joy. And the future always seems brighter.

Finally, I am blessed for my best friend and steady Tim Dussinger. Thank you for all the all.

About the Author

Farnoosh Torabi is a personal finance expert, author, speaker, and TV personality. *The New York Times* calls her advice "perfectly practical." Her first book, *You're So Money*, was widely acclaimed for its candid, tell-all advice for young adults seeking financial independence.

Farnoosh's latest television work includes SOAPnet's *Bank of Mom & Dad*, where she coaches young women struggling with debt. She was also the resident finance expert on TLC's *REAL SIMPLE. REAL LIFE*.

You've seen Farnoosh on *Larry King Live*, *The View*, *Today*, *Good Morning America*, *The Early Show*, *Tyra*, *Fox News*, *MSNBC*, and *CNN*. She was formerly a Senior Financial Correspondent and host of *Wall Street Confidential* with Jim Cramer for TheStreet.com TV.

Farnoosh's work and advice have been profiled in *The New York Times*, *The New York Post*, *Real Simple*, *Glamour*, *Marie Claire*, *Seventeen*, *Cosmopolitan*, *Money Magazine*, *AOL*, *People*, and *Entrepreneur Magazine*.

Farnoosh attended Pennsylvania State University, graduating with honors in finance and international business. She also holds an M.S. in journalism from Columbia University.

Preface

The arrival of this book and its message, I suspect, could not have been better timed. We're more than two years into this great recession, and many of us are more confused than ever about our personal finances. With the financial and employment landscapes evolving before us, it's difficult to return to the old, prescriptive advice we've grown accustomed to. Emotionally, we've got a lot going on; we're angry, hurt, confused, and we've lost confidence. Our emotions have (and continue to) run high. By now we recognize that we need to change our ways, but not in a knee-jerk, reactionary way. After all, economic volatility is cyclical and will likely return in a new form in the near future. What's needed is advice that doesn't just stem from the rules and regulations of the banking, credit, and financial world but is rooted in our behavior and habits. We need to understand ourselves, get honest, and make money one of the most personal issues and biggest priorities of our lives. If we can get a tighter hold on our minds, our actions, and our belief systems, we can be in control of anything, most importantly our financial lives.

When I first started developing this book, I struggled to succinctly describe its idea to my colleagues, friends, and family. Not because I hadn't a clue, but because my mind was racing. Only until I was deep into my writing could I possibly narrow it down, and even then my summary ran wild. "It's about how our emotions complicate our financial lives and hinder us from making the best financial decisions…It's about the complications of money and how it's actually never about the money…*ramble ramble ramble*…It's about how we have the ability to make better financial decisions, but rarely do…It's…well, it's complicated," went my usual rant (followed by awkward silence). My sympathetic listeners often responded with generous nods and smiles. They said they couldn't wait to read it, even though they weren't quite sure what the heck I was talking about!

This book has been an incredible learning process and has been, by far, my most challenging project. It's been a couple years since I've authored a book. The first was a financial guide for young adults, and as my readers and I matured, we reached a place where we demanded a deeper understanding and explanation of money. We wanted to get a better handle on our financial commitments and our future goals. We wanted to better understand our mistakes and learn how to lay a foundation for personal wealth down the road, especially with the recent financial crisis. This book teaches us how to stop second-guessing ourselves, how to differentiate what is financially right and wrong, and how to actually make the best decisions on our own terms.

Fortunately, I've always had a deep curiosity for understanding why we do the silly things we do with money, so researching the *why* for this book was quite entertaining at times. The behavioral research was available in abundance, thanks to some economic pioneers. Without them and their brilliant minds, this book would be just 50% complete. As for me, my promise was to provide the *what now* to readers. What do we do, now that we know we have irrational tendencies when it comes to money? How do we actually begin to embrace the *M* word in a more honest, personal, and rational way?

Finding solutions to these questions has been a journey of discovery. Looking back, it was a trip I believe that was launched long before I began developing the notion behind *Psych Yourself Rich*. It started when I began entering people's homes, watching them spend money and hearing them talk about their goals. There's nothing like the face to face. Participating in shows such as TLC's *Real Simple. Real Life* and SOAPnet's *Bank of Mom & Dad* allowed me to see and hear actual people struggling with money. Through them, I discovered how our emotions and our biases can deeply influence our financial decisions. And getting to the root of your emotions—and realizing you can control them—is the first *what now* step toward financial freedom. Along the way, I've learned and taught that financial freedom is also about respecting yourself, having a deep understanding of what you want and *don't* want in life, and of course, living within your means.

In the chapters that follow, I'll help you develop the discipline, behaviors, and habits that will lead you to make positive choices about your financial life. I'll help you dig into what's keeping you from being motivated and taking positive action, and look at the behaviors that make people "money zombies." Once those ingrained behaviors are exposed, we can explore the positive habits and the discipline necessary to build a secure financial future.

The methods in this book will enable you to pursue personal and professional goals and will result in achieving financial security, now, five years from now, and long into the future.

Your journey starts now.

Introduction

Being decisive about money can be a crapshoot. By the time you finish reading this book, you'll find out why and what you can do about it.

Ask yourself: Why is it that even the best, most coherent, and logical financial advice does little to mobilize us into thinking about or taking control of our money in a meaningful way? Rarely does a lecture on retirement savings and life insurance inspire us to build a path toward improved security and financial well-being. When it comes to making decisive financial choices, there's a visible disconnect between our mind and our actions.

Between earning money and spending lies a world of uncertainty—a gray area. We lose sleep over finding the right answers to questions such as: *How much should I really spend on a house? Maybe I should just rent? Do I put more money into stocks? Where is my money best invested? Why can't I kick the credit card habit? How do I budget for uncertain times? Why do I make impulsive purchases? What was I thinking when I bought this Vespa? And why do I feel the need to keep giving money to mooching friends? Why, when I know better?*

Do you see yourself up there in that swirl of hows, whys, and wheres?

Psych Yourself Rich is based on the principal that our financial lives—much like life in general—are powered and transformed by personal choices and behaviors, both of which are rooted in our values, perspectives, goals, and financial means. Rarely, though, do we really consider all of these key variables when making a purchase, investing in stocks, building savings, or charging against a credit card. Sometimes we just look at price tags and shrug in compliance, or perhaps we're so narrow-minded about our goals we miss great financial opportunities. In other cases, we can't even get to the point of making any decisions. We feel paralyzed and stop dead in our tracks. Emotions prevent us from getting the right help. So instead, poor decisions are made, or worse, nothing at all is done.

A Behavioral Bubble

Emotions play an enormous role when managing personal finances. Many behavioral experts will go so far as to say that our emotions can potentially *destroy* the ability to make sound financial moves. The most recent recession is one such example of bad financial decision making. Finance and economic experts, including Curtis Faith and Dan Ariely (both best-selling authors), have told me that human behavior played a great role in the financial crisis that began in 2008 and continues to this day. Many were caught in a "behavioral bubble"—thinking and acting irrationally, expecting that home prices would rise generously year after year. This behavioral phenomenon was introduced in 2002 by Princeton University psychology professor Daniel Kahneman, who won the Nobel Memorial Prize in Economics for his work into how individuals approach uncertainty.[1] Kahneman's research sheds new light on the theory that investors are prone to behave irrationally. His argument debunked the traditional economic theory that investors make rational and calculated decisions when the stakes are high, that they learn from their mistakes, and are able to adapt to changes over time.

Since the 1970s, a growing group of economists have explored this fringe viewpoint of irrational investing, but it was Kahneman who brought it to the forefront of modern finance and gave a whole new momentum to what we now popularly discuss as *behavioral economics* or *behavioral finance*.

Behavioral finance has struck a major chord within the financial community—so much so that the big investment firms have begun to help their risk-averse clients regain confidence in the markets with internal teams of behavioral finance experts—Barclays Wealth in Europe, to name one. As the bank sees it, different individuals have a predisposition to their own type of investing that makes them more comfortable with that approach over time (i.e., they do what feels emotionally good). Greg Davies, the head of Behavioral Analytics at Barclays Wealth, explains in a bank report that "Everyone sees the world from a perspective which is uniquely theirs, and investing is no different. People have individual goals, requirements, desires, fears and hopes for their wealth. We all have different habits, different people we trust for advice, and different beliefs about the right decision on any occasion."[2]

We're only human, right? Our emotions play a massive role in practically all facets of life…why not money management? The trouble is that emotions often restrict us from making sound financial decisions. Jay Ritter, the Cordell Professor of Finance at the University of Florida and an expert on behavioral finance, recently told me that he believes we are all afflicted by "cognitive biases." Translation: mental barriers. We lean toward following easy, but not always helpful, rules of thumb. Some individuals (especially men) are overconfident about their decision-making abilities, which can manifest in investing excessively and not asking for help when it's really needed. I found this to be true, while doing research in 2009 on the trading strengths of women. A study[3] of 30,000 single male and female investors found that women's portfolios performed a slight 1.4% better than men's.

To learn why, I called Terrance Odean, coauthor of the study and the Rudd Family Foundation Professor of Finance at the Haas School of Business at the University of California, Berkeley. Odean told me that being too bold doesn't always pay off in the investment world. "We hypothesized men would trade more actively than women because of their greater overconfidence in trading ability…and this trading would hurt their returns. We were exactly right," he said. And not only are some of us too confident, we're sometimes too optimistic, a byproduct of human nature and an American culture that emphasize positive thinking.

According to Ritter, we tend to rely more on short-term patterns rather than long-term patterns, which can prove detrimental when making decisions that concern certain financial moves like investing in the stock market or buying real estate. "People tend to put too much weight on recent experiences," says Ritter. Just think about the latest housing bubble and how many of us were convinced real estate prices would never slow down. In addition to recency bias, another behavioral tendency that plagues us is "group think." For example, many individuals believed—and were told by experts—that high returns were normal and should continue. Humans are prone to trusting conventional wisdom, the actions of crowds, and staying on the beaten path.

Ritter, who also teaches a course on financial decision making, says another reason it's often hard for individuals to make money decisions is because they're not trained to think about things like mortgages, car loans, and investments on a *daily* basis. These topics are largely foreign until we are forced to deal with them. But what about spending, I asked? We certainly do that on a day-to-day basis, but still many times without really thinking about the consequences. "That's a matter of people putting more weight on current gratification versus thinking about the future." As humans, we emotionally prefer to live in the now and deal with tomorrow when it arrives. This explains well my irrational Vespa purchase in 2006. (Don't worry, Mom. I returned it.)

One study that really surprised me was a 2005 report published in the *Journal of Psychological Science*. Researchers from Carnegie

Mellon University, the Stanford Graduate School of Business, and the University of Iowa discovered that brain-damaged people with an inability to experience emotions made better financial choices. After completing a basic investment game that required math and logic, the mentally impaired individuals actually ended up with 43% more money than the mentally healthier participants. The conclusion: If you just stick to the facts and figures and take the emotion out of it, you'll have a better potential to make money.

But, of course, that was just a game. Interestingly, the study also discovered that while the brain-damaged were better at this one game, the healthier participants were better at dealing with day-to-day financial issues. So, emotions can come in handy. Intuition can be an important weapon in making healthy financial choices. As Ritter tells me, having a fishy feeling or thinking something is too good to be true is an example of tapping into your emotions. "You may just call that being skeptical, too," he says. And those intuitions can sometimes keep your money out of trouble.

To achieve the things you want, you need to understand your relationship with money, your belief system, and why you act the way you do.

The goal of *Psych Yourself Rich* is to help you become accountable for your financial decisions and to manage the behaviors that either bring you closer to or distract you from reaching your life goals.

That's the notion behind the title of this book. To "psych" yourself rich means to develop the brainpower—the mental discipline and positive behaviors—you need to traverse volatile times, build wealth, and secure your financial well-being.

You're in Control

The fact that you hold the power to control your financial destiny can be intimidating. But, it's indecision that is the real enemy. The fear of making the wrong decisions is paralyzing and can potentially jeopardize your security, finances, happiness, and health. After all, financial choices affect how well you can provide for your family, how early you can retire, how much house you can afford, and whether you can start your own business some day. But, the truth is, when it comes to finances, we all possess the ability to control the way we think, behave, and act.

My Story: The Fight to Mobilize

When I first began digging into the inner workings of personal finance and learning the techniques of smart money management about ten years ago, I wasn't convinced I had the chops. Even with a degree in finance and a Master's in journalism, I had serious insecurities. How would I fare as a reporter whose weekly assignments included the lowdown of no-load mutual funds and mortgage-backed securities? I daydreamed about meeting the editor of Time *in the elevators and how she, very impressed with my research on the underground culture in Iran, would lure me away from the thirty-second floor at* Money *magazine and allow me to enter the world of politics, international relations, and current affairs at the* Time *news desk.*

I admit I had my sights set on sexier assignments like journeying to the Middle East and reporting on freedom fighters in Iran (where my parents grew up). I wanted to travel the world and share important stories of poverty, crime, war, and injustice. Little did I know financial reporting would end up being a battlefield all its own.

> *I made the decision to stay in New York City, the heart of the financial world, and learned to love the craft of financial and business reporting. It was a conscious effort that involved whipping my brain into shape and convincing myself that the subject matter was, in fact, fascinating. I truly trusted that if I dug deep enough and wrote creatively enough, my stories would alter the minds and lives of readers for the better. As my journalism professor used to say (when she really thought an idea was hopeless): It was quite* ambitious.
>
> *Month after month, I dove into assignments, which had at the very least, promising titles such as "How to Make Your Fortune Now" and "Best Mutual Funds to Buy." It wasn't long until I started to wonder whether I was really making a difference. I knew from the complimentary letters to the editor that some Americans were picking up on the advice and saving more, investing more wisely, building their retirement savings, and so on. Was that most people or was that just the savvy* Money *magazine reader? The thought stuck.*

As a journalist who covered this area, I hoped everyone would agree that his or her personal finances were a priority and would want and need guidance in this department just as much as with issues pertaining to health, relationships, and careers. But while I was closing issue after issue of the magazine, growing more convinced that there was no end to giving away financial prescriptions, consumers were not quite tuning into the money-savvy messages spilled all over the media. In fact, many were in a major financial rut.

A decade later, the stats speak volumes about our long-running reckless ways:

- The average household carries roughly $10,000 in credit card debt, according to the Federal Reserve.
- Foreclosure experts at RealtyTrac predict four million homes will receive a foreclosure notice in 2010, about the same as in 2009.
- Expect more than a million individuals to file for bankruptcy in 2010.
- The Census Bureau estimates that by the end of 2010, there will be nearly 181 million credit card users in the United States, an increase from 159 million at the start of the millennium.
- Our collection of credit cards, when piled up, can physically reach more than 70 miles into space, and be as high as more than a dozen Mount Everests, according to researchers at CreditCards.com.

It's not a delightful picture. Financial advisors and journalists have tried hard to boost financial literacy, but have people been really listening or trying? I can see that our work has helped *educate* people on how to save more, spend less, and make wiser choices with their money. But can we execute on what we know? We still struggle to mobilize ourselves, to turn knowledge into action. Despite colorful lessons about credit scores, annual percentage rates, and the perils of overdraft fees, we're still a debt-ridden nation (especially younger adults). We tend to repeat our mistakes and perpetuate the cycle of debt. Why as a group are we such money zombies? And what does it take to really get a grip on your financial life?

Facing the Enemy

Behavioral finance experts have made it crystal clear that when it comes to managing money, we're irrational. Our decisions are influenced by deep-rooted emotions and perceptions that are hard to overcome. I've seen this while working with people in debt, and what I've learned is that one's lack of financial empowerment has a great deal to do with his or her personal insecurities, fears, lack of confidence, overconfidence, false perceptions, and misguided goals. As Napoleon Hill wrote in the classic book *Think and Grow Rich,* "Both poverty and riches are the offspring of thought."

My Story: Finding My Financial Persona

In my early 20s, I made more money mistakes than I'm willing to admit. But thanks to my constant exposure to all-things money and access to experts and professionals in every financial field, I was able to reverse those mistakes. This access alone wasn't what gave me the motivation or the drive to stick to a sound financial regimen.

For me, my financial confidence and empowerment was an emotional and psychological journey more than anything else. I discovered that you can learn all you can about the do's and don'ts of money management, but unless you have the mindset and the right behaviors in place, it's very hard to make intelligent moves. What were the emotions I channeled to help me find this strength?

First, I felt obligated *to be a financial do-gooder. I believed that if I was put in a position to offer people savings advice, I, for one, should not be in debt.*

I also knew I had no excuse but to make healthy choices with my money. Looking back at how my parents, who journeyed to the United States with two suitcases and very little money, managed to build their finances and create a comfortable life for their family, I really had no justification *for getting into financial difficulty.*

I assumed control *of the situation. I was also, frankly, a bit afraid of the consequences of* not *getting my act together. I knew that my parents wouldn't bail me out if I ended up over my head in credit card debt. (More on the benefits of scaring yourself straight in order to take control of your money in a later chapter.)*

And I felt a little obsessed with my money, wanting to make sure I never lived beyond my means.

Finally, I recognized I had milestones and goals *to achieve, and therefore I had the desire to become financially fit. I remember graduating from college and driving away from Penn State thinking, "My life starts now. No more waiting for when I 'grow up,'" and with that came immediate financial responsibilities. With everything having a price tag in life, I knew the earlier I started thinking and saving toward my goals, the more likely I could achieve them. Once I crossed that emotional and mental bridge, I was then able to execute on what I knew were sound financial methods. I never let go of these forceful emotions.*

Searching for answers as to why personal finance is so difficult to digest, so tough to triumph, has been a preoccupation and intellectual pursuit of mine for the past couple of years. Almost immediately after my first book hit the market, the economy went into a fetal position. We slid into a recession, and many of us felt we had gone back to the drawing board. We didn't just lose money. We lost our bearings. Many of the goals we had identified, chased after, and hoped for, vanished. For me, it was an extremely busy time, fulfilling editorial assignments, answering people's questions on- and offline, and going on TV to break down the stock market crash, the housing debacle, and to offer shreds of positive news in this wretched economic environment. I interviewed economists, fund advisors, investors, entrepreneurs, cab drivers, therapists, and, most important, everyday Americans for their insight into where we went wrong, what they wish they'd known, and their hopes for the future.

Sure enough, consumers could tell you exactly where they went wrong. They hadn't paid enough attention to the "signs," they trusted the wrong people, they didn't work hard enough, they got scammed, they were lied to, they had too much optimism, and so forth. But why bother with the past? Putting the pieces back together was the main issue at task now for most people.

To do this, you need to understand the behavioral and disciplinary commitments needed to build a financial foundation based on reason and personal aspirations. At this stage in one's life, years after college and working the grind, making plenty of mistakes, learning the hard way, and experiencing the real world first hand, your financial curiosities have evolved and tend to be more philosophical and open ended than technical. It's not so much about definitions or calculators. You're wondering how to move into a more elevated world of managing your money to bring security for today and the rest of your life. It is about money, but it's more about you.

My Story: Lessons from Reality

I was recently able to test this thinking on SOAPnet's Bank of Mom & Dad. *In 2009, I was intimately involved in this pioneering television series that revealed the financial skeletons in the participants' closets, making them come face to face with their financial hardships, their debt, and overspending. It was a far cry from the top-rated reality shows big networks backed season after season, like* American Idol *or* The Biggest Loser. *It was a risky show, not exactly escapist television. This was in-your-face, real-life drama about the one thing we, as a society, have yet to openly and wholeheartedly discuss: our money conflicts.*

My task each week was to provide the participants—women in their late 20s and early 30s—with solid advice that we hoped would give them the necessary tools to resolve their financial messes. In return, I received an education as to some of the reasons we, as a society and particularly women, overspend and compile debt. In many cases, these women were highly educated, came from supporting families, and made above-average salaries. So why were they $20,000, $30,000, or $60,000 in debt? It was not because they failed to understand the slippery slope of credit card usage, that spending $1,000 on boots was beyond their means, or that their daily $4 Starbucks latte destroyed their ability to save for a rainy day. The problem ran much deeper than that. To get to *the root of the issue, I needed to take money out of the equation, at least at first. Instead of beginning our meetings with lengthy sermons about sound money management, I dug into their childhood a bit, into their personal relationships, their goals, and what in life made them happy. I had to know, where's your head at? What do you want? Where do you see yourself in five years? What would Dr. Phil ask?*

I really got under people's skin for the first time in my career as I tried to open the emotional and mental floodgates and encourage these individuals to face their fears, weaknesses, and dependencies. My theory was if I could get them to care about their lives and their personal goals first, then suddenly making the right financial choices would not be so difficult or so detestable a task. And I was proved right.

The emotional baggage on Bank of Mom & Dad *ran the gamut—from poor self-esteem to strained personal relationships, dependency on others, and a reluctance to just "grow up."*

For some women, their money (or borrowed money, as it usually was) had become a substance that they abused to make themselves feel better and live their ideal life (or what they perceived *to be ideal).*

Shameeka, a 29-year-old nurse from Brooklyn, New York, came on the show, desperate to rein in her $60,000 of debt and begin a new chapter in her life that included marriage and family. Granted, most people may not be *in as dire straights as Shameeka. (In fact, viewers would write in to me, relieved to know that their financial mess wasn't as bad as the women on* Bank of Mom & Dad.*) That said, the show had significant takeaways for people experiencing difficult financial circumstances. Money aside, many viewers could still relate to Shameeka. She was the girl next door, a hardworking nurse with a beautiful smile. She was your friend who always dressed perfectly and gave the best restaurant recommendations. But beneath the Louis Vuitton handbag and Tory Burch flats, Shameeka was an emotional mess who used money like a pill. Spending money made her feel better, but only for a short while, just until her underlying pain resurfaced. She knew enough to realize there was a better life out there for her, but didn't know how to cross that bridge and start building her financial life. She just wanted to be happy.*

As was usually the case with the participants on Bank of Mom & Dad, *their drama was never over the money. Their behavioral issues with money stemmed from deep-rooted emotional struggles. Shameeka, for example, had an extremely strained relationship with her mom. Just as much as she wanted to be debt free and have a clean financial start, she wanted to develop a closer bond with her mother. In our first meeting, she confessed that she wished she had a healthier relationship with her mom and that until that was achieved, she couldn't imagine getting out of her rut. She filled the void in her heart by filling her closet with high-end clothes and shoes and by taking expensive vacations. Her bond with her mom was cordial at best, volatile at worst. Some background: Mom had Shameeka when she was just a teenager, and it was decided that Shameeka's grandmother would assume the role of Shameeka's primary caretaker. As a result, that mother-daughter bond never quite formed, and now almost 30 years later, Shameeka desperately longed for a deeper connection with her young mother. But the two often failed to see eye to eye, and knowing Shameeka's money troubles, her mom was openly critical, which didn't do much to help her daughter's confidence.*

Their relationship continues to be a work in progress. But after coming to terms with the ultimate root of her financial mismanagement and confronting her mom and getting her feelings out on the table, Shameeka felt a huge weight lifted and was compelled to finally change her behavior and begin building a foundation for a secure financial life, with or without her mom's companionship. Her mom didn't quite give her the support she was hoping for, and although Shameeka felt lonely, she somehow found it within herself to commit to change, to dedicate herself to her future, and to ignore the hurt feelings stemming from her past. Shameeka accepted that she is the only one responsible for her actions and must therefore face reality on her own.

Psych It Up

Just like when you're trying to become more physically fit, sure you need to count calories and fat grams, but you need to *psych yourself* into it first. You need to accept your current weight and your bad habits, understand why you are having difficulties, commit to goals, and get into the right eating and exercising habits for long-term health. The same is true of turning the corner with your finances. It is critical that you first establish and learn how to maintain certain behaviors in order to secure your finances now and ensure future wealth building throughout life.

To psych yourself rich, you need willpower, a confident spirit, intuition, a commitment to your personal and professional goals, and sometimes a little thinking outside the box.

It's not enough to examine pie charts, pay your bills on time, clip coupons, and subscribe to the *Wall Street Journal.* That's all wonderful, but building a sound financial foundation that will last for your entire life is a mental and behavioral journey, not unlike trying to live healthier, transitioning to a new job, or preparing for a marathon. When you find yourself stuck answering questions like…

Should I buy or rent?
How do I make extra money?
Where to invest my money?

…you'll only have to refer back to your personal financial philosophy, your goals, and your strengths and weaknesses to give you most if not all of the answers you need. This book will give you the right tools to understand and address key issues from your relationship to money to your personal and financial obligations.

[1] Daniel Kahneman and Amos Tversky, "Prospect Theory: An Analysis of Decision Under Risk," *Econometrica* 47(2), 1979.

[2] Barclays Wealth, "Behavioural Finance, The Psychology of Financial Decision Making," 2008.

[3] Brad Barber and Terrence Odean, "Boys Will Be Boys: Gender, Overconfidence and Common Stock Investment," *Quarterly Journal of Economics,* February 2001.

Part I

Draft Your Financial Blueprint

1

Personalize *Rich*

*"Rich is some sh*t you could lose with a crazy summer and a drug habit."*

Chris Rock, comedian

My first recollection of the term *rich* dates back to around Halloween 1984. While my other 4-year-old friends dressed up as ghosts, witches, and Snow White, my costume was Richie Rich, "The richest kid in the world."

Hanna-Barbera's Richie Rich was a cartoon series about a fictitious little boy whose animated life couldn't have been further from my childhood truth. Whereas this young boy summered on a gold-painted yacht, I elbowed my way around the sandpit at Elm Park in Worcester, Massachusetts. Richie had a butler and a maid, as well as a room full of stuffed animals, video game machines, an outdoor tennis court, and shiny blonde hair. I did not have such luxuries. From this show's viewpoint, rich meant having lots of stuff, countless dollar bills, and a smile locked on your face.

Fortunately, my education of what constitutes rich didn't end there, but it was a memorable influence. For many of us, our initial introduction to *rich* goes back to childhood and usually focuses on the material aspects. This is not only an incomplete picture; it doesn't quite speak to personal needs and goals. What about the kind of rich that leads to personal gratification?

Rich: Up Close and Personal

How you perceive your own wealth is really a function of behavioral leanings, life experience, and, most important, personal philosophy. I contend that to be rich, you should also feel fulfilled. Interestingly enough, many individuals whom the government would classify as rich (at an annual salary of $250,000 and higher) think of themselves as quite the opposite: bereft of happiness and satisfaction. A study published in the *Journal of Research in Personality* reported that recent college graduates earning more money than their fellow grads of equal standing had greater systems of depression than their peers.[1] Even more surprising, a highly referenced study about the correlation between lottery winners and accident victims found that there was no difference between the happiness level of 22 lottery winners and comparison samples of average people or paraplegics.[2] The takeaway here is that money doesn't lead to happiness or fulfillment—being rich and feeling richly fulfilled are two separate concepts. The *Journal of Research in Personality* study went on to hypothesize that the reason financially rich people don't have better attitudes on life is because they're too narrow-minded. They focus on the goals of being materially rich as opposed to the deeper values and goals in life such as committed relationships, having a family, leading a healthful life, making plans for your future, and working in a job you love.

Although wealth doesn't correlate with happiness, it helps maintain one's lifestyle and drive future opportunities. Harvard professor David Gilbert and the author of *Stumbling on Happiness* wrote in his book that "wealth increases human happiness when it lifts people out of abject poverty and into the middle class...but it does little to increase happiness thereafter." So, it's true that a level of happiness does come with the ability to afford basic needs. Beyond that, however, happiness evolves from the quality of your personal, professional, and financial relationships.

Rich *as used in the title of this book is not about chasing a dollar figure or accumulating more and more wealth—that's not the end game.*

Rich: A Paradigm Shift

In the thick of the recession, I called up my friend and economist Joseph Brusuelas to get his take on this and to see whether, in fact, the rich were changing their ways. Joe theorized that the negative impact on the wealthy during the recession may have triggered a long-term cultural shift that has changed how the rest of the country spends and values wealth.

Wealth in this country became not just about accumulation. In early 2010, Sallie Krawcheck, the head of Bank of America's global wealth and investment management division and one of *Forbes* magazine's "most powerful women," explained a paradigm shift among the bank's clientele on CNBC. Based on the bank's newest survey results,[3] the wealthy in this country are less concerned with accumulating a certain *amount* of wealth for retirement. Instead, these investors are searching for a certain quality of life and a way to make the most of their time. "People are cutting back on luxuries to spend more time with their families," said Sallie.

We're seeing the new definition of rich playing out at all tiers of society; it is punctuated by security, savings, enjoying life, and an emphasis on value and quality over quantity.

Your Formula for Rich

So, given the aftermath of the recession, the Fed figures, and the Richie Rich lifestyle, what's rich *to you*? What does being *and* feeling rich, together at the same time, constitute? What is being *holistically* rich? Let's focus on the emotions that will be foundation of your formula. For starters, feeling rich is mainly about feeling *secure.* So, let me ask you: What does security mean in your life? Is it knowing that you're doing all you can in your power to protect your health, house, income, savings, investments, and the security of your loved ones? How about having money to donate and to be generous to others? Is rich being secure at work and in your career?

Maybe you can't buy everything you want right now without comparing price tags and cutting coupons, but you sure *feel* rich because you know you have a firm financial foundation that's working for you today and in the future. Feeling rich is a better goal, in my mind, and a far more achievable ideal than actually being *numerically* rich. Rich is, in addition to security, the quality and value of our possessions, friends and relationships.

Getting Started: Covering All Bases

Covering your financial bases means you are prepared for the unexpected (job loss, surprise baby number two, a broken dishwasher) as well as the expected (annual doctor visits, your mortgage, your retirement). Your bases may not get covered all at once, but hitting these marks early on will enable you to build a foundation for a comfortable financial life. Here's a summary of the ten most critical bases you need to secure to achieve peace of mind, gain control over your money, and keep your lifestyle in check:

1. **Sufficient earnings.** You need to make money. How much? At the bare minimum, enough to cover your necessities from food to housing, transportation, heat, clothing, and medical insurance. If you want a child, you'll need to boost your earnings or retire from dining out and shopping. Like my childhood friend Targol, who just became a new mom, tells me, "Babies cost a fortune—not only do you need to spend a lot of money for diapers, healthcare, clothes, and such, but now you have someone

else's future to save for." Babycenter.com estimates the average first-year baby costs at more than $10,000. To cope, Targol and her husband John have a separate savings account for baby Cameron's expenses, in addition to starting a college savings fund. That's what's known as *milestone savings* (explained later in this list).

2. **Savings.** The recession has turned us back into savers. In 2006—when life was merry and people's homes were appreciating 25% a quarter—the savings rate was a fat 0%. Today, after the threat of not being able to make ends meet or losing a job, the savings rate has reversed to a near a 15-year high of around 5%. Targol and John (the new parents) have about six months of savings resting in a liquid account. John was briefly unemployed before Cameron's arrival, and that was enough to make rainy-day savings a priority. A simple way of structuring your savings is to automatically deduct a portion of your biweekly or monthly paycheck into an account. Using your earnings, allocate a weekly or monthly amount to a liquid (i.e., readily converted into cash) savings account. Do so until you have at least six months to nine months of savings tucked away in case of an unexpected setback like a job loss. Bear in mind that during this recession it is taking the unemployed roughly 30 weeks to find a new job, and sometimes it isn't an equal or higher paying one. Having said that, research shows we hate seeing our paychecks shrink. A small trick to motivate yourself to save is to, as Richard Thaler and Cass Sustein, behavioral experts and authors of the best-seller *Nudge*, state, "Save More Tomorrow." Their theory is that if you precommit to saving a portion of a future salary hike toward retirement or rainy-day savings, you'll save more over time and feel less pain doing so. If you expect you'll get a $5,000 raise, precommit to saving half of that. Or, the next time you get an unexpected cash bonus or surprise lump sum of money, commit to putting at least half of it into a savings account right away.

3. **Retirement savings.** 401k plans and individual retirement accounts (IRAs) dominate the world of retirement savings tools. Like rainy-day savings, automatically investing a fraction of your earnings into these accounts helps add to your financial security. Remember that the younger you are, the more aggressive you want to be. In my 20s, I put about 10% of my income toward my 401k and mostly in stock funds. In addition, I max out my IRA contribution allowance every year. Now that I'm self-employed and no longer have access to a 401k, I've set up a SEP IRA, which is a type of IRA strictly for the self-employed and small business owners that lets you be more aggressive than a traditional IRA. With a SEP, I can tuck away up to $49,000 a year (if I could). With a traditional IRA, I'm limited to $5,000 a year.
4. **Milestone savings.** What's on your wish list in the next five years? Hoping to buy a house? Get married? Start a family? Build a business? Send a child to private school? It's going to cost you, but it won't be as daunting if you start socking away money in advance. Even if you're not certain you'll hit these milestones in five years, ten years, or ever, it's smart to have goals and look forward to your future. At the least, your goals will motivate you to get out of bed in the morning.
5. **Debt elimination.** Rich people don't have debt. They may have credit cards and use them to score points, but they certainly don't carry balances beyond 30 days. They pay in full each month. You can't afford a fulfilling life with debt on your personal balance sheet.
6. **Sufficient insurance.** From health to disability to home and life, you're not secure unless you have proper insurance. Although the healthcare situation in the United States is in transition, this shouldn't deter you from putting some of your income toward a simple health insurance plan that will cover

the basics like doctor checkups, prescriptions, and x-rays. And why is disability insurance important? If you become disabled and a doctor says you can't work in your profession (or any job for that matter) and you don't have proper disability insurance, you won't be able to continue collecting a paycheck from your employer. And being disabled doesn't just mean breaking your arms. It can also mean a psychological or emotional condition that prevents you from working. According to the Insurance Information Institute (III), at age 35, people have a 45% chance of being disabled for 90 days or longer before their sixty-fifth birthday. And among those people, there's a 70% chance of being disabled for another two years.

7. **Home equity.** If you don't own a home, you can skip to the next base, although I encourage you to consider buying a home if you plan to work and live somewhere for more than five years. Is your house really an asset? Or a liability? Home equity has helped make a lot of people wealthy and simultaneously many people very poor over the past five years. You could earn $200,000 a year and have several of these bases covered, but if your mortgage is greater than the current market value of your house—with no appreciation in sight and a rate that's set to adjust higher in the next year or two—your net worth may be approaching a loss. To cover this base, you need to find ways to end up house *rich* at the end of the month rather than house *poor*—actions like refinancing, renting out the basement, and investing in smart home upgrades that will offer a positive return on investment. (We also explore walking away from your mortgage in Chapter 4, "Embrace Your Relationship with Money.") No doubt you'll have better years than others, as housing prices fluctuate, but if you consistently pay down your principal, history shows you should be in the black in the long run, primed to cash out when time comes to sell.

8. **Defined financial responsibilities in your relationship.** Who's in charge of the bills? How do you decide on big purchases? Do you have a separate savings account and a joint savings account (you should)? Having open communication in your relationship as it pertains to your financial obligations and goals is one base you can't afford not to cover. In their marriage, Targol takes care of the finances. They're both numbers people, both have MBAs, but they find it's easier to allocate the day-to-day responsibilities to one person. Occasionally, they may switch off to give the other person some familiarity with how the gas and heat get paid, but the couple has defined their responsibilities, and that adds to their security, a big rich factor. "Our system is that I am in control of our finances," says Targol. "The budgeting, saving, bill paying, planning, etc. Of course, I consult him when needed, but we've mutually decided that I'm just 'better at it,' I have more time to do it and, frankly, more interest in controlling it!" (Targol is a self-described Type A control freak.)
9. **Money that *works*.** When asked what defines being rich, many of the respondents in a survey I took answered "having your money work for you so that you can pursue what you love and not be stressed." Of course, this base can get covered only when you have enough money to put to work, which is why it's covered later in this list. At some point, once all other bases are covered, you should start to be more aggressive in getting your money to work for you. Now, technically, putting money in a traditional savings account or certificate of deposit is "working" for you. It's yielding, at last check, anywhere from 1% to 2%. But that's not really what I'm getting at here. Good work is when money earns you annual average returns of more than 5%, 6%, 7%, and higher from working in stocks and mutual funds. *Great* work is when you put your money in *alternative* (albeit riskier) investments that may possibly yield even higher

returns (for example, real estate, a business plan, and let's not forget, you). Investing in yourself to advance your skills is one of the greatest ways to put your money to work, something we delve into later in this book.

10. **Charitable giving.** Social psychologists conducted a study in 2005 and found spending on others, being charitable and philanthropic, boosts happiness.[4] The survey tested college students' happiness levels before and after an experiment in which half the participants were given money to spend on themselves and the other half of the participants were given money to spend on others (for example, a charitable contribution). In the end, those who spent money on others admitted to having a greater level of happiness. But beyond the selfish pleasure that follows charitable giving, it's important to give back because it's good karma and it makes you appreciate and be thankful for what you have. My mom always said one of the keys to a satisfied life was not to keep your head in the skies but to be mindful of the less fortunate. Having an awareness of what you have and what others have *not* keeps you grounded, appreciative, and respectful. It reminds you to embrace all that is good and positive in your life, your riches.

[1] C. P. Niemiec, R. M. Ryan, and E. L. Deci, "The Path Taken: Consequences of Attaining Intrinsic and Extrinsic Aspirations in Post-College Life," *Journal of Research in Personality*, 2009.

[2] Philip Brickman, Dan Coates, and Ronnie Janoff-Bulman, "Lottery Winners and Accident Victims: Is Happiness Relative?" *Journal of Personality and Social Psychology* 36(8), 1978.

[3] *Merrill Lynch Quarterly Affluent Insight Survey*, January 2010.

[4] Elizabeth Dunn, Lara Aknin, and Micahel Norton. "Spending Money on Others Promotes Happiness," University of British Columbia, Harvard Business School, 2005.

2

Establish Goals

"The quest for money is a misguided goal."

Joseph J. Luciani, *The Power of Self-Coaching*

Let me tell you about a young woman who came to me for financial help last year. She was 24, mostly unemployed—except for a few one-off promotional jobs here and there—and living with her boyfriend rent free. She had some $20,000 in debt, was struggling to make ends meet, and had come to New York City to pursue modeling and acting. "What are your goals," I asked at our first meeting. "To be a famous actress and make millions of dollars," she said, with an innocent sparkle in her eye. She would refuse to listen to her naysaying mom and friends who explained she had a one-in-a-billion chance of becoming the next Angelina Jolie. You need to find an alternative career path, they pleaded with her. But the young woman refused to focus on anything else. For that, I guess you have to give her some kudos for being strong willed and adamant about her goals. But, really, what about a backup plan? Or let's say she does become the next Hollywood starlet. What happens if and when she strikes it rich? After all, just because you have money and fame doesn't mean you'll know how to manage it. This is someone who racked up $20,000 in debt. What's to say she's not going to fall into the debt trap again? What's going to keep her from falling off the millionaire wagon? Or, let's be fair, what if she never gets on the wagon to begin with?

The goal to have boatloads of cash—but not having a plan or roadmap to protect said money—is something I wouldn't wish on my worst enemy. It's practically a curse. Think of the people in this country who are linked to giant sums of money upfront, such as professional athletes, lottery winners, and celebrities, and you'll see that these rich folks are quite prone to financial ruin. Reports show one-third of lotto winners file for bankruptcy within the first five years after their win.[1] Four out of five professional football players in the NFL go bankrupt within two years of retirement.[2] And celebs have their own share of woes. In 2009, the IRS reportedly filed a multi-million-dollar tax lien against actor Nick Cage.[3] And New York socialite Veronica Hearst faced foreclosure on her $45-million Florida residence that same year.[4]

So let's forget about money for the next few pages. I find that when we focus on our utmost desires, our dreams and aspirations first, we elegantly find our way back to the topic of money in a positive and accepting way. Having goals and pursuing them almost inevitably means having a firm grip on your money. The idea of starting a family, building a house, or planning a wedding can motivate us to be financially responsible. But thinking about saving when you don't really know what you're saving for can seem pointless and uninspiring.

Goals keep the rest of your financial life in order. When you desire to have a house and you make this dream a constant thought in your day-to-day life, when you think about furnishing the house, living in the house, raising your family in the house, growing old in the house and the memories you will create there, the house becomes a sought-after passion and encourages you to follow your course in life in a healthy path toward the finish line. Along the way, you don't overspend on frivolous things, you start saving well and consciously for a down payment, you research interest rates, you explore neighborhoods, and you spend time talking to realtors and on other activities that support this goal, as opposed to spending time and money on other things that distract you from buying the house of your dreams.

This is not to say that all the wealthy folks mentioned at the beginning of the chapter (the athletes, the celebs) fell into financial difficulties because they did not have goals or ambitions. I'm absolutely certain they did or else they wouldn't have become so successful in their careers. As they built and sustained their careers, they somehow became misguided, and that negatively affected their financial situations. Some might have gotten carried away with the trappings of success, whereas others entrusted their money to the wrong people. Others just overlooked the fact that their money wouldn't last forever. As for the lottery winners? They, too, may have had great goals at one point, but their sudden encounter with vast sums of money made them lose their grip on reality and forget what was really important.

The more certain and specific our goals are,
the better able we are to be productive, stay the course,
and sniff out trouble.

An important reason why goals are so vital in life is that they help us to commit to the hierarchy of our personal needs and wants. With defined ambitions, we suddenly don't need or want many things that we previously may have coveted. The phrase *having it all* doesn't literally mean having every material thing in the universe. It means having what you need and some things that you want and overall feeling very pleased and content with your life and your relationships in the long run. You've heard it before—it's about quality, not quantity.

Finally, goals help define and shape our lives and give us something to work toward. Whatever your goals—whether it's to live as healthy a life as possible, to earn a black belt in karate, be the "perfect" parent, start your own clothing company, buy a home, buy a second home, or to travel the country on your motorbike—you must realize that all goals carry price tags, both emotional and financial. Similarly, all goals have tradeoffs. If you want to upgrade to a larger home in the next two years, you might need to shore up a down payment, and doing so might require living on less for some time. The key is to keep those price tags and tradeoffs in mind while mainly focusing on the *behavioral* changes you need to make to achieve your goals.

Goal Ambivalence

Fighting goal ambivalence is the longest and trickiest part of the process, but once you defeat it, there should be few barriers between you and the accomplishment of your goals. To be clear, *goal ambivalence* refers to those who don't care enough to or have any clues about identifying what's important to them and where they want to be in the next three months, let alone the next three, five, ten years of life.

On my television program, *The Bank of Mom & Dad*, I worked with Stacey, a 23-year-old part-time preschool teacher who had yet to finish college. She'd been in and out of school since graduating from high school, uncertain about the direction she wanted to take (despite the fact that her parents were willing to pay for her education). Frankly, I don't think her future was a serious consideration for her at that time. She was living for the moment, teaching by day, shopping by afternoon, and hanging out with friends by night. She spent all that she made on day-to-day expenses, with none going toward savings. She had also managed to rack up a considerable amount of credit card debt along the way.

Stacey's story raises these questions: At what point do you need to start getting serious? How do you get over financial indifference and become committed to change?

Ask yourself these questions:

- What's keeping you from getting off your seat?
- Do you know what your reality is and that there's a better reality waiting for you if only you identify it and make a plan to work toward it?
- Why don't you desire to hit certain milestones?

- Do you feel that life is unpredictable and perhaps that uncertainty is making you feel out of control of your life?
- Do you know what makes you happy?
- Are you trapped by your debt and don't think you can focus on your future yet?
- Are you financially dependent on someone else, and is that dependence keeping you from charting your own course?

These are all valid questions, and the resulting emotions can cause goal ambivalence, but at some point you need to assume responsibility and make plans for your life.

For Stacey, a significant part of her goal ambivalence was that she didn't need to have a grasp on her reality. She didn't know what it was like in the real world. After all, she lived in a nurturing bubble where her parents and friends seemed to always be around to bail her out or support her when times got financially rough. She had no inspiring role models and no real understanding of how a college degree can boost earnings potential. (Average annual earnings for a high school graduate are about $30,000 a year, whereas those with a Bachelor's degree earn on average $50,000 a year [based on census data].)

To snap Stacey out of this, her parents and I had her volunteer to help others who were less fortunate. To really overcome her goal ambivalence, she needed to understand not only her reality but an alternate reality, one of near-poverty and one where family doesn't exist. We sent her to a local soup kitchen to meet with older adults who had had financial setbacks and who had no family or close friends to give them a helping hand. That experience helped her realize how fortunate she was and how she was taking her family for granted. She saw how necessary it is to be able to stand on your own two feet and why it's helpful to set goals for yourself. In addition, we used a bit of a scare tactic. We forced Stacey to confront her grandmother, who had cosigned on a car loan for Stacey that had become delinquent. Their relationship had been greatly strained as a result of Stacey's financial negligence. Apologizing and hearing directly from her grandma how her behavior had ruined her credit, as well as her trust in her, was an enormous wakeup call for Stacey.

Taking personal responsibility and having goals (even if she doesn't map out every last detail of what she wants to do in life) will help motivate Stacey out of a state of laziness and unaccountability, where she's been for most her young adult life. The first sign that you've conquered goal ambivalence is that you feel mobilized and ready to make a plan. Today, Stacey is back in school and has managed to find a place of her own. The next goal? To find a full-time job after college and pay down her debt.

Mastering Goal Ambivalence

So, how can you defeat goal ambivalence? First, you need to do some homework and soul searching. Translation: You need to stop whatever you're doing and take a time out—anywhere from an hour to a long weekend away—to analyze the direction your life is headed and your feelings about that. Bring a journal, bring music, go down memory lane to when you were a child, and think about what your goals were back then. Your instincts are very good when you're a kid because your thoughts and perceptions have yet to be muddied. As a kid, you think simply and innocently. So, if you remember wanting to be a fireman when you were just 8 years old, there may actually be some truth to that. Perhaps your true calling is not to be a firefighter per se, but perhaps a problem solver and humanitarian.

In addition to your journals, your iPod, and childhood memories, find a mentor, talk to friends and family, and talk to people who've been in your shoes and have struggled with the concept of happiness and wealth. Who are your happiest and most balanced friends? Give them a call and grab some coffee.

My Story: Soul Searching

In 2005, I went to the Bahamas (on a budget) with my best friend Kate. It was my first serious vacation as an independent adult. The timing was good because I was feeling pretty rundown at work and was sort of going through a quarter-life crisis (being about 26 years old at the time). I was asking myself introspective questions, such as: Where is my life headed? What makes me happy? Will I ever make enough money to really save? I hustled my way through the corporate world and was still trying to figure out my Zen place.

My inspiration for getting out of the rut was the fact that I wanted to really amp up my career and earn more money. I felt I'd hit a wall at work and wanted to be more excited about my job. I also wanted to start saving and investing aggressively. During my soul searching, I remembered thinking how I didn't really have much of an excuse to not *push harder since that's what my parents always did to provide a great life for us and they had far less than I did at my age. My parents also taught me that little in life is ever handed to you. If you want something badly, you need to go grab it yourself. Holding onto that lesson, I quickly started networking when I got back to New York. Within a month I had landed a new job. I also began a personal project—outside of my 9 to 5—drafting a book proposal about how to make the most of your financial life in your 20s. Two years later,* You're So Money *hit bookstore shelves and marked a turning point in my career and personal life.*

Finally, you have to commit to your goals: mind, body, and soul. Imagine what life will be like. How will you feel? The goal has to come out of your head and permeate your senses, travel to your heart and your being. It's known as *visualization,* something humans are inherently good at. According to Dan Ariely, author of *Predictably Irrational* and the James B. Duke Professor of Behavioral Economics at Duke University, "We do more vision more hours of the day than we do anything else...and we're good at it." "What's more," says Ariely, "when it comes to visual illusions, we can see the mistakes." Visualization will enable your whole body and brain to understand how this accomplishment may (or may not) resonate in your life. Even professional athletes, who often deal with extreme pressure and sometimes suffer a great deal of anxiety, use visualization to control and perhaps enhance their performance.

Of course, you don't need to go to the Bahamas to triumph over goal ambivalence or indecisiveness (although the sandy beaches and crystal-clear waters are a nice touch). I could have easily gotten revved up after a weekend at home, running, reading, and talking through my concerns with family and close friends. Everyone has his or her own process. The important thing is that you acknowledge you want and need to move forward and accomplish your goals and that you're willing to work hard and do what it takes to achieve those goals. Don't get overwhelmed, either. The objective is to create a viable goal that you can focus on and accomplish in the near term. If you can set goals that apply from now through eternity, go for it, with the understanding that you can change your mind as life goes on. For now, though, based on where you are today and where you want to be in, say, five years, what are your goals? To answer this, you must come to understand the type of person you are, the kind of life you want, and try to focus on the positive (while being realistic).

Finding Your Will and Your Way

You won't beat goal ambivalence by pulling goals out of thin air or leaving them open ended. The spirit or the will is necessary to have, but what about the way? What about the strategy and the follow through? Here are seven steps to help establish your willpower and follow through:

Step 1: Own up to your obligations. What do you absolutely, unequivocally need to address in your life? How must you stay the course in order to accomplish goals? An obligation is different from a goal. An obligation is something that you need to do to survive, plain and simple. Often, people chase their goals while forgetting or not recognizing their obligations, like earning money, paying rent, paying your bills, and if you have a family, providing and caring for them. Chasing a dream without assuming responsibility for your obligations is like buying the car of your dreams and not having the means to pay down the loan. Or still another example: Getting in your car and driving out West to find a job in Hollywood while ditching your lease back on the East Coast. When you think of what your obligations are, think of what you are *required* to do: legally, financially, and morally. In some cases, your obligations are plain and simple. For example, make enough money to pay your rent on time. In others, your obligations are very personal. For instance, devote time to your ailing parents who could use your assistance. Jonas, a 34-year-old marketing consultant from New York, says his obligations are providing for his family, protecting his home, saving for retirement, growing his career, and of course, enjoying life. (Yes, enjoying life should be a requirement.) Knowing his obligations has helped Jonas better manage his money and his goals, which include adding two more kids to the family. "I find myself managing my money a lot more conservatively than I have in the past," Jonas said. "I'm also questioning myself on purchases and trying to understand my current needs over my wants."

Step 2: Identify opportunities. Part of recognizing your goals and understanding how you can accomplish them involves identifying the opportunities that surround you. You may have an idea for a business and a friend who's interested in the same thing. This might be your opportunity to collaborate and get your goals off the ground. You might live close to a university and have been thinking about going back to school. There's a potential opportunity to get that elevated degree you always wanted and get a raise at work. You may have an idea for a book and have a friend who can refer you to a literary agent. That's one big opportunity to bounce your ideas off a professional and market your idea to different publishers. Or how about this: The country's in the midst of a recession, and you want to take advantage of markdowns and make a smart bet. Keeping your eyes and ears open during a financial crisis is a great way to seize opportunities. In 2008, my friend Lydia and her husband Rick did what few Americans dared to do at that time. When the news was all about foreclosure and falling home values, the couple decided to seize the moment and scoop up a second home to serve as their family's vacation spot. In that year, the number of people purchasing a second home—either a vacation home or an investment property to rent out—dropped by 30% from 2007, based on recent data from the National Association of Realtors.[5] In the meantime, the median price of a vacation home fell 23% in 2008, from $195,000 to $150,000. It was always a goal of theirs to have a home away from home, and with more inventory and fallen prices, they figured it was a smart time to make the move. In the end, they believe they saved 20% off the 2007 market price. "It seemed like the perfect time to invest," said Lydia, who hopes their new investment will, over time, offset the recent losses in their retirement portfolios.

I like to use the Web for inspiration. When I was a sophomore in college interning at an online media firm in New York City, I, like most interns, had some free time on my hands. Curious to identify my ideal job, I began looking up people I admired on the Internet, from various accomplished journalists, to authors, television hosts, and producers. I examined their biographies to see what opportunities they grasped and how I might be able to replicate them in some way myself. I learned about the advantages they had via higher education, through living in New York City, via working in challenging environments, and through being entrepreneurial. Sometimes—for these men and women—opportunities arose while being at the right place at the right time. But, they were there *and* aware enough to seize the opportunities, weren't they? It was an inspiring exercise then and one that I still do from time to time when I am considering the next steps in my career and personal life.

Step 3: Analyze price tags. All of your goals, whether personal or professional, have a financial denominator. Everything in life has a price tag, a cost more or less. If one of your goals is to build a house in the next three years, you have to consider the cost of the land, the architect, and building materials. Also, what expenses may have to take a backseat while you save up and pay for this house? What changes are you willing to make to fit these goals into your life's picture? The same goes for starting a family.

While there's never a perfect time to have kids, according to my friend Michael who has five children under the age of 12, there are ways to be financially prepared for the arrival of a new life, and it starts by understanding all the costs that go into having a child (at least for the first year), including examinations, formula, diapers, clothing, and childcare. Your life will change—for the better, I hope—when you have a family, especially your financial life. It's interesting to hear my expecting friends say things like "this will be my last big clothing purchase for myself before my baby arrives." Meaning, once the baby enters the picture, the family's financial focus turns to the baby and providing for him or her. For some, having a baby means that the days of splurging on Prada are temporarily over. And it's totally worth it.

Step 4: Get specific and aim high. So, now you know what your goals are. Where to next? Well, how specific are your goals? How detail oriented are they? In other words, do you describe one of your goals as "go back to school" or as "go back to school for a Master's degree in sociology, a school located close enough to work so that I can still work part time and study part time?" Is your goal to "buy a home in two years" or "buy a five-bedroom home within a ten-mile radius of our current location, with the goal of putting down 25% in two years."

The more specific your goals, the better you can narrow them down and start working toward them. Knowing you need a 25% down payment may mean you have to adjust your saving strategy. And, obviously, you can only get so specific because some things are simply not up to you. Not everything's a guarantee, no matter how much you plan, set goals, and follow the course. You might want to further your education at a particular school, but doing so will depend on the admissions board. However, knowing in advance the required qualifications, you can try your best to meet the board's expectations and along the way shoot high enough that admission to your second- and third-choice schools become slam dunks. And while you have your heart set out on a colonial-style home, the inventory may be limited in your desired neighborhoods. But knowing you want a five-bedroom home of some sort will encourage you to save more aggressively than you might otherwise for a smaller-sized property, even if it's not in your first-choice design. Always aim high, I guess, is the moral of that story.

Step 5: Raise your goal karma. Now that you understand your obligations, your goals, and their price tags, design a path that will help you track your savings and keep your goals in check. This roadmap should be filled with your obligations and your goals first. Along the way, you may find room for extra fillers (such as dinners out, a new wardrobe, a new bike). As long as you keep your eye on your obligations and your goals, you shouldn't fall off track. As part of your roadmap, it's critical that you take along one or a few buddies. A buddy system is where you share your goals with a close friend or relative and use each other's guidance and support as motivation to stay the course. I joke (although it's kind of true) that I insist on calling my mom and getting her opinion on financial things because, for me, it's one way to make sure I don't screw up and buy something frivolous. My mom, I know, will tell me like it is. She wants only the best for me, too, so I know her advice is coming from a good and loving place.

Step 6: Constantly motivate. The New Year is typically a time for people to reexamine their goals and identify what they would like to accomplish or change. But once a year is not enough to really motivate yourself and follow through on your goals. Like a promise to quit smoking or to lose ten pounds, if we only check in once a year on that promise, we're less likely to stay on track.

Goal setting and goal achieving should be an ongoing process, and you want to set up a system to check in with yourself and your goals on a regular basis. One way to do this is to make your goals visual and omnipresent. Begin by writing down your goals on paper and on your computer. I have goals written down in my cell phone, believe it or not. Read and review them at least a few times a week when you have downtime. Having my goals in my cell phone allows for easy access when riding on the subway or when I need something to distract myself with. And by the way, it's okay to modify your goals as much as you want. Better to do this throughout the year than once a year. If you wait until that once-a-year checkup, you might "waste" days, weeks, or even months without realizing that your goals have changed from what you initially set out to accomplish.

The next best way to check in with your goals and motivate yourself is to share your goals with people in your life whom you respect and admire. Surround yourself with people who you know will support you in your dreams. Finally, chart your progress. There are several online tools to help us chart and monitor our financial goals. Most banks and credit unions will let you set up separate savings accounts for personal goals. The online banking site SmartyPig.com, in fact, was set up precisely for goal setters. There, you can create a savings account for your goal (a new kitchen, a new car, a wedding) and invite friends and family to donate money to your account. Once you've reached the finish line, you can redeem your cash either on a debit card or on various gift cards or transfer it to another bank account. The site even has a calculator to help you figure out the ballpark estimate of how much you may need to save.

Step 7: Diversify your goals. Our goals fall into primarily two key areas of life. One the one hand, we have our professional goals, which involve our careers and jobs. On the other, we have personal goals, which are related to health, relationships, and personal development. It's important to have goals in both of these main categories to help fulfill that "richness" in life we explored in the first chapter.

If nothing else, getting in the habit of evaluating your priorities, wishes, and wants is an effective way to make money more tangible and less abstract. By giving your money a purpose, you give your financial life more meaning. In the following chapter, we take this relationship a step further.

[1] *Eagle Tribune*, October 28, 2007.

[2] *Sports Illustrated*, March 23, 2009.

[3] *Detroit News*, July 31, 2009.

[4] Forbes.com, June 3, 2009.

[5] National Association of Realtors, Investment and Vacation Home Buyers Survey, 2009.

3

Craft Your Money Philosophy

"If a man is proud of his wealth, he should not be praised until it is known how he employs it."

Socrates

Everyone has his or her own philosophical theories on various aspects of life, from relationships to staying healthy to work and family—some are more firmly established than others. What are your money philosophies? I agree with Socrates: Your money is practically worthless until you put it to work and have something valuable and honorable to show for it.

Whatever your view, money philosophies are essential because they reemphasize and nourish our goals, in addition to keeping financial obligations in check. They serve as a compass of sorts, helping to guide us through the countless money-related obstacles life presents. In this chapter, I will help you define your financial philosophy and make it a part of your conscious life. Trust that if you can develop a personal money mission statement, it will help lead you to goals, to answers, shed light on what to do with your money, and help you figure out how to make more of it.

The Journey to Creating a Financial Philosophy

Your money philosophy is a basic statement about how you should manage your financial life: how you should save, spend, invest, donate, and control it, in addition to your backup plan should money become tight. This philosophy isn't created in a vacuum. The experiences and behaviors we've previously discussed figure prominently into how financial matters are explicitly or subconsciously managed. It's important to be in tune with these experiences and behaviors because that is often the genesis of our philosophies.

My Story: Unexpected Opportunities

After almost three years working as a correspondent for TheStreet.com, a financial news site, I was laid off along with 20 or so other employees from the already lean-staffed web company in spring 2009. I was stunned and confused, but mostly just sad, especially after my last stop in Jim Cramer's office to thank him for all his support and encouragement over the years. Jim was a co-founder of the company (in addition to being the host of CNBC's Mad Money *and author of numerous books.) Jim was and continues to be a mentor and a friend to me. He generously wrote the foreword and investing section for my first book and later publicly supported it when* You're So Money *was published. He was not involved with the downsizing decisions that spring, he told me, and I believe him.*

On my last day, I expressed my gratitude for his unconditional support. I sort of lost it after our goodbye hug—though, not in front of him. Oh, never.

Instead, I fell into Debbie's arms, his longtime assistant, my waterproof mascara spilling down my cheeks and onto her button-down sweater. Get it together, Torabi, I could hear my high school track coach yelling at me. But I couldn't help it. And at that moment, I felt really, really crappy.

In retrospect, I should have been celebrating my independence. The night before, I was having an early dinner with my friend John-Paul when I learned of my layoff. John-Paul, a serial entrepreneur, raised his glass and made a toast to my newfound freedom. I knew what he meant and I appreciated it. Still, I was depressed.

To get over this, I needed to change my way of thinking, or maybe it was just that I had to remind myself of my goals, who I was and wanted to be. But that might not have been enough. I needed to also concentrate on my philosophy—the substance behind those goals.

The alternative (feeling sorry for myself and sleeping in until noon) would have been a lot easier. And for the record, yes, I did do that for about five days (maybe six); after all, it was a necessary part of my healing process. You have to allow yourself some time off. But soon you need to take the reins and deal with the situation. You need to psych yourself back into getting out there, finding a job, being professionally relevant, and creating a new momentum.

For me, being given a pink slip was a reason to pursue a different career path—working for myself. I had considered leaving the company voluntarily on and off for this purpose, but I don't think I would have done it as early if I hadn't been caught in this particular layoff. It was unpleasant and unplanned, but it was the kick in the pants I needed to take my career to a new level.

The next month I appeared on the NBC Today Show *to offer personal finance advice for a segment on careers, during which I talked about how young professionals can bounce back after a layoff, much to the chagrin of others who thought telling six million viewers I was laid off may mean I was not "good enough." Bull. The unemployment rate was creeping toward 10% at the time and amazing, talented, highly qualified workers were in unemployment lines. A layoff was no longer a stigma. I wanted to share my story and wore my unemployment like a badge with honor because with it came a new beginning.*

All this to say that my encounter with sudden unemployment, which some of you may relate to, could have easily put me in an indefinite stage of self-doubt, trepidation, and weakness. My goals were put to the test. Could I actually still succeed in my profession as a journalist without a full-time employer? Could I save enough money to buy a house in the next couple of years, as I'd hoped? Could I now still save as aggressively for retirement? I guessed so...but recognizing my goals, alone, didn't seem quite enough to get me out of my quasi-uncertain phase. I needed philosophies for life, money, and career that I could latch onto for reaffirmation.

The upshot? Viewers wrote in to say how much they appreciated my candor on the Today Show *and that it offered them hope that there is life after losing your day job. That year, I won the distinguished Alumni Achievement Award from the Smeal College of Business at Penn State. Addressing the faculty and staff at the ceremony, I said that it's funny how you can be handed a pink slip and be honored for great achievement in the same year.*

Putting Philosophy to the Test

My layoff caused me to address my own beliefs head on. During this time, I became more convinced that the five philosophies that I had put in place years earlier would carry me through this rough patch and keep me on the path toward achieving my goals. I shared these perspectives with Meredith Viera during that same morning I appeared on the *Today Show*:

Philosophy 1: When it comes to your career, you have to be entrepreneurial, stay in charge of your income somehow, sometimes think creatively, and always find value in your experiences to help get you to the next step.

Philosophy 2: I, along with 10% of the U.S. workforce at that time, could now vouch that a full-time job was no guarantee. So, you have to hope for the best and prepare for the worst. If you can't afford your lifestyle while working toward future goals with one job, you need a second or a third.

Philosophy 3: The more you have to do, the more you get done. Having a few jobs kept me busy and helped me stay organized and responsible.

Philosophy 4: Pursue what makes you happy; work hard and trust that the money will somehow follow. After all, I didn't stay up all night filing stories from 2004 to 2008 for *AM New York* on the side because of the $75 per article they gave me (which amounted to less than 15 cents per word). It was because I valued the opportunity and hoped it would lead to bigger things, which it absolutely did. Your salary notwithstanding, if you're happy with your career and you feel in control of your career destiny, you'll feel fulfilled in ways money can't provide.

Philosophy 5: Know what you're worth and honestly evaluate your strengths. If you feel like you're getting a raw deal from the big cheese and nothing else, let it be known and seek change.

In the years prior to being laid off, I wrote a book to be a bit creative and help strengthen my personal brand. I started doing more television segments and even dabbled in radio. I joined Facebook and started Tweeting. All this helped me remain relevant, boost my revenue stream, make me competitive in my professional realm, and enhance my network. Until my setback, however, I didn't recognize all of my behavior was actually part of a bigger personal philosophy on work and money. Once I was able to define it and lock it down, it was much easier to think about the future and feel empowered.

Guidelines for Crafting Your Financial Philosophies

When you feel fear or are in doubt about money or work, share those feelings with people you trust. The answers won't arrive at your front door unannounced.

A self-respecting person doesn't neglect credit card debt.

Save first, spend second.

A sale is not always a friend.

Some of the best things in life are free.

Money should be enjoyed (responsibly).

Opportunities to make money and advance your career are everywhere, but it's up to you to grab them.

Live beyond your means but spend within them.

Nobody cares about your money more than you.

The best investment is often a personal investment.

If you lend money, accept that you'll never see it returned.

Your generosity will pay off...with dividends.

Crafting Your Personal Money Philosophies

When crystallizing your own money beliefs, don't think that you have to limit each philosophy to one thought or one sentence. Clearly, I have many thoughts and points of view on the subject of money. Your philosophy or money mantra can be as short as a few bullets or pamphlet sized. It can be a combination of words and images. Your personal beliefs about money should reflect you, your values, and your sensibilities and strengths.

The three steps to crafting and maintaining your money philosophy are as follows:

> **Step 1:** Recognize your values, which are often the same values you grew up with. These come from both nature and nurture. Our values are also ingrained in the commitments we deem most important to us in life, like family, marriage, career, staying healthy, and a commitment to our personal development and growth.
>
> I asked one of my fiscally responsible friends and former colleague Allison, 33 and married, for her earliest childhood memory about money. What did she learn and why was it memorable?
>
> *I remember being so embarrassed as a child when my mom would drag us to the supermarket with her. We'd have a ridiculously full cart and head toward the checkout, where she'd whip out a stack of coupons (to be doubled, of course) and her checkbook. The line behind us would get longer and longer, and even as a kid I could read the body language of the people waiting impatiently behind us. It used to mortify me, and I remember barely being tall enough to reach the items on the counter, but I'd start bagging everything to speed the process along and end the embarrassment as fast as my little body would allow.*
>
> *These memories are significant to me because when I entered college, no job, no car, no money, I realized that the best way to save money and still get the groceries that I needed was to use coupons and store membership programs. Now, as an adult, I've adopted it into my lifestyle, saving everywhere I can. I am an avid coupon clipper, surfing the fliers for sales and discounts, matching them up to the coupons that I have, knowing which stores will double the values (or sometimes triple!), and many times, getting all my household necessities for free or pennies. I don't allow us to carry any credit card debt.*

Part of Allison's financial philosophy—which is to always look for deals, live below your means, and save whenever possible—is rooted in her upbringing. Her financial nurturing has also brought on other financial philosophies such as *don't allow thoughts of money to consume you* and *pay attention to the little things since they can add up.* She has chosen to see the benefits of being frugal, as opposed to holding on to the embarrassment as a child.

And that is the key takeaway with Allison's story. No matter how you were raised as a child around money, the adult thing to do is to look at it for what it was worth. What were the lessons it taught you, good and bad? What choices can you make now that you are in control of your own financial path to correct or build on the lessons ingrained in you as a kid? Allison continues by saying that "my parents and grandparents worked hard for their money. They scrimped and saved everywhere they could in order to splurge where it mattered. I adopted their philosophy on money and savings—and I'm really proud of it."

Allison describes her life as "financially stable" thanks to a deep-rooted and established belief system about money and how to manage it. She and her husband are committed to sticking to their mission statements. It's probably why Allison admits she is flirting with the idea of leaving her job. Someone without the security of savings and a commitment to her financial responsibilities wouldn't easily be able to do such a thing.

Conversely, memories and experiences from our childhood may not be how to properly craft financial philosophies. Sarah, a young 20-something retail associate, a subject on the *Bank of Mom & Dad,* remembers she and her mother always going on shopping sprees as a child. Very often, Sarah got what she wanted and would throw gigantic fits when she didn't. At one point, her mom remembers she had to drag her daughter out of the mall because she refused to buy her a dress.

Fast-forward 20-some years and Sarah is a self-described shopaholic (although she is recovering). One of her financial philosophies is that you have to "look the part in order to earn the part." She wants to be a professional designer and believes she needs to wear well-made and designer (i.e., expensive) clothing to make an impression on clients. I can see how appearances can make a positive difference in the workplace, but if you're like Sarah and you're racking up credit card debt to do so, you're not being responsible. You're not really fulfilling your philosophy. So the lesson here is that you may think you have established viewpoints, but do they work for you or against you? And if your perspective is causing you to fall into debt, how does that fit into your goals?

Step 2: Recognize your goals in life, everything to do with family, work, personal achievements, and relationships.

Step 3: Now tie in your working definition of *rich,* which you may still be pondering since reading the first chapter.

Now you're ready to develop as many personal *tenets* as you desire to help guide your decisions throughout your financial life. You'll find that some of your philosophies might not apply during the toughest of times, such as a divorce, a job loss, or a stock market crash, which is why it's helpful to have a few in your back pocket and refer to the ones that make the most sense given the circumstances.

At the same time, you must accept that your philosophies may transform over the course of your life. No matter how firm your views on money and no matter how well they're working for you, sometimes you need to make adjustments or commit to a backup philosophy. When you're younger, you may be more likely to embrace risk. As you age, however, you recognize the value in being more prudent and reserved with your cash. You should leave room for minor adjustments and growth because, after all, life (and our place in it) changes as time goes on.

For example, you may be someone who believes that you should splurge on what makes you happy. But if you lose your job and your income, you might need to put those splurges on hold for awhile, at least until you get back on your feet. During my unemployment hiatus, which ended up lasting a month or so, I used my time off to really buckle down and think about what I wanted to do, not what I *needed* to do. It was an opportunity to soul search (again!) at age 29 and reexamine my personal, professional, and financial ambitions. Thankfully, my finances weren't totally squeezed at that time—as I had sufficient savings—but an anxious voice in the back of my head kept asking, "What if you don't get steadily back on your feet in the next six months?" and more important, "What will you have to show for your time off?" Basically, my conscience was begging to know what my backup plan was, my Plan B. Well, my financial philosophy has one addendum that says "if all else fails, you can cash out the equity in your apartment and cast a wide net of jobs across a broad swath of fields and positions." What's important is that through a downturn, don't ever lose sight of your goals and try to "stay in the game" as much as possible.

4

Embrace Your Relationship with Money

"Money is not the most important thing in the world. Love is. Fortunately, I love money."

Jackie Mason, comedian

In any kind of relationship, you want to be confident and in control. You want to make sure you're being heard. You want clarity (and rightly so). Your relationship with money should be no different, yet this is something with which many of us struggle. And it's simple to see why. Money has been a taboo topic in our country for centuries.

Our upbringing influences how close we get with money and how honest our relationship with it becomes as adults. First impressions, as they turn out, hugely impact our subsequent decisions, including those related to money. If your parents never talked about money openly and never introduced you to the principles of saving, you may have a very disconnected relationship with money. From a macro perspective, too, money has yet to become a totally acceptable topic for wide-open discussion in our culture. We are more prone to talk about disease, sex, and marital conflict in the media than price tags, salaries, and credit card debt. The lack of financial literacy in schools and in homes is still another factor of this relationship weakness. And finally, because we encounter money issues somewhat infrequently (i.e., we don't deal with mortgages, car loans, and IRAs every day), it's hard to stay in touch and develop a level of comfort around finances.

The Money Heebie Jeebies

If you ask folks about their feelings toward money, their emotional response to even just the word *money* is a mix of anxiety, fear, desperation, and confusion. I have found this to be true even among those who make good salaries, have savings, and own a home.

In a recent poll, I asked people how money made them feel. The responses were largely negative, and many felt out of control. Jeff, a treasurer for an oil and gas company, says, "When I have a large amount of money, I feel warm and happy. When it's dwindling from spending, I get butterflies and feel disgusted and sick." Polly, a magazine editor, writes, "Money gives me excitement and lust for stuff when it comes my way… but overall fear that I'll mismanage it or that there won't be enough!" Michael, a teacher, says money makes him anxious. "Very anxious."

Partly to blame for this is our latest economic slide, no doubt. This dismal financial period in our country from late 2007 to the present has resulted in a near 10% unemployment rate, depleted investment accounts, millions of home foreclosures, and a lack of trust in institutions. How could we not be somewhat frightened? How can money make us feel safe when it could all be lost overnight?

But if we're being honest, our money emotions date further back than the latest economic slowdown. The recession may have just cemented existing fears and uncertainties about personal finance. Think back to your first job, your first paycheck, your first credit card statement, and the day you found out you didn't have enough financial aid to go to your dream college. What conversations about money did you have with your parents? With your friends? Most times, we deal and connect with money only when times are tough, when we need more of it, when we can't afford something. Therefore, when we go down memory lane, we remember the ugly stuff. But what about the good times?

After almost a decade of researching, writing, reporting, and coaching about money, I believe that we are still a long way from really finding the positive emotions related to money. We feel at a loss with our finances and indecisive at best, when actually the circumstances could be much, much better. Our money woes are not the result of an inability to understand budgeting pie charts or the evils of compound interest on a credit card. We know that our credit reports take a hit when we pay our bills late and that a little bit of savings here and there really adds up. The calculations and the mathematical reasoning behind sound financial management are available and widely known. So what gives? Why are we still a nation that can't get a grip on its finances?

There is something else holding us back, and for many of us it's not having the proper mindset or discipline to take money by the reins and establish the kind of financial life that we want. And then there's the emotional baggage.

Money Zombies

Gradually now, perhaps by force, we're getting better at our money relationships. With the recent flood of layoffs, investment losses, and foreclosures, Americans feel attacked by the financial world, and consumer confidence continues to lag. Through it all, we've been valiantly voicing our concerns and fighting to get a better handle on our finances. I call that both a silver lining and a work in progress. We're not totally at peace yet. Many of our emotional reactions to money and the thoughts surrounding our "money relationships" are negative, and that negativity is turning us into zombies. Here's why:

Lack of confidence. There's a severe lack of confidence when it comes to dealing with money, and that, in turn, becomes a huge psychological and emotional barrier as we try to get help, find solutions, and win our financial freedom. Money zombies are part of the "I'm not good at this stuff and I never will be" crowd. As a result, many of us do nothing; we become paralyzed and end up living paycheck to paycheck because we just don't have the confidence to take control of our finances and aim higher. The fact is, there's a lot of shame around money, and so long as we continue to believe we're not good enough or we're not capable enough to help ourselves, the further we drown in our shame and the more susceptible we become to damaging our finances.

Apathy. Those who are apathetic often think "why bother?" These are the people inflicted with a sense of defeat before any financial move takes place, folks who in their minds just can't win when it comes to championing their finances. They see no point in doing so either since they can't fight "the system." *Why bother* investing money in the stock market if it's all going to dissolve in the next recession? *Why bother* paying off my credit card if they're just going to settle pennies on the dollar? *What's in it for me?*

My Story: Bad Credit...So What!

At Loyola University in Chicago, during one of my college visits this year, a brazen senior sitting in the back row of the auditorium raised his hand to ask, "Why bother paying off my credit cards? What's the worst that'll happen? Is it just that it will get reported on my credit report?" Just? *Wasn't that consequence enough? I couldn't tell whether this guy just wanted to put me on the spot or if he was seriously questioning why he should follow the rules.*

I played along. "Your credit report will be stained for about seven years if you default on your credit cards, which will make it tougher for you to borrow money for a car, a house, or a business in the future," I explained to him and to the crowd. That's bad enough, right?

The young man in the back was not impressed. He wanted to hear about potential torture and pain, the possibility of losing your house, losing your car, serious and painful consequences. Would he prefer American Express take his firstborn child in the event of being 60 days past due? (Sometimes I wish those were *the terms. I happen to think fear plays an effective role for some in getting their financial act together. More on that later.)*

On the one hand, this apparent-masochist had a point. Credit card companies don't necessarily come after you for the wrinkle-free khakis you charged on your Gap card and never paid off. They don't drive to your house and take away your college diploma (since 30% of students are now carrying tuition balances on credit cards). But if push comes to shove, you could very well get sued in some cases for neglecting to pay your debt. You might have legal costs on top of your other financial troubles to deal with. And who wants that? A show of hands? Masochist Mickey quieted down and left early. He didn't even grab a free book or some cookies. I'm hoping it was because he was so anxious to get back to his dorm to make an overdue Visa payment online.

Addiction. Then there are money addicts. These aren't people who are addicted to *making* money. It's actually just the opposite: people who are addicted to spending money to reach an emotional or psychological high they need and fill a void in their life. Addicts don't usually think they're addicts (the first sign of being an addict). With money addicts, the first tell-tale sign is thinking they're not the only one who has a spending or a savings problem. They rationalize what they're doing by saying, "Well, I'm not the only one having a hard time." That's according to Terri Ciochetti, a licensed psychotherapist and financial counselor in Southern California for the past decade. She specializes in studying people's relationships with their money. During the recession, she noticed more of her clients coming to her confessing their financial difficulties, but with the attitude that "well, the world is having a hard time," so it's not just me. They frighteningly believed their overspending and undersaving was just a phase, despite years and years of the same struggles. "That's a common addict's approach," says

Terri, "the it's not me, it's them mentality." For addicts, taking ownership of their problems and coming to terms with their reality is the first step toward recovery.

Money Harmony

Constructing a Healthier Connection

A colleague of mine, Atefeh, a CFA with a degree in psychology, tells me in all honesty that "money makes me anxious because I always fear it will run out…I have the need to both make money and save it, so I never end up enjoying it…I know there has to be a happy medium."

Well, there is a happy medium. Just as in any relationship, there are compromises. Married folks, like my parents, will tell you this. But as long as there is a commitment to the relationship, a willingness to work hard, be patient, and make careful decisions, your relationship can be a healthy one. As we know in so many other realms of life, the mind that says "I can do it" can help us achieve anything, including financial bliss.

Identifying What's Not *Working*

Since so many of us are in the dumps about money, it's important to first isolate what about the relationship is troubling you. If you don't feel in control, what needs to change? If you're anxious, what do you need to do feel more certain about? If you don't feel confident, why are you insecure?

To know the details of your money picture is to know yourself. First, you need to understand what your lifestyle is today and what you want it to be in the future. What is, in fact, your mission statement for life? What are your values, your hopes, your dreams? What ethics do you follow? What inspires you? What do you know about yourself (your strengths and weaknesses)? This process of identifying what's not working is similar to your thought process before entering a serious relationship with another person. It helps to know what you want out of it, what you're going to give back, and how you plan to keep the relationship thriving.

Reconnecting

You can reestablish your relationship with money in the following four ways:

1. **Focus on the good.** Feeling appreciative of your financial situation, despite some of the possible setbacks you're facing, is one way to improve your relationship with money. Terri says this is a behavioral exercise that often helps her clients. "I'm hearing people having a little bit more appreciation for the fact that they have a job, they have a home and live indoors. As people have more appreciation, feelings of depravation can diminish." If you're trying to feel more appreciative of your money and develop a closer relationship in that sense, it's important to surround yourself with people who share your beliefs and values.
2. **Reflect on earlier years.** To transition out of any of bad relationships with money, Terri agrees with me that the first step is to explore our earliest connections with money. How did our upbringing leave an impression? What did our parents teach us (or neglect to teach us) about money? What do you want to change about the past? Just as we did this to formulate our philosophy on money, it's important to do so when trying to find peace with your relationship with money.
3. **Roll up your sleeves.** To connect with your money, you need to do it on a regular basis and in as many ways as possible. "Until people get very hands on with their money—tracking it, keeping account of how it's spent, analyzing where their money's gone, their values and expectations—they're stuck," Terri says.
4. **Let fear make you stronger.** Fear is a major emotion when it comes to our finances. Some of us fear failure (losing our jobs),

some fear dependency (being in a marriage and not having any financial knowledge or wherewithal), and some fear the unknown (a sudden market crash). And I dare say that having a little fear in your money relationship can go a long, long way. At the least, it may prevent you from making the choices that will lead you to your worst nightmare.

In general, we never want to imagine bad things happening. We want to think that some supernatural force will protect us from evil. But in life, the unexpected happens. And although "preparing for the unexpected" may sound oxymoronic, you can, in fact, ensure that you have various options available when the "unforeseen" becomes the "seen." And wouldn't you like to be prepared to deal with or possibly even avoid the negative ramifications of life's difficulties?

The same is true when it comes to money. We'd like to think that our jobs will always be there, that our savings will be protected forever, that our homes will only appreciate in value. But people do lose their jobs and their savings, they get robbed, scammed, divorced, they fall sick without health insurance, all things with major financial repercussions. A little fear can help you face these possible realities and prepare for the worst. It can inspire you to take control and change bad financial habits.

I expect some of you disagree with my notion about fear and money. We know that fear can get in the way of us getting ahead in life. But fear of financial disaster can yield positive results when it is coupled with awareness: a wakefulness to the potential tough times that are the consequences of certain actions and choices. You want to get to a place where you can say, "I would never want that to happen to me!" After that, you will be prompted to take more responsible action. For what it's worth, Terri agrees with my theory on fear. Channeling your fear is sometimes very helpful, she tells me, because "you're imagining hitting rock bottom and what it feels like to be stuck and really in trouble."

My Story: Facing Up to Reality

In one of my episodes of Bank of Mom & Dad, *I worked with a sweet young woman named Julie. Julie was a former NFL cheerleader who had a serious amount of debt—close to $30,000—stemming from an over-the-top car loan, unpaid bills, and of course, credit card debt from clothes, eating out, and jewelry she couldn't necessarily afford.*

While a cheerleader, Julie was accustomed to the "good life," but she also had a boyfriend who paid for most of her expenses. Despite the fact that her cheering days and open-wallet boyfriend were over, 28-year-old Julie insisted on holding on to the past. Even though she was earning a smaller salary at her part-time dental assistant job, she continued to charge ahead (literally) with her previous lifestyle and tastes.

Less than a year into her post-cheerleading life, she was begging her mom and her older brother for some financial SOS, and for a while, they obliged. Mom took money out of her pension to assist Julie with her bills. Chad, her older brother, let Julie live in his apartment rent free.

Julie's goals included becoming financially independent, but she didn't have a plan. I suspect it was because she was banking on marrying a wealthy man and becoming a housewife, like some of her cheerleader girlfriends had. Julie admitted this during the show, and even her mom and brother acknowledged that Julie had dependency issues on men that kept her from seeking her own financial independence. But Prince Charming isn't coming, we all explained to Julie. And if he does, that will just be icing on top. In the meantime, you still need to get your financial act together and assume responsibility in your life.

What Julie didn't quite realize at the time is the help you get from friends and family has limits. It's only temporary. At some point, family and friends will get fed up with our mooching ways. And that's exactly what happened to Julie. Her mother and brother came on the show to say they would not be able to continue helping her out. I asked Julie to consider some scary consequences: What are you going to do when the money stops coming in from your mom? What's going to happen when Chad says you can't sleep on his couch anymore? What if your knight in shining armor with his fat bank account never comes to rescue you? It's going to get really ugly, I explained.

So let's imagine the consequences. How would she like to sleep in her car? What would it feel like to declare bankruptcy? The thoughts hadn't ever entered Julie's head, and so this sudden encounter with fear first made her cry (and made me feel really bad). But then it led her to face her responsibilities once and for all.

Did she change overnight? Of course not. But the progress reports I've been getting from both Julie and her mom suggest she's truly beginning to pick up the financial pieces in her life and actually enjoying the process. She has found the motivation to make better choices that will steer her away from complete financial ruin. She has found a second part-time job, moved into her own apartment (with an ugly, used couch, but nonetheless "it's my *couch," she writes), and has completely paid off one of her credit cards. She's not out of the woods entirely yet, but she now realizes that she is the only one who is going to get herself out of the ugly mess she created (and has the will to do so).*

Moral Obligations in Your Relationship?

Some of you might immediately roll your eyes at this topic: morality and money. Do the two even belong in the same sentence? Do you have any moral or ethical obligations to the financial choices you make? This is not something we think about often. However, your views about such influence your decision making, especially during tough times. So, you want to know what your views are, right?

One way to analyze this is to consider a hot topic: your home mortgage (and think of that as a subrelationship to the overall relationship you have with your money at large). Lots of Americans locked themselves into risky mortgages over the past decade, and as home values depreciated over the past few years, many began to question the benefits to staying in a financial relationship in which they felt they were getting a raw deal. Should you just walk away or continue to make payments on a depreciated asset? You understand that your credit will take a hit for seven years or so, and securing any further loans will be pretty much impossible in the near future. But if your mortgage is eating away at your ability to live a stable life and fulfill your other financial obligations, is this a relationship you should kick to the curb?

Last year, I received that very question from a distressed reader, Michael, who was wondering whether he should stay or just give up and walk away from his three-bedroom home in Detroit, Michigan. His main gripe—like some eight million Americans at the time—was that his home was valued much lower than the amount of his mortgage. So, should he just stop paying and let the bank deal with it since he isn't building any equity and probably won't at any point in the foreseeable future? Apparently, most Americans would stay put, according to a recent survey of 1,000 U.S. homeowners; only 15% of Americans believe financial distress is a good enough reason to walk away from their underwater mortgages.[1] Those who would stay put would consider other options, like trying to modify their loan, selling the property, and renting out a room to help make ends meet. In that same survey, a third of respondents said moral obligations would convince them to continue paying an underwater mortgage.

In Michael's situation, he had an extremely high interest rate of 8.6%, making his monthly principal plus interest payment roughly $1,850 (more than half his monthly income). In addition, Detroit was suffering from the highest unemployment and foreclosure rates in the country at the time, so the chances of a quick market recovery there were not likely. "The area is starting to decline due to many vacant or vandalized homes, with several break-ins, three for myself," he wrote to me. Michael's credit was already poor (hence the 8.6% rate), but on the flip side he no longer used his credit cards. He and his wife were on a cash diet.

More middle-of-the-road homeowners are grappling with the same issue as Michael, not necessarily because they can't *afford* their monthly payments, but because they are "underwater," owing more on their mortgage than the home is currently worth. They're not building any equity, and when time comes to sell, they'll probably be in the hole. The IRS has also made it less of a tax pain to give up on your mortgage by now offering special tax relief for financially strapped borrowers who lose their home due to foreclosure. Prior to this, so-called forgiven debt was considered taxable income.

The Fixed-Income Team at Credit Suisse noted at the end of 2009 that "should the downward spiral in home prices, neighborhood condition, and equity deterioration continue, more and more mainstream borrowers are likely to walk away from their homes." Credit Suisse also predicted that more than eight million mortgages would enter into foreclosure over the next four years. That's about 16% of all mortgages.

In Michael's case, it's obvious he should definitely move to a safer neighborhood. Three break-ins in one month is more than enough reason to leave. But should he *abandon* his mortgage? I asked some experts to weigh in with some analysis: Wall Street economist Joe Brusuelas; Gerri Detweiler, a credit advisor for Credit.com; and Jon Maddux, CEO and co-founder of YouWalkAway.com, a site that helps distressed homeowners learn about their alternatives, such as ditching their mortgage. For a $1,000 fee, YouWalkAway guides you through the process. Before getting started, the website offers an online calculator that helps you mathematically decide whether it's a good idea to walk away from your mortgage. To them, some financial commitments justifiably call for a split.

Joe said that in general he was not a fan of walking away from a mortgage, but in certain cases he said abandoning your mortgage sometimes make sense. It's an exception, not a rule, and sometimes you'll find, after close examination, that it's not even a matter of ethics. "There may be a narrow range of conditions under which walking away from a home that is so far underwater, it's absolutely rational," Joe tells me.

Breaking Up

Here are some of the factors our experts say are extremely important to consider before deciding to walk away from this specific money relationship. And in any sticky situation like this, you may want to get legal help from a bankruptcy attorney.

Your bank won't help. The bottom line is, banks don't want to go through another foreclosure process. It takes time and money. But if playing scared and saying you desperately need to modify your loan or *else* fails to earn you any material help, consider it a sign you have to take matters into your own hands, which may require walking away. And before you do, make sure your bank also has no plans to chase you down and sue you for "deficiency" claims, says Gerri Detweiler of Credit.com, which, depending on your situation, could end up costing thousands and thousands of dollars. Some states, such as California and Florida, now prohibit deficiency claims, and in other states some lenders are choosing not to go after defaulted borrowers because they've got too much else on their plates. But, "until the statute of limitations is expired, I wouldn't think I was in the clear," says Detweiler. "The lenders may come after you in a couple of years after taking a deep breath." Some attorneys recommend getting a signed letter from your bank stating it won't sue you for deficiency claims.

You're not able to save or address your other immediate money relationships. Of the 5,000+ members (at the time of this writing) who've so far signed on to YouWalkAway.com, many have decided to forgo their mortgage because they say they're no longer able to save any money. "They see [their home] as a major drain to their savings and cash flow in general. They don't want to keep bleeding, basically," says CEO Jon Maddox. If every payment on your mortgage is a step backward from achieving your other top financial goals, like saving, putting food on the table for your family, and paying down your other debt, a foreclosure, he says, may be a suitable path, especially if you don't see the area appreciating in value in the next five, seven, or ten years.

You're okay with damaging your credit. A foreclosure stains your credit report for seven years, much like Chapter 13 bankruptcy, which is a partial debt repayment plan. A Chapter 7 bankruptcy, which eliminates your debt entirely, sits on your credit report for ten years. Despite foreclosures becoming more common, don't expect any lender to cut you a break. "Ultimately, lenders make decision based on risk," says Detweiler. "Lenders really shy away from serious negative items like foreclosure and bankruptcy." It will take at least a few years before you can qualify for a new loan, and your rates will be extremely high. To put it in economic terms, "Your credit score is going to limit your opportunities for consumption and your choice matrix," says Brusuelas. Another tip: Don't let the potential consequences on your credit report decide between filing for a foreclosure or a bankruptcy. They're both quite ugly. Instead, examine the bigger picture. Determine what your future goals are and what the best personal strategy may be for you. And talk to a bankruptcy attorney to weigh all your options. "The homeowner needs to focus on what is the best financial strategy for the next, say, five years, versus trying to beat the credit scoring system," says Detweiler.

You're otherwise "okay" with it. This is where your conscience can potentially take the steering wheel. The decision to walk away from your home has been chastised in some press for being "immoral." A contract is a promise, some critics argue, and therefore should be upheld no matter what. It's an obligation, plain and simple. What's more, foreclosing on your home potentially lowers the value of the neighborhood and hurts the value of your neighbor's home and the stability of the overall economy. Are you okay with that? University of Arizona law school professor Brent T. White wrote in a controversial paper titled "Underwater and Not Walking Away: Shame, Fear and the Social Management of the Housing Crisis," that if it was in their best financial interests, homeowners should consider ditching their mortgage and not worry about the "moral hazard."

Maddox agrees, telling me there's no moral obligation to keeping an unfavorable mortgage, considering if all the above holds true. Desperate mortgage holders should do what they can to help themselves get out of a painful situation, especially when their bank won't compromise or modify the loan. That means considering all alternatives: renting out a room, selling the house for a loss, and yes, even walking way. After all, he says, banks have no problem breaking contracts or writing off assets. "If banks cut their bottom line by, for example, firing workers, they get applauded by shareholders. But guys struggling to pay for their kids' college because their mortgage is too high, those guys get thrown under the bus and we say they're deadbeats, unethical, and immoral."

Breaking up is never easy. Before parting ways—whether it's with a mortgage, a financial advisor, or a particular bank—you need to evaluate the pros and cons, as well as the consequences on your finances and on your stability.

Family, Friends, and Money

Friends and family can be a serious money drain, and it helps to be able to stand up for yourself when the pressure's on to lend. Experts Jeanne Fleming and Leonard Schwarz, *Money* magazine columnists and authors of *Isn't It Their Turn to Pick Up the Check?*, have done a great deal of research on the subject. They found 60% of the public admitted that in every family, there's always someone who's constantly asking for money, the "serial borrowers." As times get tougher, they will see this "as a golden opportunity to do what they always do, namely put their hands out and whine," say the authors.

Here's how to stay in control of the situation:

Be open-minded. Being an advocate for your money in scenarios where you are asked to lend money doesn't mean always saying no. It means, first and foremost, assessing the situation and the potential borrower. If this certain someone has lent you money in the past, you're sort of obligated to try to return the favor. Consider a few things, including the closeness of your relationship, how likely it is you'll get the money back, and why this person needs money in the first place. Is it to help pay a mortgage? Or to buy a new cell phone (when he already has two)? Knowing how your money will be spent should be a big determining factor for you, the potential lender.

Be okay with never seeing the money returned. It's never a good idea to lend money that you can't afford to live without. Fleming and Schwarz's research shows that 43% of the largest loans people make in their lives are not repaid in full, and with 27% of them, the lender gets nada. Before lending anyone money, think about whether you can realistically and emotionally afford to make the loan a gift.

For big loans, get a contract. For amounts that exceed, say, $500, or an amount that you absolutely, unequivocally need to get back in the near future, have a contract that lists the borrower's and lender's information, including names, addresses, social security numbers, and so forth. Then describe the loan agreement: the dollar amount of the loan, the repayment schedule, and any interest you may want to charge. VirginMoney.com is the largest social loan facilitator in the country and helps contract and manage private loans between peers. They've processed more than $450 million in social loans since launching in 2007. If you have a loan with a family member, friend, or a business partner, and it's at least a few hundred dollars, Virgin Money's services (starting at around $99) might make sense. You can also enlist the help of an attorney you pay by the hour to draft the contract and set up the repayment process. Working with a third-party—either online or offline—not only keeps you organized, but it helps to take some emotion out of the deal.

If the answer is no, present alternatives. It's hard to say no, but remember that the conversation doesn't need to abruptly end at N-O. There are alternatives to cash. Direct them to peer-to-peer lending sites like LendingClub.com, where you can apply for an individual loan in the public marketplace. Or perhaps you know a financial advisor who can help them acquire a loan from a local bank, or maybe go with them to apply for a loan. If your friend or family member gets rejected, don't stop there. Make a plan to visit at least three banks and credit unions. Another alternative to giving money is to offer your help in the form of time and services. If your cousin or best friend needs $500 to make ends meet this month, offer to cook dinners, drive her to work, or watch her kids for free. If she needs a new suit for an interview, let her shop in your closet. There are numerous ways to help without actually writing a check.

When Love Strikes

Whether you are dating, in a partnership, or married, money can play an enormous role in the union. Couples say spending is the cause of the most serious conflicts in marriage, specifically lack of communication (including not discussing goals or knowing each other's money habits, both good and bad). Married couples have about a 45% chance of divorcing over money-related issues, according to the *New York Times*.[2] More likely than not, your partner will have a different relationship with money than you do...and that's okay. Terri, who meets with couples on a regular basis, explains that the important thing is that you both recognize your similarities and your differences as early on as possible, agree to common goals, and accept that you will both do what you have to do support those goals. "If we don't talk about it and instead just make assumptions, that makes for a very difficult road." And just like sex, she adds, if you can't talk about it, you shouldn't do it.

In a MyFico.com survey, one-third of respondents said that a lack of financial responsibility hurt their relationships more than being unfaithful (22%), a lack of affection (21%), or a lack of a sense of humor (16%).[3] Problems paying bills late was cited as often as problems with in-laws or relatives as the most stressful situations that put pressure on a relationship. Credit.com's Gerri Detweiler, my go-to credit expert, says the stats speak volumes about how important it is to be on the same financial page as your partner. And the sooner the better. She says 20% of divorces occur within the first five years of a marriage. "Clearly, a good income and financial stability can help a marriage, and the opposite can hurt it. While some couples draw closer together during times of crisis, many won´t survive financial woes," says Gerri. "Going into a marriage with different views about money can spell disaster." She cites a few studies with glaring evidence. One from the University of California found that money was the major source of disagreement for close to 250 newlywed couples in their first and third years of marriage.[4] And based on a survey by researchers at Utah State University, tying the knot before clearing yourself of debt has a harmful impact on "newlywed levels of marital quality."[5]

You should try everything you can to get financially in sync, and I'll be the first to say that's easier said than done. How to come out and just discuss money? For starters, you don't have to be so direct about it (at first). Terri offers us some easy exercises to, as she explains, "meet *around* money." For example, consider reading a money book together (maybe this one!) or going to a seminar and sharing your notes afterward.

If after much discussion and perhaps even therapy you find that your goals are not aligned and never will be and that is weighing on your happiness and your ability to live your life, you have to seriously think about whether you can afford *this relationship.*

Before you commit, before walking down the aisle and signing that marriage license, you should know each other's money strengths and weaknesses, as well as your short- and long-term goals. Admittedly, while dating, it might not feel all that appropriate to ask personal questions about money.

Here are my favorite icebreakers to help open discussions as the respondent begins to go down memory lane:

How did you pay your way through college? Or, how did you afford college?

You may discover you both have tens of thousands of dollars in student loans or a great big credit card bill that's carrying debt from college. Maybe he or she skipped college and has no debt at all. Dig deeper and discover how both of you are dealing with your loans and how you are managing to find work without a degree. After about six months of dating, my boyfriend and I disclosed our "debt" loads, and it started with a conversation about college loans, which was the easiest to talk about since nearly everyone with a college degree has dealt with this at some point. I discovered he had paid off his loans already like I had. He didn't have all that much when he graduated and aggressively paid off the remaining amount within the first few years after graduating. I had used a lump sum of cash from my first book advance to pay down all my remaining student loans both from Penn State and Columbia, where I went to grad school.

What is your earliest memory of money?

This is a great question because it could provide some insight into this person's perception or value of money and his or her nurtured influence. My friend Dave, a 34-year-old dad of two, remembers growing up in a very financially conservative household. At age 7, his parents explained to the kids what "basic necessities" were: food, shelter, and clothing. Anything above and beyond that would have to come out of an allowance, which as Dave recalls, "didn't amount to much week over week." This led him to become extremely patient with money and learn how to delay gratification. He remembers obsessing over a Transformers action figure and having to wait months before he could afford it. "The reason this is so memorable," he says, "is because that's a tough lesson to learn from the point of view of a child…To save took a lot of dedication and drive." As an adult, Dave's saving skills protected his family when he became unemployed in 2009 for almost an entire year. "I always pay myself first by putting the most I can manage into a savings account and losing the account number at least until the next paycheck!"

Do you rent or do you own?

A conversation about real estate is often one of the best ways to get into some serious money conversations. If the answer is "I rent," ask whether he or she has ambitions to ever own a home and why or why not. It's a loaded question that may bring up signs of financial stability or insecurities about the market and their own finances. If this person has tackled the real estate market and owns a property, that's a pretty impressive sign, assuming he or she is current with the mortgage (by the way, a good thing to find out).

Where do you want to be in a few years?

It's a perfectly natural question to want to know the direction your partner is headed or *wants* to lead. For example, do you want to save up for a house, a big trip, your own business? All of these milestones have price tags, and it's important to know whether you would support these goals once in a committed relationship with this person.

What's your number?

And I don't mean phone digits. I mean, what would be a comfortable salary for you to live on? This might not be first-date conversation, but as you two grow closer, this may be a strategic way to open a dialogue about what it means to be "financially comfortable." Use this question as a gateway to then talk further about money values, long-term goals, and what it means to feel rich.

What's your credit like?

This is probably the most important question...but it's not kosher to ask this straight out on date one or even date number two. This is a topic you want to gauge when you feel the relationship is getting serious or if you see the two of you investing in or purchasing anything together. And if you want my advice: Hold off on cosigning anything for each other until you're married and/or prepared to accept the risk that your partner may not follow through on your joint financial obligations.

My friend Karina is married and house hunting, but has decided not to apply for a mortgage jointly with her husband Sam. The reason? Sam has poor credit, and the couple is worried his less-than-stellar track record might weigh down their chances of getting a good interest rate. The downside is that they will not qualify for as big of a loan because the bank will base it on Karina's salary alone. They figure they'll live in a smaller house until Sam improves his credit score and then try again down the road for a new, bigger home.

And after all those questions and answers, still keep your eyes open!

Finally, be observant about how your partner spends and manages money. Is he or she using cash or plastic all the time? Does your partner track his or her spending at all? Good tipper or bad tipper? Generous with his or her money? Does your partner talk about money so much it makes you want to scream? Or the opposite, which also makes you wonder?

It's easy to overlook money issues when you are in love because talking about money is not romantic. Also, it's not something that we as a culture talk very openly about. We're more likely to disclose intimate details about previous relationships, our health, and our jobs than our credit score or the number of loans under our name. So, the best advice here is when you want to combine your money relationships, be straightforward about it as much as you can, but in a nonthreatening way and when you're both in a good mood. If you start feeling strain on the financial relationship you share, go first to each other for guidance. See what adjustments each may need to make to spending and saving. Designate one person (the one who's most organized) to be the chief financial officer in the household. All the while, keep the other partner involved. And trade responsibilities once in a while so that no one's kept in the dark.

And a final thought from Terri: "Best to do all of this before kids enter the picture."

[1] Fannie Mae National Housing Survey, April 2010.

[2] Ron Leiber, "Money Talks to Have Before Marriage," *New York Times*, October 23, 2009.

[3] MyFico.com and The Heart/Credit Connection, "Personal Shortcomings" survey, 2006.

[4] Jean Roggins, "Topics of Marital Disagreement Among African-American and Euro-American Newlyweds," University of California at San Francisco, 2003.

[5] Lisa Skogrand, David Schramm, James Marshall, and Thomas Lee, "The Effects of Debt on Newlyweds and Implications for Education," Utah State University, 2005.

Part II

Psych It Up

5

Organize. Don't Agonize

"Once you have a clear picture of your priorities—that is values, goals, and high-leverage activities—organize around them."

Stephen Covey, author of *The 7 Habits of Highly Effective People*

Why do I invest so much time and money at the Container Store? Why do I feel like I "need" a Lazy Susan turntable and another shoe rack? As a society, many of us strive to get our lives neatly organized, as evidenced by our spice racks, DVD shelves, and tax folders. Spring cleaning in the winter? I'm so there. But does all this organization really create Zen?

Well, have you ever been to the Container Store? For me, I can honestly say it's a form of heaven on earth. I can (and have) spent hours cruising through the chain store's glorious aisles of Elfa installation components and desktop organizers, imagining how they'll bring peace and serenity to my life. And when my bed is made and my kitchen is clean, I certainly do feel more at ease. And I'm not alone. My friend and organization professional Jodi Watson, the founder of Supreme Organization, tells me that organization helps us stay balanced, clear, and focused. Not to mention, it makes us more self-confident and efficient in our day-to-day lives. (Just as long as your Container Store addiction doesn't deplete your bank account.)

Getting Squared Away

Messiness is distracting. Benjamin Franklin wisely said that "for every minute spent organizing, an hour is earned." Conversely, a lack of organization can stir up anxiety, confusion, and a feeling of helplessness. When it comes to your finances, a lack of a system or strategy is nearly ten times worse because you're not only sacrificing your peace of mind but you're potentially sacrificing your financial well-being.

The four words I hear most commonly from people inundated with bills and credit card statements are these: *Where do I begin?* That is, how do I start taking care of this mess and turn it into something that makes clear sense and is easy to reference?

My Story: Junk Drawer Diaries

Danielle, a great case study on Bank of Mom & Dad, *was raised by a very organized mom who had a system for all her financial paperwork and bills, yet Danielle struggled to manage her own finances. She couldn't tell you how much her cable bill was last month because she lost the statement or never even opened the bill. She had a disastrous kitchen drawer of unopened envelopes from creditors, in addition to crinkled-up receipts. It had become so overwhelming that Danielle just opted to ignore it. She became a financial zombie. As a result, bills got paid late or never at all. Along the way, she struggled to make ends meet for herself and for her family. Her money would run out before the end of the month (and without her having a clue as to where it all went). Interestingly enough, Danielle was an extremely talented woman when it came to managing and organizing other aspects of her life, from caring for her baby daughter to growing her small fashion business. When it came to money, however, she just didn't know, to put it in her words, where to begin. She felt defeated before ever making any real effort to solve the problem.*

Luckily for Danielle and everyone else who feels lost, three clear-cut steps can help you put your financial life in order (and they're primarily mental). First and foremost, take a mental inventory of your life and understand your obligations and goals. Second, cut the clutter from your life; *clutter* here refers to the emotional distractions that keep you from addressing your obligations and goals. The difficulty, of course, is that humans have a tough time letting go of most things. Dan Ariely, behavioral economist and author of *Predictably Irrational,* says the reason for this is that we simply prefer to keep our options open. "It's very hard to close doors," Ariely tells me. Choosing what should stay and what should go from our lives is not easy. "Closing a door is saying here's an option that I'll never have for life. It's a very hard choice," he says. The final piece in achieving an organized financial life is to establish the right habits and stay committed. Let's examine how these steps play out in reality.

Step 1. Take Inventory: Priorities and Goals

Whenever you feel like you've lost a grip on your finances, stop and remind yourself of your obligations and goals. Maybe you've fallen off course, racked up a bit of debt, and now find yourself asking how you get here. And more important, you might be asking, how do I get out of this mess? To address this problem, you must first remember who you are and what you want in life.

If you were to organize your inventory of obligations and goals, what would the list look like? I asked my friend Dave for his list. You met him in the previous chapter. He's the married father of two whose early days of saving up for a Transformer taught him how to delay gratification.

Dave's Personal Priorities:

1. Provide for and protect my family: wife and kids (have money for food, clothes, health expenses, saving, and so on).
2. Protect our home (pay the mortgage and real estate taxes).
3. Save for our retirement (invest in our 401k, IRA, and other retirement savings vehicles).
4. Enjoy life (have enough money for fun like eating out, travel, entertainment, and so forth).

Dave's Professional Priorities:

1. Understand and fulfill the requirements at work.
2. Grow my career as well as the business of the company.
3. Watch for opportunities and focus on professional areas that may be beyond my current understanding.

Dave's Personal Goals:

1. Travel more, specifically to Ireland, Greece, Italy, and St. Barts.
2. Expand my family and have a couple more kids.

Dave's Professional Goals:

1. Move up the corporate ladder to become an officer of a company.
2. Continue to grow a side career in real estate.
3. Start my own business in real estate.

Knowing where you currently stand with obligations and goals and where you eventually want to stand will allow you to build an organizational structure to help realize those aspirations. It all goes back to the notion that if you understand your goals and consciously and actively strive for them to become reality, you'll more easily guide your money toward the appropriate channels. For example, with his inventory of priorities and goals established, Dave is unlikely to invest all his savings toward starting his own business in real estate, even though it's a top goal, before he has addressed his mortgage and his retirement savings. As Dave says, "In order to accomplish my goals, I find myself managing my money a lot more conservatively than I have in the past and trying to understand my needs versus my wants."

Step 2. Clear the Clutter

The next step is to clear the clutter out of your life. And I'm not talking about clutter such as two-year-old receipts from the now-defunct Circuit City and your tax forms from 1992. To cut the clutter out of your financial life, you need to eliminate the conscious and unconscious distractions that do absolutely nothing to support your financial obligations and your goals. From mooching friends to unstable relationships to peer pressure and social expectations to look and act a certain way, clutter is all around us, and it is not helping you in the financial department.

What's the unnecessary drama that's preventing you from putting your life in perspective, from getting a hold on your finances and making sense out of it all? You want to identify it and get it out of your system.

Part of Danielle's clutter was a lack of self-esteem. She had just gotten laid off from her dream job working for a fashion design house in New York City and had no new job prospects. The layoff had forced her move back to her hometown of Hartford, Connecticut, where life was more affordable. There she was struggling to re-create her New York City life with her husband and 2-year-old daughter. Depression was eating away at her ability to properly manage her financial house. How did she ultimately snap out of it? Well, she wasn't exactly in denial of her disorganized ways. She also knew she was having a hard time dealing with unemployment. So, she was very much aware of her financial problems. For Danielle, visualization and seeking a mentor were the two vital forces that helped her change her ways.

First, she began to set up visual reinforcements of her goals around her home. Because she is a creative person, this was a fun exercise for her, and she took it really far. She created a board of visual elements to remind herself why it's important to stay financially on track. She included pictures of her baby daughter, her family, fabric swatches, and a list of bills she needed to address right away. She left the board hanging in her kitchen, knowing people would ask her about it and that she'd be prompted to share…and down the road she would feel accountable to those people and would want to make them proud. Another helpful technique was to seek the mentorship of Byron Lars, a designer she had always looked up to. Danielle had always admired his success but never quite knew the sweat and tears behind the scenes. Getting in touch with him and sharing her goals, as well as her financial struggles, earned her a much-needed advocate and a trusted source to help her follow through on her goals.

Understanding the Signs

Jack, a 29-year-old aspiring fitness guru, spent almost $11,000 last year on his image: athletic clothing, sneakers, and tanning. That's in addition to money he spent on marketing, rental space at athletic facilities, and training equipment. He argued the clothes and the tan were a necessary investment to project a certain image that would score clients. Okay, I understand that. But did he have to buy $150 sneakers every three months? And really, $500 a month for tanning? Although he might have had a great tan to show for it all at the end of the month, his business wasn't growing that much. What was growing, however, was his debt. Jack looked amazing on the outside but was a financial mess on the inside. What was really driving his compulsive shopping, as it turns out, was not so much the desire to boost his business, but the need to feed his self-confidence and self-image. I understand that self-confidence and image are components of a successful business, but I don't accept that they have to come at an annual expense of $11,000 for material things that ultimately keep you in a cycle of debt.

The fact was, Jack's obsession with appearance was clutter. It was fogging up his ability to focus on what really mattered, which was building relationships with clients, getting his certifications, and of course, getting out of debt so that he could manage a profitable business sooner rather than later. To cut this clutter, he needed to think long term and accept that at this rate of spending he would not be able to get his business off the ground.

The Working-Mother Dilemma

Another example of how clutter or inner drama can damage one's ability to organize financial obligations and goals is the mother who works full-time and rarely says no to her kids' wishes. She's put their needs and wants before hers, which ends up causing a lot of financial drama in this mom's life.

One of my clients, let's call her Rita, feels she neglects her kids during the week, working 60 hours at her PR office and arriving home in time just to give baths and read bedtime stories. Her guilt translates into not being able to say no to her children, even while knowing she should teach them to delay gratification. On weekends, it's constant pampering, toy store visits, and dessert before dinner. Money just pours out of her wallet to make up for lost time and attention during the week. It's safe to say Rita is not organized in terms of having a firm grip on her goal and priorities. Certainly a goal is not to raise spoiled children. And although one of her goals has been to begin saving money to afford a vacation sometime soon, all her disposable income has been going toward the kids' expenses. Rita's not alone. Women generally fail to put themselves (and their financial needs) first.

Marcia Brixey, author of *The Money Therapist,* told me, "Women are nurturers and caregivers. We take care of everyone else but ourselves and it hinders us later in life." So how can Rita and other mothers get their financial lives in order and kill this guilt?

First, they must alter their perspective and focus on the positive aspects of having their kids see them as the ultimate multitasker, which Rita certainly is. If this is you, you need to change the way you view your decision to be a mom who works full time. Be proud of the fact that you are able to provide for your family. Second, communicate your message by explaining your choice to work to your family and children. Describe what you do at work and introduce the family to your 9 to 5 so that they can grow up understanding why it's so important and so cool that "mommy works." Third, try to seek flexibility on the job. Maybe you can work from home one or two days a week and spend more time with your kids. Eliminating the guilt will inevitably free up your financial outlook on your life and your family's life. You'll be able to better organize your priorities, including providing for the kids and for yourself. Finally, spend time, not money. Instead of going to the toy store on the weekends, spend time in the park or have your children's friends over. The important thing is to follow through on your personal goal to allocate money toward savings and give your kids the time they don't normally get with you during the week. That's a memory they'll cherish and respect, more than the $15 toy you would have bought them.

Remember, to cut the clutter you must first identify the emotional barriers that are keeping you from getting a grip on what's important to you. They could be embedded in a relationship, or perhaps you're struggling with your own personal insecurity. Next, understand that this clutter does not benefit your bottom line and how it's distracting you from leading an organized financial life. Finally, commit to eliminating the drama and returning to your priorities and goals. That leads us to the last step, practicing good habits.

Step 3. Practice Good Habits

After you've worked through Steps 1 and 2, it's time to create and follow through on certain habits that will keep you committed to an organized financial life. Here are the top six habits to secure good financial organization:

1. **Deal with it right away.** Save yourself aggravation and deal with any financial issues as they arise. When a letter from your bank arrives, don't just stick in your junk drawer. It might have helpful information, or it may be a bill. Either way, if you shrug it off, it may come back to haunt you. The ten minutes you spend sorting through mail can be a way to reinforce good, consistent behaviors toward financial organization. Whether it's a credit card statement or a messy drawer full of receipts, addressing all aspects of your financial life in a timely fashion is an effective habit that will earn you the benefit of not having to worry or feel at a loss down the road. For those who are self-employed, invoice right away upon completion of a job to ensure fast payment.
2. **Create your own deadlines.** Even the best of us are forgetful. Forgetting about your financial goals and obligations can end up being a costly slip-up. The most effective way to get people to stick to deadlines is to be, in some ways, dictatorial about it. Like, "You must pay on the fifteenth or we will shut off your water." That should be enough to get someone to pay on time. But it doesn't always work. So, one way to lessen our tendency to miss deadlines is to create our *own* deadlines—a precomittment. If your phone bill is due at the end of the month, make a point to pay it on the 25th of each month. Give yourself the wiggle room and pay early. It not only makes you

more efficient; it will give you peace of mind. Not to mention, you'll feel more in control. Duke Professor and author Dan Ariely conducted an experiment with his students in which he let one class choose their own deadlines for three papers. In another class, he told students they needed to submit the three papers by the end of the semester, with no rewards for turning in their work early. In a third class, he used a dictatorial approach and said students must submit the three papers at the fourth, eighth, and twelfth weeks of class—or else! Which class performed the best? Well, the class that received dictatorial treatment earned the highest marks. But the class that made their own deadlines showed improved grades, too. As Ariely writes, "the biggest revelation is that simply offering the students a tool by which they could precommit to deadlines helped them achieve better grades."

In your financial world, where you may have dozens of deadlines and no clear system for organizing bills and payments, you might find it helpful to set your own deadlines. For example, if your mortgage is technically due on the fifteenth of every month, set a deadline of, say, the tenth of every month to ensure you never fall behind. To reinforce the deadline, lock it into your calendar and set alarms on your phone and PDA to remind you of the approaching deadline. Or, arrange for the payment to be deducted automatically from your checking account.

Do you want to save but seem to come up dry at the end of the month? A precommitment to paying yourself first and saving automatically in your employer's 401k plan before you get your paycheck will ensure that you save well. A precommitment is extremely beneficial, Ariely says, "otherwise... we keep on falling for temptation."

You may also be able to request that your bank send e-mail alerts regarding your account balances and your savings goals. As for keeping to the organization of your goals and priorities, it's helpful to share them with others you trust so that they, too, can help you reinforce what's important to you in your life. Call it a "money buddy." My money buddy is my mom. She knows my goal is to save up for a family and house in a few years. So, if I'm obsessing over a pair of $250 shoes, she'll flat out tell me, "It's not in your plan, Farnoosh. Stick to your plan!"

3. **Stay consistent.** Associated with Step 2, setting deadlines, is staying consistent. The best way to do this is to automate as many of your financial responsibilities as possible so that you never fall behind. For example, electronically link your checking account to your mortgage collector, the town treasurer (who collects taxes), the heating company, and your healthcare provider. You never have to be unsure about when to pay bills because they'll be automatically addressed each month. As for savings, decide on a percentage of your income to be automatically deposited into a savings account bearing the highest interest rate you can find.
4. **Seek balance.** Our financial lives can easily get complicated and convoluted if we don't constantly try to get rid of the white noise. There are lots of changes you'll make to your financial life as you age and hit various milestones in life. The best thing to keep in mind is that while the ideal may be to "have it all," that doesn't mean having it all "at once." When your world becomes overwhelming, make sure you go back to the first step of cutting the clutter and eliminating stress. Physically it's also important to cut the clutter. If you have too much "stuff," too many old statements, old receipts, old forms, just shred them if you don't need them. Become comfortable with detaching yourself from the clutter. And when a new expense enters your

life, a new child or a new house, it's important to reevaluate your life to re-create financial balance. For example, if the mortgage on your new house is an extra $300 a month more than your previous home loan, how can you find that $300 from another area of your life?

5. **Keep tabs.** Behavioral experts tell me the key to getting out of bad spending habits is to track your behavior. Did you know that our messy money habits net thousands of lost dollars per year? Men are the worst at forgetting how they spent their cash. Visa USA found that men 34 and under spent close to $60 a week on things they couldn't account for, totaling more than $3,000 a year.[1] Women, meantime, lost an average $2,700 a year on miscellaneous buys. The solution is to track your spending for one week. Although some financial experts advise keeping a strict budget and writing down all that you purchase for one month to learn your spending habits, that's not at all practical. David Bach, the best-selling author of the *Finish Rich* series, tells me that seven days of tracking should be enough monitoring. "It's an honest snapshot of how you spend money," says Bach. "The key is to not change the way you spend money. Don't become a better person on the third or fourth day." In his research, Bach has found that on average many people spend 50% more a day than they actually think they're spending. Sites like Bach's AutomaticMoneyManager.com and Mint.com can help trace your spending.

   In addition, ever year, quarter, month, week, and day, you can be doing some activity to ensure everything is going smoothly—that all your bills and other financial paperwork are in their place and that you're current with any updates in your financial life. Here's a checklist of smart follow-ups to make throughout the year.

Every Year

A new year offers a new beginning, a chance to set a fresh personal finance agenda and to end the bad behaviors of the past year. Start with getting your free credit report. You are entitled to one from each of the three major credit reporting bureaus: Experian, TransUnion, and Equifax. My preference is to download a free copy from one and stagger the other two through the year to track my progress. All are available for free through AnnualCreditReport.com. Also, in early January, start collecting your tax statements from the various entities that paid you in the previous year and agencies to which you paid taxes. You'll know from the envelopes because they'll usually say "Important Tax Forms Enclosed." Expect mail from your employer, your student loan organization, your municipality (if you paid real estate taxes), and maybe even your bank, plus any other firms where you have investments (if you earned interest on any savings). In early February or March (depending on how soon you want to start filing your taxes), start logging all your itemized expenses into a spreadsheet or some sort of accessible software to help you as you prepare your taxes in April. In December, make sure you've received all the receipts from the various charities to which you donated throughout the year. These will come in handy for the next tax-filing season since some donations are tax deductible!

Every Quarter

You want to review your investment statements—from your 401k to your IRA, child's 529 plan, and stock portfolio—at least once every quarter to make sure you are staying balanced and diversified. Every quarter you also want to schedule a time to recap your goals with your partner or spouse, to make sure you're on the right path and schedule to financially afford your goals. This is a good time to bring up any concerns, and it's best to do it when you're both in a good mood. Schedule a time when you can both comfortably recap the last three months.

Every Month

Every 30 days, you want to review your billing statements for credit cards and other monthly expenses like cable, phone, and utilities. Make sure you haven't been charged erroneously.

Every Week

Empty out your wallet and dump out receipts older than 45 days. Unless the store has a limit-free returns policy, you probably don't need this receipt anymore, and your wallet is just carrying extra cargo. Cut this clutter out of your life! (One exception: warranty receipts. Keep them for the life of the warranty.)

Every Day

Just like you may step on a scale each day to check your weight and remind yourself why you shouldn't have that piece of pie after dinner, check your bank balance each day to remind yourself of where you stand financially. Knowing you have, say, $800 left in checking with two weeks left to go in the month may, or may not, give you the assurance to eat out a couple nights this week, depending on how much of your obligations have been accounted for at that point. In other words, are your bases covered? If the mortgage and car payments have already been paid and the credit card bill has been paid, you may figure that a couple nights out on the town won't break the bank. But it always helps to double check, daily! At the end of the day, I like to empty out my change purse and dump any and all loose change into a mason jar on my desk. It's just a habit that has kept me conscious and consistent with savings. Of course, I do have other savings tools, like CDs and money market accounts, but a coin jar is a nice added bonus that's a visual reminder of the importance to save. A few more months of coin collecting and my daily habit could translate into dinner and a movie. Okay, maybe just dinner. But still!

6. **Create personal rules of thumb.** As Jay Ritter, the Cordell professor of finance at the University of Florida, tells me, humans are creatures of habit. We thrive when we have rules of thumb ways to guide us. Like your money philosophies, you need to devise rules of thumb that offer parameters and speak to your personal organization needs and goals. It's best to start with your biggest problem areas. If you are having difficulty paying your bills on time, a rule of thumb that might work is this: "I pay my bills every first Monday of the month." If you tend to lose receipts and get burned when trying to return things, create a rule of thumb for yourself like this: "I always keep my receipts for 45 days in this box." The same helps with dieting, says Ritter. If your weakness is midnight snacking, for example, committing to a parameter like "I don't eat after 8 p.m." may make it easier to avoid the fridge.

Let's Get Physical!

Now that you understand the psychological underpinnings of sound financial practices, let's look at your physical surroundings. I know you've been dying to discuss color-coordinated storage folders for all your paperwork, haven't you? Good. So have I. But not all your finances are best-managed offline. There are fabulous online resources to help guide you through the maze of money. Let's start there.

Online Assistance

Budgeting tools. Free personal finance software sites like Mint.com, Wesabe.com, and Thrive.com offer a way to manage many of our financial accounts, from savings and checking to our home mortgage and credit cards.

Spending trackers. Various smart phone applications can help us better track our expenses. If you like having mobile access to your spending records, there are applications you can download from iTunes for $1 to $5. The most popular ones are BillTracker, AceBudget, iExpenseIt, and Xpense Tracker.

Free bank help. Your bank will likely have a variety of online and mobile services to keep your finances organized. For example, Bank of America customers can receive free text alerts regarding their bank account balances. Online, you can also track your spending by reviewing debit and credit card purchases.

Offline Assistance

Receipt box. Because I freelance and have my own business, it's important that I keep a record of all my work-related expenses, from travel to stationary to office equipment and transportation, for tax purposes. In February, I usually dump this box out and start logging my expenses to guide me through my tax filing in April.

Storage for paper trails. I have two accordion folders purchased from Staples ($12.99 each), one for my taxes and one for everything else. The one for my taxes includes the past three years of statements and returns, because that's usually the longest the IRS waits to audit you. In the other folder, I have the following categories of paperwork: mortgage, deed to home, utility statements, insurance (health and home), investment statements, agency contracts, warranties, employment records, cable, and pay stubs.

Safety box. Your passport, birth certificate, and any other hard-to-replace valuables should be stored in a fire-proof safety lock box in your home.

Shredder. A shredder represents your best protection against identity theft. In my kitchen, I have a basket into which all my junk mail travels. At the end of each week, I open up those envelopes and shred all the documents that include my personal information.

Goal-supportive visuals. It's not cheesy to put your goals in visual perspective. Creating a colorful board of images, magazine cutouts, photographs, and so on depicting your future goals is a great investment of your time, as it will serve as a constant reminder and reinforcement of what your "good life" is all about. Place the board somewhere you'll notice it daily. You can also create screen savers on your computer to visualize a goal. Right now on my MacBook, I have a lovely photo of the Eiffel Tower, symbolic of my goal to return to Paris for vacation in the next year or two.

Security account. You want to have a hardcopy list of all your usernames and passwords for your various online accounts (for example, frequent flier programs, banks, credit card companies, cable company, utilities, and health insurer). So that you have a backup, e-mail the list to your personal e-mail account and file it there. Don't leave it on your hard drive, in case your computer or laptop gets hacked into.

Remember, the key to an organized life (and one that's moving forward)—whether it relates to your finances, your relationships, or career—is to maintain your composure and not get overwhelmed. To remain on top of your financial plan, revisit your goals, clear the clutter, and stick to good habits. Consistency really pays off in this department.

[1] Visa USA Survey, 2007.

6

Be Your Biggest Advocate

"Insist upon yourself."

Ralph Waldo Emerson

I absolutely love to hear stories about people negotiating their way to better interest rates, reduced fees, and getting their money back. (Is that weird?) On *Bank of Mom & Dad,* I worked with a young woman and helped her convince her bank to lower the interest rate on a credit card, which ultimately helped reduce her minimum monthly payments from $1,800 a month to $400 a month. We ran the math and found that if she continued to pay $1,800 a month with the new lower interest rate, she'd be out of debt in less than 5 years, versus 30. It was so incredible a moment, she nearly cried in disbelief. Even I was shocked by how much the bank helped. And no, it wasn't because it was for a TV show. The bank actually had a special program for struggling borrowers that we only learned about once she called asking for help. I call this being your own advocate.

Being an advocate for yourself is critically important because no person or institution cares more about your money than you. That's not just my personal philosophy. That's a proven fact. That's why there's 8-point font on the back of credit card statements. That's why retailers aren't always upfront about their return policies and why there are more than 27 million victims of identity fraud in this country. Banks don't give you a courtesy call to say when you're close to running on empty. Instead, they hope you go over your limit so that they can rack up overdraft fees. Fees and other noninterest income made up nearly $40 billion in bank revenues in 2009,[1] and according to the *New York Times*, the average customer paid a dozen overdraft or insufficient-fund charges that same year, at $30 a ding.[2]

Fortunately, current law requires financial institutions to be clearer and more transparent about their rules and regulations. The Credit Card Act of 2009 prohibits credit card companies from jacking up interest rates without fair warning. And if you're a card holder with a consistent history of paying on time, your rate cannot increase on any outstanding balance, unless your rate was a "teaser" (i.e., promotional) rate or unless you hold a variable rate credit card. And those pesky overdraft fees? Since July 2010, banks are also required to get permission from customers before letting their debit card transactions go through when there isn't enough money in the account to cover the charge.

I mentioned a few new regulations that favor consumers, but banks still continue to find ways to impose fees. We still live in a world of *them* against us. Them being the financial institutions, the retailers, even sometimes our friends and family who tug away at our purse strings and try to get access to our hard-earned money. If we are conscious about this and take the role of advocate, we can better reclaim control of our money. Unless we speak up and make some behavioral changes, no one is going to volunteer to help us out. And worse, we risk losing our financial bearings and we risk not accomplishing our goals.

The Art of Personal Advocacy

True financial advocacy requires self-determination and self-awareness. The average person often remains on the sidelines even when getting into the game means the chance for a better deal or rate. We come up with excuses to avoid change and thus reinforce the status quo. Professor Jay Ritter explains that "people make decisions once, and unless there's a strong reason to change things, that's where they tend to remain." He calls it lethargy. I call it lazy. Banks, credit card companies, and cable and cell phone companies actually depend on our lazy butts, hoping we'll go years without changing what we signed up for.

Combating lethargy and being an active advocate means six things:

1. Being committed
2. Knowing your rights
3. Exercising common sense
4. Having persistence
5. Identifying helpful resources
6. And always, always, assuming there are risks to everything

The Composite of Self-Advocate

Here's more on what an effective self-advocate looks like:

Self-determination. Having self-determination in the context of your financial life basically means having the freedom to be in charge of financial decisions. If you depend on someone else's financial means, it is difficult to be an advocate for your financial well-being. That's why it's important that you do what it takes to earn your own money, even if you're a stay-at-home mom. And if you are in a single-income household, take responsibility for the organization and bill paying so that you have a current and working knowledge of your household finances. Never be in the dark. And, agree with your partner that even though there's just one income, both of you have the power and vested interest to be advocates for your family's money.

Self-awareness. Awareness of your history—from a credit and purchasing perspective—can greatly enhance your ability to be a financial self-advocate. For example, a clean bill of credit and a high credit score (for example, higher than 740) will, in most cases, earn you the best interest rate on a bank loan. Knowing this, you advocate for yourself during a loan application process, in case the bank returns with a higher-than-expected rate. In contrast, if you have a bad credit report and you're up for a job where your credit is being checked, the employer may perceive this as a red flag. By knowing your track record, you can be an advocate for yourself. Be upfront and clear about how your credit got tarnished and specifically what you are doing to clean up the mess. Maybe your credit took a hit because of a divorce or health-related expenses. Many employers will respect that you are working to improve your situation.

Know your rights. Understand what you are legally entitled to, whether it is a plane ticket that you purchased from Expedia, a municipal bond you bought through your brokerage, or flowers you ordered from the Internet. You need to understand all the terms and conditions (including risks).

Exercise common sense. Exercising common sense is all about being realistic and boiling things down to a "let me get this straight" place. Legal jargon and fine print aside, do you feel you're being taken advantage of in some way? Can you articulate this in a way so that the person at the other end of the line or across the counter can empathize and enforce (or maybe even bend) the rules for you?

My Story: What Being an Advocate Looks Like

My parents recently rented a van from Enterprise Rent-a-Car to help move my brother to college (from San Francisco to Irvine, California, about 400 miles away). About an hour before they arrived in Irvine, the van broke down on a Los Angeles freeway (in the middle of the night!). A tow truck took them and the broken-down vehicle to the nearest Enterprise office at LAX airport. Enterprise employees at that facility told my family that because they had rented the car from an independently owned and operate Enterprise location in San Francisco, their rental records were not showing up in the system at LAX. Contractually, this LAX office was not obligated to help my parents get a new van free of charge or help them in any other way.

Here is how you get to the bottom line: So, let me see whether I understand this correctly (say this with a smile, always): I rented a car from a company bearing your same name (even though it is not the same operator), the car dies on us in the middle of the freeway where we could have gotten run over, and now you are telling me that there's nothing, absolutely nothing you can do? Believe me, we would go back and deal with this problem in San Francisco, but that's about 400 miles away. It's midnight, and my son needs to check into his dorm tomorrow. What's our alternative?

Suddenly, common sense kicks in and the attendant realizes the company's rules are not humanely applicable in this situation. Apparently, there was something she could do, and at that moment she was convinced enough to take action. She handed my parents the keys to a new van and booked them a hotel room at the nearby Marriot where they could rest overnight and continue their drive in the morning. As for the old broken-down van? "We'll send that up to San Francisco in the morning for an inspection; no worries," she told my parents.

Be persistent. Persistence pays. Check your bank statements at least once a month, check mortgage rates every week, and always read the fine print on everything. These are all persistent behaviors of a money advocate and can help you save money.

Reference helpful resources. Ideally, you want to handle the situation yourself, without involving other advocates. But it's worth identifying resources that can support your claim or cause, because sometimes it helps to have backup. Here are a few to consider:

If you're in debt, one great advocacy partner is the National Foundation for Credit Counseling (www.nfcc.org), a nonprofit that connects people who are in debt or have other financial problems with credit counselors in their area.

The Better Business Bureau (www.bbb.org, and enter your ZIP code for the bureau nearest you) is a great resource if you want some additional help when battling with a local business. The mere threat to contact the BBB is sometimes enough to get owners to cooperate, since a negative review from the BBB can sometimes really hurt a business.

Be aware of risks. There's no such thing as risk free. We need to think of all the possible outcomes before committing to any financial decision. We already understand that investing in the stock market has its risks. But there's more. Not to frighten you, but there is also a risk (albeit a smaller one) in opening a bank account, donating to a charity, working with a financial consultant, renting a house, and in some cases, even paying off your mortgage too quickly.

Assume accountability. To be a great personal advocate, you need to remain accountable for all your financial responsibilities and goals. Yes, banks and consumer laws promise us certain protections, but accountability is a two-way street, and many of us (as evidenced by the personal financial losses in the recession) have not been as active in this lane. As a society, we fell out of touch with this very important behavior during the boom years before the recent recession.

I appeared on the *Today Show* to discuss then-presidential hopeful John McCain's explanation to voters as to the cause of the financial collapse in 2008. It was simply "Wall Street greed," he explained. "Is he right?" Matt Lauer asked me. Well, I replied, if he was talking to an audience of 5-year-olds, McCain's answer might be acceptable. After all, children don't quite yet understand the complexities of the world we live in. Sure, greed is to blame, but there's much more to this recession than a bunch of white-collar bad guys. What about those consumers who signed on to risky mortgages with adjustable rates that they knew would adjust higher and so face potentially higher monthly bills? And those who purchased homes wildly out of their league? At the end of the day, whose fault is it when we spend more than we earn? I'm no political theorist, but I suppose telling prospective voters that they were partly to blame for the stock market and housing market calamities was too risky a move. But the grave reality is that consumers share the blame with those fat cat bankers for not assuming accountability for their financial decisions.

Some people emerged from the recession relatively unscathed. These individuals put their money to work (safely). They didn't wait for their financial planner to call the shots. People like my tax accountant, for example, who boasted at our last meeting that his retirement account actually earned 3% in 2008 while most 401k accounts tumbled by 40%. It wasn't his best year, but he is just thankful he didn't lose money like the majority of investors. "How did you see it coming?" I asked. "I'm 60 years old. I've seen it all before, and I can tell when a market's about to collapse. The signs were all there. There was too much exuberance, and our portfolio had earned double-digit percentage gains for the last five years straight. So, a year before the stock market crashed, when signs were pointing toward a bursting bubble, we put most of our retirement money in bonds and the money market." That smart and rational preemptive strike helped preserve their savings.

To lower financial risk, you need to be aware of all details of your current financial involvements. When calling a credit card company to ask for a lower rate, you don't want to be caught off guard when the agent tells you that you are ineligible because of recent missed payments. Read all the fine print, stay organized, and don't be afraid or embarrassed to get answers to your questions from your bank, your credit card company, and anywhere else you involve your money. These are all the top attributes of strong accountants. Along the way, it also helps to stay accountable and have a "money buddy" or a support group.

More on Accountability

As a sidebar to staying accountable, here is a list of professionals who can help you better understand and manage your various financial accounts. I don't want to send the message that trusting professionals is dangerous. On the contrary, getting the right help is critical in some cases. But because you want to assume accountability, you don't want to blindly trust these people can do it all (and without failure). The following paragraphs identify what you need to know about the limits of each professional's services.

Your bank rep. The cost is free to enlist the help of this person. You can expect him to help you open a new savings or checking account, explain confusing fees, transfer money to various funds you hold at the bank, cut you a break on an overdraft fee (if you're convincing!), update you on new offers with better interest rates within the bank, and explain how your account is affected in the event of a bank merger or bankruptcy. A bank rep won't tell you tell you if you can get a better interest rate elsewhere or whether you can truly "afford" a loan.

Your 401k plan administrator. If you are enrolled in a 401k plan offered through your employer, the plan administrator is at your service for free. He or she will help craft a retirement portfolio based on your risk tolerance and time horizon, update you on your account balance and investment options, explain any taxes and penalties if you withdraw money, plus any other fees, and walk you through your statements and help you roll your account over if you leave your job. This person cannot guarantee that your investments won't depreciate or tip you off that the market is crashing.

Your accountant. The cost of hiring an accountant depends on how complex your taxes are. If you are an individual (not a small business), the cost will be about $400 for a basic return, approximately $200 for two hours. Your accountant will file your annual tax returns, help reduce your taxable income by deducting allowable expenses, advise you on paperwork to keep (and for how long), and advise you about how changes in income (job loss, inheritance, business start-ups) may affect your taxes.

He won't tell you that you're paying for some work that you could actually do yourself, such as organizing receipts and paperwork and itemizing deductions. Chances are, he won't store any of your receipts for you, either. You'll have to organize that for yourself. Accountants also won't just offer their personal background check for your reassurance. Sure, the diploma's on the wall, but what about previous experience? Choose wisely by partnering with a certified public accountant with at least five years' experience. Do a background check and double-check credentials. Ask whether any clients were audited in the past five years and how it went. Ask for certified board or association memberships. Finally, copy everything for yourself.

Your financial adviser. The cost of hiring a financial adviser runs the gamut. Some charge by the hour, whereas others require a retainer fee. Still others earn their income by taking a percentage of your portfolio. Typically, a certified financial adviser will help you construct and manage a financial portfolio, including investments, insurance, your will, college savings, and retirement, and will normally give you a free first meeting.

And remember, your financial adviser can't read your mind. You have to speak up and say if you're not comfortable with certain investments or if you have new financial goals. Also, financial advisers don't guarantee investment returns. Your financial adviser might have an MBA and be a certified financial analyst, but don't assume that he or she can guess where the market is headed any better than you can. Financial advisers also can't help you budget. That's up to you. They can diversify your investment accounts, but your personal day-to-day finances are your responsibility to manage. Stay accountable by choosing a fee-based adviser, not one who earns commissions on your business. Fees can be hourly (starting at around $150/hour), a flat rate, or a percentage of your assets under management. Interview several financial advisers before signing with any one in particular. It's a chance for you to ask a zillion questions to see whether a person is a good fit. Consider interviewing a CFA in your area through the National Association of Personal Financial Advisers (NAPFA) or the Financial Planning Association (FPA).

Your health insurance agent. The cost is free under your health insurance plan. Agents will explain medical bills and your insurance policy. They'll answer questions about what a procedure costs and what your policy covers for doctor visits, emergency room care, prescriptions, and out-of-hospital care. Expect them to also explain your flex spending or health saving accounts and tell you how much of your annual benefits are left and which doctors are in your network. What an agent won't be able to provide is availability 24 hours a day, which can be annoying during emergencies. They also cannot resolve every issue, and you might need to get your doctor or healthcare agent involved in a bill dispute.

My Story: 360° Financial Advocacy

I worked with a woman named Amy, whom I met during a financial counseling session in 2008. In the midst of a divorce, the 29-year-old was struggling with unpaid bills, an underwater mortgage, overdue credit card bills, and worst of all, no job! After seven months of marriage, things started to crumble between her and her then-husband. Feeling dejected, she came to me asking for financial help.

My goal was to gather as much information as I could about her financial records, her goals, and her personality so that I could devise a way to get her back on track. I learned that over the course of a couple years, she had racked up close to $44,000 in credit card debt (debt she was planning to pay down with her husband's income). She was currently unemployed and didn't know how to start making a dent in these obligations. In addition, she owned a home in Florida with a mortgage that was worth more than the home was currently then worth on the market. In a few months, the divorce settlement (and about $17,000) would arrive, but Amy's financial drama would continue to haunt her, unless she learned how to help herself and be her own advocate.

Amy's financial mess was a combination of her own poor decision making and the strains inherent in the recession. She also believed her ex to be a culprit, the "jerk" who let her spend freely and now refused to pay her credit card bills (charges she made during the marriage).

I explained to Amy that she could point fingers all she wanted, but the reality was that this financial debacle was all hers. I laid out her two choices: She could own up to the situation or she could waste time feeling sorry for herself and hope to get bailed out (the latter not a reality).

Amy had to accept that she is the only one in the world who cares about her financial life. Her parents love her, but they're not going to pay off her debt. Her husband said he loved her, and we know how that turned out. No husband, no parent, no bank, no broker, no divorce attorney is ever going to give a you-know-what about her money. Our meeting motivated Amy to take control of the situation. After all, she was only 29. She had her whole life ahead of her. Relatively speaking, she could have it a lot worse.

She promptly moved in with her parents for several months (a tough decision, but a rational one) to save money. Next, she began phoning her credit card companies and asking for settlements. She articulated over the phone that she was currently out of a job and desperately needed to pay down her debt, but that the current finance charges were preventing her from reducing the principal on her balances. It took some time on the phone, but Amy was able to settle her debt by paying less than 50% of the current balances. This would hurt her credit score, but for Amy, the more important thing was cleaning the slate and getting the collection agents off her back.

With her divorce settlement, she would be able to pay off these settlements in full and quickly. By taking the initiative and convincing her creditors to help resolve her debt, Amy had opened a new chapter in her life. A few months later, I followed up with Amy and learned that she was is in talks with an attorney to help get her own small business off the ground. Later, I learned she did get her event planning firm, Lucia Paul Design, up and running (and has subsequently won numerous clients and awards). She's so empowered she wants to help other young women in her community become more financially savvy. It wasn't easy, but the fact that she resolved her debt on her own made her feel in control (which is what you always want to be when it comes to your money).

Sweat the Small Stuff

Part of being a powerful self-advocate is to know which battles are worth fighting. And you might be surprised to discover how the little things can really add up. Here's a list of everyday expenses we can potentially lower by being advocates:

Your home insurance. The latest figures from the Insurance Information Institute show the average homeowner's insurance premium is about $700 a year. Play advocate by calling your insurance provider and asking about every available discount. If you don't immediately qualify, mention any improvements you've made to the home. If you upgraded plumbing or electrical, added a security system, smoke detectors, and so on, all that can shave 10% to 20% off your premium. A phone call to your insurance company could save you more than $100 annually.

Your car insurance. The average cost for auto insurance in the United States is roughly $800 per year. You might be able to save a bit on that, though. For instance, perhaps you work from home now and drive less, or maybe you're taking public transportation more often, or bought a safer car, or took the keys away from your teenager. In these scenarios, it's definitely worth your time to call your car insurance company and let them know about any changes that may affect your premium rate. Some changes lower your risk as a client, and so they won't charge as much to insure you as they did before. If you can shave off even just 15% because you are using your car less, that's a $120 savings with just one phone call.

Your cell phone bill. Ask about friends and family deals. The term *friends and family* has become loosely defined over the years, and some carriers will accept a roommate or your third cousin removed as a "friend or family" member. You basically share a plan and make calls to each other for free. For two people on a shared plan, the monthly cost may be only $50 rather than $80 when you pay for each line separately. In a year, that's $360 savings.

Tuition. Experts at FinAid.org, a financial aid website for college students, say that if you have had any changes to your financial situation in the past year (e.g., job loss/cutback), you should call to ask about getting extra financial aid from your or your child's university. If you have less money coming in than a year ago, or even six months ago, you should call the school's financial aid office and ask for what's called a "professional judgment review," in which the school reassesses (factoring in your new circumstances) your need for financial aid. They'll want documents, a copy of your layoff notice, and a list of circumstances that have changed. The savings? Potentially thousands of dollars. More than 90% of colleges responding to a 2009 survey by the National Association of Independent Colleges and Universities said they were increasing their financial aid budgets. Michigan State University, where students were hit hardest by the collapse of the auto industry, set up a $500,000 fund for financially troubled families. A financial aid spokesperson at Michigan State told me they awarded needy students anywhere from $900 to $7,000 per student, but it was ultimately up to the students and parents to speak up and ask for help. If you find yourself in a financial bind, FinAid.org says you can potentially get an additional $2,000 to $5,000 in financial aid by seeking a review of your application.

Your cable, TV, and Internet bills. New deals and sign-up incentives are always around for new customers, but even if you're an existing customer, call and ask whether you qualify for these new deals. If not, mention that you are considering canceling your premium channels. That usually earns you a discount. Bring up a better offer, and say you plan to switch. They'll likely make some concessions. Ask about any triple-play bundles of TV, Internet, and voice service. If you're already paying for all three separately, perhaps you can save money by bundling them into one deal.

If it doesn't work, ask one more time, politely. The key here is let them know you've been a long-standing customer. This way, you're in a good place to negotiate and ask for some wiggle room. The last-ditch effort is to simply threaten to cancel. Discounts vary from provider to region to each individual customer, but expect at least $10 off your monthly bill for six months. That's $60 right away. If you have an even more expensive plan, you can save as much as $20 per month for over six months. That's up to $120 total for the year.

Being your own financial advocate means standing up for your rights and protecting your money. Once you embrace this, you are ready to discover the ways to make the kind of personal financial decisions that will reap dividends now and in the future, the money choices that are truly worth it (to you).

[1] 2009 Moebs Services Survey.

[2] Ron Lieber, "Free Checking Could Go the Way of Free Toasters," *New York Times*, January 22, 2010.

7

Make Your Money Count

"Try not to become a man of success, but rather try to become a man of value."

Albert Einstein

As Einstein saw it, pursuing a life of value is the greatest goal. A life of value has more to offer you and the world around you than a life of success. After all, a life of value keeps on giving. It inspires and teaches, offers happiness, and ultimately leaves a legacy.

This chapter explains how to pursue a financial life with an emphasis on value, how to make the most of your money in a way that reaps dividends down the road, and have it ultimately live up to be a sound and wise investment. In short, how to make financial moves that we can proudly say are "worth it." Just because something is affordable doesn't make it *worthy*.

I've examined this from several angles—both from my own experiences and that of others—and in this chapter, you'll find a formula for determining what a worthy expense looks like, no matter how big or small the financial move. The formula is broken down into the following critical factors:

Comfortable affordability. After weighing all of your finances, you are confident and secure in paying for this particular item or event, whether it means paying for it all in cash or via a loan.

Good utility. The financial move should have satisfying purpose and benefits, financially, psychologically, or both. What are you receiving in exchange for your money? What's the *quality* of the return?

Manageable risks. Examine the potential drawbacks of the financial move and how well you're prepared and able to deal with them. What will this purchase cost you *in practice.* And what if things don't go as you presume? In other words, what are the *opportunity costs?* For instance, how will spending $50,000 on a wedding affect the first few years of your marriage? A financial move that's worth it may have risks, but they are *manageable*—meaning you are ready, willing, and able to handle the potential downside.

If you discover that you're financially and emotionally confident in all of these three areas, don't be held back. Whether it's starting a business, going back to school, buying property, throwing a huge wedding, or so forth, chances are it's worth it to you if all these variables are answered in the positive.

What "Worthy" Looks Like

"Worthy" can be an extremely relative point of view. We may be biased as to the meaning of *worthy* based on past experiences, our goals, and our ability to spend. Let's take that out of the equation and examine the notion of *worth* as objectively as possible. A few key areas need to be examined, beginning with an understanding of affordable versus unaffordable.

Affordable vs. Unaffordable

When you are considering the affordability of an item or event, it's important to see whether your top bases are covered. Remember the bases from the first chapter, the obligations we need to fulfill to go on to achieve our version of rich? The most important ones include sufficient earnings, a variety of savings (rainy day and retirement), and no revolving debt. Have you addressed these? That's a good first question to ask when considering whether you can afford a specific financial decision. Someone *without* a stated money plan, in contrast, might make the purchase by tapping into an emergency nest egg, stretching the monthly paycheck, or paying thousands in interest over the next few years by using a credit card (and all the while without putting any money aside for retirement).

From there, look at how readily and easily you can afford the purchase. If the money is sitting in your bank account, you're a step ahead of the game. But purchasing it with a credit card may just get you into a debt trap—and works against the affordability of the expense. A bank loan can be equally troubling. Although you don't have the complications of accruing credit card debt, you do have to pay the loan. And those monthly payments may have to come out of your savings plan.

What constitutes unaffordable? If you find yourself carrying revolving debt to purchase discretionary items, you may be living way beyond your means and need to reevaluate your goals and your budget. Squeezing in more purchases that'll only add to your debt is an unaffordable move. It may be more appropriate to use revolving credit to pay for large-ticket items and stretch out those payments. For purchases of $1,000 or less, however, it makes more sense to use cash rather than credit, given all the interest you'll be paying.

For years I've been saying that cash helps us save because it has real financial limitations as compared to a credit card. Once the cash is gone, you can't spend anymore. Credit cards give people a false license to shop above their means. In fact, credit experts, including Gerri Detweiler of Credit.com and Gail Cunningham of the National

Foundation for Credit Counseling, tell me that credit cards lead us to overspend by 20%.

But my perspective runs much deeper: You should use cash not only because it's practical, but because it's the *right* thing to do. Economist Dan Ariely's research finds that "cash keeps us honest." By using cash instead of credit, we will be prompted to make smarter purchasing decisions that more closely match our actual needs. Credit cards cue people to make rash purchasing choices and spend more than they have, simply because they can. "When we deal with cash, we are primed to think about our actions as if we had just signed an honor code," Dan tells me.

Easier said than done, I realize. We struggle to pay with cash because it's painful, Dan tells me. In economic terms, he calls this the "pain of pain." He tells me to imagine going to a nice meal and at the end of the dinner paying with either a credit card or cash. Which feels better? For most people, it's paying with a credit card. Why? "When the timing of consumption and spending coincide, we enjoy the experience less," he says. For this reason, we also gravitate to unlimited monthly deals and bill-me-later options—even it means we end up paying more than we would if we opted for a pay-as-you-go plan.

"If you want to save money, you should opt to do things that have more 'pain of pain,'" suggests Dan. And as it happens, today consumers are opting for the "pain of pain" plan, as evidenced by Visa's latest earnings report in which the company said more consumers are making debit transactions (i.e., using cash in their checking accounts) instead of relying on credit.[1]

I asked Dan if there was a cheerier name for this strategy, but he just laughed. Bottom line, he advised, you want to choose financial options that make you much more conscious of your money, especially if saving is a priority. According to Dan, "If you want to give it a good name, say that you want to make more thoughtful decisions… be deliberative."

Pursuing a Credit-Free Life

Although it's not advised that you ditch the use of credit cards entirely (after all, you need them to help establish credit so that you can later qualify for a mortgage, a car loan, a personal loan, or even a job in some cases), it is possible to live mainly off your hard-earned cash. Some may want to pursue this plan because they want to stay on a strict budget and don't trust themselves with credit cards. For others, the purpose is to help get out of existing credit card debt. Here are my top tips for living credit free:

Build savings. Credit cards are often used in emergency situations, when your car breaks down, a water leak leaves your basement flooded, or you need to quickly book a flight. But if you want to live credit free, you must rely on your savings in such situations. To do this, it's imperative that you have a healthy amount of savings. Stay as liquid as possible. A savings cushion linked to a different debit card or checkbook may be one helpful solution.

Keep constant tabs on your money. This is something everyone should do no matter what. We talked about this in the chapter on staying organized. And for those who opt for a cash-based existence, getting e-mail or text alerts from your bank with your daily balance is especially helpful, as is signing up online for a free personal finance software that can help you track spending.

Connect checking with savings. As a further step to reduce the chances of bounced check or insufficient fund fees, link your checking and savings accounts at your bank. This way, if there's a shortfall in your checking account next time you swipe your debit card at the store, the money in your savings account can cover the gap. This is usually a free service, although in some cases banks may charge a small transfer fee for linked accounts.

Keep credit cards open and active *enough.* Although it might seem logical and even cathartic to close an old credit card account, doing so may end up damaging your credit score. Your credit score, as determined by Fair Isaac Corporation (FICO), factors in heavily your credit history and the amount of credit in your name. The longer the history and the more credit you have, the better. Closing an account will wipe out the history of that card and erase that line of credit in your name, which may knock points off your credit score. Gail Cunningham, my trusted source at the National Foundation of Credit Counselors, suggests keeping your existing credit card accounts "active" by charging a small amount to them each month for, say, only fixed expenses, like cable or car insurance, and linking those cards to a checking account that pays off the balances in full automatically each month.

The Credit Card Accountability Responsibility and Disclosure Act of 2009 (effective early 2010), enacted by the federal government to benefit cardholders, says consumers must opt-in for overdraft service. In the past, overdraft services had just been provided by banks (at their discretion) and marketed as a "benefit" to consumers who went over an account's limit. Instead of rejecting the transaction, the bank would approve it, despite insufficient funds. It saved the consumer some embarrassment, but the fee for overdraft protection could be up to $35 each time. By connecting checking with savings, you may not need to opt-in for this service and you may save a great deal of money.

Measuring Utility

Once you've come to the confident conclusion that a purchase is affordable—the math works and your bases are covered—you need to identify the use and benefits of the purchase. *Utility* is a measure of the purpose and benefits of a particular financial decision.

Something with great utility is reassuring because we feel we're making the most of our money, exchanging it for something that will offer a great return either financially or psychologically or, in the best-case scenario, both. Like, *the market's rocky right now but buying this beach house today at a discounted price will prove to be a great investment down the road, and it's comforting to know I can retire here someday. It's worth it.* Or, *getting my MBA will take me two years and $100,000 in student loans to complete the degree, but given that I'll probably be able to increase my rank and salary by 50% right after school, it'll totally be worth it.*

Understanding utility can help us justify (or not) expensive financial decisions. When you attach high value to a purchase or financial move, there's less chance of having buyer's remorse, and you are more inclined to maintain it and perhaps even build more value in to it (like the beach house).

But determining utility can be tricky. Behaviorally, people tend to mistake high price and fancy marketing for quality and utility. Studies show that when we pay *more* for something, it makes us feel better, and we in turn think that the item is *necessarily* better. A recent study by researchers at California Institute for Technology found that when presented with two identical wines, people preferred the taste of the more expensive wine.[2]

Also, people are more likely to make irrational purchasing decisions when they're in a hurry or feel pressured. That's why infomercials make so much money. A study by *Consumer Reports* recently concluded that there's a science behind infomercials that creates brain waves that compel us to buy.[3] In fact, infomercials are perfectly written and produced to excite the dopamine levels (i.e., happiness levels) in the brain. After the loud and insisting commercials end, our dopamine levels typically drop within five to six minutes, but of course, we're encouraged to *buy now*… and often we do. Infomercials are a $150 billion industry.[4]

All this behavioral data raises these questions: How do we properly measure something's utility and value without being clouded by our brain? How can we be more in control of our money decisions? I find that the following three techniques work best:

Globalize your scope of relatively. Take the time to understand and measure how this purchase compares not just to other similar options on the market but also to everything else in your life. We tend to measure things in small relative parameters, which can muddy our perspective on whether something is really worthy. In Dan's book, he uses the example of how we might have no problem spending $3,000 to upgrade to leather seating for a car we're buying for $25,000. It seems like a small amount to spend relative to the $25,000. What's another 10%, right? But funny enough, we hesitate to spend that same $3,000 on a new sofa, despite the fact that it may offer more utility.[5] The trick here is to think about how else you spend your money, and that way you'll be better able to draw a conclusion as to the relative value, worth, and utility of a particular purchase.

Narrow your options. It's a proven behavioral fact that too many options that run the gamut causes confusion, whether items on a menu or mutual funds for your 401k. One way to deal with this phenomenon is to identify a price range you're comfortable with and stick to it. When debating what kind of a car to buy, and you know you want to spend only $28,000 to $30,000 soup to nuts, stick to reviewing a few vehicles in that price range. Don't cross the $30,000 threshold. Stick to your guns. When you look at cars that cost more than $30,000, temptation kicks in and you may try to justify spending more than initially planned.

It's no coincidence that Greg Rapp, a restaurant menu engineer, sometimes puts an outrageously expensive item on the menu. He does this to cause patrons to think that the less-expensive (although still pricey) menu items are a better value. I first learned about Rapp during a segment on the *Today Show* in which I gave advice about how to save money when eating out. Rapp was introduced in the first half of the segment as a sort of "menu psychologist" who helped restaurant owners increase profits by manipulating their menu design and layout.

Detach. Remember what you learned earlier in this chapter about making financial decisions under time pressure, such as when viewing an infomercial? Here's a way to counter this behavioral trait. Take a breather. Give yourself at least 10 minutes to disassociate your brain from the commercial's or salesperson's fanfare. You'll be able to make a better decision after your dopamine levels calm down. Chances are, without the sense of urgency or all the pressure around you to buy, you can make a sounder decision and you won't feel that you missed an opportunity if you skip it.

Mitigating Risks

After you determine the affordability and utility of the purchase, you then need to examine the *effects* of this financial move. Will it compromise your comfort level in life? Does this purchase make sense in a financial and *personal* way? What risks and compromises might you need to make to fulfill this purchase? What are the opportunity costs?

Measuring drawbacks can be somewhat subjective. For example, you're not going to get everyone to agree that going back to school for a higher degree is necessarily purposeful or beneficial. It depends on the degree, it depends on the likelihood you'll find a higher-paying job, and it depends on *you*. The thought of a six-figure loan is enough for many to shy away from quitting a paid job and going back to school. It may be too big of a risk not knowing whether you'll have a job available when you graduate. For others, however, no matter the debt load, they may be willing to go back to school because they consider it an investment in themselves that will reap rewards, both tangible and intangible, down the road.

The last piece of this analysis is meant to determine your capacity to handle your appetite for risk. For example, you might have enough now to buy a new house and you're convinced it will offer great financial benefits, but is it something you can truly afford with potential layoffs happening at your company? Do you have a Plan B in case things go awry?

Investing in Yourself

Investing in yourself is one of the most *worthwhile* things you can do. As Ralph Waldo Emerson said, *"Make the most of yourself, for that is all there is of you."* To invest in yourself is to invest in the activities, relationships, and challenges that will pay off not just financially but also psychologically. From joining the gym to traveling the world, starting a side business to taking extra courses, to moving to a neighborhood with a better school system for your kids, these are all potential actions that offer added personal incentives. It's my favorite money philosophy because it empowers us to believe that we can reach our greatest potential and that we can actually take control of what it means to be "rich."

This, of course, is not to dismiss the value of investing in real estate, the stock market, or your 401k. Those incredible moneymaking vehicles definitely deserve our attention. But when all is said and done, you can expect much better returns when you invest in yourself. How do you decide whether such an investment is worthwhile? These three steps will help:

1. **Recap what it means to be and feel fulfilled and satisfied in your life.** What kind of financial and emotional stability are you looking for, and how will this personal investment, whether it's going back to school, starting a new relationship, or launching a business, be a complement?

2. **Revisit your goals.** Understand how this personal endeavor can support your short- and long-term goals. Also make sure you understand if and how this personal investment may compromise any of your goals.
3. **Figure out how to make the most of the investment.** This is the best part about investing in yourself: You can control the outcome far more than the outcome of, say, investing in stocks or real estate. If you can visualize how to take the knowledge and experience of this investment and turn it into a positive difference in your life, it might be worth it.

Worthy Banking: Making the Most of Your Earnings

Making worthy financial decisions relates not only to how you spend, but also to how you save and invest. I got my first savings account with the help of my dad when I was a teenager. We opened it at the local credit union where my parents did their banking, and I don't even remember if we discussed interest rates. We probably did, but I don't think I quite understood the importance of earning a few pennies on the dollar. But the truth is, by making small adjustments, you can significantly improve savings. The following three adjustments will offer immediate results.

Adjustment 1: Land the Best Rate

You might think there's no difference between earning 1.5% or 1.75% on a savings account, but rest assured, a little bit can go a very long way. Suppose, for instance, you start the year off with $10,000 in an account earning 1.5%, and your friend begins with $10,000 in an account earning 1.75%. You each diligently add $5,000 a year to your accounts for the next five years. By 2015, your friend will be $2,000 richer, and all because he did some research and secured a better rate.

Adjustment 2: Ladder CDs

Are you familiar with certificates of deposit? Different CDs carry different maturities and interest rates. Typically, the longer the maturity date, the greater the interest rate. For example, a one-year CD may carry a 2.5% interest rate, a two-year CD a 3.0% interest rate, and a three-year CD a 3.50% interest rate. It may seem logical to want to put all your money in the three-year CD because it earns the highest rate. But actually there's a better strategy. By *laddering* your CDs, you spread out your savings into multiple CDs with various maturities and interest rates. Every time a CD expires, you redeposit that money into whichever CD has the longest maturity in your original CD ladder. In this case, it would be a new three-year CD, which may have an even higher rate of return at this point. By staggering out the savings, you can potentially maximize your rate of return and boost liquidity. By rolling from one CD to another, you also avoid the risk of locking into one single rate. If interest rates rise, you can still benefit from them. There are online calculators, such as at Bankrate.com, Bankingmyway.com, and CalculatorPlus.com, that can help you crunch the numbers.

Adjustment 3: Avoid Fees

Banks earn most of their revenue just from fees (billions of dollars a year, from overdraft fees, minimum balance requirement fees, ATM fees, transfer fees, and so forth). ATM fees alone are enough to eat up hundreds of dollars a year from your savings account. Do you even earn hundreds of dollars in interest in that account? Probably not, which means you are definitely getting a raw deal. To make your money work harder for you, sign up for fee-free checking accounts, link your checking and savings account together to lessen the risk of having insufficient funds, and learn the locations of your bank's fee-free ATMs between work and home to avoid paying usage fees at nonmember banks.

My Story: When Having Debt Is Worth It

One of my readers wrote into my website at Farnoosh.TV desperate to understand why her husband opted not to pay down the mortgage ahead of schedule. He had explained it was because he could get a better return investing that money in the stock market. But for her, paying down the mortgage seemed like a more secure thing to do. Another perplexed reader asked me whether he should pay off his $5,000 car loan, which had a historically low 3.9% APR. He mentioned he was only earning .01% in his savings account.

What both readers fundamentally wanted to know is this: Are some debts good (worthy) *debts? The answer is yes, some are, but that depends on the type of debt and the pros and cons of paying it off early. For instance, a con would be any penalties that might apply for paying off the debt early. Keep in mind that the pros and cons can be both financial and psychological. To make an informed decision, use the same analysis as when considering a big-ticket purchase. You must first determine affordability and then consider utility and risks.*

Let's tackle both reader questions:

Should I Pay Off My Mortgage Early?

Let's throw out some numbers to give this question more context. The couple has a $200,000, 30-year mortgage *with a 5.5% fixed interest rate. Monthly payments, interest plus principal, total $1,135. At the end of 30 years, the couple will have paid a total of $408,000 to the bank.*

The couple has an excess cash flow of $1,000 a month for saving and investing. The norm is for the husband to take $500 of that and invest in the couple's retirement portfolio each month, which currently holds $75,000. The expectation is an average 8% return over the long run. The other $500 goes into a rainy-day fund that's already enough for eight-months of living expenses, or close to $40,000. The interest rate on that savings account is about 2%.

Pros to paying down the mortgage early: If the couple reroutes $500 toward the mortgage principal, they could save close to $115,000 in interest fees and own their home in half as many years, 15 instead of 30 years. The financial burden will be lifted in half the time, and the couple can sleep better at night knowing the roof over their heads is theirs and not the bank's. By putting money toward the mortgage, the couple also avoids paying additional income tax on any interest earned in a savings account.

What are the cons? If the couple neglects to put $500 toward savings, they miss out on their rainy-day savings account reaching $158,000 in 15 years or $319,000 in 30 years, assuming an average 2% return rate over time. Would they prefer to stay liquid? As for the investment *portfolio, if $500 was rerouted from that account to the mortgage, the couple misses out on a buildup of more than $413,000 in just 15 years at that 8% rate.*

The Verdict

My advice is to keep investing $500 a month in their retirement portfolio. The interest there is unbeatable in the long run and best addresses the couple's retirement needs. Meantime, they should reroute the other $500 from savings to the mortgage principal. The couple already has a fat cushion for a rainy day; the possibility of being relieved of their mortgage in just 15 years is both financially and emotionally cathartic. And by the way, if the couple wants to continue saving in their rainy-day fund and put just one extra payment a year toward the principal, that would still go a long way. By doing this, they would save more than $40,000 in interest and be able to retire their mortgage five years sooner!

Should I Pay Down My Car Early?

My reader says he has only $5,000 left on his car loan with a 3.9% interest rate. He's been paying the loan down since 2006. Monthly payments total $290. He has 18 more payments left. I ask him about his liquidity. "$15,000," he says. "If I suddenly lost my job and needed an emergency fund, I think I'd be okay since I could use the remaining $10,000 and use my 0% interest credit card (a teaser rate for the first 12 months)." He also has *no credit card debt. Should he pay down his car loan early?*

Pros and cons: The pros are pretty clear. If he pays down the car loan, he immediately frees up an extra $290 a month that he could add to his liquid savings. He'd also save $220 in interest by paying the loan down immediately. In addition, his credit score—which is already at 780, he tells me—would benefit even further from reducing this outstanding debt. On the con side, the interest rate is so low on this car loan that he's only paying an extra $220 for stretching out the payments five more years. Is that better than taking a huge stash of money out of his savings account, which might leave him vulnerable in an emergency? True, he may be able to resort to a 0% APR credit card, but that's still a risk since he'd have to pay that back at some point and the interest rate will jack up after 12 months.

The Verdict

My advice to the reader is to pay down the car early. His finances are pretty stable, and getting this liability off his personal balance sheet is comforting. I advise him to continue to act like he still has a car payment, though, and pay himself to make up for the $5,000 hole in his rainy-day savings. And that .01% rate? He can do a whole lot better by moving his account to an online bank where savings rates are generally much higher.

"Worthy" in Action

Let's put this formula to the test with a couple of hypothetical cases. Because "worthy" choices have an element of subjectivity, I'm not going to conclude each case study with a definite "worthy" or "unworthy" stamp. The point is to walk through all the necessary analysis and consider both options—and even potential modifications.

Case Study 1

Charles and Mary are married, in their early 30s, and live in Northern California. Both are full-time faculty members at a university. Charles teaches political science. Mary teaches statistics. Their joint monthly take-home pay is roughly $8,000 a month, and their expenses average $6,500 a month. Net: $1,500 a month.

They've been hacking away at their credit card debt since getting married and have reduced it to approximately $5,000 from $15,000 in less than two years. Their goal is to be debt free in the next eight months, which means they need to allocate at least $650 a month toward that credit card debt, including interest and principal. They plan to use their excess cash flow of $1,500 to afford the fast payoff. Fortunately, they have no other debt besides their mortgage. Rainy-day savings equal $40,000. Retirement savings: $75,000. Job security? Both work in higher education, and although there's been some downsizing recently at their university, they have not been affected and don't expect to be.

Would buying a new SUV for $30,000 be worth it to them? Let's use our equation of comfortable affordability + good utility + manageable risks.

Comfortable Affordability?

What's their income security? No one can ever really be too certain about the safety of a job, but Charles and Mary believe they're not in as risky an industry as real estate or retail, which have seen greater rates of downsizing in their region recently. Mary has a little craft business on the Web and earns about $500 a month selling homemade jewelry on Etsy.com. She always thought if she lost her job, she'd try to make more out of that hobby and use the earnings to pay down their mortgage. It's not a certifiable backup plan, but the money does come in handy for impromptu expenses like baby shower gifts, restaurant dining, and the occasional parking ticket. In short, the couple's income security is above average.

Are they living below their means? Yes. They are netting $1,500 a month after their monthly expenses, with the goal of putting $650 of that toward credit card debt for the next eight months. The rest of their excess cash is used for discretionary things like vacations, clothes, and *maybe a new car.* We'll see....

Do they have enough savings? Yes. The couple has about six months of living expenses socked away in an online savings account earning a top rate (excellent!) and $75,000 in their combined retirement accounts, to which they add monthly from their pretax earnings.

How will they financially afford it? What's the plan? Charles plans on trading in his sedan (which he's had for seven years and finished paying off four years ago) for the new SUV. The blue book value of his car is about $7,000, so that should bring down the cost of the SUV to $23,000, plus another $3,000 for sales tax, title, and registration costs. They plan to finance the $26,000 total with a loan from their local credit union. With a 48-month, 6.4% auto loan, the couple's looking at $615 a month in car payments for the next four years. This expense will come out of their monthly net of $1,500.

With $1,500 disposable income each month, the money is certainly available to pay down the loan in four years and help pay down outstanding debt, one of the couple's priorities. If the numbers came up short, they would know to stop right here and start considering more affordable alternatives to the $30,000 SUV.

Good Utility?

What are the benefits of the new car? They love that it has twice the cargo room, which comes in handy since both are sporty and carry around golf clubs and tennis racquets in their current smaller trunks. The couple also goes on ski trips in the winter, and it would be nice to fit all their gear in the car—not to mention plow through the snow. And if they ever get a pet (or have a baby), the extra space in the car will certainly help out then, as well. They also decide that money spent would outweigh the benefits of any other purchases in this price range.

Manageable Risks?

Financial downsides? Financially the car isn't going to help them save any money—especially when you factor in the added gas and maintenance. But the couple feels confident this won't stretch their budget much. And if it does, they'll drive it less and carpool in Mary's hybrid car.

How does this expense potentially interfere with future planned expenses, and how do they plan to offset the interference? They think this one through and confess wanting to start a family in the next two years. They understand the expenses related to having a newborn can be at least $10,000 in the first year. They also want to renovate their kitchen in the next five years, and estimate that at $30,000. They also want to continue saving and, once again, be debt free from credit cards before anything else. Buying a new car now and paying an estimated $615 a month may slow down their current savings rate, but the couple believes they can allocate their entire year-end bonuses over the next few years toward saving for the baby and the renovations. Typically, they'd use all their year-end bonus money on vacations, but understanding that the new car will eat up some disposable income, they're committed to saving their bonus money (usually $10,000 total) for these short-term savings goals.

The Final Verdict for Charles and Mary

For this couple, buying a $30,000 car won't affect their finances too much. It's arguably *affordable,* but whether it's *worth it* is really a question of whether or not they'd like to use that extra money at the end of the month toward something else. We know their goals over the next few years include starting a family and renovating the kitchen. Would they rather save that $615 a month and speed up their kitchen renovation project? Maybe have two kids rather than one in the next few years? Skipping the car will also mean having more freedom to spend and use their year-end bonuses on vacations. Charles's car is only seven years old and has fewer than 100,000 miles on it. Surely, it can run smoothly for another few years. Do they really need the new car?

At this point, there's no right or wrong answer. Whether the couple decides yes or no, they'll have made a more conscious and educated decision...and that's a really good thing.

Keep in mind that sometimes the final answer doesn't have to be a flat out no. Sometimes financial moves aren't worth it *at the moment* but might be down the road. What about the couple waiting a year to buy the car? Or just waiting until they're free of debt in eight months, at which point they might qualify for a lower interest rate on the car and thus reduce their monthly payments? By then, too, one of them might be making more money to help make the payments. In the meantime, they could just use Mary's car so that Charles's car doesn't add more mileage or wear and tear. If they were to do that, they could still sell it for about $7,000 in a year's time. What's more, if they can even save an extra $500 a month in an interest-bearing account specifically for the new car, they'll have close to another $6,000, totaling about $13,000 for a down payment. Their monthly payments at that point (with even the same financing) would just be around $400, including sales tax and title and registration costs. The takeaway? *Sometimes waiting makes it all the more worthwhile. Call it delayed gratification.*

Case Study 2

Laura is a 29-year-old financial analyst from Boston, Massachusetts. After six years working for a large investment firm, she wants to quit the finance industry and go to nursing school to become an RN. She knows she won't necessarily make as much money in that line of work but is looking for more job security and has always been quietly fascinated by the medical field. Through some research, she's discovered she can go on an accelerated path toward achieving the degree. The Accelerated BSN (Bachelor of Science in Nursing) programs are available for those who already have a Bachelor degree or higher degree in another field and who are interested in moving into nursing quickly, like Laura, and typically last 12 to 18 months. Laura figures the faster she can get out of school, the faster she can start making money and paying off her student loans.

Will the leap to nursing school and the transition from one industry to another be worth it for Laura in the end? Let's dig.

Comfortable Affordability?

How much will the Accelerated BSN cost Laura? Tuition and fees alone average out to about $30,000. Does Laura have debt? At present, she has no credit card debt. Her salary has afforded her a comfortable life, and she has consistently tucked money away each month. She also has no student loans or a mortgage; she's currently renting her apartment.

What's her savings? Right now, she has $30,000 in liquid savings and another $30,000 in retirement savings.

Good Utility

What are the benefits? After seeing so many colleagues laid off over the past two years, Laura questions the long-term security of the financial services industry, an industry she's not even that passionate about. For her, a transition to nursing offers several psychological benefits. First, it offers peace of mind, knowing the industry is stable.

As boomers retire and the demand for healthcare soars, the number of nursing jobs is expected to increase through 2016, with an additional 587,000 new jobs (or 23% growth) over that period, according to the Department of Labor. That's higher than the national average of all other occupations, which are expected to show 7% to 13% growth. (She's clearly done her research.) Beyond that, becoming a nurse would make her happier, plain and simple. Her desk job at the financial firm is slowly but surely eating away at her happiness. Laura is someone who prefers to interact with and help others. Plus, she's always been curious about the medical world. And although her current job pays a generous salary, she's not attached to the lifestyle it affords.

Manageable Risks?

Would Laura be willing to move cities? There are no accelerated nursing programs in the Boston area, and this may be a red flag. To manage this risk, Laura must accept that if she wants to find work right away, she might need to be flexible and willing to move, especially to far-off regions in Arizona, Texas, and the Midwest, where nursing staff are in relatively short supply. Northeast hospitals, meanwhile, have plenty of applicants and few spots to offer to new graduates. Of course, once her career gets going, jobs will be open, regardless of the locale. Laura doesn't have a family or other dependents at this point, and so she decides she is willing to move to where the best job openings are.

Can she adjust to a lower salary? At present, Laura earns $120,000 a year plus a bonus of roughly $20,000 annually. In the nursing world, the pay is solid, but not as lucrative—at least not immediately. RNs earned, on average, a little more than $56,000 in 2007. The highest 10% brought home an average annual income of $83,000.

Can she handle the stress? Many nurses will tell you their jobs are not easy. Some may even compare the stress level to that of working at a trading desk on Wall Street; instead of people's money, however, you're responsible for people's lives. Although Laura might find this career more interesting, she won't exactly be leaving the pressure of her finance job behind.

The Final Verdict for Laura

Laura has many potential risk factors to weigh and consider here. She wonders whether she's underestimating how well she can manage after school with student loans, a lower-paying job, the stress of nursing, and possibly moving to another state. Did the recession just scare her to the point of wanting to ditch her current industry? Switching careers would be a huge game changer for Laura. While she can ultimately "afford" the cost of tuition, she wonders if she'll miss her current life too much? The goal here is not to scare Laura into staying put (discussed as "paralysis" in previous chapters). The goal of this exercise, as it was with Charles and Mary, is to fully examine the potential realities of a financial decision, both positive and negative. Laura's decision will ultimately depend on her personality, her tolerance for risk, and her commitment to achieving this goal. Perhaps what she needs is more time to think, more time to talk to her current boss to consider other responsibilities she might pursue if her current track is unfulfilling. Feeling insecure about a job or an industry is common, especially during a recession. During the recession of the late 2000s, the unemployment rate soared to 10%. In the midst of it all, I'll never forget former President Bill Clinton's appearance on one of the Sunday morning political programs. On that program, he recommended out-of-work Americans, especially recent grads, to consider investing in themselves by going back to school. As Clinton explained, it would be a great way to acquire new skills and boost their hiring and salary potential, and might even lead them to switch industries. For Laura, she might want to speak with more nurses, especially those who have transitioned from different careers so that she can understand what they see as pros and cons and get a sense of how they all cope. In the end, she'll come to a clear choice with few regrets, if any, and all because she took the time to aim for a *worthy* decision.

For all others considering grad school, remember that it isn't for everyone: It might cost too much money, it might be unnecessary in your field, or maybe you just don't feel like studying (or all of the above). It's no secret, after all, that continuing your education costs a lot of dough, unless you score a scholarship or your employer pays. According to the College Board, graduate students on average assume close to $13,000 a year in federal loans, and it's not uncommon for law and business school students to pile on more than $100,000 in debt.

So, how can you determine whether a financial move is worth it? If it complements your goals and you can find a way to make it work—financially and practically—it's probably worth every bit of your time and dime.

[1] Phone interview with Dan Ariely.

[2] Antonio Rangel, "Marketing Actions Can Modulate Neural Representations of Experienced Pleasantness," *Proceedings of the National Academy of Sciences,* January 2008.

[3] "Should You Buy This Now?" *Consumer Reports,* January 15, 2010.

[4] Electronic Retailing Association

[5] Dan Ariely, *Predictably Irrational* (HarperCollins, 2008), p. 20.

8

Think Five Years Ahead

"A good plan today is better than a perfect plan tomorrow."

General George S. Patton

When it comes to our life savings, we often refer to two primary buckets: rainy day and retirement. We save for short-term emergencies such as a layoff, car accident, or sudden medical procedure. For retirement, we have 401ks, IRAs, and other investment portfolios to help aggressively build savings for the future. At best, we live in the now, plan for the uncertainties, and invest for life 20, 30, or 40 years down the road. But what about everything else in between? What about all those tremendous milestones that help shape the purpose and meaning of life? Events such as starting a family, buying a home, changing careers, getting married (and divorced), and a sudden loss in the family? For those events, we tend to just fly by the seat of our pants and hope we'll have the means and resources to handle them when they occur. It's true that people prepare for some events—like a wedding or a baby—a year in advance, but they often still feel a bit uncomfortable when the time arrives.

Dealing with life's personal finances shouldn't have to feel like a 911 emergency, but extreme situations are not uncommon. Managing your finances in emergency situations—paying down debt after a sudden job loss, dealing with student loans, getting back on track after a pricey divorce—is not ideal. You need a plan that is ready to go if and when something bad happens to your finances. Neglecting to prepare as best we can for both the potential positive and *negative* outcomes of a given situation can prove unnecessarily stressful and burdensome, emotionally and financially.

To that end, we need a good in-between measure, a point of view that can help us better plan and prepare for our goals and when life *happens,* a thought strategy that's not as immediate as six-months down the road and not as intangible or distant as retirement.

The answer: *a five-year lens*. By now, we should know ourselves well enough to predict what we may need and want personally and professionally over the next five years. And if we're not 100% sure, we can at least make some pretty good guesses. For example, at the moment, I'm 30 years old and unmarried. I know I want to tie the knot and start a family in the next five years, and so far I'm on a hopeful track. My boyfriend and I have been together for almost four years. We've discussed marriage and agree we're going to make the leap soon (and yes, as a couple, not separately). If all goes as expected, our future, including marriage, children, and a Labrador Retriever, will no doubt be a complete life and financial game changer. So with that in mind, what can I do now to ensure these events won't startle my bank account and my savings? What risks can I expect in the meantime as I strive to hit my five-year marks?

You think this is unnecessary premeditation? You like to live life a bit more spontaneously, you say? Well, here's the thing. A proper five-year compass is not designed to be a buzz kill. It's simply a useful strategy to prepare you for the expected and unexpected. A five-year strategy lets you manage your money and your goals at a more consistent and tangible pace. Even if you don't hit all your goals in the next five years, the discipline and focus you gain from sticking to a five-year plan will ensure your money stays safe and well managed.

Know Where You Stand

The money meetings on *Bank of Mom & Dad* begin by covering the first step in conquering your goals: to get real and accept responsibility for your financial life. Own up to it and don't be afraid to learn that you *haven't* yet been doing the best job.

To start, evaluate your current financial picture by answering the following questions:

- How much savings do I have right now? Know every penny.
- How much debt do I have right now? Again, know every penny.
- What's my credit score? (Clue: 740 and above is terrific; anything lower and you may want to work at boosting your score by consistently paying bills on time and paying down debt.)
- What is my job security at this moment? Be honest and consider your industry and your performance.
- What are my problem areas when it comes to managing my money and why? Do I often pay bills late? Do I have recurring debt? What are my money drains and what am I doing (if anything) to combat them? If I'm sinking in debt, am I seeking professional help? Have I made more payments toward debt? Do I see a light at the end of the tunnel?

Know Where You Want to Go

From there, list your five-year personal, financial, and professional goals as specifically as you can. This is similar to the practice from the second chapter, but this time you want to think about explicit milestones you want to cross five years out. What would you like to see change for the better? Do you want to make more money? How much more? Do you want to switch careers? If so, what do you want to transition toward? Will you want to help support an older family member, like a parent or grandparent? How much time and money might that cost? Do you hope to get married? Have children? Move to a new part of town? A bigger house? Granted, again, you might not be able to draw out a descriptive five-year map of goals. You may not know whether you absolutely want to raise a family in the next few years or if you will stay at your current job, but being conscious of and prepared for the *possibilities* can still help as you manage your money and your five-year compass.

Be Pessimistic *Enough*

As you imagine your life in the next five years, it's important to consider all the possibilities, the good and the bad. I'm going to disagree with my mother here for a moment (the eternal optimist) and say that sometimes in life you have to acknowledge potential hardships and risks that may come your way. Pessimism, in some ways, can pay off. Barbara Ehrenreich, the best-selling author of *Nickel and Dimed,* recently published a new book titled *Bright-Sided,* which criticizes the highly marketed ideology and industry of "positive thinking." She posits that all the smiley-faced hype has kept individuals from considering negative outcomes and, in turn, they become victims of their own overzealousness. It's a valid point, and she provides strong examples to support her theory (ahem, our recent housing and stock market crash).

For your financial house to be completely in order, it's critical to be somewhat, even slightly, pessimistic. I don't want you to let pessimism cloud your journey or keep you from exploring new opportunities. The hope is that a little pessimism can serve as a shield against some of life's real risks because it ensures preparedness.

In a 2002 interview with *Forbes* magazine, Nobel laureate Daniel Khaneman, around the time he was awarded his prize for his work on irrationality, discussed his thinking about optimism, saying that it was a wonderful thing. "There are contexts where optimism helps. Generally where it helps is in executing plans. It keeps you on track. It gives you energy to overcome obstacles...It keeps you healthy and it keeps you resilient." But personally, he said, he would not want his financial advisor to be optimistic. "I'd like him to be as realistic as possible."[1]

His reasoning was that there's no harm in understanding the odds of a particular decision. In our own lives, too much optimism can sometimes lead to overconfidence and a false sense of security when taking on real risks.

Now, about those risks: The two primary types are the sort you control and the sort you can't. The risks we can control are those we bring upon ourselves...when we sign on to an adjustable rate mortgage, neglect to stick to a budget, or fail to pay down debt aggressively. In the example scenarios, we risk staying in a cycle of debt and damaging our credit. The biggest, perhaps, is failing to save on a consistent basis and not having enough money in an emergency or to fulfill our goals. Separately, some risks are *beyond* our control, such as a stock market crash, an unexpected illness that forces you to pay out of pocket, or a job loss.

What follows is an approach that will help protect you from both types of risks.

Develop Your Strategy

Your financial strategy is a plan of attack against risk and unforeseen events, plotted against goals, wants, and needs (for today through to a specified time in the future). With your financial reality firmly grasped, you can begin to lay the foundation of a viable financial future. Be sure to set up detours and preemptive strikes to deal with potential risks from a job loss to a recession to your own overspending. Know how you will pay down debt and save, and how you'll measure and keep tabs on your progress.

Indiscriminating Five-Year Risk: The Next Recession

Before we get too deep into our five-year plans, let's recognize some highly probably risks we will face (sometimes more than once): The first is a recession, or at the least a "market correction." The need for a five-year plan was reinforced during the recent downturn in our economy, a downturn that, looking back, we really should have anticipated. But instead, when the stock market crashed and unemployment soared, panic and a contagion of fear broke out. Uncertain as to how to react, many Americans made some poor choices. They pulled out of the stock market, quit investing in their 401k plans, and lost confidence in all that they'd built up over the previous five years. Their emotions got the better of them and to the better of their money.

My Story: When Does Cashing Out Make Sense?

One of the best pieces of advice I heard occurred on Monday, October 6, 2008, on the Today Show. *It came from Jim Cramer, who told America that if they had any money in the stock market that they absolutely needed in the next five years, whether to help send their kids to college or retire, they should to turn it to cash. For those who could afford to withstand the turmoil in the market (for example, parents with 529 college savings plans that still had ten years until maturity), Cramer said to go ahead and "ride it out."*

The media was up in arms over Cramer's directions. So, during our daily show, Wall Street Confidential *on TheStreet.com TV, I asked Jim for some clarification, because much of the mainstream media was interpreting his statement as a call for all people to flee the stock market. But, of course, that's not what he meant. Jim explained, if you lost your job tomorrow and saw your stock portfolio plummet in the next few weeks, would you still be able to get by and hit your five-year goals with your investments? Rising unemployment and stock market losses were risks Americans were likely facing, and so Cramer's advice was to think ahead by five years. If you were dependent on the profits from your stock market investments between now and the next five years for any major goals such as college tuition or a down payment on a home, he suggested taking a less-risky approach and shifting those investments to safer havens like cash or bonds.*

Cramer was right to be cautious. The days that followed would mark the worst week in stock market history. Between Monday, October 6 and Friday, October 10, 2008, the Dow Jones Industrial Average plunged 1,874 points, losing nearly 20% of its value. It took more than a year for the Dow—and the overall stock market—to bounce back, but the market is still an unpredictable beast. I'm not sure anyone who followed Cramer's advice really regrets holding on to their cash as they watched the market deteriorate in the days, weeks, and months that followed. Maybe they needed that money to send a child to college in the upcoming year. Maybe they needed the money for a down payment on a new home in a couple of years. How might their five-year goals have changed if all that money was tied up in the stock market?

As history has proven, our economy is not done with recessions. We've averaged a downturn about every five or so years since the Panic of 1797. According to the National Bureau of Economic Research, a trusted resource on recessions among economists, policy makers, and academia, a recession is defined as "a significant decline in economic activity spread across the country, lasting more than a few months."[2] Always count on a recession in your five-year plan. Don't take too much risk with your investments, especially if they're meant to cover short-term goals. There are several ways to play the cash card (e.g., U.S. Treasury bills, certificates of deposit, money market mutual funds). Investors embraced this approach over the past two years, distinctly transitioning away from equities and over to the cash market. In June 2008, researchers at Merrill Lynch found investors moved away from the stock market at a record rate. Twenty seven percent of fund managers were "underweight" stocks, the most in ten years. The same month, 42% of money managers were "overweight" cash, up from 31% in May.[3]

Todd Harrison, the founder of Minyanville.com, told me that in times of great financial difficulty, the winning formula includes discipline, not so much conviction. In other words, stay rational. Don't take risks that might jeopardize your near-term goals. The best strategy during volatile financial times is to stay calm and focused.

When markets are too good to be true, know that those happy days are likely to end soon and won't return for some time. Although it's almost impossible to precisely anticipate these downturns, the five-year lens should be helpful enough when mapping out your financial strategy. Just because the economy decides to take a breather doesn't mean your goals have to.

Indiscriminating Five-Year Risk: A Job Loss

At the height of the recent unemployment crisis in our country, you had about a one in ten chance of finding yourself out of work, and probably higher if your job was in real estate, finance, or in a mall.

And the scariest thing about layoffs is that you're often completely blindsided. In fact, a 2009 survey by Harris Interactive found that employees usually think the guy or gal in the nearby cubicle is more likely to get the axe than them. During one of my college internships, a manager told me that a sure sign of layoffs approaching is when the top boss alerts the entire staff to an impromptu "mandatory meeting" in a conference room.

I don't need to explain how getting laid off can be a deeply emotional experience, but I do need to remind you to not let your feelings get in the way of protecting your finances. A layoff or sudden firing is a fact of life, and regaining your financial footing can take several months. In 2009, the average job hunt lasted six to seven months. That is why I and other financial experts emphasize the importance of having at least a six-month rainy-day savings cushion.

Your five-year strategy should include doing all that you can to secure employment and prepare for an unfortunate turn of events. Having the savings cushion is integral. In addition, here are some other protective measures you should be prepared to take quickly in case of a layoff:

Know your rights. If your employer offers you a severance package, remember that you can negotiate before signing. Keep in mind, too, that you are legally allowed to receive any and all accrued vacation time. Keep your employee guidebook handy to refer to your employee rights. As for any vested stock options you own, you typically have 3 months or 90 days after the date you got laid off to exercise those options. Some companies may even extend that period. If you are a contract employee, go through your paperwork to understand your rights. Perhaps you had a three-year contract and you only worked at the company for one year. The contract may have a clause that protects you from early termination, and you may be able to earn compensation for the remaining time on your contract. Hiring a labor attorney for a couple hours of her time to review your severance package and your contract may be money well spent, especially if you feel you're getting a raw deal.

Apply for unemployment benefits ASAP. During times of high unemployment, when many more individuals are applying for unemployment insurance from the state, there may be a wait of several weeks from when you apply to when you actually start receiving your benefits. The good news is that once you start collecting unemployment, the payout is retroactive from the date you applied. In most states, you can apply over the phone or online. Visit the Department of Labor's website at www.dol.gov for details on eligibility requirements, as well as where to apply for benefits.

Secure health insurance. Again, do this as soon as possible. You need to notify your healthcare provider that you want to enroll in COBRA within 30 days of getting laid off. If your former employer was sponsoring your health insurance plan and continues to sponsor health insurance for its existing employees, you can apply for COBRA, which provides up to 18 months of health insurance to those who've been laid off or left their jobs voluntarily and under good terms. If you got fired under bad terms or laid off because your company went bankrupt, you more than likely won't be eligible for COBRA. Your company's human resources department should have the application information or you can go to www.dol.gov. A note of caution: COBRA can be pricey because you have to pay the entire cost your employer pays plus a 2% administrative fee. Monthly COBRA premiums can easily run up to $400 for single coverage and $1,200 for family coverage. For some more affordable alternatives, check with your spouse or partner. If your wife, husband, or partner is getting insurance from his or her employer, see whether you can piggyback. If you don't fall into that category but you're still young and healthy, consider an individual policy by shopping online and comparing rates at sites like eHealthInsurance.com and Esurance.com. Beyond that, there are ways to get health insurance with group discounts through union membership or by going through a professional organization. Still others have been known to take courses part time at a local school, where you may be able to get group health insurance. If you have kids, contact your state's children's health insurance program to see whether they are eligible for coverage at www.chipmedicaid.org.

Protect your 401k. You might be tempted to cash it out, but remember that your 401k is for the golden years and not to pay for living expenses now. Significant tax penalties apply to an early withdrawal from your 401k before age 59 1/2. The best thing to do is to either leave your money in the existing account until you get another job and roll the money into your new employer's 401k plan or roll that money penalty free through a direct transfer into an individual retirement account or IRA.

Milestone Math

What can happen during the five-year allotment runs the gamut from weddings to first-borns, buying a new home, starting a business, and going back to school. Here's what these milestones roughly cost—on average—and what you need to know ahead of time.

Wedding and Marriage

The average cost of a wedding in the United States is between $21,000 and $24,000, according to the Association for Wedding Professionals International. That's not including the rings or the honeymoon. Meantime, in fancy ZIP codes like Manhattan and San Francisco, wedding costs can easily be more than double the national average. The earlier you start planning, the earlier you can commit to saving for the big day and your new life together. My advice to engaged couples is to consider living on one partner's salary for a few months up to the wedding to not only help pay for the bash but also to start building a joint nest egg. And just as important as saving, you want to pay off those towering credit card balances, too. If you have bad credit or high levels of debt, commit to improving your financial mess before marriage. In 2009, I heard from a distraught reader who—only after marrying her beau—discovered his credit score was in the 500s (out of 850). Ouch. Now as the couple plans to buy their first home, they're hitting roadblocks. If they file jointly for a mortgage, banks will likely reject them based on his poor credit or slap them with an exorbitant interest rate. But if she files alone for a mortgage, they won't be able to qualify for as big of a loan because the bank will consider only her income. Their plans to buy a home are now on the back burner as the couple plays catch up in the credit arena. Had this been discussed before marriage, the couple could have invested their time and money more wisely to avoid this hurdle.

Your First House

At last check, the median price of a single-family home in the United States was roughly $178,000, according to data from the National Association of Realtors. Since the credit crisis, banks have not been as open-armed with loans, in particular with mortgages. That means borrowers need to be extra squeaky-clean and secure when applying for credit. You want to show that you have cash in the bank, a secure income, and a clean bill of credit. Before the recession, a 0% down payment was not unheard of. Today, expect to have 15% to 20% in cash to put down, with an additional cash reserve in your savings account totaling the first year's property taxes. If you work for yourself, banks like to see two years of steady income (likewise, if you are employed by a company). As for your credit, the best mortgage rates go to borrowers with credit scores in the 700s. Depending on your savings and your credit status, you may need to begin getting your act together a year or two in advance of applying for a mortgage. Six months before beginning your home search, get preapproved for a mortgage to know how much banks will lend you. Keep in mind that 99% of the time—even still in this post-recession era—you'll prequalify for more than you'll be comfortable spending. A safe rule of thumb: Avoid borrowing more than two-and-a-half times your annual income.

New Set of Wheels

Want to finance a $40,000 Beemer on a $55,000 salary? Think again.

Monthly payments for a new car plus its insurance and gas shouldn't exceed 15% to 20% of one's take-home pay. As with mortgages, banks prefer to give the best loan rates to borrowers with credit scores at least in the 700s. A 1% or 2% difference in your interest rate can save you thousands of dollars in interest payments over the life of the loan. A reliable car, safe neighborhood, and sound driving record can also lower the insurance rate. Another tip: Don't assume you have to finance the car through the auto dealership. Consumers can opt to use a less-expensive, third-party lender such as a local bank or credit union.

Baby

In year one, babies, on average cost $7,700, according to researchers at BabyCenter.com, a site for new and expecting parents. That doesn't include childcare, which can easily run an extra $1,000 a month. With the use of BabyCenter.com's handy online calculator, I discovered that if I were to have a baby tomorrow, I'd need about $39,000, including the cost of childcare, to take care of my newborn for the first 12 months. Yeesh. The first financial must before parenthood: Wipe out any and all credit card debt. Try to start parenthood with a clean slate, since you're likely to incur a heap of additional costs preparing for and raising a child. Not to mention, if you need to take on any loans over the next few years (perhaps for a bigger home or a bigger car), banks prefer borrowers with a small credit-utilization ratio. That ratio is equal to your level of outstanding debt over your total available credit. Keep that ratio to less than 30% and pay all your bills on time to really polish your credit score. Next, don't worry about moving right away to a bigger space. Perhaps the biggest misconception about having a baby is that expectant parents need more room to provide for the child. False. Save your time, energy, and money while pregnant. The experts at BabyCenter.com tell me that an infant can probably sleep in a bassinet in the parents' room for the first six months, especially if being breastfed. If money's tight, don't worry about splurging on a fancy nursery, either. Instead, start a savings nest egg for all the day-to-day food and diaper costs in the first year. As soon as you learn that you're pregnant, consider putting aside as much as you can afford every week or month to help at least make it through your maternity leave. Another important preemptive strike against child costs is to know your healthcare rights, to fully understand the terms and conditions of your health insurance policy. Know whether your health care provider covers pre-natal to post-partum. In addition, at least six months before your scheduled delivery, sit down with your human resources manager to clarify how much you will be paid during your maternity leave (if at all). In some states, new moms can qualify for short-term disability, but that's also very limited pay. Finally, a great way to avoid many unnecessary costs related to pregnancy is to take care of you. Eating a healthful diet, taking vitamins, cutting back on caffeine, exercising throughout your pregnancy, and having a preconception checkup can all help reduce health risks.

Grad School

Priya Dasgupgta, GRE program manager at Kaplan Test Prep and Admissions, told me over 70% of students preparing for the GRE said they were "very" or "somewhat" concerned about taking on debt from grad school tuition and its related costs. That's based on a 2007 survey by Kaplan. It figures, since, on average, grad students owe about $30,000 upon completing a Master's program—also according to Kaplan. Begin by exhausting all financial resources. A year before the start of enrollment, fill out the FAFSA (Free Application for Federal Student Aid) at fafsa.ed.gov, which is the gateway to a large chunk of financial aid awarded to students.

Even though banks are getting out of the business of offering private student loans, that's no excuse to quit your search for funding. Talk to your local community bank or credit union that hasn't suffered from severe write-downs for available loan programs. Ask the student aid office in your graduate school for applications for private scholarships, school fellowships, and teaching assistantships. Also consider peer-to-peer lending websites, such as Prosper.com and Lending.com, which eliminate banks as middlemen and directly connect individual borrowers and lenders. Another savings strategy is to structure your schedule to work and go to school part time. It may be more time consuming and challenging, but it also eases the blow of graduate school tuition. Some employers may even contribute tuition expenses, if you agree to return to the same company full time upon graduation for a minimum number of years. The federal government actually encourages this with a special tax code letting employers pay as much as $5,250 a year in tuition for courses pertaining to your profession. Check with your human resources manager to learn about your company's education benefits program, often called the employer assistance program.

In the final two chapters of this book, we look at some alternative paths you might take to enhance your personal and financial satisfaction—and it all starts with getting out of your comfort zone.

[1] Forbes, "Nobel Laureate Debunks Economic Theory," November, 6, 2002.

[2] National Bureau of Economic Research, "Determination of the December 2007 Peak in Activity," December 11, 2008.

[3] Merrill Lynch Fund Manager Survey, June 18, 2008.

Part III

Raise the Bar

9

Break from the Norm

"Do one thing every day that scares you."

Eleanor Roosevelt

As my mom often says to my brother and me when we are too hesitant to try something new, "You'll never know your true potential unless you get out of your comfort zone." My mom and the brainy folks at Google think alike. Engineers at the search engine giant dedicate 20% of their time, or one day per week, pursuing projects that take them down a whole new path, extracurricular assignments that pique their interests, separate from their normal responsibilities at work. Google calls its philosophy "Innovative Time Off" or "20% Time" and boasts the initiative has led to major corporate product launches from Gmail to AdSense. In all, the company estimates about half of its new products launched in the last six months of 2005 stemmed from this emphasis to be "creative" at work.[1]

At the core of Google's 20% rule is the theory that you can potentially boost your bottom line by exploring new thoughts and strategies. How might our personal lives improve if we actively dedicate a fraction of our time and resources to creative interests or alternative projects?

What if we were to adopt a way of thinking that encourages us to explore unconventional paths? It doesn't have to be grandiose. It can be something small, a minor tweak or a slight derailment that can help create even more financial momentum. Some risk may apply, but the long-term benefits might end up outweighing the costs.

Pursue something new. For example, pick up a few shares of dicey stock, invest in a small business, start your own business (more about that in Chapter 10, "Embrace the Entrepreneurial Spirit"), or even write a book. Such endeavors are personally satisfying and have the potential of building financial momentum. But what are the obstacles?

Overcoming Risk Aversion

Breaking from the norm requires that you assume some risk. There may be opportunity costs or financial risks. So, how does one get over the fear of risk? It's not simple, say the experts, because people are hardwired to avoid risk. Curtis Faith, a successful entrepreneur and trader for the past 20 years and best-selling author of *Way of the Turtle* and *Trading from Your Gut,* explained to me that society encourages us toward safe decision making and following the rules. "As a society, we beat risk taking out of people," Curtis told me. "Look at our school system. If you're a nonconformist, the system is against you from the beginning. You risk detention and teachers hating you. Teachers like kids who don't cause a fuss. And when you get out to a world beyond school, most people continue being pushed slowly toward this risk-averse idea that if you follow this prescribed 'path' that we set out for you, then your life will turn out wonderful. In reality, that's not the case." He explained that this is a 70-year-old mentality that goes back to the time our country's school system became officially formalized. But as society evolves, more uncertainty is naturally unleashed, and maintaining a risk-averse attitude can actually be a dangerous thing. What you once considered to be risk free is in fact no longer the case, whether it be investing in blue-chip stocks or taking a corporate job at a well-established firm. The key takeaway is that we must accept that there's no such thing as risk free, especially as our society and the economy changes. Pay attention to the potential for risk in all decisions, but don't miss important opportunities because you fear the risks.

Strategies for mastering risk that Curtis recommends include the following:

1. Embrace the fact that risk, in various forms, is everywhere.
2. Be prepared (financially and psychologically) to minimize risk by staying on top of things. Have a Plan B and be prepared to go to it if circumstances warrant.

Investing is still a sore spot for many Americans as we climb out of the recession, and understandably so. Many of our 401k portfolios got sliced in half, earning a new name: the 201k. If you ask Curtis, he'll tell you that the strategy of buy and hold, where you put *x* amount of money in stocks, bonds, and funds and ride out the market until retirement, is no longer the best way to manage risk (for obvious reasons). Instead, investors need to be willing to shift their allocations periodically to address the risks in the marketplace, while addressing their own personal needs.

If you want to beat the curve, review your investments once a month. If you are heavily invested in stocks and see that the S&P 500 keeps bouncing around a high level (say, 1,500, as it did in late 2008 before the market crashed), and you know you will need the cash currently tied up in shares for something critical sometime in the next five years, you should manage risk by adjusting away from high-risk investments to lower-risk instruments such as cash and bonds. When you're examining your portfolio each month, "Pay attention to long-term cycles, too," Curtis advises. That might be a lot to ask of us, since we tend to analyze short-term patterns, as some behavioral economists have concluded.

But, as Curtis reminded me, if you pay attention to historical trends, you should never really be caught by surprise. "It was apparent to anyone who was paying attention to the real estate market that the rise was unsustainable," says Curtis. "What's more," he says, "Lots of people were talking about it." So read the news and talk to older investors you know who can give their perspective on trends.

Finally, to manage risk, you have to be willing to lose (at least a little). "Any time you make a financial decision around uncertainty (i.e., risk), you have to be willing to be wrong," says Curtis. For example, you might see the trend reports on real estate and deduce that the gains cannot be sustained for much longer. You sell your condo, and for the next year or two, prices continue to go up. You feel like an utter loser. You have seller's remorse. That's a risk you might need to take, but in the long run it should pay off. In other words, be okay to leave the party early. "When you deal with uncertain outcomes, the right decision doesn't always result the way you expected it to. You have to play for the long run," says Curtis.

Timing Is Everything

Warren Buffet famously said that a key to investing well is to "be greedy when others are fearful."[2] And he's right. Opportunities present themselves when people are running for the hills. This signals a great time to consider alternative paths. Don't fear being contrary.

"A lot of major successful companies started during times of great stress, recession, and depression," says Victoria Colligan, founder of Ladies Who Launch. I interviewed Victoria in 2009 regarding the rising trend in female entrepreneurship during the recession. She wasn't surprised at all by the movement and referenced the Great Depression as an example of how individuals can embark on once-in-a-lifetime opportunities in down periods. Victoria reminded me that several blue chip companies got their start during the Great Depression, from Hewlett-Packard to McDonald's and United Technologies.

For some, breaking from the norm in hard times has partly to do with the "what do I have to lose" mentality, a mentality that can actually encourage people to take a chance. For others, a recession or depression presents fewer barriers to entry (e.g., bigger talent pool willing to work for less pay because of layoffs, cheaper real estate and technology, and more flexible ways of transacting business, such as bartering).

When 30-something moms Emily Meyer and Leigh Rawdon cofounded their children's clothing line, Tea Collection, it was right after the dot-com bust in the heart of Silicon Valley. "People said it was a crazy time to start," says Rawdon. "But looking back, timing was everything...A recession makes you incredibly disciplined about how you spend your money," she told me. "We thought 'if you can start a business now, imagine how stronger we'll be when the economy comes back.'" Today their clothing line is available worldwide.

Aside from starting a business, consumers snatched up deals during the recession—from homes at heavily discounted prices to beaten-down stocks that should one day afford them a more secure retirement. In fact, if you bought any of the depressed financial stocks at the depth of the recession, you probably made a nice profit less than a year later. Second-home market experts say a market slowdown and low interest rates create buying opportunities.

All said, breaking from the norm may require that you jump through a few extra hoops. While prices are down during a recession, banks might not be as willing to lend because of tight credit markets and the fear of defaulting borrowers. Banks are normally tough on second-home borrowers no matter the market conditions, but in a recession the standards are even higher. They assume if the borrower runs into financial hardship, the second home is likely the first property they'll default on. When preparing to buy a second home, ensure that you have maintained a particularly strong credit history, that you have a credit score well into the 700s, and can put down at least a 20% of the cost of the property as an initial payment.

Other options to consider when banks stop lending are to turn to peer-to-peer (P2P) lending websites or the "bank of friends and family." Research firm Celent reported that the overall P2P market will climb to $5.8 billion in loans in 2010, up 800% from 2009.[3] P2P is not only a creative way to borrow money and secure an interest rate that is probably lower than what financial institutions are offering, but it's also a way for lenders to earn more interest than leaving money in a savings account. Sure there are risks when lending to people, but the established sites like VirginMoney.com, Prosper.com, and LendingClub.com are set up to encourage both parties to fulfill their contractual promises.

The recession also encouraged bartering, or the swapping of goods and services, as strapped individuals and business owners strove to spend less money in the new economy. I discussed this on the *Today Show* in 2009, picking up on a rise in new Internet sites catering to this rebirth of bartering. Sites such as Swaptree, U-Exchange, SwapGiant, and FavorPals were just a handful of new web businesses capitalizing on our renewed interest in bartering. Granted, bartering is not a "new" strategy, but to see a boom during hard times is evidence that people are creatively breaking from the norm. They're figuring out ways to get what they want without relying on the traditional methods (like paying cash or using a credit card), and both parties to the transaction get what they need.

To break from the norm is to simply get out of your comfort zone and open yourself up to a bigger world of opportunity in your personal, financial, and professional life. If we can commit to creativity, at least once a week as the Google folks do, we have a great chance of accomplishing our furthest goals in good times and especially in bad. Along the way, we also gain self-confidence and enhance our problem-solving skills.

Alternative Places for Your Investments

Investing in a Friend's Business

As we enter a new post-recession wave of entrepreneurship and as financial institutions continue to struggle with a tight credit market and restricted lending, you may be approached more and more to invest in a friend's or relative's business. When handing money to a friend or relative, you need to consider some key risks, including the impact on your relationship if things don't work out as planned. With good planning and execution, however, it's possible to mitigate risks, make a sound profit, and most important, keep your relationship intact.

The first step, before jumping into a business deal with someone close to you, is to understand the role you will play. Be clear about your motivations. Do you want an active role in the business and be involved in day-to-day decisions or do you want to be a silent partner? Do you care how your money gets invested? I interviewed an unhappy investor who complained that the $100,000 he gave to his friend for his start-up actually paid for the company car. He had hoped it would go toward hiring employees or establishing the storefront. Again, be clear about your expectations.

The next step is to do your due diligence. Go through your friend's business plan with a fine-tooth comb and read closely the sections on market size, competition, and the exit strategy. Call other friends and business contacts who have more knowledge of the type of business you're considering investing in. What are the barriers to entry, and why might your friend's business be in a good position to combat those hurdles? Review the financial strategy. If the numbers are too much to digest, call your finance friends or a small business counselor at Score.org for free advice.

Another topic to pursue is who will be in charge of the business. Your friend may have a brilliant business idea and plan, but he's not one to execute a bachelor party, let alone a full-on business.

Find out the number of investors involved in this business. Who else besides you is forking over money for the start-up? Ask whether he's gotten any bank loans. If he has, that may also be a positive indicator that this business plan has some legs. Even better is if your friend, himself, is putting in a significant portion of money, say 20% of the overall costs.

Finally, put everything in writing. Get legal help. The National Venture Capital Association, www.nvca.org, has free samples of legal documents, from term sheets to investor rights agreements.

Investing in Gold

Gold has become all the rage over the last decade, as more investors drool over this commodity's insane returns. By the start of 2010, the price of gold had rallied to more than $1,100 an ounce, compared to just $270 an ounce in 2001.

I wrote about gold for *Entrepreneur* and TheStreet.com—probably more than I would have liked—and learned there is a whole underground world of gold enthusiasts. So, what is it with all the *amour d'or?* For one, gold is considered to be a "safe-haven investment." It's viewed as a means to store value when all other financial instruments are depreciating (e.g., stocks, funds, the U.S. dollar). The price of gold tends to go up amid rising inflation, a weak U.S. dollar, and higher oil prices. What's more, gold insiders tell me, the precious metal has something going for it that other financial instruments don't in that it's not based on a government's or financial institution's promise; that is, it's not backed by debt. Instead, it's a tangible investment. You can hold it in your hands and it stays intact. The one great risk, of course, is that the price of gold is highly volatile. It can easily run up or down because of its small market supply.

Simon Constable, a former colleague of mine at TheStreet.com, is a bona-fide gold expert. Simon tells me that buying gold bullion coins is like buying financial insurance for your portfolio. It's basically acting as a hedge against catastrophic events occurring. If something bad happens, like a depression or financial catastrophe, gold should greatly appreciate in value. What if conditions suddenly improve, Simon? Is gold a complete bust at that point? "If nothing bad happens, then the gold will be a bad investment," he tells me. "But, hey, everything else will be superb," he quickly points out.

How does one go about buying gold? The Gold American Eagle Coin is the most widely traded gold bullion coin. The U.S government guarantees it by weight, content, and purity. There is a bit of a markup from the spot price of gold, mainly so the dealer can cover its costs. You can buy gold in more affordable ways. For example, you can purchase the Gold American Eagle coin in a fraction, as small as one-tenth. Retailers include Kitco.com, BlanchardGold.com, and UsaGold.com. There are also gold funds, which you can buy online through various brokerage sites.

As with all of these untraditional investments, you want to keep your exposure to gold limited, around 5% of a diversified portfolio, for the reasons we covered earlier. Also, this is a buy and hold investment. You want to keep gold for the long term, not to get rich quick. Gold experts don't usually recommend selling back your entire gold investments unless you really have to—somewhat like life insurance. It may be wiser to rebalance your exposure by selling a bit here and there when the market goes awry.

Investing in Private Equity

Michael Lazerow is a serial entrepreneur. The 34-year-old father of three has created at least four companies since his college days at Northwestern University, where he launched University Wire, a network of college newspapers, from his dorm room. He then sold the company to CBS, and soon after launched Golf.com, which would later be bought by Time Inc. Next, he started Lazerow Consulting and his newest venture, Buddy Media, an application development firm that works with social networking websites like Facebook.

If you're a risk taker like Lazerow, then investing in private equity might be your thing. It certainly has been a lucrative strategy for him. Briefly, investing in private equity means investing in companies that seize other companies and later sell them for a profit (at least that's the plan).

When I first dove into the inner workings of private equity, I suspected it was just a game for the rich to get richer. And it sure used to be. Traditionally, it was an exclusive society of high net-worth (i.e., more than $1 million in the bank) and in-the-know individuals like Lazerow and institutional investors, pension plans, and university endowments. Lazerow, himself, calls it a "clubby" investment.

But recently this members-only club opened its doors to invite the financial B-listers (i.e., the <$1 million in the bank crowd) to the party. Vista Research and Management has issued the Listed Private Equity Plus Fund (ticker: PRIVX), an open-end mutual fund that tracks private equity firms. You can begin investing with a minimum $1,000. To learn more, visit vrmfunds.com.

The PowerShares Global Listed Private Equity Portfolio (ticker: PSP) is another way to get in. The portfolio tracks the Red Rocks Listed Private Equity exchange-traded fund, which consists of 40 to 60 publicly traded companies tied to private equity.

With all these new ways to invest in private equity, it's still risky business. These should be considered long-term investments that you want to hold for an average five to ten years.

[1] Marissa Mayer, VP of Google Search Product and User Experience, Presentation at Stanford University, June 30, 2006.

[2] Warren Buffet, "Buy American, I Am." *New York Times*, October 16, 2008.

[3] Celent, "Top Tech Trends in Banking: 2008."

10

Embrace the Entrepreneurial Spirit

"Choose a job you love and you will never have to work a day in your life."

Confucius

Throughout the past decade while working in financial news, I've interviewed hundreds and hundreds of entrepreneurs, from domestic doyenne Martha Stewart to billionaire media maverick Mark Cuban to Ali and Hash Hafizi, the young, immigrant brothers who've run the "Good Morning America" coffee pushcart on Wall Street for almost 10 years. Their specialty buck-twenty-five brew is the morning must-have on Wall Street, with the brothers selling about 100 cups every hour—enough to help support their family of nine, including their mom, dad, and brothers and sisters, who all live under one roof just over the bridge in New Jersey. It's not confirmed, but I suspect the success of the Hafizi brothers' cart had something to do with the sudden closings of the competing Starbucks and Dunkin Donuts across the street.

At present, I am fascinated with 28-year-old Megan Faulkner Brown, the married young mom who just recently started in 2009 the successful Sweet Tooth Fairy Bake Shop in Provo, Utah. The gourmet bake shop's specialty is cupcakes. I sampled only her award-winning double-fudge cake bites, and I'm pretty sure I died and went to heaven for a few seconds. I discovered her business while reporting on how to launch a cupcakery (truth be told, a personal aspiration of mine, too) and found her start-up journey quite compelling. Faulkner left her day job in marketing, depleted her savings account, and got a loan from her grandmother to open the store. And all during a recession, no less. Risky? You bet, since some critics say the nationwide cupcake bubble will soon go the way of the dinosaur or the Krispy Kreme doughnut. And why leave the luxury of a job (i.e., a guaranteed salary and benefits) with so much uncertainty in the market?

Megan understood the high risks, but her entrepreneurial spirit and hard work eventually paved the way to profits in less than a year. As it turned out, a recession was a fabulous time to start a cupcake shop. As Megan explained to me, people were willing to still spend money on small luxuries that made them feel good. "Sure, maybe no vacation to Hawaii, but they'll pay $2.25 for a cupcake," she laughed.

There's a lot we can learn from entrepreneurs, and it's not just how to, say, launch a Fortune 500 company or a bakery in the Midwest. It's not always about following a path toward making millions or billions of dollars. Rather, it's about pursuing their passion for creativity, strong work ethic, independence, appetite for risk, and willingness to go the extra mile and down the road less traveled. Theirs are the attributes and behaviors we should all embrace for the great sake of enriching our lives and our bank accounts.

For my parting chapter in *Psych Yourself Rich,* I've chosen to introduce this idea of embracing the entrepreneurial mind and spirit and to examine how to be a pioneer in life. Bottom line: It all starts with your willingness to take a chance.

A New Era of Entrepreneurship

Why are more and more Americans starting their own businesses or, at the minimum, taking more ownership of their revenue streams? A key variable in keeping your financial foundation solid is earning enough money to keep your bases covered and to achieve your goals. Best-selling author and behavioral expert Dan Pink describes in his book *A Whole New Mind* that "artistry, empathy, taking the long view, pursuing the transcendent...will increasingly determine who soars and who stumbles." He describes it as a revolution. Before, "left-brained" or binary thinking, also known as SAT- and CPA-style aptitude, "drove the world." Why the transition now? Abundance, Asia, and automation have diminished the importance of left-brain thinking, says Pink. In other words, we have so much that we now have a heightened sense of "need," we face fierce competition, and the electronic world is diminishing the value of left-brained skills. The world around us is changing, and we need to adapt.

The once-stable career path of working for one company and cashing out at age 65 is no longer a likelihood. Day jobs have become unpredictable. A job loss can seriously set you back *unless* you have set some protocols in place, one of which is entrepreneurship.

In a conversation with Richard Bolles, author of the famous career guide *What Color Is Your Parachute* and the new book *The Job-Hunter's Survival Guide*, he tells me that there is no such thing as an "essential" employee. The recession taught us that much, at least. "There is no safety in the structure of company or job market," says Bolles. "There are too many different waves of change in the market to make any person's job indispensable."

Having an entrepreneurial project is also food for the soul. Our day jobs may not offer enough money or the right kind of emotional fulfillment. Therefore, to really be financially secure, you have to put some or all of your earnings potential into your own hands. It helps to have a stream of revenue that you can control—either in lieu of or in addition to your traditional 9 to 5 income.

But, what if you have no fear of losing your job. Instead, you're worried that an annual raise and a bonus are not on the horizon. In that case, you might want to seek this alternative route to fulfilling your earnings aspirations. Perhaps you want extra money for a down payment on a second home, to renovate your existing kitchen and bathrooms, you may want to boost your retirement savings, send your children to private school; making some money on the side is a strategy you can control.

What if you want to transition out of your current job altogether and pursue running your own business full time—which could not only bring in more money, it will make you happier. Baby steps in entrepreneurship can build that bridge. It's not false to believe that entrepreneurship will make us happier human beings. That's not just my intuition talking. An early 1990s study conducted by researchers at Dartmouth College and the London School of Economics titled "Entrepreneurship, Happiness and Supernormal Returns," concluded that "the self-employed report significantly higher levels of well-being than employees." Why is that?

For one, when you are your own boss, you don't have the same fears as when you are employee number 4,352. Namely, the fear of job security goes away. Sure, start-ups and small businesses fail, but knowing you have the power and control to turn things around helps keep your spirits high and your focus clear. I'll never forget what one young, daring entrepreneur told me in 2009, in the heat of the recession, as she was transitioning from pink slip recipient to full-time, self-employed caterer. Passion for food was one motivator. Fear was the other. "I have a huge fear of failure," she said. "So I know I'll work as hard as I can to not fail. I have no other choice." And that's the truth.

More and more people transition to entrepreneurship because they are seeking a higher purpose and more happiness in life. As the market begins to settle, becoming your own boss may be less an economic choice and more a decision based on how you want to live your life.

When the economy came to a shrieking halt during the previous recession, entrepreneurship went full speed ahead for both men and women, as discussed earlier in this book. Men continued to start businesses in droves while women set records with their trailblazing (and now constitute more than 50% of new start-ups). Ladies Who

Launch, a savvy network that attracts young female entrepreneurs (both budding and established), boasts more than 70,000 registered subscribers in the United States and Canada. That's up from just 500 in 2005 when the group launched.

We've been over the *why* behind this trend. When companies are laying people off and the job market is weak, becoming your own boss is a viable alternative fully within your control. Now let's explore the *how* to transition to entrepreneurship and begin taking control of your career.

The Part-Time Entrepreneur

Anyone can be a part-time entrepreneur. After all, that role doesn't require that you leave your day job. And as uncertain as the job market is, one could argue that it's pretty crazy to leave a stable job while unemployment is setting generational records. Dr. Patricia Greene, the F.W. Olin Distinguished Chair in Entrepreneurship at Babson College, explained to me that "entrepreneurship is leadership." It doesn't mean dropping your corporate life to start a jewelry business or a restaurant. It may or may not mean owning a business at all. In its purest form, an entrepreneur is one who takes initiative, creates his or her own opportunities, and accepts some risks. It's somebody who wants to be in charge and earn freedom, flexibility, and control over his or her career and finances. And being entrepreneurial can lead you to a more fulfilling life and secure future.

So in this section, let's look at keeping the day job while pursuing something more interesting (and entrepreneurial) on the side. You'll know when you're ready to make the full transition to You Inc. (which we explore later, as well). In the meantime, here's how to get started.

Step 1: Remember Who You Were

Earlier this year, I went on the CBS *Early Show* with my tips on how to "monetize your skills." We all have skills and passions, I explained, but we don't bank on them as much as we can. Life gets so hectic that we forget what we really enjoy doing, what our hobbies once were, and what we're actually really talented at doing. So to begin, think about what you enjoyed doing in high school. Were you in the school play? Did you play saxophone? Did you volunteer? The first step toward entrepreneurship is self-rediscovery. It's recognizing what you truly enjoy doing (i.e., your passion), which is often rooted in childhood and adolescence, when the world was a simpler place.

By following through with something you really enjoy, you will perceive it less as a "job" and more of a "lucrative hobby." I had the pleasure of meeting Erika Weltz Prafder, a *New York Post* columnist and author of a terrific book called *Keep Your Paycheck, Live Your Passion.* After years of writing about entrepreneurs and small business owners, Erika was able to brilliantly translate that entrepreneurial *je ne sais quoi* for the masses. It's hard to pursue your dreams full time, she explains, but a part-time commitment is far more doable and can just as well fulfill your creativity and lead you to making more money. She will tell you that a big part of discovering your "passion" is tapping into your earliest memories. She asks people to examine what they enjoyed doing back then. What were your aspirations? Was it to be a dancer, a singer, an actor? What were your extracurricular activities? And more important, what were your dreams? It's time to pay attention, she says, because dreams—what she calls "windows to our souls"—are a lot more telling than we might think.

All said, some people are perfectly happy pursuing a side gig that just functions as a way to pay the bills and nothing more. My high school friend Allison is one such example. Allison works full time as an analyst for a web firm, and in her spare time offers social media help to promote musical companies and their national tours. She doesn't see herself turning this into a full-time career, but she's committed to the job because it brings in an extra $10,000 a year and helps her pay down debt and afford large purchases like new tires or ski passes.

Fair enough. Keeping things strictly business is definitely an aspect of entrepreneurship. The ideal, however, is to make extra money and be passionate about what you're doing. But if you find a job that you can do, that fits well into your schedule, and that pays well...don't let me be the one to stop you!

Step 2: Channel the Urge

To incorporate entrepreneurship into your life, you need to get some *fire in the belly.* You need a purpose, a reason to pursue this goal. A layoff, dissatisfaction at work, a need to make more money to either pay for your needs (rent, utilities, debt, savings) or your wants (vacations, a new car, more clothes) are all stimuli for rethinking the composition of your work life. Imagine how as you create more opportunities for yourself your life might change for the better. Channel those thoughts of gaining financial security and happiness in your work life and stoke those flames of ingenuity.

Dr. Greene describes this fiery urge to be our own boss as "necessity entrepreneurship." On the one hand, it may be, "I lost my job and I have to do something," she explains. On the other hand, if you still have your job, you may feel unfulfilled or not earn as much money as you need, she says. In those cases, too, people are "needing" entrepreneurship to fill the gap.

In 2004, 29-year-old Amanda Cox began doubling as a chocolate maker and a marketing coordinator for a manufacturing firm in Cambridge, Ohio. Can you guess which was her day job? Chocolate has always been her passion. "I made it growing up," she said. "My whole family made chocolates." Following college, Amanda lived in an Amish county, where she gained more experience, and soon she began monetizing her skills, while choosing to keep her full-time job at the factory (for the much-needed income, health benefits, and paid vacation). Amanda managed her side gig online through her website NothingButChocolate.com. On weekends, she worked at festivals and events; she picked up a few wholesale clients mainly through word of mouth. For her, this part-time entrepreneurial endeavor served a couple of purposes: extra revenue to pay the bills and a passionate escape from her daily corporate responsibilities. Continue reading to learn what happened next!

Step 3: Make It Work

As *Project Runway*'s fashion consultant Tim Gunn would say, "Make it work!" For budding entrepreneurs, it's about putting your passion to work and pursuing it in such a way that you manage your time and money well. It might also mean "leaving the door open" for the possibility of turning your side business into a full-time business someday.

So, now that you've identified a list of things you enjoy doing, which of those activities can you realistically pursue in your free time? How you can turn it into a worthwhile extra revenue stream, all while maintaining your professional 9 to 5? I find that networking on Facebook, Twitter, and LinkedIn is a great way to start a word-of-mouth alert about the kind of work you're seeking. My friend Tim just started teaching English as a second language to young kids in the Toronto area. Full time, he runs his own magazine called *Corduroy*—so I guess that makes him a double entrepreneur?

Entrepreneur Tim: Corduroy and ELS

Here is how my hard-working friend is "making it work," in his own words:

I knew I wanted something flexible that allowed me to be my own "boss" and also something that paid well. With that in mind, I ruled out serving tables, retail, office jobs, etc. I've always loved working with kids (ever since my early days as a camp counselor during summers off in high school), and I have a ton of experience and education in writing, so I figured I would make a good English tutor.

I posted a couple ads online (Craigslist and such), but most of my students have come from referrals from family and friends. I also find it helps to be proactive: I'm not ashamed to tell people I'm tutoring or to ask them for referrals when I'm out for dinner, at church, at the mall, even at the bar! And believe it or not, someone will always know someone who knows someone. The trick is to talk up your experience (I find having a magazine and a Master's degree from Columbia University helps!) and also stay firm on your rate. I charge $40/hour. And because I don't waver or give discounts, people think/know that I'm worth it and they have confidence in my abilities.

Right now I have 10 students, which puts an extra $400 into my wallet at the end of every week. It's not that much work either... 10 hours of actual teaching and then a couple hours preparing worksheets, lesson plans, readings, etc. I schedule the sessions around my magazine workload and it's worked out pretty well so far. Since kids don't normally get home from school until after 3 p.m., I have the whole morning to work on Corduroy *and then spend the evenings tutoring.*

Whether you have one or a few side jobs, time management is really important. Some, like my friend Barrie, say you almost need to be "compulsive" about planning your time well. Barrie works full-time as an academic administrator and spends her nights, weekends, and summers directing theater. "The trick," she says, "is to be a compulsive planner and have a fantastic system for organizing your schedule, your long-term calendar, and your to-do lists. It sounds boring and utterly unromantic to say that following your passions takes responsibility and practicality, but it is true."

To help make it work, keep these following things in mind:

Avoid discussing your side gig at your real job in the presence of managers. Of course, you might need to get some clearance before starting a particular side job, depending on the type of work it is. Make sure there are no conflicts of interest. For example, I needed to get the okay from my boss at the news station to be a columnist at a local paper, because I'd be working for two media companies that cover similar stories. In the end, I was allowed because my byline in the paper would mention I was an NY1 producer—free marketing for the station.

Once you're working this side job, don't blab about it at your 9 to 5. If your boss starts to sense that it's taking away from your focus at work, your next review might suffer. Bottom line: Do your best to keep the two worlds separate.

Keep track of your side earnings. The IRS requires that we claim all income, including any earnings from freelance work. So, in a separate folder, tuck away a record of any checks or cash that you receive so that you have that information available at tax time. In addition, to help reduce your taxable income, make sure to save all receipts for any purchases made to support your side gig—whether it's a computer, camera, stationery, baking utensils, and even gas to put in your car for side-gig-related travel.

Take advantage of the Web. Tim mentioned how he used Craigslist to market his business. That's just one example of how the Internet can help you get your side gig off the ground.

I recently interviewed Maria Thomas, the CEO of Etsy.com, an extremely popular online marketplace for hand-made goods, from jewelry to paintings to bags, pottery, and more. Using Etsy's existing templates, the site lets sellers showcase and sell their work online in a professional manner. Maria tells me that the Internet has officially broken down a lot of the barriers to entrepreneurship. In fact, with so much technical support and access from e-commerce sites like Etsy, Shopify, eBay, and Amazon and marketing platforms like Twitter and Facebook, it's more practical than ever to start a business online.

Online Entrepreneurship

Whether as a side or full-time occupation, the Internet is becoming the modern-day place for work. In a conversation with Elance.com CEO Fabio Rosati, I learned just how much freelance work is shifting online. His company is a thriving online job community where hirers and job seekers can connect on myriad web-based project assignments. The company's latest data shows Americans earned 45% more money online in 2009 than the previous year. "For millions of professionals, traditional career paths and even full-time employment are becoming less attractive and viable," says Fabio. "At the same time, technology, competitive pressures, and economic necessity are making online work increasingly attractive to businesses."

The top-earning skills on Elance are information technology, creative (design, multimedia, writing, translation), marketing (search engine optimization, branding), and operations (administrative support, data entry). A company report from January 2010 shows Elance has more than 100,000 active employers and more than 300,000 jobs posted in the previous 12 months.[1]

When it comes to taking the reins of your career path, think big and leverage the Web, Fabio tells me. "Those individuals who invest in keeping their skills up-to-date and learn how to effectively market their talent in this global online marketplace will thrive in the future."

Full-Time Online Freelancing

Twenty-eight year-old William Meeks from Pittsburgh, Pennsylvania, has been a full-time freelancer since 2008, running MeeksMixedMedia.com single-handedly and finding and executing 100% of his work online. Many of his opportunities arrive through Elance.com. He says his need to make more money to support his family prompted him to take his revenue streams into his own hands and the Web offered the quickest solutions.

Between having a second child and moving to a new home, he and his wife had exhausted most of their credit cards and nest egg just to keep the rent and bills current. He says his previous web design and video production job at a manufacturing company barely allowed him to make ends meet. He was only earning $11 an hour (with the promise of a raise in three months). When six months passed and that promise remained unfulfilled, he started exploring evening and weekend side jobs. He quickly found short-term web design projects on sites like FreelanceSwitch.com, Scriptlance.com, and Elance.com. The gigs paid about $15 an hour, almost 50% more than his day job. After some easy math, he and his wife decided he'd be better off quitting his day job, transitioning to full-time freelancing, and using the Internet as his vehicle to find consistent work.

The switch, he says, has been both professionally and personally rewarding. "For better or worse, it's all on me now," says William. "I don't have that constant fear of being fired for a silly mistake anymore. I also love the flexibility of my schedule. If my kids get sick or even if I just feel like taking a day off, as long as I meet my deadlines, I can do pretty much whatever I want. I will never have to choose between my loyalty to my family and my loyalty to my job." Working on a variety of projects has also given him more career confidence. "My portfolio is strong enough now that most of the time my clients give me quite a bit of creative control. They trust me."

And the best part about freelancing full-time? "There are a lot of perks, but I think the biggest one is that you never get bored," says William. "Sometimes when you are working one job at one company for years, the most creative part of your mind can stagnate from the repetitive tasks and goals as they recur quarter after quarter."

Julie Babikan would agree. The 37-year-old graphic design professional has been freelancing full time for the past year, right from her computer in her Chicago home. She admits that she wasn't convinced it was the best long-term approach to a career, mainly because she could hear her parents' nudging. "I have had the idea that people must have 'real jobs' ingrained into my head since I was very young.

Although my parents never discouraged me from being an artist, I was still told in a roundabout way that a job in a company with benefits, steady salary, and a future was the way to go." A layoff in 2008 from her corporate job was the turning point for Julie, and she began to view employment in a whole new light. "I think we are shifting toward an individual-based economy," said Julie, "turning away from corporate conglomerates that evolved after the industrial revolution, going back to our roots of individual-based services." She, too, began her online job hunt on Elance, receiving the first project she bid on, a PowerPoint presentation for a Harvard professor. "I started getting really creative with the presentations, adding animation and sound effects, turning them into educational entertainment versus your typical corporate boring PowerPoint presentations." She had found her niche and rapidly began winning more assignments.

"I love being my own boss...I no longer have to be on a train at 5 a.m. for the city, and not return until 7 or 8 p.m. My rush-hour traffic is two socks and a dust bunny. I can take a break and visit my family. My nieces and nephews know me.

"And who says the Internet keeps you isolated? It is definitely not lonely. I use Skype frequently, as it is very cost friendly for my international clients. I have made friends in Australia, Ireland, and France, as well as all over the United States. The Internet also lets Julie select quality assignments. "It's not about getting as many projects as I can. It's about choosing the right projects. It's about working for causes I believe in (like nonprofit agencies, children's welfare speakers, environmental causes, and animal rights). These projects keep me going. I am not without a loss for work now.

"Also, I am no longer afraid when my current project is nearing completion," says Julie. "The more I work, the more I get the opportunity to work. The harder I work, the better projects I receive. This has been the best, most exciting, adventurous year of my life."

Transitioning to You, Inc.

Going from employee to self-employed is not a straightforward journey, and it may seem there's no "perfect" time to launch. Perhaps the most important things you will need at this time are willpower, resourcefulness, and cold hard cash.

For some, the official transition happens after a layoff. In January 2009, Amanda, the owner of NothingButChocolate.com, lost her full-time marketing job. She recalls a moment of paralysis followed by clear determination. Instead of finding a new full-time position, she took her severance (which was only two weeks of unused vacation time) and mustered the courage to turn her hobby into a full-time home-based business. "Chocolate is recession-proof," she says. "Plus, I'm happier." Is the money flowing in? Not really, but she's finally driven to pursue an occupation, and that will be her ticket to success.

Jessi Walter, a fellow casualty of the 2009 wave of layoffs, can relate. After getting her pink slip from the now-defunct Bear Stearns, the 27-year-old took her severance and her savings to launch Cupcake Kids!, hosting cooking events for New York City children. "My business was born out of a major life change for me," says Walter. "If Bear Stearns hadn't been bought by JP Morgan, I'm not sure Cupcake Kids! would exist today."

Theirs is that transition Dr. Greene would call a "necessity," and as these women became more entrenched in their businesses full time, they would soon realize the endless opportunities their businesses engendered. A month into her business full time, orders for Amanda's treats began flowing in. "Before [when working full time], I was too bogged down to follow up on potential orders," she says. "Being laid off was the answer to my prayers… It was a blessing in disguise."

Still, for other full-time entrepreneurs, quitting their day job is the only way out. But it needn't be a rash decision. For Sarah Farzam, it took more than a few years of paltry pay and sleeping on her brother's pull-out couch for the 26-year-old California native to change gears and become the CEO of her own small business. Bilingual Birdies, the company she founded in 2007, offers foreign language classes to toddlers and young kids and teaches through song and dance. While she broke from the norm and quit her job to pursue her own business, her move was a calculated one.

Born and raised in Los Angeles, Sarah flew to New York City fresh out of UCLA in 2006 to become a school teacher in one of Brooklyn's crowded high schools, where hallway metal defectors and bloody schoolyard brawls were a way of life. Admittedly, she was pretty nervous about moving across the country and starting a job in a city where she had no friends.

Sarah made the trip, despite the potential drawbacks and $28,000 a year salary, to be a public school teacher in New York City. When it all was said and done and taxes were paid, her paycheck amounted to a paltry $400 a week—practically destitute for a young 20-something-year-old woman in the most expensive city in the country. How to pay bills, save, eat, and maintain a social life? Thankfully, her older brother, along with his wife, was generous in allowing her to stay with them for as long as she needed. Their house came with a built-in alarm clock called 2-year-old twins who would wake Sarah up in the morning by bouncing on her makeshift bed.

Fast-forward one year into Sarah's teaching life and we discover she is—to no surprise—burnt out, fed up, and broke. Instead of inspiring her students with the words of Shakespeare and instilling college ambitions, her days—as she feared—were spent playing disciplinarian to emotionally unstable kids and searching for enough pencils, textbooks, and chalk to get through her classes. The New York public school system is, in many ways, a broken system, she would later tell me. It would not be Sarah's fate to change the system, and certainly not while earning her tiny salary.

Months passed, and Sarah felt like she was just going through the motions of life—and not much more. Get up, eat breakfast, subway to school, get frustrated with students, earn measly pay. Repeat.

Sarah's life would change for the better but only after the night she spilled her guts to a friend over a plate of enchiladas at a local Mexican dive. Tired and frustrated, Sarah began imagining what sort of day-to-day job *would* make her happy, and more important, what kind of job would give her the motivation to rise out of bed (assuming the twins weren't enough of a wake-up call). She still wanted to teach, perhaps just not in the traditional classroom-type way. What would help her get off her brother's couch, and what kind of work would fulfill her goal to be financially stable and educate kids?

It took a few hours of soul searching, but in that crowded village café, Sarah began drafting the beginnings of what would ultimately be professional and financial independence. Her ideal job, she concluded, would let her integrate her existing skills of teaching, dance, foreign languages (she speaks English, Farsi, Spanish, and Hebrew), and work with young kids. Integration was key.

Now how to make the transition? She was flat broke and couldn't afford to quit her job at that point. Luckily, New York City is awake at all hours of the day, and Sarah still had her late-night college body-clock ticking. She put her energy to good use, and for the next six months Sarah continued teaching at the high school while bartending in the evenings. She managed to earn hundreds of dollars a night in tips, and with that extra revenue stream, she aggressively saved close to $15,000 in four months—enough to give her the financial confidence to quit her day job and focus on her business idea. It was also, more excitingly, enough to help her move out of her brother's living room.

Her financial instincts were right. As Rich Sloan, the co-founder of StartUpNation.com tells me, you don't need tens of thousands of dollars to launch a company. "It's not correct that it's expensive to start a business. The average requires $10,000 to get off the ground," he tells me, and that includes the storefront and materials. And with so many start-ups setting up shop on the Web to start, you might not even need as much.

What's more important to have is the fortitude and willingness to wear many hats. Today, Sarah is the CEO of Bilingual Birdies, teaching toddlers foreign languages through song and dance in rented spaces throughout New York City. She hopes to expand the business to other cities and grow the curriculum to include more languages. Sarah's days, of course, can be quite stressful—as she's in charge of the operations, marketing, and overall business strategy of Bilingual Birdies. She does it all. She'll never forget the time the elevator didn't work in the building of one of her rental spaces. She had to help parents carry strollers and babies up five flights of stairs. "But it's totally worth it," Sarah shrugs. "I'm so happy because I actually love what I'm doing."

Ironing Out the Finances

So now you've caught the small business bug. You want to turn your freelance work or side job into a full-time occupation where you call the shots. You've saved up $10,000, more or less. And mentally, you're there. My advice? Don't assume you have to quit your day job right away. After all, you may have savings to support the business, but do you also have savings to support yourself? Remember Sarah bartended her way to extra revenue to eventually help venture out of the teaching grind and off her brother's couch. I would never encourage you to quit working your corporate job if that would mean entering a world of financial uncertainties. Things may be going great for your weekend event planning business or catering gig, but do you have the financial means to be a full-time entrepreneur? Can you afford health insurance if you quit? These are just some areas worth thinking about.

Yes, entrepreneurship requires risk, but you can still be successful with prudence. Elizabeth Soule, 29, managed to launch her photography business on the side while working full time as a project manager at a design firm. After building a six-month nest egg, she gained the confidence to quit her day job and officially launched her business in late 2007, but it was only when she had her financial ducks in a row that she followed through on her exit strategy.

It's no fun having to live in your car, not unless you think it will make you stronger. That was the case with young entrepreneur John-Paul Lee, the 32-year-old Korean American founder of Tavalon Tea. In 2001, John-Paul fled from his management-consulting job in D.C. with the burning desire to launch his own tea company. Did he act in haste? If you call selling your condo, car, and stock options in one week, in addition to liquidating your 401k retirement savings and pulling out seven credit cards as hasty, then sure. "I think I took a more aggressive approach, and if I had to do it all over again, I would've started with a stronger and larger 'cash war chest,'" says John-Paul. "Money gets used up much quicker than you think in the world of business... The last thing any entrepreneur wants to do is get into a cash strap situation which can lead to poor decisions based on desperation."

But sometimes—even John-Paul will admit—there are invaluable lessons in taking risks and experiencing "rock bottom," as we've gone over in earlier chapters. It depends on your capacity and tolerance for risk, as well as your dedication to a Plan B (perhaps even Plan C). John-Paul was okay living out of his car for a while. Would you be? I once heard a saying that there is a certain luxury you gain when you know what it's like to be poor. Part of that luxury is to inherently know what it means to appreciate the things others so often take for granted in life. There is also the luxury of an unquestionable work ethic.

For some, that financial strain and desperation you experience as a result of breaking fast and loose from the corporate world to start a business may end up being what ultimately drives them toward success. As John-Paul reflects more on his journey, "I definitely learned this the hard way, but it did coerce me to be more creative, and it brought out the best in me." It also turned Tavalon into a multi-million-dollar brand in under five years.

Tips for Making the Leap to Full-Time Entrepreneur

Seek affordable loans. "Don't be intimidated that if you don't have a lot of money you're not going to be able to get off the ground," says StartupNation.com's Sloan. Banks might not be as generous as they once were with providing start-ups with ample capital. Friends and family represent one possible alternative resource. You can contract agreements with individuals with the help of a peer-to-peer lending site like VirginMoney.com. Second, he says the Small Business Administration at SBA.com is absolutely determined to provide loans. You may also want to consider tapping into the peer-to-peer market for micro loans. Sites like Prosper.com and LendingClub.com are pioneers in this alternative lending market.

Barter. It's not just a handy system from the Middle Ages. A *New York Times* story in 2008 titled "The Cash Strapped Turn to Barter" cited a more than 50% growth in membership at companies that facilitate barters, like the Itex Corporation and U-Exchange.com.[2] Remember, however, that the IRS does require you to record the fair market value of bartered goods and services. So, if a friend designs you a website for your business in exchange for you painting a room in his house, you must report the fair market value of what you receive as income (and what you pay [through barter] as an expense).

Establish emergency savings. One of the biggest questions I get from small business owners is this: How much should I pocket in case things get ugly? My advice is to save at least 10% of your earnings into a savings account until you have at least three months of your business overhead costs covered. Because entrepreneurs don't generally have a steady cash flow, save as much as possible and do it on autopilot, putting an automatic percentage into your bank account each month.

Scale back. Back to Amanda Cox, the owner of NothingButChocolate.com: While attempting to make her young business thrive, Amanda earns less income, which means she needs to cut out as many little expenses as possible. Small sacrifices can mean big returns. And because she's single, she says the stress is more manageable. "I have the stress of whether I'm going to pay the mortgage or gas bill or electric bill, but it's my stress only," she rationalizes. To simplify her finances, she canceled her Netflix and gym memberships. She began cooking more, clipping coupons, and stretching her dollars as much as possible. Her baking supplies? They come from Wal-Mart, the discounting giant. She's also keeping her car in the garage more, since living downtown offers easy walking access to most stores. She's even adjusted the thermostat in her house to 62 from 65 degrees during the winter (which also helps cool the chocolate faster). "A dollar here and a dollar there, it all adds up. It's about readjusting how you do things and they way you think."

[1] *Elance Quarterly Talent Report*, January–March 2010.

[2] Mickey Meece, "Cash-Strapped Turn to Barter," *New York Times*, November 12, 2008.

Conclusion

It almost goes without saying that we don't enjoy delaying gratification. We're a culture that desires the quick fix, the microwaveable meal, and five-minute abs. And while this book offers a long-term approach to building financial independence and wealth, I know some of you may still hope for a crib sheet edition, so in the spirit of kindness, I give you *Psych Yourself Rich...by Friday*:

1. **Clean out your desk.** Remember the most common phrase when it comes to getting organized and clearing the financial clutter in your life: Where do I begin? Although there's a whole mental aspect to this, you can start by addressing the physical space in your home where you pay your bills and store your files: Clean out your desk. Start with the easy stuff. Keep receipts for big-ticket items attached to warranties for as long as the warranty covers (at least a year). Trash receipts for small purchases after a year. Shred documents that you no longer need that contain any personal information.
2. **Make a money buddy.** It's key to have a partner in your financial life who can knock some sense into you when you feel the impulse to spend. For me, this person is usually my mom. For others, it might be your best friend, sibling, or parent. Get this person's phone number on autodial in your cell phone. Relay your goals to this person so that he or she can help remind you of them when your judgment gets cloudy while gazing at those $400 boots.

3. **Reflect on the risks you've taken.** Examine the previous year and all that you've accomplished. Believe it or not, even the easiest decisions you made carried *some* risks. Take the time to acknowledge what those risks were and how you overcame them, from taking on a particular job to moving to investing. Life may become a little less frightening after you do this. At the least, realizing how we can navigate risk will help us make better, more confident financial choices the next time around.
4. **Create one personal rule of thumb.** As discussed earlier at the beginning of this book, we love rules of thumb. An absolute rule can sometimes help make the most complicated decision easier. Just like those on a diet might make a rule of thumb preaching "no sweets after dinner," having a financial rule of "no jeans above 75 bucks," for instance, can help keep you out of the designer denim boutiques and help keep your money where it belongs.
5. **Use cash.** Unlike credit cards, where the financial transaction is paperless and invisible, when we see money disappear from our wallets, we're less likely to spend frivolously and impulsively. This practice can save you an average 20% a year, according to credit experts.
6. **Call up a close relative.** Ask questions about what you were like when you were a kid. What were your interests? What was one of the funniest things you did? What was your temperament? What was the craziest stunt you ever pulled? What did the other relatives say about you? Understanding what makes us happy, how we define *rich,* and the type of "financial" personality we have—these things are often rooted in childhood and growing-up experiences. In addition to channeling your memories, it's sometimes helpful to see yourself through the eyes of others.

7. **Automate.** Psych yourself rich by leaving the math to someone (or something) else. If your company is not automatically depositing your paychecks into a bank account, get help from human resources to do so. If you aren't automatically paying bills every month, set up autopayments with your bank so that you never miss a payment deadline. If you aren't saving automatically every month, link your checking account to a savings account and make a regular contribution every time you get paid.
8. **Track your spending.** With so many mobile applications out there to help us track our spending, this should really take just minutes to set up. The benefits of tracking your spending are priceless. Understanding how you spend and how much you spend is critical to understanding how you can better save your money. You may suddenly realize you're going to the ATM four times a week and paying $12 each week in fees, which might prompt you to look for fee-free ATMs in your neighborhood (and whaddayaknow, there's one a few blocks from your home). Or, you may see that you're spending $50 a month sending faxes from the local FedEx when you could just buy a fax machine for $100 and break even in two months.
9. **Get visual.** To see it is to believe it. Set up visual reminders of your goals and aspirations to help prevent detours along your financial track. If you really want to have fun with this, make a collage board of all the things that represent what's important to you: family photos, travel destinations, a bank statement showing your savings, and so on. In addition, use computer and phone screen savers that show your goals so that you are often visually reminded of why it's important to stick to your course!
10. **Identify your top three creative skills.** This is a tip taken from the last chapter on turning a hobby into a revenue stream. To get this show on the road, start by jotting down three skills

or hobbies you have that you are passionate about. Your passion for skiing can turn into giving skiing lessons once a week at your local ski range. A love of travel could lead to travel writing or a blog that offers travel tips. Your cooking skills could turn into a catering gig on the weekends.

And there you have it. Voilà!

Index

Symbols

D

E

F

M

N

O

P

Q

R

S

T

X-Y-Z

FT Press
FINANCIAL TIMES